Autodesk® 3ds Max® 2013
BIBLE

Autodesk® 3ds Max® 2013
BIBLE

Kelly L. Murdock

WILEY

John Wiley & Sons, Inc.

Autodesk® 3ds Max® 2013 Bible

Published by
John Wiley & Sons, Inc.
10475 Crosspoint Boulevard
Indianapolis, IN 46256
www.wiley.com

Copyright © 2012 by John Wiley & Sons, Inc., Indianapolis, Indiana

Published by John Wiley & Sons, Inc., Indianapolis, Indiana

Published simultaneously in Canada

ISBN: 978-1-118-32832-3

Manufactured in the United States of America

10 9 8 7 6 5 4 3 2 1

For general information on our other products and services or to obtain technical support, please contact our Customer Care Department within the U.S. at (877) 762-2974, outside the U.S. at (317) 572-3993 or fax (317) 572-4002.

Library of Congress Control Number is available from the publisher.

Trademarks: Wiley and the Wiley logo are trademarks or registered trademarks of John Wiley & Sons, Inc., in the United States and other countries, and may not be used without written permission. Autodesk and 3ds Max are registered trademarks of Autodesk, Inc. All other trademarks are the property of their respective owners. John Wiley & Sons, Inc. is not associated with any product or vendor mentioned in this book.

Viewpoint 3D models are copyright Digimation, Inc. All rights reserved.

John Wiley & Sons, Inc. also publishes its books in a variety of electronic formats and by print-on-demand. Some content that appears in standard print versions of this book may not be available in other formats. For more information about John Wiley & Sons, Inc. products, visit us at www.wiley.com.

About the Author

Kelly Murdock has been authoring computer books for many years now and still gets immense enjoyment from the completed work. His book credits include various 3D, graphics, multimedia, and Web titles, including eleven previous editions of this book, *3ds Max Bible*. Other major accomplishments include *Google SketchUp Bible, Edgeloop Character Modeling for 3D Professionals Only, Maya 6 and 7 Revealed, LightWave 3D 8 Revealed, The Official Guide to Anime Studio, Poser 6, 7, and 8 Revealed, 3D Game Animation For Dummies, gmax Bible, Adobe Atmosphere Bible, Master VISUALLY HTML and XHTML, JavaScript Visual Blueprint,* and co-authoring duties on two editions of the *Illustrator Bible* (for versions 9 and 10) and five editions of the *Adobe Creative Suite Bible*.

With a background in engineering and computer graphics, Kelly has been all over the 3D industry and still finds it fascinating. He's used high-level CAD workstations for product design and analysis, completed several large-scale visualization projects, created 3D models for feature films and games, worked as a freelance 3D artist, and even did some 3D programming. Kelly's been using 3D Studio since version 3 for DOS. Kelly has also branched into training others in 3D technologies. He currently works as a freelance graphic artist and video game producer.

In his spare time, Kelly enjoys playing basketball and collecting video games.

Credits

Senior Acquisitions Editor
Stephanie McComb

Project Editor
Martin V. Minner

Technical Editor
Jon McFarland

Copy Editor
Gwenette Gaddis

Editorial Director
Robyn Siesky

Business Manager
Amy Knies

Senior Marketing Manager
Sandy Smith

Vice President and Executive Group Publisher
Richard Swadley

Vice President and Executive Publisher
Barry Pruett

Project Coordinator
Patrick Redmond

Graphics and Production Specialists
Carrie A. Cesavice
Jennifer Creasey
Joyce Haughey
Sennett Vaughan Johnson

Quality Control Technician
Melissa Cossell

Proofreading
Evelyn Wellborn

Indexing
BIM Indexing & Proofreading Services

Vertical Websites Project Manager
Laura Moss-Hollister

Vertical Websites Associate Producer
Marilyn Hummel

We all have a brother or some crazy aunt,
whose movie obsession, understand we just can't.
Be it Star Wars, or Star Trek, or Lord of the Rings,
The movie's praises they loudly do sing.
They keep a count of the times they've seen each show,
and to see the latest movies, they'll wait hours in the snow.
They live as their heroes and quote famous movie lines,
and they cover their rooms with posters and signs.
They play all the games and chat with other fans online,
and their bathroom is decorated to look like a shrine.
They have boxes that are filled with collectibles galore,
with so much stuff you can't even open the door.
They look forward all year for the time of Halloween,
Because the costumes they wear are straight off the screen.
I can't understand all these the super fan views,
Just don't touch my limited edition basketball shoes.

To Kerry and Donna, the obsession rages on
2013

Contents

Contents

Contents

Contents

Contents

Contents

Contents

Contents

Contents

Contents

Contents

Contents

Contents

Contents

Contents

Preface

Every time I enter the computer room (which my wife calls the dungeon), my wife still says that I am off to my "fun and games." I, as always, flatly deny this accusation, saying that it is serious work that I am involved in. But later, when I emerge with a twinkle in my eye and excitedly ask her to take a look at my latest rendering, I know that she is right. Working with the Autodesk® 3ds Max® 2013 software is pure "fun and games."

My goal in writing this book was to take all my fun years of playing and working in 3D and boil them down into something that's worthwhile for you, the reader. This goal was compounded by the fact that all you 3ds Max-heads out there are at different levels. Luckily, this book is thick enough to include a little something for everyone.

The audience level for the book focuses on the beginner, with a smattering of intermediate and advanced topics for the seasoned user. If you're new to 3ds Max, then you'll want to start at the beginning and move methodically through the book. If you're relatively comfortable making your way around 3ds Max, then review the Table of Contents for sections that can enhance your fundamental base. If you're a seasoned pro, then you'll want to watch for coverage of the features new to Release 2013.

As this book has come together, I've tried to write the type of book that I'd like to read. I've tried to include a variety of scenes that are infused with creativity. It is my hope that these examples will not only teach you how to use the software but also provide a creative springboard for you in your own projects. After all, that's what turns 3D graphics from work into "fun and games."

The Growth of 3ds Max?

One way we humans develop our personalities is to incorporate desirable personality traits from those around us. The personality of the 3ds Max software is developing as well: Every new release has incorporated a plethora of desirable new features. Many of these features come from the many additional plug-ins being developed to enhance 3ds Max. With each new release, 3ds Max has adopted many features that were available as plug-ins for previous releases. Several new features have been magically assimilated into the core product, such as the Character Animation Toolkit (CAT) and the Hair and Fur system. These additions make the software's personality much more likable, like a human developing a sense of humor.

Other personality traits are gained by stretching in new directions. 3ds Max and its developers have accomplished this feat as well. Many of the new features are completely new, not only to 3ds Max, but also to the industry. As 3ds Max grows up, it will continue to mature by adopting new features and inventing others. I just hope 3ds Max doesn't experience a midlife crisis in the next version.

Along with adopted features and new developments, the development teams at Autodesk have sought feedback from 3ds Max users. This feedback has resulted in many small tweaks to the package that enable scenes to be created more quickly and easily.

Some additional factors have appeared in the software's house that certainly affect its development. First is the appearance of the software's adopted brother, Maya. There are other siblings in the Autodesk household (including MotionBuilder, Softimage, and AutoCAD), but Maya is closest in age to 3ds Max, and its personality likely will rub off in different ways.

3ds Max also has a split personality with two different versions. The standard 3ds Max 2013 is intended for the entertainment markets, and the 3ds Max Design 2013 package is intended for visualization and architecture users. The differences between these two versions are subtle.

About This Book

Let me paint a picture of the writing process. It starts with years of experience, which are followed by months of painstaking research. There were system crashes and personal catastrophes and the always-present, ever-looming deadlines. I wrote into the early hours of the morning and during the late hours of the night—burning the candle at both ends and in the middle all at the same time. It was grueling and difficult, and spending all this time staring at the 3ds Max interface made me feel like . . . well . . . like a 3d artist.

Sound familiar? This process actually isn't much different from what 3D artists, modelers, and animators do on a daily basis, and, like you, I find satisfaction in the finished product.

Tutorials aplenty

I've always been a very visual learner—the easiest way for me to gain knowledge is by doing things for myself while exploring at the same time. Other people learn by reading and comprehending ideas. In this book, I've tried to present information in a number of ways to make the information usable for all types of learners. That is why you see detailed discussions of the various features along with tutorials that show these concepts in action.

The tutorials appear throughout the book and are clearly marked with the "Tutorial" label in front of the title. They always include a series of logical steps, typically ending with a figure for you to study and compare. These tutorial examples are provided on the book's CD to give you a firsthand look and a chance to get some hands-on experience.

I've attempted to "laser focus" all the tutorials down to one or two key concepts. All tutorials are designed to be completed in 10 steps or less. This means that you probably will not want to place the results in your portfolio. For example, many of the early tutorials don't have any materials applied because I felt that using materials before they've been explained would only confuse you.

I've attempted to think of and use examples that are diverse, unique, and interesting, while striving to make them simple, light, and easy to follow. I'm happy to report that every example in the book is included on the CD along with the models and textures required to complete the tutorial.

The tutorials often don't start from scratch but instead give you a starting point. This approach lets me "laser focus" the tutorials even more, and with fewer, more relevant steps, you can learn and experience the concepts without the complexity. On the book's CD, you will find the 3ds Max files that are referenced in Step 1 of most tutorials.

In addition to the starting-point files, every tutorial has been saved at the completion of the tutorial steps. These files are marked with the word *final* at the end of the filename. If you get stuck in a tutorial, simply open the final example and compare the settings.

I've put lots of effort into this book, and I hope it helps you in your efforts. I present this book as a starting point. In each tutorial, I've purposely left out most of the creative spice, leaving room for you to put it in—you're the one with the vision.

Twelfth time around

This book is now in its 12th edition, and the editors have requested a major shake-up. In this day of mobile devices and tablets, carrying around a huge 1,200-page book is just too much. So, we've opted for a streamlined 800-page book covering all the necessary basics. But, for complete coverage, we're also making an Expanded Edition e-book available that has many more chapters, tutorials, and projects. And the nice part about the e-book is that it doesn't have a page limit, so if you're reading the e-book version, stand squarely in front of the fire hose because there's a lot of information coming your way.

Also for this edition, we've updated the tutorials to reflect the latest 3ds Max features. I've also included a new Quick Start.

How this book is organized

Many different aspects of 3D graphics exist, and in some larger production houses, you might be focused on only one specific area. However, for smaller organizations or the general hobbyist, you end up wearing all the hats—from modeler and lighting director to animator and post-production compositor. This book is organized to cover all the various aspects of 3D graphics, regardless of the hat on your head.

If you're so excited to be working with 3ds Max that you can't decide where to start, then head straight for the Quick Start. The Quick Start is a single chapter-long tutorial that takes you through the creation and animation of an entire scene. For those of you who were too anxious to wade through a mountain of material before you could create something, this Quick Start is for you.

The book is divided into the following parts:

- **Quick Start**—This single chapter (which is actually a chapter in Part I) is an entire animation project presented in several focused tutorials. It is designed to whet your appetite and get you up to speed and producing animations immediately.

- **Part I: Getting Started with Autodesk 3ds Max 2013**—Whether it's understanding the interface, working with the viewports, or dealing with files, the chapters in this part get you comfortable with the interface so you won't get lost moving about this mammoth package.

- **Part II: Manipulating Objects**—3ds Max objects can include meshes, cameras, lights, Space Warps, and anything that can be viewed in a viewport. This part starts by introducing the various primitive objects and also includes chapters on how to reference, select, clone, group, link, and transform these various objects.

- **Part III: Modeling 3D Assets**—3ds Max includes several different ways to model objects. This part includes chapters covering the basic modeling methods and constructs including working with spline shapes, meshes, and polys. It also introduces modifiers and the Modifier Stack.

- **Part IV: Applying Materials and Textures**—This part shows how to apply basic materials and textures to objects including maps using the Slate Material Editor.

- **Part V: Working with Cameras, Lighting, and Rendering**—This part delves into using cameras and lights. It then shows how to render out images using Quicksilver and mental ray, how to use atmospheric and render effects, and ends with some coverage of compositing.

- **Part VI: Animating Objects and Scenes**—The simplest animation features include keyframing, constraints, and controllers. With these topics, you'll be able to animate scenes. It also covers some advanced techniques, including animation layers and modifiers, wiring parameters, and the Track View.

- **Part VII: Working with Characters**—This part covers creating and working with bone systems, rigging, skinning, and the CAT system.

- **Part VIII: Dynamic Animation**—This part covers creating animation sequences using physics calculations. It includes coverage of particles and Space Warps.

- **Appendixes**—At the very end of this book, you'll find two appendixes that cover the new features of 3ds Max 2013 and the contents of the book's CD.

Using the book's icons

The following margin icons are used to help you get the most out of this book:

NOTE

Notes highlight useful information that you should take into consideration.

TIP

Tips provide additional bits of advice that make particular features quicker or easier to use.

CAUTION

Cautions warn you of potential problems before you make a mistake.

NEW FEATURE

The New Feature icon highlights features that are new to the 2013 release.

ON THE CD

This icon points you toward related material on the book's CD.

 Watch for the Cross-Reference icon to learn where in another chapter you can go to find more information on a particular feature.

The book's CD

Computer-book CD-ROMs are sometimes just an afterthought that includes a handful of examples and product demos. This book's CD, however, includes a diverse selection of 3D models that you can use in your projects if you choose. Many of these models are used in the tutorials. The CD also includes the 3ds Max files for every tutorial.

Acknowledgments

I have a host of people to thank for their involvement in this major work. The order in which they are mentioned doesn't necessarily represent the amount of work they did.

Thanks as always to my dear wife, Angela, and my sons, Eric and Thomas, without whose support I wouldn't get very far. They are my QA team and my brainstorming team who always provide honest feedback on my latest example. We have had many family sessions to think of good tutorial examples, and I'm always amazed with what they come up with. One of my favorites that hasn't been implemented yet is a tutorial of a group of bicycles chasing an ice cream truck.

In the first edition, the task at hand was too big for just me, so I shared the pain with two co-authors—Dave Brueck and Sanford Kennedy (both of whom have gone on to write books of their own). I still thank them for their work, which, although overhauled, retains their spirits. In a later edition, I again asked for help, a request that was answered by Sue Blackman. Sue provided several excellent examples that show off the power of the Track View interface. Thanks for your help, Sue.

Major thanks to the editors and personnel at Wiley. I'd like to specifically thank Stephanie McComb, who has managed the whole project and as always done a great job. Her encouragement, dedication, and positive attitude have made a big difference as I've faced some tough deadlines. Huge thanks to Marty Minner (the double M), who has once again managed the entire editing process, and to Gwenette Gaddis for her excellent copyediting input. Marty's comments during the review cycle always crack me up.

I'd also like to thank Jon McFarland for taking on the technical editing. Additional thanks go out to Laura Moss-Hollister and her co-workers in the Media Development department for chasing down the required permissions and for compiling the resources for the CD, and finally, to the entire staff at Wiley who helped me on this journey. Of particular note are the cover designers who have been delightfully stuck on reptiles and amphibians for the covers to the last several editions. I'm starting to refer to the titles by their cover creature; that is, "hand me the frog book next to the lizard book."

The various people who work in the graphics industry are amazing in their willingness to help and support. I'd like to thank first of all Rob Hoffman, Brittany Bonhomme, and the entire Autodesk team for their timely support and help. I'd also like to thank the talented people at Zygote Media, Curious Labs, and Viewpoint Digital Media for many of their models, which make the examples much more interesting. (You can only do so much with the teapot after all.) Additional thanks go out to David Mathis, Sue Blackman, and Chris Murdock for completing models used in some of the tutorials.

Part I

Getting Started with Autodesk 3ds Max 2013

Falling from a Tightrope

IN THIS CHAPTER

Planning the production

Creating and positioning objects

Adding a camera and lights

Rendering a preview

Animating with keyframes

Running a MassFX simulation

Rendering the final animation

When you first sat down to use the Autodesk® 3ds Max® 2013 software, you were probably focused on one goal—creating cool 3D images and animations. I know that many of you bought 3ds Max to make money, claim a tax write-off, earn a way to Hollywood, or impress your girlfriend or boyfriend, but I'll just ignore those reasons for now. The goal is to create something cool.

If you've perused this book's Table of Contents or thumbed through its many pages, you've seen sections on modeling, materials, dynamics, and other topics. But if you're like me, you don't want to wade through tons of material before you have something to show off to Mom. (Actually, if you're like me, you opened straight to the special effects section, in which case you won't be reading this.)

The purpose of this Quick Start is to give you a taste of what 3ds Max can do. This soaring view of the software from 20,000 feet is intended to show you the big picture before you delve into the details. It exposes you to some of the most common features and, I hope, whets your appetite for the more in-depth chapters to follow.

This part of the book is intended for those new to the software. If you're an experienced user, then your mom no doubt is already impressed with your work, so you can happily advance to whichever chapter appeals to you. (Forgive me for catering to the newbie, but we were all beginners once.)

Planning the Production

For this Quick Start, we'll take a trip to the circus to see a character on the tightrope that really shouldn't be there. But don't worry, because the plan is not to have him stay around long. In this example, you'll use the ragdoll feature in the MassFX system to automate the spectacular fall. This gives you a chance to set up a scene, create and position some primitive objects and lights, and work with the MassFX system to animate the untimely accident.

The first thing to consider is setting up the scene. For this sequence, we need some simple cylinders to create the tightrope and the balancing pole. We also need a spot light aimed right at the character, and we need a character. For the character, we're going to use a simple default biped character. After the objects and lights are in place, we can turn our attention to the animation process. We'll start by animating the character struggling to keep its balance for about 30 frames, then we'll turn control over to the MassFX system and let it compute the remaining motions of the fall.

ON THE CD

After each of the following tutorials, I saved the scene file. You can find these files in the Quick Start directory on the book's CD.

Setting Up the Scene

This section on setting up is divided into several simple tutorials. The first step in the production is to create all the objects we need. Then we can position them where we need them.

After the models are in place, we can create the ground plane, and then we're ready to add a camera and light.

Tutorial: Creating the objects

Your first step begins with creating and positioning the tightrope and the balance pole. Then we can create the biped skeleton and position it at its initial location. To create and position the objects, follow these steps:

1. Reset the interface with the Application Button ⇨ Reset menu command. Answer Yes in the warning box that appears to confirm the reset.

2. In the Command Panel, click the Cylinder button, drag in the Front viewport to create a circular base, and then click and drag again to define the cylinder's height. In the Parameters rollout, set the Radius to **2** and the Height to **500**. Then type the name **Tightrope** in the Name field in the Name and Color rollout.

NOTE

This Quick Start uses Generic Units. You can change the units using the Units Setup dialog box, which you open using the Customize ⇨ Units Setup menu command.

3. Click the Select and Move button on the main toolbar, and drag the red X-axis to the left in the Left viewport to center the tightrope about the origin. Then drag the green Y-axis upward in the Left viewport to move the tightrope above the ground plane.

4. Drag on the ViewCube in the Perspective viewport until the view changes so that the tightrope object runs diagonally through the viewport.

The tightrope is positioned, as shown in Figure QS.1.

FIGURE QS.1

The tightrope is now in place.

Tutorial: Balancing the biped

The next object to add is the biped, which we need to balance on the tightrope.

To position the balanced biped on the tightrope, follow these steps:

1. Select the Create ⇨ Systems ⇨ Biped menu command, and drag in the Top viewport to create a biped skeleton. The height of the biped should be about half the height from the ground to the tightrope.

2. Using the Select and Move tool in the main toolbar, drag the green Y-axis in the Left viewport upward to position the biped so its feet are just above the tightrope.

3. Select the biped's right foot, and move it in the Front viewport to be centered over the tightrope and in the Left viewport to be behind the left foot. Then repeat similar moves for the right foot until the body is balanced with the left foot in front of the right foot standing on the tightrope.

4. With the biped's feet in place, select and move the tightrope upward until it just touches the bottoms of both feet.

5. Click the Select and Rotate tool in the main toolbar, and rotate the left and right upper arms until they stick straight out from the body on either side.

The biped skeleton is now balancing nicely on the tightrope, as shown in Figure QS.2. He'll be alright as long as he doesn't try to move.

FIGURE QS.2

The biped is balanced on the tightrope.

Tutorial: Adding a balance pole

Next we'll add a balance pole to the scene. This should make the biped feel safer, but actually we just want to have another object that will be falling along with our character.

To add a balance pole, follow these steps:

1. Click the Geometry button in the Command Panel, and click the Cylinder button. Then click and drag in the Left viewport to set the circular base and again to set the cylinder height. Create a cylinder that runs parallel to the biped's arms. Set the Radius value to **1** and the Height to **200**.

2. Click the Hierarchy panel in the Command Panel, click the Affect Pivot Only button in the Adjust Pivot rollout. Then click the Center to Object button, and click the Affect Pivot Only button again to exit pivot mode. This moves the pivot point to the center of the balance pole.

3. Move the cylinder in the Left viewport so it's in front of the biped, and center it on the tightrope in the Top viewport.

4. Select and rotate the upper arms in the Top viewport toward the balance pole about 15 degrees and then downward in the Front viewport about 15 degrees also. Then select and rotate the lower arm until the hands are over the balance pole in the Top viewport.

5. Finally, select and move the balance pole upward in the Left viewport until it is just under the hands.

The balance pole is now in place, as shown in Figure QS.3.

FIGURE QS.3

The balance pole surely makes the biped feel more comfortable.

Adding a Camera and Light

The modeling phase, which usually is quite time-consuming, went really quickly when we used the default primitives, and because we're not adding materials, we can jump straight to the placement of a camera and lights.

Tutorial: Adding a camera and light

We'll use only a single camera, but we want a camera to follow the biped's fall down. If the viewport view was used, we wouldn't have control over following the fall.

To add single camera to the scene, follow these steps:

1. Click in the Perspective viewport, and select the Views ⇨ Create Camera from View menu command to automatically create a camera that is positioned to create this same view.

2. Select the Create ⇨ Lights ⇨ Standard Lights ⇨ Target Spotlight and drag from the top-right corner of the Left viewport to the center of the biped.

3. Select the Create ⇨ Lights ⇨ Standard Lights ⇨ Omni menu command, and click in the Left viewport. Then position the Omni light underneath and to the side of the biped. In the Intensity/Color/Attenuation rollout, set the Multiplier value to **0.5** and make sure the Shadows On option in the General Parameters rollout is disabled. This secondary light provides some additional lighting to the scene.

The viewports by default render with a black background, so with the camera and lights in place, we have a scene setup complete. Figure QS.4 shows the light and camera positions.

FIGURE QS.4

With the camera and lights in position, the scene is ready to go.

Tutorial: Rendering a test preview

Before moving to animation, you can render the scene now that lights have been added. Rendering is configured using the Render Setup dialog box accessed from the Rendering menu.

To render a preview of the tightrope biped, follow these steps:

1. Select the Camera001 viewport.

2. Choose the Rendering ⇨ Render menu command (or press the F9 key).

The scene is rendered in the Rendered Frame Window, as shown in Figure QS.5, includes the lighting.

FIGURE QS.5

A test render shows that the lights are working fine.

Animating the Great Fall

With the test render complete and the scene looking good, we can move to the animation phase. This phase starts with some simple keyframe animation and then uses the MassFX tools to create a dynamic animation for the final fall.

Tutorial: Creating animation keys

When creating animation keys, we can simply turn on the Auto Key feature and all the keys are set every time when make a change for each new frame we select. We want to animate using keyframes from the start to frame 25. We want the fall to be at frame 25, so we use the MassFX system at this point.

To create some simple animation keys, follow these steps:

1. Click the Auto Key button at the bottom of the interface. Notice that the button turns red to remind us that it is enabled.

2. Drag the Time Slider to frame 10, and select and lift the front foot upward in the Left viewport.

3. Drag the Time Slider back to frame 8, select the one of the middle spine bones, and barely rotate it to the left in the Front viewport to create a key. Then drag the Time Slider to frame 10, and rotate the middle spine bone about 5 degrees to create another key.

4. Drag the Time Slider to frame 12, and move the front foot back to the tightrope in the Left viewport.

5. Drag the Time Slider to frame 15, and rotate the middle spine bone to the right in the Front viewport about 10 degrees.

6. Drag the Time Slider to frame 20, and rotate the middle spine bone to the left in the Front viewport about 15 degrees.

7. Drag the Time Slider to frame 25, and rotate the middle spine bone to the right in the Front viewport about 20 degrees.

8. Click the Auto Key button again to disable Auto Key mode.

Figure QS.6 shows the scene after the keyframes have been set.

FIGURE QS.6

All keyframes for the selected object show up on the Track Bar under the Time Slider.

Tutorial: Linking objects

If you play through the animation, you'll notice it seems odd that the balance pole doesn't move with the biped; we can easily fix that with a link.

To animate the balance pole by linking, follow these steps:

1. Select the balance pole object, click the Select and Link button on the main toolbar, and then drag from the balance pole to the middle spine bone to create a link.

2. Drag the Time Slider through the animated frames, and notice how the pole now moves with the biped but that the hands are off.

3. Enable the Auto Key button again, drag the Time Slider to frame 0, and move the right and left hands in the Front viewport to be positioned on the balance pole. Repeat this step for frames 10, 12, 15, 20, and 25.

4. Click the Auto Key button again to disable Auto Key mode.

Figure QS.7 shows the rotating balance pole and the hands that move with it.

FIGURE QS.7

A link between the balance pole on the rotating spine makes the pole rotate also.

Tutorial: Animating with MassFX

Now that we have some simple keyframe animation, we can set up the MassFX system and let it create the falling motions using physics.

To animate the final fall using MassFX, follow these steps:

1. Right-click the toolbar away from the buttons, and select MassFX from the pop-up menu to open the MassFX toolbar.

2. Select the balance pole, and click the Set Selected as Dynamic Rigid Body button in the MassFX toolbar.

3. Select the tightrope object, and click the Set Selected as Static Rigid Body button (which is a flyout under the Dynamic Rigid Body button).

4. Double-click the biped's pelvis to select the entire biped hierarchy, and then click the Create Dynamic Ragdoll button in the MassFX toolbar.

5. Click the Time Configuration button near the Play button at the lower-right corner of the interface, set the Start Time to **26**, and click OK.

6. In the MassFX toolbar, click the Start Simulation button. Let the simulation run to frame 100.

7. Open the Simulation Tools panel in the MassFX Tools dialog box by clicking its button in the MassFX toolbar located as a flyout under the World Parameters button, and then click the Bake All button to add all the keys for the simulation to the Track Bar.

8. Open the Time Configuration dialog box again, and set the Start Time back to **0**.

9. Click the Play button to see the result animation with the keyframe and dynamic animations combined.

Figure QS.8 shows one frame of the tragic fall, compliments of the MassFX system.

FIGURE QS.8

The final animation includes both keyframe and dynamic animations.

Tutorial: Rendering the final animation

When the simulation looks good in the viewport, you are ready to render the final animation. This is a process that you can start by specifying the animation format. Once started, 3ds Max automatically proceeds through all the frames of the animation and notifies you when it is completed.

To render the final animation, follow these steps:

1. Select the Rendering ⇨ Render Setup menu command to open the Render Setup dialog box.
2. At the top of the dialog box, enable the Active Time Segment so that all 100 frames of the animation are rendered. Then set the Output Size to 640x480.
3. In the Render Output section, click the Files button to open a file dialog box. Set the format as AVI, give the file a name such as Tightrope fall, and click the Save button. In the AVI Compression Setup dialog box that appears, simply select the default and click OK.
4. At the very bottom of the Render Setup dialog box, make sure the Camera001 view is selected and click the Render button.

3ds Max then renders each frame of the animation and shows its progress in a dialog box. When completed, the final animation file is saved with the filename you entered. You then can locate and play it. Figure QS.9 shows a frame of the final animation.

FIGURE QS.9

The final animation includes rendered results of each frame.

Summary

I hope you're happy with your first footsteps into 3ds Max. This chapter exposed you to a number of important aspects of 3ds Max, including the following:

- Setting up a scene
- Creating and positioning objects
- Adding a camera and lights
- Rendering test previews
- Animating using keyframes
- Linking objects
- Running dynamic simulations using MassFX
- Rendering the final animation

But hold onto your seats, because so much of the software lies ahead. In Chapter 1, you start easily with an in-depth look at the 3ds Max interface. If you feel ready for more advanced challenges, review the Table of Contents and dive into any topic that looks good.

Exploring the Interface

IN THIS CHAPTER

Learning the interface elements

Previewing the menu commands

Becoming familiar with the toolbars

Using the Command Panel

Examining the Lower Interface Bar

Interacting with the interface

Defining workspaces

Getting help

W ell, welcome to the latest version of the Autodesk® 3ds Max® 2013 software, and the first question on the minds of existing users is, "Did the interface change?" The answer is a happy "very little." Most serious users would rather go through root canal surgery than have their user interface (UI) change, and Autodesk has learned and respected this valued opinion by keeping the interface changes to a minimum.

As you look around the new interface, you'll see that everything is still there, but that 3ds Max has a few new additions. You may find yourself saying, as you navigate the interface, "Where did that come from?" But, just like encountering a new house in your neighborhood, over time you'll become accustomed to the addition and may even meet some new friends.

Why is the software interface so important? Well, consider this: The interface is the set of controls that enable you to access the program's features. Without a good interface, you may never use many of the best features of the software or you may spend a frustrating bit of time locating those features. A piece of software can have all the greatest features, but if the user can't find or access them, then the software won't be used to its full potential. 3ds Max is a powerful piece of software with some amazing features, and luckily the interface makes these amazing features easy to find and use, but the interface can be a little daunting to new users.

The interface's purpose is to make the software features accessible, and in 3ds Max you have many different ways to access the features. Some of these access methods are faster than others. This design is intentional because it gives beginning users an intuitive command and advanced users direct access. For example, to undo a command, you can choose Edit⇔Undo (requiring two mouse clicks), but as you gain more experience, you can simply click the Undo icon on the Quick Access toolbar (only one click); an expert with his hands on the keyboard can press Ctrl+Z without having to reach for the mouse at all. All three of these methods have the same result, but you can use the one that is easiest for you.

Has the 3ds Max interface succeeded? Yes, to a degree, but like most interfaces, it always has room for improvement, and we hope that each new version takes us closer to the perfect interface (but I'm still looking for the "read my thoughts" feature). Autodesk has built a loophole into the program to cover anyone who complains about the interface—customization. If you don't like the current interface, you can change it to be exactly what you want.

This chapter examines the latest incarnation of the 3ds Max interface and presents some tips that make the interface feel comfortable, not cumbersome.

> **NOTE**
>
> When 3ds Max starts, the default color scheme uses dark gray colors with white text. Although this scheme works great for artists who stare at a computer monitor for long periods of time with little or no background light, it isn't the ideal setting for printing. All the figures in this book use the alternate lighter gray color scheme. You can easily switch between the different color schemes using the Customize ⇨ Custom UI and Defaults Switcher menu command.

Learning the Interface Elements

If you're new to the 3ds Max interface, the first order of business is to take a stroll around the block and meet the neighbors. The interface has a number of elements that neatly group all the similar commands together. For example, all the commands for controlling the viewports are grouped together in the Viewport Navigation Controls found in the lower-right corner of the interface.

> **NOTE**
>
> If all the details of every interface command were covered in this chapter, it would be an awfully long chapter. So for those commands that are covered in more detail elsewhere, I include a cross-reference to the chapter where you can find their coverage.

The entire interface can be divided into six easy elements. Each of these interface elements, in turn, has groupings of sub-elements. The six main interface elements are listed here and shown separated in Figure 1.1:

- **Title bar and menus:** This is the default source for most commands, but also one of the most time-consuming interface methods. The title bar and menus are found along the top edge of the 3ds Max window.
- **Toolbars:** 3ds Max includes several toolbars of icon buttons that provide single-click access to features. These toolbars can float independently or be docked to an interface edge. The main toolbar and the Viewport Layout toolbar are visible by default.
- **Modelingribbon:** Located under the main toolbar, the Modeling ribbon provides quick access to the polygon modeling features, including the Graphite Modeling Tools. It is populated with panels, buttons, and menus when a modeling object is selected.

- **Viewports:** Four separate views into the scene show the scene from different points of view including Top, Front, Left, and Perspective.
- **Command Panel:** The major control panel located to the right of the four viewports, it has six tabbed icons at its top that you can click to open the various panels. Each panel includes rollouts containing parameters and settings. These rollouts change, depending on the object and tab that is selected.
- **Lowerinterfacebar:** Along the bottom edge of the interface window is a collection of miscellaneous controls for working with animations and navigating the viewports.

NEW FEATURE
The Viewport Layout toolbar is new to 3ds Max 2013.

FIGURE 1.1

3ds Max includes six main interface elements.

In addition to these default elements are several additional interface elements that aren't initially visible when 3ds Max is first loaded. These additional interface elements include the following:

- **Floating toolbars:** Several additional toolbars are available as floating toolbars. You access them by choosing Customize ⇨ Show UI ⇨ Show Floating Toolbars or by selecting them from the main toolbar's right-click pop-up menu.

- **Quad menus:** Right-clicking the active viewport reveals a pop-up menu with up to four panes, referred to as a quad menu. *Quad menus* offer context-sensitive commands based on the object or location being clicked and provide one of the quickest ways to access commands.

- **Caddy settings:** When modeling, you can open Caddy settings. This group of settings floats in a simple dialog box near the current selection and offer several settings that are immediately updated in the viewport.

- **Dialog boxes and editors:** Some commands open a separate window of controls such as the Array dialog box or the Material Editor. These dialog boxes may contain their own menus, toolbars, and interface elements.

Using the Menus

The pull-down menus at the top of the 3ds Max interface include most of the features available in 3ds Max and are a great place for beginners to start. Several of the menu commands have corresponding toolbar buttons and keyboard shortcuts. To execute a menu command, you can choose it from the menu with the mouse cursor, click its corresponding toolbar button if it has one, or press its keyboard shortcut.

The main menu includes the following options: Application Button, Edit, Tools, Group, Views, Create, Modifiers, Animation, Graph Editors, Rendering, Customize, MAXScript, and Help. Unlike some other programs, these menu options do not disappear if not needed. The list is set, and they are always there when you need them.

The File menu commands are located under a button that displays the 3ds Max logo. This is called the Application Button. Some of the more common commands have been located on the Quick Access toolbar for quick access, as shown in Figure 1.2.

FIGURE 1.2

The 3ds Max title bar includes the Application Button, the Quick Access toolbar, and the InfoCenter toolbar.

If a keyboard command is available for a menu command, it is shown to the right of the menu item. If an ellipsis (three dots) appears after a menu item, that menu command causes a separate dialog box to open. A small black arrow to the right of a menu item indicates that a submenu exists. Clicking the menu item or holding the mouse over the top of a menu item makes the submenu appear. Toggle menu options (such as Views ⇨ Show Ghosting) change state each time they are selected. If a toggle menu option is enabled, a small check mark appears to its left; if disabled, no check mark appears.

You also can navigate the menus using the keyboard by pressing the Alt key by itself. Doing so selects the Edit menu, and then you can use the arrow keys to move up and down and between menus. With a menu selected, you can press the keyboard letter that is underlined to select and execute a menu command. For example, pressing and holding down the Alt and then E (for Edit) and then pressing U (for Undo) executes the Edit ⇨ Undo command; or you can press Alt, use the down arrow to select the Undo command, and press the Enter key.

TIP

By learning the underlined letters in the menu, you can use the keyboard to quickly access menu commands, even if the menu command doesn't have an assigned keyboard shortcut. And because you don't need to stretch for the Y key while holding down the Ctrl key, underlined menu letters can be faster. For example, by pressing and holding Alt, then pressing the G, and U keys successively, you can access the Group ⇨ Ungroup menu command. The keyboard buffer remembers the order of the letters you type regardless of how fast you key them, making it possible to quickly access menu commands using the keyboard. Over time, you can learn patterns to help you remember how to access certain menu commands, such as Alt, C, H, E for creating an ellipse.

Not all menu commands are available at all times. If a menu command is unavailable, then it is grayed out, as shown in Figure 1.3, and you cannot select it. For example, the Clone command is available only when an object is selected, so if no objects are selected, the Clone command is grayed out and unavailable. After you select an object, this command becomes available.

FIGURE 1.3

All menus feature visual clues.

> **TIP**
> If you right-click the menu bar, you can access a pop-up command to hide the menu bar. If you accidentally dismiss the menu bar, you can recover it clicking on the menu arrow located at the right end of the Quick Access toolbar and choosing the Show Menu Bar command.

Using the Toolbars

Now that you've learned the menu two-step, it is time for the toolbar one-step. The main toolbar appears by default directly under the menus at the top of the 3ds Max window. Using toolbars is one of the most convenient ways to execute commands because most commands require only a single click.

Docking and floating toolbars

By default, the main toolbar is docked along the top edge of the interface just below the menus, but you can make any docked toolbar (including the main toolbar) a floating toolbar by clicking and dragging the two vertical lines on the left (or top) end of the toolbar away from the interface edge. After you separate it from the window, you can resize the floating toolbar by dragging on its edges or corners. You can then drag and dock it to any of the window edges or double-click the toolbar title bar to automatically dock the toolbar to its latest docked location. Figure 1.4 shows the main toolbar as a floating panel.

If you right-click any floating toolbar away from the buttons, you can access a pop-up menu that includes options to dock or float the current toolbar, access the Customize User Interface window, or show or hide any of the toolbars or the Command Panel. The main toolbar can be hidden and made visible again with the Alt+6 keyboard shortcut toggle.

FIGURE 1.4

The main toolbar includes buttons and drop-down lists for controlling many of the most popular 3ds Max functions.

If you select the Customize ⇨ Show UI ⇨ Show Floating Toolbars menu command, several additional toolbars appear. These are floating toolbars. You also can make them appear by selecting them individually from the toolbar right-click pop-up menu. These floating toolbars include Viewport Layout Tabs, Axis Constraints, Layers, Extras, Render Shortcuts, Snaps, Animation Layers, Containers, MassFX Toolbar, and Brush Presets.

The Quick Access toolbar and the InfoCenter toolbar, located on the title bar at the top of the interface, don't act like the other toolbars and cannot be pulled away from the title bar.

Using tooltips and flyouts

All icon buttons (including those found in toolbars, the Command Panel, and other dialog boxes and windows) include tooltips, which are identifying text labels. If you hold the mouse cursor over an icon button, the tooltip label appears. This feature is useful for identifying buttons. If you can't remember what a specific button does, hold the cursor over the top of it and the tooltip gives you its name.

All toolbar buttons with a small triangle in the lower-right corner, such as the Rectangular Selection Region button, are flyouts. A *flyout* is a single toolbar button that expands to reveal additional buttons. Click and hold on the flyout to reveal the additional icons, and drag to select one. Figure 1.5 shows the flyout for the Align button on the main toolbar.

FIGURE 1.5

Flyout menus bundle several toolbar buttons together.

Flyout menu

> **NOTE**
>
> The General panel of the Preference Settings dialog box contains an option for setting the number of milliseconds to wait before the flyout appears.

Using the Quick Access toolbar

Located next to the Application Button on the title bar is the Quick Access toolbar. This mini toolbar includes icons for the following commands: New Scene, Open File, Save File, Undo Scene Operations, Redo Scene Operations, and Project Folder. A drop-down list also allows you to change the Workspace layout. If you click the down-arrow icon on the right end of the toolbar, you can access a menu with options to hide any one of the icons or the menus. You also can select to show the toolbar beneath the Ribbon.

Learning the main toolbar

On smaller-resolution screens, the main toolbar is too long to be entirely visible. To see the entire main toolbar, you need to set your monitor resolution to be at least 1280 pixels wide. To scroll the toolbar to see the end, position the cursor on the toolbar away from the buttons, such as below one of the drop-down lists (the cursor changes to a hand); then click and drag the toolbar in either direction.

Using the hand cursor to scroll also works in the Command Panel, Material Editor, and any other place where the panel exceeds the given space.

> **TIP**
> The easiest way to scroll the main toolbar is to drag with the middle mouse button because you can click anywhere on the toolbar and drag.

Toolbar buttons that open dialog boxes such as the Layer Manager, Material Editor, and Render Setup buttons are toggle buttons. When the dialog box is open, the button is highlighted, indicating that the dialog box is open. Clicking a highlighted toggle button closes the dialog box. Corresponding menus (and keyboard shortcuts) work the same way, with a small check mark appearing to the left of the menu command when a dialog box is opened.

Table 1.1 lists the controls found in the main toolbar. Buttons with flyouts are separated with commas.

TABLE 1.1   Main Toolbar Buttons

Toolbar Button	Name	Description
	Select and Link	Establishes links between objects.
	Unlink Selection	Breaks links between objects.
	Bind to Space Warp	Assigns objects to be modified by a space warp.
	Selection Filter drop-down list	Limits the type of objects that can be selected.
	Select Object (Q)	Chooses an object.
	Select by Name (H)	Opens a dialog box for selecting objects by name.
	Rectangular Selection Region, Circular Selection Region, Fence Selection Region, Lasso Selection Region, Paint Selection Region (Ctrl+F to cycle)	Determines the shape used for selecting objects in the viewport.
	Window/Crossing Toggle	Specifies whether an object must be crossed or windowed to be selected.
	Select and Move (W)	Selects an object and allows positional translations.
	Select and Rotate (E)	Selects an object and allows rotational transforms.

Toolbar Button	Name	Description
	Select and Uniform Scale, Select and Non-uniform Scale, Select and Squash (R to cycle)	Selects an object and allows scaling transforms using different methods.
View ▼	Reference Coordinate System drop-down list	Specifies the coordinate system used for transforms.
	Use Pivot Point Center, Use Selection Center, Use Transform Coordinate Center	Specifies the center about which rotations and scaling are completed.
	Select and Manipulate	Selects an object and allows parameter manipulation via a manipulator.
	Keyboard Shortcut Override Toggle	Allows keyboard shortcuts for the main interface and the active dialog box or feature set to be used when enabled. Only main interface shortcuts are available when disabled.
	Snap Toggle 2D, Snap Toggle 2.5D, Snap Toggle 3D (S)	Specifies the snap mode. 2D snaps only to the active construction grid, 2.5D snaps to the construction grid or to geometry projected from the grid, and 3D snaps to anywhere in 3D space.
	Angle Snap Toggle (A)	Causes rotations to snap to specified angles.
	Percent Snap (Shift+Ctrl+P)	Causes scaling to snap to specified percentages.
	Spinner Snap Toggle	Determines the amount a spinner value changes with each click.
	Edit Named Selection Sets	Opens a dialog box for creating and managing selection sets.
New Set ▼	Named Selection Sets drop-down list	Lists and allows you to select a set of named objects.
	Mirror	Creates a mirrored copy of the selected object.
	Align (Alt+A), Quick Align, Normal Align (Alt+N), Place Highlight, Align Camera, Align to View	Opens the alignment dialog box for positioning objects, allows objects to be aligned by their normals, determines the location of highlights, and aligns objects to a camera or view.
	Manage Layers	Opens the Layer Manager interface where you can work with layers.
	Graphite Modeling Tools	Opens the Graphite Modeling Tools panel.

continued

TABLE 1.1   *(continued)*

Toolbar Button	Name	Description
	Curve Editor (Open)	Opens the Function Curves Editor.
	Schematic View (Open)	Opens the Schematic View window.
	Compact Material Editor (M), Slate Material Editor (M)	Opens either the Compact Material Editor window or the Slate Material Editor window.
	Render Setup (F10)	Opens the Render Setup dialog box for setting rendering options.
	Rendered Frame Window	Opens the Rendered Frame Window.
	Render Production, Render Iterative, ActiveShade	Produces a quick test rendering of the current viewport without opening the Render Setup dialog box using the production settings, the iterative render mode, or the ActiveShade window.

Using the Modeling Ribbon

The Modeling Ribbon interface is a deluxe toolbar with many different tool sections. It currently is populated with a variety of modeling tools that are collectively called the Graphite Modeling Tools. You can turn the Modeling Ribbon on and off using the Graphite Modeling Tools button on the main toolbar. When enabled, tabs for the Graphite Modeling Tools, Freeform, Selection, and Object Paint are displayed.

 Most Modeling Ribbon buttons are visible only when an Editable Poly object is selected. You can learn more about Editable Poly objects and the Graphite Modeling Tools in Chapter 11, "Modeling with Polygons," and Chapter 12, "Using the Graphite Modeling Tools."

Using the Minimize Ribbon button at the right end of the Ribbon, you can switch the display mode to minimize to only the tabs, only the panel titles, or only the panel buttons, or to enable the Minimize button to cycle through each of the modes. You also can double-click the Ribbon tabs to minimize the Ribbon or to cycle through the minimized modes.

Right-click the Ribbon title bar to access menu options to show or hide specific tabs or panels, customize the ribbon, save or load a custom ribbon configuration, switch between horizontal and vertical orientations, reset the ribbon to its default, or enable tooltips. Figure 1.6 shows the different Ribbon display modes.

The entire Ribbon, as well as each individual panel of buttons, can be made into a floating control by dragging the Ribbon title bar or the lower panel bar away from the rest of the buttons. When a panel is made into a floating panel, like the one in Figure 1.7, the icons in the upper right of the floating panel let you return the panel to the Ribbon or toggle the orientation between vertical and horizontal. You also can move the floating panel about by dragging on the gray bar on either side of the panel.

FIGURE 1.6

The Ribbon can be set to be displayed using several different modes.

Ribbon Tabs display mode   Minimize Ribbon button

Panel Titles display mode

Panel Buttons display mode

Full Ribbon display mode

FIGURE 1.7

Ribbon panels can float independent of each other.

Return panel to Ribbon

Toggle Orientation

Using the Viewports

The four viewports make up the largest area of the entire interface and provide a way of viewing the objects within the scene. Each of the viewports is configurable and can be unique from the others.

 Understanding how to work with the viewports is vital to accomplishing tasks with 3ds Max, so viewports have an entire chapter dedicated just to them—Chapter 2, "Controlling the Viewports."

Using the Command Panel

If there is one place in 3ds Max, besides the viewports, where you'll spend all your time, it's the Command Panel (at least until you're comfortable enough with the quad menus). The Command Panel is located to the right of the viewports along the right edge of the interface. This is where all the specific parameters, settings, and controls are located. The Command Panel is split into six panels, each accessed via a tab icon located at its top. These six tabs are Create, Modify, Hierarchy, Motion, Display, and Utilities.

You can pull away the Command Panel from the right window edge as a floating dialog box, as shown in Figure 1.8, by clicking the open space to the right of the tabbed icons at the top of the Command Panel and dragging away from the interface edge. You also can dock it to the left window edge, which is really handy if you're left-handed. While it's a floating panel, you can resize the Command Panel by dragging on its edges or corners (but its width remains constant).

After you've pulled the Command Panel or any of the toolbars away from the interface, you can redock them to their last position by double-clicking their title bar. You also can right-click the title bar to access the pop-up menu of floating toolbars, but the pop-up menu also includes options to Dock (either Left or Right for the Command Panel or Left, Right, Top, or Bottom for toolbars), Float, and Minimize.

FIGURE 1.8

The Command Panel includes six separate panels accessed via tab icons.

The right-click pop-up menu for the Command Panel also includes a Minimize command. If enabled, the Command Panel collapses to the edge of the interface, but moving the mouse near the interface where the Command Panel is minimized expands the Command Panel again. Moving the mouse away from the Command Panel makes it collapse to the interface edge again. You can take the Command Panel out of Minimize mode by selecting one of the Dock commands.

Working with rollouts

Most of the controls, buttons, and parameters in the Command Panel are contained within sections called rollouts. A *rollout* is a grouping of controls positioned under a gray, boxed title, as shown in Figure 1.9. Each rollout title bar includes a plus or minus sign (a minus sign indicates that the rollout is open; a plus sign shows closed rollouts). Clicking the rollout title opens or closes the rollout. You also can reposition the order of the rollouts by dragging the rollout title and dropping it above or below the other rollouts.

> **NOTE**
>
> You cannot reposition some of the rollouts, such as the Object Type and the Name and Color rollouts, found in the Create panel.

FIGURE 1.9

Open and close rollouts by clicking the rollout title.

— Opened rollout

— Closed rollout

Right-clicking away from the buttons in a rollout presents a pop-up menu where you can select to close the rollout you've clicked in, Close All, Open All, or Reset Rollout Order. The pop-up menu also lists all available rollouts within the current panel with a check mark next to the ones that are open.

Expanding all the rollouts often exceeds the screen space allotted to the Command Panel. If the rollouts exceed the given space, then a small vertical scroll bar appears at the right edge of the Command Panel. You can drag this scroll bar to access the rollouts at the bottom of the Command Panel, or you can click away from the controls when a hand cursor appears. With the hand cursor, click and drag in either direction to scroll the Command Panel. You also can scroll the Command Panel with the scroll wheel on the mouse or by dragging with the middle mouse button.

Increasing the Command Panel's width

The Command Panel can be doubled or tripled (or any multiple, as long as you have room) in width by dragging its left edge toward the center of the interface. The width of the Command Panel is increased at the expense of the viewports. Figure 1.10 shows the Command Panel double its normal size.

FIGURE 1.10

Increase the width of the Command Panel by dragging its left edge.

Tutorial: Rearranging the interface for lefties

I used to work for a company that required that all computers have the mouse to the left of the keyboard. We swapped computers often, and the boss hated having to move the mouse to the other side of the keyboard (and you thought your work environment was weird). The reality is that some people like it on the left and others prefer it on the right, and 3ds Max can accommodate both.

With the Command Panel on the right side of the interface, the default interface obviously favors right-handers, but with the docking panels, you can quickly change it to be friendly to lefties.

To rearrange the interface for lefties, follow these steps:

1. Click the Command Panel on the empty space to the right of the last tab (the Utilities tab), and drag toward the center of the interface. As you drag the Command Panel away from the right edge, the cursor changes.

2. Continue to drag the Command Panel to the left edge, and the cursor changes again to indicate that it will be docked when released. Release the mouse button, and the Command Panel docks to the left side.

3. For an even easier method, you can right-click the Command Panel's title bar and select Dock ⇨ Left from the pop-up menu.

Figure 1.11 shows the rearranged interface ready for all you southpaws.

> **TIP**
>
> If you've made changes to the interface that you want to keep, try saving a workspace using the Quick Access toolbar. Workspaces can be immediately recalled using the drop-down list. Workspaces are covered later in this chapter.

FIGURE 1.11

Left-handed users can move the Command Panel to the left side.

Using the Lower Interface Bar Controls

The last major interface element isn't really an interface element but just a collection of several sets of controls located along the bottom edge of the interface window. These controls cannot be pulled away from the interface like the main toolbar, but you can hide them using Expert Mode (Ctrl+X). These controls, shown in Figure 1.12, include the following, from left to right:

- **Time Slider:** The Time Slider, located under the viewports, enables you to quickly locate a specific animation frame. It spans the number of frames included in the current animation. Dragging the Time Slider moves you quickly between frames. Clicking the arrow buttons on either side of the Time Slider moves to the previous or next frame (or key).

- **Track Bar:** The Track Bar displays animation keys as color-coded rectangles with red for positional keys, green for rotational keys, and blue for scale keys. Parameter change keys are denoted by gray rectangles. Using the Track Bar, you can select, move, and delete animation keys. The button at the left end of the Track Bar is the Open Mini Curve Editor button. It provides access to the animation function curves.

- **Status Bar:** The Status Bar is below the Track Bar. It provides valuable information, such as the number and type of objects selected, transformation values, and grid size. It also includes the Selection Lock Toggle, Transform Type-In fields, and the value of the current Grid size.

- **Prompt Line:** The Prompt Line is text located at the bottom of the window. If you're stuck as to what to do next, look at the Prompt Line for information on what 3ds Max expects. The Prompt Line also includes buttons for enabling Progressive Display and adding and editing Time Tags, which are used to name specific animation frames.

- **Key Controls:** These controls are for creating animation keys and include two different modes—Auto Key (keyboard shortcut, N) and Set Key (keyboard shortcut, '). Auto Key mode sets keys for any changes made to the scene objects. Set Key mode gives you more precise control and sets keys for the selected filters only when you click the Set Keys button (keyboard shortcut, K).

- **Time Controls:** Resembling the controls on an audio or video device, the Time Controls offer an easy way to move through the various animation frames and keys. Based on the selected mode (keys or frames), the Time Controls can move among the first, previous, next, and last frames or keys.

- **Viewport Navigation Controls:** In the lower-right corner of the interface are the controls for manipulating the viewports. They enable you to zoom, pan, and rotate the active viewport's view.

> Most of the controls on the lower interface bar—including the Time Slider, the Track Bar, and the Key and Time Controls—deal with animation. You can learn more about these controls in Chapter 24, "Understanding Animation and Keyframes." The Viewport Navigation Controls are covered in Chapter 2, "Controlling the Viewports."

FIGURE 1.12

The lower interface bar includes several sets of controls.

Interacting with the Interface

Knowing where all the interface elements are located is only the start. 3ds Max includes several interactive features that make the interface work. Learning these features makes the difference between an interface that works for you and one that doesn't.

Gaining quick access with the right-click quad menus

Quad menus are pop-up menus with up to four separate sections that surround the cursor, as shown in Figure 1.13. Right-clicking in the active viewport opens these quad menus. The contents of the menus depend on the object selected.

> **TIP**
>
> Many of the real pros use quad menus extensively. One reason is that they can access the commands from the mouse's current location using a couple of clicks without having to go all the way to the Command Panel to click a button.

FIGURE 1.13

Quad menus contain a host of commands in an easily accessible location.

Clicking with the left mouse button away from the quad menu closes it. For each menu, the text of the last menu item selected is displayed in blue. To quickly access the blue menu item again, simply click the gray-shaded bar for the quadrant that contains the blue menu item. Using Customize ⇨ Customize User Interface, you can specify which commands appear on the quad menus, but the default options have just about everything you need.

If you press and hold the Alt, Ctrl, and Shift keys while right-clicking in the active viewport, you can access specific sets of commands; Shift+right-click opens the Snap options, Alt+right-click opens Animation commands, Ctrl+right-click opens a menu of primitives, Shift+Alt+right-click opens a menu of MassFx commands, and Ctrl+Alt+right-click opens a menu of rendering commands.

Using Caddy controls

Quad menus are great for accessing specific commands, but changing the settings for the various features still requires that you visit the Command Panel. This is where the Caddy controls help. Certain modeling features such as Bevel and Extrude let you open a select set of controls, known as a Caddy, overlaid over the selected object, as shown in Figure 1.14. Changing any of these settings updates the selection and lets you see if the change is what you want. If you're happy with the setting, you can accept the change and dismiss the Caddy control.

A key benefit of the Caddy controls is that they stay near the selected subobject even if you change the viewport. In addition to several settings that are updated immediately, there are buttons to accept and commit the current change, to apply the change and continue to work with the tool, or to cancel. Using the Apply and Continue button keeps the tool around for more work.

FIGURE 1.14

Caddy controls appear above the selection and let you try several different settings.

Understanding the button color cues

The interface uses color cues to help remind you of the current mode. When a button is yellow, it warns that it has control of the interface. For example, if one of the subobject buttons in the Command Panel is selected, it turns yellow, and the ability to select another object is disabled until this subobject mode is turned off. Knowing what the current mode is at all times can keep you out of trouble.

Another common button color is red. When either the Auto Key or Set Key button is active, it turns red. The edge of the active viewport being animated along with the Time Slider also turns red. This reminds you that any modifications will be saved as a key.

Toggle buttons can be turned on and off. Example toggle buttons include the Snap buttons. When a toggle button is enabled, it also turns yellow (or light gray depending on the color scheme). Toggle buttons highlighted in blue are nonexclusive, but they notify you of a mode that is enabled, such as the Key Mode Toggle or the Affect Pivot Only button.

Using drag-and-drop features

Dialog boxes that work with files benefit greatly from the software's drag-and-drop features. The Material Editor, Background Image, View File, and Environmental Settings dialog boxes all use drag and drop. These dialog boxes let you select a file or a material and drag it on top of where you want to apply it. For example, with the Maps rollout in the Material Editor open, you can drag a texture image filename from Windows Explorer or the Asset Manager and drop it on the Map button. You can even drag and drop 3ds Max files from Windows Explorer into the interface to open them.

Controlling spinners

Spinners are those little controls throughout the interface with a value field and two small arrows to its right. As you would expect, clicking the up arrow increases the value and clicking the down arrow decreases the value. The amount of the increase or decrease depends on the setting in the General tab of the Preference Settings dialog box. Right-clicking the spinner resets the value to its lowest acceptable value. Another way to control the spinner value is to click the arrows and drag with the mouse. Dragging up increases the value, and dragging down decreases it.

The effect of the spinner drag is shown in the viewport if the Update During Spinner Drag menu option is enabled in the Views menu. If the cursor is located within a spinner, you can press Ctrl+N to open the Numerical Expression Evaluator, which lets you set the value using an expression. For example, you can set a spinner value by adding numbers together as you would if using a calculator. An expression of 30+40+35 sets the value to 105.

Understanding modeless and persistent dialog boxes

Many dialog boxes in 3ds Max are *modeless,* which means that the dialog box doesn't need to be closed before you can work with objects in the background viewports. The Material Editor is an example of a modeless dialog box. With the Material Editor open, you can create, select, and transform objects in the background. Other modeless dialog boxes include the Material/Map Browser, the Render Scene dialog box, Caddy controls, the Video Post dialog box, the Transform Type-In dialog box, the Display and Selection Floaters, the Array dialog box and the various graph editors. Pressing the Ctrl+~ keyboard shortcut closes all open dialog boxes. Pressing the same keyboard shortcut again reopens the dialog boxes that were previously closed.

Another feature of many, but not all, dialog boxes is *persistence,* which means that values added to a dialog box remain set when the dialog box is reopened. This feature applies only within a given session. Choosing the File ⇨ Reset command button or exiting and restarting 3ds Max resets all the dialog boxes.

Using Workspaces

If you've rearranged the various interface elements or customized different aspects of the interface, the Workspaces drop-down list located in the Quick Access toolbar at the top of the interface, lets you save the changes for quick recall. Workspaces let you create a unique interface environment for several different tasks. For example, if you are modeling, you can create an interface with a double-wide control panel and another with the control panel hidden for animating.

NEW FEATURE
The ability to define and switch between workspaces is new to 3ds Max 2013.

All the custom workspaces that are saved are available for instant recall in the Workspaces drop-down list. When 3ds Max is exited and reloaded, the last workspace that was open is automatically loaded. If you change a saved workspace, you can return it to its saved setting using the Reset to Default State menu also found in the drop-down list.

To save a custom interface setup, simply select the Manage Workspaces from the Workspace drop-down list and the dialog box shown in Figure 1.15 opens.

FIGURE 1.15

The Manage Workspaces dialog box lets you save custom interfaces for immediate recall.

All the current defined workspaces are shown in a list to the left of the Manage Workspaces dialog box. You can delete any defined workspace by clicking the red X next to it. Clicking the Save as New Workspace button opens another dialog box where you can enter the workspace's name. For the selected workspace, you also can select which interface elements to include and even specify a MaxScript to run when the workspace loads or is exited.

Getting Help

If you get stuck, 3ds Max won't leave you stranded. You can turn to several places in 3ds Max to get help. The Help menu is a valuable resource that provides access to references and tutorials. The 3ds Max Help and MAXScript Help are comprehensive help systems. They are HTML pages that are accessible through the Autodesk.com website. Selecting Autodesk 3ds Max Help from the Help menu opens a web browser and loads the help files. This ensures that the latest and most up-to-date help files are available. Additional Help presents help systems for any external plug-ins that are loaded. The Tutorials command loads the tutorials, which offer a chance to gain valuable experience.

If you are working with 3ds Max offline, you can download and access a local copy of the help files. The Help panel in the Preference Settings dialog box, lets you specify whether to use the online or the local help files.

TIP

If you choose to use the online help files, you may find yourself waiting for the pages to load, which can be annoying if you are anxious to get an answer. I find that downloading and using a local copy is much quicker than the online version.

Using the InfoCenter toolbar

With all the various help files, sometimes it can be tough to know exactly which one to look in for the information you need. To help with this, 3ds Max includes an InfoCenter toolbar located at the right end of the title bar.

When you enter a keyword in the InfoCenter toolbar, 3ds Max performs a search and presents a list of information on where the keyword is found in all the various help files, including documentation and online resources.

TIP

You can use wildcards when searching for keywords. The asterisk (*) replaces one or more characters, the question mark (?) replaces a single character, and the tilde (~) looks for prefixes and/or suffixes added to the word. For example, con* finds controller, construct, and contour; sta? finds star and stat; ~lit finds prelit and relit; and limit~ finds limited and limitless.

Clicking the Search icon located to the right of the search text field (which looks like a tiny pair of binoculars) starts the search. The InfoCenter toolbar also includes buttons for accessing the Subscription Center, Communication Center, and Favorites. For each of these buttons, a pop-up dialog box appears that includes icon buttons in the upper right for closing the dialog box and for opening the InfoCenter Settings dialog box. The InfoCenter Settings dialog box includes settings for configuring the Communication Center, which is a resource for getting information and announcements from Autodesk. You can configure the Communication Center to inform you when updates are available, display product support issues, and even include RSS feeds from Autodesk.

TIP

Within the InfoCenter Settings dialog box is an option to disable those annoying balloon notifications that frequently pop up, or you can make them semitransparent.

Viewing the Essential Skills Movies

When the software first loads, users are greeted with a Welcome to 3ds Max dialog box, shown in Figure 1.16, which includes several Essential Skills Movies. These simple movies explain the basics of working with 3ds Max.

The Welcome to 3ds Max dialog box also includes links to What's New and to the YouTube Learning Channel, which are pages where you can find more tutorials and resources. If you get tired of this appearing every time the software starts, you can disable the Show this dialog at startup option to prevent this dialog box from appearing the next time you start 3ds Max. You can access the Essential Skills Movies dialog box at any time using the Help menu. This dialog box is also helpful in that it presents buttons to create a new scene or open a file, and a list of recently opened files.

> **NOTE**
> The Essential Skills Movies require an installation of Flash.

FIGURE 1.16

The Welcome to 3ds Max dialog box includes video clips showing the basic skills you need for working with 3ds Max.

Using the online reference guides

Within the Help menu, the Autodesk 3ds Max Help, What's New, MAXScript Help, and Tutorials are all loaded within a Web browser. An organized list of topics is available in the left navigation pane, as shown in Figure 1.17, and the right side includes a pane where the details on the selected topic are displayed. Across the top are several toolbar buttons used to control the interface. The Show in Contents button opens the selected help page in the Contents navigation list. The Add to Favorites button adds the current help page to the Favorites drop-down list accessible in the InfoCenter toolbar at the top of the interface. The Home: 3ds Max Help button returns to the first page of the Help file. The Share button lets you e-mail the selected page. The Back, Up, and Forward buttons move to the last, above, or previous page in the navigation.

> **TIP**
> You also can use the web browser buttons to move back and forth between the last-visited and next-visited pages.

FIGURE 1.17

The 3ds Max Reference includes panels for viewing the index of commands and searching the reference.

Above the left navigation pane are four tabs that open separate panels when selected. The Contents panel displays a list of topics; the Index panel lists all topics alphabetically, the Search panel includes a text field where you can search for specific keywords, and the Favorites panel keeps a list of bookmarks to topics you add to the list.

Throughout the textual descriptions, keywords linked to other related topics are highlighted in blue and underlined.

Using the rest of the Help menu

The Help ➪ Keyboard Shortcut Map displays an interactive interface for learning all the keyboard shortcuts. The Help ➪ Data Exchange Solutions menu opens a web page that explains how to use the FBX format to exchange files with other software packages. The Help ➪ Customer Involvement Program provides an interface where you can send feedback to Autodesk regarding 3ds Max. The program lets you send feedback anonymously or you can include your e-mail. If you notice a problem with the software, you can report it with the Report a Problem feature.

The Help ⇨ 3ds Max on the Web options (The AREA, Online Support, Updates, Resources, Partners, Training, and so on) automatically open a web browser and load the Autodesk Support web pages or look for updates. The AREA website is another excellent resource for help. It is the community site for 3ds Max users.

> **TIP**
>
> If you need help from something more personable than a Help file, the AREA website is a 3ds Max community sponsored by Autodesk. It has some awesome help worth looking into.

The License Borrowing option lets you borrow and return the current license for use on another computer. The About 3ds Max command opens the About 3ds Max dialog box, which displays the serial number, the version number and information about your license.

Summary

You should now be familiar with the interface elements for 3ds Max. Understanding the interface is one of the keys to success in using the software. 3ds Max includes a variety of different interface elements. Among the menus, toolbars, and keyboard shortcuts, you have several ways to perform the same command. Discover the method that works best for you.

This chapter covered the following topics:

- Learning the interface elements
- Viewing and using the pull-down menus
- Working with toolbars
- Accessing the Command Panel
- Learning the lower interface controls
- Interacting with the 3ds Max interface
- Managing workspaces
- Getting additional help

In this chapter, I've skirted about the viewports covering all the other interface elements, but in Chapter 2, you're going to hit the viewports head-on.

CHAPTER

2

Controlling the Viewports

IN THIS CHAPTER

Understanding 3D space

Using the ViewCube and the SteeringWheels

Navigating with the mouse and the Viewport Navigation Control buttons

Changing the visual style of the viewports

Changing viewport layouts and adding information to the viewports

Displaying materials, lighting, and shadows

Loading a viewport background image

Although the Autodesk® 3ds Max® 2013 software consists of many different interface elements, such as panels, dialog boxes, and menus, the viewports are the main areas that will catch your attention. The four main viewports make up the bulk of the interface. You can think of the viewports as looking at the television screen instead of the remote. Learning to control and use the viewports can make a huge difference in your comfort level with 3ds Max. Nothing is more frustrating than not being able to rotate, pan, and zoom the view.

The viewports have numerous settings and controls that you can use to provide thousands of different ways to look at your scene, and beginners can feel frustrated at not being able to control what they see. 3ds Max includes several handy little gizmos that make navigating the viewports much easier. This chapter includes all the details you need to make the viewports reveal their secrets.

Understanding 3D Space

It seems silly to be talking about 3D space because we live and move in 3D space. If we stop and think about it, 3D space is natural to us. For example, consider trying to locate your kids at the swimming pool. If you're standing poolside, the kids could be to your left or right, in front of you or behind you, or in the water below you or on the high dive above you. Each of these sets of directions represents a dimension in 3D space.

Now imagine that you're drawing a map that pinpoints the kid's location at the swimming pool. Using the drawing (which is 2D), you can describe the kid's position on the map as left, right, top, or bottom, but the descriptions of above and below have been lost. By moving from a 3D reference to a 2D one, the number of dimensions has decreased.

The conundrum that 3D computer artists face is this: How do you represent 3D objects on a 2D device such as a computer screen? The answer that 3ds Max provides is to present several views, called *viewports*, of the scene. A viewport is a small window that displays the scene from one perspective. These viewports are the windows into the software's 3D world. Each viewport has numerous settings and viewing options.

Learning Axonometric versus Perspective

When it comes to views in the 3D world, two different types exist: axonometric and perspective. Axonometric views are common in the CAD world where the viewer is set at an infinite distance from the object such that all parallel lines remain parallel. A perspective view simulates how our eyes actually work and converges all points to a single location off in the distance.

You can see the difference between these two types of views clearly if you look at a long line of objects. For example, if you were to look down a long row of trees lining a road, the trees would eventually merge on the horizon. In axonometric views, lines stay parallel as they recede into the distance. Figure 2.1 shows this example with the axonometric view on the left and the perspective view on the right.

FIGURE 2.1

Axonometric and perspective views

Learning orthographic and isometric views

If you dig a little deeper into axonometric views, you find two different types: orthographic and isometric. Orthographic views are displayed from the perspective of looking straight down an axis at an object. This reveals a view in only one plane. Because orthographic viewports are constrained to one plane, they show the actual height and width of the object, which is why the CAD world uses orthographic views extensively. Isometric views are not constrained to a single axis and can view the scene from any location, but all dimensions are still maintained. The words Isometric and Orthographic are often interchanged, but they refer to a view that has consistent dimensions.

Discovering the viewports in 3ds Max

Available orthographic viewports in 3ds Max include Front, Back, Top, Bottom, Left, and Right. 3ds Max starts up with the Top, Front, and Left orthographic viewports visible. The center label in the top-left corner of the viewport displays the viewport name. This label is called the Point-of-View viewport label. The fourth default viewport is a perspective view. Only one viewport, known as the *active viewport*, is enabled at a time. A yellow border highlights the active viewport.

Figure 2.2 shows the viewports with a Viewpoint Datalabs model of a PT-328 U.S. torpedo boat. You can see the model from a different direction in each viewport. If you want to measure the boat's length from aft to stern, you could get an accurate measurement using the Top or Left viewport, whereas you can use the Front and Left viewports to measure its precise height. Using these different viewports, you can accurately work with all object dimensions.

Isometric views in 3ds Max are called Orthographic viewports. You can create an Orthographic viewport by rotating any of the default non-perspective views.

FIGURE 2.2

The 3ds Max interface includes four viewports, each with a different view.

> **TIP**
>
> 3ds Max includes several keyboard shortcuts for quickly changing the view in the active viewport, including T (Top view), B (Bottom view), F (Front view), L (Left view), C (Camera view), $ (Spotlight view), P (Perspective view), and U (Orthographic User view). Pressing the V key opens a quad menu that lets you select a new view.

Using the Navigation Gizmos

One of the key advantages of working in 3D is that you can view your models from an endless number of viewpoints, but you won't be able to switch to these endless viewpoints until you learn to navigate the viewports. Being able to quickly navigate the viewports is essential to working in 3ds Max and one of the first skills you should master.

To make the process of navigating within the viewports and switching among the various views easier, 3ds Max has some navigation gizmos that make this chore easy. These semitransparent gizmos hover in the upper-right corner of each viewport and provide a way to change the view without having to access a tool, select a menu, or even use a keyboard shortcut.

Working with the ViewCube

The ViewCube consists of a 3D cube that is labeled on each side and centered in a ring aligned with the ground plane. Its purpose is to show the current orientation of the viewport, but it is also interactive and provides a way to quickly move among the different views.

If you drag the cursor over the top of the ViewCube, shown in Figure 2.3, you'll notice that the cube's faces, corners, and edges are highlighted as the cursor moves over them. If you click when any of the cube's parts are highlighted, the viewport is animated and moves to the new view so it's positioned as if it's pointing at the selected part. By slowly animating the transition to the new view, you get a better idea of the size and shape of the model. It also makes it easy to reorient the model if it gets twisted around to an odd angle. For example, if you click the cube's face labeled Top, then the view moves from its current view to the same orientation as the top view.

FIGURE 2.3

The ViewCube lets you quickly change the current view.

Go to home view

The ViewCube also lets you click and drag on the cube to rotate the view around. The scene rotates along with the ViewCube. You also can click and drag on the base ring to spin the model about its current orientation. When you hover over the ViewCube, a small house icon appears. Clicking this icon changes the view to the defined home view. You can set the Home view by right-clicking the ViewCube and selecting the Set Current View as Home option from the pop-up menu. These same menu options also are available in the Views ➪ ViewCube menu and as an option in the General Viewport label (the small plus sign located in the upper-left corner of each viewport). If the ViewCube isn't visible, you can enable it using the Views ➪ ViewCube ➪ Show For Active View. Another option is to Show For All Views.

Other pop-up menu options let you switch the view between orthographic and perspective views. You also can set the current view as Front, reset the Front view, and open the ViewCube panel that is located in the Viewport Configuration dialog box with the Configure option.

The ViewCube panel in the Viewport Configuration dialog box includes settings for turning the ViewCube on and off In All Views in Active Layout or In Only the Active View. You also can set the ViewCube size and its inactive opacity.

> **TIP**
>
> If you like the ViewCube but feel that it takes up too much of the viewport, you can change its size to Small or Tiny or you can set its inactive opacity to 0. When its inactive opacity is set to 0, the ViewCube isn't visible at all until you move the cursor over its location, causing it to appear.

The ViewCube panel in the Viewport Configuration dialog box also has options to control what happens when you click or drag the ViewCube. You can snap to the closest view when dragging the ViewCube, and you have options to automatically make the models fit to the view when the view changes, to use animated transitions, and to keep the scene upright. If you find that the view keeps ending up at odd angles when you drag the ViewCube, try enabling the Keep Scene Upright option. Finally, you have an option to display the compass under the ViewCube and a setting for the Angle of North so you can change the compass' orientation. The compass is helpful in being able to spin the model around, but if your model is something like a planet that doesn't have a top or bottom, disabling the compass makes sense.

Using the SteeringWheels

The ViewCube is great for switching between the default views and for rotating the current view, but there are many additional navigation tools that aren't covered with the ViewCube. To handle many of these other navigation tools, such as zooming and panning, 3ds Max includes the SteeringWheels, another gizmo for navigating the viewports.

When 3ds Max is first started, the SteeringWheels are turned off, but you can enable this gizmo with the Views ➪ SteeringWheels ➪ Toggle SteeringWheels menu or by pressing the Shift+W shortcut. The SteeringWheels menu also is found in the General Viewport label located in the upper-left corner of the viewport. Once enabled, this gizmo follows your mouse cursor around as it moves about the viewport, and different parts of the wheel are highlighted when you move over them. If you click and drag while a section of the SteeringWheels is highlighted, then you can access that control. Right-clicking at any time will toggle the SteeringWheels off again.

There are several different modes for the SteeringWheels in both full-size and mini versions, including the Full Navigation Wheel, with all commands; the View Object Wheel, with commands for navigating about objects; and the Tour Building Wheel, for walking through buildings. The Full Navigation Wheel, shown in Figure 2.4, includes the following modes:

FIGURE 2.4

The SteeringWheel gizmo includes several different ways to navigate the viewports.

- **Zoom:** This causes the view to zoom in and out of the scene about the pivot. The pivot is set by holding down the Ctrl key while clicking.
- **Orbit:** This causes the view to orbit about the pivot. The pivot is set by holding down the Ctrl key while clicking.
- **Pan:** This causes the view to pan in the direction that you drag the cursor.
- **Rewind:** As you change the scene, 3ds Max remembers each view where you stop and keeps these views in a buffer. The Rewind mode displays these views as small thumbnails, as shown in Figure 2.5, and lets you move through them by dragging the mouse. This allows you to rewind and move forward through the buffered views.

> **TIP**
>
> Moving between the buffered thumbnail views with the Rewind feature gradually animates the transition between adjacent thumbnails and allows you to click to change the view to one that is between two buffered views.

- **Center:** This lets you click an object to be the pivot center for zooming and orbiting.
- **Walk:** This moves you forward through the scene as if you were walking through it. Holding down the Shift key lets you move up and down.
- **Look:** This causes the camera to rotate side to side as if looking to the side.
- **Up/Down:** This moves the view up and down from the current location.

> **NOTE**
>
> It is covered later in the chapter, but you can maximize the active viewport by clicking the Maximize Viewport Toggle button (the button in the lower-left corner of the interface) or by pressing Alt+W.

In the upper-right corner of the wheel is a small X icon. This icon is used to close the SteeringWheels gizmo. In the lower-right corner of the wheel is a small down arrow. This icon opens a pop-up menu. Using the pop-up menu, you can select a different wheel type, go to the Home view as defined by the ViewCube, increase or decrease the walk speed, restore the original center, or open the SteeringWheels panel in the Viewport Configuration dialog box. These same options are also available in the Views ⇨ SteeringWheels menu and in the General viewport label, along with an option to Toggle the SteeringWheels on and off (Shift+W).

Using the SteeringWheels panel in the Viewport Configuration dialog box, you can set the size and opacity of the SteeringWheels. Settings for controlling many of the different modes are available as well.

FIGURE 2.5

Rewind mode lets you move back and forth through recent views.

Tutorial: Navigating the active viewport

Over time, navigating the viewports becomes second nature to you, but you need to practice to get to that point. In this tutorial, you get a chance to take the viewports for a spin—literally.

To practice navigating a viewport, follow these steps:

1. Open the Bruce the dog.max file from the Chap 02 directory on the CD.

   This file includes a model of a dog (affectionately named Bruce) created by Viewpoint Datalabs. It provides a reference as you navigate the viewport. The active viewport is the Perspective viewport.

2. Click the Maximize Viewport Toggle button (or press Alt+W) to make the Perspective viewport fill the space of all four viewports.

3. Click the Front face in the ViewCube to transition the view to the front view. Then move the cursor over the upper-right corner of the ViewCube, and click to return the view to an angled view.

4. Select the Views⇨SteeringWheels⇨Toggle SteeringWheels; then hold down the Ctrl key and click Bruce's head to set the pivot. Then move the cursor over the Zoom button, and drag until Bruce's head fills the viewport.

5. With the SteeringWheels still active, move the cursor over the Pan button and drag the window until Bruce's head is centered evenly in the viewport, as shown in Figure 2.6. Right-click in the viewport to toggle the SteeringWheels gizmo off.

FIGURE 2.6

The Perspective viewport is zoomed in on the dog's head using the Zoom and Pan controls.

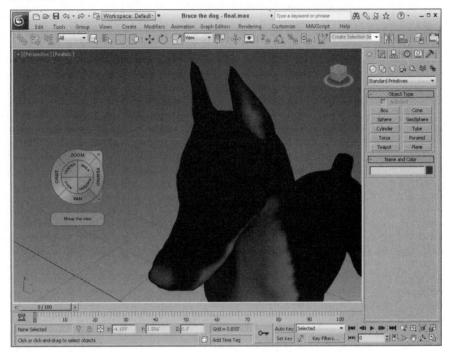

Controlling Viewports with a Scroll Wheel Mouse

Now that I've explained the viewport navigation gizmos, I'll explain another easy way to control the viewports. Often, the quickest way to control the viewports is with the mouse. To really get the benefit of the mouse, you need to use a mouse with a scroll wheel (which also acts as a middle mouse button).

Rolling the scroll wheel in the active viewport zooms in to and out of the viewport by steps just like the bracket keys ([and]). You can zoom gradually by holding down the Ctrl and Alt keys while dragging the scroll wheel.

Clicking and dragging the scroll wheel button pans the active viewport. Clicking and dragging with the Alt button held down rotates the active viewport. If the scroll wheel isn't working, check the Viewports panel in the Preference Settings dialog box, found at the bottom of the Customize menu.

You can select to use the scroll wheel control to pan and zoom in the viewports or to define and use Strokes, which is a feature for defining shortcuts using the mouse.

CAUTION

Be careful when zooming in with the scroll wheel. If you zoom in too far, the zooming becomes unstable. If this happens, you can select the Views ➪ Undo View Change (Shift+Z) menu command to undo the zoom or use the Zoom Extents button.

Using the Viewport Navigation Controls

Although the ViewCube, the SteeringWheels, and the scroll wheel make navigating the viewports easy, you can still use the standard navigation tools located in the bottom-right corner of the interface. The standard viewports show you several different views of your current project, but within each viewport, you can zoom in on certain objects, pan the view, or rotate about the center of the viewport. Clicking a viewport with any of the Viewport Navigation Controls automatically makes the selected viewport the active viewport. In Table 2.1, the keyboard shortcut for each button is listed in parentheses next to its name.

TABLE 2.1 **Viewport Navigation Controls**

Toolbar Button	Name	Description
	Zoom (Alt+Z or [or])	Moves closer to or farther from the objects in the active viewport by dragging the mouse or zooming by steps with the bracket keys.
	Zoom All	Zooms in to or out of all the viewports simultaneously by dragging the mouse.
	Zoom Extents (Ctrl+Alt+Z), Zoom Extents Selected (Z)	Zooms in on all objects or just the selected object until it fills the active viewport.
	Zoom Extents All (Ctrl+Shift+Z), Zoom Extents All Selected	Zooms in on all objects or just the selected object until it fills all the viewports.
	Field-of-View, Zoom Region (Ctrl+W)	The Field-of-View button (available only in the perspective view) controls the width of the view. The Zoom Region button zooms in to the region selected by dragging the mouse.
	Pan View (Ctrl+P or I), Walk Through (Up arrow)	Moves the view to the left, to the right, up, or down by dragging the mouse or by moving the mouse while holding down the I key. The Walk Through feature moves through the scene using the arrow keys or a mouse like a first-person video game.
	Orbit (Ctrl+R), Orbit Selected, Orbit SubObject	Rotates the view around the global axis, selected object, or subobject by dragging the mouse.
	Maximize Viewport Toggle (Alt+W)	Makes the active viewport fill the screen, replacing the four separate viewports. Clicking this button a second time shows all four viewports again.

> **CAUTION**
>
> When one of the Viewport Navigation buttons is selected, it is highlighted yellow. You cannot select, create, or transform objects while one of these buttons is highlighted. Right-clicking in the active viewpoint or clicking the Select Objects tool reverts to select object mode.

Zooming a view

You can zoom into and out of the scene in several ways. Clicking the Zoom (Alt+Z) button enters zoom mode where you can zoom in to and out of a viewport by dragging the mouse. This works in whichever viewport you drag in. To the right of the Zoom button is the Zoom All button, which does the same thing as the Zoom button, only to all four viewports at once. If you hold down the Ctrl key while dragging in Zoom mode, the zoom action happens more quickly, requiring only a small mouse movement to get a large zoom amount. Holding down the Alt key while dragging in Zoom mode has the opposite effect; the zoom happens much more slowly, and a large mouse move is required for a small zoom amount. This is helpful for fine-tuning the zoom.

The Zoom Extents (Ctrl+Alt+Z) button zooms the active viewport so that all objects (or the selected objects with the Zoom Extents Selected button) are visible in the viewport. A Zoom Extents All (Ctrl+Shift+Z) button is available for zooming in all viewports to all objects' extents; the most popular zoom command (and the easiest to remember) is Zoom Extents Selected (Z), which is for zooming in to the extents of the selected objects in the active viewport.

You can use the brackets keys to zoom in ([) and out (]) by steps. Each key press zooms in (or out) another step. The Zoom Region (Ctrl+W) button lets you drag over the region that you want to zoom in on. If you select a non-orthogonal view, such as the Perspective view, the Zoom Region button has a flyout called the Field-of-View. Using this button, you can control how wide or narrow the view is. This is like using a wide angle or telephoto lens on your camera. This feature is different from zoom in that the perspective is distorted as the Field-of-View is increased.

Field of View is covered in more detail in Chapter 18, "Configuring and Aiming Cameras."

Panning a view

The Viewport Navigation Controls also offer two ways to pan in a viewport. In Pan View mode (Ctrl+P), dragging in a viewport pans the view. Note that this doesn't move the objects, only the view. The second way to pan is to hold down the I key while moving the mouse. This is known as an *interactive* pan. In addition, the Ctrl and Alt keys can be held down to speed or slow the panning motions.

Walking through a view

The Walk Through button (Up arrow), found as a flyout button under the Pan View button, allows you to move through the scene in the Perspective or Camera viewport using the arrow keys or the mouse just as you would if you were playing a first-person computer game. When this button is active, the cursor changes to a small circle with an arrow inside it that points in the direction you are moving. You need to first click in the viewport before you can use the arrow keys.

CAUTION
The Pan View button is a flyout only if the Perspective view or a Camera view is selected.

The Walk Through feature includes several keystrokes for controlling the camera's movement. The arrow keys move the camera forward, left, back, and right (or you can use the W, A, S, and D keys). You can change the speed of the motion with the Q (accelerate) and Z (decelerate) keys or with the [(decrease step size) and] (increase step size) keys. The E and C keys (or the Shift+up and Shift+down arrows) are used to move up and down in the scene. The Shift+spacebar key causes the camera to be set level. Dragging the mouse while the camera is moving changes the direction in which the camera points.

A handy alternative to Walk Through mode is the Walkthrough Assistant, which is found on the Animation menu. This utility opens a dialog box that includes buttons for creating and adding a camera to a path. It also has controls from turning the view side to side as the camera moves along the path.

 The Walkthrough Assistant is covered in more detail in Chapter 25, "Animating with Constraints and Simple Controllers."

Rotating a view

Rotating the view can be the most revealing of all the view changes. When the Orbit (Ctrl+R) button is selected, a rotation guide appears in the active viewport, as shown in Figure 2.7. This rotation guide is a circle with a square located at each quadrant. Clicking and dragging the left or right squares rotates the view side to side; the same action with the top and bottom squares rotates the view up and down. Clicking within the circle and dragging rotates within a single plane, and clicking and dragging outside of the circle rotates the view about the circle's center either clockwise or counterclockwise. If you get confused, look at the cursor, which changes depending on the type of rotation. The Ctrl and Alt keys also can speed and slow the rotating view.

NOTE
The Orbit keyboard shortcut (Ctrl+R) selects whichever Orbit tool was the last to be used.

NOTE
If you rotate one of the default non-perspective views, it automatically becomes an orthographic view, but you can undo the change using the Views ⇨ Undo View Change command or the Shift+Z shortcut.

Maximizing the active viewport

Sooner or later, the viewports will feel too small. When this happens, you have several ways to increase the size of your viewports. The first trick to try is to change the viewport sizes by clicking and dragging any of the viewport borders. Dragging on the intersection of the viewports resizes all the viewports. Figure 2.8 shows the viewports after being dynamically resized.

TIP
You can return to the original layout by right-clicking any of the viewport borders and selecting Reset Layout from the pop-up menu.

FIGURE 2.7

The rotation guide appears whenever the Orbit tool is selected.

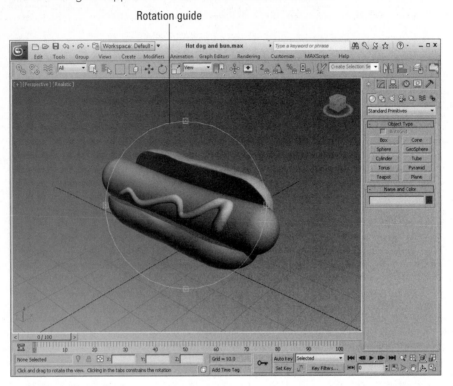

The second trick is to use the Maximize Viewport Toggle (Alt+W) to expand the active viewport to fill the space reserved for all four viewports. Clicking the Maximize Viewport Toggle (or pressing Alt+W) a second time returns to the defined layout.

Maximizing the viewport helps temporarily, but you can take another step before convincing your boss that you need a larger monitor. You can enter Expert Mode by choosing Views ⇨ Expert Mode (Ctrl+X). It maximizes the viewport space by removing the main toolbar, the Command Panel, and most of the lower interface bar.

With most of the interface elements gone, you'll need to rely on the menus, keyboard shortcuts, and quad menus to execute commands. To re-enable the default interface, click the Cancel Expert Mode button in the lower right of the 3ds Max window (or press Ctrl+X again). Figure 2.9 shows the interface in Expert Mode.

FIGURE 2.8

You can dynamically resize viewports by dragging their borders.

Controlling camera and spotlight views

You can set any viewport to be a camera view (C) or a spotlight view ($) if a camera or a spotlight exists in the scene. When either of these views is active, the Viewport Navigation Control buttons change. In camera view, controls for dolly, roll, truck, pan, orbit, and field of view become active. A light view includes controls for the falloff and hotspots.

Chapter 18, "Configuring and Aiming Cameras," and Chapter 19, "Using Lights and Basic Lighting Techniques," cover these changes in more detail.

FIGURE 2.9

Expert Mode maximizes the viewports by eliminating most of the interface elements.

Setting the navigation controls to match Maya

In many studios, you'll find both 3ds Max and Maya. These software packages have different navigation controls, but you can set 3ds Max to mimic the Maya controls using the Interaction Mode panel in the Preference Settings dialog box. This panel includes a simple drop-down box for switching the viewport navigation controls between 3ds Max and Maya. If you make the change, the designated controls will be used automatically the next time you start up the software.

NEW FEATURE

The ability to switch viewport navigation controls to mimic the Maya controls is new to 3ds Max 2013.

Table 2.2 shows the basic keyboard and mouse navigation controls for both 3ds Max and Maya.

TABLE 2.2   Viewport Navigation Controls for 3ds Max and Maya

Viewport Navigation Control	3ds Max	Maya
Rotate view	Alt + middle mouse button	Alt + left mouse button
Pan view	middle mouse button	Alt + middle mouse button
Zoom view	scrub scroll wheel	Alt + right mouse button

Viewport Navigation Control	3ds Max	Maya
Zoom Extents Selected	Z	F
Zoom Extents All	Shift+Ctrl+Z	A
Maximize viewport	Alt + W	Spacebar
Undo/Redo Viewport Change	Shift+Z/Shift+Y	Alt+Z/Alt+Y

Changing the Viewport Display

Although the Viewport Navigation Controls are focused on controlling what is visible in the viewports, a number of useful commands are available in the Views menu and in the viewport labels at the top-left corner of each viewport that directly affect the viewports. The three viewport labels, shown in Figure 2.10, include the General viewport label (which is a simple plus sign), the Point-of-View viewport label, and the Shading viewport label. The last two labels show the current setting.

Undoing and saving viewport changes

If you get lost in your view, you can undo and redo viewport changes with Views ⟹ Undo View Change (Shift+Z) and Views ⟹ Redo View Change (Shift+Y). These same commands also are available at the bottom of the Point-of-View viewport label. These commands are different from the Edit ⟹ Undo and Edit ⟹ Redo commands, which can undo or redo geometry changes.

You can save changes made to a viewport by using the Views ⟹ Save Active Viewport menu command. This command saves the Viewport Navigation settings for recall. To restore these settings, use Views ⟹ Restore Active Viewport.

FIGURE 2.10

Viewport labels in the upper-left corner of each viewport hold settings for that particular viewport.

General viewport label

Point-of-View viewport label

Shading viewport label

> **NOTE**
>
> The Save and Restore Active Viewport commands do not save any viewport configuration settings, just the navigated view. Saving an active view uses a buffer, so it remembers only one view for each viewport.

Disabling and refreshing viewports

If your scene gets too complicated, you can experience some slow-down waiting for each viewport to be updated with changes, but fear not, because several options will come to your rescue. The first option to try is to disable a viewport.

You can disable a viewport by clicking the General viewport label and selecting the Disable View menu command from the pop-up menu, or you can press the keyboard shortcut, D. When a disabled viewport is active, it is updated as normal; when it is inactive, the viewport is not updated at all until it becomes active again. Disabled viewports are identified by the word "Disabled," which appears next to the viewport's labels in the upper-left corner.

Another trick to increase the viewport update speed is to disable the Views ⇨ Update During Spinner Drag menu option. Changing parameter spinners can cause a slowdown by requiring every viewport to update as the spinner changes. If the spinner is changing rapidly, it can really slow even a powerful system. Disabling this option causes the viewport to wait for the spinner to stop changing before updating.

Sometimes when changes are made, the viewports aren't completely refreshed. This typically happens when dialog boxes from other programs are moved in front of the viewports or as objects get moved around, because they often mask one another and lines disappear. If this happens, you can force 3ds Max to refresh all the viewports with the Views ⇨ Redraw All Views (keyboard shortcut, `) menu command. The Redraw All Views command refreshes each viewport and makes everything visible again.

Setting the viewport visual style

Complex scenes take longer to display and render. The renderer used for the viewports is highly optimized to be very quick, but if you're working on a huge model with lots of complex textures and every viewport is set to display the highest quality view, updating each viewport can slow the program to a crawl.

By default, all the orthographic views are set to wireframe and only the perspective view is set to show shading, but the Shading viewport label includes several options that let you set the visual style settings for the current viewport.

> **TIP**
>
> If you ever get stuck waiting for 3ds Max to complete a task, such as redrawing the viewports, you can always press the Escape key to suspend any task immediately and return control to the interface.

> **NOTE**
>
> These settings have no effect on the final rendering specified using the Rendering menu. They affect only the display in the viewport.

The Rendering Level options include the following:

- **Realistic:** Shows smooth surfaces with lighting highlights
- **Shaded:** Shows smooth surfaces without any lighting effects
- **Consistent Colors:** Shows the entire object with minimal lighting
- **Edged Faces:** An option applied in addition to the shading method that shows all edge segments
- **Facets:** Shows each face as a flat surface without smoothing the edges
- **Hidden Line:** Shows only polygon edges facing the camera
- **Wireframe:** Shows all polygon edges only
- **Bounding Box:** Shows a box that would enclose the object
- **Clay:** Shows the surface as red modeling clay, which is helpful for seeing deformations

NEW FEATURE
The Facets and Clay rendering methods are new to 3ds Max 2013.

Although it really isn't a rendering method, the Edged Faces option shows the edges for each face when a shaded rendering method is selected. You can enable and disable this option with the F4 keyboard shortcut. Figure 2.11 shows, side by side, all the various viewport rendering methods applied to a simple sphere.

FIGURE 2.11

The viewport rendering methods are shown from left to right. First row: Realistic, Shaded, Consistent Colors, Facets, and Hidden Line. Second row: Wireframe, Bounding Box, Clay, and Edged Faces applied to Shaded.

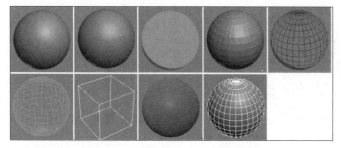

The Realistic shading method uses any applied textures and high-quality lighting and shadows. The Shaded method is similar, but it uses a quick shading method called Phong shading. The Consistent Color method displays the entire object using a single color without any shading. The simplest rendering setting that represents the shape of the object is Wireframe. It gives a good representation of the object while redrawing very quickly. By default, the Top, Front, and Left viewports are set to Wireframe, and the Perspective viewport is set to Realistic. The Bounding Box method shows only the limits of the object as a rectangular-shaped box.

Viewing stylized scenes

Stylized non-photorealistic effects often are not as computationally complex as realistic renderings, and as such, they can be enabled and displayed within the viewports as well as rendered images. Although you probably would not want to work in one of these stylized display modes, you can use the Shading viewport label to access a menu of available stylized display options.

The options include Graphite, Color Pencil, Ink, Color Ink, Acrylic, Pastel, and Tech. Figure 2.12 shows the gingerbread house model with the Color Ink option.

The various stylized display options also can be set in the Visual Style & Appearance panel in the Viewport Configuration dialog box.

FIGURE 2.12

The gingerbread house scene is displayed using the Colored Ink display style.

Enhancing the Viewport

In addition to changing the viewport display, several options allow for changing the viewport layout or adding information that will help during modeling and animating such as xView, clipping view, and safe frames. These enhancements help the viewports to be even more helpful by presenting information that you need.

Changing the viewport layout

So far, we've used only the default four-pane layout and the maximized viewport, but you can change the viewport layout to have one, two, three, or four panes orientated on top of each other or side by side. The easiest way to switch between the different layouts is with the Viewport Layout Tabs toolbar.

NEW FEATURE

The Viewport Layout Tabs toolbar is new to 3ds Max 2013.

This toolbar is opened by right-clicking any toolbar and selecting it from the pop-up menu. The toolbar appears by default vertically at the left edge of the viewports, as shown in Figure 2.13. Clicking the Create a New Viewport Layout Tab button opens a panel of several layout options. Selecting one switches the current layout and places the selected layout in the toolbar where it can quickly be selected again.

FIGURE 2.13

The Viewport Layout Tabs toolbar lets you quickly change between different layouts.

Create a New Viewport Layout Tab

For more options, including the ability to change the view type for each pane, open the Viewport Configuration dialog box using the Views menu and select the Layout panel.

Displaying Safe Frames

The Viewport Configuration dialog box includes a panel called Safe Frames that lets you display guidelines within the viewports. These guidelines show the render boundaries and areas where the action and titles won't be clipped. You also can enable a user-defined set of guides. Once configured in the Safe Frames panel, you can turn them on and off using the Point-of-View viewport label option or with the Shift+F shortcut.

Using clipping planes

Clipping planes define an invisible barrier beyond which all objects are invisible. For example, if you have a scene with many detailed mountain objects in the background, working with an object in the front of the scene can be difficult. By setting the clipping plane between the two, you can work on the front objects without having to redraw the mountain objects every time you update the scene. This affects only the viewport, not the rendered output.

Enabling the Viewport Clipping option in the viewport Point-of-View label menu places a yellow line with two arrows on the right side of the viewport, as shown in Figure 2.14. The top arrow represents the back clipping plane, and the bottom arrow is the front clipping plane. Drag the arrows up and down to set the clipping planes.

Tutorial: Viewing the interior of a heart with clipping planes

You can use the Viewport Clipping option in the Point-of-View viewport label to view the interior of a model, such as this heart model created by Viewpoint Datalabs.

To view the interior of a heart model, follow these steps:

1. Open the Heart interior.max file from the Chap 02 directory on the CD.
2. In the Point-of-View viewport label in the upper-left corner of the viewport, enable the Viewport Clipping option.
3. The clipping plane markers appear along the right edge of the viewport. The top marker controls the back clipping plane, and the bottom marker controls the front clipping plane. Drag the bottom clipping plane marker upward to slice through the heart model to reveal its interior, as shown in Figure 2.15.

Locating mesh problems with xView

When modeling or importing mesh objects, a number of problems with the geometry can cause rendering artifacts such as flipped normals, overlapping faces, and open edges. Locating these problem areas can be tricky, requiring multiple renders to get it right. Within the viewports is a powerful analysis feature for locating a number of specific problem areas. This feature is called xView, and you can access it from the Views menu and the General viewport label.

FIGURE 2.14

The clipping planes can be used to show the interior of this car model.

Far Clipping Plane marker

Near Clipping Plane marker

The xView analysis tool can locate and highlight the following anomalies:

- **Show Statistics (7):** Displays the number of Polys, Tris, Edges, Verts, and Frames per Second (FPS) for the entire scene and for the selected object.
- **Face Orientation:** Highlights the back side of the faces in the current selection to quickly identify faces with flipped normals.
- **Overlapping Faces:** Highlights any faces that are stacked on top of each other, which can cause render problems.
- **Open Edges:** Identifies unwanted holes in the geometry.
- **Multiple Edges:** Checks for edges that are stacked on each other. Each edge should be connected to only two faces.
- **Isolated Vertices:** Highlights vertices that aren't connected to anything. These vertices just take up space.
- **Overlapping Vertices:** Flags vertices that are within a given tolerance.

FIGURE 2.15

By using clipping planes, you can reveal the interior of a model.

- **T-Vertices:** Highlights vertices where three edges meet. This can terminate an edge loop.
- **Missing UVW Coordinates:** Shows any faces that have no UVW coordinates for applying textures.
- **Flipped UVW Faces:** Highlights any faces that are flipped with opposite-pointing normals.
- **Overlapping UVW Faces:** Displays any faces where the textures are overlapping.

Whichever option is selected is listed at the bottom of the viewport in green along with the number of offending subobjects, such as Isolated Vertices: 12 Vertices. The menu also includes options to Select the Results, which provides to a way to quickly select and delete problem subobjects like isolated vertices. If the selected option has a setting such as the Tolerance of overlapping edges, you can select the Configure option to set this setting or click the Click Here to Configure text at the bottom of the viewport. Additional menu options allow you to See Through the model, Auto Update the results, and display the results at the top of the viewport.

> **TIP**
>
> If any xView data is displayed in the viewport, you can click it to select another data option. This lets you quickly view all the potential problems with the current object.

By enabling the Show Statistics option, the selected statistics are overlaid on the active viewport, as shown in Figure 2.16. This is helpful to know how complex your model is and how many polygons it includes.

FIGURE 2.16

The active viewport can be set to display the selected statistics.

Displaying Materials, Lighting, and Shadows in the Viewport

The difference between what is seen in the viewport and the final render that is output is often the details like materials, lighting, and shadows. Over time, the viewport has gotten stronger and better at being able to display these details without slowing down the system, especially with the Nitrous display drivers. If you are working on a complex scene, you can turn down or turn off these details in order to work faster with the scene.

Viewing materials in the viewports

The Views menu and the Shading viewport label also include several commands for making scene details such as materials, lighting, and shadows visible in the viewports. Each of these options can slow down the refresh rate, but they provide immediate feedback, which is often helpful.

Texture maps also can take up lots of memory. The Views⇨Show Materials in Viewport As⇨Shaded Materials with Maps command shows all applied texture maps in the viewports. If you don't need to see the texture maps, then switching to Views⇨Show Materials in Viewport As⇨Shaded Materials without Maps will speed up the display. The option to use Realistic Materials without Maps and Realistic Materials with Maps uses the video card's memory to display the applied textures.

The Views⇨Show Materials in Viewport As menu also includes a toggle to Enable Transparency in the viewport.

TIP

The options for enabling materials in the viewports also are available as a submenu under the Shading viewport label.

 More on applying texture maps is covered in Chapter 15, "Adding Material Details with Maps."

Displaying lighting and shadows in the viewports

Options for enabling lighting and shadow effects within the viewports are located in the Shading viewport label menu. By default, both shadows and ambient occlusion are enabled when the Realistic shading mode is selected, but you can disable them using the toggle menu options under the Lighting and Shadows menu. You also have an option to Illuminate the scene using Scene Lights or Default Lights. Default Lights are simply one or two lights added to the scene if no other lights are present to make sure the scene objects are visible. Figure 2.17 shows an example of viewport shadows and Ambient Occlusion.

Ambient Occlusion is a lighting effect that adds to the realism of a scene by making objects cast shadows on surrounding objects based on how they block the light. Objects that are close to one another spread a soft shadow onto nearby objects. Figure 2.18 gives a good example. The columns in the left viewport have ambient occlusion turned off, but the right columns have it turned on. Notice how the columns on the right cast a light shadow onto the walls and onto the areas around the column caps.

FIGURE 2.17

Viewport Shading shown with shadows enabled

> **CAUTION**
>
> Displaying shadows in the viewport requires Direct3D 9.0 to be installed on your system, and your video card must support Shader Model 2.0 or Shader Model 3.0. If your computer doesn't support either of these Shader models, then the options will be disabled in the viewport shading label menu and in the Viewport Configuration dialog box. You can check the capabilities of your video card using the Help ⬦ Diagnose Video Hardware command.

FIGURE 2.18

Ambient Occlusion can often be used as an alternative to full shadows.

To enable and configure lighting and shadows in the viewports, follow these steps:

1. Open the Foot bones.max file from the Chap 02 directory on the CD.

   This file includes a set of foot bones created by Viewpoint Datalabs. An Omni light is added to the scene as well.

2. Click in the Shading viewport label, and check the Lighting and Shadows ⇨ Shadows option to make sure it is enabled. Then select the Configure option from the same menu to access the Visual Style & Appearance panel in the Viewport Configuration dialog box.

> **CAUTION**
>
> If you don't see the Visual Style & Appearance panel in the Viewport Configuration dialog box, then you probably have a different display driver enabled.

   Enable the Ambient Occlusion setting with a Radius of 10 and an Intensity/Fade value of 1. Select the Point Lights/Soft-Edged Shadows option in the Lighting and Shadows Quality slider. Then click the OK button.

3. Click the Select and Move toolbar button, and drag the light object about the scene.

   The shadows under the foot bones are automatically updated as the light is moved, as shown in Figure 2.19. Notice how the shadows are soft.

FIGURE 2.19

Lights and shadows are updated in real time when the light is moved about the scene.

Working with Viewport Backgrounds

Remember in grade school when you realized that you could immediately draw really well using tracing paper (where all you needed to do was follow the lines)? Well, it's not quite tracing paper, but you can load background reference images into a viewport that can help as you create and position your objects.

Changing the viewport background

The Views⇨Viewport Background menu command includes submenus for switching the viewport background between a gradient and solid color. You also have options to display the Environment Background or a custom image file. These same commands also are available in the Shading viewport label.

NEW FEATURE

The ability to load gradient backgrounds and the inclusion of the Background panel in the Viewport Configuration dialog box are new to 3ds Max 2013.

The default gradient is set to display dark gray at the top of the viewport that gradually changes to a lighter gray at the bottom. You can alter the displayed colors using the Colors panel in the Customize User Interface dialog box opened using the Customize menu. Look for the Viewport Background, Viewport Gradient Background Bottom, and Viewport Gradient Background Top entries.

Loading viewport background images

To create a background image to be rendered along with the scene, you need to choose the Environment Background option and specify the background in the Environment dialog box, opened using the Rendering ⇨ Environment (keyboard shortcut, 8) menu command. If an environment map is already loaded into the Environment dialog box, you can simply click the Use Environment Background option. Keep in mind that the background image will not be rendered unless it is used as an Environment map.

Environment maps are covered in Chapter 20, "Rendering a Scene and Enabling Quicksilver."

To load images into the viewport background, select the Custom Image File option in the Views ⇨ Viewport Background menu or in the Shading viewport label, and then use the Views ⇨ Viewport Background ⇨ Configure Viewport Background menu command (Alt+B) to open a dialog box, shown in Figure 2.20, in which you can select an image or animation to appear behind a viewport. Each viewport can have a different background image. The displayed background image is helpful for aligning objects in a scene, but it is for display purposes only and will not be rendered.

FIGURE 2.20

The Background panel in the Viewport Configuration dialog box lets you select a background source image or animation.

The Files button in the Background panel of the Viewport Configuration dialog box opens the Select Background Image dialog box, where you can select the image to load. Once an image is selected, its path is added to the Background panel of the Viewport Configuration dialog box. You can remove the designated file path by clicking the Remove button. The Aspect Ratio section offers options for setting the size of the background image. You can select to Match Viewport, Match Bitmap, or Match Rendering Output.

The Lock Zoom/Pan option is available if either the Match Bitmap option or the Match Rendering Output option is selected. This option locks the background image to the geometry, so that when the scene is zoomed or panned, the background image follows. You'll want to make sure your scene objects are in place before enabling the Lock Zoom/Pan option.

> **CAUTION**
>
> When the Lock Zoom/Pan option is selected, the background image is resized when you zoom in on an object. Resizing the background image fills the virtual memory, and if you zoom in too far, the background image could exceed your virtual memory. If this happens, a dialog box appears to inform you of the problem and gives you the option of not displaying the background image.

Loading viewport background animations

The Animation Synchronization section of the Background panel lets you set which frames of a background animation sequence are displayed. The Use Frame and To values determine which frames of the loaded animation are used. The Step value trims the number of frames that are to be used by selecting every Nth frame. For example, a Step value of 4 would use every fourth frame.

> **TIP**
>
> Loading an animation sequence as a viewport background can really help as you begin to animate complex motions, like a running horse. By stepping through the frames of the animation, you can line up your model with the background image for realistic animations.

The Start At value is the frame in the current scene where this background animation would first appear. The Sync Start to Frame value is the frame of the background animation that should appear first. The Start and End Processing options let you determine what appears before the Start and End frames. Options include displaying a blank, holding the current frame, and looping. Make sure to enable the Animate Background option in order to play the background animation when the animation plays.

You can set the Apply to All Views in the Active Layout Tab or the Apply to Active View option to display the background in All Views or in the active viewport only.

Tutorial: Loading reference images for modeling

When modeling a physical object, you can get a jump on the project by taking pictures with a digital camera of the front, top, and left views of the object and then loading them as background images in the respective viewports. The background images can then be a reference for your work. This is especially helpful with models that need to be precise. You can even work from CAD drawings.

To load the background images of a brass swan, follow these steps:

1. Choose Application button⇨New (or press Ctrl+N) to open a blank scene file. Select New All in the New Scene dialog box.

2. Right-click the Front viewport to make it the active viewport, and choose Views⇨Viewport Background⇨Configure Viewport Background (or press Alt+B).

   The Background panel of the Viewport Configuration dialog box opens.

3. Enable the Use Files option, click the Files button, and in the Select Background Image dialog box that opens, select the Brass swan-front view.jpg image from the Chap 02 directory on the CD, then click Open.

4. Select the Match Bitmap, Lock Zoom/Pan, and Apply to Active View options, and click OK to close the dialog box.

   The image now appears in the background of the Front viewport.

5. Repeat Steps 2 through 4 for the Top and Left viewports.

6. Zoom and pan each view until the image is centered in the background.

Figure 2.21 shows the 3ds Max interface with background images loaded in the Front, Top, and Left viewports.

FIGURE 2.21

Adding a background image to a viewport can help as you begin to model objects.

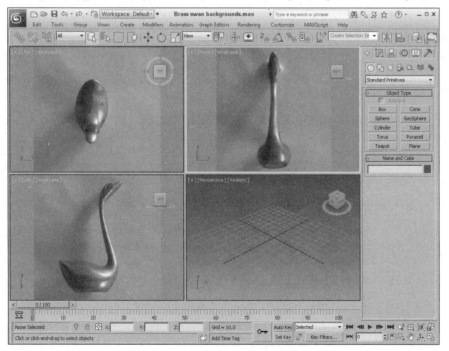

Summary

Viewports are the window into the 3ds Max world. Remember that if you can't see it, you can't work with it, so you need to learn to use the viewports. You also can configure viewports to display just the way you desire.

This chapter covered the following topics:

- Understanding 3D space and the various viewport points-of-view
- Navigating with the ViewCube, the SteeringWheels, and the scroll wheel
- Using the various Viewport Navigation Control buttons
- Changing the Visual Style of the viewport
- Changing the viewport layout, safe frames, clipping planes, and xView information
- Turning materials, lighting, and shadows on and off in the viewport
- Working with viewport background colors, gradients, and images

In the next chapter, you find out all the details about working with files, including loading, saving, and merging scene files. The next chapter also covers the import and export formats for interfacing with other software packages.

CHAPTER 3

Working with Files

IN THIS CHAPTER

Saving, opening, merging, and archiving files

Exporting objects and scenes

Importing objects from external packages

Working with file utilities

Accessing scene files' information

C omplex scenes can end up being a collection of hundreds of files, and misplacing any of them will affect the final output, so learning to work with files is critical. This chapter focuses on working with files, whether they are object files, texture images, or background images. Files enable you to move scene pieces into and out of the Autodesk® 3ds Max® 2013 software. You also can export and import files to and from other packages.

This chapter also includes perhaps the most important feature in 3ds Max, the Save feature, which I suggest you use often. Remember the mantra: Save Early, Save Often.

Working with 3ds Max Scene Files

Of all the different file types and formats, you probably will work with one type of file more than any other—the 3ds Max format. 3ds Max has its own proprietary format for its scene files. These files have the .max extension and allow you to save your work as a file and return to it at a later time. 3ds Max also supports files saved with the .chr extension used for character files.

Using the Application Button

All the various file commands are located by clicking the 3ds Max logo in the upper-left corner. This logo is called the Application Button. The Application Button menu, shown in Figure 3.1, presents its menu options as icons. Several shortcuts also are presented on the Quick Access toolbar located to the right of the Application Button.

FIGURE 3.1

The Application Button menu holds all the various file commands.

The right half of the Application Button menu displays an extensive list of recently opened 3ds Max files. This list holds 10 recently opened filenames, but it can hold up to 50 filenames, as set in the Files panel of the Preference Settings dialog box. The most recently accessed files are organized by last date opened, but clicking the pushpin icon to the right of the filename causes the selected file to remain on the list. In this way, you can keep an important file around for easy access regardless of how old it is.

The icon button at the top of the Recent Documents list lets you change the size of the display icons. The options include Small Icons, Large Icons, Small Images, and Large Images.

> **TIP**
> The image options display a thumbnail of the 3ds Max file.

To the right of the Application Button is the Quick Access toolbar, shown in Figure 3.2. This bar contains icons for the following commands: New Scene, Open File, Save File, Undo Scene Operations, Redo Scene Operations, and Set Project Folder. It also holds a drop-down list of available workspaces.

The arrows to the right of the Undo Scene Operations and Redo Scene Operations icons present a list of buffered commands, and you can select one to undo or redo all commands up to the selected one.

The current workspace is listed at the right end of the Quick Access bar. If you click on the current workspace name, you can select another workspace from the list or access a command to Manage Workspaces, where you can create new workspaces. Clicking the small arrow icon at the right end of the toolbar presents a menu where you can toggle the visibility of each icon. Additional options allow you to hide the menu bar and to move the Quick Access toolbar below the Ribbon.

FIGURE 3.2

The Quick Access toolbar offers quick access for opening and saving files. It also holds the Undo Scene Operations and Redo Scene Operations buttons.

Using the Welcome Screen

When 3ds Max first starts, the Welcome Screen appears, as shown in Figure 3.3. The Welcome Screen includes Essential Skill Movies that show the basics of 3ds Max. It also includes buttons to create a new scene, open an existing scene, and open a recently opened scene.

TIP

If you're new to the software, don't skip the Essential Skills Movies. They are brief and worth taking a minute or so to watch.

FIGURE 3.3

The Welcome Screen includes buttons for opening files and creating new scene files.

If the Show This Welcome Screen at Startup option is disabled, the Welcome Screen won't appear when 3ds Max starts, but you can access it at any time using the Help⇨Essential Skills Movies menu command.

Starting new

When 3ds Max starts, a new scene opens. You can start a new scene at any time with the button on the Quick Access toolbar or with the Application Button⇨New (Ctrl+N) command. Although each instance of 3ds Max can have only one scene open at a time, you can open multiple copies of 3ds Max, each with its own scene instance, if you have enough memory.

Starting a new scene deletes the current scene, but if you've made changes to the current scene, then a dialog box appears asking if want to save your changes. Then, 3ds Max gives you options to keep the objects and hierarchy, keep the objects, or make everything new. These options are available as sub-menu options if you use the Application Button or as a dialog box, shown in Figure 3.4, if the Quick Access toolbar icon or the keyboard shortcut is used.

FIGURE 3.4

When creating a new scene, you can keep the current objects or select New All.

Starting a new scene maintains all the current interface settings, including the viewport configurations, any interface changes, viewport backgrounds, and any changes to the Command Panel. To reset the interface, choose Application Button⇨Reset. When reset, all interface settings return to their default states, but interface changes aren't affected.

Saving files

After you start up 3ds Max, the first thing you should learn is how to save your work. After a scene has changed, you can save it as a file. Before a file is saved, the word "Untitled" appears in the title bar; after you save the file, its filename appears in the title bar. Choose the Save File icon on the Quick Access toolbar or Application Button⇨Save (Ctrl+S) to save the scene. If the scene hasn't been saved yet, then a Save File As dialog box appears, as shown in Figure 3.5. You also can make this dialog box appear using the Application Button⇨Save As command. After a file has been saved, using the Save command saves the file without opening the Save File As dialog box. Pretty simple—just don't forget to do it often.

Within the Save File As dialog box is an option in the Save as Type field to save the file as a 3ds Max file, a 3ds Max 2010 file, a 3ds Max 2011 or a 3ds Max 2012 file. Files saved using a format for a previous version of 3ds Max can be opened only within the designated version or any version newer than that version. Be aware that any new features included in 3ds Max 2013 are not included in the saved file using an older format. For example, if the current file uses a newer feature, and you save the file to an older format, then support for the new feature is lost.

CAUTION

Be aware that 3ds Max files beyond 3ds Max 2010 are not backward-compatible. A .max file saved using 3ds Max 2013 cannot be opened in an earlier version of 3ds Max. The solution to compatibility issues is to export the file using the FBX format and then import it in the older version of 3ds Max.

FIGURE 3.5

Use the Save File As dialog box to save a scene as a file.

Go up one directory

Create a new folder

Go to last folder visited   View Options

Save a numbered version

The Save File As dialog box keeps a history list of the last several directories that you've opened. You can select these directories from the History drop-down list at the top of the dialog box. The buttons in this dialog box are the standard Windows file dialog box buttons used to go to the last folder visited, go up one folder, create a new folder, and to view a pop-up menu of file view options.

NOTE

If you try to save a scene over an existing scene, 3ds Max presents a dialog box confirming this action.

Clicking the button with a plus sign to the right of the Save button automatically appends a number onto the end of the current filename and saves the file. For example, if you select the myScene.max file and click the plus button, a file named myScene01.max is saved.

TIP

Use the auto increment file number and Save button to save progressive versions of a scene. This is an easy version control system. If you need to backtrack to an earlier version, you can.

The Application Button ⇨ Save As submenu includes options to Save As, Save Copy As, Save Selected, and Archive. The Application Button ⇨ Save As ⇨ Save Copy As menu command lets you save the current scene to a different name without changing its current name. The Application Button ⇨ Save As ⇨ Save Selected option saves the current selected objects to a separate scene file. If you create a single object that you might use again, select the object and use the Save Selected option to save it to a directory of models.

> **TIP**
>
> Another useful feature for saving files is to enable the Auto Backup feature in the Files panel of the Preference Settings dialog box. This dialog box can be accessed with the Customize ⇨ Preferences menu command or by clicking the Options button at the bottom of the Application Button menu.

Archiving files

By archiving a 3ds Max scene along with its reference bitmaps, you can ensure that the archived file includes all the necessary files. This is especially useful if you need to send the project to your cousin to show off or to your boss and you don't want to miss any ancillary files. Choose Application Button ⇨ Save As ⇨ Archive to save all scene files as a compressed archive. The default archive format is .zip (but you can change it to use whichever compression program you want in the Files panel of the Preference Settings dialog box to use whatever archive format you want).

Saving an archive as a ZIP file compiles all external files, such as bitmaps, into a single compressed file. Along with all the scene files, a text file is automatically created that lists all the files and their paths.

Opening files

When you want to open a file you've saved, you may do so by choosing the Open File icon on the Quick Access toolbar or Application Button ⇨ Open (Ctrl+O), which opens a file dialog box that is similar to the one used to save files. 3ds Max can open files saved with the .max and .chr extensions. 3ds Max also can open VIZ Render files that have the .drf extension. Selecting a file and clicking the plus button opens a copy of the selected file with a new version number appended to its name.

If 3ds Max cannot locate resources used within a scene (such as maps) when you open a 3ds Max file, then the Missing External Files dialog box, shown in Figure 3.6, appears, enabling you to Continue without the file or to Browse for the missing files. If you click the Browse button, the Configure External File Paths dialog box opens, where you can add a path to the missing files.

> **NOTE**
>
> If 3ds Max cannot locate missing files, a similar warning dialog box also appears when you try to render the scene with missing files.

FIGURE 3.6

The Missing External Files dialog box identifies files for the current scene that are missing.

If you open a file saved using a previous version of 3ds Max that includes features that have changed since the previous version, then 3ds Max presents an obsolete data format warning statement. Resaving the file can fix this problem. However, if you save a file created with a previous version of 3ds Max as a 3ds Max 2013 scene file, then you won't be able to open the file again in the previous versions of 3ds Max.

TIP

You can disable the Obsolete File Message in the Files panel of the Preference Settings dialog box.

NOTE

You can also open files from the command line by placing the filename after the executable name, as in 3dsmax.exe myFile.max. You can also use the –L switch after the executable name to open the last file that was opened.

Setting a Project Folder

By default, the software's Open File dialog box opens to the Scenes folder in the Documents\3dsMax directory, but you can set a project folder that may be located anywhere on your local hard drive or on the network. All file dialog boxes will then open to the new project folder automatically. The Set Project Folder icon on the Quick Access toolbar or the Application Button ⇨ Manage ⇨ Set Project Folder menu opens a dialog box where you can select a project folder. After a project folder is selected, the folder is automatically populated with a series of resource folders.

Within the project folder's root is a file with the .mxp extension named the same as the project folder. This file is a simple text file that can be opened within a text editor. Editing this file lets you define which subfolders are created within the project folder. The defined project folder also is visible within the title bar if the interface is wide enough to display it.

Merging and replacing objects

If you happen to create the perfect prop in one scene and want to integrate the prop into another scene, you can use the Merge menu command. Choose Application Button ⇨ Import ⇨ Merge to load objects from another scene into the current scene. Using this menu command opens a file dialog box that is exactly like the Open File dialog box, but after you select a scene and click the Open button, the Merge dialog box, shown in Figure 3.7, appears. This dialog box displays all the objects found in the selected scene file. It also has options for sorting the objects and filtering certain types of objects. Selecting an object and clicking OK loads the object into the current scene.

NOTE

Using the Merge command places a copy of the object into the current scene. The object maintains no links to the previous scene and can be edited. XRefs are different from merged objects in that they do maintain a link to the previous scene, which allows them to be updated when the original is changed.

FIGURE 3.7

The Merge dialog box lists all the objects from a merging scene.

If you ever get involved in a modeling duel, then you'll probably be using the Application Button ⇨ Import ⇨ Replace menu command at some time. A modeling duel is when two modelers work on the same rough model of named objects and the animator (or boss) gets to choose which object to use. With the Replace command, you can replace a named object with an object of the same name in a different scene. The objects are selected using the Replace dialog box, which is identical to the Merge dialog box, but only the objects with identical names in both scene files display. If no objects with the same name appear in both scene files, a warning box is displayed.

> **TIP**
>
> When working with a team, one person, such as an environment modeler, can add a dummy object to the scene that shares the name of a more detailed model, such as "furniture." When the detailed model is completed, the Replace command adds the detailed model to the scene. This lets the environment modeler work, even though the detailed models aren't completed yet.

Getting out

As you can probably guess, you use the Application Button ⇨ Exit 3ds Max command in the lower-right corner to exit the program, but only after it gives you a chance to save your work. Clicking the window icon with an X on it in the upper right has the same effect (but I'm sure you knew that).

Importing and Exporting

If you haven't noticed, 3ds Max isn't the only game in town. A number of different 3D packages exist, and exchanging files between them is where the importing and exporting menu commands come in. You can find both of these commands in the Application Button menu.

Importing supported formats

Choose Application Button ⇨ Import ⇨ Import to open the Select File To Import dialog box. This dialog box looks like a typical Windows file dialog box. The real power comes with the various Import Settings dialog boxes that are available for each format. These dialog boxes appear after you select a file to import. The settings in the Import Settings dialog box are different for the various format types.

3ds Max can import several different formats. All acceptable files are automatically displayed in the file dialog box, or you can filter for a specific format using the Files of Type drop-down list at the bottom of the file dialog box. The available import formats include the following:

- Autodesk (FBX)
- 3D Studio Mesh, Projects, and Shapes (3DS, PRJ, SHP)
- Adobe Illustrator (AI)
- Autodesk Packet File (APF)
- Pro/ENGINEER ASM (ASM)
- Pro/ENGINEER (PRT)
- CATIA V5 (CARPART, CGR, CATPRODUCT)
- CATIA V4 (MODEL, DLV4, DLV3, DLV, EXP, SESSION, MDL)
- Collada (DAE)
- LandXML/DEM/DDF (DEM, XML, DDF)
- AutoCAD and Legacy AutoCAD (DWG, DXF)
- Flight Studio OpenFlight (FLT)
- Motion Analysis (HTR, TRC)

3

- Initial Graphics Exchange Standard (IGE, IGS, IGES)
- Autodesk Inventor (IPT, IAM)
- JT Open (JT)
- OBJ Material and Object (OBJ)
- Unigraphics-NX (PRT)
- ACIS SAT (SAT)
- Google SketchUp (SKP)
- StereoLitho (STL)
- STEP (STP, STEP)
- Autodesk Alias (WIRE)
- VIZ Material XML Import (XML)

NEW FEATURE
Using the Autodesk DirectConnect utility, many additional CAD formats including CATIA, JT Open, Pro/ENGINEER, Solidworks, STEP, and Unigraphics-NX can now be imported into 3ds Max 2013.

NOTE
Be aware that these formats are used for different types of data. For example, Adobe Illustrator files typically hold only 2D data, and Motion Analysis files hold motion capture data for animations.

Import preference

The Files panel of the Preference Settings dialog box has a single option dealing with importing—Zoom Extents on Import. When this option is enabled, it automatically zooms all viewports to the extent of the imported objects. Imported objects can often be scaled so small that they aren't even visible. This option helps you to locate an object when imported. This option also helps if the imported objects aren't located near the other scene objects.

Exporting supported formats

In addition to importing, you'll sometimes want to export 3ds Max objects for use in other programs. You access the Export command by choosing Application Button ⇨ Export ⇨ Export. You also have the option to Export Selected (available only if an object is selected) and Export to DWF. DWF files use the Design Web Format, which enables them to be viewed by others that don't have access to 3ds Max. The files are compressed and can be viewed and navigated using the Autodesk Design Review program.

3ds Max can export to several different formats, including the following:

- Autodesk (FBX)
- 3D Studio (3DS)
- Adobe Illustrator (AI)
- ASCII Scene Export (ASE)
- AutoCAD (DWG, DXF)
- Collada (DAE)

- Initial Graphics Exchange Standard (IGS)
- Flight Studio OpenFlight (FLT)
- Motion Analysis (HTR)
- Publish to DWF (DWF)
- OBJ Material and Object (OBJ)
- PhysX and APEX (PXPROJ)
- ACIS SAT (SAT)
- StereoLithography (STL)
- Shockwave 3D Scene Export (W3D)
- Autodesk Alias (WIRE)
- VRML97 (WRL)

NEW FEATURE

The ability to export to PhysX and APEX, Shockwave 3D, and Alias is new to 3ds Max 2013.

Moving files to other Suite packages

3ds Max is available as a standalone product, but it also ships within a Creative Suite of applications offered by Autodesk. These suites can include Maya, Softimage, MotionBuilder, and Mudbox, and you can easily move the current 3ds Max scene file to one of these other applications using the Application Button ➪ Send To menu. For each application, you can send the scene as a New Scene, Update the Current Scene, Add to the Current Scene, or Select the Previously Sent Objects.

Manually moving files to and from Maya

Maya is Autodesk's sister to 3ds Max, so you may find yourself having to move scene files between 3ds Max and Maya at some time. If you are not using the Send To command, then the best format to transport files between 3ds Max and Maya is the FBX format. Autodesk controls this format and has endowed it with the ability to seamlessly transport files between these packages.

TIP

The FBX format also is the format to choose when transferring files back and forth with 3ds Max files in older versions of 3ds Max.

The FBX format includes support for all the scene constructs, including animation, bone systems, morph targets, and animation cache files. It has an option to embed textures with the export file or to convert them to the TIF format. Other import and export settings deal with the system units and world coordinate orientation. You also have the ability to filter specific objects.

TIP

When exporting a file for use in Maya, be sure to set the Up Axis to Y-up, or the models will show up rotated.

The FBX format is being continually updated, but the FBX Export dialog box lets you select which FBX version to use. If you need to export a 3ds Max file for use in an older version of 3ds Max, be sure to select an older FBX version in the Version drop-down list.

Using the File Utilities

A single scene can include multiple files including model files, textures, environment lighting, script files, and so on. With all these various files floating around, 3ds Max has included several utilities that make working with them easier. The Utilities panel of the Command Panel includes several useful utilities for working with files. You can access these utilities by opening the Utilities panel and clicking the More button to see a list of available utilities.

Using the Asset Browser utility

The Asset Browser utility is the first default button in the Utilities panel. Clicking this button opens the Asset Browser window. The Asset Browser resembles Windows Explorer, except that it displays thumbnail images of all the supported formats contained within the current directory. Using this window, shown in Figure 3.8, you can browse through directory files and see thumbnails of images and scenes.

> **NOTE**
>
> Even though thumbnails aren't visible in Windows Explorer on Vista or Windows 7, thumbnails are visible when you use Asset Browser.

FIGURE 3.8

The Asset Browser window displays thumbnails of the files in the current directory.

The supported file types include AVI, BMP, CIN, DDS, EXR, GIF, HDRI, IFL, JPEG, MPEG, PNG, PSD, MOV, RGB, RLA, RPF, SGITGA, TIF, and YUV. These types are the same ones that the Rendering menu⇨View Image File command can open. All files with these extensions are viewable within the Asset Browser. You can select to view only a certain type of file using the Filter menu. You also can view and filter MAXScript and AutoCAD DWG files.

> **TIP**
> Open and display the Asset Browser within a viewport by clicking the viewport Point-of-View label and choosing Extended Viewports ⇨ Asset Browser from the pop-up menu.

You also can drag and drop files from the Asset Browser window to 3ds Max. Drag a scene file, and drop it on the software's title bar to open the scene file within 3ds Max. You can drop image files onto the map buttons in the Material Editor window or drop an image file onto a viewport to make a dialog box appear, which lets you apply the image as an Environment Map or as a Viewport Background, respectively.

The Asset Browser window is modeless, so you can work with the 3ds Max interface while the Asset Browser window is open. Double-clicking an image opens it full size in the Rendered Frame Window.

The Asset Browser also can act as a Web browser to look at content online. When the Asset Browser first opens, a dialog box reminds you that online content may be copyrighted and cannot be used without consent from the owner.

The Display menu includes three panes that you can select. The Thumbnail pane shows the files as thumbnails. You can change the size of these thumbnails using the Thumbnails menu. The Explorer pane displays the files as icons the same as you would see in Windows Explorer. The Web pane displays the web page for the site listed in the Address field.

To view websites, you need to be connected to the Internet. The Asset Browser can remember your favorite websites using the Favorites menu. The Asset Browser window also includes the standard web browser navigation buttons, such as Back, Forward, Home, Refresh, and Stop. You also can find these commands in the Browse menu.

3ds Max keeps thumbnails of all the images you access in its cache. The *cache* is a directory that holds thumbnails of all the recently accessed images. Each thumbnail image points to the actual directory where the image is located. Choose File⇨Preferences to open the Preferences dialog box, in which you can specify where you want the cache directory to be located. To view the cached files, choose Filter⇨All in Cache. The Preferences dialog box also includes options to define how to handle dropped files. The options include Always Merge/Import the File, Always XRef the File, or Ask Me Each Time.

Choose File⇨Print to print the file view or web window.

Finding files with the Max File Finder utility

Another useful utility for locating files is the Max File Finder utility, which you get to by using the More button in the Utilities panel of the Command Panel. When you select this utility, a rollout with a Start button appears in the Utilities panel. Clicking this button opens the MAXFinder dialog box. Using MAXFinder, you can search for scene files by any of the information listed in the File Properties dialog box.

> **TIP**
>
> You also can access the MAXFinder dialog box using the MaxFind icon located in the same folder where 3ds Max is installed.

You can use the Browse button to specify the root directory to search. You can select to have the search also examine any subfolders. Figure 3.9 shows the MAXFinder dialog box locating all the scene files that include the word *blue*.

FIGURE 3.9

You can use the MAX File Finder utility to search for scene files by property.

Collecting files with the Resource Collector utility

When a scene is created, image and object files can be pulled from several different locations. The Resource Collector utility helps you consolidate all these files into one location. The settings for this utility appear in the Parameters rollout in the Utilites panel of the Command Panel, as shown in Figure 3.10. The Output Path is the location where the files are collected. You can change this location using the Browse button.

FIGURE 3.10

The Resource Collector utility can compile all referenced files into a single location.

The utility includes options to Collect Bitmaps/Photometric Files, to include the 3ds Max scene file, and to compress the files into a compressed MaxZip/WinZip file. The Copy option makes copies of the files, and the Move option moves the actual file into the directory specified in the Output Path field. The Update Materials option updates all material paths in the Material Editor. When you're comfortable with the settings, click the Begin button to start the collecting.

Accessing File Information

As you work with files, several dialog boxes in 3ds Max supply you with extra information about your scene. You can use this information to keep track of files and record valuable statistics about a scene.

Displaying scene information

If you like to keep statistics on your files (to see whether you've broken the company record for the model with the greatest number of faces), you'll find the Summary Info dialog box useful. Use the Application Button ⇨ Properties ⇨ Summary Info menu command to open a dialog box that displays all the relevant details about the current scene, such as the number of objects, lights, and cameras; the total number of vertices and faces; and various model settings, as well as a Description field where you can describe the scene. Figure 3.11 shows the Summary Info dialog box.

FIGURE 3.11

The Summary Info dialog box shows all the basic information about the current scene.

The Summary Info dialog box also includes a Save to File button for saving the scene summary information as a text file.

Viewing file properties

As the number of files on your system increases, you'll be wishing you had a card catalog to keep track of them all. 3ds Max has an interface that you can use to attach keywords and other descriptive information about the scene to the file. The Application Button ⇨ Properties ⇨ File Properties menu command opens the File Properties dialog box. This dialog box, shown in Figure 3.12, includes three panels: Summary, Contents, and Custom. The Summary panel holds information such as the Title, Subject, and Author of the 3ds Max file and can be useful for managing a collaborative project. The Contents panel holds information about the scene, such as the total number of objects and much more. Much of this information also is found in the Summary Info dialog box. The Custom panel, also shown in Figure 3.12, includes a way to enter a custom list of properties such as client information, language, and so on.

> **NOTE**
>
> You also can view the File Properties dialog box information while working in Windows Explorer by right-clicking the file and selecting Properties. Three unique tabs are visible: Summary, Contents, and Custom. The Summary tab holds the file identification information, including the Title, Subject, Author, Category, Keywords, and Comments.

FIGURE 3.12

The File Properties dialog box contains workflow information such as the scene author, comments, and revision dates.

Viewing files

Sometimes looking at the thumbnail of an image isn't enough to help you decide whether you have the right image. For these cases, you can quickly load the image in question into a viewer to look at it closely. The Rendering ⇨ View Image File menu command opens the View File dialog box shown in Figure 3.13. This dialog box lets you load and view graphic and animation files using the Rendered Frame Window or the default Media Player for your system.

FIGURE 3.13

The View File dialog box can open an assortment of image and animation formats.

The Rendered Frame Window is discussed in more detail in Chapter 20, "Rendering a Scene and Enabling Quicksilver."

The View File dialog box includes several controls for viewing files. The Devices and Setup buttons let you set up and view a file using external devices such as video recorders. The Info button lets you view detailed information about the selected file. The View button opens the file for viewing while leaving the View File dialog box open. The Open button opens the selected file and closes the dialog box. At the bottom of the View File dialog box, the statistics and path of the current file are displayed.

The View File dialog box can open many types of files, including Microsoft videos (AVI), MPEG files, bitmap images (BMP), Kodak Cineon images (CIN), Combustion files (CWS), Graphics Interchange Format images (GIF), Radiance HDRI image files (HDR), Image File List files (IFL), JPEG images (JPG), OpenEXR image files (EXR, FXR), Portable Network Graphics images (PNG), Adobe Photoshop images (PSD), QuickTime movies (MOV), SGI images (RGB), RLA images, RPF images, Targa images (TGA, VST), Tagged Image File Format images (TIF), Abekas Digital Disk images (YUV), and DirectDraw Surface (DDS) images.

You use the Gamma area on the View File dialog box to specify whether an image uses its own gamma settings or the system's default setting, or whether an override value should be used.

Summary

If you look into the different commands located in the Application Button and in the Quick Access toolbar, you'll find commands that let you save your work, share it with others, and reload it for more work. There are also commands to import and export files and several utilities for viewing, accessing and getting information about the file's contents.

This chapter covered the following topics:

- Creating, saving, opening, merging, and archiving files
- Understanding the various import and export types
- Working with the file utilities, such as the Asset Browser
- Using the Summary Info and File Properties dialog boxes to keep track of scene files

Part II, "Manipulating Objects," is next. The first chapter covers the primitive objects and gets some objects into a scene for you to work with.

Part II

Manipulating Objects

Creating and Editing Primitive Objects

IN THIS CHAPTER

Setting system units

Creating primitive objects

Naming objects and setting object colors

Using creation methods

Setting object parameters

Using helper objects and utilities

S o what exactly did the Romans use to build their civilization? The answer is lots and lots of basic blocks. The basic building blocks in the Autodesk® 3ds Max 2013® software are called *primitives*. You can use these primitives to start any modeling job. After you create a primitive, you can then bend it, stretch it, smash it, or cut it to create new objects, but for now, you'll focus on using primitives in their default shape.

This chapter covers the basics of using primitive object types and introduces the various primitive objects, including how to accurately create and edit them by changing some simple parameters. You also use these base objects in the coming chapters to learn about selecting, cloning, grouping, and transforming.

Modeling is covered in depth in Part III, but first you need to learn how to create some basic blocks and move them around. Later, you can work on building a civilization. I'm sure workers in Rome would be jealous.

Selecting System Units

One of the first things you'll want to set before beginning a project is the scene units. Units can be as small as millimeters or as large as kilometers, or they can be generic, which means they have meaning only relative to the other parts of the scene. 3ds Max offers a large array of available units, and you can even define your own.

The system units have a direct impact on modeling and define the units that are represented by the coordinate values. Units directly relate to parameters entered with the keyboard. For example, with the units set to meters, a sphere created with the radius parameter of 2 would be 4 meters across.

3ds Max supports several different measurement systems, including Metric and U.S. Standard units. You also can define a Custom units system. (I suggest parsecs if you're working on a space scene.) Working with a units system enables you to work with precision and accuracy using realistic values.

TIP
Most game engines work with meters, so if you're building assets for a game, set the units to meters.

To specify a units system, choose Customize ➪ Units Setup to display the Units Setup dialog box, shown in Figure 4.1. For the Metric system, options include Millimeters, Centimeters, Meters, and Kilometers. The U.S. Standard units system can be set to the default units of Feet or Inches displayed as decimals or fractional units. You also can select to display feet with fractional inches or feet with decimal inches. Fractional values can be divided from $1/1$ to $1/100$ increments.

FIGURE 4.1

The Units Setup dialog box lets you choose which units system to use. Options include Metric, U.S. Standard, Custom, and Generic.

Using Custom and Generic units

To define a Custom units system, modify the fields under the Custom option, including a units label and its equivalence to known units. The final option is to use the default Generic units. Generic units relate distances to each other, but the numbers themselves are irrelevant. You also can set lighting units to use American or International standards. Lighting units are used to define Photometric lights.

At the top of the Units Setup dialog box is the System Unit Setup button. This button opens the System Unit Setup dialog box, also shown in Figure 4.1. This dialog box enables you to define the measurement system used by 3ds Max. Options include Inches, Feet, Miles, Millimeters, Centimeters, Meters, and Kilometers.

For example, when using 3ds Max to create models that are to be used in the Unreal game editor, you can use the Custom option to define a unit called the Unreal Foot unit that sets 1 Uft equal to 16 units, which matches the units in the Unreal editor just fine.

A multiplier field allows you to alter the value of each unit. The Respect System Units in Files toggle presents a dialog box whenever a file with a different system units setting is encountered. If this option is disabled, all new objects are automatically converted to the current units system.

The Origin control helps you determine the accuracy of an object as it is moved away from the scene origin. If you know how far objects will be located from the origin, then entering that value tells you the Resulting Accuracy. You can use this feature to determine the accuracy of your parameters. Objects farther from the origin have a lower accuracy.

CAUTION

Be cautious when working with objects that are positioned a long way from the scene origin. The farther an object is from the origin, the lower its accuracy and the less precisely you can move it. If you are having trouble precisely positioning an object (in particular, an object that has been imported from an external file), check the object's distance from the origin. Moving it closer to the origin should help resolve the problem.

Handling mismatched units

Imagine designing a new ski resort layout. For such a project, you'd want to probably use kilometers as the file units. If your next project is to design a custom body design on a race car, then you'll want to use meters as the new units. If you need to reopen the ski resort project while your units are set to meters, then you'll get a File Load: Units Mismatch dialog box, shown in Figure 4.2.

This dialog box reminds you that the units specified in the file that you are opening don't match the current units setting. This also can happen when trying to merge in an object with a different units setting. The dialog box lists the units used in both the file and the system and offers two options. The Rescale the File Objects to the System Unit Scale option changes the units in the file to match the current system units setting. The second option changes the system units to match the file unit settings.

TIP

If you rescale the file object to match the system file units setting, then the objects will either appear tiny or huge in the current scene. Use the Zoom Extents All button to see the rescaled objects in the viewport.

FIGURE 4.2

The File Load: Units Mismatch dialog box lets you synch up units between the current file and the system settings.

4

Rescaling world units

If you discover halfway through your scene that you're working with the wrong units, you can use the Rescale World Units utility to scale up the entire scene or just selected objects. To access this utility, click the Utilities panel and then the More button. In the utilities list, select the Rescale World Units utility and click OK. Then click the loaded Rescale button in the Command Panel to open the Rescale World Units dialog box.

The Rescale World Units dialog box has a Scale Factor value, which is the value by which the scene or objects are increased or decreased. If your world was created using millimeter units and you need to work in meters, then increasing by a Scale Factor of 1000 will set the world right. You also can select to scale the entire Scene or just the Selection.

Creating Primitive Objects

3ds Max is all about creating objects and scenes, so it's appropriate that one of the first things to learn is how to create objects. Although you can create complex models and objects, 3ds Max includes many simple, default geometric objects—called *primitives*—that you can use as a starting point. Creating these primitive objects can be as easy as clicking and dragging in a viewport.

Using the Create menu

The Create menu offers quick access to the buttons in the Create panel. All the objects that you can create using the Create panel you can access using the Create menu. Selecting an object from the Create menu automatically opens the Create panel in the Command Panel and selects the correct category, subcategory, and button needed to create the object. After selecting the menu option, you simply need to click in one of the viewports to create the object.

Using the Create panel

The creation of all basic 3ds Max objects, such as primitive spheres, shapes, lights, and cameras, starts with the Create panel (or the Create menu, which leads to the Create panel). This panel is the first in the Command Panel, indicated by a star icon.

Of all the panels in the Command Panel, only the Create panel—shown in Figure 4.3—includes both categories and subcategories. After you click the Create tab, seven category icons are displayed. From left to right, they are Geometry, Shapes, Lights, Cameras, Helpers, Space Warps, and Systems.

The Create panel is the place you go to create objects for the scene. These objects could be geometric objects such as spheres, cones, and boxes or other objects such as lights, cameras, or Space Warps. The Create panel contains a huge variety of objects. To create an object, you simply need to find the button for the object that you want to create, click it, click in one of the viewports—and *voilà*—instant object.

After you select the Geometry category icon (which has an icon of a sphere on it), a drop-down list with several subcategories appears directly below the category icons. The first available subcategory is Standard Primitives. After you select this subcategory, several text buttons appear that enable you to create some simple primitive objects.

> **NOTE**
> The second subcategory is called Extended Primitives. It also includes primitive objects. The Extended Primitives are more specialized and aren't used as often.

FIGURE 4.3

The Create panel includes categories and subcategories.

Create panel

Category icons

Subcategory drop-down list

As an example, click the button labeled Sphere (not to be confused with the Geometry category, which has a sphere icon). Several rollouts appear at the bottom of the Command Panel: These rollouts for the Sphere primitive object include Name and Color, Creation Method, Keyboard Entry, and Parameters. The rollouts for each primitive are slightly different, as well as the parameters within each rollout.

If you want to ignore these rollouts and just create a sphere, simply click and drag within one of the viewports, and a sphere object appears. The size of the sphere is determined by how far you drag the mouse before releasing the mouse button. Figure 4.4 shows the new sphere and its parameters.

4

FIGURE 4.4

You can create primitive spheres easily by dragging in a viewport.

When an object button, such as the Sphere button, is selected, it is highlighted (in yellow or gray depending on your color scheme). This color change reminds you that you are in creation mode. Clicking and dragging within any viewport creates an additional sphere. While in creation mode, you can create many spheres by clicking and dragging several times in one of the viewports. To get out of creation mode, right-click in the active viewport, or click the Select Object button or one of the trans-form buttons on the main toolbar.

After you select a primitive button, several additional rollouts magically appear. These new rollouts hold the parameters for the selected object and are displayed in the Create panel below the Name and Color rollout. Altering these parameters changes the most recently created object.

Naming and renaming objects

Every object in the scene can have both a name and a color assigned to it. Each object is given a default name and random color when first created. The default name is the type of object followed by a number. For example, when you create a sphere object, 3ds Max labels it "Sphere001." These default names aren't very exciting and can be confusing if you have many objects. You can change the object's name at any time by modifying the Name field in the Name and Color rollout of the Command Panel.

> **NOTE**
>
> 3ds Max gives each newly created object a unique name. 3ds Max is smart enough to give each new object a different name by adding a sequential number to the end of the name.

Names and colors are useful for locating and selecting objects, as you find out in Chapter 5, "Selecting Objects and Using Layers."

The Tools ⇨ Rename Objects menu command opens a dialog box that lets you change the object name of several objects at once. The Rename Objects dialog box, shown in Figure 4.5, lets you set the Base Name along with a Prefix, a Suffix, or a number. These new names can be applied to the selected objects or to the specific objects that you pick from the Select From Scene dialog box.

FIGURE 4.5

The Rename Objects dialog box can rename several objects at once.

Assigning colors

The object color is shown in the color swatch to the right of the object name. This color is the color that is used to display the object within the viewports and to render the object if a material isn't applied. To change an object's color, just click the color swatch next to the Name field to make the Object Color dialog box appear. This dialog box, shown in Figure 4.6, lets you select a different color or pick a custom color.

The Object Color dialog box includes the standard 3ds Max palette and the AutoCAD ACI palette. The AutoCAD palette has many more colors than the 3ds Max palette, but the 3ds Max palette allows a row of custom colors. Above the Cancel button is the Select by Color button. Click this button to open the Select Objects dialog box, where all objects that match the selected color are highlighted.

With the Object Color dialog box, if the Assign Random Colors option is selected, then a random color from the palette is chosen every time a new object is created. If this option is not selected, the color

4

of all new objects is the same until you choose a different object color. Making objects different colors allows you to more easily distinguish between two objects for selection and transformation.

FIGURE 4.6

You use the Object Color dialog box to define the color of objects displayed in the viewports.

Select by Color button

The Object Color dialog box also includes a button that toggles between By Layer and By Object, which appears only when an object is selected. Using this button, you can cause objects to accept color according to their object definition or based on the layer of which they are a part.

You can select custom colors by clicking the Add Custom Colors button. This button opens a Color Selector dialog box, shown in Figure 4.7. Selecting a color and clicking the Add Color button adds the selected color to the row of Custom Colors in the Object Color palette. You can also open the Color Selector by clicking on the Current Color swatch. The current color can then be dragged to the row of Custom Colors.

TIP

You can fill the entire row of Custom Colors by clicking repeatedly on the Add Color button.

FIGURE 4.7

The Color Selector dialog box lets you choose new custom colors.

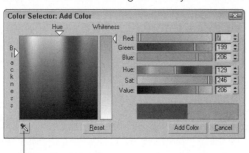

Sample screen color

The Color Selector dialog box defines colors using the RGB (red, green, and blue) and HSV (hue, saturation, and value) color systems. Another way to select colors is to drag the cursor around the rainbow palette on the left. After you find the perfect custom color to add to the Object Color dialog box, click the Add Color button. This custom color is then available whenever the Object Color dialog box is opened.

Object colors are also important because you can use them to select and filter objects. For example, use the Edit⇨Select by⇨Color menu (or click the Select by Color button in the Object Color dialog box) to select only objects that match the selected color.

NOTE

You can set objects to display an object's Object Color or its Material Color. These options are in the Display Color rollout under the Display panel (the fifth tab from the left in the Command Panel with an icon of a monitor). You can set them differently for Wireframe and Shaded views.

The Sample Screen Color tool, located at the bottom of the Color Selector dialog box, lets you select colors from any open 3ds Max window, including the Rendered Frame Window. This gives you the ability to sample colors directly from a rendered image. To use this tool, simply click it and drag around the screen. The cursor changes to an eyedropper. If you click and drag around the window, the color is instantly updated in the Color Selector dialog box. If you hold down the Shift key while dragging, then the selected colors are blended together to create a summed color.

TIP

The Sample Screen Color tool can be used to sample any desktop color, but you need to start dragging in the 3ds Max window first before moving to another one.

Using the Color Clipboard

The object color is one of the first places where colors are encountered, but it certainly won't be the last. If you find a specific color that you like and want to use elsewhere, you can use the Color Clipboard utility to carry colors to other interfaces. You can access this utility using the Tools⇨Color Clipboard menu command, which opens the Utilities panel, as shown in Figure 4.8.

FIGURE 4.8

The Color Clipboard utility offers a way to transport colors.

When selected, the Color Clipboard appears as a rollout in the Utilities panel and includes four color swatches. These color swatches can be dragged to other interfaces such as the Material Editor. Clicking on any of these swatches launches the Color Selector. The New Floater button opens a floatable Color Clipboard that holds 12 colors, shown in Figure 4.9. Right-clicking the color swatches opens a pop-up menu with Copy and Paste options. Using this clipboard, you can open and save color configurations. The files are saved as Color Clipboard files with the .ccb extension.

FIGURE 4.9

The Color Clipboard floating palette can hold 12 colors.

Using different creation methods

You actually have a couple of ways to create primitive objects by dragging in a viewport. With the first method, the first place you click sets the object's initial position. You then need to drag the mouse to define the object's first dimension and then click again to set each additional dimension, if needed. Primitive objects with a different number of dimensions require a different number of clicks and drags.

For example, a sphere is one of the simplest objects to create. To create a sphere, click in a viewport to set the location of the sphere's center, drag the mouse to the desired radius, and release the mouse button to complete. A Box object, on the other hand, requires a click-and-drag move to define the base (width and depth), and another click to set the height. If you ever get lost when defining these dimensions, check the Prompt Line to see what dimension the interface expects next.

When you click a primitive object button, the Creation Method rollout appears and offers different methods for creating the primitives. For example, click the Sphere button, and the Creation Method rollout displays two options: Edge and Center. When you choose the Edge method, the first viewport click sets one edge of the sphere, and dragging and clicking again sets the diameter of the sphere. The default Center creation method defines the sphere's center location; dragging sets the sphere's radius. The creation method for each primitive can be different. For example, the Box primitive object has a creation method for creating perfect cubes, which require only a single click and drag. Table 4.1 shows the number of clicks required to create an object and the creation methods for each primitive object.

TIP

If you're dragging to create a primitive object and halfway through its creation you change your mind, you can right-click to eliminate the creation of the object.

TABLE 4.1 Primitive Object Creation Methods

Primitive Object	Primitive Object Name	Number of Viewport Clicks to Create	Default Creation Method	Other Creation Method
	Box	2	Box	Cube
	Cone	3	Center	Edge
	Sphere	1	Center	Edge

Primitive Object	Primitive Object Name	Number of Viewport Clicks to Create	Default Creation Method	Other Creation Method
	GeoSphere	1	Center	Diameter
	Cylinder	2	Center	Edge
	Tube	3	Center	Edge
	Torus	2	Center	Edge
	Pyramid	2	Base/Apex	Center
	Teapot	1	Center	Edge
	Plane	1	Rectangle	Square
	Hedra	1	-	-
	Torus Knot	2	Radius	Diameter
	ChamferBox	3	Box	Cube
	ChamferCyl	3	Center	Edge
	OilTank	3	Center	Edge
	Capsule	2	Center	Edge
	Spindle	3	Center	Edge
	L-Ext	3	Corners	Center
	Gengon	3	Center	Edge
	C-Ext	3	Corners	Center
	RingWave	2	-	-
	Hose	2	-	-
	Prism	3	Base/Apex	Isosceles

NOTE

Some primitive objects, such as the Hedra, RingWave, and Hose, don't have any creation methods.

Using the Keyboard Entry rollout for precise dimensions

When creating a primitive object, you can define its location and dimensions by clicking in a viewport and dragging, or you can enter precise values in the Keyboard Entry rollout, located in the Create panel. Within this rollout, you can enter the offset XYZ values for positioning the origin of the primitive and the dimensions of the object. The offset values are defined relative to the active construction plane that is usually the Home Grid.

When all the dimension fields are set, click the Create button to create the actual primitive. You can create multiple objects by clicking the Create button several times. After a primitive is created, altering the fields in the Keyboard Entry rollout has no effect on the current object, but you can always use the Undo feature to try again.

Altering object parameters

The final rollout for all primitive objects is the Parameters rollout. This rollout holds all the various settings for the object. Compared to the Keyboard Entry rollout, which you can use only when creating the primitive, you can use the Parameters rollout to alter the primitive's parameters before or after the creation of the object. For example, increasing the Radius value after creating an object makes an existing sphere larger. This works only while the primitive mode is still enabled and the object is still selected.

The parameters are different for each primitive object, but you can generally use them to control the dimensions, the number of segments that make up the object, and whether the object is sliced into sections. You can also select the Generate Mapping Coordinates option (which automatically creates material mapping coordinates that are used to position texture maps) and the Real-World Map Size option (which lets you define a texture's dimensions that are maintained regardless of the object size).

NOTE

After you deselect an object, the Parameters rollout disappears from the Create tab and moves to the Modify tab. You can make future parameter adjustments by selecting an object and clicking the Modify tab.

Recovering from mistakes and deleting objects

Before going any further, you need to be reminded how to undo the last action with the Undo menu command. The Edit ⇨ Undo (Ctrl+Z) menu command will undo the last action, whether it's creating an object or changing a parameter. The Redo (Ctrl+Y) menu command lets you redo an action that was undone.

NOTE

A separate undo and redo feature for undoing and redoing a view change is available in the Views menu. The Views ⇨ Undo View Change (Shift+Z) and Views ⇨ Redo View Change (Shift+Y) applies to any viewport changes like zooming, panning, and rotating the view.

You can set the levels of undo in the General panel of the Preference Settings dialog box. If you click on the small arrow to the left of either the Undo Scene Operation button or the Redo Scene Operation button on the Quick Access toolbar, a list of recent actions appears. You can select any action from this list to be undone, but all actions up to the selection are undone.

> **TIP**
>
> Another way to experiment with objects is with the Hold (Ctrl+H) and Fetch (Alt+Ctrl+F) features, also found in the Edit menu. The Hold command holds the entire scene, including any viewport configurations, in a temporary buffer. You can recall a held scene at any time using the Fetch command. This is a quick alternative to saving a file.

The Edit ⇨ Delete menu command removes the selected object (or objects) from the scene. (The keyboard shortcut for this command is, luckily, the Delete key, because anything else would be confusing.)

Tutorial: Exploring the Platonic solids

Among the many discoveries of Plato, an ancient Greek mathematician and philosopher, were the mathematical formulas that defined perfect geometric solids. A perfect geometric solid is one that is made up of polygon faces that are consistent throughout the object. The five solids that meet these criteria have come to be known as the Platonic solids.

Using 3ds Max, you can create and explore these interesting geometric shapes. Each of these shapes is available as a primitive object using the Hedra primitive object. The Hedra primitive object is one of the Extended Primitives.

To create the five Platonic solids as primitive objects, follow these steps:

1. Open the Create panel, click the Geometry category button, and select Extended Primitives from the subcategory drop-down list. Click the Hedra button to enter Hedra creation mode, or select the Create ⇨ Extended Primitives ⇨ Hedra menu command.

2. Click in the Top viewport, and drag to the left to create a simple Tetrahedron object.

   After the object is created, you can adjust its settings by altering the settings in the Parameters rollout.

> **CAUTION**
>
> Primitive parameters are available in the Create panel only while the new object is selected. If you deselect the new object, then the parameters are no longer visible in the Create panel, but you can access the object's parameters in the Modify panel.

3. Select the Tetra option in the Family section of the Parameters rollout, set the P value in the Family Parameters section to **1.0**, and enter a value of **5** for the Radius. Be sure to press the Enter key after entering a value to update the object. Enter the name **Tetrahedron** in the Name and Color rollout.

4. Click and drag again in the Top viewport to create another Hedra object. In the Parameters rollout, select the Cube/Octa option, and enter a value of **1.0** in the Parameters P field and a value of **5** in the Radius field. Name this object **Octahedron**.

5. Drag in the Top viewport to create another object. The Cube/Octa option is still selected. Enter a value of **1.0** in the Parameters Q field this time, and set the Radius to **5**. Name this object **Cube**.

6. Drag in the Top viewport again to create the fourth Hedra object. In the Parameters rollout, select the Dodec/Icos option, enter a value of **1.0** in the P field, and set the Radius value to **5**. Name the object **Icosahedron**.

4

7. Drag in the Top viewport to create the final object. With the Dodec/Icos option set, enter **1.0** for the Q value, and set the Radius to **5**. Name this object **Dodecahedron**.

8. To get a good look at the objects, click the Perspective viewport, press the Zoom Extents button, and maximize the viewport by clicking the Maximize Viewport Toggle (or press Alt+W) in the lower-right corner of the window.

Figure 4.10 shows the five perfect solid primitive objects. Using the Modify panel, you can return to these objects and change their parameters to learn the relationships among them.

FIGURE 4.10

The octahedron, cube, tetrahedron, icosahedron, and dodecahedron objects; Plato would be amazed.

Using Modeling Helpers

Before leaving the discussion on primitive objects, let's take a look at some modeling helpers. In the Create panel (and the Create menu) is a category of miscellaneous objects called *helpers* (the icon looks like a tape measure). These objects are useful in positioning objects and measuring dimensions.

Using Dummy and Point objects

The Dummy object is a useful object for marking specific locations in the scene with an object that isn't included in the final render. A Dummy object appears in the viewports as a simple cube with a pivot point at its center, but the object will not be rendered and has no parameters. It is used only as an object about which to transform objects. For example, you could create a Dummy object that the camera could follow through an animation sequence. Dummy objects are used in many examples throughout the remainder of the book.

The Point object is very similar to the Dummy object in that it also is not rendered and has minimal parameters. A Point object defines a point in space and is identified as a Cross, an Axis Tripod, or a simple Box. The Center Marker option places an X at the center of the Point object (so X really does mark the spot). The Axis Tripod option displays the X-, Y-, and Z-axes, the Cross option extends the length of the marker along each axis, and the Box option displays the Point object as a Box. The Size value determines how big the Point object is. You can display several of these options at once.

> **TIP**
>
> The Size parameter actually makes Point helpers preferable over Dummy helpers because you can parametrically change their size.

The Constant Screen Size option keeps the size of the Point object constant, regardless of how much you zoom in or out of the scene. The Draw On Top option draws the Point object above all other scene objects, making it easy to locate. The main purpose for the Point object is to mark positions within the scene.

> **CAUTION**
>
> Point objects are difficult to see and easy to lose. If you use a point object, be sure to name it so you can find it easily in the Select From Scene dialog box.

Measuring coordinate distances

The Helpers category also includes several handy utilities for measuring dimensions and directions. These are the Tape, Protractor, and Compass objects. The units are all based on the current selected system units.

Using the Measure Distance tool

In the Tools menu is a command to Measure Distance. This tool is easy to use. Just select it and click at the starting point and again at the ending point; the distance between the two clicks is shown in the Status Bar at the bottom of the interface. Measure Distance also reports the Delta values (the amount of change for each dimension) in the X, Y, and Z directions. You can use this tool with the Snap feature enabled for accurate measurements.

Using the Tape helper

You use the Tape helper object to measure distances. To use it, simply drag the distance that you would like to measure and view the resulting dimension in the Parameters rollout. You can also set the length of the Tape object using the Specify Length option. You can move and reposition the end points of the Tape object with the Select and Move tool, but the Rotate and Scale transforms have no effect.

Using the Protractor helper

The Protractor helper object works in a manner similar to the Tape object, but it measures the angle between two objects. To use the Protractor object, click in a viewport to position the Protractor object. (The Protractor object looks like two pyramids aligned point to point and represents the origin of the angle.) Then click the Pick Object 1 button, and select an object in the scene. A line is drawn from the Protractor object to the pivot point of the selected object. Next, click the Pick Object 2 button and select another object. A second line is drawn from the Protractor object and the pivot point of the second object. The Protractor object and the two lines form an angle and its value is displayed in the Parameters rollout. The value changes when either of the selected objects or the Protractor is moved.

> **NOTE**
>
> All measurement values are presented in gray fields within the Parameters rollout. This gray field indicates that the value cannot be modified.

Using the Compass helper

The Compass helper object identifies North, East, West, and South positions on a planar star-shaped object called a Compass Rose. You can drag the Compass object to increase its size or change its Radius value. The Show Compass Rose option lets you turn the compass on and off.

Using the Measure utility

In the Utilities panel is another useful tool for getting the scoop on the current selected object: the Measure utility. You can open the Measure utility as a floater dialog box, shown in Figure 4.11. This dialog box displays the object's name along with its Surface Area, Volume, Center of Mass, Length (for shapes), and Dimensions. It also includes an option to lock the current selection.

FIGURE 4.11

The Measure dialog box displays some useful information.

Tutorial: Testing the Pythagorean Theorem

I always trusted my teachers in school to tell me the truth, but maybe they were making it all up, especially my math teacher. (He did have shifty eyes, after all.) For my peace of mind, I want to test one of the mathematical principles he taught us, the Pythagorean Theorem. (What kind of name is that anyway?)

If I remember the theorem correctly, it says that the sum of the squares of the sides of a right triangle equals the hypotenuse squared. So, according to my calculations, a right triangle with a side of 3 and a side of 4 has a hypotenuse of 5. Because 3ds Max is proficient at drawing shapes such as this one, we test the theorem by creating a box with a width of 4 and a height of 3 and then measuring the diagonal.

To test the Pythagorean Theorem, follow these steps:

1. **Start by setting the scene units. Select the Customize ⇨ Units Setup to open the Units Setup dialog box. Select the Metric option with the Meters selection from the drop-down list and click OK.**

2. **Select the Create ⇨ Standard Primitives ⇨ Box menu command, and drag and click in the Top viewport to create a Box object. Change its parameters to 4 for the Length, 3 for the Width, and 1 for the Height values.** Then right-click in the active viewport to exit Box creation mode, and press the Z key to zoom in on the Box object.

3. **Right-click the Snaps Toggle on the main toolbar to open** the Snap and Grid Settings dialog box, select the Snaps panel, and set the Snap feature to snap to vertices by clicking the Clear All button and then selecting the Vertex option. Close the Grid and Snap Settings dialog box, and enable the 3D Snap feature by clicking on the Snaps Toggle button in the main toolbar (or by pressing S).

4. Select the Create ⇨ Helpers ⇨ Tape Measure menu command.

5. In the Top viewport, move the cursor over the upper-left corner of the object, and click on the blue vertex that appears. Then drag down to the lower-right corner, and click the next blue vertex that appears. Note the Length value in the Parameters rollout.

Well, I guess my math teacher didn't lie about this theorem, but I wonder whether he was correct about all those multiplication tables. Figure 4.12 shows the resulting box and measurement value.

FIGURE 4.12

I guess old Pythagoras was right. (Good thing I have 3ds Max to help me check.)

Summary

Primitives are the most basic objects and often provide a starting point for more ambitious modeling projects. The two classes of primitives—Standard and Extended—provide a host of possible objects. This chapter covered the following topics:

- Handling system units
- Creating primitives by both dragging and entering keyboard values
- Naming objects and set and change the object color
- Using the various creation methods for all the primitive objects
- Using helper objects and measuring distances

Now that you know how to create objects, you can focus on selecting them after they're created, which is what the next chapter covers. You can select objects in numerous ways. Organizing objects into layers is also discussed.

CHAPTER

5

Selecting Objects and Using Layers

IN THIS CHAPTER

Selecting objects using toolbars and menus

Using named selection sets

Hiding and freezing objects

Working with layers

Exploring the Scene Explorer

Now that you've learned how to create objects and had some practice, you've probably created more than you really need. To eliminate, move, or change the look of any objects, you first have to know how to select the object. Doing so can be tricky if the viewports are all full of objects lying on top of one another. Luckily, the Autodesk® 3ds Max® software offers several selection features that make looking for a needle in a haystack easier.

3ds Max offers many different ways to select objects. You can select by name, color, type, and even material. You also can use selection filters to make only certain types of objects selectable. And after you've found all the objects you need, you can make a selection set, which will allow you to quickly select a set of objects by name.

Another way to organize objects so they are easier to locate and select is to use layers. The Object Layer features in 3ds Max allow you to collect several objects together. Once established, a layer can quickly hide or freeze many scene objects at once with a single command. Now where is that needle?

Selecting Objects

3ds Max includes several methods for selecting objects—the easiest being simply clicking the object or dragging over it in one of the viewports. Selected objects turn white and are enclosed in brackets called *selection brackets*.

In addition to turning white and displaying selection brackets, several options allow you to mark selected objects. You can find these options in the Viewport Configuration dialog box (which you access with the Views ⇨ Viewport Configuration menu command); they include selection brackets (keyboard shortcut, J) and edged faces. Either or both of these options can be enabled, as shown in Figure 5.1. Another way to detect the selected object is that the object's axes appear at the object's pivot point. The Views⇨Shade Selected command turns on shading for the selected object in all viewports including Wireframe viewports.

TIP
If clicking on an object isn't working, it may be that you have another tool selected. Try right-clicking in the viewport to release the current tool or click the Select Object button in the main toolbar.

CAUTION
The Viewport Configuration dialog box also includes an option to Shade Selected Faces (F2), but this option shades only selected subobject faces.

FIGURE 5.1

Selected objects can be highlighted with selection brackets (left), edged faces (middle), or both (right).

With many objects in a scene, clicking directly on a single object, free from the others, can be difficult, but persistence can pay off. If you continue to click an object that is already selected, then the object directly behind the object you clicked is selected. For example, if you have a row of spheres lined up, you can select the third sphere by clicking three times on the first object.

TIP
In complicated scenes, finding an object is often much easier if it has a relevant name. Be sure to name your new objects using the Name and Color rollout. If a single object is selected, its name appears in the Name and Color rollout.

Selection filters

Before examining the selection commands in the Edit menu, I need to tell you about Selection Filters. With a complex scene that includes geometry, lights, cameras, shapes, and so on, selecting the exact object that you want can be difficult. Selection filters can simplify this task.

A selection filter specifies which types of objects can be selected. The Selection Filter drop-down list is located on the main toolbar to the left of the Select Object button. Selecting Shapes, for example, makes only shape objects available for selection. Clicking a geometry object with the Shapes Selection Filter enabled does nothing.

The available filters include All, Geometry, Shapes, Lights, Cameras, Helpers, and Warps. If you're using Inverse Kinematics, you also can filter by Bone, IK Chain Object, Point, and CAT Bone.

The Combos option opens the Filter Combinations dialog box, shown in Figure 5.2. From this dialog box, you can select combinations of objects to filter. These new filter combinations are added to the drop-down list. For example, to create a filter combination for lights and cameras, open the Filter Combinations dialog box, select Lights and Cameras, and click Add. The combination is listed as LC in the Current Combinations section, and the LC option is added to the drop-down list.

FIGURE 5.2

The Filter Combinations dialog box enables you to create a custom selection filter.

The Filter Combinations dialog box also includes a list of additional objects. Using this list, you can filter very specific object types, such as a Boolean object or a Box primitive. In fact, the Bone, IK Chain Object, Point, and CAT Bone filters that appear in the default main toolbar drop-down list all come from this additional list.

Select buttons

On the main toolbar are several buttons used to select objects, shown in Table 5.1. The Select Object button looks like the arrow cursor over a box. The other three buttons select and transform objects. They are Select and Move (W), Select and Rotate (E), and Select and Scale (R). These commands also are available on the quad menu. The final selection button is the Select and Manipulate button. With this button, you can select and use special helpers such as sliders.

5

TABLE 5.1 Select Buttons

Button	Description
	Select Object (Q)
	Select and Move (W)
	Select and Rotate (E)
	Select and Scale (R)
	Select and Manipulate

 See Chapter 6, "Transforming Objects, Pivoting, Aligning, and Snapping," for more details on the Select and Transform buttons.

Selecting with the Edit menu

The Edit menu includes several convenient selection commands. The Edit ➪ Select All (Ctrl+A) menu command does just what you would think it does: It selects all unfrozen and unhidden objects in the current scene of the type defined by the selection filter. The Edit ➪ Select None (Ctrl+D) menu command deselects all objects. You also can simulate this command by clicking in any viewport away from all objects. The Edit ➪ Select Invert (Ctrl+I) menu command selects all objects defined by the selection filter that are currently not selected and deselects all currently selected objects.

The Edit ➪ Select Similar (Ctrl+Q) command selects all objects that are similar to the current selection. Select Instances selects all instances of the current object. Instances are copies of an object that have a link to the original so that changing one automatically changes the other. If multiple objects are selected, the Select Similar command selects the objects that meet the criteria for being similar to each of the selected objects. Objects are similar if they meet one of the following criteria:

- Same object type such as lights, helpers, or Space Warps
- Same primitive object such as Sphere, Box, or Hedra
- Same modeling type such as Editable Spline, Editable Poly, or Editable Patch
- Imported objects from an AutoCAD DWG file that have the same style applied
- Same applied material
- Objects existing on the same layer

Figure 5.3 shows a treasure chest of Hedra gems. With a single object selected, choosing Edit ➪ Select Similar (Ctrl+Q) causes all Hedra primitive objects to be selected.

An instanced object is one that is a copy of another object in the scene, but it maintains a link to the previous object so that changing one automatically changes its instance. If an instanced object is selected, you can use the Edit ➪ Select Instances menu to quickly select all other instances of the current object.

FIGURE 5.3

The Select Similar command selects all Hedra objects.

Select by Name

Choosing Edit ⇨ Select By ⇨ Name opens the Select From Scene dialog box, which is a version of the Scene Explorer dialog box, except that you can't change any parameters. Clicking the Select by Name button on the main toolbar, positioned to the right of the Select Object button, or pressing the keyboard shortcut, H, also opens this dialog box. The Scene Explorer dialog box is covered in detail later in this chapter.

You select objects by clicking their names in the list and then clicking OK, or by simply double-clicking a single item. To pick and choose several objects, hold down the Ctrl key while selecting. Holding down the Shift key selects a range of objects.

Select by Layer

The Layer Manager lets you separate all scene objects into layers for easy selection. The Edit ⇨ Select By ⇨ Layer command opens a simple dialog box listing the defined layers and lets you select a layer. All objects in the selected layer are then selected. The Layer Manager is covered in detail later in this chapter.

Select by Color

Choosing Edit ⇨ Select By ⇨ Color lets you click a single object in any of the viewports. All objects with the same color as the one you selected are selected. Even if you already have an object of that color selected, you still must select an object of the desired color. Be aware that this is the object color, not the applied material color. This command, of course, does not work on any objects without an associated color, such as Space Warps. This same command is also accessible as a button in the Object Color dialog box.

5

111

Select by Region

The Edit ⇨ Selection Region command lets you select from one of two different methods for selecting objects in the viewport using the mouse. First, make sure that you're in select mode, and then click away from any of the objects and drag over the objects to select. The first method for selecting objects is Window Selection. This method selects all objects that are contained completely within the dragged outline. The Crossing Selection method selects any objects that are inside or overlapping the dragged outline. You also can access these two selection methods via the Window/Crossing toggle button found on the main toolbar and shown in Table 5.2.

TIP

If you can't decide whether to use the Crossing or Window selection method, you can select to use both. The General panel of the Preference Settings dialog box provides an option to enable Auto Window/Crossing by Direction. When this option is enabled, you can select a direction, and the Crossing selection method is used for all selections that move from that direction. The Window selection method is used for all selections that move from the opposite direction. For example, if you select Left to Right for the Crossing selection method, then moving from Left to Right uses the Crossing selection method, and selecting from Right to Left uses the Window selection method.

TABLE 5.2 Window Selection Buttons

Button	Description
	Window
	Crossing

You also can change the shape of the selection outline. The Selection Region button on the main toolbar to the left of the Selection Filter drop-down list includes flyout buttons for Rectangular, Circular, Fence, Lasso, and Paint Selection Regions, shown in Table 5.3.

TABLE 5.3 Shape-Shifting Selection Region Buttons

Button	Description
	Rectangular
	Circular
	Fence
	Lasso
	Paint

The Rectangular selection method lets you select objects by dragging a rectangular section (from corner to corner) over a viewport. The Circular selection method selects objects within a circle that grows from the center outward. The Fence method lets you draw a polygon-shaped selection area by clicking at each corner. Simply double-click to finish the fenced selection. The Lasso method lets you draw by freehand the selection area. The Paint method lets you choose objects by painting an area. All objects covered by the paint brush area are selected.

Pressing the Q keyboard shortcut selects the Select Object mode in the main toolbar, but repeated pressing of the Q keyboard shortcut cycles through the selection methods. Figure 5.4 shows the first four selection methods.

FIGURE 5.4

The drill's front is selected using the Rectangular, Circular, Fence, and Lasso selection methods.

Selecting multiple objects

As you work with objects in 3ds Max, you'll sometimes want to apply a modification or transform to several objects at once. You can select multiple objects in several ways. Using the Edit ⇨ Select By ⇨ Name command, the Select by Name main toolbar button, or by pressing the H key, you can open the Select From Scene dialog box. With the Select From Scene dialog box open, you can choose several objects from the list using the standard Ctrl and Shift keys. Holding down the Ctrl key selects or deselects multiple list items, but holding down the Shift key selects all consecutive list items between the first selected and the second selected items.

The Ctrl key also works when selecting objects in the viewport using one of the main toolbar Select buttons. You can tell whether you're in select mode by looking for a button that's highlighted. If you hold down the Ctrl key and click an object, then the object is added to the current selection set. If you drag over multiple objects while holding down the Ctrl key, then all items in the dragged selection are added to the current selection set.

The Alt key deselects objects from the current selection set, which is opposite of what the Ctrl key does.

If you drag over several objects while holding down the Shift key, then the selection set is inverted. Each item that was selected is deselected, and vice versa.

Object hierarchies are established using the Select and Link button on the main toolbar. You can select an entire hierarchy of objects by double-clicking its parent object. You also can select multiple objects within the hierarchy. When you double-click an object, any children of that object also are selected. When an object with a hierarchy is selected, the Page Up and Page Down keys select the next object up or down the hierarchy.

5

Hierarchies and linking objects are covered in Chapter 8, "Grouping, Linking and Parenting Objects."

Another way to select multiple objects is by dragging within the viewport using the Window and Crossing Selection methods discussed previously in the "Select by Region" section.

> **CAUTION**
>
> Although the Move, Rotate, and Scale buttons also may be used to select objects, they can cause problems when selecting multiple objects. If you are selecting multiple objects with the Select and Move tool and you accidentally drag the mouse while moving to the next item, then the entire selection is moved out of place. You can use the Undo feature to return it to its original position. To prevent this from happening, use the Select Object tool when selecting multiple objects.

Using the Paint Selection Region tool

The Paint Selection Region tool is the last flyout button under the Selection Region button. Using this tool, you can drag a circular paint brush area over the viewports, and all objects or subobjects underneath the brush are selected.

The size of the Paint Selection brush is shown as a circle when the tool is selected and may be changed using the Paint Selection Brush Size field in the General panel of the Preference Settings dialog box. Right-clicking the Paint Selection Region button on the main toolbar automatically opens the Preference Settings dialog box. Figure 5.5 shows how the Paint Selection Region may be used to select several spheres by dragging over them.

FIGURE 5.5

The Paint Selection Region tool makes it easy to select spheres by dragging.

Paint Selection Region button   Paint Selection brush

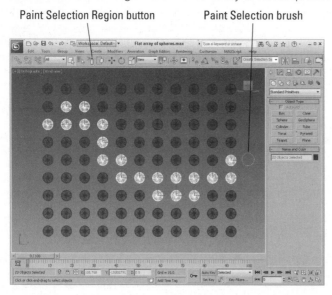

Tutorial: Selecting objects

To practice selecting objects, you'll work with a simple model of the lion toy. When you're finished, you can throw this model to your dog for a chew toy.

To select objects, follow these steps:

1. Open the Lion toy.max scene, which you can find in the Chap 05 directory on the CD.

2. Click the Select Object button (or press the Q key), and click the lion's body in one of the viewports.

   In the Command Panel, the name for this object, lion, is displayed in the Name and Color rollout and the lion's body is selected and highlighted in white.

3. Click the Select and Move button (or press the W key), click the lion's body, and drag in the Perspective viewport to the right.

   Moving the selected body separates it from the rest of the model's objects.

4. Choose Edit ➪ Undo Move (or press Ctrl+Z) to undo the move and to piece the lion back together.

5. With the Select and Move tool still selected, drag an outline around the entire lion in the Top view to select all the lion parts, and then click and drag the entire lion.

   This time, the entire lion moves as one entity, and the name field displays 9 Objects Selected.

6. Open the Select From Scene dialog box by clicking the Select by Name button on the main toolbar (or by pressing the H key).

   All the individual parts that make up this model are listed.

7. Select the nose object listed in the dialog box and click OK.

   The Select From Scene dialog box automatically closes, and the nose object becomes selected in the viewports.

Figure 5.6 shows our lion friend with just its nose object selected. Notice that the name of the selected object in the Name and Color rollout says "nose."

5

FIGURE 5.6

A lion cartoon character with its selected nose

Using named selection sets

With a group of selected objects, you can establish a named selection set. After it's established as a named selection set, you can recall this group of selected objects at any time by selecting its name from the Named Selection Sets drop-down list on the main toolbar or by opening the Named Selection Sets dialog box, shown in Figure 5.7.

You can access this dialog box using the Edit Named Selection Sets button on the main toolbar or by selecting the Edit ➪ Manage Selection Sets menu command. To establish a selection set, type a name in the Named Selection Set drop-down list toward the right end of the main toolbar or use the dialog box.

You also can create named selection sets for subobject selections. Be aware that these subobject selection sets are available only when you're in subobject edit mode and only for the currently selected object.

TIP

Anytime you spend a lot of time selecting a bunch of objects like trees in the landscape scene, you should create a selection set.

Editing named selection Sets

After you've created several named selection sets, you can use the Named Selections Sets dialog box to manage the selection sets. The buttons at the top let you create and delete sets, add or remove objects from a set, and select and highlight set objects. You also can move an object between sets by dragging its name to the set name to which you want to add it. Dragging one set name onto another set name combines all the objects from both sets under the second set name. Double-clicking a set name selects all the objects in the set.

FIGURE 5.7

The Named Selection Sets dialog box lets you view and manage selection sets.

Subtract Selected Objects

Add
Selected
Objects

Select
Objects
in Set

Remove

Select by Name

Create
New
Set

Highlight
Selected
Objects

Locking selection sets

Another alternative to creating a selection set is to lock the current selection. If you've finally selected the exact objects you want to work with, you can disable any other selections using the Selection Lock Toggle button on the status bar. (It looks like a lock.) When this button is enabled, it is highlighted, and clicking objects in the viewports won't have any effect on the current selection. The keyboard shortcut toggle for this command is the spacebar.

> **CAUTION**
> In Photoshop and Illustrator, the spacebar is the keyboard shortcut to pan, but in 3ds Max it locks the current selection. If you accidentally lock the current selection, you can't select any other objects until the lock is removed.

Isolating the current selection

The Tools ⇨ Isolate Selection (Alt+Q) menu command hides all objects except for the selected object. This command is also available by clicking the Isolate Selection Toggle button located on the status bar at the bottom of the interface. It also zooms to extents on the object in the active viewport. The

Isolate Selection Toggle button is highlighted when enabled. Clicking this button or selecting the Isolate Selection command again exits isolation mode and displays all the objects again.

NEW FEATURE
The Isolate Selection Toggle button is new to 3ds Max 2013.

Isolate Selection mode is very convenient for working on a certain area. Figure 5.8 shows the Isolate Selection mode for a selection set that includes all elements of the lion toy's face.

FIGURE 5.8

Isolated Selection mode lets you focus on the details of the selected object.

Selection Lock toggle
Isolate Selection toggle

Selecting objects in other interfaces

In addition to selecting objects in the viewports, you can use many of the other interfaces and dialog boxes to select objects. For example, the Material Editor includes a button that selects all objects in a scene with the same material applied.

 The Select by Material button opens the Select Object dialog box with all objects that use the selected material highlighted.

Another interface that you can use to select objects is the Schematic View, which is opened using the Graph Editors⇨New Schematic View menu command. It offers a hierarchical look at your scene and displays all links and relationships between objects. Each object in the Schematic View is displayed as a rectangular node.

To select an object in the viewport, find its rectangular representation in the Schematic View and simply click it. To select multiple objects in the Schematic View, you need to enable Sync Selection mode with the Select ⇨ Sync Selection command in the Schematic View menu and then drag an outline over all the rectangular nodes that you want to select.

The Schematic View also includes the Select by Name text field for selecting an object by typing its name.

The Material Editor is covered in detail in Chapter 14, "Creating and Applying Standard Materials with the Slate Material Editor."

Setting Object Properties

After an object is selected, you can change its property values using the Object Properties dialog box, shown in Figure 5.9. This dialog box is opened using the Edit ⇨ Object Properties menu. The settings located in this dialog box are different from the parameters found in the Command Panel. Parameters are used to change the resulting look and shape of the object, and object properties are used only to set how the object is displayed and rendered.

FIGURE 5.9

The Object Properties dialog box provides information about the selected object and sets how it is displayed and rendered.

The top portion of the Object Properties dialog box includes information about the selected object including its name, color, position, layer, material, parent, and the number of vertices and faces it has.

TIP

Knowing how many faces an object has is an important piece of information, especially when working with games where you need to know how much memory the object will take. The Object Properties dialog box is an easy place to find this information.

5

The bottom portion of the Object Properties dialog box includes settings for defining how the object is displayed within the viewports and how it is rendered. For example, the See-Through option makes the object appear semi-transparent in the viewports, which is helpful to see how it lines up with other objects. Another helpful setting is the Visibility value. This value can be animated over time to make the object slowly disappear or reappear.

Hiding and Freezing Objects

Hidden and frozen objects cannot be selected, and as such they cannot be moved from their existing positions. This becomes convenient when you move objects around in the scene. If you have an object in a correct position, you can freeze it to prevent it from being moved accidentally or you can hide it from the viewports completely. A key difference between these modes is that frozen objects are still rendered, but hidden objects are not.

You can hide and freeze objects in several ways. You can hide or freeze objects in a scene by selecting the Hide or Freeze options in the Object Properties dialog box. You also can hide and freeze objects using the Display Floater dialog box, which you access by choosing Tools ⇨ Display Floater. You also can hide and freeze objects using the quad menu commands.

> **TIP**
> Several keyboard shortcuts can be used to hide specific objects. These shortcuts are toggles, so one press makes the objects disappear and another press makes them reappear. Object types that can be hidden with these shortcuts include cameras (Shift+C), geometry (Shift+G), grids (G), helpers (Shift+H), lights (Shift+L), particle systems (Shift+P), shapes (Shift+S), and Space Warps (Shift+W).

The Hide option makes the selected object in the scene invisible, and the Freeze option turns the selected object dark gray (if the Show Frozen in Gray option in the Object Properties dialog box is enabled) and doesn't allow it to be transformed or selected. You cannot select hidden objects by clicking in the viewport.

> **NOTE**
> When you use the Zoom Extents button to resize the viewports around the current objects, hidden objects aren't included.

Using the Display Floater dialog box

The Display Floater dialog box includes two tabs: Hide/Freeze and Object Level. The Hide/Freeze tab splits the dialog box into two columns, one for Hide and one for Freeze. Both columns have similar buttons that let you hide or freeze Selected or Unselected objects, By Name or By Hit. The By Name button opens the Select Objects dialog box (which is labeled Hide or Freeze Objects). The By Hit option lets you click in one of the viewports to select an object to hide or freeze. Each column also has additional buttons to unhide or unfreeze All objects, By Name, or in the case of Freeze, By Hit. You also can select an option to Hide Frozen Objects.

> **NOTE**
> Other places to find the same buttons found in the Display Floater are the Hide and Freeze rollouts of the Display panel of the Command Panel and in the right-click quad menu.

The Object Level panel of the Display Floater lets you hide objects by category such as All Lights or All Cameras. You also can view and change many of the Display Properties that are listed in the Object Properties dialog box.

Figure 5.10 shows the Hide/Freeze and Object Level panels of the Display Floater dialog box.

FIGURE 5.10

The Display Floater dialog box includes two panels: Hide/Freeze and Object Level.

Using the Display panel

If you took many of the features of the Display Floater and the Object Properties dialog box and mixed them together, the result would be the Display panel. You access this panel by clicking the fifth icon from the left in the Command Panel (the icon that looks like a monitor screen).

The first rollout in the Display panel, shown in Figure 5.11, is the Display Color rollout. This rollout includes options for setting whether Wireframe and Shaded objects in the viewports are displayed using the Object Color or the Material Color.

FIGURE 5.11

The Display panel includes many of the same features as the Display Floater and the Object Properties dialog box.

The panel also includes a **Hide by Category** rollout. Using this rollout, you can add new categories that will appear in the Object Level panel of the Display Floater. To add a new category, click the Add button of the Hide by Category rollout. **The Add Display Filter** list appears, as shown in Figure 5.12. From this list, you can choose specific object categories to add to the Hide by Category list.

FIGURE 5.12

From this dialog box, you can add new categories to the Hide by Category list.

The Display panel also includes Hide and Freeze rollouts that include the same buttons and features as the Hide/Freeze panel of the Display Floater. You also find a Display Properties rollout that is the same as the list found in the Display Floater's Object Level panel and the Object Properties dialog box.

The Link Display rollout at the bottom of the Display panel includes options for displaying links in the viewports. Links are displayed as lines that extend from the child to its parent object. Using the Link Replaces Object option, you can hide the objects in the viewport and see only the links.

Tutorial: Hidden toothbrushes

In this example, I've hidden several toothbrushes in the scene, and your task is to find them. To find the hidden objects, follow these steps:

1. Open the Toothbrushes.max scene file.

   This file appears to contain only a single toothbrush, but it really contains more. Can you find them? The toothbrush model was created by Viewpoint Datalabs. You can find it in the Chap 05 directory on the CD.

2. Locate the hidden object in the scene by opening the Display Floater (choose Tools ⇨ Display Floater).

3. In the Display Floater, select the Hide/Freeze tab. In the Unhide section, click the By Name button.

   The Unhide Objects dialog box appears, which lists all the hidden objects in the scene.

4. Select the green toothbrush object from the list, and click the Unhide button.

   The Unhide Objects dialog box closes, and the hidden object become visible again.

NOTE
Notice that the Display Floater is still open. That's because it's modeless. You don't need to close it to keep working.

5. To see all the remaining objects, click the All button in the Unhide section of the Display Floater.

Figure 5.13 shows the finished scene with all toothbrushes visible.

FIGURE 5.13

Here are toothbrushes for the whole family; just remember which color is yours.

Using Layers

So what does 3ds Max have in common with a wedding cake? The answer is layers. Layers provide a way to separate scene objects into easy-to-select and easy-to-work-with groupings. These individual layers have properties that can then be turned on and off.

Using the Layer Manager

You create, access, and manage layers through the Layer Manager dialog box, shown in Figure 5.14. This dialog box is a floater that can remain open as you work with objects in the viewports. You can access the Layer Manager using the Tools ⇨ Manage Layers menu command, by clicking the Layer Manager button on the main toolbar, or by clicking the same button in the Layers toolbar.

These layers are different from Animation Layers that are used to break an animation sequence into several different parts that can be blended together. Animation Layers are covered in Chapter 26, "Using Animation Layers and Animation Modifiers."

FIGURE 5.14

The Layer Manager lists all the layers and the objects contained within each layer.

After you've set up your layers, you can control them using the Layers toolbar, shown in Figure 5.15, rather than having the Layer Manager open. You can access the Layers toolbar by right-clicking the main toolbar away from the buttons and selecting the Layers toolbar from the pop-up menu or by selecting the Customize ⇨ Show UI ⇨ Floating Toolbars menu command.

FIGURE 5.15

Use the Layers toolbar to set the active layer.

Set Current Layer to Selection's Layer
   Select Objects in Current Layer
  Add Selection to Current Layer
     Create New Layer

Manage Layers
  Layer Selection drop-down list

Table 5.4 lists the buttons found in the Layer Manager.

TABLE 5.4 **Layer Manager Buttons**

Button Icon	Name	Description
	Create New Layer (Containing Selected Objects)	Creates a new layer that includes the selected objects
	Delete Highlighted Empty Layers	Deletes a layer if the layer is highlighted and empty
	Add Selected Objects to Highlighted Layer	Adds any selected objects to the current highlighted layer

Button Icon	Name	Description
	Select Highlighted Objects and Layers	Selects in the viewports any highlighted layers or objects
	Highlight Selected Objects' Layers	Highlights the layer of the viewport's selected object in the Layer Manager
	Hide/Unhide All Layers	Toggles between hiding and unhiding all layers
	Freeze/Unfreeze All Layers	Toggles between freezing and unfreezing all layers

With the Layer Manager open, you can create new layers by clicking the Create New Layer (Containing Selected Objects) button. This adds a new layer to the manager, names it "Layer001," and includes any selected objects as part of the layer. If you click the layer's name, you can rename it. Layer 0 is the default layer to which all objects are added, if other layers don't exist. Layer 0 cannot be renamed.

NOTE

Although you can rename layers in the Layer Manager, you cannot use the Layer Manager to rename objects. To rename an object from the Layer Manager, simply click the object's icon to open the Object Properties dialog box, where you can change the object's name.

Creating a new layer automatically makes the new layer the current layer as denoted by the check mark in the first column of the Layer Manager. All new objects that are created are automatically added to the current layer. Only one layer can be current at a time, but several layers or objects can be highlighted. To highlight a layer, click it in the Layer Manager. Highlighted layers are highlighted in yellow.

A highlighted layer can be deleted with the Delete Highlighted Empty Layers button, but only if it is not the current layer and it doesn't contain any objects.

Newly created objects are added to the current layer (the one marked with a check mark in the first column of the Layer Manager). If you forget to select the correct layer for the new objects, you can select the objects in the viewports, highlight the correct layer, and use the Add Selected Objects to Highlighted Layer button to add the objects to the correct layer.

NOTE

Every object can be added only to a single layer. You cannot add the same object to multiple layers.

The Select Highlighted Objects and Layers button selects the highlighted layers (and objects) in the viewports. This provides a way to select all the objects on a given layer. If an object in the viewports is selected, you can quickly see which layer it belongs to with the Highlight Selected Object's Layers button.

If you expand the layer name in the Layer Manager, you see a list of all the objects contained within the layer. If you click the Layer icon (to the left of the layer's name), the Layer Properties dialog box,

5

shown in Figure 5.16, opens. Clicking the Object icon opens the Object Properties dialog box. You also can open either of these dialog boxes by right-clicking the layer name and selecting either from the pop-up menu.

FIGURE 5.16

The Layer Properties dialog box is similar to the Object Properties dialog box, but it applies to the entire layer.

Using the layer list

The main section of the Layer Manager (and repeated in the Layers toolbar) is the layer list and its columns, which allow you to turn certain properties on and off. The properties in the columns include Hide, Freeze, Render, Color, and Radiosity. If a property is enabled, a simple icon is displayed; if disabled, a dash is displayed. If an object is set to get its property from the layer (by clicking the ByLayer button in the Object Properties dialog box), then a dot icon is displayed. Individual objects within a layer can have different properties. You can sort the column properties by clicking the column head.

You can toggle these properties on and off by clicking them. You also can set these properties in the Layers toolbar. The Hide toggle determines whether the layer's objects are visible in the viewports. The Freeze toggle makes objects on a layer unselectable. The Render toggle enables the layer's objects to be rendered. The Color toggle sets the layer color. Layer 0 is set to assign random colors and cannot be changed. The Radiosity toggle includes the layer's objects in the radiosity calculations.

The Layer Manager also includes a right-click pop-up menu that includes many of the same commands found as buttons, but a unique set of commands found in the right-click pop-up menu are the Cut and Paste commands. With these commands, you can select objects in one layer to cut and paste into another layer.

CAUTION

If multiple objects are selected within the Layer Manager, then right-clicking an object's name deselects all the selected objects. To maintain the current selection, right-click within the Layer Manager, away from the Layers column.

Tutorial: Dividing a scene into layers

As a scene begins to come together, you'll start to find that it is difficult to keep track of all the different pieces. This is where the layers interface can really help. In this example, you take a simple scene and divide it into several layers.

To divide a scene into layers, follow these steps:

1. Open the Elk on hill layers.max scene file.

   You can find it in the Chap 05 directory on the CD. This file includes an Elk model created by Viewpoint Datalabs.

2. Select Tools ⇨ Manage Layers to open the Layer Manager.

3. With no objects selected, click the Create New Layer (Containing Selected Objects) button and name the layer **Hill and trees**. Click the Create New Layer (Containing Selected Objects) button again, and name this layer **Elk**. Click the Create New Layer (Containing Selected Objects) button again, and create a layer named **Background and light**. The Layer Manager now includes four layers, including Layer 0.

4. In the Layer Manager, click the Selection column for the Elk layer to make it the current layer. With the Edit ⇨ Select All (Ctrl+A) menu command, select all objects in the scene and click the Add Selected Objects to Highlighted Layer button in the Layer Manager.

5. Expand the Elk layer by clicking the + icon to the left of its name.

   This displays all the objects within this layer.

6. Select all the trees and the hill objects by holding down the Ctrl key and clicking each object's name in the Layer Manager. Then right-click away from the names, and select Cut from the pop-up menu. Then select the Hill and trees layer, and select Paste from the right-click pop-up menu.

7. Select the background and light objects from within the Elk layer, and click the Select Highlighted Objects and Layers button. Then select the Background and light layer, and click the Add Selected Objects to Highlighted Layer button to move the background and light objects to the correct layer.

You can now switch between the layers, depending on which one you want to add objects to or work on, and you can change properties as needed. For example, to focus on the elk object, you can quickly hide the other layers using the Layer Manager. Figure 5.17 shows the various layers and the objects in each layer.

5

FIGURE 5.17

All objects assigned to a layer can be viewed in the Layer Manager dialog box.

Using the Scene Explorer

The Scene Explorer is a one-stop shop for all scene objects and display properties. It displays all the objects in the scene in a hierarchical list along with various display properties. It allows you to filter the display so you can see just what you want and customize the display so only those properties you want to see are visible. The Scene Explorer also lets you select, rename, hide, sort, freeze, link, and delete objects and change the object color.

A Scene Explorer dialog box, shown in Figure 5.18, is opened using the Tools ⇨ New Scene Explorer menu command (Alt+Ctrl+O). Each subsequent Scene Explorer view is numbered, but these individual views also can be named using the View field at the top of each Scene Explorer window. Each new or named view can be recalled with the Tools ⇨ Saved Scene Explorers menu, and the Tools ⇨ Manage Scene Explorers opens a simple dialog box where you can Load, Save, Delete, and Rename the saved views.

> **NOTE**
> Scene Explorer views are automatically saved and reloaded with the 3ds Max file.

All scene objects in the Scene Explorer are listed in hierarchical order with children objects indented under their parent objects. You can expand or contract children objects by clicking the plus (+) or minus (–) icon to the left of the parent object.

FIGURE 5.18

The Scene Explorer dialog box displays all scene objects and their display properties.

Object Filter buttons

Display Containers
Display Hidden Objects
Display None
Enable Advanced Filtering
Lock Cell Editing
Configure Advanced Filtering

Display Frozen Objects
Display All
Invert Display
Select All

Filter Selection Set
Sync Selection
Select Invert
Select None

Selecting and filtering objects

If you click an object in the Scene Explorer dialog box, the object row is highlighted. Holding down the Ctrl key lets you click to select multiple objects, or you can use the Shift key to select a range of adjacent objects. Selected objects also can be removed from the current selection with the Ctrl key held down.

The Select menu also includes options for selecting objects. The Select All (Ctrl+A), Select None (Ctrl+D), and Select Invert (Ctrl+I) menu commands work as expected, selecting all objects, deselecting all objects, and selecting the inverse of the current selection. You also can access these commands using the buttons at the bottom of the dialog box.

The Select Children (Ctrl+C) option causes all children objects to automatically be selected when the parent is selected. The Select Influences option selects all influence objects that are attached to the selected objects. An influence object is an object that controls or shapes another object. For example, when a sphere is constrained to follow an animation path, the path is an influence object to the sphere. Another example is a skin mesh being influenced by a biped rig. The Select Dependants option selects any objects that are dependent on the selected object, such as an instance and reference.

5

When the Select ⇨ Sync Selection option is enabled, any objects selected in the Scene Explorer dialog box are automatically selected in the viewports also. This also works in reverse, causing any objects selected in the viewport to be selected in the Scene Explorer dialog box.

The Scene Explorer recognizes any defined Selection Sets and lets you select these sets from the drop-down list at the bottom of the interface.

The Display toolbar includes several object type icons. The yellow icons are selected and allowed to be viewed in the Scene Explorer. To filter out a specific object type, disable its icon, and then all objects of that type are no longer displayed in the list. These same commands are available in the Display ⇨ Object Types menu.

The Display menu includes some additional commands for displaying children, influences, and dependants. You also have an option to Display in Track View. This option opens the Track View with the selected object's tracks visible.

The Track View interface is covered in more detail in Chapter 28, "Editing Animation Curves in the Track View."

Finding objects

You also can use the Find field to search the hierarchy for a specific object by name. All objects that match the typed characters are selected. If you enable the Select ⇨ Find Case Sensitive option, upper-case characters are distinguished from lowercase characters.

If the Select ⇨ Find Using Wildcards option is selected, you can use wildcards to locate objects. Acceptable wildcards include an asterisk (*) for multiple characters in a row and a question mark (?) for single characters. For example, an entry of **hedra*** selects all objects beginning with "hedra," regard-less of the ending and **hedra?1** finds "hedra01" and "hedra11" but not "hedra02" or "hedra0001."

The Select ⇨ Find Using Regular Expressions option provides yet another way to search for specific objects. Regular expressions are commonly used in various scripting languages and require specific syntax in order to locate objects. Table 5.5 lists some common regular expression characters.

TABLE 5.5   Common Regular Expression Syntax

Character	Description	Example
[htk]	Used to define a group of search characters	Matches all objects beginning with the letters *h*, *t*, and *k*
eye|light|key	Used to separate words to search for	Matches all objects beginning with eye, light, or key
\w	Used to identify any letter or number, just like the ? wildcard	Matches any number or letter
\s	Used to identify any white space	Matches any space between words, no matter the length
\d	Used to identify any single digit number	Matches any single-digit number, 0 through 9

Character	Description	Example
[^geft]	Used to match all objects except for the ones inside the brackets	Matches all objects except for those that begin with g, e, f, or t
t.*1	Used to match multiple letters in between two specified characters	Matches all objects that begin with the letter t and end with the number 1

If regular expressions seem confusing, you also can search using the Advanced Search dialog box, shown in Figure 5.19. This dialog box is opened using the Select ⇨ Search menu command or by clicking the Configure Advanced Filter button. In the Property field, you can search by Name, Type, Color, Faces, or any of the other available columns. In the Condition, the options include Starts With, Does Not Start With, Contains String, Does Not Contain String, Regular Expression Matches, and Inverse Regular Expression Matches. Multiple criteria can be added to the search list.

FIGURE 5.19

The Advanced Search dialog box lets you select search criteria using drop-down lists.

Editing in the Scene Explorer

Any of the display properties listed in the Scene Explorer can be enabled by simply clicking the check box to enable the property. If multiple objects are selected when a property is enabled or disabled, the same property is enabled or disabled for all the selected objects at the same time.

> **NOTE**
> If the Lock Cell Editing button is enabled, none of the properties can be changed.

If you click the column name, you can sort all the listed objects either in descending or ascending order. Click the column name once to sort in ascending order and again to sort in descending order. You also can right-click and select the sorting order from the pop-up menu. For example, if you click the Faces column, all the objects are sorted so the objects with the smallest number of faces are listed at the top of the interface and the objects with the most faces are listed at the bottom.

You also can rearrange the columns by dragging and dropping them to a new location. Selecting the Customize ⇨ Configure Columns menu opens the Configure Columns dialog box, shown in Figure 5.20. This dialog box lists all the available remaining display property columns. To add one to the Scene Explorer, simply select it from the Configure Columns dialog box and drop it where you want it.

5

The Configure Columns dialog box includes a large number of properties that can be added as columns to the Scene Explorer including Revit Category, Revit Family, Revit Level, Revit Type, and Application Origin.

> **TIP**
> The width of each column can be altered by dragging on either side. To reset all column widths, right-click a column name and choose Best Fit (all columns) from the pop-up menu.

FIGURE 5.20

The Configure Columns dialog box holds all the display properties not currently available in the Scene Explorer.

Using the Edit menu, you also can cut, copy, and paste selected objects, called nodes. Pasting objects opens the Clone Options dialog box. The Customize menu also includes options to hide various toolbars and a choice to lay out the window using horizontal or vertical icons.

Summary

Selecting objects enables you to work with them, and 3ds Max includes many different ways to select objects. You also learned how to work with selection sets, hide and freeze objects, and divide the scene into layers. The Scene Explorer dialog box also was covered. In this chapter, you've done the following:

- Learned how to use selection filters
- Selected objects with the Edit menu by Name, Layer, Color, and Region
- Selected multiple objects and used a named selection set to find the set easily
- Selected objects using other interfaces
- Learned how to hide and freeze objects
- Separated objects using layers
- Used the Scene Explorer dialog box

Now that you've learned how to select objects, you're ready to move them about using the transform tools, which are covered in the next chapter.

Transforming Objects, Pivoting, Aligning, and Snapping

IN THIS CHAPTER

Transforming objects

Controlling transformations with the Transform Gizmos

Using the Transform Type-Ins, and the Transform Managers

Working with pivot points and axis constraints

Aligning objects with the align tools

Using grids and snapping objects to common points

Although a *transformation* sounds like something that would happen during the climax of a superhero film, transformation is simply the process of "repositioning" or changing an object's position, rotation, or scale. So moving an object from here to there is a transformation. Superman would be so envious.

The Autodesk® 3ds Max® 2013 software includes several tools to help in the transformation of objects, including the Transform Gizmos, the Transform Type-In dialog box, and the Transform Managers.

This chapter covers each of these tools and several others that make transformations more automatic, such as the alignment, grid, and snap features.

Translating, Rotating, and Scaling Objects

So you have an object created, and it's just sitting there—sitting and waiting. Waiting for what? Waiting to be transformed. To be moved a little to the left or rotated around to show its good side or scaled down a little smaller. These actions are called transformations because they transform the object to a different state. Transformations are different from modifications. Modifications change the object's geometry, but transformations do not affect the object's geometry at all.

The three different types of transformations are translation (which is a fancy word for moving objects), rotation, and scaling.

Translating objects

The first transformation type is *translation*, or moving objects. This is identified in the various transform interfaces as the object's Position. You can move objects along any of the three axes or within the three planes. You can move objects to an absolute coordinate location or move them to a certain offset distance from their current location.

To move objects, click the Select and Move button on the main toolbar (or press the W key), select the object to move, and drag the object in the viewport to the desired location. Translations are measured in the defined system units for the scene, which may be inches, centimeters, meters, and so on.

Rotating objects

Rotation is the process of spinning the object about its Transform Center point. To rotate objects, click the Select and Rotate button on the main toolbar (or press the E key), select an object to rotate, and drag it in a viewport. Rotations are measured in degrees, where 360 degrees is a full rotation.

Scaling objects

Scaling increases or decreases the overall size of an object. Most scaling operations are uniform, or equal in all directions. All Scaling is done about the Transform Center point.

To scale objects uniformly, click the Select and Uniform Scale button on the main toolbar (or press the R key), select an object to scale, and drag it in a viewport. Scalings are measured as a percentage of the original. For example, a cube scaled to a value of 200 percent is twice as big as the original.

Non-uniform scaling

The Select and Scale button includes two additional flyout buttons for scaling objects non-uniformly, allowing objects to be scaled unequally in different dimensions. The two additional tools are Select and Non-Uniform Scale, and Select and Squash, shown in Table 6.1. Resizing a basketball with the Select and Non-Uniform Scale tool could result in a ball that is oblong and taller than it is wide. Scaling is done about whatever axes have been constrained (or limited) using the Axis Constraint buttons on the Axis Constraints toolbar.

Squashing objects

The Squash option is a specialized type of non-uniform scaling. This scaling causes the constrained axis to be scaled at the same time that the opposite axes are scaled in the opposite direction. For example, if you push down on the top of a basketball by scaling the Z-axis, the sides, or the X- and Y-axes, it bulges outward. This simulates the actual results of such materials as rubber and plastic.

> **TIP**
> You can cycle through the different Scaling tools by repeatedly pressing the R key.

Figure 6.1 shows a basketball that has been scaled using uniform scaling, non-uniform scaling, and squash modes.

FIGURE 6.1

These basketballs have been scaled using uniform, non-uniform, and squash modes.

> **NOTE**
> It is also important to be aware of the order of things. Transformations typically happen after all object properties and modifiers are applied. So, if you scale an object, it happens after the deforming modifier is applied.

Using the transform buttons

The three transform buttons located on the main toolbar are Select and Move, Select and Rotate, and Select and Uniform Scale, as shown in Table 6.1. Using these buttons, you can select objects and transform them by dragging in one of the viewports with the mouse. You can access these buttons using three of the big four keyboard shortcuts: Q for Select Objects, W for Select and Move, E for Select and Rotate, and R for Select and Uniform Scale.

TABLE 6.1   Transform Buttons

Toolbar Button	Name	Description
	Select and Move (W)	Enters move mode where clicking and dragging an object moves it.
	Select and Rotate (E)	Enters rotate mode where clicking and dragging an object rotates it.
	Select and Uniform Scale (R), Select and Non- uniform Scale, Select and Squash	Enters scale mode where clicking and dragging an object scales it.

Working with the Transformation Tools

To help you in your transformations, you can use several tools to transform. These tools include the Transform Gizmos, the Transform Type-In dialog box (F12), Status Bar Transform Type-In fields, and the Transform Managers.

Working with the Transform Gizmos

The Transform Gizmos appear at the center of the selected object (actually at the object's pivot point) when you click one of the transform buttons. The type of gizmo that appears depends on the transformation mode that is selected. You can choose from three different gizmos, one for each transformation type. Each gizmo includes three color-coded arrows, circles, or lines representing the X-, Y-, and Z-axes. The X-axis is colored red, the Y-axis is colored green, and the Z-axis is colored blue. Figure 6.2 shows the gizmos for each of the transformation types—move, rotate, and scale.

FIGURE 6.2

The Transform Gizmos let you constrain a transformation to a single axis or a plane.

If the Transform Gizmo is not visible, you can enable it by choosing Views ➪ Show Transform Gizmo or by pressing the X key to toggle it on and off. You can use the – (minus) and = (equal) keys to decrease or increase the gizmo's size.

Using the interactive gizmos

Moving the cursor over the top of one of the Transform Gizmo's axes in the active viewport selects the axis, which changes to yellow. Dragging the selected axis restricts the transformation to that axis only. For example, selecting the red X-axis on the Move Gizmo and dragging moves the selected object along only the X-axis.

> **NOTE**
> The transformation gizmos provide an alternate (and visual) method for constraining transformations along an axis or plane. This reduces the need for the Axis Constraint buttons, which are found on a separate floating toolbar. Learning to use these gizmos is well worth the time.

The Move Gizmo

In addition to the arrows for each axis, in each corner of the Move Gizmo are two perpendicular lines for each plane. These lines let you transform along two axes simultaneously. The colors of these lines match the various colors used for the axes. For example, in the Perspective view, dragging on a red and blue corner would constrain the movement to the XZ plane. Moving the cursor over the top of one of these lines highlights it. At the center of the Move Gizmo is a Center Box that marks the pivot point's origin.

The Rotate Gizmo

The Rotate Gizmo surrounds the selected object in a sphere that is made up of colored lines, one for each axis and each circles the surrounding sphere. As you select an axis and drag, an arc is highlighted that shows the distance of the rotation along that axis and the offset value is displayed in text above the object. Clicking within the sphere away from the axes lets you rotate the selected object in all directions. Dragging on the outer gray circle causes the selected object to spin perpendicular to the viewport.

The Scale Gizmo

The Scale Gizmo consists of two triangles and a line for each axis. Selecting and dragging the center triangle uniformly scales the entire object. Selecting a slice of the outer triangle scales the object along the adjacent two axes, and dragging on the axis lines scales the object in a non-uniform manner along a single axis.

TIP
To keep the various gizmo colors straight, simply remember that RGB = XYZ.

Additional settings that control how the transformation gizmos work are located in the Gizmo panel of the Preference Settings dialog box, opened using the Customize menu. These settings control the size and thresholds of the various gizmos. If you find that the gizmos are cumbersome, try tweaking these settings.

Using the Transform Toolbox

The Transform Toolbox, shown in Figure 6.3, is a pop-up panel that offers quick access to the most common transformation operations. You can open this panel using the Edit ⇨ Transform Toolbox menu command. The panel can be docked to the side of the interface by dragging it near the window border.

FIGURE 6.3

The Transform Toolbox provides quick access to the most common transformation operation.

Rotate Counter-clockwise
Degrees drop-down list
Rotate Clockwise
Reset XForm
Get size of object
Put current size in spinner

The Transform Toolbox is divided into four sections—Rotate, Size, Align Pivot, and Object. The Rotate section includes buttons for rotating the current selection by a set number of degrees in a clockwise or counterclockwise direction based on the current view. The drop-down list includes rotation values ranging from 1, 5, and 10 up to 180 and 240.

The Size section includes controls for scaling objects. The Set Size button scales the current object to the designated Size value along the specified axis or uniformly if the All option is selected. The R button resets the object transform by automatically applying the XForm modifier and then collapsing the stack to its base object. This sets the scaling values back to 100 percent for all axes. The Get button opens a small pop-up panel that lists the scale values for each of the axes, and the Put Current Size In Spinner button places the scale value for the selected object in the Size field for the specified axis.

The Align Pivot section changes the location of the selected object's pivot without having to open the Hierarchy panel. Using the Min, Max, Center, and Origin options, you can move the pivot's origin for the X, Y, or Z axes or you can use the Center and Origin buttons to move it for all three axes. Center moves the pivot to the object's center, and Origin moves the pivot to the center of the current scene.

The Object section includes only two buttons. The Center button moves the entire object to the world's origin. The QClone button, which stands for Quick Clone, creates a duplicate object and moves it to the side of the original object.

More information on the Quick Clone feature is available in Chapter 7, "Cloning Objects and Creating Object Arrays."

Using the Transform Type-In dialog box

The Transform Type-In dialog box (F12) lets you input precise values for moving, rotating, and scaling objects. This command provides more exact control over the placement of objects than dragging with the mouse.

The Transform Type-In dialog box allows you to enter numerical coordinates or offsets that can be used for precise transformations. Open this dialog box by choosing Edit ⇨ Transform Type-In or by pressing the F12 key.

TIP
Right-clicking any of the transform buttons opens the Transform Type-In dialog box for the transform button that is clicked.

The Transform Type-In dialog box is modeless and allows you to select new objects as needed or to switch between the various transforms. When the dialog box appears, it displays the coordinate values for the pivot point of the current selection if the Move tool is selected, rotation values in degrees if the Rotate tool is selected, or Scale percentages in the Absolute: World column.

Within the Transform Type-In dialog box are two columns. The first column displays the current Absolute coordinates. Updating these coordinates transforms the selected object in the viewport. The second column displays the Offset values. These values are all set to 0.0 when the dialog box is first opened, but changing these values transforms the object along the designated axis by the entered value. Figure 6.4 shows the Transform Type-In dialog box for the Move Transform.

6

FIGURE 6.4

The Transform Type-In dialog box displays the current Absolute coordinates and Offset values.

Using the Status Bar Type-In fields

The Status Bar includes three fields labeled X, Y, and Z for displaying transformation coordinates. When you move, rotate, or scale an object, the X, Y, and Z offset values appear in these fields. The values depend on the type of transformation taking place. Translation shows the unit distances, rotation displays the angle in degrees, and scaling shows a percentage value of the original size.

When you click the Select Object button, these fields show the absolute position of the cursor in world coordinates based on the active viewport.

You also can use these fields to enter values, as with the Transform Type-In dialog box. The type of transform depends on which transform button you select. The values that you enter can be either absolute coordinates or offset values, depending on the setting of the Transform Type-In toggle button that appears to the left of the transform fields. This toggle button lets you switch between Absolute and Offset modes, as shown in Table 6.2.

TABLE 6.2 Absolute/Offset Buttons

Button	Description
	Absolute mode
	Offset mode

Understanding the Transform Managers

To keep track of the position of every object in a scene, internally 3ds Max records the position of the object's vertices in reference to a Universal Coordinate System (UCS). This coordinate system defines the vertex position using the X, Y, and Z coordinates from the scene's origin.

However, even though 3ds Max uses the UCS to internally keep track of all the points, this isn't always the easiest way to reference the position of an object. Imagine a train with several cars. For each individual train car, it is often easier to describe its position as an offset from the car in front of it.

The Transform Managers are three types of controls that help you define the system about which objects are transformed. These controls, found on the main toolbar and on the Axis Constraints toolbar, directly affect your transformations. They include the following:

- **Reference Coordinate System:** This defines the coordinate system about which the transformations take place.
- **Transform Center settings:** The Use Pivot Point Center, Use Selection Center, and Use Transform Coordinate Center settings specify the center about which the transformations take place.
- **Axis Constraint settings:** These allow the transformation to happen using only one axis or plane. These buttons are on the Axis Constraints toolbar.

Understanding reference coordinate systems

3ds Max supports several reference coordinate systems based on the UCS, and knowing which reference coordinate system you are working with as you transform an object is important. Using the wrong reference coordinate system can produce unexpected transformations.

Within the viewports, the UCS coordinates are displayed as a set of axes in the lower-left corner of the viewport, and the Transform Gizmo is oriented with respect to the reference coordinate system.

To understand the concept of reference coordinate systems, imagine that you're visiting the Grand Canyon and standing precariously to the edge of a lookout. To nervous onlookers calling the park rangers, the description of your position varies from viewpoint to viewpoint. A person standing by you would say you are next to him. A person on the other side of the canyon would say that you're across from her. A person at the floor of the canyon would say you're above him. And a person in an airplane would describe you as being on the east side of the canyon. Each person has a different viewpoint of you (the object), even though you have not moved.

3ds Max recognizes the following reference coordinate systems:

- **View Coordinate System:** A reference coordinate system based on the viewports; X points right, Y points up, and Z points out of the screen (toward you). The views are fixed, making this perhaps the most intuitive coordinate system to work with.
- **Screen Coordinate System:** Identical to the View Coordinate System, except the active viewport determines the coordinate system axes, whereas the inactive viewports show the axes as defined by the active viewport.
- **World Coordinate System:** Specifies X pointing to the right, Z pointing up, and Y pointing into the screen (away from you). The coordinate axes remain fixed regardless of any transformations applied to an object. For 3ds Max, this system matches the UCS.
- **Parent Coordinate System:** Uses the reference coordinate system applied to a linked object's parent and maintains consistency between hierarchical transformations. If an object doesn't

have a parent, then the world is its parent and the system works the same as the World Coordinate System.

- **Local Coordinate System:** Sets the coordinate system based on the selected object. The axes are located at the pivot point for the object. You can reorient and move the pivot point using the Pivot button in the Hierarchy panel.
- **Gimbal Coordinate System:** Provides interactive feedback for objects using the Euler XYZ controller. If the object doesn't use the Euler XYZ controller, then this coordinate system works just like the World Coordinate System.
- **Grid Coordinate System:** Uses the coordinate system for the active grid.
- **Working Coordinate System:** Lets you transform the selected object about the scene's Working Pivot as defined in the Hierarchy panel.
- **Pick Coordinate System:** Lets you select an object about which to transform. The Coordinate System list keeps the last four picked objects as coordinate system options.

> **TIP**
> Most of the time, you'll just stick with the View Coordinate System, but the World Coordinate System is useful if you need to match your scene to a real-world location. Parent and Local Coordinate Systems are helpful for positioning objects relative to their parent or to move an object such as a cylinder along its own center axis.

All transforms occur relative to the current reference coordinate system as selected in the Referenced Coordinate System drop-down list found on the main toolbar.

Each of the three basic transforms can have a different coordinate system specified, or you can set it to change uniformly when a new coordinate system is selected. To do this, open the General panel in the Preference Settings dialog box and select the Constant option in the Reference Coordinate System section.

Using a transform center

All transforms are done about a center point. When transforming an object, you must understand what the object's current center point is, as well as the coordinate system in which you're working.

The Transform Center flyout consists of three buttons: Use Pivot Point Center, Use Selection Center, and Use Transform Coordinate Center, which are shown in Table 6.3. Each of these buttons alters how the transformations are done. The origin of the Transform Gizmo is always positioned at the center point specified by these buttons.

TABLE 6.3 **Transform Center Buttons**

Button	Description
	Use Pivot Point Center
	Use Selection Center
	Use Transform Coordinate Center

Pivot Point Center

Pivot points are typically set to the center of spherical objects and at the base of box-shaped and cylinder-shaped objects when the object is first created, but they can be relocated anywhere within the scene including outside of the object. Relocating the pivot point allows you to change the point about which objects are rotated. For example, if you have a car model that you want to position along an incline, moving the pivot point to the bottom of one of the tires allows you to easily line up the car with the incline.

If you select the Use Pivot Point Center button, then the Select and Rotate tool rotates about the pivot point for the selected object, which can be located anywhere in the scene.

NOTE
Pivot points are discussed in detail in the next section.

Selection Center

The Use Selection Center button sets the transform center to the center of the selected object or objects regardless of the individual object's pivot point. If multiple objects are selected, then the center is computed to be in the middle of a bounding box that surrounds all the objects.

Transform Coordinate Center

The Use Transform Coordinate Center button uses the center of the Local Coordinate System. If the View Coordinate System is selected, then all objects are transformed about the center of the viewport grid. If an object is selected as the coordinate system using the Pick option, then all transformations are transformed about that object's center.

When you select the Local Coordinate System, the Use Transform Coordinate Center button is ignored and objects are transformed about their local axes. If you select multiple objects, then they all transform individually about their local axes. Grouped objects transform about the group axes.

For example, the default pivot point for a cylinder object is in the middle of the cylinder's base, so if the Transform Center is set to the Use Pivot Point option, then the cylinder rotates about its base pivot point. If the Use Selection Center option is selected, then the cylinder rotates about its center point. If the Use Transform Coordinate Center option is selected for the View Coordinate System, then the cylinder is rotated about the grid origin.

Figure 6.5 shows a simple cylinder object in the Left viewport using the different transform center modes. The left image shows the Pivot Point Center mode, the middle image shows the Selection Center mode with both objects selected, and the right image shows the Transform Coordinate Center mode. For each mode, notice that the Rotate Gizmo is located at different locations.

FIGURE 6.5

The Rotate Gizmo is located in different places, depending on the selected Transform Center mode.

Selecting Axis Constraints

Three-dimensional space consists of three basic directions defined by three axes: X, Y, and Z. If you were to stand on each axis and look at a scene, you would see three separate planes: the XY plane, the YZ plane, and the ZX plane. These planes show only two dimensions at a time and restrict any transformations to the two axes. These planes are visible from the Top, Left, and Front viewports.

TIP

If you use the transformation gizmos, then these constraints are used automatically without having to mess with the Axis Constraints toolbar.

By default, the Top, Left, and Front viewports show only a single plane and thereby restrict transformations to that single plane. The Top view constrains movement to the XY plane, the Left or Right side view constrains movement to the YZ plane, and the Front view constrains movement to the ZX plane. This setting is adequate for most modeling purposes, but sometimes you might need to limit the transformations in all the viewports to a single plane. In 3ds Max, you can restrict movement to specific transform axes using the Constrain Axis buttons in the Axis Constraints toolbar. You access this toolbar, shown in Figure 6.6, by right-clicking the main toolbar (away from the buttons) and selecting Axis Constraints options from the pop-up menu.

FIGURE 6.6

The Axis Constraints toolbar includes buttons for restricting transformations to a single axis or plane.

The first four buttons on this toolbar are Constrain axes buttons: Constrain to X (F5); Constrain to Y (F6); Constrain to Z (F7); and the flyout buttons, Constrain to XY, YZ, and ZX Plane (F8). The last button is the Snaps Use Axis Constraints Toggle button. The effect of selecting one of the Constrain axes buttons is based on the selected coordinate system. For example, if you click the Constrain to X button and the reference coordinate system is set to View, then the object always transforms to the right because, in the View Coordinate System, the X-axis is always to the right. If you click the Constrain to X button and the coordinate system is set to Local, the axes are attached to the object, so transformations along the X-axis are consistent in all viewports (with this setting, the object does not move in the Left view because it shows only the YZ plane).

CAUTION

If the axis constraints don't seem to be working, check the Preference Settings dialog box and look at the General panel to make sure that the Reference Coordinate System option is set to Constant.

Additionally, you can restrict movement to a single plane with the Constrain to Plane flyouts consisting of Re Constrain strict to XY, Constrain to YZ, and Constrain to ZX. (Use the F8 key to cycle quickly through the various planes.)

NOTE

If the Transform Gizmo is enabled, then the axis or plane that is selected in the Axis Constraints toolbar initially is displayed in yellow. If you transform an object using a Transform Gizmo, then the respective Axis Constraints toolbar button is selected after you complete the transform.

Locking axes transformations

To lock an object's transformation axes on a more permanent basis, go to the Command Panel and select the Hierarchy tab. Click the Link Info button to open the Locks rollout, shown in Figure 6.7. The rollout displays each axis for the three types of transformations: Move, Rotate, and Scale. Make sure that the object is selected, and then click the transformation axes that you want to lock. Be aware that if all Move axes are selected, you won't be able to move the object until you deselect the axes.

NOTE

Another option is to use the Display floater to freeze the object.

Locking axes is helpful if you want to prevent accidental scaling of an object or restrict a vehicle's movement to a plane that makes up a road.

The Locks rollout displays unselected X, Y, and Z check boxes for the Move, Rotate, and Scale transformations. By selecting the check boxes, you limit the axes about which the object can be transformed. For example, if you check the X and Y boxes under the Move transformation, the object can move only in the Z direction of the Local Coordinate System.

NOTE

These locks work regardless of the axis constraint settings.

FIGURE 6.7

The Locks rollout can prevent any transforms along an axis.

Tutorial: Landing a spaceship in port

Transformations are the most basic object manipulation that you will do and probably the most common. This tutorial includes a spaceship object and a spaceport. The goal is to position the spaceship on the landing pad of the spaceport, but it is too big and in the wrong spot. With a few clever transformations, you'll be set.

To transform a spaceship to land in a spaceport, follow these steps:

1. Open the Transforming spaceship.max file from the Chap 06 directory on the CD.

2. To prevent any extraneous movements of the spaceport, select the spaceport by clicking it. Open the Hierarchy panel, and click the Link Info button. Then in the Locks rollout, select all nine boxes to restrict all transformations so that the spaceport won't be accidentally moved.

3. To position the spaceship over the landing platform, select the Spaceship object and click the Select and Move button in the main toolbar (or press the W key). The Move Gizmo appears in the center of the Spaceship object. If you don't see the Move Gizmo, press the X key. Make sure that the Reference Coordinate System is set to View and that the Use Selection Center option is enabled. Right-click the Left viewport to make it active, select the red X-axis line of the gizmo, and drag to the right until the center of the spaceship is over the landing pad. Zoom out of the view if you can't see the spaceship fully.

4. Right-click the Front viewport, and drag the red X-axis gizmo line to the left to line up the spaceship with the center of the landing pad.

5. Click the Select and Uniform Scale button (or press the R key until it appears). Place the cursor over the center gizmo triangle, and drag downward until the spaceship fits within the landing pad.

6. Click the Select and Move button again (or press the W key), and drag the green Y-axis gizmo line downward in the Front viewport to move the spaceship toward the landing pad.

7. Click the Select and Rotate button (or press the E key). Right-click the Top viewport, and drag the blue Z-axis gizmo circle downward to rotate the spaceship clockwise so that its front end points away from the buildings.

Figure 6.8 shows the spaceship correctly positioned.

FIGURE 6.8

Transformation buttons and the Transform Gizmos were used to position this spaceship.

Using Pivot Points

An object's pivot point is the center about which the object is rotated and scaled and about which most modifiers are applied. Pivot points are created by default when an object is created and are usually created at the center or base of an object. You can move and orient a pivot point in any direction, but repositioning the pivot cannot be animated. Pivot points exist for all objects, whether or not they are part of a hierarchy.

> **CAUTION**
>
> Try to set your pivot points before animating any objects in your scene. If you relocate the pivot point after animation keys have been placed, all transformations are modified to use the new pivot point.

Positioning pivot points

To move and orient a pivot point, open the Hierarchy panel in the Command Panel and click the Pivot button. At the top of the Adjust Pivot rollout are three buttons; each button represents a different mode. The Affect Pivot Only mode makes the transformation buttons affect only the pivot point of the current selection. The object does not move. The Affect Object Only mode causes the object to be transformed, but not the pivot point. The Affect Hierarchy Only mode allows an object's links to be moved.

The pivot point is easily identified as the place where the Transform Gizmo is located when the object is selected, as shown in Figure 6.9.

FIGURE 6.9

The Transform Gizmo is located at the object's pivot point.

> **NOTE**
> Using the Scale transformation while one of these modes is selected alters the selected object but has no effect on the pivot point or the link.

Aligning pivot points

Below the mode buttons are three more buttons that are used to align the pivot points. These buttons are active only when a mode is selected. The buttons are Center to Object/Pivot, Align to Object/Pivot, and Align to World. The first two buttons switch between Object and Pivot, depending on the mode selected. You may select only one mode at a time. The button turns light blue when selected.

The Center to Object button moves the pivot point so it is aligned with the object center, and the Center to Pivot button moves the object so it is centered on its own pivot point. The Align to Object/Pivot button rotates the object or pivot point until the object's Local Coordinate System and the pivot point are aligned. The Align to World button rotates either the object or the pivot to the World Coordinate System. For example, if the Affect Object Only mode is selected and the object is separated from the pivot point, clicking the Center to Pivot button moves the object so its center is on the pivot point.

Under these three alignment buttons is another button labeled Reset Pivot, which you use to reset the pivot point to its original location.

Using the Working Pivot

Below the Adjust Pivot rollout is the Working Pivot rollout. Working Pivots are handy if you want to position an object using a temporary pivot without having to change the default object pivot. To position a Working Pivot, click the Edit Working Pivot button. This enters a mode just like the Affect Pivot Only button described previously, except it works with the working pivot.

After the Working Pivot is in place, you can select to use it instead of the object pivot by clicking the Use Working Pivot button. The Working Pivot stays active until you disable it in the Hierarchy panel. The Working Pivot works for all objects in the scene. When the Working Pivot is active, reminder text "USE WP" appears in all the viewports under the viewport name; when the Edit Working Pivot mode is enabled, this text reads, "EDIT WP."

TIP

You can quickly enable the Working Pivot by selecting the Working option from the Reference Coordinate System drop-down list in the main toolbar.

The Working Pivot rollout includes several buttons to help position the Working Pivot. The Align To View button reorients the Working Pivot to the current view. The Reset button moves the Working Pivot to the object pivot location of the selected object or to the view center if no object is selected.

NOTE

There is only one working pivot that you can use, but it can be used by any selected object.

The View button enters a mode identified by "EDIT WP" in the viewports that lets you place the Working Pivot anywhere in the current viewport by simply clicking where it should be. This is great for eyeballing the Working Pivots location. The Surface button (also identified by the EDIT WP text in the viewport) enters a mode where you can position the Working Pivot on the surface of an object by interactively dragging the cursor over the object surface. The cursor automatically reorients itself to be aligned with the surface normal. If the Align to View option is selected, then the Working Pivot is automatically aligned to the current view.

Transform adjustments

The Hierarchy panel of the Command Panel includes another useful rollout labeled Adjust Transform. This rollout includes another mode that you can use with hierarchies of objects. Clicking the Don't Affect Children button places you in a mode where any transformations of a linked hierarchy don't affect the children. Typically, transformations are applied to all linked children of a hierarchy, but this mode disables that.

The Adjust Transform rollout also includes two buttons that allow you to reset the Local Coordinate System and scale percentage. These buttons set the current orientation of an object as the World coordinate or as the 100 percent standard. For example, if you select an object, move it 30 units to the left, and scale it to 200 percent, these values are displayed in the coordinate fields on the status bar. Clicking the Reset Transform and Reset Scale buttons resets these values to 0 and 100 percent.

6

You use the Reset Scale button to reset the scale values for an object that has been scaled using non-uniform scaling. Non-uniform scaling can cause problems for child objects that inherit this type of scaling, such as shortening the links. The Reset Scale button can remedy these problems by resetting the parent's scaling values. When the scale is reset, you won't see a visible change to the object, but if you open the Scale Transform Type-In dialog box while the scale is being reset, you see the absolute local values being set back to 100 each.

TIP

If you are using an object that has been non-uniformly scaled, using Reset Scale before the item is linked saves you some headaches if you plan on using modifiers.

Using the Reset XForm utility

You also can reset transform values using the Reset XForm utility. To use this utility, open the Utilities panel and click the Reset XForm button, which is one of the default buttons. The benefit of this utility is that you can reset the transform values for multiple objects simultaneously. This happens by applying the XForm modifier to the objects. The rollout for this utility includes only a single button labeled Reset Selected.

Tutorial: A bee buzzing about a flower

By adjusting an object's pivot point, you can control how the object is transformed about the scene. In this example, you position the pivot point for the bee's wings and then reposition the pivot point for the entire bee so it can rotate about the flower object.

To control how a bee rotates about a flower, follow these steps:

1. Open the Buzzing bee.max file from the Chap 06 directory on the CD.

   This file includes a bee created from primitives and a flower model created by Zygote Media.

2. Click the bee's body object to select it, and press Z to zoom in on it.

3. Select the right wing, and click the Select and Rotate button on the main toolbar. Notice how the gizmo axes are centered on the wing. Then open the Hierarchy panel, and click the Affect Pivot Only button. Select the Local coordinate system from the list in the main toolbar. This orients the Transform Gizmo to match the pivot's orientation. Drag the wing's pivot point along its X-axis with the Select and Move tool to place the pivot where the wing contacts the body object. Then disable the Affect Pivot Only button. Then select and repeat this step for the left wing. Select each wing and rotate it about with the Select and Rotate tool to see how it moves relative to the body.

CAUTION

Be sure you select the Rotate tool before changing the pivot. Because each transform tool can have its own pivot and coordinate system, if you don't select the Rotate tool, you'll change the pivot for the Move tool instead.

 Working with the Track View is beyond the scope of this chapter, but you can find more information on the Track View in Chapter 28, "Editing Animation Curves in the Track View."

4. Select all parts that make up the bee in the Top viewport, select Group ⇨ Group, and name the object **bee**. Then select the bee and the flower in the Left viewport, and press Z to zoom in on them.

5. With the bee group selected and the Select and Rotate tool enabled, click the Affect Pivot Only button in the Hierarchy panel and move the pivot point to the center of the flower using the Select and Move tool in the Top and Front viewports. Click the Affect Pivot Only button again to disable it.

> **NOTE**
> If you don't want to move the object pivot in Step 5, you can use the Working Pivot to rotate the bee around the flower, or you could select the Pick coordinate system and select the flower.

6. Enable the Auto Key button (N) at the bottom of the interface, and drag to frame 35. With the Select and Rotate button (E), rotate the bee in the Top viewport a third of the way around the flower. Drag the Time Slider to frame 70, and rotate the bee another third of the way. With the Time Slider at frame 100, complete the rotation. Click the Auto Key button again to display key mode.

7. Click the Play Animation button (/) to see the final rotating bee.

Figure 6.10 shows the bee as it moves around the flower where its pivot point is located.

FIGURE 6.10

By moving the pivot point of the bee, you can control how it spins about the flower.

Using the Align Commands

The Align commands are an easy way to automatically transform objects. You can use these commands to line up object centers or edges, align normals and highlights, align to views and grids, and even line up cameras.

Aligning objects

Any object that you can transform, you can align, including lights, cameras, and Space Warps. After selecting the object to be aligned, click the Align flyout button on the main toolbar or choose Tools ⇨ Align ⇨ Align (or press Alt+A). The cursor changes to the Align icon. Now, click a target object with which you want to align all the selected objects. Clicking the target object opens the Align Selection dialog box with the target object's name displayed in the dialog box's title, as shown in Figure 6.11.

FIGURE 6.11

The Align Selection dialog box can align objects along any axes by their Minimum, Center, Pivot, or Maximum points.

The Align Selection dialog box includes settings for the X, Y, and Z Positions to line up the Minimum, Center, Pivot Point, or Maximum dimensions for the selected or target object's bounding box. As you change the settings in the dialog box, the objects reposition themselves, but the actual transformations don't take place until you click Apply or OK.

 Another way to align objects is with the Clone and Align tool, which is covered in Chapter 7, "Cloning Objects and Creating Object Arrays."

Using the Quick Align tool

The first flyout tool under the Align tool in the main toolbar (and in the Tools menu) is the Quick Align tool (Shift+A). This tool aligns the pivot points of the selected object with the object that you click without opening a separate dialog box. This is much quicker than the Align tool, which causes a separate dialog box to open.

Aligning normals

You can use the Normal Align command to line up points of the surface of two objects. A Normal vector is a projected line that extends from the center of a polygon face exactly perpendicular to the surface. When two Normal vectors are aligned, the objects are perfectly adjacent to one another. If the two objects are spheres, then they touch at only one point.

To align normals, you need to first select the object to move (this is the source object). Then choose Tools ➪ Align ➪ Normal Align, or click the Normal Align flyout button under the Align button on the main toolbar (or press Alt+N). The cursor changes to the Normal Align icon. Drag the cursor across the surface of the source object, and a blue arrow pointing out from the face center appears. Release the mouse when you've correctly pinpointed the position to align.

Next, click the target object, and drag the mouse to locate the target object's align point. This is displayed as a green arrow. When you release the mouse, the source object moves to align the two points and the Normal Align dialog box appears, as shown in Figure 6.12.

FIGURE 6.12

The Normal Align dialog box allows you to define offset values when aligning normals.

When the objects are aligned, the two points match up exactly. The Normal Align dialog box lets you specify offset values that you can use to keep a distance between the two objects. You also can specify an Angle Offset, which is used to deviate the parallelism of the normals. The Flip Normal option aligns the objects so their selected normals point in the same direction.

Objects without any faces, like Point Helper objects and Space Warps, use a vector between the origin and the Z-axis for normal alignment.

Tutorial: Aligning a kissing couple

Aligning normals positions two object faces directly opposite one another, so what better way to practice this tool than to align two faces?

To connect the kissing couple using the Normal Align command, follow these steps:

1. Open the Kissing couple.max file from the Chap 06 directory on the CD.

   This file includes two extruded shapes of a boy and a girl. The extruded shapes give you flat faces that are easy to align.

2. Select the girl shape, and choose the Tools ➪ Align ➪ Normal Align menu command (or press Alt+N). Then click and drag the cursor over the extruded girl shape until the blue vector points out from the front of the lips, as shown in Figure 6.13.

3. Then click and drag the cursor over the boy shape until the green vector points out from the front of the lips. This vector pointing out from the face is the surface normal. Then release the mouse, and the Normal Align dialog box appears. Enter a value of **5** in the Z Position Offset field, and click OK.

Figure 6.13 shows the resulting couple with normal aligned faces.

FIGURE 6.13

Using the Normal Align feature, you can align object faces.

 In the Align button flyout are two other common ways to align objects: Align Camera and Place Highlight (Ctrl+H). To learn about these features, see Chapter 18, "Configuring and Aiming Cameras," and Chapter 19, "Using Lights and Basic Lighting Techniques," respectively.

Aligning to a view

The Align to View command provides an easy and quick way to reposition objects to one of the axes. To use this command, select an object and choose Tools ⇨ Align ⇨ Align to View. The Align to View dialog box appears, as shown in Figure 6.14. Changing the settings in this dialog box displays the results in the viewports. You can use the Flip command for altering the direction of the object points. If no object is selected, then the Align to View command cannot be used.

FIGURE 6.14

The Align to View dialog box is a quick way to line up objects with the axes.

153

The Align to View command is especially useful for fixing the orientation of objects when you create them in the wrong view. All alignments are completed relative to the object's Local Coordinate System. If several objects are selected, each object is reoriented according to its Local Coordinate System.

> **NOTE**
>
> Using the Align to View command on symmetrical objects like spheres doesn't produce any noticeable difference in the viewports.

Using Grids

When 3ds Max is started, the one element that is visible is the Home Grid. This grid is there to give you a reference point for creating objects in 3D space. At the center of each grid are two darker lines. These lines meet at the origin point for the World Coordinate System where the coordinates for X, Y, and Z are all 0.0. This point is where all objects are placed by default.

In addition to the Home Grid, you can create and place new grids in the scene. These grids are not rendered, but you can use them to help you locate and align objects in 3D space.

The Home Grid

You can turn the Home Grid on and off by choosing Tools ⇨ Grids and Snaps ⇨ Show Home Grid. (You also can turn the Home Grid on and off for the active viewport using the G key.) If the Home Grid is the only grid in the scene, then by default it is also the construction grid where new objects are positioned when created.

You can access the Home Grid parameters (shown in Figure 6.15) by choosing Tools ⇨ Grids and Snaps ⇨ Grid and Snap Settings. You also can access this dialog box by right-clicking the Snap, Angle Snap, or Percent Snap toggle buttons located on the main toolbar.

> **TIP**
>
> Right-clicking the Spinner Snap Toggle opens the Preference Settings dialog box.

FIGURE 6.15

The Home Grid and User Grids panels of the Grid and Snap Settings dialog box let you define the grid spacing.

In the Home Grid panel of the Grid and Snap Settings dialog box, you can set how often Major Lines appear, as well as Grid Spacing. (The Spacing value for the active grid is displayed on the status bar.) You also can specify to dynamically update the grid view in all viewports or just in the active one.

The User Grids panel lets you activate any new grids when created.

Creating and activating new grids

In addition to the Home Grid, you can create new grids. To create a new Grid object, select the Create⇨Helpers⇨Grid menu command, or open the Create panel, select the Helpers category, and click the Grid button. In the Parameters rollout are settings for specifying the new grid object's dimensions, spacing, and color, as well as which coordinate plane to display (XY, YZ, or ZX).

You can designate any newly created grid as the default active grid. To activate a grid, make sure it is selected and choose Tools⇨Grids and Snaps⇨Activate Grid Object. Keep in mind that only one grid may be active at a time and that the default Home Grid cannot be selected. You also can activate a grid by right-clicking the grid object and selecting Activate Grid from the pop-up menu. To deactivate the new grid and reactivate the Home Grid, choose Tools⇨Grids and Snaps⇨Activate Home Grid, or right-click the grid object and choose Activate Grid⇨Home Grid from the pop-up quad menu.

You can find further grid settings for new grids in the Grid and Snap Settings dialog box on the User Grids panel. The settings include automatically activating the grid when created and an option for aligning an AutoGrid using World space or Object space coordinates.

Using AutoGrid

You can use the AutoGrid feature to create a new construction plane perpendicular to a face normal. This feature provides an easy way to create and align objects directly next to one another without manually lining them up or using the Align features.

The AutoGrid feature shows up as a check box at the top of the Object Type rollout for every category in the Create panel. It becomes active only when you're in Create Object mode.

To use AutoGrid, click the AutoGrid option after selecting an object type to create. If no objects are in the scene, then the object is created as usual. If an object is in the scene, then the cursor moves around on the surface of the object with its coordinate axes perpendicular to the surface that the cursor is over. Clicking and dragging creates the new object based on the precise location of the object under the mouse.

The AutoGrid option stays active for all new objects that you create until you turn it off by unchecking the box.

> **TIP**
> Holding down the Alt key before creating the object makes the new construction grid visible, disables the AutoGrid option, and causes all new objects to use the new active construction grid. You can disable this active construction grid by enabling the AutoGrid option again.

Tutorial: Creating a spyglass

As you begin to build objects for an existing scene, you find that working away from the scene origin is much easier if you enable the AutoGrid feature for the new objects you create. This feature enables you to position the new objects on (or close to) the surfaces of the nearby objects. It works best with objects that have pivot points located at their edges, such as Box and Cylinder objects.

In this example, you quickly create a spyglass object using the AutoGrid without needing to perform additional moves.

To create a spyglass using the AutoGrid and Snap features, follow these steps:

1. Before starting, click the Left viewport and zoom way out so you can see the height of the spyglass pieces.

2. Select Create ⇨ Standard Primitives ⇨ Cylinder, and drag from the origin in the Top viewport to create a Cylinder object. Set the Radius value to **40** and the Height value to **200**. Then enable the AutoGrid option in the Object Type rollout.

3. Drag from the origin again in the Top viewport to create another Cylinder object. Set its Radius to **35** and its Height to **200**. Repeat this step three times, reducing the Radius by 5 each time.

Figure 6.16 shows the resulting spyglass object.

FIGURE 6.16

This spyglass object was created quickly and easily using the AutoGrid option.

Using Snap Options

Often, when an object is being transformed, you know exactly where you want to put it. The Snap feature can be the means whereby objects get to the precise place they should be. For example, if you are constructing a set of stairs from box primitives, you can enable the Edge Snap feature to make each adjacent step align precisely along the edge of the previous step. With the Snap feature enabled, an object automatically moves (or snaps) to the specified snap position when you place it close enough. If you enable the Snap features, they affect any transformations that you make in a scene.

Snap points are defined in the Grid and Snap Settings dialog box that you can open by choosing Tools⇨Grids and Snaps⇨Grid and Snap Settings or by right-clicking any of the first three Snap buttons on the main toolbar. (These Snap buttons have a small magnet icon in them.) Figure 6.17 shows the Snaps panel of the Grid and Snap Settings dialog box for Standard and Body objects. An option for configuring NURBS snapping also is available. NURBS stands for Non-Uniform Rational B-Splines. They are a special type of object created from spline curves.

FIGURE 6.17

The Snaps panel includes many different points to snap to, depending on the object type.

After snap points have been defined, the Snap buttons on the main toolbar activate the Snap feature, or you can press the S key. The first Snaps button consists of a flyout with three buttons: 3D Snap toggle, 2.5D Snap toggle, and 2D Snap toggle. The 2D Snap toggle button limits all snaps to the active construction grid. The 2.5D Snap toggle button snaps to points on the construction grid as well as projected points from objects in the scene. The 3D Snap toggle button can snap to any points in 3D space.

When snapping is enabled, a small circle appears at the center of the pivot point. This circle is a visual reminder that snapping is enabled. When you move an object while snapping is enabled, you can either drag the small circle to move the object freely between snapping points or drag the Move tool's controls to constraint the object's movement.

As you drag an object, the starting position is marked and a line is drawn between this starting point and the destination point. Available snapping points are marked with a set of cross-hairs. If you release the object, it snaps to the highlighted set of cross-hairs. The line connecting the start and end points and the snapping point cross-hairs are colored green when the object is over an available snapping point, and yellow when not.

In addition to the small circle icon and the Move tool controls, you can move the mouse over the object and any available snapping points on the object are highlighted. For example, if the Vertex option in the Grid and Snap Settings dialog box is enabled, moving the mouse over one of a box object's corners highlights the corner with a set of yellow cross-hairs. Dragging while a vertex's cross-hair is highlighted lets you snap the selected corner to another position.

Tutorial: Creating a 2D outline of an object

The 2.5D snap can be confusing. It limits snapping to the active construction grid, but within the active grid, it can snap to 3D points that are projected onto the active grid. You can create a 2D representation of a 3D object by snapping to the vertices of the suspended object.

To create a 2D outline of a cylinder object, follow these steps:

1. Select the Create⇨Standard Primitives⇨Cylinder menu to create a simple cylinder object.
2. Select and rotate the cylinder so it is suspended and rotated at an angle above the construction grid.
3. Click and hold the Snap toggle button, and select the 2.5D Snap flyout option. Then right-click the Snap toggle, and select only the Vertex option in the Snaps panel. Then close the Grid and Snap Settings dialog box.
4. Choose the Create⇨Shapes⇨Line menu, and create a line in the Top viewport by snapping to the points that make the outline of the cylinder.

Figure 6.18 shows the projected outline. Using this method, you can quickly create 2D projections of 3D objects.

FIGURE 6.18

The 2.5D snap feature snaps to vertices of 3D objects projected onto the active grid.

These Snap buttons control the snapping for translations. To the right are two other buttons: Angle Snap toggle and Percent Snap. These buttons control the snapping of rotations and scalings.

> **NOTE**
> The keyboard shortcut for turning the Snap feature on and off is the S key.

Setting snap points

The Snaps tab in the Grid and Snap Settings dialog box has many points that can be snapped to in several categories: Standard, Body Snaps, and NURBS. The Standard snap points (previously shown in Figure 6.17) include the following:

- **Grid Points:** Snaps to the Grid intersection points
- **Grid Lines:** Snaps only to positions located on the Grid lines
- **Pivot:** Snaps to an object's pivot point
- **Bounding Box:** Snaps to one of the corners of a bounding box
- **Perpendicular:** Snaps to a spline's next perpendicular point
- **Tangent:** Snaps to a spline's next tangent point
- **Vertex:** Snaps to polygon vertices
- **Endpoint:** Snaps to a spline's end point or the end of a polygon edge
- **Edge/Segment:** Snaps to positions only on an edge
- **Midpoint:** Snaps to a spline's midpoint or the middle of a polygon edge
- **Face:** Snaps to any point on the surface of a face
- **Center Face:** Snaps to the center of a face

The Body Snaps category includes a subset of the above list, including Vertex, Edge, Face, End Edge, and Edge Midpoint.

Several snap points specific to NURBS objects, such as NURBS points and curves, are also shown in Figure 6.17. These points include:

- **CV:** Snaps to any NURBS Control Vertex subobject
- **Point:** Snaps to a NURBS point
- **Curve Center:** Snaps to the center of the NURBS curve
- **Curve Normal:** Snaps to a point that is normal to a NURBS curve
- **Curve Tangent:** Snaps to a point that is tangent to a NURBS curve
- **Curve Edge:** Snaps to the edge of a NURBS curve
- **Curve End:** Snaps to the end of a NURBS curve
- **Surf Center:** Snaps to the center of a NURBS surface
- **Surf Normal:** Snaps to a point that is normal to a NURBS surface
- **Surf Edge:** Snaps to the edge of a NURBS surface

Setting snap options

The Grid and Snap Settings dialog box holds a panel of Options, shown in Figure 6.19, in which you can set the marker size and whether they display. The Snap Preview Radius defines the radial distance from the snap point required before the object that is being moved is displayed at the target snap point as a preview. This value can be larger than the actual Snap Radius and is meant to provide visual feedback on the snap operation. The Snap Radius setting determines how close the cursor must be to a snap point before it snaps to it.

The Angle and Percent values are the strengths for any Rotate and Scale transformations, respectively. The Snap to Frozen Objects lets you control whether frozen items can be snapped to. You also can cause translations to be affected by the designated axis constraints with the Use Axis Constraints option. The Display Rubber Band option draws a line from the object's starting location to its snapping location.

FIGURE 6.19

The Options panel includes settings for marker size and color and the Snap Strength value.

Within any viewpoint, holding down the Shift key and right-clicking in the viewport can access a pop-up menu of grid points and options. This pop-up quad menu lets you quickly add or reset all the current snap points and change snap options, such as Transformed Constraints and Snaps to Frozen Objects.

Using the Snaps toolbar

As a shortcut to enabling the various snapping categories, you can access the Snaps toolbar by right-clicking the main toolbar away from the buttons and selecting Snaps from the pop-up menu. The Snaps toolbar, shown in Figure 6.20, can have several toggle buttons enabled at a time. Each enabled button is highlighted in yellow.

FIGURE 6.20

The Snaps toolbar provides a quick way to access several snap settings.

Tutorial: Creating a lattice for a methane molecule

Many molecules are represented by a lattice of spheres. Trying to line up the exact positions of the spheres by hand could be extremely frustrating, but using the Snap feature makes this challenge . . . well . . . a snap.

One of the simpler molecules is methane, which is composed of one carbon atom surrounded by four smaller hydrogen atoms. To reproduce this molecule as a lattice, you first need to create a tetrahedron primitive and snap spheres to each of its corners. The hedra isn't shown as part of the molecule, but only used to place the spheres where they need to be.

To create a lattice of the methane molecule, follow these steps:

1. Right-click the Snap toggle button in the main toolbar to open the Grid and Snap Settings, and enable the Grid Points and Vertex options. Then click the Snap toggle button (or press the S key) to enable 2D Snap mode.

2. Select the Create⇨Extended Primitives⇨Hedra menu command, set the P Family Parameter to **1.0**, and drag in the Top viewport from the center of the Home Grid to the first grid point to the right to create a Tetrahedron shape.

3. Click and hold the Snap toggle button, and select the 3D Snap flyout option. Select the Create⇨Standard Primitives⇨Sphere menu command. Right-click in the Left viewport, and drag from the top-left vertex to create a sphere. Set the sphere's Radius to **25**.

4. Create three more sphere objects with Radius values of 25 that are snapped to the vertices of the Tetrahedron object.

5. Finally, create a sphere in the Top viewport using the same snap point as the initial tetrahedron. Set its Radius to **80**.

Figure 6.21 shows the finished methane molecule.

FIGURE 6.21

A methane molecule lattice drawn with the help of the Snap feature

Summary

Transforming objects in 3ds Max is one of the fundamental actions you can perform. The three basic ways to transform objects are moving, rotating, and scaling. 3ds Max includes many helpful features to enable these transformations to take place quickly and easily. In this chapter, you learned these features:

- Using the Move, Rotate, and Scale buttons and the Transform Gizmos
- Transforming objects precisely with the Transform Type-In dialog box and Status Bar fields
- Using Transform Managers to change coordinate systems and lock axes
- Aligning objects with the align tool, aligning normals, and aligning to views
- Manipulating pivot points and using a Working Pivot
- Working with grids
- Setting up snap points
- Snapping objects to snap points

In the next chapter, you work more with multiple objects by learning how to clone objects. Using these techniques, you could very quickly have too many objects (and you were worried that there weren't enough objects).

Cloning Objects and Creating Object Arrays

IN THIS CHAPTER

Cloning objects

Understanding copies, instances, and references

Using the Mirror and Snapshot tools

Spacing clones along a path with the Spacing tool

Using the Clone and Align tool

Creating object arrays

Using the Ring Array system

The only thing better than one perfect object is two perfect objects. Cloning objects is the process of creating copies of objects. These copies can maintain an internal connection (called an instance or a reference) to the original object that allows them to be modified along with the original object. For example, if you create a school desk and clone it multiple times as an instance to fill a school room, then changing the parameter of one of the desks automatically changes it for all the other desks also. This is a huge timesaver and helps keep multiple scene objects up to date.

Another common way to create copies is with the Array dialog box. An *array* is a discrete set of regularly ordered objects. So creating an array of objects involves cloning several copies of an object in a pattern, such as in rows and columns or in a circle.

I'm sure you have the concept for that perfect object in your little bag of tricks, and this chapter lets you copy it over and over after you get it out.

Cloning Objects

You can clone objects in the Autodesk® 3ds Max® 2013 software in a couple of ways (and cloning luckily has nothing to do with DNA or gene splices). One method is to use the Edit ⇨ Clone (Ctrl+V) menu command, and another method is to transform an object while holding down the Shift key. You won't need to worry about these clones attacking anyone (unlike *Star Wars: Episode II*).

Using the Clone command

You can create a duplicate object by choosing the Edit ⇨ Clone (Ctrl+V) menu command. You must select an object before the Clone command becomes active, and you must not be in a Create mode. Selecting this command opens the Clone Options dialog box, shown in Figure 7.1, where you can give the clone a name and specify it as a Copy, Instance, or Reference. You also can copy any animation controllers associated with the object as a Copy or an Instance.

> **CAUTION**
> The Edit menu doesn't include the common Windows cut, copy, and paste commands because many objects and subobjects cannot be easily pasted into a different place. However, you will find a Clone (Ctrl+V) command that can duplicate a selected object.

FIGURE 7.1

The Clone Options dialog box defines the new object as a Copy, Instance, or Reference.

> **NOTE**
> The difference between Copy, Instance, and Reference is discussed in the "Understanding Cloning Options" section in this chapter.

When a clone is created with the Clone menu command, it is positioned directly on top of the original, which makes distinguishing it from the original difficult. To verify that a clone has been created, open the Select From Scene dialog box by pressing H and look for the cloned object (it has the same name, but an incremented number has been added). To see both objects, click the Select and Move button on the main toolbar and move one of the objects away from the other.

Using the Shift-clone method

An easier way to create clones is with the Shift key. You can use the Shift key when objects are transformed using the Select and Move, Select and Rotate, and Select and Scale commands. Holding down the Shift key while you use any of these commands on an object clones the object and opens the Clone Options dialog box. This Clone Options dialog box is identical to the dialog box previously shown, except it includes a spinner to specify the number of copies.

Performing a transformation with the Shift key held down defines an offset that is applied repeatedly to each copy. For example, holding down the Shift key while moving an object 5 units to the left (with the Number of Copies set to 5) places the first cloned object 5 units away from the original, the second cloned object 10 units away from the original object, and so on.

Tutorial: Cloning dinosaurs

The story behind *Jurassic Park* is pretty exciting, but in 3ds Max you can clone dinosaurs without their DNA. You also don't need to worry about them chasing you.

To investigate cloning objects, follow these steps:

1. Open the Cloning dinosaurs.max file found in the Chap 07 directory on the CD.

2. Select the dinosaur object by clicking it in one of the viewports.

3. With the dinosaur model selected, choose Edit ⇨ Clone (or press Ctrl+V).
   The Clone Options dialog box appears.

4. Name the clone **First clone**, select the Copy option, and click OK.

5. Click the Select and Move button (or press the W key) on the main toolbar. Then in the Top viewport, click and drag the dinosaur model to the right.
   As you move the model, the original model beneath it is revealed.

6. Select each model in turn, and notice the name change in the Create panel's Name field.

7. With the Select and Move button still active, hold down the Shift key, click the cloned dinosaur in the Top viewport, and move it to the right again. In the Clone Options dialog box that appears, select the Copy option, set the Number of Copies to **3**, and click OK.

8. Click the Zoom Extents All button (or press Shift+Ctrl+Z) in the lower-right corner to view all the new dinosaurs.
   Three additional dinosaurs have appeared, equally spaced from each other. The spacing was determined by the distance that you moved the second clone before releasing the mouse. Figure 7.2 shows the results of our dinosaur cloning experiment. (Now you'll need to build a really strong fence.)

FIGURE 7.2

Cloning multiple objects is easy with the Shift-clone feature.

Using Quick Clone

Within the Transform Toolbox is a QClone button. This Quick Clone button creates a clone of the selected object and places it to the side of the selected object. The placement is exactly half the width of the selected object so the cloned object just touches the original. Placement also depends on the active viewport, if the Front or Left viewports are active, then the clone is placed to the original's right and if the Top viewport is active, then the object is placed above the original object. Holding down the Shift key creates an Instanced copy, and holding down the Alt key creates two copies. This provides a quick and easy way to clone and move the object at the same time.

Understanding Cloning Options

When cloning in 3ds Max, you're offered the option to create the clone as a copy, an instance, or a reference. This is true not only for objects but for materials, modifiers, and controllers as well.

Working with copies, instances, and references

When an object is cloned, the Clone Options dialog box appears. This dialog box enables you to select to make a copy, an instance, or a reference of the original object. Each of these clone types is unique and offers different capabilities.

A copy is just what it sounds like—an exact replica of the original object. The new copy maintains no ties to the original object and is a unique object in its own right. Any changes to the copy do not affect the original object, and vice versa.

Instances are different from copies in that they maintain strong ties to the original object. All instances of an object are interconnected, so any geometry modifications (done with modifiers or object parameters) to any single instance changes all instances. For example, if you create several instances of a mailbox and then use a modifier on one of them, all instances also are modified.

> **NOTE**
>
> Instances and references can have different object colors, materials, transformations (moving, rotating, or scaling), and object properties.

References are objects that inherit modifier changes from their parent objects but do not affect the parent when modified. Referenced objects get all the modifiers applied to the parent and can have their own modifiers as well. For example, suppose you have an apple object and a whole bunch of references to that apple. Applying a modifier to the base apple changes all the remaining apples, but you also can apply a modifier to any of the references without affecting the rest of the bunch.

 Instances and references are tied to the applied object modifiers, which are covered in more detail in Chapter 9, "Introducing Subobjects and Modifiers and Using the Modifier Stack."

At any time, you can break the tie between instanced and referenced objects with the Make Unique button in the Modifier Stack. The Views⇨Show Dependencies command shows in magenta any objects that are instanced or referenced when the Modify panel is opened. This means that you can easily see which objects are instanced or referenced from the current selection.

Tutorial: Creating instanced doughnuts

Learning how the different clone options work will save you lots of future modifications. To investigate these options, you'll take a quick trip to the local doughnut shop.

To clone some doughnuts, follow these steps:

1. Create a doughnut using the Torus primitive by selecting Create⇨Standard Primitives⇨Torus, dragging and clicking to set the doughnut's radius, and then dragging and clicking a second time to set the cross-section radius in the Top viewport to create a torus object.

2. With the doughnut model selected, click the Select and Move button (or press the W key). Hold down the Shift key, and in the Top viewport, move the doughnut upward. In the Clone Options dialog box, select the Instance option, set the Number of Copies to **5**, and click OK. Click the Zoom Extents All (or press the Shift+Ctrl+Z key) button to widen your view.

3. Select all objects with the Edit⇨Select All (Ctrl+A) command, and then Shift+drag the doughnuts in the Top viewport to the right. In the Clone Options dialog box, select the Instance option again, set **3** for the Number of Copies, and click OK. This creates a nice array of two dozen doughnuts. Click the Zoom Extents All button (or press the Ctrl+Shift+Z key) to see all the doughnuts.

4. Select a single doughnut, and in the Parameters rollout of the Modify panel, set Radius1 to **20** and Radius2 to **10**.

   This makes a nice doughnut and changes all doughnuts at once.

5. Select the Modifiers⇨Parametric Deformers⇨Bend command. Then in the Parameters rollout of the Command Panel, enter **25** in the Angle field and select the X Bend Axis.

   This adds a slight bend to the doughnuts.

You can use modifiers to alter geometry. You can learn about using modifiers in Chapter 9, "Introducing Subobjects and Modifiers and Using the Modifier Stack."

Figure 7.3 shows the doughnuts all changed exactly the same. You can imagine the amount of time it would take to change each doughnut individually. Using instances made these changes easy.

FIGURE 7.3

Two dozen doughnut instances ready for glaze

Tutorial: Working with referenced apples

Now that you have filled your bellies with doughnuts, you need some healthful food for balance. What better way to add balance than to have an apple or two to keep the doctor away?

To create some apples using referenced clones, follow these steps:

1. Open the Referenced Apples.max file from the Chap 07 directory on the CD.
2. Select the apple, and Shift+drag with the Select and Move (W) tool in the Top viewport to create a cloned reference. Select the Reference option in the Clone Options dialog box. Then click OK to close the Clone Options dialog box.
3. Select the original apple again, and repeat Step 2 until several referenced apples surround the original apple.
4. Select the original apple in the middle again, and choose the Modifiers⇨Subdivision Surfaces⇨MeshSmooth command. In the Subdivision Amount rollout, set the number of Iterations to **2**.

   This smoothes all the apples.
5. Select one of the surrounding apples, and apply the Modifiers⇨Parametric Deformers⇨Taper command. Set the Amount value to **0.5** about the Z-axis.
6. Select another of the surrounding apples, and apply the Modifiers⇨Parametric Deformers⇨Squeeze command. Set the Axial Bulge Amount value to **0.3**.
7. Select another of the surrounding apples, and apply the Modifiers⇨Parametric Deformers⇨Squeeze command. Set the Radial Squeeze Amount value to **0.2**.
8. Select another of the surrounding apples, and apply the Modifiers⇨Parametric Deformers⇨Bend command. Set the Angle value to **20** about the Z axis.

> **NOTE**
>
> As you apply modifiers to a referenced object, notice the thick, gray bar in the Modifier Stack. This bar, called the Derived Object Line, separates which modifiers get applied to all referenced objects (below the line) and which modifiers get applied to only the selected object (above the line). If you drag a modifier from above the gray bar to below the gray bar, then that modifier is applied to all references.

Using referenced objects, you can apply the major changes to similar objects but still make minor changes to objects to make them a little different. Figure 7.4 shows the apples. Notice that they are not all exactly the same.

FIGURE 7.4

Even apples from the same tree should be slightly different.

Mirroring Objects

Have you ever held the edge of a mirror up to your face to see half of your head in the mirror? Many objects have a natural symmetry that you can exploit to require that only half an object be modeled. The human face is a good example. You can clone symmetrical parts using the Mirror command.

> **TIP**
>
> The Symmetry modifier lets you model only half of an object. It automatically applies the modeling changes to the opposite side of the model.

Using the Mirror command

The Mirror command creates a clone (or No Clone, if you so choose) of the selected object about the current coordinate system. To open the Mirror dialog box, shown in Figure 7.5, choose Tools ⇨ Mirror, or click the Mirror button located on the main toolbar. You can access the Mirror dialog box only if an object is selected.

FIGURE 7.5

The Mirror dialog box can create an inverted clone of an object.

Within the Mirror dialog box, you can specify an axis or plane about which to mirror the selected object. You also can define an Offset value. As with the other clone commands, you can specify whether the clone is to be a Copy, an Instance, or a Reference, or you can choose No Clone, which flips the object around the axis you specify. The dialog box also lets you mirror IK (inverse kinematics) Limits, which reduces the number of IK parameters that need to be set.

Learn more about inverse kinematics in Chapter 29, "Understanding Rigging, Kinematics, and Working with Bones."

Tutorial: Mirroring a robot's leg

Many characters have symmetry that you can use to your advantage, but to use this symmetry, you can't just clone one half or the cloned object would be oriented just like the original. Consider the position of a character's right ear relative to its right eye. If you clone the ear, then the position of each ear will be identical, with the ear to the right of the eye, which would make for a strange-looking creature. What you need to use is the Mirror command, which clones the object and rotates it about a selected axis.

In this example, you have a complex mechanical robot with one of its legs created. Using Mirror, you can quickly clone and position its second leg.

To mirror a robot's leg, follow these steps:

1. Open the Robot mech.max file from the Chap 07 directory on the CD.
    This file includes a robot with only one leg.

2. Select all objects that make up the robot's leg in the Left viewport (which is easy because they are all grouped together), and open the Mirror dialog box with the Tools ⇨ Mirror menu command.

3. In the Mirror dialog box, select X as the Mirror Axis and Instance as the Clone Selection. Change the Offset value until the cloned leg is in position, which should be at around **–2.55.**

> **NOTE**
> The mirror axis depends on the viewport, so make sure the Left viewport is selected.

Any changes made to the dialog box are immediately shown in the viewports.

4. Click OK to close the dialog box.

> **NOTE**
> By making the clone selection an instance, you can ensure that any future modifications to the right half of the figure are automatically applied to the left half.

Figure 7.6 shows the resulting robot, which won't be falling over now.

FIGURE 7.6

A perfectly symmetrical robot, compliments of the Mirror tool

Cloning over Time

Another useful way to create multiple copies of an object is to have an object be created based on its position during a specific frame of an animation. This cloning at specific times is accomplished with the Snapshot feature.

Using the Snapshot command

The Snapshot command creates static copies, instances, references, or even meshes of a selected object as it moves along an animation path. For example, you could create a series of footprints by animating a set of footprints moving across the screen from frame 1 to frame 100, and then choose Tools⇨ Snapshot and enter the number of steps to appear over this range of frames in the Snapshot dialog box. The designated number of steps is created at regular intervals for the animation range. Be aware that the Snapshot command works only with objects that have an animation path defined.

You can open the Snapshot dialog box by choosing Tools ⇨ Snapshot or by clicking the Snapshot button (under the Array flyout on the Extras toolbar). Snapshot is the second button in the flyout. In the Snapshot dialog box, shown in Figure 7.7, you can choose to produce a single clone or a range of clones over a given number of frames. Selecting Single creates a single clone at the current frame.

> **NOTE**
>
> When you enter the number of Copies in the Snapshot dialog box, a copy is placed at both the beginning and end of the specified range, so if your path is closed, two objects are stacked on top of each other. For example, if you have a square path and you want to place a copy at each corner, you need to enter a value of 5.

FIGURE 7.7

The Snapshot dialog box lets you create clones as a Copy, Instance, Reference, or Mesh.

> **TIP**
>
> The Snapshot tool also can be used with particle systems.

Tutorial: Creating a path through a maze

The Snapshot tool can be used to create objects as a model is moved along an animated path. In this example, you create a series of footsteps through a maze.

To create a set of footprints through a maze with the Snapshot tool, follow these steps:

1. Open the Path through a maze.max file from the Chap 07 directory on the CD. This file includes a set of animated footprints that travel to the exit of a maze.
2. Select both footprint objects at the entrance to the maze.
3. Choose the Tools ⇨ Snapshot menu to open the Snapshot dialog box. Select the Range option, set the number of Copies to **20**, and select the Instance option. Then click OK.

Figure 7.8 shows the path of footsteps leading the way through the maze, which are easier to follow than breadcrumbs.

FIGURE 7.8

The Snapshot tool helps to build a set of footprints through a maze.

Spacing Cloned Objects

The Snapshot tool offers a convenient way to clone objects along an animation path, but what if you want to clone objects along a path that isn't animated? The answer is the Spacing tool. The Spacing tool can position clones at regular intervals along a path by either selecting a path and the number of cloned objects or by picking two points in the viewport.

Using the Spacing tool

You access the Spacing tool by clicking a button in the flyout under the Array button on the Extras toolbar. (The Extras toolbar can be made visible by right-clicking the main toolbar away from the buttons.) You also can access it using the Tools⇨Align⇨Spacing Tool (Shift+I) menu command. When accessed, it opens the Spacing Tool dialog box, shown in Figure 7.9. At the top of this dialog box are two buttons: Pick Path and Pick Points. If a path is selected, its name appears on the Pick Path button.

You also can specify Count, Spacing, Start Offset, and End Offset values. The drop-down list offers several preset options, including Divide Evenly, Free Center, End Offset, and more. These values and preset options are used to define the number and spacing of the objects. The spacing and position of the objects depend on the values that are included. For example, if you include only a Count value, then the objects are evenly spaced along the path including an object at each end. If an offset value is included, then the first or last item is moved away from the end by the offset value. If a Spacing value is included, then the number of objects required to meet this value is included automatically.

FIGURE 7.9

The Spacing Tool dialog box lets you select how to position clones along a path.

The Lock icons next to the Start and End Offset values force the Start or End Offset values to be the same as the Spacing value. This has the effect of pushing the objects away from their end points.

Before you can use either the Pick Path or Pick Points buttons, you must select the object to be cloned. Using the Pick Path button, you can select a spline path in the scene, and cloned objects are regularly spaced according to the values you selected. The Pick Points method lets you click to select the Start point and click again to select an end point. These points don't have to be objects, they are just locations selected on the construction grid in the viewport where you click. The cloned objects are spaced in a straight line between the two points.

The two options for determining the spacing width are Edges and Centers. The Edges option spaces objects from the edge of its bounding box to the edge of the adjacent bounding box, and the Centers option spaces objects based on their centers. The Follow option aligns the object with the path so the object's orientation follows the path. Each object can be a copy, instance, or reference of the original. The text field at the bottom of the dialog box displays for your information the number of objects and the spacing value between objects.

> **TIP**
> Lining up objects to correctly follow the path can be tricky. If the objects are misaligned, you can change the object's pivot point so it matches the viewport coordinates. This makes the object follow the path with the correct position.

You can continue to modify the Spacing Tool dialog box's values while the dialog box is open, but the objects are not added to the scene until you click the Apply button. The Close button closes the dialog box.

Tutorial: Stacking a row of dominoes

A good example of using the Spacing tool to accomplish something that is difficult in real life is to stack a row of dominoes. It is really a snap in 3ds Max, regardless of the complexity of the path.

To stack a row of dominoes using the Spacing tool, follow these steps:

1. Open the Row of dominoes.max file from the Chap 07 directory on the CD.

   This file includes a single domino and a wavy spline path.

2. Select the domino object, and open the Spacing tool by selecting the Tools ⇨ Align ⇨ Spacing Tool menu or with the flyout button under the Array button on the Extras toolbar (or by pressing Shift+I).

3. In the Spacing Tool dialog box, click the Pick Path button and select the wavy path.

   The path name appears on the Pick Path button.

4. From the drop-down list in the Parameters section of the Spacing Tool dialog box, enable the Count option with a value of **35**.

   This is the same as the Divide Evenly, Objects at Ends option in the drop-down list.

5. Select the Edges Context option, check the Follow check box, and make all clones Instances. Click Apply when the result looks right, and close the Spacing Tool dialog box.

Figure 7.10 shows the simple results. The Spacing Tool dialog box remains open until you click the Cancel button.

FIGURE 7.10

These dominoes were much easier to stack than the set in my living room.

Using the Clone and Align Tool

Imagine you're working on a production team and the modeler assigned to the project says he needs some more time to make the building columns "something special." Just as you prepare to give him the "deadlines don't die" speech, you remember the Clone and Align tool. Using this tool, you can place proxy objects where the detailed ones are supposed to go. Then, when the detailed object is ready, the Clone and Align tool lets you clone the detailed object and place it where all the proxies are positioned. This, of course, makes the modeler happy and doesn't disrupt your workflow. It's another production team victory.

Aligning source objects to destination objects

Before selecting the Tools ⇨ Align ⇨ Clone and Align tool, you need to select the detailed object that you want to place. This object is referred to as the source object. Selecting the Clone and Align tool opens a dialog box, shown in Figure 7.11. From this dialog box, you can pick the proxy objects that are positioned where the source objects are supposed to go. These proxy objects are referred to as destination objects. The dialog box shows the number of source and destination objects that are selected.

The Align tool is covered in Chapter 6, "Transforming Objects, Pivoting, Aligning, and Snapping."

The Clone and Align dialog box also lets you select whether source objects are cloned as copies, instances, or references. In the Align Parameters rollout, you can specify the object's position and orientation using the same controls that are used to align objects, including any Offset values.

As you make changes in the Clone and Align dialog box, the objects are updated in the viewports, but these changes don't become permanent until you click the Apply button. The Clone and Align dialog box is *persistent*, meaning that, after being applied, the settings remain until they are changed.

FIGURE 7.11

The Clone and Align dialog box lets you choose which objects mark the place where the source object should go.

Tutorial: Cloning and aligning trees on a beach

To practice using the Clone and Align tool, you'll open a beach scene with a single set of grouped trees. Several other box objects have been positioned and rotated about the scene. The trees will be the source object, and the box objects will be the destinations.

To position and orient several high-res trees using the Clone and Align tool, follow these steps:

1. Open the Trees on beach.max file from the Chap 07 directory on the CD.

   This file includes a beach scene created by Viewpoint Datalabs.

2. Select the tree objects that have been grouped together, and open the Clone and Align dialog box by selecting the Tools ⇨ Align ⇨ Clone and Align menu command.

> **NOTE**
>
> The Clone and Align dialog box remembers the last settings used, which may be different from what you want. You can reset all the settings with the Reset All Parameters button at the bottom of the dialog box.

3. In the Clone and Align dialog box, click the Pick button and select each of the box objects in the scene.

4. In the Align Parameters rollout, enable the X and Y axes for the Positions and the X, Y, and Z axes for the Orientation. Then click the Apply button.

Figure 7.12 shows the simple results. Notice that the destination objects have not been replaced and are still there, but if you use dummy objects as the destination objects, then you won't need to remove them because they won't be rendered.

FIGURE 7.12

Using the Clone and Align dialog box, you can place these trees to match the stand-in objects' position and orientation.

Creating Arrays of Objects

Now that you've probably figured out how to create arrays of objects by hand with the Shift-clone method, the Array command multiplies the fun by making it easy to create many copies instantaneously. The Array dialog box lets you specify the array dimensions, offsets, and transformation values. These parameters enable you to create an array of objects easily.

Access the Array dialog box by selecting an object and choosing Tools ⇨ Array or by clicking the Array button on the Extras toolbar. Figure 7.13 shows the Array dialog box. The top of the Array dialog box displays the coordinate system and the center about which the transformations are performed.

The Array dialog box is *modeless*, which means that you can still access and change the selected object or view in the viewports while the dialog box is open. The Array dialog box is also *persistent*, which means that it remembers the values you enter for the next time you open it. You can reset all the values at once by clicking the Reset All Parameters button within the Array dialog box. You also can preview the current array settings without actually creating an array of objects using the Preview button. The Display as Box option lets you see the array as a bounding box to give you an idea of how large the array will be.

NEW FEATURE
The modeless nature of the Array dialog box is new to 3ds Max 2013.

FIGURE 7.13

The Array dialog box defines the number of elements and transformation offsets in an array.

Linear arrays

Linear arrays are arrays in which the objects form straight lines, such as rows and columns. Using the Array dialog box, you can specify a positional offset along the X-, Y-, and Z-axes at the top of the dialog box and define this offset as an incremental amount or as a total amount. To change between incremental values and total values, click the arrows to the left and right of the Move, Rotate, and Scale labels. For example, an array with 10 elements and an incremental value of 5 will position each successive object a distance of 5 units from the previous one. An array with 10 elements and a total value of 100 will position each element a distance of 10 units apart by dividing the total value by the number of clones.

The Move row values represent units as specified in the Units Setup dialog box. The Rotate row values represent degrees, and the Scale row values are a percentage of the selected object. All values can be either positive or negative values.

Clicking the Re-Orient check box causes the coordinate system to be reoriented after each rotation is made. If this check box isn't enabled, then the objects in the array do not successively rotate. Clicking the Uniform check box to the right of the Scale row values disables the Y and Z Scale value columns and forces the scaling transformations to be uniform. To perform non-uniform scaling, simply deselect the Uniform check box.

The Type of Object section lets you define whether the new objects are copies, instances, or references, but unlike the other cloning tools, the Array tool defaults to Instance. If you plan on modeling all the objects in a similar manner, then you will want to select the Instance or Reference options.

In the Array Dimensions section, you can specify the number of objects to copy along three different dimensions. You also can define incremental offsets for each individual row.

Tutorial: Building a white picket fence

To start with a simple example, you'll create a white picket fence. Because a fence repeats, you need to create only a single slat; then you'll use the Array command to duplicate it consistently.

To create a picket fence, follow these steps:

1. Open the White picket fence.max file from the Chap 07 directory on the CD.
2. With the single fence board selected, choose Tools⇨Array or click the Array button on the Extras toolbar to open the Array dialog box.
3. In the Array dialog box, click the Reset All Parameters button to start with a clean slate. Then enter a value of **50** in the X column's Move row under the Incremental section. (This is the incremental value for spacing each successive picket.) Next, enter **20** in the Array Dimensions section next to the 1D radio button. (This is the number of objects to include in the array.) Click OK to create the objects.

4. Click the Zoom Extents All button (or press Shift+Ctrl+Z) in the lower-right corner of the 3ds Max window to see the entire fence in the viewports.

Figure 7.14 shows the completed fence.

FIGURE 7.14

Tom Sawyer would be pleased to see this white picket fence, created easily with the Array dialog box.

Circular arrays

You can use the Array dialog box for creating more than just linear arrays. All transformations are done relative to a center point. You can change the center point about which transformations are performed using the Use Selection Center button on the main toolbar. The three flyout options are Use Pivot Point Center, Use Selection Center, and Use Transform Coordinate Center.

For more about how these settings affect transformations, see Chapter 6, "Transforming Objects, Pivoting, Aligning, and Snapping."

Tutorial: Building a Ferris wheel

Ferris wheels, like most of the rides at the fair, entertain by going around and around, with the riders seated in chairs spaced around the Ferris wheel's central point. The Array dialog box also can create objects around a central point.

In this example, you use the Rotate transformation along with the Use Transform Coordinate Center button to create a circular array.

To create a circular array, follow these steps:

1. Open the Ferris wheel.max file from the Chap 07 directory on the CD.

This file has the Front viewport maximized to show the profile of the Ferris wheel.

2. Click the Use Pivot Point Center button on the main toolbar, and drag down to the last icon, which is the Use Transform Coordinate Center button.

   The Use Transform Coordinate Center button becomes active. This button causes all transformations to take place about the axis in the center of the screen. Navigate the scene view so the center of the ferris wheel is in the center of the viewport.

3. Select the light blue seat object, and open the Array dialog box by choosing Tools ⇨ Array or by clicking the Array button on the Extras toolbar. Before entering any values into the Array dialog box, click the Reset All Parameters button.

4. Between the Incremental and Totals sections are the labels Move, Rotate, and Scale. Click the arrow button to the right of the Rotate label. Set the Z column value of the Rotate row to **360** degrees, and make sure that the Re-Orient option is disabled.

   A value of 360 degrees defines one complete revolution. Disabling the Re-Orient option keeps each chair object from gradually turning upside down.

5. In the Array Dimensions section, set the 1D spinner Count value to **8 and** click OK to create the array.

6. Next, select the green strut, and open the Array dialog box again with the Tools ⇨ Array command. Select the Re-Orient option, and leave the rest of the settings as they are. Click OK to create the array.

Figure 7.15 shows the resulting Ferris wheel. You can click the Min/Max toggle in the lower-right corner to view all four viewports again.

FIGURE 7.15

A circular array created by rotating objects about the Transform Coordinate Center

Working with a Ring Array

You can find the Ring Array system by opening the Create panel and selecting the Systems category. Clicking the Ring Array button opens a Parameters rollout. In this rollout are parameters for the ring's Radius, Amplitude, Cycles, Phase, and the Number of elements to include.

You create the actual array by clicking and dragging in one of the viewports. Initially, all elements are simple box objects surrounding a green dummy object.

The Amplitude, Cycles, and Phase values define the sinusoidal nature of the circle. The Amplitude is the maximum distance that you can position the objects from the horizontal plane. If the Amplitude is set to 0, then all objects lie in the same horizontal plane. The Cycles value is the number of waves that occur around the entire circle. The Phase determines which position along the circle starts in the up position.

Tutorial: Using Ring Array to create a carousel

Continuing with the theme park attractions motif, this example creates a carousel. The horse model comes from Poser but was simplified using the MultiRes modifier.

To use a Ring Array system to create a carousel, follow these steps:

1. Open the Carousel.max file from the Chap 07 directory on the CD.

   This file includes a carousel structure made from primitives along with a carousel horse.

2. Open the Create panel, select the Systems category, and click the Ring Array button. Drag in the Top viewport from the center of the carousel to create a ring array. Then enter a Radius value of **250**, an Amplitude of **20**, a Cycles value of **3**, and a Number value of **6**. Then right-click in the active viewport to deselect the Ring Array tool.

> **NOTE**
> If the Ring Array object gets deselected, you can access its parameters in the Motion panel, not in the Modify panel.

3. Select the Ring Array's center Dummy object in the Left viewport, select the Tools ⇨ Align ⇨ Align menu command, and then click the center cylinder. The Align Selection dialog box opens. Enable the X, Y, and Z Position options, choose the Center options for both the Current and Target objects, and click the OK button. This aligns the ring array to the center of the carousel.

4. Select the horse object, and choose the Tools ⇨ Align ⇨ Clone and Align menu command. In the Clone and Align dialog box that opens, select the Instance option along with the X, Y, and Z Position and Orientation options. Then click the Pick button, and click each of the boxes in the ring array. Set the Y-axis Orientation Offset value to 90 and the Z-axis Orientation Offset to -90, and then raise the whole set with a value of 100 for the Z-axis Position Offset to move the horses under the rooftop. Then click the Apply button, and close the Clone and Align dialog box.

Figure 7.16 shows the finished carousel. Notice that each horse is at a different height. After the horses are placed, you can delete or hide the Ring Array object.

FIGURE 7.16

The horses in the carousel were created using a Ring Array system.

Summary

Many ways to clone an object are available. You can use the Clone command under the Edit menu or the Shift-clone feature for quickly creating numerous clones. Clones can be copies, instances, or references. These methods differ in how they retain links to the original object. You can also clone using the Mirror, Snapshot, and Spacing tools.

Arrays are another means of cloning. You can use the Array dialog box to produce clones in three different dimensions, and you can specify the offset transformations.

This chapter covered the following cloning topics:

- Cloning objects and Shift-cloning
- Understanding copies, instances, and references
- Using the Mirror, Snapshot, Spacing, and Clone and Align tools
- Building linear and circular arrays of objects
- Using the Ring Array system

In the next chapter, you learn to group objects and link them into hierarchies. Then you'll be able to organize into structures all the objects that you've learned to create. These hierarchies become important as you prepare to animate the scene.

Grouping, Linking, and Parenting Objects

IN THIS CHAPTER

Grouping objects

Understanding root, parent, and child relationships

Linking and unlinking objects

Now that you've learned how to select and clone objects, you'll want to learn how to group objects in an easily accessible form, especially as a scene becomes more complex. The grouping features in the Autodesk® 3ds Max® 2013 software enable you to organize all the objects that you're dealing with, thereby making your workflow more efficient.

Another way of organizing objects is to build a linked hierarchy. A *linked hierarchy* attaches, or links, one object to another and makes it possible to transform the attached object by moving the object to which it is linked. The arm is a classic example of a linked hierarchy: When the shoulder rotates, so do the elbow, wrist, and fingers. Establishing linked hierarchies can make moving, positioning, and animating many objects much easier.

Working with Groups

Grouping objects organizes them and makes them easier to select and transform. Groups are different from selection sets in that groups exist like one object. Selecting any object in the group selects the entire group, whereas selecting an object in a selection set selects only that object and not the selection set. You can open groups to add, delete, or reposition objects within the group. Groups also can contain other groups. This is called *nesting groups*.

Creating groups

The Group command enables you to create a group. To do so, simply select the desired objects and choose Group ⇨ Group. A simple Group dialog box opens and enables you to give the group a name. The newly created group displays a new bounding box that encompasses all the objects in the group.

> **TIP**
> You can easily identify groups in the Select From Scene dialog box by using the Groups display toggle. Groups appear in bold in the Name and Color rollout of the Command Panel.

Ungrouping objects

The Ungroup command enables you to break up a group (kind of like a poor music album). To do so, simply select the desired group and choose Group ⇨ Ungroup. This menu command dissolves the group, and all the objects within the group revert to separate objects. The Ungroup command breaks up only the currently selected group. All nested groups within a group stay intact.

> **CAUTION**
> If you animate a group and then later use the Ungroup command, then all the keys created for the whole group are lost when you ungroup.

The easiest way to dissolve an entire group, including any nested groups, is with the Explode command. This command eliminates the group and the groups within the group and makes each object separate.

Opening and closing groups

The Open command enables you to access the objects within a group. Grouped objects move, scale, and rotate as a unit when transformed, but individual objects within a group can be transformed independently after you open a group with the Open command.

To move an individual object in a group, select the group and choose Group ⇨ Open. The white bounding box changes to a pink box. Then select an object within the group, and move it with the Select and Move button (keyboard shortcut, W). Choose Group ⇨ Close to reinstate the group.

Attaching and detaching objects

The Attach and Detach commands enable you to insert or remove objects from a group without dissolving and recreating the group. To attach objects to an existing group, you select an object, select the Attach menu command, and click the group to which you want to add the object. To detach an object from a group, you need to open the group and select the Detach menu command. Remember to close the group when finished.

Tutorial: Grouping a plane's parts together

Positioning objects relative to one another takes careful and precise work. After spending the time to place the wings, tail, and prop on a plane exactly where they need to be, transforming each object by itself can misalign all the parts. By grouping all the objects together, you can move all the objects at once.

For this tutorial, you can get some practice grouping all the parts of an airplane together. Follow these steps:

1. Open the T-28 Trojan plane.max file from the Chap 08 directory on the CD. This file includes a model created by Viewpoint Datalabs.

2. Click the Select by Name button on the main toolbar (or press the H key) to open the Select From Scene dialog box. In this dialog box, notice all the different plane parts. Click the Select All button to select all the separate objects, and click OK to close the dialog box.

3. With all the objects selected, choose Group⇨Group to open the Group dialog box. Give the group the name **Plane**, and click OK.

4. Click the Select and Move button (or press W), and click and drag the plane. The entire group now moves together.

Figure 8.1 shows the plane grouped as one unit. Notice how only one set of brackets surrounds the plane in the Perspective viewport. The group name is displayed in the Name field of the Command Panel instead of listing the number of objects selected.

FIGURE 8.1

The plane moves as one unit after its objects are grouped.

Alternatives to grouping

Grouping objects together makes them easier to transform about the scene, but they are limited in their functionality and can cause some headaches when animating. One alternative to grouping objects is to combine them together into a single object using the Attach command for editable objects. Editable objects, like the Editable Poly, also can make use of an Attach feature, but attaching objects to an editable object permanently combines the objects together. Another alternative is to use the Container feature, which allows the grouped assets to be saved as an external file where they can be shared with other team members.

Understanding Parent, Child, and Root Relationships

3ds Max uses several terms to describe the relationships between objects. A *parent object* is an object that controls any secondary, or child, objects linked to it. A *child object* is an object that is linked to and controlled by a parent. A parent object can have many children, but a child can have only one parent. Additionally, an object can be both a parent and a child at the same time. Another way to say this is:

- Child objects are linked to parent objects.
- Moving a parent object moves its children with it.
- Child objects can move independently of their parents.

A hierarchy is the complete set of linked objects that includes these types of relationships. Ancestors are all the parents above a child object. Descendants are all the children below a parent object. The root object is the top parent object that has no parent and controls the entire hierarchy.

Each hierarchy can have several branches or subtrees. Any parent with two or more children represents the start of a new branch.

The default hierarchies established using the Select and Link tool are referred to as forward kinematics systems, in which control moves forward down the hierarchy from parent to child. In forward kinematics systems, the child has no control over the parent. An inverse kinematics system (covered in Chapter 29, "Understanding Rigging, Kinematics, and Working with Bones") enables child objects to control their parents.

All objects in a scene, whether linked or not, belong to a hierarchy. Objects that aren't linked to any other objects are, by default, children of the *world object*, which is an imaginary object that holds all objects.

> **NOTE**
> You can view the world object, labeled Objects, in the Track View. Individual objects are listed under the Objects track by their object name.

You have several ways to establish and edit hierarchies using 3ds Max. The simplest method is to use the Select and Link and Unlink Selection buttons found on the main toolbar. You can find these buttons in the Schematic View window as well. The Hierarchy panel in the Command Panel provides access to valuable controls and information about established hierarchies.

Building Links between Objects

The main toolbar includes two buttons that you can use to build and edit a hierarchy: Select and Link and Unlink Selection. The order of selection defines which object becomes the parent and which becomes the child.

Linking objects

The Select and Link button always links children to the parents. To remind you of this order, remember that a parent can have many children, but a child can have only one parent.

To link two objects, click the Select and Link button. This places you in Link mode, which continues until you turn it off by selecting another button, such as the Select Object button or one of the Transform buttons. When you're in Link mode, the Link button is highlighted.

With the Link button highlighted, click an object, which will be the child, and drag a line to the target parent object. The cursor arrow changes to the link icon when it is over a potential parent. When you release the mouse button, the parent object flashes once and the link is established. If you drag the same child object to a different parent, the link to the previous parent is replaced by the link to the new parent.

Once linked, all transformations applied to the parent are applied equally to its children about the parent's pivot point. A *pivot point* is the center about which the object rotates and scales.

Unlinking objects

The Unlink Selection button is used to destroy links, but only to the parent. For example, if a selected object has both children and a parent, clicking the Unlink button destroys the link to the parent of the selected object but not the links to its children.

To eliminate all links for an entire hierarchy, double-click an object to select its entire hierarchy and click the Unlink Selection button.

Tutorial: Linking a family of ducks

What better way to show off parent-child relationships than with a family? I could have modeled my own family, but for some reason, my little ducks don't always like to follow me around.

To create a linked family of ducks, follow these steps:

1. Open the Linked duck family.max file from the Chap 08 directory on the website. This file includes several simple ducks lined up in a row.

2. Click the Select and Link button in the main toolbar, and drag a line from the last duck to the one just in front of it.

TIP

You can link several objects at once by highlighting all the objects you want to link and dragging the selected objects to the parent object. This procedure creates a link between the parent object and each selected object.

3. Continue to connect each duck to the one in front of it.

4. Click the Select and Move button (or press the W key), and move the Mommy duck object. Notice how all the children move with her.

Figure 8.2 shows the duck family as they move forward in a line. The Select and Link button made it possible to move all the ducks simply by moving the parent duck.

FIGURE 8.2

Linked child ducks inherit transformations from their parent duck.

Displaying Links and Hierarchies

The Display panel includes a rollout that lets you display all the links in the viewports.

After links have been established, you can see linked objects listed as a hierarchy in several places. The Select From Scene dialog box, opened with the Select by Name button (or with the H key), can display objects in this manner, as well as the Schematic and Track Views.

Displaying links in the viewport

You can choose to see the links between the selected objects in the viewports by selecting the Display Links option in the Link Display rollout of the Display panel. The Display Links option shows links as lines that run between the pivot points of the objects with a diamond-shaped marker at the end of each line; these lines and markers are the same color as the object.

> **NOTE**
>
> The Display Links option can be enabled or disabled for each object in the scene. To display the links for all objects, use the Edit ⇨ Select All (Ctrl+A) command and then enable the Display Links option.

The Link Display rollout also offers the Link Replaces Object option, which removes the objects and displays only the link structure. This feature removes the complexity of the objects from the viewports and lets you work with the links directly. Although the objects disappear, you can still transform the objects using the link markers.

Viewing hierarchies

The Select From Scene dialog box, the Scene Explorer and the Schematic and Track Views can display the hierarchy of objects in a scene as an ordered list, with child objects indented under parent objects.

Clicking the Select by Name button (H) on the main toolbar opens the Select From Scene dialog box; select the Display ⇨ Display Children menu to see all the children under the selected object. Click on the small plus sign next to the parent to see its children. Figure 8.3 shows the Select From Scene dialog box with the Display Children menu enabled.

 You can learn more about the Scene Explorer dialog box in Chapter 5, "Selecting Objects and Using Layers."

FIGURE 8.3

The Select From Scene dialog box indents all child objects under their parent.

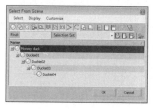

The Schematic View (opened with the Graph Editors ⇨ New Schematic View menu command) presents a graph in which objects are represented by rectangle nodes with their hierarchical links drawn as lines running between them.

The Track View (opened with the Graph Editors ⇨ New Track View menu command) displays lots of scene details in addition to the object hierarchy. In the Track View, you can easily expand and contract the hierarchy to focus on just the section you want to see or select.

 For more information on using the Track View, see Chapter 28, "Editing Animation Curves in the Track View."

Working with Linked Objects

If you link some objects together and set some animation keys, and the magical Play Animation button starts sending objects hurtling off into space, chances are good that you have a linked object that you didn't know about. Understanding object hierarchies and being able to transform those hierarchies are the keys to efficient animation sequences.

All transformations are done about an object's pivot point. You can move and reorient these pivot points as needed by clicking the Pivot button under the Hierarchy panel.

Several additional settings for controlling links are available under the Hierarchy panel of the Command Panel (the Hierarchy panel tab looks like a mini-organizational chart). Just click the Link Info button. This button opens two rollouts if a linked object is selected. You can use the Locks and Inherit rollouts to limit an object's transformations and specify the transformations that it inherits.

 I present more information on object transformations in Chapter 6, "Transforming Objects, Pivoting, Aligning, and Snapping."

Locking inheriting transformations

The Inherit rollout, like the Locks rollout, includes check boxes for each axis and each transformation, except that here, all the transformations are selected by default. By deselecting a check box, you specify which transformations an object does not inherit from its parent. The Inherit rollout appears only if the selected object is part of a hierarchy.

For example, suppose that a child object is created and linked to a parent and the X Move Inherit check box is deselected. As the parent is moved in the Y or Z directions, the child follows, but if the parent is moved in the X direction, the child does not follow. If a parent doesn't inherit a transformation, then its children don't either.

Using the Link Inheritance utility

The Link Inheritance utility works in the same way as the Inherit rollout of the Hierarchy panel, except that you can apply it to multiple objects at the same time. To use this utility, open the Utilities panel and click the More button. In the Utilities dialog box, select the Link Inheritance (Selected) utility and click OK. The rollout for this utility is identical to the Inherit rollout discussed in the previous section.

Selecting hierarchies

You need to select a hierarchy before you can transform it, and you have several ways to do so. The easiest method is to simply double-click an object. Double-clicking the root object selects the entire hierarchy, and double-clicking an object within the hierarchy selects it and all of its children.

After you select an object in a hierarchy, pressing the Page Up or Page Down keyboard shortcut selects its parent or child objects. For example, if you select the Mommy duck object and press Page Down, the first baby duck object is selected and the Mommy duck object is deselected. Selecting any of the baby duck objects and pressing Page Up selects the duck object in front of it.

Linking to dummies

Dummy objects are useful as root objects for controlling the motion of hierarchies. By linking the parent object of a hierarchy to a dummy object, you can control all the objects by moving the dummy.

To create a dummy object, select Create ➪ Helpers ➪ Dummy, or open the Create panel, click the Helpers category button (this button looks like a small tape measure), and select the Standard category. Within the Object Type rollout is the Dummy button; click it, and then click in the viewport where you want the dummy object to be positioned and drag to set its size. Dummy objects look like wireframe box objects in the viewports, but dummy objects are not rendered.

Tutorial: Circling the globe

When you work with complex models with lots of parts, you can control the object more easily if you link it to a dummy object and then animate the dummy object instead of the entire model. To practice doing this, you'll create a simple animation of an airplane flying around the globe. To perform this feat, you create a dummy object in the center of a sphere, link the airplane model to it, and rotate the dummy object. This alternative doesn't require that you move any pivot points. This tutorial involves animating objects, which are covered in other chapters.

The basics of animation are covered in Chapter 24, "Understanding Animation and Keyframes."

To link and rotate objects using a dummy object, follow these steps:

1. Open the Circling the globe.max file found in the Chap 08 directory on the website.

   This file includes a texture mapped sphere with an airplane model positioned to the side of it. The airplane model was created by Viewpoint Datalabs.

2. Select Create ⇨ Helpers ⇨ Dummy, and then drag in the center of the Sphere to create a dummy object. With the dummy object selected, choose the Tools ⇨ Align ⇨ Align menu command (or press the Alt+A shortcut) and click the globe. In the Align Selection dialog box, enable the X, Y, and Z Position options along with the Center options and click OK to align the centers of the dummy and globe objects.

3. Because the dummy object is inside the sphere, creating the link between the airplane and the dummy object can be difficult. To simplify this process, select and right-click the sphere object, and then select Hide Selection from the pop-up quad menu.

   This hides the sphere so you can create a link between the airplane and the dummy object.

4. Click the Select and Link button on the main toolbar, and drag a line from the airplane to the dummy object.

5. Click the Auto Key button (or press N) to enable animation key mode, and drag the Time Slider to frame 100. Then click the Select and Rotate button on the main toolbar (or press E), and select the dummy object. Then rotate the dummy object about its X-axis one full revolution, and notice how the linked airplane also rotates over the surface of the sphere. Click the Auto Key button again to disable auto key mode.

6. Right-click to access the pop-up quad menu. Then select the Unhide All menu command to make the sphere visible again. Then click the Play button to see the plane fly about the globe.

By linking the airplane to a dummy object, you don't have to worry about moving the airplane's pivot point to get the correct motion. Figure 8.4 shows a frame from the final scene.

FIGURE 8.4

With a link to a dummy object, making the airplane circle the globe is easy.

Summary

As scenes become more complex, the name of the game is organization. You can organize objects within the scene in several ways, including grouping, linking, and building hierarchies.

In this chapter, you've done the following:

- Grouped objects using the Group menu and learned to work with groups
- Learned about parent, child, and root relationships
- Created a hierarchy of objects using the Select and Link and Unlink Selection buttons
- Viewed links in the viewport
- Learned how to create a link to a dummy object

In the next chapter, you jump headfirst into modeling by covering the basics of modeling and working with subobjects, modeling modifiers, and using the Modifier Stack.

Part III

Modeling 3D Assets

IN THIS PART

Introducing Subobjects and Modifiers and Using the Modifier Stack

IN THIS CHAPTER

Understanding the modeling types

Using normals

Working with subobjects

Using Soft Selection

Introducing Modifiers

Using the Modifier Stack to manage modifiers

Learning to work with modifier gizmos

Modeling is the process of pure creation. Whether it is sculpting, building with blocks, construction work, carving, architecture, or advanced injection molding, you can create objects in many different ways. The Autodesk® 3ds Max® 2013 software includes many different model types and even more ways to work with them.

This chapter introduces the various modeling methods in 3ds Max. It also explains the common modeling components, including normals and subobjects. The purpose of this chapter is to whet your whistle for modeling and to cover some of the general concepts that apply to all models. More specific details on the various modeling types are presented in the subsequent chapters, so onward into the realm of creation.

Think for a moment of a woodshop with all its various (and expensive) tools and machines. Some tools, like a screwdriver or a sander, are simple, and others, like a lathe or router, are more complex, but they all change the wood (or models) in different ways. In some ways, you can think of modifiers as the tools and machines that work on 3D objects.

Each woodshop tool has different parameters that control how it works, such as how hard you turn the screwdriver or the coarseness of the sandpaper. Likewise, each modifier has parameters that you can set that determine how it affects the 3D object.

Modifiers can be used in a number of different ways to reshape objects, apply material mappings, deform an object's surface, and perform many other actions. Many different types of modifiers exist. This chapter introduces you to the concept of modifiers and explains the basics on how to use them. The chapter concludes by exploring some of the common modifiers that are used to deform geometry objects.

Exploring the Model Types

You can climb a mountain in many ways, and you can model one in many ways too. You can make a mountain model out of primitive objects like blocks, cubes, and spheres, or you can create one as a polygon mesh. As your experience grows, you'll discover that some objects are easier to model using one method, and some are easier using another. 3ds Max offers several different modeling types to handle various modeling situations.

Parametric objects versus editable objects

All geometric objects in 3ds Max can be divided into two general categories: parametric objects and editable objects. *Parametric* means that the geometry of the object is controlled by variables called parameters. Modifying these parameters modifies the geometry of the object. This powerful concept gives parametric objects lots of flexibility. For example, the sphere object has a parameter called Radius. Changing this parameter changes the size of the sphere. Parametric objects in 3ds Max include the primitive objects found in the Create menu.

Editable objects do not have this flexibility of parameters, but they deal with subobjects and editing functions. The editable objects include Editable Spline, Mesh, Poly, Patch, and NURBS (Non-Uniform Rational B-Splines). Editable objects are listed in the Modifier Stack with the word *Editable* in front of their base object (except for NURBS objects, which are simply called NURBS Surfaces). For example, an editable mesh object is listed as Editable Mesh in the Modifier Stack. This identifies it as an object that is edited by adjusting its subobjects.

> **NOTE**
>
> Actually, NURBS objects are a different beast altogether. When created using the Create menu, they are parametric objects, but after you select the Modify panel, they are editable objects with a host of subobject modes and editing functions.

Editable objects aren't created; instead, they are converted or modified from another object. When a primitive object is converted to a different object type like an Editable Mesh, it loses its parametric nature and can no longer be changed by altering its base parameters. Editable objects do have their advantages, though. You can edit subobjects such as vertices, edges, and faces of meshes—all things that you cannot edit for a parametric object. Each editable object type has a host of functions that are specific to its type. These functions are discussed in the coming chapters.

> **NOTE**
>
> Several modifiers enable you to edit subobjects while maintaining the parametric nature of an object. These include Edit Patch, Edit Mesh, Edit Poly, and Edit Spline.

3ds Max includes the following model types:

- **Primitives:** Basic parametric objects such as cubes, spheres, and pyramids. The primitives are divided into two groups consisting of Standard and Extended Primitives. The AEC Objects also are considered primitive objects. A complete list of primitives is covered in Chapter 4, "Creating and Editing Primitive Objects."

- **Shapes and splines:** Simple vector shapes such as circles, stars, arcs, and text, and splines such as the Helix. These objects are fully renderable. The Create menu includes many parametric shapes and splines. These parametric objects can be converted to Editable Spline objects for more editing. These are covered in Chapter 10, "Drawing and Editing 2D Splines and Shapes."

- **Meshes:** Complex models created from many polygon faces that are smoothed together when the object is rendered. These objects are available only as Editable Mesh objects. Meshes are covered in Chapter 11, "Modeling with Polygons."

- **Polys:** Objects composed of polygon faces, similar to mesh objects, but with unique features. These objects also are available only as Editable Poly objects. Poly objects are covered in Chapter 11, "Modeling with Polygons." The Graphite Modeling tools are designed to work on Editable Poly objects. These tools are covered in Chapter 12, "Using the Graphite Modeling Tools."

- **Patches:** Based on spline curves; patches can be modified using control points. The Create menu includes two parametric Patch objects, but most objects also can be converted to Editable Patch objects.

- **NURBS:** Stands for Non-Uniform Rational B-Splines. NURBS are similar to patches in that they also have control points. These control points define how a surface spreads over curves.

- **Compound objects:** A miscellaneous group of model types, including Booleans, loft objects, and scatter objects. Other compound objects are good at modeling one specialized type of object such as Terrain or BlobMesh objects. The Compound objects are presented in Chapter 13, "Working with Compound Objects."

- **Body objects:** Solid objects that are imported from an SAT file produced by a solid modeling application like Revit have the concept of volume. 3ds Max mesh objects typically deal only with surfaces but can be converted to Body objects.

- **Particle systems:** Systems of small objects that work together as a single group. They are useful for creating effects such as rain, snow, and sparks. Particles are covered in Chapter 32, "Creating Particles."

- **Hair and fur:** Modeling hundreds of thousands of cylinder objects to create believable hair would quickly bog down any system, so hair is modeled using a separate system that represents each hair as a spline.

- **Cloth systems:** Cloth — with its waving, free-flowing nature — behaves like water in some cases and like a solid in others. 3ds Max includes a specialized set of modifiers for handling cloth systems.

> **NOTE**
> Hair, fur, and cloth are often considered effects or dynamic simulations instead of modeling constructs, so their inclusion on this list should be considered a stretch.

With all these options, modeling in 3ds Max can be intimidating, but you learn how to use each of these types the more you work with 3ds Max. For starters, begin with primitive or imported objects and then branch out by converting to editable objects. A single 3ds Max scene can include multiple different object types.

9

Converting to editable objects

Of all the commands found in the Create menu and in the Create panel, you won't find any menus or subcategories for creating editable objects.

To create an editable object, you need to import it or convert it from another object type. You can convert objects by right-clicking the object in the viewport and selecting the Convert To submenu from the pop-up quad menu, or by right-clicking the base object in the Modifier Stack and selecting the object type to convert to in the pop-up menu.

Once converted, all the editing features of the selected type are available in the Modify panel, but the object is no longer parametric and loses access to its common parameters such as Radius and Segments. However, 3ds Max also includes specialized modifiers such as the Edit Poly modifier that maintain the parametric nature of primitive objects while giving you access to the editing features of the Editable object. More on these modifiers is presented in the later modeling chapters.

> **CAUTION**
>
> If a modifier has been applied to an object, the Convert To menu option in the Modifier Stack pop-up menu is not available until you use the Collapse All command.

The Modifier Stack pop-up menu includes options to convert to editable mesh, editable poly, deformable gPoly, editable patch, and NURBS. If a shape or spline object is selected, then the object also can be converted to an editable spline. Using any of the Convert To menu options collapses the Modifier Stack.

> **NOTE**
>
> Objects can be converted between the different types several times, but each conversion may subdivide the object. Therefore, multiple conversions are not recommended.

Converting between object types is done automatically using the software's best guess, but if you apply one of the Conversion modifiers to an object, several parameters are displayed that let you define how the object is converted. For example, the Turn to Mesh modifier includes an option to Use Invisible Edges, which divides polygons using invisible edges. If this option is disabled, then the entire object is triangulated. The Turn to Patch modifier includes an option to make quads into quad patches. If this option is disabled, all quads are triangulated.

The Turn to Poly modifier includes options to Keep Polygons Convex, Limit Polygon Size, Require Planar Polygons, and Remove Mid-Edge Vertices. The Keep Polygons Convex option divides any polygon that is concave, if enabled. The Limit Polygon Size option lets you specify the maximum allowable polygon size. This can be used to eliminate any pentagons and hexagons from the mesh. The Require Planar Polygons option keeps adjacent polygons as triangles if the angle between them is greater than the specified Threshold value. The Remove Mid-Edge Vertices option removes any vertices caused by intersections with invisible edges.

All Conversion modifiers also include options to preserve the current subobject selection (including any soft selection) and to specify the Selection Level. The From Pipeline option uses the current subobject selection on the given object. After a Conversion modifier is applied to an object, you must collapse the Modifier Stack in order to complete the conversion.

Understanding Normals

Before moving on to the various subobjects, you need to understand what a normal is and how it is used to tell which way the surface is facing. *Normals* are vectors that extend outward perpendicular to the surface of an object. These vectors aren't rendered and are used only to tell which way the surface face is pointing. If the normal vector points toward the camera, then the polygon is visible, but if it points away from the camera, then you are looking at the polygon's backside, which is visible only if the Backface Cull option in the Object Properties dialog box is disabled.

Several other properties also use the normal vector to determine how the polygon face is shaded, smoothed, and lighted. Normals also are used in dynamic simulations to determine collisions between objects.

Viewing normals

In all mesh subobject modes except for Edge, you can select the Show Normals option to see any object's normals and set a Scale value. Figure 9.1 shows a Plane, a Box, and a Sphere object. Each object has been converted to an Editable Mesh with all faces selected in Face subobject mode and with the Show Normals option selected.

FIGURE 9.1

The Show Normals option shows the normal vectors for each face in a Plane, a Box, and a Sphere.

Tutorial: Cleaning up imported meshes

Many 3D formats are mesh-based, and importing mesh objects sometimes can create problems. By collapsing an imported model to an Editable Mesh, you can take advantage of several of the editable mesh features to clean up these problems.

Figure 9.2 shows a model that was exported from Poser using the 3ds format. Notice that the model's waist is black when viewed using the Hidden Line viewport shading method. It appears this way because I've turned off the Backface Cull option in the Object Properties dialog box. If it were turned on, his waist would be invisible. The problem here is that the normals for this object are pointing in the wrong direction. This problem is common for imported meshes, and you'll fix it in this tutorial.

To fix the normals on an imported mesh model, follow these steps:

9

1. Open the Hailing taxi man with incorrect normals.max file from the Chap 09 directory on the CD.

2. Select the problem object—the waist on the right mesh. Open the object hierarchy by clicking the plus sign to the left of the Editable Mesh object in the Modifier Stack if it isn't already expanded, and then select Element subobject mode and click the waist area.

3. In the Selection rollout, select the Show Normals option and set the Scale value to a small number such as **0.1**.

   The normals are now visible. Notice that some of them point outward, and some of them point inward.

4. With the element subobject still selected, click the Unify button in the Surface Properties rollout and then click the Flip button until all normals are pointing outward.

This problem is fixed on the right model, and the waist object is now a visible part of the mesh. The fixed mesh on the right looks just like the original mesh on the left without being invisible (or more correctly inside-out), as shown in Figure 9.2.

FIGURE 9.2

This mesh suffers from objects with flipped normals, which makes them invisible.

Working with Subobjects

All the editable modeling types offer the ability to work with subobjects. Subobjects are the elements that make up the model and can include vertices, edges, borders, faces, polygons, and elements. These individual subobjects can be selected and transformed just like normal objects using the transformation tools located on the main toolbar. But, before you can transform these subobjects, you need to select them. You can select subobjects only when you're in a particular subobject mode. Each editable object type has a different set of subobjects.

If you expand the object's hierarchy in the Modifier Stack (by clicking the small plus sign to the left of the object's name), all subobjects for an object are displayed, as shown in Figure 9.3. Selecting a subobject in the Modifier Stack places you in subobject mode for that subobject type. You also can enter subobject mode by clicking the subobject icons located at the top of the Selection rollout or by pressing the 1 through 5 keys on the keyboard. When you're in subobject mode, the subobject title and the icon in the Selection rollout are highlighted. You can work with the selected subobjects only while in subobject mode. To transform the entire object again, you need to exit subobject mode, which you can do by clicking either the subobject title or the subobject icon, or by pressing one of the keyboard shortcuts, 1–5.

> **TIP**
>
> You also can access the subobject modes using the right-click quad menu. To exit a subobject mode, select Top Level in the quad menu.

FIGURE 9.3

Expanding an editable object in the Modifier Stack reveals its subobjects.

Subobject icons

Subobject selections can be locked with the Selection Lock Toggle (spacebar) located along the bottom edge of the interface to the left of the transform type-in fields. Subobject selections can also be made into a Selection Set by typing a name into the Named Selection Set drop-down list on the main toolbar. After a Selection Set is created, you can recall it any time you are in that same subobject mode. Named Selection Sets can then be copied and pasted between objects using the Copy and Paste buttons found in the Selection rollout for most editable objects.

Using Soft Selection

When working with editable mesh, poly, patches, or splines, the Soft Selection rollout, shown in Figure 9.4, becomes available in subobject mode. Soft Selection selects all the subobjects surrounding the current selection and applies transformations to them to a lesser extent. For example, if a face is selected and moved a distance of 2, then with linear Soft Selection, the neighboring faces within the soft selection range move a distance of 1. The overall effect is a smoother transition.

> **NOTE**
>
> The Soft Selection options are different for the various modeling types. For example, the Editable Mesh includes a standard set of options, but the Editable Poly object has more options, including a Paint Soft Selection mode.

FIGURE 9.4

The Soft Selection rollout is available only in subobject mode.

 —— Soft Selection curve

The Use Soft Selection parameter enables or disables the Soft Selection feature. The Edge Distance option sets the range (the number of edges from the current selection) that the Soft Selection will affect. If disabled, the distance is determined by the Falloff amount. The Affect Backfacing option applies the Soft Selection to selected subobjects on the backside of an object. For example, if you are selecting vertices on the front of a sphere object and the Affect Backfacing option is enabled, then vertices on the opposite side of the sphere also are selected. This provides a way to work with subobjects on both sides of an object such as a wheel.

The Soft Selection curve shows a graphical representation of how the Soft Selection is applied. The Falloff value defines the spherical region where the Soft Selection has an effect. The Pinch button sharpens the point at the top of the curve. The Bubble button has an opposite effect and widens the curve. Changing the Falloff, Pinch and Bubble values also changes the shape of the curve. Figure 9.5 shows several sample values and the resulting curve.

If you open the Customize User Interface dialog box found in the Customize menu, you'll find an Action called Edit Soft Selection in the Keyboard panel. If you assign a Hotkey to this action, then you can use that keyboard shortcut to access Edit Soft Selection mode in the viewport. This mode lets you interactively change the soft selection falloff, pinch, and bubble values by dragging in the viewports.

Once the Edit Soft Selection mode is enabled by using its assigned shortcut, the cursor changes to a custom cursor that looks like two circles. When this cursor appears, you can drag to change the Soft Selection's Falloff value. If you click, the cursor changes (to an upside-down V shape) and lets you drag to change the Pinch value. One more click and you can edit the Bubble value (the cursor looks like an upside-down U-shape for this mode), and another click returns you to the falloff edit mode. Pressing the keyboard shortcut again exits Edit Soft Selection mode.

FIGURE 9.5

The Soft Selection curve is affected by the Falloff, Pinch, and Bubble values.

Tutorial: Soft selecting a heart shape from a plane

Soft Selection enables a smooth transition between subobjects, but sometimes you want the abrupt edge. This tutorial looks at moving some subobject vertices in a plane object with and without Soft Selection enabled.

To move subobject vertices with and without Soft Selection, follow these steps:

1. Open the Soft selection heart.max file from the Chap 09 directory on the CD.

   This file contains two simple plane objects that have been converted to Editable Mesh objects. Several vertices in the shape of a heart are selected.

2. Select the left plane and you'll see that the vertices are already selected; in Vertex subobject mode, click the Select and Move button (or press the W key), move the cursor over the selected vertices, and drag upward on the Y-axis in the Left viewport away from the plane.

3. Exit subobject mode, select the right plane object, and enter Vertex subobject mode. The same vertices are again selected. Open the Soft Selection rollout, enable the Use Soft Selection option, and set the Falloff value to **40**.

4. Click the Select and Move button (or press the W key), and move the selected vertices upward. Notice the difference that Soft Selection makes.

Figure 9.6 shows the two resulting plane objects with the heart selections.

FIGURE 9.6

Soft Selection makes a smooth transition between the subobjects that are moved and those that are not.

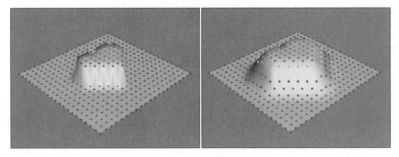

When you select subobjects, they turn red. Non-selected subobjects are blue, and soft selected subobjects are a gradient from orange to yellow, depending on their distance from the selected subobjects. This visual clue provides valuable feedback on how the Soft Selection affects the subobjects. Figure 9.7 shows the selected vertices from the preceding tutorial with Falloff values of 0, 20, 40, 60, and 80.

FIGURE 9.7

A gradient of colors shows the transition zone for soft selected subobjects.

For the Editable Poly and Editable Patch objects, the Soft Selection rollout includes a Shaded Face Toggle button below its curve. This button shades the surface using the soft selection gradient colors, as shown in Figure 9.8. This shaded surface is displayed in any shaded viewports. The cooler colors have less of an impact over the transform.

FIGURE 9.8

The Shaded Face Toggle shades the surface using the soft selection gradient colors.

For Editable Poly objects, the bottom of the Soft Selection rollout includes a Paint Soft Selection section. Clicking the Paint button presents a brush icon in the viewports. You can change the Brush Size to increase or decrease the paint brush. The Brush Strength sets the weight of the painted area. A Brush Strength of 1 sets the painted subobjects to their maximum value (which is only to orange when painting). Smaller Brush Strength values make more subtle changes and a setting of 0 makes no change when painting.

In addition to Paint mode, you can Blur the selections, which evens out the subobjects where you paint removing the high and low values. The Revert mode lets you return the selected subobjects to their previous values.

Introducing Modifiers

Modifiers are functions that you can apply to an object that allow you to change its structure without altering its base nature. For example, if you apply a Twist modifier to a cylinder, you'll still be able to change its base parameters, such as the cylinder radius and height. The Twist modifier adds additional parameters, such as the center of the twist and the amount to twist the model. Modifiers are stored separate from the object in the Modifier Stack. The Modifier Stack lets you remove, reorder, copy, and paste modifiers between objects.

Because modifiers provide an easy way to add more parameters to objects, they are used for all the different modeling types. Some specific modifiers are used on spline objects, and others are for polygon-based models. Another set of modifiers helps you animate. To keep all the various modifiers organized, 3ds Max has grouped them into several distinct modifier sets. The modifier sets, as they appear in the Modifier menu, include those listed in Table 9.1.

TABLE 9.1 Modifiers Menu Items

Menu	Submenu Items
Selection Modifiers	FFD Select, Mesh Select, Patch Select, Poly Select, Select by Channel, Spline Select, Volume Select
Patch/Spline Editing	Cross Section, Delete Patch, Delete Spline, Edit Patch, Edit Spline, Fillet/Chamfer, Lathe, Normalize Spline, Renderable Spline Modifier, Surface, Sweep, Trim/Extend
Mesh Editing	Cap Holes, Delete Mesh, Edit Mesh, Edit Normals, Edit Poly, Extrude, Face Extrude, MultiRes, Normal Modifier, Optimize, ProOptimizer, Quadify Mesh, Smooth, STL Check, Symmetry, Tessellate, Vertex Paint, Vertex Weld
Conversion	Turn to Mesh, Turn to Patch, Turn to Poly
Animation Modifiers	Attribute Holder, Flex, Linked XForm, Melt, Morpher, PatchDeform, PatchDeform (WSM), PathDeform, PathDeform (WSM), Skin, Skin Morph, Skin Wrap, Skin Wrap Patch, SplineIk Control, SurfDeform, SurfDeform (WSM)
Cloth	Cloth, Garment Maker, Welder
Hair and Fur	Hair and Fur (WSM)
UV Coordinates	Camera Map, Camera Map (WSM), MapScaler (WSM), Projection, Unwrap UVW, UVW Map, UVW Mapping Add, UVW Mapping Clear, UVW XForm
Cache Tools	Point Cache, Point Cache (WSM)
Subdivision Surfaces	HSDS Modifier, MeshSmooth, TurboSmooth
Free Form Deformers	FFD 2x2x2, FFD 3x3x3, FFD 4x4x4, FFD Box, FFD Cylinder
Parametric Deformers	Affect Region, Bend, Displace, Lattice, Mirror, Noise, Physique, Push, Preserve, Relax, Ripple, Shell, Slice, Skew, Stretch, Spherify, Squeeze, Twist, Taper, Substitute, XForm, Wave
Surface	Disp Approx, Displace Mesh (WSM), Material, Material By Element
NURBS Editing	Disp Approx, Surf Deform, Surface Select
Radiosity	Subdivide, Subdivide (WSM)
Cameras	Camera Correction

9

You can find roughly these same sets if you click the Configure Modifier Sets button in the Modifier Stack. Within this list is a single selected set. The selected set is marked with an arrow to the left of its name. The modifiers contained within the selected set appear at the very top of the Modifier List.

 Covering all the modifiers together would result in a very long chapter. Instead, I decided to cover most of the modifiers in their respective chapters. For example, animation modifiers in Chapter 26, "Using Animation Layers and Animation Modifiers"; the UV Coordinates modifiers in Chapter 17, "Unwrapping UVs"; and so on.

Exploring the Modifier Stack

All modifiers applied to an object are listed together in a single location known as the *Modifier Stack*. This Stack is the manager for all modifiers applied to an object and can be found at the top of the Modify panel in the Command Panel. You also can use the Stack to apply and delete modifiers; cut, copy, and paste modifiers between objects; and reorder them.

Understanding Base Objects

The first entry in the Modifier Stack isn't a modifier at all; it is the Base Object. The Base Object is the original object type. The Base Object for a primitive is listed as its object type, such as Sphere or Torus. Editable meshes, polys, patches, and splines also can be Base Objects. NURBS Surfaces and NURBS Curves also are Base Objects.

You also can see the Base Objects using the Schematic View window if you enable the Base Objects option in the Display floater.

Applying modifiers

An object can have several modifiers applied to it. Modifiers can be applied using the Modifiers menu or by selecting the modifier from the Modifier List drop-down list located at the top of the Modify panel directly under the object name. Selecting a modifier in the Modifiers menu or from the Modifier List applies the modifier to the current selected object. Modifiers can be applied to multiple objects if several objects are selected.

> **TIP**
> You can quickly jump to a specific modifier in the Modifier List by pressing the first letter of the modifier that you want to select. For example, pressing the T key when the Modifier List is open immediately selects the Taper modifier.

> **NOTE**
> Some modifiers aren't available for some types of objects. For example, the Extrude and Lathe modifiers are enabled only when a spline or shape is selected.

Tutorial: Bending a tree

If you have a tree model that you want to bend as if the wind were blowing, you can apply the Bend modifier. The tree then bends about its Pivot Point. Luckily, all the trees and plants found in the AEC Objects category have their Pivot Points set about their base, so bending a tree is really easy.

To bend a tree using the Bend modifier, follow these steps:

1. Select the Create ⇨ AEC Objects ⇨ Foliage menu command to access the available trees. Select a long, thin tree like the Yucca, and click in the Top viewport to add it to the scene.

2. With the tree selected, select the Modifiers ⇨ Parametric Deformers ⇨ Bend menu command to apply the Bend modifier to the tree.

3. In the Parameters rollout found in the Modify panel, set the Bend Axis to **Z** and the Bend Angle to **60**.

   The tree bends as desired.

Figure 9.9 shows the bending Yucca plant and a non-bent one behind for reference. To animate this tree bending back and forth, just set keys for the Angle parameter.

FIGURE 9.9

The Bend modifier can be used to bend trees.

Other Modifier Stack entities

Most modifiers are Object-Space modifiers, but another category called World-Space modifiers also exists. World-Space modifiers are similar to Object-Space modifiers, except they are applied using a global coordinate system instead of a coordinate system that is local to the object. More on World-Space modifiers is presented later in this chapter, but you should be aware that World-Space modifiers (identified with the initials WSM) appear at the top of the Modifier Stack and are applied to the object after all Object-Space modifiers.

In addition to World-Space modifiers, Space Warp bindings also appear at the top of the Modifier Stack.

 Space Warps are covered in Chapter 33, "Using Space Warps."

Using the Modifier Stack

After a modifier is applied, its parameters appear in rollouts within the Command Panel. The Modifier Stack rollout, shown in Figure 9.10, lists the base object and all the modifiers that have been applied to an object. Any new modifiers applied to an object are placed at the top of the stack. By selecting a modifier from the list in the Modifier Stack, all the parameters for that specific modifier are displayed in rollouts.

FIGURE 9.10

The Modifier Stack displays all modifiers applied to an object.

> **TIP**
> You can increase or decrease the size of the Modifier Stack by dragging the horizontal bar that appears beneath the Modifier Stack buttons.

Beneath the Modifier Stack are five buttons that affect the selected modifier. They are as described in Table 9.2.

TABLE 9.2 **Modifier Stack Buttons**

Button	Name	Description
	Pin Stack	Makes the parameters for the selected modifier available for editing even if another object is selected (like taking a physical pin and sticking it into the screen so it won't move).
	Show End Result On/Off Toggle	Shows the end results of all the modifiers in the entire Stack when enabled and only the modifiers up to the current selected modifier if disabled.
	Make Unique	Used to break any instance or reference links to the selected object. After you click this button, an object will no longer be modified along with the other objects for which it was an instance or reference. Works for Base Object and modifiers.
	Remove Modifier from the Stack	Used to delete a modifier from the Stack or unbind a Space Warp if one is selected. Deleting a modifier restores it to the same state it was in before the modifier was applied.
	Configure Modifier Sets	Opens a pop-up menu where you can select to show a set of modifiers as buttons above the Modifier Stack. You also can select which modifier set appears at the top of the list of modifiers. The pop-up menu also includes an option to configure and define the various sets of modifiers.

If you right-click a modifier, a pop-up menu appears. This pop-up menu includes commands to rename the selected modifier, which you might want to do if the same modifier is applied to the same object multiple times. This pop-up menu also includes an option to delete the selected modifier among other commands.

Copying and pasting modifiers

The pop-up menu also includes options to cut, copy, paste, and paste instance modifiers. The Cut command deletes the modifier from the current object but makes it available for pasting onto other objects. The Copy command retains the modifier for the current object and makes it available to paste onto another object. After you use the Cut or Copy command, you can use the Paste command to apply the modifier to another object. The Paste Instanced command retains a link between the original modifier and the instanced modifier, so that any changes to either modifier affect the other instances.

You also can apply modifiers for the current object onto other objects by dragging the modifier from the Modifier Stack and dropping it on the other object in a viewport. Holding down the Ctrl key while dropping a modifier onto an object in a viewport applies the modifier as an instance (like the Paste Instanced command). Holding down the Shift key while dragging and dropping a modifier on an object in the viewport removes the modifier from the current object and applies it to the object on which it is dropped (like the Cut and Paste commands).

9

Using instanced modifiers

When you apply a single modifier to several objects at the same time, the modifier shows up in the Modifier Stack for each object. These are *instanced modifiers* that maintain a connection to each other. If one of these instanced modifiers is changed, the change is propagated to all other instances. This feature is very helpful for modifying large groups of objects.

When a modifier is copied between different objects, you can select to make the copy an instance.

To see all the objects that are linked to a particular modifier, select an object in the viewport and choose Views⇨Show Dependencies. All objects with instanced modifiers that are connected to the current selection appear in bright pink. At any time, you can break the link between a particular instanced modifier and the rest of the objects using the Make Unique button below the Modifier Stack.

Identifying instances and references in the Modifier Stack

If you look closely at the Modifier Stack, you will notice that it includes some visual clues that help you identify instances and references. Regular object and modifier copies appear in normal text, but instances appear in bold. This applies to both objects and modifiers. If a modifier is applied to two or more objects, then it appears in italic.

Referenced objects and modifiers can be identified by a Reference Object Bar that splits the Modifier Stack into two categories—ones that are unique to the referenced object (above the bar) and ones that are shared with the other references (below the bar).

Figure 9.11 shows each of these cases in the Modifier Stack.

FIGURE 9.11

The Modifier Stack changes the text style to identify instances and references.

Referenced modifier applied to two or more objects

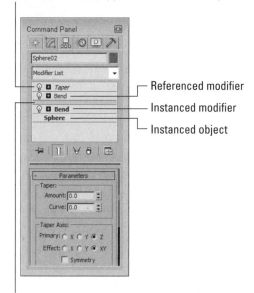

Reference object bar

Disabling and removing modifiers

Clicking the light bulb icon to the left of the modifier name toggles the modifier on and off. The right-click pop-up menu also offers options to turn the modifier off in the viewport or off for the renderer.

To remove a modifier from the Modifier Stack, just select the modifier and press the Remove Modifier from the Stack button below the stack. This button removes the selected modifier only. You can select multiple modifiers at once by holding down the Ctrl key while clicking individually on the modifiers or by holding down the Shift key and clicking the first and last modifiers in a range. This feature lets you apply and experiment with modifiers. If you try one that doesn't work, you can simply remove without altering the object.

Reordering the Stack

Modifiers are listed in the Modifier Stack with the first applied ones on the bottom and the newest applied ones on the top. The Stack order is important and can change the appearance of the object. 3ds Max applies the modifiers starting with the lowest one in the Stack first and the topmost modifier last. You can change the order of the modifiers in the Stack by selecting a modifier and dragging it above or below the other modifiers. You cannot drag it below the object type or above any World-Space modifiers or Space Warp bindings.

Tutorial: Creating a molecular chain

Whether you're working with DNA splices or creating an animation to show how molecular chains are formed, you can use the Lattice and Twist modifiers to quickly create a molecular chain. Using these chains shows how reordering the Modifier Stack can change the outcome.

To create a molecular chain using modifiers, follow these steps:

1. Select Create ➪ Standard Primitives ➪ Plane, and drag in the Top viewport to create a Plane object. Set its Length to **300**, its Width to **60**, its Length Segments to **11**, and its Width Segments to **1**.

2. With the Plane object selected, select Modifiers ➪ Parametric Deformers ➪ Lattice to apply the Lattice modifier. Enable the Apply to Entire Object option. Then set the Struts Radius value to **1.0** with **12** sides and the Joints Base Type to **Icosa** with a Radius of **6.0** and a Segments value of **6**.

3. Select Modifiers ➪ Parametric Deformers ➪ Twist, and set the Twist Angle to **360** about the Y-axis.

4. Notice that the Sphere objects have been twisted along with the Plane object creating non-spherical shaped objects. You can fix this by switching the modifier order in the Modifier Stack. Select the Lattice modifier, and drag and drop it above the Twist modifier in the Modifier Stack.

    This step corrects the elongated spheres.

Figure 9.12 shows both the original and corrected molecular chains and is a good example of how the order of the modifiers can affect the final outcome.

FIGURE 9.12

Changing the order of the modifiers in the Modifier Stack can affect the end result.

Holding and fetching a scene

Before going any further, you need to know about an important feature in 3ds Max that allows you to set a stopping point for the current scene. The Edit⇨Hold menu command saves the scene into a temporary buffer for easy recovery. After a scene is set with the Hold command (Ctrl+H), you can bring it back instantly with the Edit⇨Fetch menu command (Alt+Ctrl+F). These commands provide a quick way to backtrack on modifications to a scene or project without having to save and reload the project. If you use these commands before applying or deleting modifiers, you can avoid some potential headaches.

TIP

Along with saving your file often, using the Hold command before applying any complex modifier to an object is a good idea.

Collapsing the Stack

Collapsing the Modifier Stack removes all its modifiers by permanently applying them to the object. It also resets the modification history to a baseline. All the individual modifiers in the Modifier Stack are combined into the base object. This feature eliminates the ability to change any modifier parameters, but it simplifies the object. The right-click pop-up menu offers options to Collapse To and Collapse All. You can collapse the entire Stack with the Collapse All command, or you can collapse to the current selected modifier with the Collapse To command. Collapsed objects typically become Editable Mesh objects.

> **TIP**
>
> Another huge advantage of collapsing the Modifier Stack is that it conserves memory and results in smaller file sizes, which makes larger scenes load much quicker. Collapsing the Modifier Stack also speeds up rendering because 3ds Max doesn't need to calculate the stack results before rendering.

When you apply a Collapse command, a warning dialog box appears, shown in Figure 9.13, notifying you that this action will delete all the creation parameters. Click Yes to continue with the collapse.

> **NOTE**
>
> In addition to the Yes and No buttons, the warning dialog box includes a Hold/Yes button. This button saves the current state of the object to the Hold buffer and then applies the Collapse All function. If you have any problems, you can retrieve the object's previous state before the collapse was applied by choosing Edit⇨Fetch (Alt+Ctrl+F).

FIGURE 9.13

This warning dialog box offers a chance to Hold the scene.

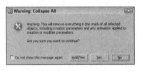

Using the Collapse utility

You also can use the Collapse utility found on the Utility panel to collapse the Modifier Stack. This utility enables you to collapse an object or several objects to a Modifier Stack Result or to a Mesh object. Collapsing to a Modifier Stack Result doesn't necessarily produce a mesh but collapses the object to its base object state, which is displayed at the bottom of the Stack hierarchy. Depending on the Stack, this could result in a mesh, patch, spline, or other object type. You also can collapse to a Single Object or to Multiple Objects.

If the Mesh and Single Object options are selected, you also can select to perform a Boolean operation. The Boolean operations are available if you are collapsing several overlapping objects into one. The options are Union (which combines geometries together), Intersection (which combines only the overlapping geometries), and Subtraction (which subtracts one geometry from another).

▷ Boolean operations also can be performed using the Boolean compound object. See Chapter 13, "Working with Compound Objects," for details on this object type.

If multiple objects are selected, then a Boolean Intersection results in only the sections of the objects that are intersected by all objects; if no objects overlap, all objects disappear.

If you use the Boolean Subtraction option, you can specify which object is the base object from which the other objects are subtracted. To do so, select that object first and then select the other objects by holding down the Ctrl key and clicking them. Figure 9.14 shows an example of each of the Boolean operations.

FIGURE 9.14

Using the Collapse utility, you can select the following Boolean operations (shown from left to right): Union, Intersection, and Subtraction.

Using gizmo subobjects

As you've worked with modifiers, you've probably noticed the orange wireframe box that surrounds the object in the viewports when you apply the modifier. These boxes are called *modifier gizmos,* and they provide a visual control for how the modifier changes the geometry. If you want, you can work directly with these gizmos to affect the modifier.

Clicking the plus sign to the left of the modifier name reveals any subobjects associated with the modifier. To select the modifier subobjects, simply click the subobject name. The subobject name is highlighted when selected. Many modifiers create *gizmo subobjects.* Gizmos have an icon usually in the shape of a box that can be transformed and controlled like regular objects using the transformation buttons on the main toolbar. Another common modifier subobject is Center, which controls the point about which the gizmo is transformed.

Tutorial: Squeezing a plastic bottle

To get a feel for how the modifier gizmo and its center affect an object, this tutorial applies the Squeeze modifier to a plastic bottle; by moving its center, you can change the shape of the object.

To change a modifier's characteristics by moving its center, follow these steps:

1. Open the Plastic bottle.max file from the Chap 09 directory on the CD.

    This file includes a plastic squirt bottle with all the parts attached into a single mesh object.

2. With the bottle selected, choose the Modifiers ⇨ Parametric Deformers ⇨ Squeeze menu command to apply the Squeeze modifier to the bottle. Set the Radial Squeeze Amount value to **1**.

3. In the Modifier Stack, click the plus sign to the left of the Squeeze modifier to see the modifier's subobjects. Select the Center subobject.

    The selected subobject is highlighted.

4. Click the Select and Move (W) button on the main toolbar, and drag the center point in the Perspective viewport upward.

Notice how the bottle's shape changes.

Figure 9.15 shows several different bottle shapes created by moving the modifier's center point.

FIGURE 9.15

By changing the modifier's center point, the bottle's shape changes.

Applying modifiers to subobject selections

Modifiers are typically applied to entire objects, but you also can apply modifiers to subobjects. If the modifier isn't available for subobjects, it is excluded from the Modifier List or disabled in the Modifiers menu.

To work in subobject selection mode, click the plus sign to the left of the object name to see the sub-objects. Several modifiers, including Mesh Select, Spline Select, and Volume Select, can select subobject areas for passing these selections up to the next modifier in the Stack. For example, you can use the Mesh Select modifier to select several faces on the front of a sphere and then apply the Face Extrude modifier to extrude just those faces.

If the selected object isn't an editable object with available subobjects, you can still apply a modifier using one of the specialized Select modifiers. These modifiers let you select a subobject and apply a modifier to it without having to convert it to a non-parametric object. These Select modifiers include Mesh Select, Poly Select, Patch Select, Spline Select, Volume Select, FFD (Free Form Deformers) Select, and Select by Channel. You can find all these modifiers in the Modifiers ⇨ Selection submenu.

After you apply a Select modifier to an object, you can select subobjects in the normal manner using the hierarchy in the Modifier Stack or the subobject icons in the Parameters rollout. Any modifiers that you apply after the Select modifier (which appear above the Select modifier in the Modifier Stack) affect only the subobject selection.

Tutorial: Applying damage to a car

In this tutorial, you use the Volume Select modifier to select the front corner of a car and then apply Noise and XForm modifiers to make the corner look like it's been damaged in a collision. With the Volume Select modifier, only the selected front portion of the car gets the damage instead of the whole car.

9

To use modifiers to make a section of a car appear damaged, follow these steps:

1. Open the Damaged car.max file from the Chap 09 directory on the CD.

   This file includes a car model created by Viewpoint Datalabs.

2. With the front end of the car selected, choose the Modifiers ⇨ Selection Modifiers ⇨ Volume Select menu command.

   This command applies the Volume Select modifier to the group.

3. In the Modifier Stack, click the plus icon to the left of the modifier name and select the Gizmo subobject. Move the gizmo in the Top viewport so only the front corner of the car is selected. In the Parameters rollout, select the Vertex option as the Stack Selection Level.

4. Choose the Modifiers ⇨ Parametric Deformers ⇨ Noise menu command to apply the Noise modifier to the selected volume. In the Parameters rollout, enable the Fractal option and set the X, Y, and Z Strength values to **30**.

5. Choose Modifiers ⇨ Parametric Deformers ⇨ XForm to apply the XForm modifier, and use its gizmo to push the selected area up and to the left in the Top viewport to make this section look dented.

Figure 9.16 shows the resulting damaged car. Notice that the rest of the object is fine and only the selected volume area is damaged.

FIGURE 9.16

The Noise and XForm modifiers are applied to just the subobject selection.

Topology dependency

When you attempt to modify the parameters of a Base Object that has a modifier applied, you sometimes get a warning dialog box that tells you that the modifier depends on topology that may change. 3ds Max is telling you that the surface of the object with that particular modifier is dependent on the subobjects that are selected, and if you change the underlying subobjects, you may change the resulting topology. For example, the CrossSection and Surface modifiers build the surface using a set of splines, but if you change the original spline, you can destroy the resulting surfaced object. You can eliminate this problem by collapsing the Modifier Stack.

You can disable the warning by selecting the "Do not show this message again" option on the dialog box or by opening the Preference Settings dialog box and turning off the Display Topology-Dependence Warning option in the General panel of the Preference Settings dialog box. Disabling the warning does not make the potential problem go away; it only prevents the warning dialog box from appearing.

Summary

Understanding the basics of modeling helps you as you build scenes. In this chapter, you've seen several different object types that are available in 3ds Max, including parametric and editable object types. Editable objects have subobjects that you can move to change the object.

With the modifiers contained in the Modify panel, you can alter objects in a vast number of ways. Modifiers can work with every aspect of an object, including geometric deformations, materials, and general object maintenance. In this chapter, you looked at the Modifier Stack and how modifiers are applied. This chapter covered the following topics:

- Understanding parametric objects and the various modeling types
- Viewing normals
- Using subobjects and soft selections
- Introducing and applying modifiers
- Working with the Modifier Stack to apply, reorder, and collapse modifiers

Now that you have the basics covered, you're ready to dive into the various modeling types. The first modeling types on the list are splines and shapes, which are covered in the next chapter.

9

CHAPTER

10

Drawing and Editing 2D Splines and Shapes

IN THIS CHAPTER

Working with shape primitives

Editing splines and shapes

Working with spline subobjects

Many modeling projects start from the ground up, and you can't get much lower to the ground than 2D. But this book is on 3D, you say? What place is there for 2D shapes? Within the 3D world, you frequently encounter flat surfaces—the side of a building, the top of a table, a billboard, and so on. All these objects have flat 2D surfaces. Understanding how objects are composed of 2D surfaces will help as you start to build objects in 3D. This chapter examines the 2D elements of 3D objects and covers the tools needed to work with them.

Working in 2D in the Autodesk® 3ds Max® 2013 software, you use two general objects: splines and shapes. A *spline* is a special type of line that curves according to mathematical principles. In 3ds Max, splines are used to create all sorts of shapes such as circles, ellipses, and rectangles.

You can create splines and shapes using the Create⇨Shapes menu, which opens the Shapes category on the Create panel. Just as with the other categories, several spline-based shape primitives are available. Spline shapes can be rendered, but they are normally used to create more advanced 3D geometric objects by extruding or lathing the spline. You can even find a whole group of modifiers that apply to splines. You can use splines to create animation paths as well as Loft and NURBS (Non-Uniform Rational B-Splines) objects, and you will find that splines and shapes, although they are only 2D, are used frequently in 3ds Max.

Drawing in 2D

Shapes in 3ds Max are unique from other objects because they are drawn in 2D, which confines them to a single plane. That plane is defined by the viewport used to create the shape. For example, drawing a shape in the Top view constrains the shape to the XY plane, whereas drawing the shape in the Front view constrains it to the ZX plane. Even shapes drawn in the Perspective view are constrained to a plane such as the Home Grid.

221

You usually produce 2D shapes in a drawing package such as Adobe Illustrator (AI) or CorelDRAW. 3ds Max supports importing line drawings using the AI format.

Whereas newly created or imported shapes are 2D and are confined to a single plane, splines can exist in 3D space. The Helix spline, for example, exists in 3D, having height as well as width values. Animation paths in particular typically move into 3D space.

Working with shape primitives

The shape primitive buttons are displayed in the Object Type rollout of the Create panel when either the Create ⇨ Shapes or the Create ⇨ Extended Shapes menu is selected. The Shapes category includes many basic shapes, including Line, Circle, Arc, NGon (a polygon where you can set the number of sides), Text, Egg, Rectangle, Ellipse, Donut, Star, Helix, and Section, as shown in Figure 10.1. The Extended Shapes category includes several shapes that are useful to architects, including WRectangle, Channel, Angle, Tee, and Wide Flange, as shown in Figure 10.2. Clicking any of these shape buttons lets you create the shape by dragging in one of the viewports. After a shape is created, several new rollouts appear.

> **NOTE**
> Within the Create menu, the various shapes are listed as Shapes and Extended Shapes, but within the Create panel of the Command Panel, the sub-categories are listed as Splines and Extended Splines. They both have the same elements, but are only called differently.

FIGURE 10.1

The shape primitives in all their 2D glory: Line, Circle, Arc, NGon, Text, Egg, Rectangle, Ellipse, Donut, Star, Helix, and Section

FIGURE 10.2

The extended shape primitives: WRectangle, Channel, Angle, Tee, and Wide Flange

Above the Shape buttons are two check boxes: AutoGrid and Start New Shape. AutoGrid creates a temporary grid, which you can use to align the shape with the surface of the nearest object under the cursor at the time of creation. This feature is helpful for starting a new spline on the surface of an object.

> For more details on AutoGrid, see Chapter 6, "Transforming Objects, Pivoting, Aligning, and Snapping."

The Start New Shape option creates a new object with every new shape drawn in a viewport. Leaving this option unchecked lets you create compound shapes, which consist of several shapes used to create one object. Because compound shapes consist of several shapes, the shapes are automatically converted to be an Editable Spline object and you cannot edit them using the Parameters rollout. For example, if you want to create a target from several concentric circles, keep the Start New Shape option unselected to make all the circles part of the same object.

Just as with the Geometric primitives, every shape that is created is given a name and a color. You can change either of these in the Name and Color rollout.

Most of the shape primitives have several common rollouts: Rendering, Interpolation, Creation Method, Keyboard Entry, and Parameters, as shown in Figure 10.3. I cover these rollouts initially and then present the individual shape primitives.

FIGURE 10.3

These rollouts are common for most of the shape primitives.

Rendering rollout

The Rendering rollout includes options for making a spline a renderable object. Making a spline a renderable object converts the spline into a 3D object that is visible when you render the scene. For renderable objects, you can choose to make the spline Radial or Rectangular. For the Radial option, you can specify a Thickness, the number of Sides, and the Angle values; for the Rectangular option, you can specify Length, Width, Angle, and Aspect values.

The Radial Thickness is the diameter of the renderable spline. The number of Sides sets the number of sides that make up the cross section of the renderable spline. The lowest value possible is 3, which creates a triangle cross section. The Length and Width values set the size along the Y-axis and the X-axis, respectively, of the rectangular sides. The Angle value determines where the corners of the cross section sides start, so you can set a three-sided spline to have a corner or an edge pointing upward. The Aspect value sets the ratio of the Length per Width. If the Lock icon to the right of the Aspect value is enabled, then the aspect ratio is locked, and changing one value affects the other.

10

You can choose different rendering values for the viewport and for the renderer using the Viewport and Renderer options above the Radial option. Each of these settings can be enabled or disabled using the Enable in Renderer and Enable in Viewport options at the top of the Rendering rollout. Renderable splines appear as normal splines in the viewport unless the Enable in Viewport option is selected. The Use Viewport Settings option gives the option of setting the spline render properties different in the viewport and the renderer.

The Auto Smooth option and Threshold value offer a way to smooth edges on the renderable spline. If the angle between two adjacent polygons is less than the Threshold value, then the edge between them is smoothed. If it is greater than the Threshold value, then the hard edge is preserved.

The Generate Mapping Coordinates option automatically generates mapping coordinates that are used to mark where a material map is placed, and the Real-World Map Size option allows real-world scaling to be used when mapping a texture onto the renderable spline.

To learn more about mapping coordinates and real-world scaling, see Chapter 15, "Adding Material Details with Maps."

Interpolation rollout

In the Interpolation rollout, you can define the number of interpolation steps or segments that make up the shape. The Steps value determines the number of segments to include between adjacent vertices. For example, a circle shape with a Steps value of 0 has only 4 segments and looks like a diamond. Increasing the Steps value to 1 makes a circle out of 8 segments. For shapes composed of straight lines (like the Rectangle and simple NGons), the Steps value is set to 0, but for a shape with many sides (like a Circle or Ellipse), the Steps value can have a big effect. Larger step values result in smoother curves.

The Adaptive option automatically sets the number of steps to produce a smooth curve by adding more interpolation points to the spline based on the spline's curvature. When the Adaptive option is enabled, the Steps and Optimize options become disabled. The Optimize option attempts to reduce the number of steps to produce a simpler spline by eliminating all the extra segments associated with the shape.

Figure 10.4 shows the number 5 drawn with the Line primitive in the Front viewport. The line has been made renderable so you can see the cross sections. The images from left to right show the line with Steps values of 0, 1, and 3. The fourth image has the Optimize option enabled. Notice that it uses only one segment for the straight edges. The fifth image has the Adaptive option enabled.

Creation Method and Keyboard Entry rollouts

Most shape primitives also include Creation Method and Keyboard Entry rollouts (Text, Section, and Star are the exceptions). The Creation Method rollout offers options for specifying different ways to create the spline by dragging in a viewport, such as from edge to edge or from the center out. Table 10.1 lists the various creation method options for each of the shapes and each of the extended shapes.

FIGURE 10.4

Using the Interpolation rollout, you can control the number of segments that make up a line.

TABLE 10.1 **Shape Primitive Creation Methods**

Primitive Object	Primitive Object Name	Number of Viewport Clicks to Create	Default Creation Method	Other Creation Method
~	Line	2 to Infinite	Corner Initial, Bézier Drag	Smooth, Initial, Corner, or Smooth Drag
○	Circle	1	Center	Edge
⌒	Arc	2	End-End-Middle	Center-End-End
⬡	NGon	1	Center	Edge
Aₐ	Text	1	none	none
-	Egg	2	none	none
△	Section	1	none	none
□	Rectangle	1	Edge	Center
◇	Ellipse	1	Edge	Center
◎	Donut	2	Center	Edge
☆	Star	2	none	none
⧦	Helix	3	Center	Edge
-	WRectangle	2	Edge	Center
-	Channel	2	Edge	Center
-	Angle	2	Edge	Center
-	Tee	2	Edge	Center
-	Wide Flange	2	Edge	Center

Some shape primitives such as Star, Text, and Section don't have any creation methods because 3ds Max offers only a single way to create these shapes.

The Keyboard Entry rollout offers a way to enter exact position and dimension values. After you enter the values, click the Create button to create the spline or shape in the active viewport. The settings are different for each shape.

The Parameters rollout includes such basic settings for the primitive as Radius, Length, and Width. You can alter these settings immediately after an object is created. However, after you deselect an object, the Parameters rollout moves to the Modify panel, and you must do any alterations to the shape there.

Line

The Line primitive includes several creation method settings, enabling you to create hard, sharp corners or smooth corners. You can set the Initial Type option to either Corner or Smooth to create a sharp or smooth corner for the first point created.

After clicking where the initial point is located, you can add points by clicking in the viewport. Dragging while creating a new point can make a point a Corner, Smooth, or Bézier based on the Drag Type option selected in the Creation Method rollout. The curvature created by the Smooth option is determined by the distance between adjacent vertices, whereas you can control the curvature created by the Bézier option by dragging with the mouse a desired distance after the point is created. Bézier corners have control handles associated with them, enabling you to change their curvature.

> **TIP**
>
> Holding down the Shift key while clicking creates points that are constrained vertically or horizontally. This makes it easy to create straight lines that are at right angles to each other. Holding down the Ctrl key snaps new points at an angle from the last segment, as determined by the Angle Snap setting.

After creating all the points, you exit Line mode by clicking the right mouse button. If the last point is on top of the first point, then a dialog box asks whether you want to close the spline. Click Yes to create a closed spline or No to continue adding points. Even after creating a closed spline, you can add more points to the current selection to create a compound shape if the Start New Shape option isn't selected. If the first and last points don't correspond, then an open spline is created.

Figure 10.5 shows several splines created using the various creation method settings. The left spline was created with all the options set to Corner, and the second spline with all the options set to Smooth. The third spline uses the Corner Initial type and shows where dragging has smoothed many of the points. The last spline was created using the Bézier option.

FIGURE 10.5

The Line shape can create various combinations of shapes with smooth and sharp corners.

In the Keyboard Entry rollout, you can add points by entering their X, Y, and Z coordinates and clicking the Add Point button. You can close the spline at any time by clicking the Close button or keep it open by clicking the Finish button.

Rectangle

The Rectangle shape produces simple rectangles. In the Parameters rollout, you can specify the Length and Width and also a Corner Radius. Holding down the Ctrl key while dragging creates a perfect square shape.

Circle

The Circle button creates—you guessed it—circles. The only adjustable parameter in the Parameters rollout is the Radius. All other rollouts are the same, as explained earlier. Circles created with the Circle button have only four vertices.

Ellipse

Ellipses are simple variations of the Circle shape. You define them by Length and Width values. Holding down the Ctrl key while dragging creates a perfect circle (or you can use the Circle shape).

Arc

The Arc primitive has two creation methods. Use the End-End-Middle method to create an arc shape by clicking and dragging to specify the two end points and then dragging to complete the shape. Use the Center-End-End method to create an arc shape by clicking and dragging from the center to one of the end points and then dragging the arc length to the second end point.

Other parameters include the Radius and the From and To settings, where you can enter the value in degrees for the start and end of the arc. The Pie Slice option connects the end points of the arc to its center to create a pie-sliced shape, as shown in Figure 10.6. The Reverse option lets you reverse the arc's direction.

FIGURE 10.6

Enabling the Pie Slice option connects the arc ends with the center of the arc.

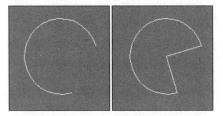

Donut

As another variation of the Circle shape, the Donut shape consists of two concentric circles; you create it by dragging once to specify the outer circle and again to specify the inner circle or vice-versa. The parameters for this object are simply two radii.

10

NGon

The NGon shape lets you create regular polygons by specifying the number of Sides and the Corner Radius. You also can specify whether the NGon is Inscribed or Circumscribed, as shown in Figure 10.7. Inscribed polygons are positioned within a circle that touches all the outer polygon's vertices. Circumscribed polygons are positioned outside of a circle that touches the midpoint of each polygon edge. The Circular option changes the polygon to a circle that inscribes the polygon.

FIGURE 10.7

An inscribed pentagon and a circumscribed pentagon

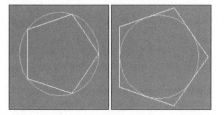

Star

The Star shape also includes two radii values; the larger Radius value defines the distance of the outer points of the Star shape from its center, and the smaller Radius value is the distance from the center of the star to the inner points. The Points setting indicates the number of points. This value can range from 3 to 100. The Distortion value causes the inner points to rotate relative to the outer points and can be used to create some interesting new star types. The Fillet Radius 1 and Fillet Radius 2 values adjust the Fillet for the inner and outer points. Figure 10.8 shows a sampling of what is possible with the Star shapes.

FIGURE 10.8

The Star primitive can be changed to create some amazing shapes.

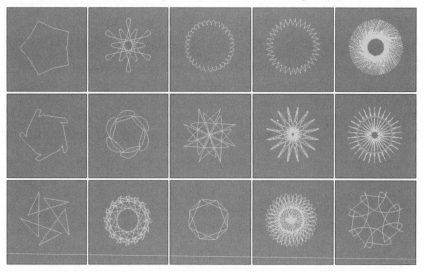

Text

You can use the Text primitive to add outlined text to the scene. In the Parameters rollout, you can specify a Font by choosing one from the drop-down list at the top of the Parameters rollout. Under the Font drop-down list are six icons, shown in Table 10.2. The left two icons are for the Italic and Underline styles. Selecting either of these styles applies the style to all the text. The right four icons are for aligning the text to the left, centered, right, or justified.

TABLE 10.2 Text Font Attributes

Icon	Description
I	Italic
U	Underline
≣	Align Left
≣	Centered
≣	Align Right
≣	Justify

> **NOTE**
>
> The list of available fonts includes only the Windows TrueType fonts and Type 1 PostScript fonts installed on your system and any extra fonts located in the font path listed in the Configure System Paths dialog box. You need to restart 3ds Max before the fonts in the font path are recognized.

The size of the text is determined by the Size value. The Kerning (the space between adjacent characters) and Leading (the space between lines of text) values can actually be negative. Setting the Kerning value to a large negative number actually displays the text backward. Figure 10.9 shows an example of some text and an example of Kerning values in the 3ds Max interface.

You can type the text to be created in the text area. You can cut, copy, and paste text into this text area from an external application if you right-click the text area. After setting the parameters and typing the text, the text appears as soon as you click in one of the viewports. The text is updated automatically when any of the parameters (including the text) are changed. To turn off automatic updating, select the Manual Update toggle. You can then update with the Update button.

If you open the Character Map application, you can see a complete list of special characters. The Character Map application, shown in Figure 10.10, can be opened in Windows by selecting Start ⇨ All Programs ⇨ Accessories ⇨ System Tools ⇨ Character Map. To enter special characters into the text area in 3ds Max, choose the special character by clicking it in the Character Map dialog box and then click the Select button. Click the Copy button to copy the character to the Windows clipboard, and in 3ds Max, use the Ctrl+V paste command to add it to the text area.

10

FIGURE 10.9

The Text shape lets you control the space between letters, known as kerning.

> **TIP**
> If the text object is selected and you click on the drop-down list to access the available fonts, you can use the up and down arrow keys to scroll through the font choices and the selected font is automatically displayed in the viewport.

FIGURE 10.10

The Character Map application shows all the special characters that are available.

Helix

A Helix is like a spring coil shape, and it is the one shape of all the Shape primitives that exists in 3D. Helix parameters include two radii for specifying the inner and outer radius. These two values can be equal to create a coil or unequal to create a spiral. Parameters also exist for the Height and number of Turns. The Bias parameter causes the Helix turns to be gathered all together at the top or bottom of the shape. The CW and CCW options let you specify whether the Helix turns clockwise or counterclockwise.

Figure 10.11 shows a sampling of Helix shapes: The first Helix has equal radii values, the second one has a smaller second radius, the third Helix spirals to a second radius value of 0, and the last two Helix objects have Bias values of 0.8 and –0.8.

FIGURE 10.11

The Helix shape can be straight or spiral shaped.

Egg

The Egg shape creates two concentric egg-shaped outlines positioned one within the other. The distance between the two shapes is defined by the Thickness value; you can eliminate the inner shape by deselecting the Outline option. The size of the egg is set by the Length and Width values, but these two values are locked so that the egg shape is maintained. The Angle value lets the shape rotate about its center, where the pivot is located.

NEW FEATURE

The Egg shape is new to 3ds Max 2013.

Section

Section stands for cross section. The Section shape is a cross section of the edges of any 3D object through which the Section's cutting plane passes. The process consists of dragging in the viewport to create a cross-sectioning plane. You can then move, rotate, or scale the cross-sectioning plane to obtain the desired cross section. In the Section Parameters rollout is a Create Shape button. Clicking this button opens a dialog box where you can name the new shape. You can use one Section object to create multiple shapes.

NOTE

You can make sections only from intersecting a 3D object. If the cross-sectioning plane doesn't intersect the 3D object, then it won't create a shape. You cannot use the Section primitive on shapes, even if it is a renderable spline.

The Section Parameters rollout includes settings for updating the Section shape. You can update it when the Section plane moves, when the Section is selected, or Manually (using the Update Section button). You also can set the Section Extents to Infinite, Section Boundary, or Off. The Infinite setting creates the cross-section spline as if the cross-sectioning plane were of infinite size, whereas the

10

Section Boundary limits the plane's extents to the boundaries of the visible plane. The color swatch determines the color of the intersecting shape.

To give you an idea of what the Section shape can produce, Figure 10.12 shows the shapes resulting from sectioning two Cone objects, including a circle, an ellipse, a parabola, and a hyperbola. The shapes have been moved to the sides to be more visible.

FIGURE 10.12

You can use the Section shape primitive to create the conic sections (circle, ellipse, parabola, and hyperbola) from a set of 3D cones.

Tutorial: Drawing a company logo

One of the early uses for 3D graphics was to animate corporate logos, and although 3ds Max can still do this without any problems, it now has capabilities far beyond those available in the early days. The Shape tools can even be used to design the logo. In this example, you'll design and create a simple logo using the Shape tools for the fictitious company named Expeditions South.

To use the Shape tools to design and create a company logo, follow these steps:

1. Create a four-pointed star by selecting the Create ⇨ Shapes ⇨ Star menu and dragging in the Top view to create a shape. Change the parameters for this star as follows: Radius1 = **60**, Radius2 = **20**, and Points = **4**.

2. Select and move the star shape to the left side of the viewport with the Select and Move tool.

3. Now click the Text button in the Command Panel, and change the font to **Impact** and the Size to **50**. In the Text area, type **Expeditions South** and include a line return and several spaces between the two words so they are offset. Click in the Top viewport to place the text.

4. Use the Select and Move button (W) to reposition the text next to the Star shape.

5. Click the Line button, and create several short highlighting lines around the bottom point of the star.

The finished logo is now ready to extrude and animate. Figure 10.13 shows the results.

FIGURE 10.13

A company logo created entirely in 3ds Max using shapes

Tutorial: Viewing the interior of a heart

As an example of the Section primitive, you'll explore a section of a Heart model. The model was created by Viewpoint Datalabs and is very realistic—so realistic, in fact, that it could be used to teach medical students the inner workings of the heart.

To create a spline from the cross section of the heart, follow these steps:

1. Open the Heart section.max file from the Chap 10 directory on the CD.

   This file includes a physical model of a heart.

2. Select Create ⇨ Shapes ⇨ Section, and drag a plane in the Front viewport that is large enough to cover the heart.

   This plane is your cross-sectioning plane.

3. Select the Select and Rotate button on the main toolbar (or press the E key), and rotate the cross-sectioning plane to cross the heart at the desired angle.

4. In the Section Parameters rollout of the Modify panel, click the Create Shape button and give the new shape the name **Heart Section**, and then click the OK button.

5. From the Select From Scene dialog box (opened with the H key), select the new section by name, separate it from the model, and reposition it to be visible.

Figure 10.14 shows the resulting model and section in a maximized viewport.

10

FIGURE 10.14

You can use the Section shape to view the interior area of the heart.

Editing Splines

After you create a shape primitive, you can edit it by modifying its parameters, but the parameters for shapes are fairly limited. For example, the only parameter for the Circle shape is Radius. All shapes can be converted to Editable Splines, or they can have the Edit Spline modifier applied to them. Doing either enables a host of editing features. Before you can use these editing features, you must convert the shape primitive to an Editable Spline (except for the Line shape). You can do so by right-clicking the spline shape in the viewport and choosing Convert to ➪ Convert to Editable Spline from the pop-up quad menu or by right-clicking the Circle base object in the Modifier Stack and selecting Convert to Editable Spline in the pop-up menu.

Editable Splines versus the Edit Spline modifier

After you convert the spline to an Editable Spline, you can edit individual subobjects within the spline, including Vertices, Segments, and Splines. The difference between applying the Edit Spline modifier and converting the shape to an Editable Spline is subtle. Applying the Edit Spline modifier maintains the shape parameters and enables the editing features found in the Geometry rollout. However, an Editable Spline loses the ability to change the base parameters associated with the spline shape.

> **NOTE**
>
> When you create an object that contains two or more splines (such as when you create splines with the Start New Shape option disabled), all the splines in the object are automatically converted into Editable Splines.

Another difference is that the shape primitive base name is listed along with the Edit Spline modifier in the Modifier Stack. Selecting the shape primitive name makes the Rendering, Interpolation, and Parameters rollouts visible, and the Selection, Soft Selection, and Geometry rollouts are made visible when you select the Edit Spline modifier in the Modifier Stack. For Editable Splines, only a single base object name is visible in the Modifier Stack, and all rollouts are accessible under it.

> **NOTE**
> Another key difference is that subobjects for the Edit Spline modifier cannot be animated.

Making splines renderable

Splines normally do not show up in a rendered image, but using the Renderable option in the Rendering rollout and assigning a thickness to the splines makes them appear in the rendered image. Figure 10.15 shows a rendered image of the Expeditions South logo after all shapes have been made renderable and assigned a Thickness of 3.0.

FIGURE 10.15

Using renderable splines with a Thickness of 3.0, the logo can be rendered.

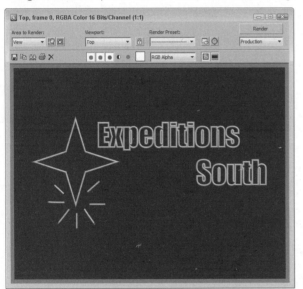

> **NOTE**
> The settings in the Rendering and Interpolation rollouts are the same as those used for newly created shapes, which were covered earlier in the chapter.

Selecting spline subobjects

When editing splines, you must choose the subobject level to work on. For example, when editing splines, you can work with Vertex (1), Segment (2), or Spline (3) subobjects. A spline object can have multiple splines as part of the single object. The Spline subobject mode lets you access the individual splines within the spline object.

Before you can edit spline subobjects, you must select them. To select the subobject type, click the small plus sign icon to the left of the Editable Spline object (or the Edit Spline modifier) in the Modifier Stack. This lists all the subobjects available for this object. Click the subobject in the Modifier Stack to select it. Alternatively, you can click the red-colored icons under the Selection rollout, shown in Figure 10.16. You also can select the different subobject modes using the 1, 2, and 3 keyboard shortcuts. When you select a subobject, the selection in the Modifier Stack and the associated icon in the Selection rollout is highlighted.

> **NOTE**
> The subobject button is highlighted when selected to remind you that you are in Subobject Edit mode. Remember, you must exit this mode before you can select another object.

FIGURE 10.16

The Selection rollout provides icons for entering the various subobject modes.

You can select many subobjects at once by dragging an outline over them in the viewports. You also can select and deselect subobjects by holding down the Ctrl key while clicking them. Holding down the Alt key removes any selected vertices from the selection set.

After selecting several vertices, you can create a named selection set by typing a name in the Named Selection Sets drop-down list in the main toolbar. You can then copy and paste these selection sets onto other shapes using the buttons in the Selection rollout.

The Lock Handles option allows you to move the handles of all selected vertices together when enabled, but each handle moves by itself when disabled. With the Lock Handles and the All options selected, all selected handles move together. The Alike option causes all handles on one side to move together.

The Area Selection option selects all the vertices within a defined radius of where you click. This is helpful for dense mesh objects with lots of vertices that are close together. The Segment End option, when enabled, allows you to select a vertex by clicking the segment. The closest vertex to the segment that you clicked is selected. This feature is useful when you are trying to select a vertex that lies near other vertices. The Select By button opens a dialog box with Segment and Spline buttons on it. These buttons allow you to select all the vertices on either a spline or segment that you choose.

The Selection rollout also has the Show Vertex Numbers option to display all the vertex numbers of a spline or to show the numbers of only the selected vertices. This can be convenient for understanding how a spline is put together and to help you find noncritical vertices. The Selected Only option displays the Vertex Numbers only for the selected subobjects when enabled.

> **NOTE**
> The vertex order is critical in determining the direction in which cross sections are swept when using the Loft and Sweep commands. You can identify the first vertex in a spline because it is yellow when one of the subobject modes is enabled.

Figure 10.17 shows a simple star shape that was converted to an Editable Spline. The left image shows the spline in Vertex Subobject mode. All the vertices are marked with small plus signs, and the starting point is marked with a small square. The middle image has the Show Vertex Numbers option enabled. For the right image, the vertex numbers are shown after the Reverse button was used (in Spline Subobject mode).

At the bottom of the Selection rollout, the Selection Information is displayed. This information tells you the number of the spline (or segment) and vertex selected, or the number of selected items and whether a spline is closed.

FIGURE 10.17

Several spline shapes displayed with vertex numbering turned on

Spline end point

Vertex marker

Controlling spline geometry

Much of the power of editing splines is contained within the Geometry rollout, shown in Figure 10.18, including the ability to add new splines, attach objects to the spline, weld vertices, use Boolean operations, Trim and Extend splines, and many more. Some Geometry buttons may be disabled, depending on the subobject type that you've selected. Many of the features in the Geometry rollout can be used in all subobject modes. Some of these features do not even require that you be in a Subobject mode. These features are covered first.

FIGURE 10.18

For Editable Splines, the Geometry rollout holds most of the features.

Create line

While editing splines, you can add new lines to a spline by clicking the Create Line button and then clicking in one of the viewports. You can add several lines at the same time, and all these new splines are part of the same object. Right-click in the viewport to exit this mode. Any new lines are their own spline, but you can weld them to the existing splines.

Break

Selecting a vertex and clicking the Break button in Vertex Subobject mode breaks the segment at the selected vertex by creating two separate end points. You also can use the Break button in Segment Subobject mode by clicking anywhere along the segment to add two separated vertices on the segment, thereby breaking the segment into two.

Attach and Attach Multiple

The Attach button lets you attach any existing splines to the currently selected spline. The cursor changes when you're over the top of a spline that can be attached. Clicking an unselected object makes it part of the current object. The Reorient option aligns the coordinate system of the spline being attached with the selected spline's coordinate system.

For example, using the Boolean button requires that all the splines be part of the same object. You can use the Attach button to attach several splines into the same object.

The Attach Mult. button enables several splines to be attached at once. When you click the Attach Mult. button, the Attach Multiple dialog box (which looks much like the Select by Name dialog box) opens. Use this dialog box to select the objects you want to attach to the current selection. Click the Attach button in the dialog box when you're finished. You can use both the Attach and Attach Mult. buttons in all three subobject modes.

> **NOTE**
> If the spline object that is being attached has a material applied to it, then a dialog box appears that gives you options for handling the materials. These options include Match Material IDs to Material, Match Material to Material IDs, or Do Not Modify Material IDs or Material. Applying materials is covered in Chapter 14, "Creating and Applying Standard Materials with the Slate Material Editor."

Cross Section

The Cross Section button works just like the Cross Section modifier by creating splines that run from one cross-section shape to another. For example, imagine creating a baseball bat by positioning circular cross sections for each diameter change and connecting each cross section from one end to the other. All the cross sections need to be part of the same Editable Spline object, and then using the Cross Section button, you can click from one cross section to another. The cursor changes when the mouse is over a shape that can be used. When you're finished selecting cross-section shapes, you can right-click to exit Cross Section mode.

The type of vertex used to create the new splines that run between the different cross sections is the type specified in the New Vertex Type section at the top of the Geometry rollout.

> **CAUTION**
> Although the splines that connect the cross sections are positioned alongside the cross section shape, they are not connected.

After the splines are created, you can use the Surface modifier to turn the splines into a 3D surface.

Auto Welding end points

To work with surfaces, you typically need a closed spline. When you enable the Automatic Welding option in the End Point Auto-Welding section and specify a Threshold, all end points within the threshold value are welded together, thus making a closed spline. This provides a quick way to close all splines in the selected object.

Insert

The Insert button adds vertices to a selected spline. Click the Insert button, and then click the spline to place the new vertex. After placing the new vertex, you can reposition the new vertex and its attached segments and then click to set it in place. A single click adds a Corner type vertex, and a click-and-drag adds a Bézier type vertex.

After positioning the new vertex, you can add another vertex next to the first vertex by dragging the mouse and clicking. To add vertices to a different segment, right-click to release the currently selected segment, but stay in Insert mode. To exit Insert mode, right-click in the viewport again or click the Insert button to deselect it.

Tutorial: Working with cross sections to create a doorknob

You can work with cross sections in several ways. You can use the Cross Section feature for Editable Splines, the Cross Section modifier, or the Loft compound object. All these methods have advantages, but the first is probably the easiest and most forgiving method.

To create a simple doorknob using the Editable Spline Cross Section button, follow these steps:

1. Select the Tools ⇨ Grid and Snaps ⇨ Grid and Snap Settings menu, and select Grid Points in the Snaps panel of the Grid and Snap Settings dialog box. Close the Grid and Snap Settings dialog box, then click the Snap toggle button on the main toolbar (or press the S key) to enable grid snapping.

2. Select the Create ⇨ Shapes ⇨ Circle menu command, and drag from the center grid point in the Top viewport to create a small circle. Repeat this step to create two more circles—one the same size and one much larger.

3. Select the Create ⇨ Shapes ⇨ Rectangle menu command, and hold down the Ctrl key while dragging in the Top viewport to create a square that is smaller than the first circle. Repeat this step to create another square the same size. Aligning the squares is easier if you select the Center option in the Creation Method rollout. Press the S key to disable snapping.

4. Click the Select and Move (W) button on the main toolbar, and drag the shapes in the Left viewport upward in this order: square, square, small circle, large circle, small circle so that the square is on the bottom and the small circle is on the top. Separate the squares by a distance equal to the width of a door, and spread the circles out to be the width of a doorknob.

5. Select the bottom-most square shape, and then right-click and select Convert To ⇨ Convert to Editable Spline in the pop-up quad menu.

6. In the Geometry rollout, click the Attach button and then select the other shapes one at a time to add them to the selected Editable Spline object. Then, right-click in the viewport to exit the Attach tool.

7. Orbit the Perspective viewport until all shapes are visible and easily selectable. Then select each and rotate each of the cross sections in the Top viewport so their first vertices (the yellow one when selected) are lined up. This helps prevent any twisting that may occur when the cross sections try to align the first vertices.

8. Select the Linear option in the New Vertex Type section in the Geometry rollout, and then click the Cross Section button. Click the lowest square shape in the Perspective viewport,

followed by the higher square shape, and then the lower small circle. This creates a spline that runs linearly between these lowest three cross-section shapes. Right-click in the Perspective viewport to exit Cross Section mode.

9. Select the Bezier option in the New Vertex Type section, and then click the Cross Section button again. Click the lowest circle shape in the Perspective viewport, followed by the larger circle shape, and then the higher small circle. This creates a spline that runs smoothly between the last three cross-section shapes. Right-click in the Perspective viewport to exit Cross Section mode.

TIP

After a spline outline is constructed, you can use the Surface modifier to add a surface to the object.

Figure 10.19 shows the splines running between the different cross sections. A key benefit to the Editable Spline approach is that you don't need to order the cross-section shapes exactly. You just need to click them in the order that you want.

FIGURE 10.19

The Cross Section feature of Editable Splines can create splines that run between several cross-section shapes.

Editing vertices

To edit vertices, click the Vertex subobject in the Modifier Stack or select the vertex icon from the Selection rollout (keyboard shortcut, 1). After the Vertex subobject type is selected, you can use the transform buttons on the main toolbar to move, rotate, and scale the selected vertex or vertices. Moving a vertex around causes the associated spline segments to follow.

With a vertex selected, you can change its type from Corner, Smooth, Bézier, or Bézier Corner by right-clicking and selecting the type from the pop-up quad menu.

Selecting the Bézier or Bézier Corner type vertex reveals green-colored handles on either side of the vertex. Dragging these handles away from the vertex alters the curvature of the segment. Bézier type vertices have both handles in the same line, but Corner Bézier type vertices do not.

Figure 10.20 shows how the Bézier and Bézier Corner handles work. The first image shows all vertices of a circle selected where you can see the handles protruding from both sides of each vertex. The second image shows what happens to the circle when one of the handles is moved. The handles for Bézier vertices move together, so moving one upward causes the other to move downward. The third image shows a Bézier Corner vertex where the handles can move independently to create sharp points. The fourth image shows two Bézier Corner vertices moved with the Lock Handles and Alike options enabled. This causes the handles to the left of the vertices to move together. The final image has the Lock Handles and All options selected, causing the handles of all selected vertices to move together.

FIGURE 10.20

Moving the vertex handles alters the spline around the vertex.

The pop-up quad menu also includes a command to Reset Tangents. This option makes the tangents revert to their original orientation before the handles were moved.

Refine

The Refine button lets you add vertices to a spline without changing the curvature, giving you more control over the details of the spline. With the Refine button selected, just click a spline where you want the new vertex, and one is added.

The Connect option adds a new segment that connects each two successive points added with the Refine tool. These segments don't actually appear until the Refine button is disabled. This provides a method for copying part of an existing spline. When the Connect option is enabled, then the Linear, Closed, Bind First, and Bind Last options become enabled. The Linear option creates Corner type vertices, resulting in linear segments. The Closed option closes the spline by connecting the first and last vertices. The Bind First and Bind Last options bind the first and last vertices to the center of the selected segment. Refine is available only for Vertex and Segment Subobject modes.

Weld and Fuse

When two end point vertices are selected and are within the specified Weld Threshold, they can be welded into one vertex and moved to a position that is the average of the welded points using the Weld button. Several vertices can be welded simultaneously. Another way to weld vertices is to move one vertex on top of another. If they are within the threshold distance, a dialog box asks whether you want them to be welded. Click the Yes button to weld them.

CAUTION
The Weld button can be used only to weld spline end points.

The Fuse button is similar to the Weld command, except that it doesn't delete any vertices. It just positions the two vertices on top of one another at a position that is the average of the selected vertices.

In Figure 10.21, the left image shows a star shape with all its lower vertices selected. The middle image is the same star shape after the selected vertices have been welded together, and the right image shows the star shape with the selected vertices fused. The Selection rollout shows five selected vertices for the fused version.

FIGURE 10.21

Using the Fuse and Weld buttons, several vertices in the star shape have been combined.

You can use the Fuse button to move the selected vertices to a single location. This is accomplished by selecting all the vertices to relocate and clicking the Fuse button. The average point between all the selected vertices becomes the new location. You can combine these vertices into one after they've been fused by clicking the Break button to make the fused points into end points and then clicking the Weld button.

Connect

The Connect button lets you connect end vertices to one another to create a new line. This works only on end vertices, not on connected points within a spline. To connect the ends, click the Connect button and drag the cursor from one end point to another (the cursor changes to a plus sign when it is over a valid end point) and release it. The first image in Figure 10.22 shows an incomplete star drawn with the Line primitive, the middle image shows a line being drawn between the end points (notice the cursor), and the third image is the resulting star.

Make First

The Show Vertex Numbers option in the Selection rollout displays the number of each vertex. The first vertex is identified by the yellow square when selected. The Make First button lets you change which vertex you want to be the first vertex in the spline. To do this, select a single vertex and click the Make First button. If more than one vertex is selected, 3ds Max ignores the command. If the selected spline is an open spline, then an end point must be selected in order to use the Make First command.

10

FIGURE 10.22

You can use the Connect button to connect end points of shapes.

> **NOTE**
> The vertex number is important because it determines the starting location for path animations and where Loft objects start.

Cycle

If a single vertex is selected, the Cycle button causes the next vertex in the Vertex Number order to be selected. The Cycle button can be used on open and closed splines and can be repeated around the spline. The exact vertex number is shown at the bottom of the Selection rollout. This is very useful for locating individual vertices in groups that are close together, such as groups that have been fused.

CrossInsert

If two splines that are part of the same object overlap, you can use the CrossInsert button to create a vertex on each spline at the location where they intersect. The distance between the two splines must be closer than the Threshold value for this to work. Note that this button does not join the two splines; it only creates a vertex on each spline. Use the Break and Weld buttons to join the splines. Figure 10.23 shows how you can use the CrossInsert button to add vertices at the intersection points of two elliptical splines. Notice that each ellipse now has eight vertices.

Fillet

The Fillet button is used to round the corners of a spline where two edges meet. To use the Fillet command, click the Fillet button and then drag on a vertex in the viewport. The more you drag, the larger the Fillet. You also can enter a Fillet value in the Fillet spinner for the vertices that are selected. The Fillet has a maximum value based on the geometry of the spline. Figure 10.24 shows the Fillet command applied to an 8-pointed star with values of 10, 15, and 20. Notice that each selected vertex has split into two.

FIGURE 10.23

The CrossInsert button can add vertices to any overlapping splines of the same object.

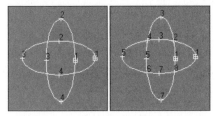

CAUTION

Be careful not to apply the fillet command multiple times to the selected vertices. If the new vertices cross over each other, then the normals will be misaligned, which will cause problems when you use modifiers.

NOTE

You can fillet several vertices at once by selecting them and then clicking the Fillet button and dragging the Fillet distance.

FIGURE 10.24

The Fillet tool can round the corners of a shape.

Chamfer

The Chamfer button works much like the Fillet button, except that the corners are replaced with straight-line segments instead of smooth curves. This keeps the resulting shape simpler and maintains hard corners. To use the Chamfer command, click the Chamfer button and drag on a vertex to create the Chamfer. You also can enter a Chamfer value in the rollout. Figure 10.25 shows chamfers applied to the same 8-pointed shape with the same values of 10, 15, and 20.

Tangent Copy and Tangent Paste

If you spend considerable time positioning the handles for the Bézier or Bézier Corner vertices just right, it can be tricky to repeat these precise positions again for other handles. Using the Tangent Copy and Tangent Paste buttons, you can copy the handle positions between different handles. To do so, simply select a handle that you want to copy and click the Copy button, and then select the vertex to which you want to copy the handle and press the Paste button. The Paste Length button copies the handle length along with its orientation, if enabled.

FIGURE 10.25

Chamfers alter the look of spline corners.

Hide/Unhide All

The Hide and Unhide All buttons hide and unhide spline subobjects. They can be used in any Subobject mode. To hide a subobject, select the subobject and click the Hide button. To unhide the hidden subobjects, click the Unhide All button.

10

Bind/Unbind

The Bind button attaches an end vertex to a segment. The bound vertex then cannot be moved independently, but only as part of the bound segment. The Unbind button removes the binding on the vertex and lets it move independently again. To bind a vertex, click the Bind button and then drag from the vertex to the segment to bind to. To exit Bind mode, right-click in the viewport or click the Bind button again.

For Figure 10.26, a circle shape is created and converted to an Editable Spline object. The right vertex is selected and then separated from the circle with the Break button. Then by clicking the Bind button and dragging the vertex to the opposite line segment, the vertex is bound to the segment. Any movement of the spline keeps this vertex bound to the segment.

FIGURE 10.26

The Bind button attaches one end of the circle shape to a segment.

Delete

The Delete button deletes the selected subobject. You can use it to delete vertices, segments, or splines. This button is available in all subobject modes. Pressing the Delete key when the subobject is selected has the same effect.

Show Selected Segments

The Show Selected Segs option causes any selected segments to continue to be highlighted in Vertex Subobject mode as well as Segment Subobject mode. This feature helps you keep track of the segments that you are working on when moving vertices.

Tutorial: Making a ninja star

If you're involved with fighting games, either creating or playing them, then chances are good that when you look at the Star primitive, you think, "Wow, this is perfect for creating a ninja star weapon." If not, then just pretend.

To create a ninja star using splines, follow these steps:

1. Select the Tools ⇨ Grid and Snaps ⇨ Grid and Snap Settings menu, and select Grid Points in the Snaps panel of the Grid and Snap Settings dialog box. Close the Grid and Snap Settings dialog box, and then click the Snaps Toggle button (or press the S key) on the main toolbar to enable grid snapping.

2. Select the Create ⇨ Shapes ⇨ Circle menu command, and drag from the center grid point in the Top viewport to create a circle.

3. Select the Create ⇨ Shapes ⇨ Star menu command, and drag again from the center of the Top viewport to center align the star with the circle. Make the star shape about three times the size of the circle, and set the number of Points to **10**.

4. With the star shape selected, right-click in the Top viewport and select Convert To ⇨ Convert to Editable Spline. In the Modify panel, click the Attach button, and click the circle shape. Then click the Vertex icon in the Selection rollout (or press 1) to enter Vertex Subobject mode.

5. Click the Create Line button in the Geometry rollout; then click the circle's top vertex and bottom vertex to create a vertical line that divides the circle, then right-click to end the line, and right-click again to exit Create Line mode.

6. Select the top vertex of the line that you just created. (Be careful not to select the circle's top vertex; you can use the Cycle button to find the correct vertex.) Right-click the vertex, and select the Bézier vertex type from the quad menu. Then drag its lower handle until it is on top of the circle's left vertex. Repeat this step for the bottom vertex, and drag its handle to the circle's right vertex to create a yin-yang symbol in the center of the ninja star.

7. While holding down the Ctrl key, click all the inner vertices of the star shape. Click the Chamfer button, and change the value until the chamfer looks like that in Figure 10.27, and click the Chamfer key again to deselect it.

Figure 10.27 shows the resulting ninja star.

FIGURE 10.27

The completed ninja star, ready for action (or extruding)

Editing segments

To edit a segment, click the Segment subobject in the Modifier Stack or select the Segment icon from the Selection rollout to enter Segment Subobject mode. Clicking again on either exits this mode. *Segments* are the lines or edges that run between two vertices. Many of the editing options work in the same way as when you're editing Vertex subobjects. You can select multiple segments by holding down the Ctrl key while clicking the segments, or you can hold down the Alt key to remove selected segments from the selection set. You also can copy segments when they're being transformed by holding down the Shift key. The cloned segments break away from the original spline, but are still a part of the Editable Spline object.

You can change segments from straight lines to curves by right-clicking the segment and selecting Line or Curve from the pop-up quad menu. Line segments created with the Corner type vertex option cannot be changed to Curves, but lines created with Smooth and Bézier type vertex options can be switched back and forth.

Connect Copy

When you create a copy of a segment by moving a segment with the Shift key held down, you can enable the Connect Copy option to make segments that join the copied segment with its original. For example, if you have a single straight horizontal line segment, dragging it upward with the Copy Connect option enabled creates a copy that is joined to the original, resulting in a rectangle. Be aware that the vertices that connect to the original segment are not welded to the original segment.

Divide

When you select a segment, the Divide button becomes active. This button adds the number of vertices specified to the selected segment or segments. These new vertices are positioned based on the curvature of the segment with more vertices being added to the areas of greater curvature. Figure 10.28 shows the diamond shape (second row, second from right) after all four segments were selected, a value of 1 was entered into the spinner, and the Divide button was clicked.

FIGURE 10.28

The Divide button adds segments to the spline.

Detach

The Detach button separates the selected subobjects from the rest of the object (opposite of the Attach button). When you click this button, the Detach dialog box opens, enabling you to name the new detached subobject. When segments are detached, you can select the Same Shape option to keep them part of the original object. The Reorient option realigns the new detached subobject to match the position and orientation of the current active grid. The Copy option creates a new copy of the detached subobject.

You can use Detach on either selected Spline or Segment subobjects.

Tutorial: Using Connect Copy to create a simple flower

Connect Copy is one of the features that you'll use and wonder how you ever got along without it. For this tutorial, you create a simple flower from a circle shape using the Connect Copy feature.

To create a simple flower using the Connect Copy feature, follow these steps:

1. Select Create ⇨ Shapes ⇨ Circle, and drag in the Top viewport to create a simple circle shape.

2. Right-click the circle, and select Convert to ⇨ Convert to Editable Spline to convert the shape.

3. In the Modifier Stack, select the Segment Subobject mode (keyboard shortcut, 2) and enable the Connect option in the Connect Copy section.

4. Select one of the circle segments, and with the Shift key held down, drag it outward away from the circle with the Move tool. Then repeat this step for each segment.

Figure 10.29 shows the results. With the Connect Copy option, you don't need to worry about the connecting lines.

FIGURE 10.29

The Connect Copy feature joins newly copied segments to the original.

Surface Properties

For segment and spline subobjects, you can access a Surface Properties rollout that lets you assign a Material ID to the subobject. These Material IDs are used with the Multi/Sub-Object Material available in the Material Editor. For example, suppose you've created a road from a bunch of splines that are part of the same object. You can assign one Material ID for the lines at the edge of the road that will be the curb and a different Material ID for the yellow lines running down the middle of the road. Separate materials then can be applied to each of the parts using the matching Material IDs.

You can find information on Material IDs in Chapter 14, "Creating and Applying Standard Materials with the Slate Material Editor."

Using the Select ID button and drop-down list, you can locate and select all subobjects that have a certain Material ID. Simply select the Material ID that you are looking for and click the Select ID button, and all segments (or splines) with that Material ID are selected. Beneath the Select ID button is another drop-down list that lets you select segments by material name. The Clear Selection option clears all selections when the Select ID button is clicked. If disabled, then all new selections are added to the current selection set.

Editing Spline subobjects

To edit a spline, click the Spline subobject in the Modifier Stack or select the Spline icon from the Selection rollout. Transforming a spline object containing only one spline works the same way in Subobject mode as it does in a normal transformation. Working in Spline Subobject mode lets you move splines relative to one another. Right-clicking a spline in Subobject mode opens a pop-up quad menu that lets you convert it between Curve and Line types. The Curve type option changes all vertices to Bézier type, and the Line type option makes all vertices Corner type. Spline Subobject mode includes many of the buttons previously discussed as well as some new ones in the Geometry rollout.

Reverse

The Reverse button is available only for Spline subobjects. It reverses the order of the vertex numbers. For example, a circle's vertices that are numbered clockwise from 1 to 4 is numbered counterclockwise after using the Reverse button. The vertex order is important for splines that are used for animation paths or loft compound objects.

Outline

The Outline button creates a spline that is identical to the one selected and offset by an amount specified by dragging or specified in the Offset value. The Center option creates an outline on either side of the selected spline, centered on the original spline. When the Center option is not selected, then an outline is created by offsetting a duplicate of the spline on only one side of the original spline. To exit Outline mode, click the Outline button again or right-click in the viewport. Figure 10.30 shows an arc that has had the Outline feature applied. In the right image, the Center option is enabled.

FIGURE 10.30

The Outline button creates a duplicate copy of the original spline and offsets it.

Boolean

Boolean operations work with two or more splines that overlap one another. Three different operations can happen: You can combine the splines to create a single spline (union), you can subtract the overlapping area from one of the splines (subtract), or you can throw away everything except the overlapping area (intersection).

 You also can use Booleans to combine or subtract 3D volumes, which are covered in Chapter 13, "Working with Compound Objects."

The Boolean button works on overlapping closed splines and has three different options—Union, Subtraction, and Intersection—shown in Table 10.3. The splines must all be part of the same object.

TABLE 10.3 Boolean Button Options

Button	Description
⬙	Union
⬙	Subtraction
⬙	Intersection

To use the Boolean feature, select one of the splines and select one of the Boolean operation options. Then click the Boolean button, and select the second spline. Depending on which Boolean operation you chose, the two areas are combined, the second spline acts to cut away the overlapping area on the first, or only the overlapping area remains. To exit Boolean mode, right-click in the viewport.

> **NOTE**
> Boolean operations can be performed only on closed splines that exist within a 2D plane.

Figure 10.31 shows the results of applying the Spline Boolean operators on a circle and star shape. The first image consists of the circle and star shapes without any Boolean operations applied. The second image shows the result of the Union feature; the third (circle selected first) and fourth (star selected first) use the Subtraction feature; and the fifth image uses the Intersection feature.

Mirror

You can use the Mirror button to mirror a spline object horizontally, vertically, or along both axes. To use this feature, select a spline object to mirror and then locate the Mirror button. To the right of the Mirror button are three smaller buttons, shown in Table 10.4, each of which indicates a direction—Mirror Horizontally, Mirror Vertically, and Mirror Both. Select a direction, and then click the Mirror button. If the Copy option is selected, a new spline is created and mirrored. The About Pivot option causes the mirroring to be completed about the pivot point axes.

FIGURE 10.31

Using the Boolean operations on two overlapping shapes

10

TABLE 10.4 Mirror Button Options

Button	Description
	Mirror Horizontally
	Mirror Vertically
	Mirror Both

Figure 10.32 shows a little critter that has been mirrored horizontally, vertically, and both. The right image was horizontally mirrored with the About Pivot option disabled. Notice that the eye spline was mirrored about its own pivot.

FIGURE 10.32

Mirroring a shape is as simple as selecting a direction and clicking the Mirror button.

Trim and Extend

The Trim button cuts off any extending portion between two overlapping splines. The splines must be part of the same object. To use the Trim feature, select the spline that you want to keep, click the Trim button, and then click the segment to trim. The spline you click is trimmed back to the nearest intersecting point of the selected object. This button works only in Spline Subobject mode. The trimming command is dependent on the viewport that is active. When the Perspective or a Camera view is active, this command uses the Top viewport to trim.

Figure 10.33 shows a circle intersected by two ellipse shapes. The Trim button was used to cut the center sections of the ellipse shapes away.

FIGURE 10.33

You can use the Trim button to cut away the excess of a spline.

The Extend button works in the reverse manner compared to the Trim button. The Extend button lengthens the end of a spline until it encounters an intersection. (There must be a spline segment to intersect.) To use the Extend command, click the Extend button and then click the segment to extend. The spline you click is extended. To exit Extend mode, right-click in the viewport or click the Extend button again.

The Infinite Bounds option works for both the Trim and Extend buttons. When enabled, it treats all open splines as if they were infinite for the purpose of locating an intersecting point. The Extend command, like Trim, is dependent on the active viewport.

Close

The Close button completes an open spline and creates a closed spline by attaching a segment between the first and last vertices. You can check which vertex is first by enabling the Show Vertex Numbers in the Selection rollout. This is similar to the Connect feature (accessible in Vertex Subobject mode), but the Connect feature can connect the end point of one spline to the end point of another as long as they are part of the same Editable Spline object. The Close feature works only in Spline Subobject mode and connects only the end points of each given spline.

Explode

The Explode button performs the Detach command on all subobject splines at once. It separates each segment into a separate spline. You can select to explode all spline objects to separate Splines or Objects. If you select to explode to Objects, then a dialog box appears asking you for a name. Each spline uses the name you enter with a two-digit number appended to distinguish between the different splines.

Tutorial: Spinning a spider's web

Now that you're familiar with the many aspects of editing splines, this tutorial will try to mimic one of the best spline producers in the world—the spider. The spider is an expert at connecting lines together to create an intricate pattern. (Luckily, unlike the spider that depends on its web for food, you won't go hungry if this example fails.)

To create a spider web from splines, follow these steps:

1. Select Create ⇨ Shapes ⇨ Circle, and drag in the Front viewport to create a large circle for the perimeter of the web (pretend that the spider is building this web inside a tire swing). Right-click the circle, and select Convert To ⇨ Convert to Editable Spline to convert the circle shape.

2. Select the Spline subobject in the Modifier Stack (or press the 3 key) to enter Spline Subobject mode.

3. Click the Create Line button in the Geometry rollout, and click in the center of the circle and again outside the circle to create a line. Then right-click to end the line. Repeat this step until 12 or so radial lines extend from the center of the circle outward.

4. Select and right-click the 2D Snaps Toggle in the main toolbar. In the Grid and Snap Settings dialog box, enable the Vertex and Edge/Segment options and close the dialog box. While you're still in Create Line mode, click the circle's center and create lines in a spiral pattern by clicking each radial line that you intersect. Right-click to end the line when you finally reach the edge of the circle. Then right-click again to exit Create Line mode.

5. Select the circle shape, and click the Trim button. Then click each line segment on the portion that extends beyond the circle. This trims the radial lines to the edge of the circle. Click the Trim button again when you are finished to exit Trim mode.

10

6. Change to Vertex Subobject mode by clicking Vertex in the Modifier Stack (or by pressing 1). Turn off the Snaps Toggle, select all the vertices in the center of the circle, and click the Fuse button.

Figure 10.34 shows the finished spider web. (I have a new respect for spiders.)

FIGURE 10.34

A spider web made from Editable Splines

Summary

As this chapter has shown, there is much more to splines than just points, lines, and control handles. Splines in 3ds Max are one of the fundamental building blocks and the pathway to advanced modeling skills.

This chapter covered the following spline topics:

- Understanding the various shape primitives
- Editing splines
- Working with the various spline subobjects

The next chapter continues your voyage down the modeling pathway with perhaps the most common modeling types—meshes and polys.

Modeling with Polygons

IN THIS CHAPTER

Creating Editable Poly objects

Working with the poly subobject modes

Editing poly geometry

Changing surface properties like NURMS

Meshes (or, more specifically, polygon meshes) are perhaps the most popular and the default model type for most 3D programs. You create them by placing polygonal faces next to one another so the edges are joined. The polygons can then be smoothed from face to face during the rendering process. Using meshes, you can create almost any 3D object, including simple primitives such as a cube or a realistic dinosaur.

Meshes have lots of advantages. They are common, intuitive to work with, and supported by a large number of 3D software packages. In this chapter, you learn how to create and edit mesh and poly objects.

Understanding Poly Objects

Before continuing, you need to understand exactly what a Poly object is, how it differs from a regular mesh object, and why it is the featured modeling type in the Autodesk® 3ds Max® 2013 software. To understand these issues, you'll need a quick history lesson. Initially, 3ds Max supported only mesh objects, and all mesh objects had to be broken down into triangular faces. Subdividing the mesh into triangular faces ensured that all faces in the mesh object were coplanar, which prevented any hiccups with the rendering engine.

Over time, the rendering engines have been modified and upgraded to handle polygons that weren't subdivided (or whose subdivision was invisible to the user), and doing such actually makes the model more efficient by eliminating all the extra edges required to triangulate the mesh. Also, users can work with polygon objects (specifically four-sided quads) more easily than individual triangular faces. To take advantage of these new features, the Editable Poly object was added to 3ds Max.

As development has continued, many new features have been added to the Editable Poly object while the Editable Mesh remained mainly for backward compatibility. But, the Editable Mesh object type still exists, and there may be times when you'll want to use each type, shown in Figure 11.1. Editable Mesh objects split all polygons into triangular faces, but the Editable Poly object maintains four-sided (or more) polygon faces. Another key difference is found in the subobjects. Editable Meshes can work with Vertex, Edge, Face, Polygon, and Element subobjects; and Editable Poly objects can work with Vertex, Edge, Border, Polygon, and Element subobjects.

FIGURE 11.1

Editable Mesh objects have triangular faces; the Editable Poly object uses faces with four or more vertices.

Editable Mesh object   Editable Poly object

Some game and render engines still require that all faces be coplanar, and for such conditions you'll want to continue to use the Editable Mesh object. Another case where the Editable Mesh object is helpful is in performing certain face-oriented operations. In addition, normal meshes have a smaller memory footprint, which enables them to render more quickly, especially if you have many of them. Regardless, 3ds Max lets you convert seamlessly between these two modeling types.

Although many of the same features are available for both object types, the advance features available for the Editable Poly object make it the preferred object type to use for mesh modeling. This chapter focuses on working with Editable Poly objects. Although the specific features of the Editable Mesh object aren't covered, most of these same commands apply equally to the Editable Mesh object. However, the Graphite Modeling tools (covered in Chapter 12, "Using the Graphite Modeling Tools") can be used only on Editable Poly objects.

Creating Editable Poly Objects

The Create panel has no method for making mesh objects—mesh objects must be converted from another object type or produced as the result of a modifier. Object types that you can convert include shapes, primitives, Booleans, patches, and NURBS. Many models that are imported appear as mesh objects, but they can easily be converted to Editable Poly objects.

NOTE

You can even convert spline shapes to Editable Poly objects, whether they are open or closed. Closed splines are filled with a polygon, whereas open splines are only a single edge and can be hard to see.

Before you can use many of the mesh editing functions discussed in this chapter, you need to convert the object to an Editable Poly object, collapse an object with modifiers applied, or apply the Edit Poly modifier.

Converting objects

11

To convert an object into an Editable Poly object, right-click the object and choose Convert To⇨ Convert to Editable Poly from the pop-up quad menu. You can also convert an object by right-clicking the object within the Modifier Stack and selecting one of the convert options from the pop-up menu.

Within the quad menu is also an option to convert the object to a Deformable gPoly. This is the hardware mesh format that displays much faster when deformed, so it's ideal for animated mesh objects that are deformed, like an animated character's skin. Because this format is optimized for display, it doesn't have any parameters and should be used only after the model work is completed.

New Feature
The Convert to Deformable gPoly feature is new to 3ds Max 2013.

Collapsing to a mesh object

When an object is collapsed, it loses its parametric nature and the parameters associated with any applied modifiers. Only objects that have had modifiers applied to them can be collapsed. Objects are made into an Editable Poly object when you use the Collapse To option available from the right-click pop-up menu in the Modifier Stack or when you use the Collapse utility found in the Utilities panel.

Most objects collapse to Editable Poly objects, but some objects, such as the compound objects, give you an option of which object type to collapse to.

Applying the Edit Poly modifier

Another way to enable the mesh editing features is to apply the Edit Poly modifier to an object. You apply this modifier by selecting the object and choosing Modifiers⇨Mesh Editing⇨Edit Poly, or selecting Edit Poly from the Modifier drop-down list in the Modify panel.

The Edit Poly modifier is different from the Editable Poly object in that, as an applied modifier, it maintains the parametric nature of the original object. For example, you cannot change the Radius value of a sphere object that has been converted to an Editable Poly, but you could if the Edit Poly modifier were applied.

Editing Poly Objects

After an object has been converted to an Editable Poly, you can alter its shape by applying modifiers, or you can work with the mesh subobjects. You can find the editing features for these objects in the Modify panel, but the better place to look for the Editable Poly features is in the Graphite Modeling tools.

This chapter presents many of the editing features found in the Modify panel. Many of these same features also are available in the Graphite Modeling Tool's Ribbon, which is covered in Chapter 12, "Using the Graphite Modeling Tools."

Editable Poly Subobject modes

Before you can edit poly subobjects, you must select them. To select a Subobject mode, select Editable Poly in the Modifier Stack, click the small plus sign to its left to display a hierarchy of subobjects, and then click the subobject type with which you want to work. Another way to select a subobject type is to click on the appropriate subobject button in the Selection rollout. The subobject button in the Selection rollout and the subobject listed in the Modifier Stack both get highlighted when selected. You also can type a number from 1 to 5 to enter Subobject mode with 1 for Vertex, 2 for Edge, 3 for Border, 4 for Polygon, and 5 for Element.

The Vertex Subobject mode lets you select and work with all vertices in the object. Edge Subobject mode makes all edges that run between two vertices available for selection. The Border Subobject mode lets you select all edges that run around an opening in the object such as a hole. The Polygon Subobject mode lets you work with individual polygon faces, and the Element Subobject mode picks individual objects if the object includes several different elements.

To exit subobject edit mode, click the highlighted subobject button again. Remember, you must exit this mode before you can select another object.

> **NOTE**
> Selected subobject edges appear in the viewports in red to distinguish them from edges of the selected object, which appear white when displayed as wireframes.

After you're in a Subobject mode, you can click on a subobject (or drag over an area to select multiple subobjects) to select it and edit the subobject using the transformation buttons on the main toolbar. You can transform subobjects just like other objects.

 For more information on transforming objects, see Chapter 6, "Transforming Objects, Pivoting, Aligning, and Snapping."

When working with Editable Poly objects in Subobject mode, you can use Press and Release keyboard shortcuts. These shortcuts are identified in bold in the Editable Poly group of the Keyboard panel of the Customize User Interface dialog box. When using these keyboard shortcuts, you can access a different editing mode without having to exit Subobject mode. For example, if you press and hold Alt+C while in Polygon Subobject mode, you can make a cut with the Cut tool, and when you release the keyboard keys you'll return to Polygon Subobject mode.

You can select multiple subobjects at the same time by dragging an outline over them. You can also select multiple subobjects by holding down the Ctrl key while clicking them. Holding down the Alt key removes any selected vertices from the current selection set.

With one of the transform buttons selected, hold down the Shift key while clicking and dragging on a subobject to clone it. During cloning, the Clone Part of Mesh dialog box appears, enabling you to Clone to Object or Clone to Element. Using the Clone to Object option makes the selection an entirely new object, and you are able to give the new object a name. If the Clone to Element option is selected, the clone remains part of the existing object but is a new element within that object.

If you hold down the Ctrl key while choosing a different Subobject mode, the current selection is maintained for the new subobject type. For example, if you select all the polygons in the top half of a model using the Polygon Subobject mode and click the Vertex Subobject mode while holding down the Ctrl key, all vertices in the top half of the model are selected. This works only for the applicable sub-objects. If the selection of polygons doesn't have any borders, then holding down the Ctrl key while clicking the Border Subobject mode selects nothing.

You also can hold down the Shift key to select only those subobjects that lie on the borders of the current selection. For example, selecting all the polygons in the top half of a model using the Polygon Subobject mode and clicking the Vertex Subobject mode with the Shift key held down selects only those vertices that surround the selection and not the interior vertices.

Subobject selection

The Selection rollout, shown in Figure 11.2, includes options for selecting subobjects. The By Vertex option is available in all but the Vertex Subobject mode. It requires that you click a vertex in order to select an edge, border, polygon, or element. It selects all edges and borders that are connected to a vertex when the vertex is selected. The Ignore Backfacing option selects only those subobjects with normals pointing toward the current viewport. For example, if you are trying to select some faces on a sphere, only the faces on the side closest to you are selected. If this option is off, then faces on both sides of the sphere are selected. This option is helpful if many subobjects are on top of one another in the viewport.

> **TIP**
> The select commands in the Edit menu also work with subobjects. For example, in Vertex Subobject mode, you can select Edit ⇨ Select All (or press Ctrl+A) to select all vertices.

FIGURE 11.2

The Selection rollout includes options for determining which subobjects are selected.

Vertex subobject mode

Edge subobject mode

Border subobject mode

Polygon subobject mode

Element subobject mode

The By Angle option selects adjacent polygons that are within the specified threshold. The threshold value is defined as the angle between the normals of adjacent polygons. For example, if you have a terrain mesh with a smooth, flat lake area in its middle, you can select the entire lake area if you set the Planar Threshold to 0 and click the lake.

The Selection rollout also includes four buttons. These buttons include Shrink, Grow, Ring, and Loop. Use the Grow button to increase the current selection around the perimeter of the current selection, as shown in Figure 11.3. Click the Shrink button to do the opposite.

FIGURE 11.3

Using the Grow button, you can increase the subobject selection.

The Ring and Loop buttons are available only in Edge and Border Subobject modes. Use Ring and Loop to select all adjacent subobjects lined up horizontally and vertically around the entire object. Ring selection looks for parallel edges, and Loop selection looks for all edges around an object that are lined up end to end as the initial selection. For example, if you select a single edge of a sphere, the Ring button selects an entire row of edges going around the sphere that are lined up parallel to each other, and the Loop button selects the entire line of edges lined up around the sphere.

Next to the Ring and Loop buttons is a set of up/down arrows. These arrows are used to shift the current ring and/or loop selection to the immediate adjacent ring or loop. Holding down the Ctrl key adds the adjacent ring or loop to the current selection, and holding down the Alt key removes the adjacent selection. Figure 11.4 shows how the Ring and Loop buttons work. The first sphere shows a selection made using the Ring button; the second sphere has increased this selection by holding down the Ctrl key while clicking the up arrow next to the Loop button. The third sphere shows a selection made using the Loop button; the fourth sphere has increased this selection by holding down the Ctrl key while clicking the up arrow next to the Ring button.

FIGURE 11.4

The Ring and Loop buttons can select an entire row and/or column of edges.

> **NOTE**
>
> For Editable Poly objects, the Hide Selected, Unhide All, Copy, and Paste buttons are located at the bottom of the Edit Geometry rollout.

 The Soft Selection rollout allows you to alter adjacent nonselected subobjects when selected subobjects are moved, creating a smooth transition. For the details on this rollout, see Chapter 9, "Introducing Subobjects and Modifiers and Using the Modifier Stack."

Tutorial: Modeling a clown head

Now that you know how to select subobjects, you can use the transform tools to move them. In this example, you'll quickly deform a sphere to create a clown face by selecting, moving, and working with some vertices.

To create a clown head by moving vertices, follow these steps:

1. Select Create ⇨ Standard Primitives ⇨ Sphere, and drag in the Front viewport to create a sphere object. Then right-click the sphere and select Convert To ⇨ Editable Poly in the pop-up quad menu.

2. Open the Modify panel. Now make a long, pointy nose by pulling a vertex outward from the sphere object. Click the small plus sign to the left of the Editable Poly object in the Modifier Stack, and select Vertex in the hierarchy (or press the 1 key). This activates the Vertex Subobject mode. Enable the Ignore Backfacing option in the Selection rollout, and select the single vertex in the center of the Front viewport. Make sure that the Select and Move button (W) is selected, and in the Left viewport, drag the vertex along the X-axis until it projects outward from the sphere.

3. Next, create the mouth by selecting and indenting a row of vertices in the Front viewport below the protruding nose. Holding down the Ctrl key makes selecting multiple vertices easy. Below the nose, select several vertices in a circular arc that make a smile. Then move the selected vertices along the negative X-axis in the Left viewport.

4. For the eyes, select Create ⇨ Standard Primitives ⇨ Sphere and enable the AutoGrid option. Then drag in the Front viewport to create two eyes above the nose.

This clown head is just a simple example of what is possible by editing subobjects. Figure 11.5 shows the clown head in a shaded view.

Editing geometry

Much of the power of editing meshes is contained within the Edit Geometry rollout, shown in Figure 11.6. Features contained here include, among many others, the ability to create new subobjects, attach subobjects to the mesh, weld vertices, chamfer vertices, slice, explode, and align. Some Edit Geometry buttons are disabled depending on the Subobject mode that you select. The features detailed in this section are enabled for the Editable Poly object before you enter a Subobject mode.

FIGURE 11.5

A clown head created from an editable poly by selecting and moving vertices

FIGURE 11.6

The Edit Geometry rollout includes many general-purpose editing features.

Many of the buttons for the Editable Poly include a small icon to the right of the button that opens a settings caddy. These caddy interfaces appear around the selected subobject and allow you to change the settings and immediately see the results in the viewports. The OK button (a check mark icon) applies the settings and closes the caddy interface, and the Apply button (a plus sign icon) applies the settings and leaves the dialog box open. These caddy interfaces are included next to the buttons such as Extrude, Bevel, Outline, and Inset.

Editable Poly objects include all their common buttons in the Edit Geometry rollout and all subobject-specific buttons in a separate rollout named after the Subobject mode, such as Edit Vertices or Edit Edges.

Repeat Last

The first button in the Edit Geometry rollout is the Repeat Last button. This button repeats the last subobject command. This button does not work on all features, but it's very convenient for certain actions. For example, if you select and extrude a polygon to make it stick out from the surface, you can get other polygons to be extruded by the same amount by selecting them and clicking the Repeat Last button.

> **TIP**
> The tooltip for this button displays the last repeatable command.

Enabling constraints

The Constraints options limit the movement of subobjects to a specified subobject. The available constraints are None, Edge, Face, and Normal. For example, if you select and move a vertex with the Edge constraint enabled, then the movement is constrained to the adjacent edges. This lets you move, rotate, and scale vertices, edges, and polygons while making sure they stay with the surface of the current object.

Tutorial: Creating a quick flying saucer

Primitive shapes can be quickly changed in many ways to create other simple shapes, and the Constraints settings help keep the moved subobjects in check.

To create a simple flying saucer, follow these steps:

1. Select Create ⇨ Standard Primitives ⇨ Sphere, and drag in the Top viewport to create a Sphere object.

2. Right-click the sphere object, and select Convert To ⇨ Convert to Editable Poly in the pop-up quad menu.

3. Open the Modify panel, choose the Polygon Subobject mode, and then drag over to the select the two middle rows of polygons in the Left viewport.

4. In the Constraints section of the Edit Geometry panel, select the Normal option and drag the selected polygons outward with the Move tool in the Top viewport roughly twice the size of the sphere.

5. In the Constraints section, select the Edge option and drag the Y-axis with the Select and Scale tool downward in the Left viewport to pull the polygons close together.

6. Exit Subobject mode, and scale the entire object by dragging on the Y-axis in the Left viewport with the Select and Scale tool.

The resulting flying saucer is shown in Figure 11.7 ready to be populated with aliens.

Preserve UVs

UV coordinates define how a texture map is applied to an object's surface. These UV coordinates are tied closely to the surface subobject positions, so moving a subobject after a texture is applied moves the texture also. This could cause discontinuities to the texture map. The Preserve UVs option lets you make subobject changes without altering the UV coordinates for an existing texture.

FIGURE 11.7

The Constraints options keep the subobjects within the specified bounds.

The Settings button located to the right of the Preserve UVs option opens the Preserve Map Channels dialog box, which lets you select a Vertex Color and Texture Channel to preserve. Figure 11.8 shows two block objects with a brick texture map applied. The inner vertices on the left block were scaled outward without the Preserve UVs option selected; the right block had this option enabled.

FIGURE 11.8

The Preserve UVs option lets you make subobject changes after texture maps have been applied.

Create

The Create button lets you create new subobjects, including vertices, edges, and polygons. This is done in Vertex mode by simply clicking to place vertices. New edges are created by connecting vertices to existing vertices. When the cursor is over a vertex in Edge or Border Subobject mode, it changes to a crosshair, and you can click to create a polygon edge by clicking two vertices, one after another.

TIP
New vertices and polygons are placed by default on the construction grid, but you can specify to create new vertices and polygons on the object surface by enabling the Face or Edge snap options.

You also can use the Create button to create new polygons. To create a new polygon, click the Create button, which highlights all vertices in the selected mesh. Next, click a vertex to start the polygon; after you click two more vertices, a new face is created. You also can create a new vertex not based on any existing vertices by simply clicking to place vertices.

As you create new polygons, the normal is determined by the direction in which you create the polygon using the right-hand rule. If you bend the fingers of your right hand in the direction (clockwise or counterclockwise) that the vertices are clicked, your thumb points in the direction of the normal. If the normal is pointing away from you, then the backside of the polygon will be visible and the lighting could be off.

Polygons aren't limited to three vertices. You can click as many times as you want to add additional vertices to the polygon. Click the first vertex again, or double-click to complete the polygon.

NOTE
If you click the Create button with no Subobject mode selected, the Polygon Subobject mode is automatically selected.

Collapse

The Collapse button is used to collapse all the selected subobjects to a single subobject located at the averaged center of the selection. This button is similar to the Weld button, except that the selected vertices don't need to be within a Threshold value to be combined. This button works in all Subobject modes.

Attach and Detach

The Attach button is available with all Subobject modes, even when you are not in a Subobject mode. Use the Attach button to add objects to the current Editable Poly object. You can add primitives, splines, patch objects, and other mesh objects. Any object attached to a mesh object is automatically converted into an Editable Poly and inherits the object color of the object to which it is attached. Any objects added to a poly object can be selected individually using the Element Subobject mode.

CAUTION
If you attach an object that is smoothed using NURMS, the NURMS are lost when the object is attached.

To use this feature, select the main object and click the Attach button. Move the mouse over the object to be attached; the cursor changes over acceptable objects. Click the object to select it. Click the Attach button again or right-click in the viewport to exit Attach mode.

> **NOTE**
>
> If the object that you click to attach already has a material applied that is different from the current Editable Poly object, then a dialog box appears giving you options to Match Material IDs to Material, Match Material to Material IDs, or Do Not Modify Material IDs or Material. Materials and Material IDs are discussed in more detail in Chapter 14, "Creating and Applying Standard Materials with the Slate Material Editor."

Clicking the Attach List button opens the Attach List dialog box (which looks just like the Select From Scene [H] dialog box) where you can select from a list of all the objects to attach. The list contains only objects that you can attach.

Attaching objects is different from grouping objects because all attached objects act as a single object with the same object color, name, and transforms. You can access individual attached objects using the Element Subobject mode.

Use the Detach button to separate the selected subobjects from the rest of the object. To use this button, select the subobject and click the Detach button. The Detach dialog box opens, enabling you to name the new detached subobject. You also have the options to Detach to Element or to Detach as Clone.

Slicing and cutting options

The Slice Plane button lets you split the poly object along a plane. When you click the Slice Plane button, a yellow slice plane gizmo appears on the selected object. You can move, rotate, and scale this gizmo using the transform buttons. After you properly position the plane and set all options, click the Slice button to finish slicing the mesh. All intersected faces split in two, and new vertices and edges are added to the mesh where the Slice Plane intersects the original mesh.

The Slice Plane mode stays active until you deselect the Slice Plane button or until you right-click in the viewport; this feature enables you to make several slices in one session. The Slice Plane button is enabled for all Subobject modes. A Reset Plane button is located next to the Slice Plane button. Use this button to reset the slice plane to its original location. You use the Split option to double the number of vertices and edges along the Slice Plane, so each side can be separated from the other. When used in Element mode, the Split option breaks the sliced object into two separate elements.

> **CAUTION**
>
> Although the Slice Plane feature can be used in all Subobject modes, cuts are made only to the object in Vertex, Edge, and Border modes.

The QuickSlice button lets you click anywhere on an Editable Poly object where you want a slicing line to be located. You can then move the mouse, and the QuickSlice line rotates about the point you clicked on. When you click the mouse again, a new vertex is added at every place where the QuickSlice line intersects an object edge. This is a very convenient tool for slicing objects because the slice line follows the surface of the object, so you can see exactly where the slice will take place.

For the QuickSlice and Cut tools, you can enable the Full Interactivity option (located near the bottom of the Edit Geometry rollout). With this option enabled, the slice lines are shown as you move the mouse about the surface. With Full Interactivity disabled, the resulting lines are shown only when the mouse is clicked.

For Editable Poly objects, the Cut button is interactive. If you click a polygon corner, the cut edge snaps to the corner, and a new edge extends from the corner to a nearby corner. The cursor changes when you are over corners and edges and within the polygon interior. As you move the mouse around, the edge moves until you click where the edge should end. If you click in the middle of an edge or face, new edges appear. The Cut tool lets you add successive connected edges by clicking new end-points. If you right-click once, the current cut is released, allowing you to start a new cut. Click in a new position to create a new cut, or right-click a second time to exit the Cut tool. The Cut tool is great for cutting holes into an existing object.

Tutorial: Combining, cutting, and separating a car model

When dealing with a model that includes interior parts, you may want to slice the object and separate a portion to reveal the interior. Although this can be accomplished using a camera or viewport clipping plane, a more permanent solution uses the QuickSlice and Detach operations.

To combine, slice, and detach a car model, follow these steps:

1. Open the Sliced car.max file from the Chap 11 directory on the CD.

2. Before you can slice the car, you'll need to combine the entire car into a single Editable Poly object. Select one of the body parts, right-click on it, and select the Convert To ⇨ Convert to Editable Poly in the pop-up quad menu.

3. Open the Modify panel, and click on the small button icon next to the Attach button in the Edit Geometry rollout to open the Attach List dialog box.

4. In the Attach List dialog box that opens, click the Select All button (or use the Ctrl+A short-cut) and select the Attach button. In the Attach Options dialog box that appears, select the Match Material IDs to Material option, you can leave the Condense Materials and IDs option checked, and then click OK.

   All objects are now combined into a single Editable Poly object.

5. Click the QuickSlice button, which is also in the Edit Geometry rollout, and click in the Top viewport at the point where you want to slice the car. Then drag to align the slicing plane, and click again to make the slice. Click on the QuickSlice button again to exit QuickSlice mode.

6. Select the Polygon Subobject mode, and drag over all the polygons below the slice line in the Top viewport. Then click the Detach button in the Edit Geometry rollout. In the Detach dialog box, enter the name **Car Front** and click OK.

7. Disable Polygon Subobject mode, and use the Select and Move tool to separate the car front from the rest of the car.

Figure 11.9 shows the separated car front.

FIGURE 11.9

Using the Attach, QuickSlice, and Detach features, you can slice and separate mode parts.

MSmooth

Both the MSmooth and Tessellate buttons have caddy interfaces, as shown in Figure 11.10. The MSmooth setting for Smoothness rounds all the sharp edges of an object.

FIGURE 11.10

The Caddy interfaces for the MSmooth and Tessellate buttons let you interactively set the Smoothness and Tension values.

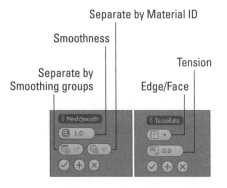

The MSmooth button can be used to smooth the selected subobjects in the same way as the MeshSmooth or TurboSmooth modifiers. This button can be used several times, but each time the density of the polygons is increased. The Smoothness value determines which vertices are used to smooth the object. The higher the value, the more vertices are included and the smoother the result. You can also select that the smoothing is separated by Smoothing Groups or by Materials.

Figure 11.11 shows a simple diamond-shaped hedra that has been MeshSmoothed using the MSmooth button and then tessellated three consecutive times.

FIGURE 11.11

Using MSmooth reduces the sharp edges, and tessellating adds more editable faces.

Tessellate

Tessellation is used to increase the density of the object's faces or edges. When modeling, you may want more details in a select area. This is where the tessellation command comes in. Tessellation can be applied to individual selected subobjects or to the entire object.

You can use the Tessellate button to increase the resolution of a mesh by splitting a face or polygon into several faces or polygons. You have two options to do this: Edge and Face.

The Edge method splits each edge at its midpoint. For example, a rectangular face would be split into four smaller rectangles, one at each corner. The Tension spinner to the right of the Tessellate button specifies a value that is used to make the tessellated face concave or convex.

The Face option creates a new vertex in the center of the face and also creates new edges, which extend from the center vertex to each original vertex. For a square polygon, this option would create four triangular faces. Figure 11.12 shows the faces of a cube that has been tessellated once using the Edge option and then again using the Face-Center option.

FIGURE 11.12

A cube tessellated twice, using each option once

Make Planar

A single vertex or two vertices don't define a plane, but three or more vertices do. If three or more vertices are selected, you can use the Make Planar button to make these vertices coplanar (which means that all vertices are on the same plane). Doing so positions the selected vertices so they lie in the same plane. This is helpful if you want to build a new polygon face or if you need to flatten an area that is deformed. Polygonal faces need to be coplanar for most rendering and game engines. This button works in all Subobject modes. The X, Y, and Z buttons let you collapse the current object or subobject selection to a single plane lying on the specified axis.

View and Grid Align

The View and Grid Align buttons move and orient all selected vertices to the current active viewport or to the current construction grid. These buttons can also be used in all Subobject modes. This causes all the selected face normals to point directly at the grid or view.

Relax

The Relax button works just like the Relax modifier by moving vertices so they are as far as possible from their adjacent vertices according to the Amount value listed in the Relax caddy interface. The caddy interface also includes an Iterations value, which determines the number of times the operation is performed. You also can select to hold all Boundary and Outer points from being moved. This is a great feature for removing any pinching or areas where the vertices are too close together to work with.

Hide, Copy, and Paste

The Hide button hides the selected subobjects. You can make hidden objects visible again with the Unhide All button.

After selecting several subobjects, you can create a named selection set by typing a name in the Named Selection Sets drop-down list in the main toolbar. You can then copy and paste these selection sets onto other shapes.

At the bottom of the Selection rollout is the Selection Information, which is a text line that automatically displays the number and subobject type of selected items.

Editing Vertex subobjects

When working with the Editable Poly objects, after you select a Vertex Subobject mode (keyboard shortcut, 1) and select vertices, you can transform them using the transform buttons on the main toolbar. All vertex-specific commands are found within the Edit Vertices rollout, shown in Figure 11.13.

FIGURE 11.13

When the Vertex Subobject mode is selected, these vertex commands become available.

Remove

The Remove button lets you delete the selected vertices or other subobjects. You also can delete the selected subobjects with the Delete key, but there is a big difference between the two. The Delete key removes the selected subobjects and all the polygons that are attached to them, thereby creating a hole in the object. The Remove key eliminates the subobject while keeping the surrounding polygons. The Remove button automatically adjusts the surrounding subobjects to maintain the mesh integrity.

Figure 11.14 shows a sphere object with several vertex subobjects selected. The middle image is an Editable Mesh that used the Delete feature, and the right image is an Editable Poly that used the Remove feature.

FIGURE 11.14

Deleting vertices also deletes the adjoining faces and edges, but Remove maintains the mesh.

The Remove button also is available in Edge Subobject mode. If you hold down the Ctrl key when clicking the Remove button when an edge is selected, vertices at either end of the deleted edge are also removed.

Break

You use the Break button to create a separate vertex for adjoining faces that are connected by a single vertex.

In a normal mesh, faces are all connected by vertices: Moving one vertex changes the position of all adjoining faces. The Break button enables you to move the vertex associated with each face independent of the others. The button is available only in Vertex Subobject mode.

Figure 11.15 shows a hedra object. The Break button was used to separate the center vertex into separate vertices for each face. After the Break button is used, the face vertices can be manipulated independently, as the figure shows.

Extrude

The Extrude button copies and moves the selected subobject perpendicular to the surface a given distance and connects the new copy with the original one. This works in several Subobject modes. For example, extruding a single vertex raises a spike off the surface, extruding four edges forms a fenced area like a box with no lid, and extruding a four-sided polygon raises a box from the surface. To use this feature, select a subobject, click the Extrude button, and then drag in a viewport. The cursor changes when it's over the selected subobject. Release the button when you've reached the desired distance. To exit Extrude mode, click the Extrude button again or right-click in the viewport.

Alternatively, you can click the small button next to the Extrude button to open the caddy settings. These settings include extrusion Height and Width values. The Height defines how far from the surface the vertex, edge, border, or polygon is raised; the Width value defines how far the base of the extrusion spreads out at the base. The Height value also can be negative to push the subobject toward the center of the object, creating a dimple.

FIGURE 11.15

You can use the Break button to give each face its own vertex.

Several options are available if a polygon selection is made. The Group option extrudes all selected polygons in the direction of the average of all the normals for the group (the normal runs perpendicular to the face); the Normal Local option moves each individual polygon along its local normal. You can extrude By Polygons, which extrudes each individual polygon along its normal as a separate extrusion.

Figure 11.16 shows a GeoSphere object with all edges selected and extruded. The Group Normal option averages all the normals and extrudes the edges in the averaged direction. The Local Normal option extrudes each edge along its own normal.

FIGURE 11.16

Subobjects can be extruded along an averaged normal or locally.

Weld and Chamfer

Vertices and edges that are close to or on top of one another can be combined together into one using the Weld command. The Weld and Chamfer buttons both have caddy settings that you can access. The Weld caddy includes settings for the weld Threshold value and displays the number of vertices before and after the welding process, which is very useful to check whether a weld was successful.

TIP

If the Weld feature isn't working because its Threshold value is too low, try using the Collapse button.

The Target Weld button lets you click on a single vertex and move the cursor over an adjacent vertex. A rubber band line stretches from the first selected vertex to the target weld vertex and the cursor changes to indicate that the vertex under the cursor may be selected. Clicking on the target vertex welds the two vertices together.

NOTE

When two vertices are welded, the new vertex is positioned at a location that is halfway between both vertices, but when Target Weld is used, the first vertex is moved to the location of the second.

The Chamfer button—which is enabled in Vertex, Edge, and Border Subobject modes—lets you cut the edge off a corner and replace it with a face. Using the caddy settings, you can interactively specify a Chamfer Amount and the number of segments. The caddy settings also include an Open Chamfer option, which cuts a hole in the polygon face instead of replacing it with a new polygon. Figure 11.17 shows two plane objects that have been chamfered with the Open option enabled. The left plane had all its interior vertices selected, and the right plane had a selection of interior edges selected.

FIGURE 11.17

Enabling the Open Chamfer option in the caddy interface removes a polygon instead of replacing it.

Connect

The Connect button can be used to add new edges to subobjects. In Vertex Subobject mode, the Connect button connects selected vertices on the opposite side of a face. If the selected vertices don't share a face, then nothing happens. This provides a quick way to tessellate a selected area.

In Edge and Border Subobject mode, the Connect button adds new edges that connect the two selected edges within a shared face. It also includes a small icon that makes the caddy settings available, which includes the Segments setting. This value is the number of edge segments to add between the selected edges or borders. It also includes Pinch and Slide values. The Pinch value moves the segments closer or farther away from each other; the Slide value moves the segments along the original edge.

Remove Isolated and Unused Map Vertices

The Remove Isolated Vertices button deletes all isolated vertices. Vertices become isolated by some operations and add unneeded data to your file. You can search and delete them quickly with this button. Good examples of isolated vertices are those created using the Create button but never attached to an edge.

The Remove Unused Map Vertices button removes any leftover mapping vertices from the object.

Weight and Crease

The Weight settings control the amount of pull that a vertex has when NURMS subdivision or a MeshSmooth modifier is used. The higher the Weight value, the more resistant a vertex is to smoothing. For edge and border subobjects, the Weight value is followed by a Crease value that determines how visible the edge is when the mesh is smoothed. A value of 1.0 ensures that the crease is visible.

> **NOTE**
> The Crease value is available only in Edge and Border Subobject modes.

Editing Edge subobjects

Edges are the lines that run between two vertices. Edges can be *closed*, which means that each side of the edge is connected to a face, or *open*, which means that only one face connects to the edge. When a hole exists in a mesh, all edges that are adjacent to the hole are open edges. Mesh edges, such as those in the interior of a shape that has been converted to a mesh, can also be *invisible*. These invisible edges appear as dotted lines that run across the face of the polygon. These invisible edges are found only in Editable Mesh objects; Editable Poly objects don't have these invisible edges because each polygon face can have any number of edges.

You can select multiple edges by holding down either the Ctrl key while clicking the edges or the Alt key to remove selected edges from the selection set. You can also copy edges using the Shift key while transforming the edge. The cloned edge maintains connections to its vertices by creating new edges.

Many of the Edge subobject options work in the same way as the Vertex subobject options. Figure 11.18 shows the Edit Edges rollout.

FIGURE 11.18

All the Edge specific commands are available when the Edge Subobject mode is enabled.

Split and Insert Vertex

The Split button adds a new vertex at the middle of the edge and splits the edge into two equal sections. This button is handy when you need to increase the resolution of a section quickly.

The Insert Vertex button lets you add a new vertex anywhere along an edge. The cursor changes to crosshairs when it is over an edge. Click to create a vertex. When in Edge, Border, Polygon, or Element Subobject mode, this button also makes vertices visible.

Bridge Edges

The Bridge button for edges allows you to create a new set of polygons that connect the selected edges. If two edges are selected when the Bridge button is pressed, then they are automatically connected with a new polygon. If no edges are selected, then you can click the edges to bridge after clicking the Bridge button. The selected edges on either side of the bridge can be different in number.

You also can access the caddy settings for the Bridge feature. This caddy offers the options to Use Specific Edges or to Use Edge Selection. The Use Specific Edges option has two buttons for each edge. If you click one of these buttons, you can select an edge in the viewport. The Use Edge Selection option lets you drag a marquee in the viewport to select the edges. The Bridge Edges caddy also includes options for setting the number of Segments, the Taper, Bias, and Smooth values, and a Bridge Adjacent value, which increases the triangulation for angles above the given threshold. A Reverse Triangulation option also is available. For Edge selection, there is only the Smooth value and for a Border selected, two Twist values rotate the bridge segments clockwise or counterclockwise relative to the connected edge and border selections.

Figure 11.19 shows a simple example of some edges that have been bridged. The letters before bridging are on the top and after bridging on the bottom.

Create Shape from Selection

The Create Shape from Selection button creates a new spline shape from selected edges. The Create Shape dialog box appears, shown in Figure 11.20, enabling you to give the new shape a name. You can also select options for Smooth or Linear shape types.

FIGURE 11.19

Selecting two opposite edges and clicking the Bridge button in Edge Subobject mode creates new connecting polygons.

FIGURE 11.20

The Create Shape dialog box lets you name shapes created from selected edge subobjects.

Edit Triangulation

For the Editable Poly object, the Edge, Border, Polygon, and Element subobjects include the Edit Triangulation button, which is labeled Edit Tri. The Edit Triangulation button shows the triangulation edges for all polygon faces and lets you change the internal edges of the polygon by dragging from one vertex to another. When this button is clicked, all hidden edges appear. To edit the hidden edges, just click a vertex and then click again where you want the hidden edge to go. If you're dealing with multiple four-sided polygons, then the Turn button is quicker.

Turn

The Turn button rotates the hidden edges that break up the polygon into triangles (all polygonal faces include these hidden edges). For example, if a quadrilateral (four-sided) face has a hidden edge that runs between vertices 1 and 3, then the Turn button changes this hidden edge to run between vertices 2 and 4. This affects how the surface is smoothed when the polygon is not coplanar.

This button is available for all Subobject modes except Vertex. When enabled, all subobjects that you click on are turned until the button is disabled again. Figure 11.21 shows the top face of a Box object with a hidden edge across it diagonally. The Turn button was used to turn this hidden edge.

TIP
Surfaces can deform only along places where there are edges, so as you create your models be aware of where you place edges and how the edges flow into one another. When building characters, it is important to have the edges follow the muscle flow to deform properly.

FIGURE 11.21

The Turn feature is used to change the direction of edges.

Editing Border subobjects

Editable Poly objects do not need the Face subobject that is found in the Editable Mesh objects because they support polygon faces. Instead, they have a Border subobject. Border subobjects are polygons with no faces that are actually holes within the geometry. The Border rollout is shown in Figure 11.22.

FIGURE 11.22

Many of the Border subobject commands are the same as those for Edges.

Cap

The Cap button causes the existing border selection to be filled in with a single coplanar polygon. After using this feature, the Border subobject is no longer identified as a Border subobject. Be aware that capping a large hole may create a polygon face with multiple edges. Once capped, you may want to use the Connect tool to subdivide the new face into many smaller polygons.

Bridge

The Bridge feature joins two selected Border subobjects with a tube of polygons that connect the two borders. The two selected borders must be part of the same object and need not have an equal number of segments.

The Bridge dialog box, shown in Figure 11.23, lets you specify twist values for each edge, the number of segments, and the Taper, Bias, and Smooth values.

FIGURE 11.23

The Bridge caddy interface for edges lets you specify options such as the number of segments, the Taper, and whether the bridge twists.

Tutorial: Bridging a forearm

The Bridge tool is great for working with two border selections, allowing you to create a smooth set of polygons that flow between them. For this example, you'll create a forearm by bridging a hi-res hand model with a simple cylinder. The polygons of the hand and the cylinder that are to be joined have already been removed.

To create a forearm object by bridging a cylinder with a hand model, follow these steps:

1. Open the Forearm bridge.max file from the Chap 11 directory on the CD.
2. With the body parts selected, open the Modify panel, and select the Border Subobject mode. Then press and hold the Ctrl key, and click on the borders for the hand and cylinder elements.
3. With both facing Border subobjects selected, click the settings icon next to the Bridge button in the Edit Borders rollout.
4. In the Bridge caddy, select the Use Border Selection option and set the Segments value to **6**. Then click the green check mark to accept the settings.

Figure 11.24 shows the resulting forearm object.

FIGURE 11.24

The Bridge feature can be used to quickly connect body parts such as this forearm.

Editing Polygon and Element subobjects

Like the other Subobject modes, Editable Polys can be edited at the polygon and element subobject level. The buttons for these modes are found in the Edit Polygons and Edit Elements rollouts. Figure 11.25 shows the Edit Polygon rollout.

FIGURE 11.25

The Polygon subobjects commands are found in the Edit Polygons rollout.

Insert Vertex

In Polygon and Element Subobject mode, the Insert Vertex button adds a vertex on the surface of the object where you clicked and automatically connects it with edges of the adjacent faces.

Outline and Inset

The Outline button (in Polygon Subobject mode) offsets the selected polygon a specified amount. This increases (or decreases) the size of the selected polygon. The Inset button creates another polygon set within the selected polygon and connects their edges. For both these buttons, caddy settings are available that includes the Outline or Inset Amount values. If multiple polygons are selected, you can inset the selection as a Group or by individual polygons.

Bevel

The Bevel button extrudes the Polygon subobject selection and then lets you size the extruded polygon face. To use this feature, select a polygon, click the Bevel button, drag up or down in a viewport to the Extrusion height, and release the button. Drag again to specify the polygon's outline value. The Outline amount determines the relative size of the extruded face. If multiple polygons are selected, you can apply this feature to the group, to the group using the Local Normal or to individually to each polygon with the By Polygon option.

Figure 11.26 displays a poly dodecahedron. Each face has been locally extruded with a value of 20 and then locally beveled with a value of –10.

FIGURE 11.26

The top faces of this dodecahedron have been individually extruded and beveled.

Flip

The Flip button flips the normal vectors for the selected subobjects. The Flip button is available only in Polygon and Element Subobject modes.

Retriangulate

The Retriangulate button automatically computes all the internal edges for you for the selected subobjects.

Hinge From Edge

The Hinge From Edge button rotates a selected polygon as if one of its edges were a hinge. The angle of the hinge depends on the distance that you drag with the mouse, or you can use the available caddy settings. In the caddy settings, shown in Figure 11.27, you can specify an Angle value and the number of segments to use for the hinged section.

FIGURE 11.27

The Hinge From Edge caddy interface lets you select a hinge.

By default, one of the polygon's edges will be used as the hinge about which the section rotates, but in the caddy settings, you can click the Pick Hinge button and select an edge (which doesn't need to be attached to the polygon). Figure 11.28 shows a sphere primitive with four polygon faces that have been hinged around an edge at the sphere's center.

FIGURE 11.28

Several polygon faces in the sphere have been extruded along a hinge.

Extrude Along Spline

The Extrude Along Spline button can be used to extrude a selected polygon along the spline path. The caddy settings, shown in Figure 11.29, includes a Pick Spline button that you can use to select the spline to use. You can also specify the number of segments, the Taper Amount and Curve, and a Twist value. You also have an option to Align the extrusion to the face normal or to specify the amount to rotate about the normal.

FIGURE 11.29

The Extrude Polygons Along Spline settings dialog box

Taper Curve

Segments   Taper amount

Twist

Rotation

Pick Spline

Extrude Along Spline Align

Tutorial: Building an octopus

The one thing about an octopus that makes it unique is the fact that it has eight tentacles. Creating these tentacles can be easily accomplished with the Extrude Along Spline feature.

To create an octopus using the Extrude Along Spline feature, follow these steps:

1. Open the Octopus.max file from the Chap 11 directory on the website.

    This file includes the base of an octopus created from a squashed sphere primitive that has been converted to an Editable Poly. Eight splines surround the object.

2. Select the octopus object to automatically open the Modify panel. In the Selection rollout, click the Polygon subobject button (keyboard shortcut, 4) and enable the Ignore Backfacing option in the Selection rollout.

3. Click the Shading viewport label, and select the Edged Faces option from the pop-up menu (or press the F4 key).

    This makes the polygons easier to see.

4. Click a single face object at the base of the sphere object that is close to one end of the splines, and click the Extrude Along Spline caddy settings button to open the Extrude Along Spline caddy interface.

5. Click the Pick Spline button, and select the spline to the side of the face. Set the Segments to **6** and the Taper Amount to **−1.0.** Make sure that the Extrude Along Spline Align option isn't selected, and click the green check mark to accept the settings.

6. Repeat Steps 4 and 5 for each spline surrounding the octopus.

7. In the Subdivisions Surface rollout, enable the Use NURMS Subdivision option and set the Display Iterations value to **2** to smooth the entire octopus.

Figure 11.30 shows the resulting octopus.

FIGURE 11.30

The tentacles of this octopus were created easily with the Extrude Along Spline feature.

Surface properties

Below the Edit Geometry rollout are several rollouts of options that enable you to set additional properties such as vertex colors, material IDs, Smoothing Groups, and Subdivision Surface.

Vertex Surface properties

The Vertex Properties rollout in Vertex Subobject mode lets you define the Color, Illumination, and Alpha value of object vertices. The color swatches enable you to select Color and Illumination colors for the selected vertices. The Alpha value sets the amount of transparency for the vertices. After you assign colors, you can then recall vertices with the same color by selecting a color (or illumination color) in the Select Vertices By section and clicking the Select button. The RGB (red, green, and blue) values match all colors within the Range defined by these values.

Polygon and Element Surface properties

For Polygon and Element subobjects, the rollouts shown in Figure 11.31 include Material IDs, Smoothing Groups, and Vertex Colors options. The Material IDs settings are used by the Multi/Sub-Object material type to apply different materials to faces or polygons within an object. By selecting a polygon subobject, you can use these option settings to apply a unique material to the selected polygon. The Select ID button selects all subobjects that have the designated Material ID, or you can select subobjects using a material name in the drop-down list under the Select ID button.

You can find more information on the Multi/Sub-Object material type in Chapter 16, "Creating Compound Materials and Using Material Modifiers."

FIGURE 11.31

Polygon and Elements subobjects includes settings for Material IDs, Smoothing Groups, and Vertex Colors.

You use the Smoothing Groups option to assign a polygon or multiple polygons to a unique smoothing group. To do this, select a polygon and click a Smoothing Groups number. The Select By SG button, like the Select By ID button, opens a dialog box where you can enter a Smoothing Groups number, and all subobjects with that number are selected. The Clear All button clears all Smoothing Groups number assignments, and the Auto Smooth button automatically assigns Smoothing Groups numbers based on the angle between faces as set by the value to the right of the Auto Smooth button.

The Vertex Colors rollout also includes options for setting vertex Color, Illumination, and Alpha values for the selected subobject.

Subdivision Surface

Editable Poly objects include an extra rollout called Subdivision Surface that automatically smoothes the object when enabled. The Subdivision Surface rollout, shown in Figure 11.32, applies a smoothing algorithm known as NURMS, which stands for Non-Uniform Rational MeshSmooth. It produces similar results to the MSmooth button but offers control over how aggressively the smoothing is applied; the settings can be different for the viewports and the renderer.

FIGURE 11.32

The Subdivision Surface rollout includes controls for NURMS subdivision.

Cage Selection color

Cage color

To enable NURMS subdivision, you need to enable the Use NURMS Subdivision option. The Smooth Result option places all polygons into the same smoothing group and applies the MeshSmooth to the entire object. Applying NURMS with a high Iterations value results in a very dense mesh, but the Isoline Display option displays a simplified number of edges, making the object easier to work with. The process of smoothing adds many edges to the object, and the Isoline Display option displays only the isolines. The Show Cage option makes the surrounding cage visible or invisible. The two color swatches to the right of the Show Cage option let you set the color of the cage and the selection.

The Iterations value determines how aggressive the smoothing is. The higher the Iterations value, the more time it takes to compute and the more complex the resulting object. The Smoothness value determines how sharp a corner must be before adding extra faces to smooth it. A value of 0 does not smooth any corners, and a maximum value of 1.0 smoothes all polygons.

CAUTION

Each smoothing iteration quadruples the number of faces. If you raise the number of Iterations too high, the system can become unstable quickly.

The two check boxes in the Render section can be used to set the values differently for the Display and Render sections. If disabled, then both the viewports and the renderer use the same settings. The smoothing algorithm can be set to ignore smoothing across Smoothing Groups and Materials.

If the Show Cage option is enabled (at the bottom of the Edit Geometry rollout), an orange cage surrounds the NURMS object and shows the position of the polygon faces that exist if NURMS is disabled. This cage makes selecting the polygon faces easier.

Tutorial: Modeling a tooth

If you've ever had a root canal, then you know how much pain dental work can cause. Luckily, modeling a tooth isn't painful at all, as you'll see in this example.

To model a tooth using NURMS, follow these steps:

1. Select Create ⇨ Standard Primitives ⇨ Box, and drag in the Top viewport to create a Box object. Set its dimensions to **140 × 180 × 110** with Segments of **1 × 1 × 1**. Then right-click, and select Convert To ⇨ Convert to Editable Poly from the pop-up quad menu.

2. Click the Polygon icon in the Selection rollout to enable Polygon Subobject mode. Then select the Top viewport, and press B to change it to the Bottom viewport. Then click the box's bottom polygon in the Bottom viewport.

3. Click the Select and Scale button (R), and scale the bottom polygon down by 10 percent.

4. Drag over the entire object to select all polygons, and click the Tessellate button in the Edit Geometry rollout once to divide the polygon into more polygons. Then select Edit ⇨ Region ⇨ Window (or click the Window/Crossing button in the main toolbar) to enable the Window selection method, and drag over the bottom of the Box object in the Left viewport to select just the bottom polygons. Click the Tessellate button again.

5. Select the Vertex Subobject mode in the Selection rollout, press and hold the Ctrl key, and select the vertices at the center of each quadrant. Then move these vertices downward in the Left viewport a distance about equal to the height of the Box.

6. Select the Bottom viewport, and press T to change it back to the Top viewport. Select the single vertex in the center of the polygon with the Ignore Backfacing option enabled in the Selection rollout, and drag it slightly downward in the Left viewport.

7. Disable the Ignore Backfacing option in the Selection rollout, and select the entire second row of vertices in the Left viewport. With the Select and Scale tool, scale these vertices toward the center in the polygon in the Top viewport.

8. In the Subdivision Surface rollout, enable the Use NURMS Subdivision option and set the Iterations value to **2**.

Figure 11.33 shows the completed tooth.

FIGURE 11.33

The organic look for this tooth is accomplished with NURMS.

Summary

Meshes are probably the most common 3D modeling types. You can create them by converting objects to Editable Meshes or Editable Poly objects or by collapsing the Stack. Editable Poly objects in 3ds Max have a host of features for editing meshes, as you learned in this chapter. More specifically, this chapter covered the following topics:

- Creating Editable Poly objects by converting other objects or applying the Edit Poly modifier
- The features for editing Editable Poly objects
- How to select and use the various mesh subobject modes
- Editing mesh objects using the various features found in the Edit Geometry rollout
- Changing surface properties using features like NURMS

This chapter provided an introduction to mesh and polygon objects and showed how to edit them, but the next chapter steps it up with coverage of the Graphite Modeling tools, which work only with Editable Poly objects.

Using the Graphite Modeling Tools

IN THIS CHAPTER

Working with the Graphite Modeling tools

Using the Freeform tools

Selecting specific subobjects

Painting with objects

The previous chapter covered everything you need to know about modeling with polygons, but the problem with the polygon workflow is the ping-pong effect of moving back and forth between the current model and the Command Panel. Although you can float the Command Panel or even use the quad menus to access most of these commands, the Autodesk® 3ds Max® 2013 software presents an entirely new workflow based on the new Ribbon interface.

The Ribbon sits conveniently above the viewports, but you can pull off and float any of the individual panels as needed. The Ribbon panels are dynamic, so only those tools that work with the current selection are presented. This places the tools you need right in front of you when you need them.

The Ribbon is populated with all the features for working with Editable Poly objects that are found in the Command Panel, but it also includes many features that cannot be found in the Command Panel. It includes a large number of brand-new tools for selecting and working with polygon objects. These tools collectively are called the Graphite Modeling tools.

The Ribbon also is home to several additional panels of tools that allow you to paint deformations into your models, make unique selections, and select and paint with objects using brushes. The best part of these new tools is that they all eliminate the ping-pong effect. Our necks thank you, Autodesk.

Working with the Graphite Modeling Tools

The Ribbon interface, shown in Figure 12.1, can be turned on and off using a button on the main toolbar or using the Customize ⇨ Show UI ⇨ Show Ribbon menu. When enabled, the toolbar button is highlighted and the Ribbon appears in the same state it was in the last time it was opened. By double-clicking the Ribbon title bar, you can switch among these displays: just the top tabs; just the tabs and panel titles; just the tabs, panel titles, and panel buttons; or the entire panel. This is great if you want to keep the Ribbon around but hide most of the buttons.

You can learn more details on working with the Ribbon interface in Chapter 1, "Exploring the Interface."

When expanded, the Graphic Modeling Tools interface shows several panels of tools. Each of these panels can be separated from the Ribbon and floated independently. You also can rearrange the panels by dragging them to a new position on the Ribbon. If the icons displayed within a panel don't fit, a small downward-pointing arrow offers access to the additional tools.

All the panels and tools that make up the Ribbon are adaptable and change depending on the subobject mode you select. Only the relevant tools are visible, which saves space and makes it easier to locate the tool you want to use.

FIGURE 12.1

The Ribbon holds several panels of modeling tools.

If you right-click the Ribbon's title bar, you can access a pop-up menu of options to hide and show different tabs and panels. There is also a Ribbon Configuration menu that includes options for customizing the Ribbon, loading and saving custom configurations, and switching to a vertically oriented Ribbon.

Using the Polygon Modeling panel

The Graphite Modeling tools are exclusive to Editable Poly objects or objects with the Edit Poly modifier applied. If you select any other type of object with the Ribbon open, all the buttons are disabled. However, two options are available in the Polygon Modeling panel of the Graphite Modeling Tools tab. These options are to Convert to Poly and Apply Edit Poly Mod. These commands convert the selected object to an Editable Poly object or apply an Edit Poly modifier and automatically open the Modify panel.

After an Editable Poly object or an object with the Edit Poly modifier applied is selected, the subobject modes can be selected from the top of the Graphite Modeling Tools panel. The Polygon Modeling panel, shown in Figure 12.2, includes options that work with the Modifier Stack including collapsing the stack, pinning the stack, and moving up and down between modifiers. The Show End Result button lets you see the object with all stack modifiers applied. Another button in this panel lets you toggle the Command Panel off.

FIGURE 12.2

The Ribbon's Polygon Modeling panel includes options for determining which subobjects are selected.

The Polygon Modeling panel also includes buttons for turning on and off subobject selection preview and for ignoring backfacing. It has three Preview buttons, but only one can be enabled at a time. Preview Off disables preview mode. Preview Subobject causes the different subobjects to be highlighted as you move the mouse over them. The Preview Multi button highlights all subobjects regardless of the current subobject mode. For example, if Preview Multi is enabled and the Polygon Subobject mode is enabled, moving the mouse over an edge highlights that edge, and if you select it, Edge Subobject mode is enabled. This provides a nice way to select different subobjects without having to change between the different subobject modes.

The Use Soft Selection button enables you to select a feathered group of subobjects. When enabled, the Soft panel appears, as shown in Figure 12.3.

Using the Soft panel, you can enable Edit mode, which lets you interactively change the Falloff, Pinch, and Bubble settings. When the Edit button is enabled, the cursor looks like two circles. This is Falloff mode, and dragging the mouse changes the amount of falloff for the soft selection. If you click in the viewport, the cursor changes to a peak indicating Pinch edit mode. Click again to access Bubble edit mode, which looks like an upside-down letter U. Continue to click to cycle through these edit modes. These values also can be set in the Soft panel using the various spinner controls.

 Using the Soft Selection features is covered in Chapter 9, "Introducing Subobjects and Modifiers and Using the Modifier Stack."

The Paint button in the Soft panel opens the PaintSS panel, also shown in Figure 12.3, with buttons for blurring, reverting, and opening the Painter Options dialog box, which holds the brush settings. You also can set the Value, Size, and Strength of the soft selection brush.

The Use Edge Distance option lets you select adjacent edges to the current selection rather than using a falloff amount.

FIGURE 12.3

The Soft and PaintSS panels let you control how soft selections are made.

Use Backfaces
Shaded
Lock

Use Edge Distance

Generate Topology

Located at the bottom of the Ribbon's Polygon Modeling panel is an option to Generate Topology. This option opens the Topology pop-up panel showing several patterns. Selecting a pattern applies the selected pattern to the selected object or to the object's subobject selection if you hold down the Shift key.

The Size, Iterations, and Smooth values let you configure the selected pattern. The ScrapVerts button removes any vertices with two edges going to it. The Plane button creates a simple plane object where the S value sets the resolution. Figure 12.4 shows four planes with different topologies applied.

FIGURE 12.4

Changing a plane's topology gives a unique set of faces to work with.

Using the Symmetry tools

The Polygon Modeling panel also holds a link for accessing the Symmetry tools. This command opens the Symmetry Tools dialog box, shown in Figure 12.5. Using this dialog box, you can select an object with the top button and automatically copy the changes on either side of any axis to the opposite side with the + To – and – To + buttons. You also can use the Flip Symmetry button to switch the moved subobjects to the opposite side of the model.

The Copy Selected button lets you copy the position of an entire object or of just the selected vertices and paste them (with the Paste button) onto another object with the same number of vertices.

FIGURE 12.5

The Symmetry Tools dialog box lets you mirror subobject movements across an axis.

Tutorial: Building a Skateboard wheel

Starting with a simple sphere, you can quickly create a symmetrical skateboard wheel using the Symmetry tools.

To create a skateboard wheel, follow these steps:

1. Use the Create⇨ Standard Primitives⇨ Sphere menu and drag in the Front viewport to create a sphere object.
2. Open the Graphite Modeling Tools by clicking its button in the main toolbar. Then select the Convert to Poly option from the Polygon Modeling panel in the Ribbon.
3. Select the Symmetry Tools option in the Polygon Modeling panel, click the Pick Main Model button in the Symmetry Tools dialog box, and pick the sphere object.
4. Select the Vertex subobject mode in the Polygon Modeling panel and drag over the top four rows of vertices in the Top viewport. Then drag with the Select and Move tool downward in the Top viewport.
5. Back in the Symmetry Tools dialog box, enable the Z Axis and click the – To + button to symmetrically copy the moved vertices, as shown in Figure 12.6.

FIGURE 12.6

The skateboard wheel is symmetrical and ready to roll.

Using the Modify Selection panel

The Ribbon also holds tools for making Loop and Ring selections. These tools are found in the Modify Selection panel, shown in Figure 12.7. When a loop or ring is selected, there are also buttons for growing and shrinking the adjacent rows or columns. There are also tools called Loop Mode and Ring Mode that cause the entire edge loop or edge ring to be automatically selected when a single edge is picked when enabled. A text label appears in the viewport when Loop Mode is enabled. Tools called Dot Loop and Dot Ring let an edge loop and edge ring with gaps be selected. The number of loops or rings to skip is set using the Dot Gap value, where a setting of 3 selects one loop and then skips three before selecting another. As a flyout tool under the Dot Loop is Dot Loop Cylinder, which selects the top and bottom edges of a cylinder using the gap settings.

NOTE

The Modify Selection panel is only visible when a subobject mode is enabled.

FIGURE 12.7

The Ribbon's Modify Selection panel includes tools for working with loops and rings.

The Modify Selection panel also includes these tools: Outline, which selects all subobjects surrounding the current selection; Similar, which selects all subobjects that are similar to the current selection, including Edge Count, Edge Length, Face Count, Face Areas, Topology, and Normal Direction; and Fill, which selects all subobjects that are within the selected subobjects or within the current outlined selection. The Fill option lets you pick two vertices that are diagonally across from each other, and then all interior vertices between the two vertices are selected to make a square area.

The StepLoop option lets you select two subobjects within the same loop, and then all subobjects between the two are selected. When Step Mode is enabled, you can pick two subobjects in the same loop and all subobjects between the two are selected. This continues for all additional selections within the same loop until Step Mode is disabled again.

TIP

Using the Shift key, you can select loops of subobjects even more quickly. If you select a single vertex, edge, or polygon, and then hold down the Shift key and click on an adjacent subobject, the entire loop or ring of subobjects is automatically selected.

Editing geometry

When no subobject modes are selected, several Ribbon panels are available, as shown in Figure 12.8. These panels contain many of the same features that are found in the Edit Geometry rollout in the Command Panel. Features contained here include, among many others, the ability to create new subobjects, attach subobjects to the mesh, weld vertices, chamfer vertices, slice, explode, and align. These panels are available regardless of the subobject mode that is selected, but some of these tools are disabled depending on the subobject mode that you select.

Details on using many of the Ribbon tools were discussed in Chapter 11, "Modeling with Polygons."

FIGURE 12.8

The Ribbon includes many general-purpose editing features that are always available.

Many of the tools, such as Relax, MSmooth, Tessellate, PConnect, and Quadrify All, include options for accessing caddy settings by clicking the small arrow to the right of the button. You also can open the caddy settings by holding down the Shift key and clicking the Tool button. These options open a caddy of settings that are located in the viewport next to the selected subobject. These caddies allow you to change the settings and immediately see the results in the viewports. The OK (check mark icon) button applies the settings and closes the dialog box, and the Apply (plus sign icon) button applies the settings and leaves the dialog box open. Similar caddies are available for other subobject-specific buttons such as Extrude, Bevel, Outline, and Inset.

Preserve UVs

The Preserve UVs Settings option opens a dialog box that lets you select a Vertex Color and Texture Channel to preserve. Beneath the Preserve UVs button in the Edit panel is a Tweak button. This button lets you move the UVs for the given object using a paint brush. The value beneath this button is the map channel that you can adjust.

Cutting holes with Paint Connect (PConnect)

Within the Edit panel are the QuickSlice (QSlice) and Cut tools, which work the same as their Command Panel counterparts, but the Edit panel also includes several new methods for cutting and slicing objects.

Another way to slice an object is with the SwiftLoop button. This button lets you click any open space between edges to add a loop between the adjacent edges. Once placed, you can drag to slide the loop to its actual location.

Another handy Ribbon tool for cutting holes is PConnect, which stands for Paint Connect. This tool lets you paint the location of a hole on the surface. As you paint, every edge that you cross is marked, and new edges are created between adjacent marks. By holding down the Shift key, you can make the connections happen in exactly the middle of each edge. Holding down the Ctrl key lets you paint new edges between adjacent vertices. Clicking on a vertex with the Alt key held down removes the vertex, and the Ctrl+Alt keys together removes an edge. The Ctrl+Shift key is used to remove an entire edge loop, and the Shift+Alt keys are used to paint two parallel lines between edges.

TIP

Help videos are available for some tools, such as PConnect. These videos are located in the tooltips for the tool and appear when you hold the mouse over the tool.

NURMS

The Edit panel also includes a NURMS button. NURMS stands for Non-Uniform Rational MeshSmooth. It produces similar results to the MSmooth button, but offers control over how aggressively the smoothing is applied; the settings can be different for the viewports and the renderer. When NURMS is enabled, the Use NURMS panel appears, as shown in Figure 12.9. This panel holds the settings for the NURMS tool and works the same as the options found in the Command Panel.

Tutorial: Smoothing an Ice Cube

NURMS can give a general smoothing to an object, which is just what we need to build an ice cube.

To create an ice cube, follow these steps:

1. Use the Create ⇨ Standard Primitives ⇨ Box menu command and drag in the viewport to create a rectangular-shaped box object.

2. Open the Graphite Modeling Tools by clicking its button in the main toolbar. Then select the Convert to Poly option from the Polygon Modeling panel in the Ribbon.

3. Select the Vertex subobject mode and drag over the lower four vertices in the Perspective viewport. Then drag inward with the Select and Scale tool to make the base of the box smaller than the top.

4. Select the Edge subobject mode and drag over all the edges of the box object, and then Shift+click on the Chamfer button in the Edges panel to open the Chamfer caddy. Enter the value of **1** for the Edge Chamfer Amount and the Connect Edge Segments, and click the Ok button to apply the settings.

5. In the Edit panel, click the NURMS button and set the Iterations value in the Use NURMS panel to 1. This smoothes all the selected edges, as shown in Figure 12.10.

FIGURE 12.9

The Ribbon's Use NURMS panel includes controls for NURMS subdivision.

Show Cage

Isoline Display

Update

Cage Selection Color

Cage Color

FIGURE 12.10

A simple ice cube made smooth with the NURMS feature.

Quadrify All

The Ribbon's Geometry (All) panel also includes a Quadrify All tool, for converting triangles to quads. You have options to Quadrify All, Quadrify Selection, Select Edges from All, and Select Edges from Selection. This is an awesome tool if you like to work with edge loops and edge rings.

Figure 12.11 shows a face model that has been built using triangular faces on the left. Using the Quadrify All command, the face on the right is aligned to much neater rows and columns of four-sided polys. This allows the edge loop features to be used.

FIGURE 12.11

The Quadrify All command greatly simplifies this model, making it easier to work with.

Subdivision panel

MeshSmooth (MSmooth) and Tessellate within the Subdivision panel are buttons for smoothing and tessellating the object. Both the MSmooth and Tessellate tools include caddies, as shown in Figure 12.12. The MSmooth setting for Smoothness rounds all the sharp edges of an object. Tessellation can be done using Edges or Faces, and the Tension setting controls how tight the adjacent faces are.

Use Displacement

The Use Displacement tool opens the Displacement panel, shown in Figure 12.13, when enabled. Using this panel, you can specify the subdivision method that is used and the settings for the displacement.

 You can learn more about using displacement maps in Chapter 16, "Creating Compound Materials and Using Material Modifiers."

FIGURE 12.12

The caddies for the MSmooth and Tessellate buttons let you interactively set the Smoothness and Tension values.

Tension

Edge/Face option

Smoothness

Separate by Material ID

Separate by Smoothing Groups

FIGURE 12.13

The Displacement panel includes all the subdivision settings.

Editing Vertex subobjects

When working with the Editable Poly objects, after you select a Vertex subobject mode (keyboard shortcut, 1) and select vertices, you can transform them using the transform buttons on the main toolbar. All vertex-specific commands are found within the Vertices panel, shown in Figure 12.14, but some new tools also appear in the Geometry (All) panel including Collapse, Detach, and Cap Poly.

Editing Edge and Border subobjects

All the edge editing tools are located in the Edges and Borders panels, shown in Figure 12.15. Many of the Edge subobject options work in the same way as the Vertex subobject options.

FIGURE 12.14

When the Vertex subobject mode is selected, these vertex commands become available.

12

FIGURE 12.15

All the Edge specific commands are available when the Edge subobject mode is enabled. Many of the Border subobject commands are the same as those for Edges.

Insert Vertices

Editing Polygon and Element subobjects

Like the other subobject modes, Editable Polys can be edited at the Polygon and Element subobject level. The buttons for these modes are found in the Polygons and Elements panels. Figure 12.16 shows the Ribbon's Polygons and Elements panels.

FIGURE 12.16

The Polygon and Element subobjects commands are found in the Polygons and Elements panels.

Mirror Axis   Clone

GeoPoly

The GeoPoly button moves the vertices of the selected polygon to make a regular polygon whose vertices are all equally spaced. The shape of the resulting polygon depends on the number of vertices included in the polygon face.

Hinge

The Hinge button rotates a selected polygon as if one of its edges were a hinge. The angle of the hinge depends on the distance that you drag with the mouse, or you can use the available caddy. By default, one of the polygon's edges will be used as the hinge about which the section rotates, but in the caddy, you can click the Pick Hinge button and select an edge (which doesn't need to be attached to the polygon).

Tutorial: Adding a handle to a mug

Creating a cup is fairly easy using the Lathe modifier, but adding the handle is another story. It could be created as half a torus and Boolean connected to the cup, but this example shows how to use the poly modeling features to hinge the handle on.

To add a handle to a mug, follow these steps:

1. Open the Mug.max file from the Chap 12 directory on the CD.

   This file includes a simple cup created using the Lathe modifier, and it has been converted to an Editable Poly object. Open the Graphite Modeling Tools by clicking on its button in the main toolbar.

2. Select the mug object. Then select the QSlice button from the Edit panel, click in the Front viewport about one-third up from the bottom of the cup, orient the line to be horizontal, and click again to slice the mug horizontally.

3. Click the Cut button in the Edit panel, and cut edges into each corner of one of the rectangular polygon faces near the bottom of the cup to create an eight-sided polygon for the mug handle. Then cut another horizontal edge in the middle of the cup directly above the cut polygon to be the hinge edge for the handle. Right-click in the viewport to exit the Cut tool.

4. Select the Polygon subobject mode in the Polygon Modeling panel, and click the interior of the cut polygon just created. Shift-click the Hinge button in the Polygons panel to open the caddy settings. In the Hinge From Edge caddy, click the Pick Hinge button and click the midline edge that was cut above the cut polygon, set the Segments to 10 and the Angle to 185, and then click the green accept caddy button.

Figure 12.17 shows the resulting handle on the mug. You can add a NURMS command to smooth the mug handle.

Mirroring elements

Within the Elements panel are commands for mirroring the current selection about the X, Y, or Z axes. These commands move the element to the opposite side, but clicking the Clone button creates a clone of the selected element.

FIGURE 12.17

The handle for this mug was created with the Hinge feature.

Surface properties

In the Properties panel are several settings for additional properties such as vertex colors, material IDs, and Smoothing Groups. For Polygon and Element subobjects, the Properties panel, shown in Figure 12.18, includes Material IDs and Smoothing Groups options.

FIGURE 12.18

The Properties panel includes settings for Material IDs, Smoothing Groups, and Vertex Colors.

Using the Freeform Tools

The second tab in the Graphite Modeling Tools includes an assortment of Freeform tools for sculpting and modeling surfaces as if working with clay. These tools are divided into three panels—PolyDraw, Paint Deform, and Defaults. The PolyDraw panel is shown in Figure 12.19.

FIGURE 12.19

Using the PolyDraw tools

The various PolyDraw tools let you create and extend the surface subobjects using tools that work like a common drawing program.

Drag

The Drag tool lets you move selected subobjects around by simply dragging them with the mouse. Clicking a subobject automatically selects it and lets you drag it to a new position. Holding down the Shift key or the Ctrl key lets you drag edges or polygons regardless of the subobject mode that is selected. Pressing Shift+Ctrl keys together lets you drag entire edge loops, and the Alt key lets you move the subobject in a direction that is perpendicular to the view axis, which is great for dragging subobjects off to the side of an object.

Conform

The Conform brushes let you push all the vertices of the selected object toward a selected underlying object. When the Freeform panel is first accessed, you can select the Draw On: Surface option to the right of the Step Build button. When Surface is selected, the Pick button becomes active. Using this button, you can select the object to which you want the selected object to be conformed.

With the object to conform to selected, you can select the Conform button and change the options for this brush using the Conform Options panel, shown in Figure 12.20. Within the Conform Options panel, you can set the Strength, Falloff, and Conform values. The Conform value sets the rate at which the vertices move toward the conform object. Higher values make the vertices move immediately, and smaller values, such as 0.1, cause the movement to be gradual. The Strength Percent value sets how much of the full strength is applied.

FIGURE 12.20

The Conform panel holds the options for using the Conform brushes.

The Mirror option causes the vertices' movement to be applied equally on either side of the mirror axis. The Vertex Normals/View drop-down list lets you control how the vertices move. The View option causes the vertices to move toward the target into the current view, and the Vertex Normals option moves the vertices along their normals toward the conform object. You also have options to move only the selected vertices, to Ignore Backfacing vertices, to select the mirror and freeze axes, and to freeze specific selected edges so no movement happens.

Within the PolyDraw panel are four brushes for defining how the vertices are transformed. The Conform Move brush moves vertices under its brush range. Vertices also can be rotated and scaled using the Conform Rotate and Conform Scale brushes, and the Conform Relax brush smoothes the moved vertices by moving them gradually toward their original position.

Step Build

The Step Build tool lets you click to place new vertices on the surface of the object. The location of these new vertices depends on the current Grid, on the current object's Surface, or within the Selection using the On selections located to the right of the Step Build button. If you select the On: Surface option, you can use the Pick button to select the object whose surface you want to create vertices on. After freestanding vertices are created, you can hold down the Shift key and drag over these new vertices to create a polygon. The Ctrl key lets you remove polygons, and the Alt key lets you remove vertices. With these controls, you can quickly remove and rebuild polygons to create new shapes.

Extend

The Extend tool works on border subobjects and lets you add new polygons to fill the hole by dragging on the border vertices. If you press and hold the Shift key while dragging an edge, you can pull the edge away to create a new polygon. Dragging with the Shift+Ctrl keys lets you drag two adjacent edges out. The Ctrl key and a click deletes the polygon, and dragging with the Alt key held down moves the polygon perpendicular to the view axis.

Optimize

The Optimize tool quickly collapses subobjects. Click an edge with this tool to remove it and to combine its two end points into one. The Shift key is used to target weld two vertices into a single one, and the Alt key removes vertices. The Shift+Ctrl key combo can remove an entire edge loop at once.

Draw On and Pick

The Draw On drop-down list gives you three options for specifying the object that is drawn on: Grid, Surface, and Selection. If Surface is selected, you can use the Pick button to choose the surface object. You also can set an Offset, which is the distance above the surface on which the drawn objects appear.

TIP

It is best to keep a non-zero offset value when drawing on the surface of an object, especially if the drawn object overlaps an edge. This keeps the surfaces from interpenetrating.

Tutorial: Matching a road to a rolling terrain

If you've created a rough rolling landscape using a Plane object and the Noise modifier, matching a road running across the surface can be tricky if you have to select and move each individual vertex. Instead, you can use the Conform brushes to move the vertices so they match the underlying hills.

To conform a road to an underlying terrain, follow these steps:

1. Open the Conforming road.max file from the Chap 12 directory on the CD.

2. With the road selected, click the Graphite Modeling Tools button on the main toolbar to make the Ribbon appear, and select the Freeform tab.

3. Select the Draw On: Surface option from the drop-down list to the right of the Step Build button, click the Pick button, and click the hilly object. Then select the straight road object, and click the Conform button.

4. In the Conform Options panel, set the Full Strength to 10, the Falloff to 70, select the View option and change the viewport to the Top view.

5. Select the Conform Move brush, and click and slowly rotate the brush in small circles over the road object to move its vertices to conform to the hilly landscape, as shown in Figure 12.21.

FIGURE 12.21

The Conform Move brush is used to make the road match the underlying terrain.

Shapes and Solve Surface

The Shapes tool lets you draw polygonal shapes directly on the surface of an object. Figure 12.22 shows three polygons drawn on the surface of a torus. You also can delete drawn polygons with the Ctrl key. The completed polygons likely will have multiple vertices, but you can reduce the polygons to tris and quads using the Solve Surface button.

FIGURE 12.22

Using the Shapes tool, you can draw polygons that conform to the surface of the underlying object.

Splines

The Splines tool lets you draw spline objects that follow the surface of the underlying object. The Ctrl key can be used to delete drawn splines.

Surface, Topology, Strips, and Branches

The Surface tool covers the object with a mesh of quads by painting over the object. You can delete any polygon by clicking it with Ctrl key held down. The Topology tool lets you draw a series of parallel lines followed by a set of perpendicular lines to form quads. The Auto Weld option automatically welds vertices together to form a mesh. The Ctrl key extends a line from the nearest end point.

The Strips tool draws a consecutive row of quads that flow across the surface of the object. The Shift key extends the strip from the nearest edge. The Branches tool extends a tapered branch from a single polygon. For the branches, you can set a Taper amount; the Minimum Distance value sets the distance between the segments. This is useful for creating tentacles, as shown in Figure 12.23.

Tutorial: Carving a pumpkin

When carving a pumpkin for Halloween, you should follow the round curvature of the pumpkin or the face will look skewed. In 3ds Max, this is easy to accomplish using the Freeform tools and selecting the pumpkin object as the Draw-On surface.

FIGURE 12.23

Using the Branches tool, you can drag out extending arms from polygons.

To draw the face details on the surface of a pumpkin, follow these steps:

1. Open the Pumpkin face.max file from the Chap 12 directory on the CD. This simple pumpkin model has been converted to an Editable Poly object.

2. Open the Graphite Modeling tools, click the Freeform tab, and select the Surface option as the Draw-On shape by selecting it from the drop-down list to the right of the Step Build tool. Then click the Pick button located under the selected Draw-On object, and click the pumpkin object.

3. Click the Shapes button, and draw the eyes, nose, and mouth for the jack-o-lantern. Right-click to exit Shapes mode.

Figure 12.24 shows the resulting face that follows the curvature of the pumpkin.

Using the Paint Deform tools

The Paint Deform tools let you sculpt the surface of an object by pushing, pulling, and modeling the object in organic ways like it was clay. Whenever any of the tools on the Paint Deform panel, shown in Figure 12.25, are selected, its settings for the brush's Size and Strength (and sometimes Offset, depending on the tool) appear in the Paint Options panel to the side of the Paint Deform panel.

Shift/Shift Rotate/Shift Scale

The Shift tool lets you drag all subobjects within the brush radius, and all subobjects within the falloff radius are moved to a less extent. You can control the brush size and falloff in the Options panel, or you can press and hold the Ctrl key and drag to alter the brush's radius. The Shift+drag changes the brush's falloff indicated by the inner white circle.

The Shift Rotate and Shift Scale brushes are used to rotate and/or scale all the vertices within the brush's range.

FIGURE 12.24

The PolyDraw tools let you draw on the surface of an object.

FIGURE 12.25

The Paint Deform tools are used to sculpt an object's surface with gradual changes.

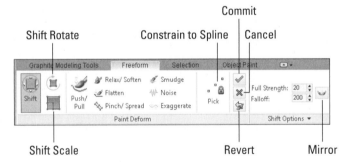

Push/Pull

The Push/Pull tool also has Size and Strength values, but it is different in that the brush follows the surface of the object. Dragging over an area pulls the vertices within the brush's radius outward, and holding down the Ctrl key pushes the vertices inward. The Shift key relaxes the area under the brush.

Relax/Soften

The Relax/Soften brush removes any extreme changes in the surface such as hard edges of a cube. The Alt key lets you relax the surface without changing its volume, and the Ctrl key causes the surface to revert to its previous state.

Flatten and Pinch/Spread

The Flatten brush pulls any bends out of the mesh causing the object to be working into a flat plane. The Ctrl key causes the object to revert to its previous state, and the Shift key accesses the Relax/ Soften brush. The Pinch/Spread tool causes vertices to be pulled in closer to each other, and holding down the Alt key has the opposite effect and pushes them away.

Smudge, Noise, and Exaggerate

The Smudge tool pushes the surrounding vertices away from the center of the brush. Dragging over the same vertices multiple times moves them each time. Holding down the Alt key causes the vertices to be moved only along the surface and not to be moved along the normal. The Noise tool randomly moves the vertices about to create a random noise pattern. The Exaggerate tool pushes vertices farther in the current direction to emphasize the details.

Constrain to Spline

If you want more control over the precise surface area that is changed using the Paint Deform tools, you can select the Constrain to Spline option and use the Pick button to select a spline near the surface area to change.

Revert

At any point, you can use the Revert tool to gradually change the object back to its last saved point. You can set a save point by clicking the Commit button, which looks like a green check mark. The Cancel button (a red X) removes the recent changes from the object.

Tutorial: Sculpting a head model

One of the huge benefits of these deformation tools is that you can quickly repurpose existing models to create a new and unique model. In this tutorial, we'll push and pull the skin of an existing head model to give it a new look.

To sculpt a head model using the Paint Deform tools, follow these steps:

1. Open the Zygote sculpt.max file from the Chap 12 directory on the CD. This is the head of a detailed Zygote character model copied once for reference and converted to an Editable Poly.

2. Open the Graphite Modeling Tools, and click the Freeform tab. Then select the right head object and choose the Shift tool in the Paint Deform panel. This makes the Shift Options panel appear. Before you begin using the tool, enable the Mirror option in the Shift Options panel and select X as the Mirror Axis. This causes the model to remain symmetrical as you work on either side.

3. With the Shift tool, set the Full Strength to **25** and the Falloff to **50**, and then slowly start to work on the model by dragging the areas around the mouth and nose toward the center axis to thin the model. Continue to work around the eyes and eyebrows to give the character a unique look.

4. After making the larger changes, select the Relax/Soften tool in the Paint Deform panel and slowly brush over the rough areas to smooth them out.

5. As a final step, apply the TurboSmooth modifier to the model to give it a smooth finish.

Figure 12.26 shows the new sculpted face, which looks much different than the original shown on the left.

FIGURE 12.26

The Paint Deform tools let you sculpt an existing model to give it a new look.

Using the Selection Tools

The next tab offers several additional Selection tools. These tools make it possible to locate specific subobjects by looking for certain criteria such as concavity, normals, and symmetry. Figure 12.27 shows the panels for this tab. These tools are only available if a subobject mode is selected.

FIGURE 12.27

The Selection tab includes panels for selecting specific subobject selections.

Selecting Tops, Open, and Non-Quads

For the Polygon and Element subobject modes, the first three tools in the Selection tab are the Tops, Open, and Non-Quads tools. The Tops tool selects all vertices resulting from the extruded sections. This quickly lets you grab all extended sections and extend or reduce them as needed. The Open tool selects all open borders, and the Non-Quads tool finds all polygons that are not quadrilaterals including all tris and all polygons with more than four corners. This is a valuable tool when working with edge loops.

For Edge and Border subobject modes, there is a Hard option that locates all edges that aren't smoothed between adjacent faces. In all subobject modes, there is also a Patterns options that selects subobjects using a pre-defined pattern such as Checker.

> **NOTE**
>
> The Non-Quads option is only available when the Polygon or Element subobject mode is selected.

Copying and pasting selections

The Stored Selections panel lets you copy a selection of subobjects into two available stores. These copied selections can be restored at any time by clicking the Paste button. Additional buttons let you combine the two selection stores, subtracting one from another and getting only the intersecting selection between the two. The Clear button removes the selection from the store.

The Copy and Paste Sets buttons, in the Sets panel, let you copy a selection set from the main toolbar and paste it as needed.

Selecting by criteria

The remaining selection criteria let you locate subobjects using a variety of different methods.

By Surface, Normal, and Perspective

The By Surface panel lets you specify a degree of concavity, and the tool locates all the concave areas in the current object. Negative values also can be used to find convex regions. Figure 12.28 shows the selected concave regions.

FIGURE 12.28

The By Surface tool can be used to find the concave regions of an object.

The By Normal panel lets you choose an axis and a value, and all subobjects within the Angle value for the selected axis are selected. This is a great way to quickly determine which polygons are facing away from the current view. The Invert button can find all normals pointing toward the negative axis side.

The By Perspective panel selects those polygons that are within the Angle value to the view axis. If the Outline button is enabled, then only the outer borders of polygons are selected. Click the Select button to see all the selected polygons meeting the criteria.

By Random, Half, and Pivot Distance

The By Random panel lets you randomly select polygons within the current object. You can set to randomly select a given number or a percentage of the total. The Select button makes the random selection, or you can randomly select within the current selection. Additional buttons grow or shrink the selection. Figure 12.29 shows a random selection.

FIGURE 12.29

The By Random tool can be used to make a random selection of polygons.

The By Half panel lets you quickly choose half of the available polygons as determined by axis. The Invert Axis button lets you choose the negative side of the axis. The By Pivot Distance chooses those polygons that are farthest away from the current pivot point, creating a circular selection area. Reducing the distance value creeps the selection closer to the pivot's location.

By View, Symmetry, and Numeric

The By View panel selects those polygons closest to the current view camera. Increasing this value extends the selection farther into the scene, as shown in Figure 12.30.

Regardless of the current selection, you can make it symmetrical about any of the three axes using the By Symmetry panel. The By Numeric panel, which is only available in Vertex and Polygon modes, lets you select all vertices that have a given number of edges or polygons that have a given number of sides. The Equal, Less Than, and Greater Than buttons are used to mathematically determine those subobjects.

By Color

The By Color panel, available in Vertex mode, lets you locate any vertices that have a given color or Illuminate vertex color setting according to the specified RGB values.

FIGURE 12.30

The By View tool is used to select those polygons closest to the current view.

Using the Object Paint Tools

The last tab is the Object Paint tab. This tab includes tools that let you select and paint with a specific object. This is great for spreading objects around a scene. The tab also includes several options for randomizing the size, orientation, and placement of the painted objects.

Selecting an object to paint with

Within the Paint Objects panel, shown in Figure 12.31, are two paint modes for painting and filling. These buttons are toggles, and they turn the paint mode on and off. While each mode is active, you can switch between objects and subobjects as needed.

FIGURE 12.31

The Paint Objects panel lets you paint or fill with objects.

Before you can begin painting with an object, you need to select an object using the Pick Object button. Simply click the Pick Object button and select an object in the scene. The selected object is highlighted and added to the list of paint objects. If you select the Pick Object button again, you can add another object to the list of paint objects. Clicking the Edit Object List button opens the list of current paint objects, as shown in Figure 12.32. Using this list, you can change the order of the items, pick new items, add items using the Select Objects dialog box, add the selected scene object, or remove the selected item from the list.

NOTE

Edits to the Paint Objects list can be made only while the Paint and Fill modes are disabled.

FIGURE 12.32

The Paint Objects list lets you manage the objects that you're painting with.

Painting with objects

After a paint object is selected, you can click the Paint button to enable Paint mode and then drag in the viewport, as shown in Figure 12.33. Each stroke drawn with the brush lays down a new curve. The Undo command can be used to remove the last stroke, but all strokes are not added to the scene until the Commit button in the Brush Settings panel is clicked. The Cancel button removes all strokes drawn since the last commit.

CAUTION

Painting with objects dramatically increases the overall polygon count of the scene, especially if you are painting with a complex object. Try to keep the paint object as simple as possible to avoid unwieldy scenes.

Before a painted set of objects is committed to the scene, you can use the settings in the Brush Settings panel, shown in Figure 12.34, to change the alignment, spacing, rotation, and scale of the objects. You have several options for randomly scattering the objects. The default alignment for the painted objects is to match the picked object, or you can align the object to the X, Y, or Z axis or flip it about the specified axis with the Flip Axis button.

FIGURE 12.33

After an object is selected, simply drag in the viewport to paint with the selected object.

FIGURE 12.34

The Brush Settings panel lets you change the position, rotation, and scale of the painted objects.

The Spacing value lets you change how far away each object is from its neighbor. The Scatter settings let you move the objects in the U, V, or W directions. The Rotation setting uniformly rotates all the objects together, or you can allow random rotations by clicking the small arrow to the right of each axis and enabling the Random option.

For the Scale settings, you can enable the Lock Axis (Uniform Scaling) option to scale all objects evenly, or you can enable the Random option to randomly scale the objects within a set range of values. The Ramp option scales the objects gradually from the start of the stroke to the end of the stroke to a given size. Figure 12.35 shows several lines of pyramids with different settings. The top line is the default. The second line has an altered spacing value, the third line is oriented about the Y axis, and the final line uses a ramp scaling.

FIGURE 12.35

Painted objects can be altered by spacing, orientation, and scaling.

Painting with multiple objects

If you have multiple objects in the Paint Objects list, you can choose which objects to paint with using the option in the Paint Objects panel. The first option is to paint with just the most recently picked object. The second option is to paint with all objects in order, and the last option is to randomly paint with all objects. Figure 12.36 shows each of these options.

Painting on objects

The Object Paint feature lets you paint on the default construction grid, on the selected object, or on the entire scene. These options are available in the Paint Objects panel. Figure 12.37 shows painting some cones on a simple sphere. The cones are aligned by default to the surface normals of the sphere.

When the Scene option is selected, the painted objects are placed on the default grid unless a scene object is encountered, and then it is placed on top of the scene object. The Offset value can be used to move the painted objects onto or off of the surface of the underlying object.

FIGURE 12.36

When painting with multiple objects, you can choose to paint the objects in order or randomly.

FIGURE 12.37

Objects also can be painted on the surface of another object in the scene.

Using the Paint Fill mode

The Paint Fill mode allows you to place the paint object at regular intervals along a selected edge. Before the Paint Fill mode is enabled, you need to have a paint object selected and an edge or an edge loop selected. Once selected, the Paint Fill button simply places the paint object along the edge. The

Fill Number value determines the number of objects that are placed along the selected edge loop. Figure 12.38 shows a sphere filled with several cone objects using this mode.

FIGURE 12.38

The Paint Fill mode places objects along a selected edge loop.

Painting with animated objects

If the object that you are painting with has some animation associated with it, you can specify an off-set for the motion of the object. The options for how the animated object plays are in the Paint Objects panel and includes Consecutive and Random options. The Consecutive options plays the animation on each painted object in order offset by the By Frames value. For example, if you have a box that spins and you set the By Frames value to 2, the first box in the painted line starts spinning at frame 0 and the second starts at frame 2, and so on. The Random option randomly starts the animation for each object.

Tutorial: Painting a scar

Although medical companies are searching for an easy way to remove scars, we're going to use the Object Paint feature to add one to our character.

To add a character scar using the Object Paint feature, follow these steps:

1. Open the Futureman with scar.max file from the Chap 12 directory on the CD.
2. Click the Graphite Modeling Tools button on the main toolbar to make the Ribbon appear, and select the Object Paint tab.
3. Click the Pick Object button in the Paint Objects panel, and then click the scar object. Select the Paint On option, and select the futureman's face object.
4. Click the Paint button, and drag across futureman's face to place the scar.

5. In the Brush Settings panel, enable the Lock Axis (Uniform Scale) button, set the Scale X value to **17**, and drag the Spacing value until the scar is equally spaced out at a value around 11.5. Figure 12.39 shows the applied scar.

6. Click the Commit button in the Brush Settings panel to apply the scar to the face.

FIGURE 12.39

Applying scars on the surface of a character is easy with the Object Paint feature.

Summary

When modeling with polygons, the Graphite Modeling tools become your best friends. With all the tools at your fingertips, you can model faster and with greater ease. In addition to the base modeling features, the Freeform modeling tools, the Selection tools, and the Object Paint features make modeling a delight. More specifically, this chapter covered the following topics:

- Accessing and using the Graphite Modeling Tools
- Modeling in the various subobject modes
- Using the Freeform tools to sculpt surfaces
- Making specific selections with the Selection tools
- Painting with objects and filling edges with the Paint Objects panel

The next chapter covers a miscellaneous set of modeling objects collectively called the Compound objects.

Working with Compound Objects

So far, we've covered a variety of modeling types, including shapes, meshes, and polys. The Compound Objects subcategory includes several additional modeling types that don't seem to fit anywhere else. As you will see in this chapter, these modeling types provide several new and unique ways to model objects, such as working with Boolean objects, morphing objects, and cutting an object into several pieces.

The compound objects would be the miscellaneous set of modeling types that are very good at one specific task. Most compound objects are identified in the Modifier Stack by the compound object name, but if the object needs more editing, you can convert it to an Editable Poly and use the various polygon tools to finish the work.

Understanding Compound Object Types

The Compound Objects subcategory includes several unique object types. You can access these object types with the Create ⇨ Compound menu or by clicking the Geometry category button in the Create panel and selecting Compound Objects in the subcategory drop-down list. All the object types included in the Compound Objects subcategory are displayed as buttons at the top of the Create panel. They include the following:

- **Morph:** Consists of two or more objects with the same number of vertices. The vertices are interpolated from one object to the other over several frames.
- **Scatter:** Randomly scatters a source object about the scene. You also can select a Distribution object that defines the volume or surface where the objects scatter.
- **Conform:** Wraps the vertices of one object onto another. You can use this option to simulate a morph between objects with different numbers of vertices.

- **Connect:** Connects two objects with open faces by joining the holes with additional faces.
- **BlobMesh:** Creates a metaball object that flows from one object to the next like water.
- **ShapeMerge:** Lets you embed a spline into a mesh object or subtract the area of a spline from a mesh object.
- **Boolean:** Created by performing Boolean operations on two or more overlapping objects. The operations include Union, Subtraction, Intersection, and Cut.
- **Terrain:** Creates terrains from the elevation contour lines like those found on topographical maps.
- **Loft:** Sweeps a cross-section shape along a spline path.
- **Mesher:** Creates an object that converts particle systems into mesh objects as the frames progress. This makes assigning modifiers to particle systems possible.
- **ProBoolean:** Replaces the original Boolean compound object with the ability to perform Boolean operations on multiple objects at a time.
- **ProCutter:** Cuts a single stock object into multiple objects using several cutter objects.

> **NOTE**
>
> When two or more objects are combined into a single compound object, they use a single object material. The Multi/Sub-Object Material type can be used to apply different materials to the various parts.

Morphing Objects

Morph objects are used to create a Morph animation by interpolating the vertices in one object to the vertex positions of a second object. The original object is called the *Base object,* and the second object is called the *Target object*. The Base and Target objects must have the same number of vertices. One Base object can be morphed into several targets.

> **CAUTION**
>
> To ensure that the Base and Target objects have the same number of vertices, create a copy of one object and modify it to be a target. Be sure to avoid such modifiers as Tessellate and Optimize, which change the number of vertices.

To morph a Base object into a Target, select the Base object and select Create ⇨ Compound ⇨ Morph. Then click the Pick Target button in the Pick Targets rollout, shown in Figure 13.1, and select a Target object in the viewport. The cursor changes to a plus sign when it is over an acceptable object. Unavailable objects (that have a different number of vertices) cannot be selected. Pick Target options include Copy, Instance, Reference, and Move. (The Move option deletes the original object that is selected.) The Target object appears under the Current Targets rollout in the Morph Targets list.

FIGURE 13.1

A Morph rollout lets you pick targets and create morph keys.

Each Morph object can have several Target objects. You can use the Pick Target button to select several targets, and the order in which these targets appear in the list is the order in which they are morphed. To delete a Target object, select it from the list and click the Delete Morph Target button. Beneath the list is a Name field where you can change the name of the selected Target object.

Creating Morph keys

With a Target object name selected in the Morph Targets list, you can drag the Time Slider to a frame and set a Morph key by clicking the Create Morph Key button found at the bottom of the rollout. This option sets the number of frames used to interpolate among the different morph states.

> **NOTE**
> If the Morph object changes dramatically, set the Morph Keys to include enough frames to interpolate smoothly.

If a frame other than 0 is selected when a Target object is picked, a Morph Key is automatically created.

Morph objects versus the Morpher modifier

The Autodesk® 3ds Max® 2013 software includes two different ways to morph an object. You can create a Morph object or apply the Morpher modifier to an existing object. The Morph object is different from the Morph modifier, but the results are the same; however, some subtle differences exist between these two.

A Morph object can include multiple Morph targets, but it can be created only once. Each target can have several Morph keys, which makes it easy to control. For example, you could set an object to morph to a different shape and return to its original form with only two Morph keys.

The Morpher modifier, on the other hand, can be applied multiple times and works well with other modifiers, but the control for each modifier is buried in the Modifier Stack. The Parameters rollout options available for the Morpher modifier are much more extensive than for the Morph object, and they include channels and support for a Morph material.

 You can find more information on the Morph modifier in Chapter 26, "Using Animation Layers and Animation Modifiers."

For the best of both worlds, apply the Morph modifier to a Morph object.

Tutorial: Morphing a woman's face

Although this example is fairly simple, it demonstrates a powerful technique that can be very helpful as you begin to animate characters. One of the key uses of morphing is to copy a character and move it about to create a new pose. You can then morph between the different poses to create smooth actions, gestures, or face motions.

To morph a woman's face, follow these steps:

1. Open the Greek woman head morph.max file from the Chap 13 directory on the CD.

    This file includes a woman's head. All objects have been attached to the facial object to make working with it easy.

2. Select the facial object, and hold down the Shift key while dragging to the right in the Top viewport. In the Clone Options dialog box that opens, select Copy and set the Number of Copies to **2**. Name one copy **frown face** and the other **smiling face**.

3. Select the object named "smiling face," and open the Modify panel. Zoom in around the mouth area, and enable Vertex subobject mode. Enable the Ignore Backfacing option in the Selection rollout, and turn on the Use Soft Selection option in the Soft Selection rollout with a Falloff value of **1.4**. Then select the vertex at the corner of the mouth, and drag it upward in the Front viewport to make the woman smile. Repeat this action for the vertex on the opposite side of the mouth. Click the Vertex subobject button again to exit subobject mode.

4. Select the original head object, and choose Create ⇨ Compound ⇨ Morph to make this object into a morph object. In the Pick Targets rollout, select the Copy option and click the Pick Target button. Then click the "frown face" object, or press the H key, and select it from the Pick Object dialog box. Then click the "smiling face" object. Both targets are now added to the list. Click the Pick Target button again to disable pick mode.

5. In the Morph Targets list, select the "frown face" object and click the Create Morph Key button. Then drag the Time Slider (below the viewports) to frame 50, select the "smiling face" object in the Morph Targets list, and press the Create Morph Key button again.

6. Click the Play Animation button (in the Time Controls section at the bottom of the 3ds Max window) to see the morph. The woman's head object morphs when you move the Time Slider between frames 0 and 50. Figure 13.2 shows different stages of the morph object.

FIGURE 13.2

A woman's face being morphed to a smile

Creating a Terrain Object

The Terrain object is a great object that enables you to create terrains from splines representing elevation contours. These contour splines can be created in 3ds Max or imported using a format like AutoCAD's DWG. If the splines are created in 3ds Max, make sure that each contour spline is a separate object. The splines all must be closed splines. If all the splines have an equal number of vertices, then the resulting terrain object is much cleaner. You can ensure this by copying and scaling the base spline.

To create a terrain, create splines at varying elevations, select all the splines, and click the Terrain button. The Terrain button is available only if closed splines are selected. You can use the Pick Operand button in the Pick Operand rollout to select additional splines to add to the Terrain object. All splines in the object become operands and are displayed in the Operands list.

The Form group includes three options that determine how the terrain is formed: Graded Surface, Graded Solid, and Layered Solid. The Graded Surface option displays a surface grid over the contour splines; the Graded Solid adds a bottom to the object; and the Layered Solid displays each contour as a flat, terraced area. The Stitch Border option causes polygons to be created to close open splines by creating a single edge that closes the spline. The Retriangulate option optimizes how the polygons are divided to better represent the contours.

The Display group includes options to display the Terrain mesh, the Contour lines, or Both. You also can specify how you want to update the terrain.

The Simplification rollout lets you alter the resolution of the terrain by selecting how many vertical and horizontal points and lines to use. Options include using all points (no simplification), half of the points, a quarter of the points, twice the points, or four times the points.

Coloring elevations

The Color by Elevation rollout, shown in Figure 13.3, displays the Maximum and Minimum Elevations for the current Terrain object. Between these is a Reference Elevation value, which is the location where the landmass meets the water. Entering a Reference Elevation and clicking the Create Defaults button automatically creates several separate color zones. You can add, modify, or delete zones using the Add, Modify, or Delete Zone buttons.

13

FIGURE 13.3

The Color by Elevation rollout lets you change the color for different elevations.

You can access each color zone from a list. To change a zone's color, select it and click the color swatch. You can set colors to Blend to the Color Above or to be Solid to Top of Zone.

Tutorial: Creating an island with the Terrain compound object

In this tutorial, you create a simple island. The Color by Elevation rollout makes distinguishing the water from the land easy.

To create an island using the Terrain object, follow these steps:

1. Select Create ⇨ Shapes ⇨ Ellipse, and drag in the Top view to create several ellipses of various sizes representing the contours of the island.

   The first ellipse you create should be the largest, and the ellipses should get progressively smaller.

2. In the Left view, select and move the ellipses up and down so the largest one is on the bottom and the smallest one is on top. You can create two smaller hills by including two ellipses at the same level.

> **NOTE**
>
> If you create the ellipses in the proper order from largest to smallest, you can use the Select All command. If not, then select the splines in the order that they'll be connected from top to bottom before clicking the Terrain button.

3. Use the Edit ⇨ Select All (Ctrl+A) menu command to select all the ellipses, and select Create ⇨ Compound ⇨ Terrain.

   The ellipses automatically join together. Joining all the ellipses forms the island.

4. In the Color by Elevation rollout, select a Reference Elevation of **5** and click the Create Defaults button.

This automatically creates color zones for the island. The elevation values for each zone are displayed in a list within the Color by Elevation rollout. Selecting an elevation value in the list displays its color in the color swatch.

5. Select each elevation value individually, and set all Zones to Blend to the Color Above option for all zones, except for the Zone with the lightest blue.

   This creates a distinct break between the sea and the land of the island.

Figure 13.4 shows the final terrain.

FIGURE 13.4

A Terrain island created with the Terrain compound object

Working with BlobMesh Objects

BlobMesh objects are simple spheres. If you have only one of them, they aren't interesting at all, but if you get them together, they run into each other much like the metal mercury. This makes them an ideal choice for modeling flowing liquids and soft organic shapes.

BlobMesh objects are used as sets of objects rather than as individual objects. If you click the BlobMesh button in the Compound Objects subcategory and then create a BlobMesh in the viewports, it appears as a sphere with the radius set using the Size parameter. The real benefit comes from clicking the Pick or Add buttons below the Blob Objects list and selecting an object in the scene.

> **NOTE**
> The Pick, Add, and Remove buttons become enabled only in the Modify panel.

The object that is picked is added to the Blob Objects list, and each vertex of the object gets a BlobMesh added to it. If the BlobMesh objects are large enough to overlap, then the entire object is covered with these objects, and they run together to form a flowing mass of blobs.

Setting BlobMesh parameters

The Size value sets the radius of the BlobMesh object. Larger sizes result in more overlapping of surrounding objects. For particle systems, the Size is discounted, and the size of the particles determines the size of the BlobMesh objects. The Tension value sets how loose or tight the surface of the BlobMesh object is. Small tension values result in looser objects that more readily flow together.

The Evaluation Coarseness value sets how dense the BlobMesh objects will be. By enabling the Relative Coarseness option, the density of the objects changes as the size of the objects changes. The Evaluation Coarseness values can be different for the viewport and the render engine.

When a BlobMesh object is selected and applied to the picked object, each vertex has an object attached to it, but if you apply a selection modifier, such as the Mesh Select modifier, to the picked object, then only the selected subobjects get a BlobMesh object. You also can use the Use Soft Selection option to select those subobjects adjacent to the selected subobjects. The Minimum Size value is the smallest-sized BlobMesh object that is used when Soft Selection is enabled.

The Large Data Optimization option is a quicker, more efficient way of rendering a huge set of BlobMesh objects. The benefit from this method comes when more than 2,000 BlobMesh objects need to be rendered. If the viewport updates are slow because of the number of BlobMesh objects, you can select to turn them Off in Viewport.

Tutorial: Creating icy geometry with BlobMesh

The BlobMesh object can be combined with a geometry object to create the effect of an object that has been frozen in ice. Using the BlobMesh's Pick feature, you can select a geometry object, and a BlobMesh is placed at each vertex of the object. I suggest using an object with a fairly limited number of vertices.

To create the effect of an object covered in ice, follow these steps:

1. Open the Icy sled.max file from the Chap 13 directory on the CD.

    This file includes a sled model created by Viewpoint Datalabs.

2. With the sled selected, choose Create ⇨ Compound ⇨ BlobMesh, and create a simple BlobMesh by simply clicking in the Top viewport. Set the Size value to **6.0**. Then right-click to exit BlobMesh mode, open the Modify panel, click the Pick button in the Parameters rollout, and select the sled object.

3. Select Rendering ⇨ Material Editor ⇨ Compact Material Editor, and select the first sample slot. Change the Diffuse color to a light blue, and set the Opacity to **20**. Then increase the Specular Level to **90** and the Glossiness to **40**, and apply the material to the BlobMesh001 object by dragging the sample slot material and dropping it on the BlobMesh001 object.

4. Render the Perspective viewport to see the final result. The sled is embedded in ice.

Figure 13.5 shows the resulting sled, all ready to be defrosted.

FIGURE 13.5

BlobMesh objects can be used to cover objects in ice.

Working with ProBoolean and ProCutter Objects

The original Boolean compound object worked well enough for combining, subtracting, and intersecting objects, but it had some limitations that have been overcome with the ProBoolean and ProCutter compound objects. The original Boolean could combine only two operands together, but the ProBoolean object can perform multiple Boolean operations simultaneously. ProBoolean also can subdivide the result into quad faces. The results of the ProBoolean and ProCutter objects are much cleaner and more accurate than the original Boolean object.

The original Boolean compound object still is available for backward compatibility, but if you perform a new Boolean operation, you really should use the ProBoolean object.

Using ProBoolean

When two objects overlap, you can perform different Boolean operations on them to create a unique object. The ProBoolean operations include Union, Intersection, Subtraction, Merge, Attach, and Insert. Two additional options are available: Imprint and Cookie.

The Union operation combines two objects into one. The Intersection operation retains only the overlapping sections of two objects. The Subtraction operation subtracts the overlapping portions of one object from another. The Merge operation combines objects without removing the interior faces and adds new edges where the objects overlap. Figure 13.6 shows the original object and the first four possible Boolean operators.

> **NOTE**
>
> Unlike many CAD packages that deal with solid objects, the Booleans in 3ds Max are applied to surfaces, so if the surfaces of the two objects don't overlap, all Boolean operations (except for Union) will have no effect.

FIGURE 13.6

Object before any operations and with Boolean operations: Union, Intersection, Subtraction, and Merge with the Imprint option enabled

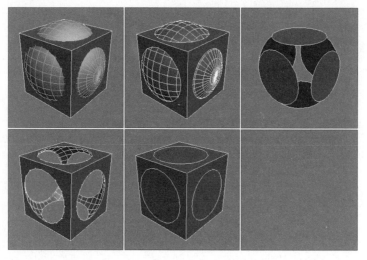

The Attach operation combines the objects like Union but keeps them as separate elements of the same compound object. For example, if you were to look inside a compound object created with Union, you would not see the interior polygons of the combined object, but with Attach, the interior polygons would still be there.

The Insert operation subtracts the second object from the first and then combines the two objects into one. If the subtracted volume makes a dent or hole into the first object, then that hole remains after the two are combined, but if the second surface has access to the first object through a hole, then the first surface covers the subtracted volume. In Figure 13.7, two tube objects have been overlapped with a box object. The left tube is capped at the bottom, forming a closed volume, but the right tube is open at the bottom. When made into a ProBoolean object with the Insert operations, the closed volume is subtracted, but the open volume is not.

The Cookie option causes the operation to cut the original object without adding any of the faces from the picked object to the original object. The Imprint option causes the outline of the operation to appear on the original object.

FIGURE 13.7

The Insert operation maintains closed volumes only when subtracted.

All Boolean operations are added in the order in which they are applied to a list in the Parameters rollout. You can select any of the operations in the list at any time and change the operation. For example, if you select the Subtraction operation from the list and then change the operation type to Union and click the Change Operation button, the Subtraction changes to a Union. With an operation selected in the list, the Extract Selected button restores the original object. When using this button, you can choose to Remove, Copy, or Instance the operation.

The order in which the operations are applied affects the result. You can reorder the operations in the list by selecting an operation, choosing its position in the list, and clicking the Reorder Ops button.

You also can apply Boolean operations to shapes using the Boolean operators available for Editable Meshes in the Geometry rollout. Chapter 10, "Drawing and Editing 2D Splines and Shapes," covers these 2D Boolean operators.

The materials that get applied to a ProBoolean result can be set to use the Operand Material or to retain the Original Material. If you use the Apply Operand Material with the subtraction operation, then the surface that touches the picked object retains the removed object's material, and the rest of the object has the original object's material. If the Retain Original Material option is selected, then the entire result gets the original object's material.

In the Advanced Options rollout are options for updating the scene and for reducing the complexity of the object. The Decimation value is the percentage of edges to remove from the result. If you plan to smooth the object or convert it to an Editable Poly object, you want to enable the Make Quadrilaterals option, which causes the polygon reduction to avoid triangles in favor of quads. You also can set the Quad Size, and you can select how planar edges are handled.

> **NOTE**
> If you plan to deform the mesh as part of a skinned object or a cloth simulation, the resulting mesh must be clean or the deformation will have problems.

Tutorial: Creating a keyhole

What was it that Alice saw when she looked through the keyhole? The ProBoolean feature is the perfect tool for cutting a keyhole through a doorknob plate.

To use the ProBoolean object to create a keyhole, follow these steps:

1. Open the Doorknob.max file from the Chap 13 directory on the CD.
2. Select the panel object, and choose the Create ⇨ Compound ⇨ ProBoolean menu command. In the Parameters rollout, select the Subtraction option.
3. In the Pick Boolean rollout, click the Start Picking button and select the Box and Cylinder objects positioned where the keyhole should be. Then right-click to exit pick mode. A keyhole has been cut into the panel object.

Figure 13.8 shows the finished keyhole.

FIGURE 13.8

A keyhole built using the ProBoolean object

Using ProCutter

The original Boolean compound object included a Cut option. This feature has been replaced with ProCutter, which offers many more features than the original option. ProCutter allows you to cut a single object (known as the Stock object) with multiple cutter objects.

You can pick both the Stock and Cutter objects using the buttons found in the Cutter Picking Parameters rollout. You have four options with each selection: Reference, Move, Copy, or Instance. The Auto Extract Mesh option automatically replaces the selected stock object with the extracted result. The Explode by Elements option works only when the Auto Extract Mesh option is enabled. It separates each cut element into an object.

Within the Cutter Parameters rollout, you can select from three Cutting Options. The Stock Outside Cutter option keeps the portion of the stock object that is on the outside of the cutter. The Stock Inside Cutter option is the opposite, keeping the stock portion inside the cutters. The Cutters Outside Stock option maintains those portions of the cutters that are outside of the stock.

All selected cutters and stock objects are added to a list in the Cutter Parameters. Using the Extract Selected button, you can restore any cutter or stock object that has been operated on as a Copy or Instance. Materials and Decimation also work the same as for ProBoolean objects.

> **TIP**
> The ProCutter features are helpful for dividing an object that will be animated exploding into pieces.

Tutorial: Creating a jigsaw puzzle

The ProCutter is useful for creating destructive scenes such as shattering glass to pieces and breaking down buildings, but it also can be used for constructive cutting, such as creating a jigsaw puzzle.

To use the ProCutter compound object to divide an object into a jigsaw puzzle, follow these steps:

1. Open the ProCutter puzzle.max file from the Chap 13 directory on the CD. This file includes a simple box mapped with a scenic image and several extruded lines that mark the jigsaw puzzle's edges.

2. Select one of the extruded lines that mark where the cuts should be (known as a cutter), and choose the Create ⇨ Compound ⇨ ProCutter menu command.

3. Then click the Pick Cutter Objects button, and select all the remaining cutter objects. In the Cutter Parameters rollout, enable the Stock Outside Cutter along with the Stock Inside Cutter options. Select the Retain Original Material option also.

4. In the Cutter Picking Parameters rollout, enable the Auto Extract Mesh and Explode By Elements options; then select the Pick Stock Objects button, and choose the Box object in the viewport. Each separate piece is given a different object color and clears its material.

5. To reapply the materials, open the Compact Material Editor and drag the image material in the first sample slot onto each puzzle piece.

> **NOTE**
> If you don't want to see the cutter lines after the puzzle is cut, you can select and hide them.

Figure 13.9 shows the final puzzle with one piece moved away from the others.

FIGURE 13.9

A puzzle cut using the ProCutter compound object

Summary

Compound objects add several additional modeling types to your bulging modeling toolkit. From morph objects to complex deformed lofts, you can use these special-purpose types to model many different objects. This chapter covered these topics:

- The various compound object types
- Morphing objects with the same number of vertices
- Creating a Terrain object using splines
- Using the BlobMesh object to simulate water
- Modeling with the ProBoolean and ProCutter objects

If you've had enough of the plain dull gray objects, then you'll be happy to get to materials in the next chapter. Finally, some color.

Part IV

Applying Materials and Textures

Creating and Applying Standard Materials with the Slate Material Editor

IN THIS CHAPTER

Understanding Material properties

Working with the Slate Material Editor

Using standard materials

Learning the various shaders

Exploring the Material rollouts

Applying materials to scene objects

Materials are used to dress, color, and paint objects. Just as materials in real life can be described as scaly, soft, smooth, opaque, or blue, materials applied to 3D objects can mimic properties such as color, texture, transparency, shininess, and so on. In this chapter, you learn the basics of working with materials and all the features of the Slate Material Editor.

After you're familiar with the Material Editor, this chapter gives you a chance to create some simple original materials and apply them to objects in the scene. The simplest material is based on the Standard material type, which is the default material type.

Understanding Material Properties

Before jumping into the Material Editor, let's take a close look at the type of material properties that you will deal with. Understanding these properties will help you as you begin to create new materials.

Until now, the only material property that has been applied to an object has been the default object color, randomly assigned by the Autodesk® 3ds Max® 2013 software. The Material Editor can add a whole new level of realism using materials that simulate many different types of physical properties.

> **NOTE**
> Many of these material properties are not visible until the scene is rendered.

Colors

Color is probably the simplest material property and the easiest to identify. However, unlike the object color defined in the Create and Modify panels, there isn't a single color swatch that controls an object's color.

Consider a basket of shiny, red apples. When you shine a bright blue spotlight on them, all the apples turn purple because the blue highlights from the light mix with the red of the apple's surface. So, even if the apples are assigned a red material, the final color in the image might be very different because the light makes the color change.

Within the Material Editor are several different color swatches that control different aspects of the object's color. The following list describes the types of color swatches that are available for various materials:

- **Ambient:** Defines an overall background lighting that affects all objects in the scene, including the color of the object when it is in the shadows. This color is locked to the Diffuse color by default so that they are changed together.
- **Diffuse:** The surface color of the object in normal, full, white light. The normal color of an object is typically defined by its Diffuse color.
- **Specular:** The color of the highlights where the light is focused on the surface of a shiny material.
- **Self-Illumination:** The color that the object glows from within. This color takes over any shadows on the object.
- **Filter:** The transmitted color caused by light shining through a transparent object.
- **Reflect:** The color reflected by a raytrace material to other objects in the scene.
- **Luminosity:** Causes an object to glow with the defined color. It is similar to Self-Illumination color but can be independent of the Diffuse color.

NOTE
Standard materials don't have Reflectivity and Luminosity color swatches, but these swatches are part of the Raytrace material.

If you ask someone the color of an object, he or she would respond by identifying the Diffuse color, but all these properties play an important part in bringing a sense of realism to the material. To get a sense of the contribution of each color, try applying very different, bright materials to each of these color swatches and notice the results.

TIP
For realistic materials, your choice of colors depends greatly on the scene lights. Indoor lights have a result different from an outdoor light like the sun. You can simulate objects in direct sunlight by giving their Specular color a yellow tint and their Ambient color a complementary, dark, almost black or purple color. For indoor objects, make the Specular color bright white and use an Ambient color that is the same as the Diffuse color, only much darker. Another option is to change the light colors instead of changing the specular colors.

Opacity and transparency

Opaque objects are objects that you cannot see through, such as rocks and trees. Transparent objects, on the other hand, are objects that you can see through, such as glass and clear plastic. The materials in 3ds Max include several controls for adjusting these properties, including Opacity and several Transparency controls.

Opacity is the amount that an object refuses to allow light to pass through it. It is the opposite of transparency and is typically measured as a percentage. An object with 0 percent opacity is completely transparent, and an object with 100 percent opacity doesn't let any light through.

Transparency is the amount of light that is allowed to pass through an object. Because this is the opposite of opacity, transparency can be defined by the opacity value. Several options enable you to control transparency, including Falloff, Amount, and Type. These options are discussed later in this chapter.

Reflection and refraction

A *reflection* is what you see when you look in the mirror. Shiny objects reflect their surroundings. By defining a material's reflection values, you can control how much it reflects its surroundings. A mirror, for example, reflects everything, but a rock won't reflect at all.

Reflection Dimming controls how much of the original reflection is lost as the surroundings are reflected within the scene.

Refraction is the bending of light as it moves through a transparent material. Think of how the background image is distorted when you look through a fishbowl full of water. The amount of refraction that a material produces is expressed as a value called the Index of Refraction. The *Index of Refraction* is the amount that light bends as it goes through a transparent object. For example, a diamond bends light more than a glass of water, so it has a higher Index of Refraction value. The default Index of Refraction value is 1.0 for objects that don't bend light at all. Water has a value of 1.3, glass a value of around 1.5, and solid crystal a value of around 2.0.

Shininess and specular highlights

Shiny objects, such as polished metal or clean windows, include highlights where the lights reflect off their surfaces. These highlights are called *specular highlights* and are determined by the Specular settings. These settings include Specular Level, Glossiness, and Soften values.

The Specular Level is a setting for the intensity of the highlight. The Glossiness determines the size of the highlight: Higher Glossiness values result in a smaller highlight. The Soften value thins the highlight by lowering its intensity and increasing its size.

A rough material has the opposite properties of a shiny material and almost no highlights. The Roughness property sets how quickly the Diffuse color blends with the Ambient color. Cloth and fabric materials have a high Roughness value; plastic and metal Roughness values are low.

> **NOTE**
> Specularity is one of the most important properties that we sense to determine what kind of material the object is made from. For example, metallic objects have a specular color that is the same as their diffuse color. If the colors are different, then the objects look like plastic instead of metal.

Other properties

3ds Max uses several miscellaneous properties to help define standard materials, including Diffuse Level and Metalness.

The Diffuse Level property controls the brightness of the Diffuse color. Decreasing this value darkens the material without affecting the specular highlights. The Metalness property controls the metallic look of the material. Some properties are available only for certain material types.

> **NOTE**
> Before proceeding, you need to understand the difference between a material and a map. A *material* is an effect that permeates the 3D object, but most *maps* are 2D images (although procedural 3D maps also exist) that can be wrapped on top of the object. Materials can contain maps, and maps can be made up of several materials. In the Material Editor, materials appear as blue nodes, and maps appear as green nodes in the View pane. Usually, you can tell whether you're working with a material or a map by looking at the default name. Maps show up in the name drop-down list as Map and a number (Map #1), and materials are named a number and Default (7- Default).

Working with the Slate Material Editor

The Material Editor is the interface with which you define, create, and apply materials. You can access the Material Editor by choosing Rendering ⇨ Material Editor ⇨ Slate Material Editor, clicking the Material Editor button on the main toolbar, or using the M keyboard shortcut.

> **NOTE**
> The M keyboard shortcut opens the Material Editor to the last mode that was used, either Slate or Compact.

The Material Editor comes in two flavors: regular and extra strength. The Material Editor from earlier versions of 3ds Max is still there, but now it is called the Compact Material Editor, and the new Material Editor interface is called the Slate interface. You can choose either from the Rendering ⇨ Material Editor menu or switch between them using the Modes menu in the Material Editor.

> **NOTE**
> Although the Slate Material Editor and the Compact Material Editor share most controls, the Slate Material Editor has more features and is the focus of our discussion. The Compact Material Editor is maintained for backward compatibility and is easier to use for existing users.

Using the Slate Material Editor controls

The Slate Material Editor, shown in Figure 14.1, consists of four panels: the Material/Map Browser panel, the Node View panel, the Navigator panel, and the Parameter Editor panel. Of these panels, only the Material View panel is open at all times. The others can be closed and reopened using the Tools menu. If you drag the panel title away from the interface, the panel floats independently. If you drag a floating panel over the interface, several arrow icons appear. Dropping a panel on one of these arrows positions the floating panel to the side of the panel in the direction of the arrow. This interface gives you the power to set up the Slate Material Editor just as you want.

> **TIP**
>
> You also can use a keyboard shortcut to show or hide the various panels: O for the Material/Map Browser, P for the Parameter Editor, and N for the Navigator panel. But note that these shortcuts work only if the Keyboard Shortcut Override Toggle is enabled on the main toolbar.

FIGURE 14.1

The Slate Material Editor has four unique panels.

At the top of the default Slate Material Editor window is a menu of options. The menu commands found in these menus offer most of the same functionality as the toolbar buttons, but the menus are often easier to find than the buttons with which you are unfamiliar.

Below the menus are several toolbar buttons. These buttons are defined in Table 14.1.

14

341

TABLE 14.1 **Slate Material Editor Buttons**

Toolbar Button	Name	Description
	Select Tool	Enables a tool for selecting, moving, and working with material trees and nodes.
	Pick Material From Object	Enables you to select a material from an object in the scene and load the material into the Node View panel.
	Put Material to Scene	If a new material is created with the same name as an applied material, then this command replaces the applied material with the new one.
	Assign Material to Selection	Applies the selected object with the selected material.
	Delete Selected	Removes any modified properties and resets the material properties to their defaults. The selected node is also deleted from the Node View panel.
	Move Children	Locks the position of the children nodes so they move with the material block. If disabled, the children nodes remain in place as the material block moves.
	Hide Unused Nodeslots	Condenses the material block so that only the nodes that are being used are visible.
	Show Shaded Material in Viewport, Show Realistic Material in Viewport	Displays 2D material maps and hardware maps on objects in the viewports.
	Show Background in Preview	Displays a checkered background image (or a custom background) behind the material, which is helpful when displaying a transparent material.
	Material ID Channel	Sets the Material ID for the selected material.
	Layout All - Vertical, Layout All - Horizontal	Aligns and places all material blocks in a vertical column or a horizontal row.
	Layout Children	Moves and orients all children nodes to be next to their respective material blocks.
	Material/Map Browser	Opens the Material/Map Browser panel, which displays all the available materials and maps.
	Parameter Editor	Toggles the Parameter Editor panel on and off.
	Select by Material	Selects all objects using the current material and opens the Select Objects dialog box with those objects selected.

Loading the Material Node View panel

When the Slate Material Editor is first opened, the Node View panel is blank. You can add material nodes to the node view by double-clicking them in the Material/Map Browser or by dragging them from the Material/Map Browser onto the Node View panel. This loads the selected node into the Node View.

If your scene has some objects with materials already applied, you can use the Material ⇨ Pick from Object menu or select the Pick Material from Object (the eyedropper) tool on the toolbar and click an object in the viewport. The applied material for that object is loaded in the Node View. If the selected object doesn't have an applied material, then nothing is loaded.

You can also get all the applied materials in the current scene using the Material ⇨ Get All Scene Materials menu. This loads all applied materials. If all the scene materials make it tough to find what you are looking for, you can use the Edit ⇨ Clear View menu to clear the Node View panel. This doesn't remove any assigned materials; it only clears the Node View panel.

Navigating the Material Node View panel

All current materials for the open scene are displayed as material node blocks in the Material Node View panel of the Slate Material Editor. At the top of each material node block are the material name and type. You can change the material name using the Name field at the top of the Parameter Editor or by right-clicking the material name and selecting Rename from the pop-up menu. Beneath the material name are all the parameters that are available for this material. Each of these parameters has a corresponding parameter in the Parameter Editor panel. These parameters are displayed when you double-click a node in the Node View panel.

If you drag the material title (where the name is located), you can move the material node block around within the Node View panel. You also can reduce the size of the material block by clicking the Hide Unused Nodeslots toolbar button. If multiple material blocks are present, you can use the Layout All buttons to align them in a column or a row. Figure 14.2 shows some material node blocks.

FIGURE 14.2

The Node View panel can hold multiple material blocks.

Minimized material node   Enlarged material preview

Material node output socket

The Navigator panel shows all the material blocks and provides a way to quickly drag to view other sets of nodes. The red outline corresponds to the viewable area in the Node View panel. Navigating the Node View panel is accomplished using the navigation tools at the lower-right corner of the Slate Material Editor. These tools include a Zoom value list, and Pan, Zoom, Zoom Region, Zoom Extents, Zoom Extents Selected, and Pan to Selected tools.

TIP

You also can pan the view by dragging with the middle mouse button and zoom by scrubbing the mouse scroll wheel, just like you can in the viewports.

In addition to the navigation tools in the lower-right corner of the Material Editor, the View menu includes several options for navigating the Node View panel, including options to Show/Hide the Grid (G), show scrollbars, and options to lay out all nodes (L).

If you right-click the Node View tab, you can access a menu to rename or delete the current view. You can also create a new view. This new view appears as another tab at the top of the Material Editor. The new view is navigated independently of the other views and can hold a completely different set of materials. With several views created, you can drag the tabs to reorder the panels as desired.

Selecting and applying materials

A material node block can be selected by simply clicking its title. When selected, the title bar is outlined in white in both the Material Node View and Navigator panels. Selecting a material node doesn't make its parameters appear in the Parameters panel, but if you double-click a material node, its parameters are loaded in the Parameters panel. This node is identified by a dashed white line in the Node View and Navigator panels.

NEW FEATURE

The ability to view the parameters for a material node that is different than the selected node is new to 3ds Max 2013.

Selected materials are applied to the object selected in the viewport using the Assign Material to Selection button in the Material Editor toolbar, using the Material⇨Assign Material to Selection (A) menu or by using the right-click pop-up menu. You can also apply a material to a scene object by dragging on the material node's output socket and dropping the material on a viewport object whether it is selected or not.

TIP

Although they aren't listed in the menu options, you can use the Undo (Ctrl+Z) and Redo (Ctrl+Y) commands to undo and redo actions done in the Slate Material Editor.

Holding down the Ctrl key while clicking material node blocks or dragging an outline over multiple nodes lets you select multiple nodes at once. When multiple nodes are selected, you can move them all together within the Node View panel. Pressing the Delete key deletes the selected material node.

The Node View panel is a temporary placeholder for materials and maps. An actual scene can have hundreds of materials. By loading a material into a material node, you can change its parameters, apply it to other objects, or save it to a library for use in other scenes. When a file is saved, all materials in the Material Editor are saved with the file.

Changing the material preview

Next to the material name is a preview of the material. If you double-click the preview, the preview is enlarged to show more detail. You can change the Sample Type object displayed in the material block to be a sphere, cylinder, or box using the Preview Object Type menu in the right-click pop-up menu.

The right-click pop-up menu also includes options to show the background in the preview, to show a backlight, and to change the preview tiling for applied maps. The Open Preview Window option opens the material preview in a separate window, as shown in Figure 14.3. Within this floating window, you can resize the preview to be larger, revealing more details. The Show End Result button shows the material with all materials and maps applied.

> **TIP**
> The Material Preview panel also can be docked to the Material Editor.

FIGURE 14.3

Material previews can be opened in a floating window.

Show End Result

When you assign a material to an object in the scene, the material becomes "hot." A *hot material* is automatically updated in the scene when the material parameters change. Hot materials have corner brackets displayed around their material preview. These brackets turn white when the object with that material is selected in the viewport. You can "cool" a material by making a copy of its material node. To copy a material node, simply drag it with the Shift key held down. This detaches the material node from the object in the scene to which it is applied, so that any changes to the material aren't applied to the object.

Whenever a material is applied to an object in the scene, the material is added to a special library of materials that get saved with the scene. Materials do not need to be seen in the Node View panel to be in the scene library. You can see all the materials included in the scene library in the Material/Map Browser by selecting the Scene Materials rollout.

Selecting objects by material

If you want to select all the objects in your scene with a specific material applied (like the shiny, gold material), select the material in the Node View panel and click the Select by Material button in the toolbar or use the Utilities ⇨ Select Objects by Material menu. This command opens the Select Objects dialog box with all the objects that have the selected material applied. Clicking the Select button selects these objects in the viewport.

Setting Slate Material Editor preferences

You open the Slate Material Editor Options dialog box, shown in Figure 14.4, by selecting the Options ⇨ Preferences menu. The top option lets you choose how the nodes are oriented. You also can select to hide the Additional Parameters and mr Connection set of parameters, use anti-aliased fonts, and set the number of default materials in a multi-subobject material and the grid spacing. The Bitmap Editor Path lets you set where to look for maps. By default, this is set to the maps directory where 3ds Max is installed, but you can change it to your current project folder.

FIGURE 14.4

The Slate Material Editor Options dialog box offers many options for controlling the Slate Material Editor window.

Removing materials and maps

If you accidentally apply an unwanted material to an object, you can replace the material with another material by applying a new material onto the object. If you want to view the object color within the viewport, open the Display panel in the Command Panel, and in the Display Color rollout, select the Object color option for Wireframe and Shaded. The Material Color options display the material color in the viewports.

If you apply a material or map to an object that doesn't look just right and tweaking it won't help, you can always return to square one by removing the material or any mappings that have been applied to the object. The tool to remove materials and maps is the UVW Remove utility. You can access this utility by clicking the More button in the Utilities panel in the Command Panel and selecting UVW Remove from the list of utilities.

This utility includes a single rollout that lists the number of objects selected. It also includes two buttons. The UVW button removes any mapping coordinates from the selected objects, and the Materials button removes any materials from the selected objects. This button restores the original object color to the selected objects. Alternatively, you can select the Set Gray option, which makes the selected object gray when the materials are removed.

Using utilities

Within the Utilities menu are several additional commands. The Render Map command lets you render out the selected map node. Once rendered, you can save the results to a file. The Render Map dialog box also lets you render out animated maps.

The Clean MultiMaterial utility removes any unused maps from the material tree and the Instance Duplicate Map identifies and uses instances of duplicate maps throughout the scene. Both these features can be used to reduce the file size of the scene file.

 More information on using the Clean MultiMaterial utility is covered in Chapter 16, "Creating Compound Materials and Using Material Modifiers." The Instance Duplicate Map utility is presented in Chapter 15, "Adding Material Details with Maps."

Using the Fix Ambient utility

Standard material types always have their Ambient and Diffuse colors locked together. If you have older files with unlocked Diffuse and Ambient colors, the Fix Ambient utility can be used to locate and fix all materials in the scene with this condition. To access this utility, open the Utilities panel, click the More button, and select the Fix Ambient utility. Clicking the Find All button opens a dialog box that lists all materials in the scene with unlocked Diffuse and Ambient color values.

Tutorial: Coloring Easter eggs

Everyone loves spring with its bright colors and newness of life. One of the highlights of the season is the tradition of coloring Easter eggs. In this tutorial, you use virtual eggs—no messy dyes and no egg salad sandwiches for the next two weeks.

To create your virtual Easter eggs and apply different colors to them, follow these steps:

1. Open the Easter eggs.max file from the Chap 14 directory on the CD.

   This file contains several egg-shaped objects.

2. Open the Slate Material Editor by choosing Rendering ⇨ Material Editor ⇨ Slate Material Editor (or press the M key).

3. Double-click the Standard material in the Material/Map Browser. Double-click the material node in the Node View, and click the Diffuse color swatch in the Parameter Editor panel. From the Color Selector that appears, drag the cursor around the color palette until you find the color you want and then click OK.

4. In any viewport, select an egg and then click the Assign Material to Selection button in the Material Editor, or you can simply drag from the material node's output socket to the viewport object.

5. Repeat Steps 3 and 4 for all the eggs.

Figure 14.5 shows the assortment of eggs that we just created.

FIGURE 14.5

These eggs have been assigned materials with different Diffuse colors.

Using the Standard Material

Standard materials are the default 3ds Max material type. They provide a single, uniform color determined by the Ambient, Diffuse, Specular, and Filter color swatches. Standard materials can use any one of several different shaders. *Shaders* are algorithms used to compute how the material should look, given its parameters.

Standard materials have parameters for controlling highlights, opacity, and self-illumination. They also include many other parameters sprinkled throughout many different rollouts. With all the various rollouts, even a Standard material has an infinite number of possibilities.

Using Shading Types

3ds Max includes several different shader types. These shaders are all available in a drop-down list in the Shader Basic Parameters rollout at the top of the Parameter Editor panel in the Material Editor. Each shader type displays different options in its respective Basic Parameters rollout. Figure 14.1 shows the basic parameters for the Blinn shader. Other available shaders include Anisotropic, Metal, Multi-Layer, Oren-Nayar-Blinn, Phong, Strauss, and Translucent Shader.

The Material/Map Browser holds all the various material types. Other material types are covered in Chapter 16, "Creating Compound Materials and Using Material Modifiers."

The Shader Basic Parameters rollout also includes several options for shading the material, including Wire, 2-Sided, Face Map, and Faceted, as shown in Figure 14.6. Wire mode causes the model to appear as a wireframe model. The 2-Sided option makes the material appear on both sides of the face and is typically used in conjunction with the Wire option or with transparent materials. The Face Map mode applies maps to each single face on the object. Faceted ignores the smoothing between faces.

> **NOTE**
> Using the Wire option or the 2-Sided option is different from the wireframe display option in the viewports. The Wire and 2-Sided options define how the object looks when rendered.

FIGURE 14.6

Basic parameter options include (from left to right) Wire, 2-Sided, Face Map, and Faceted.

Blinn shader

This shader is the default. It renders simple circular highlights and smoothes adjacent faces.

The Blinn shader includes color swatches for setting Ambient, Diffuse, Specular, and Self-Illumination colors. To change the color, click the color swatch and select a new color in the Color Selector dialog box.

> **NOTE**
> You can drag colors among the various color swatches in the Parameters panel. When you do so, the Copy or Swap Colors dialog box appears, which enables you to copy or swap the colors.

You can use the Lock buttons to the left of the color swatches to lock the colors together so that both colors are identical and a change to one automatically changes the other. You can lock Ambient to Diffuse and Diffuse to Specular.

The small, square buttons to the right of the Diffuse, Specular, Self-Illumination, Opacity, Specular Level, and Glossiness controls are shortcut buttons for adding a map in place of the respective parameter. Clicking these buttons opens the Material/Map Browser, where you can select the map type.

When a map is loaded and active, it appears in the Maps rollout, and an uppercase letter M appears on its button. When a map is loaded but inactive, a lowercase m appears. After you apply a map, these buttons open to make the map the active level and display its parameters in the rollouts. Figure 14.7 shows these map buttons.

 For more on maps and the various map types, see Chapter 15, "Adding Material Details with Maps."

14

FIGURE 14.7

The Blinn Basic Parameters rollout lets you select and control properties for the Blinn shader.

Locked maps icon

Locked colors

Inactive Map

Active Map

You can also lock the Ambient and Diffuse maps together with the lock icon to the right of the map buttons. The Ambient and Diffuse colors are locked together by default.

Self-Illumination can use a color if the Color option is enabled. If this option is disabled, a spinner appears that enables you to adjust the amount of default color used for illumination. Materials with a Self-Illumination value of 100 or a bright color like white lose all shadows and appear to glow from within. This happens because the self-illumination color replaces the ambient color, but a material with self-illumination can still have specular highlights. To remove the effect of Self-Illumination, set the spinner to 0 or the color to black. Figure 14.8 shows a sphere with Self-Illumination values (from left to right) of 0, 25, 50, 75, and 100.

FIGURE 14.8

Increasing the Self-Illumination value reduces the shadows in an object.

The Opacity spinner sets the level of transparency of an object. A value of 100 makes a material completely opaque, while a value of 0 makes the material completely transparent. Use the Show Background in Preview button on the Material Editor toolbar to enable a patterned background image to make it easier to view the effects of the Opacity setting. Figure 14.9 shows materials with Opacity values of 10, 25, 50, 75, and 90.

FIGURE 14.9

The Opacity value sets how transparent a material is.

Specular highlights are the bright points on the surface where the light is reflected at a maximum value. The Specular Level value determines how bright the highlight is. Its values can range from 0, where there is no highlight, to 100, where the highlight is at a maximum. The graph to the right of the values displays the intensity per distance for a cross section of the highlight. The Specular Level defines the height of the curve or the value at the center of the highlight where it is the brightest. This value can be overloaded to accept numbers greater than 100. Overloaded values create a larger, wider highlight.

The Glossiness value determines the size of the highlight. A value of 100 produces a pinpoint highlight, and a value of 0 increases the highlight to the edges of the graph. The Soften value doesn't affect the graph, but it spreads the highlight across the area defined by the Glossiness value. It can range from 0 (wider) to 1 (thinner). Figure 14.10 shows a sampling of materials with specular highlights. The left image has a Specular Level of 20 and a Glossiness of 10, the second image has the Specular Level increased to 80, the third image has the Specular Level overloaded with a value of 150, and the last two images have the Glossiness value increased to 50 and 80, respectively.

FIGURE 14.10

You can control specular highlights by altering brightness and size.

Phong shader

The Phong shader creates smooth surfaces like Blinn without the quality highlights, but it renders more quickly than the Blinn shader does. The parameters for the Phong shader are identical to those for the Blinn shader. The differences between Blinn and Phong are very subtle, but Blinn can produce highlights for lights at low angles to the surface, and its highlights are generally softer.

> **TIP**
> The Blinn shader is typically used to simulate softer materials like rubber, but the Phong shader is better for hard materials like plastic.

Anisotropic shader

The Anisotropic shader is characterized by noncircular highlights. The Anisotropy value is the difference between the two axes that make up the highlight. A value of 0 is circular, but higher values increase the difference between the axes, and the highlights are more elliptical.

Most of the parameters for this shader are the same as those for the Blinn shader, but several parameters of the Anisotropic type are unique. The Diffuse Level value determines how bright the Diffuse color appears. This is similar to Self-Illumination, but it doesn't affect the specular highlights or the shadows. Values can range from 0 to 400.

Compared with the Blinn shader, the Specular Highlight graph looks very different. That is because it displays two highlight components that intersect at the middle. The Specular Level value still controls the height of the curve, and the Glossiness still controls the width, but the Anisotropy value changes the width of one axis relative to the other, creating elliptical highlights. The Orientation value rotates the highlight. Figure 14.11 compares the Specular Highlight graphs for the Blinn and Anisotropic shaders.

> **TIP**
>
> Because the Anisotropy shader can produce elliptical highlights, it is often used on surfaces with strong grooves and strands, like fabrics and stainless steel objects.

FIGURE 14.11

The Specular Highlight graph for the Blinn and Anisotropic shaders

Figure 14.12 shows several materials with the Anisotropic shader applied. The first three images have Anisotropic values of 30, 60, and 90, and the last two images have Orientation values of 30 and 60.

FIGURE 14.12

Materials with the Anisotropic shader applied have elliptical highlights.

Multi-Layer shader

The Multi-Layer shader includes two Anisotropic highlights. Each of these highlights can have a different color. All parameters for this shader are the same as the Anisotropic shader described previously, except that there are two Specular Layers and one additional parameter: Roughness. The Roughness parameter defines how well the Diffuse color blends into the Ambient color. When Roughness is set to a value of 0, an object appears the same as with the Blinn shader, but with higher values, up to 100, the material grows darker.

Figure 14.13 shows several materials with a Multi-Layer shader applied. The first two images have two specular highlights, each with an Orientation value of 60 and Anisotropy values of 60 and 90. The third image has an increased Specular Level of 110 and a decrease in the Glossiness to 10. The fourth image has a change in the Orientation value for one of the highlights to 20, and the final image has a drop in the Anisotropy value to 10.

> **TIP**
> The Multi-Layer shader is useful to give a material a sense of surface depth. For example, it can give the illusion of a layer of shellac on wood or a layer of wax on tile.

FIGURE 14.13

Materials with a Multi-Layer shader applied can have two crossing highlights.

Oren-Nayar-Blinn shader

The Oren-Nayar-Blinn shader is useful for creating materials for matte surfaces such as cloth and fabric. The parameters are identical to the Blinn shader, with the addition of the Diffuse Level and Roughness values.

Metal shader

The Metal shader simulates the luster of metallic surfaces. The Highlight curve has a shape that is different from that of the other shaders. It is rounder at the top and doesn't include a Soften value. It can also accept a much higher Specular Level value (up to 999) than the other shaders. Also, you cannot specify a Specular color. All other parameters are similar to those of the Blinn shader. Figure 14.14 shows several materials with the Metal shader applied. These materials differ in Specular Level values, which are (from left to right) 50, 100, 200, 400, and 800.

> **NOTE**
> For the Metal shader, the specular color is always the same as the material's diffuse color.

FIGURE 14.14

A material with a Metal shader applied generates its own highlights.

Strauss shader

The Strauss shader provides another alternative for creating metal materials. This shader has only four parameters: Color, Glossiness, Metalness, and Opacity. Glossiness controls the entire highlight shape. The Metalness value makes the material appear more metal-like by affecting the primary and secondary highlights. Both of these values can range between 0 and 100.

> **TIP**
> The Strauss shader is often better at making metal than the Metal shader because of its smoothness value and the ability to mix colors with the Metalness property.

Translucent shader

The Translucent shader allows light to easily pass through an object. It is intended to be used on thin, flat plane objects, such as a bed sheet used for displaying shadow puppets. Most of the settings for this shader are the same as the others, except that it includes a Translucent color. This color is the color that the light becomes as it passes through an object with this material applied. This shader also includes a Filter color and an option for disabling the specular highlights on the backside of the object.

Tutorial: Making curtains translucent

The Translucent shader can be used to create an interesting effect. Not only does light shine through an object with this shader applied, but shadows also are visible.

To make window curtains translucent, follow these steps:

1. Open the Translucent curtains.max file from the Chap 14 directory on the CD.

   This file contains a simple scene of a tree positioned outside a window.

2. Open the Material Editor by choosing Rendering ⇨ Material Editor ⇨ Slate Material Editor by clicking the Material Editor button on the main toolbar or by pressing the M key.

3. In the Material/Map Browser panel of the Material Editor, double-click the Standard material, then double-click the material node, and in the Name field, name the material **Curtains**. Select the Translucent Shader from the Shader Basic Parameters rollout. Click the Diffuse color swatch, and select a light blue color. Click the OK button to exit the Color Selector.

4. Click the Translucent Color swatch, change its color to a light gray, and set the Opacity to **75**.

5. Drag the Curtains material's output node socket onto the curtain object in the Left viewport or select the curtains in the viewport and use the Assign Material to Selection button in the Material Editor toolbar.

Figure 14.15 shows the resulting rendered image. Notice that the tree's shadow is cast on the curtains.

FIGURE 14.15

These translucent window curtains show shadows.

Accessing Other Parameters

In addition to the basic shader parameters, several other rollouts of options can add to the look of a material.

Extended Parameters rollout

The Material Editor includes several settings, in addition to the basic parameters, that are common for most shaders. The Extended Parameters rollout, shown in Figure 14.16, includes Advanced Transparency, Reflection Dimming, and Wire controls. All shaders include these parameters.

FIGURE 14.16

The Extended Parameters rollout includes Advanced Transparency, Reflection Dimming, and Wire settings.

14

You can use the Advanced Transparency controls to set the Falloff to be In, Out, or a specified Amount. The In option increases the transparency as you get farther inside the object, and the Out option does the opposite. The Amount value sets the transparency for the inner or outer edge. Figure 14.17 shows two materials that use the Transparency Falloff options on a gray background and on a patterned background. The two materials on the left use the In option, and the two on the right use the Out option. Both are set at Amount values of 100.

> **TIP**
>
> If you look closely at a glass sphere, you'll notice that the glass is thicker when you look through the edge of the sphere than through the sphere's center. This can be created using the In option in the Advanced Transparency section.

FIGURE 14.17

Materials with the In and Out Falloff options applied

The three transparency types are Filter, Subtractive, and Additive. The Filter type multiplies the Filter color with any color surface that appears behind the transparent object. With this option, you can select a Filter color to use. The Subtractive and Additive types subtract from or add to the color behind the transparent object.

The Index of Refraction is a measure of the amount of distortion caused by light passing through a transparent object. Different physical materials have different Index of Refraction values. The amount of distortion also depends on the thickness of the transparent object. The Index of Refraction for water is 1.33 and for glass is 1.5. The default of 1.0 has no effect.

The Wire section lets you specify a wire size or thickness. Use this setting if the Wire option or the 2-Sided option is enabled in the Shaders Basic Parameters rollout. The size can be measured in either Pixels or Units. Figure 14.18 shows materials with different Wire values from 1 to 5 pixels.

FIGURE 14.18

Three materials with Wire values of (from left to right) 1, 2, 3, 4, and 5 pixels

Reflection Dimming controls how intense a reflection is. You enable it by using the Apply option. The Dim Level setting controls the intensity of the reflection within a shadow, and the Refl Level sets the intensity for all reflections not in the shadow.

SuperSampling rollout

Pixels are small square dots that collectively make up the entire screen. At the edges of objects where the material color changes from the object to the background, these square pixels can cause jagged edges to appear. These edges are called *artifacts* and can ruin an image. *Anti-aliasing* is the process through which these artifacts are removed by softening the transition between colors.

3ds Max includes anti-aliasing filters as part of the rendering process. SuperSampling is an additional anti-aliasing pass that can improve image quality that is applied at the material level. You have several SuperSampling methods from which to choose. The SuperSampling method can be defined in the Material Editor, or you can choose the settings in the Default Scanline Renderer rollout of the Render Setup dialog box by enabling the Use Global Settings option.

> **NOTE**
> Anti-aliasing happens before raytracing when rendering, so even if the anti-aliasing material option is enabled, the reflections and/or refractions will still be aliased unless anti-aliasing is turned on in the Render Settings.

 For more about the various anti-aliasing filters, see Chapter 20, "Rendering a Scene and Enabling Quicksilver."

SuperSampling is calculated only if the Anti-Aliasing option in the Render Setup dialog box is enabled. The Raytrace material type has its own SuperSampling pass that is required in order to get clean reflections.

> **NOTE**
> Using SuperSampling can greatly increase the time it takes to render an image.

In a SuperSampling pass, the colors at different points around the center of a pixel are sampled. These samples are then used to compute the final color of each pixel. The SuperSampling settings can be set globally in the Render Setup dialog box or for each material individually by disabling the Use Global Settings option. These four SuperSampling methods are available:

- **Adaptive Halton:** Takes semi-random samples along both the pixel's X-axis and Y-axis. It takes from 4 to 40 samples.
- **Adaptive Uniform:** Takes samples at regular intervals around the pixel's center. It takes from 4 to 26 samples.
- **Hammersley:** Takes samples at regular intervals along the X-axis, but takes random samples along the Y-axis. It takes from 4 to 40 samples.
- **Max 2.5 Star:** Takes four samples along each axis.

The first three methods enable you to select a Quality setting. This setting specifies the number of samples to be taken. The more samples taken, the higher the resolution, but the longer it takes to render. The two Adaptive methods (Adaptive Halton and Adaptive Uniform) offer an Adaptive option with a Threshold spinner. This option takes more samples if the change in color is within the Threshold value. The SuperSample Texture option includes maps in the SuperSampling process along with materials.

14

Maps rollout

A *map* is a bitmap image that is wrapped about an object. The Maps rollout includes a list of the maps that you can apply to an object. Using this rollout, you can enable or disable maps, specify the intensity of the map in the Amount field, and load maps. Clicking the Map buttons opens the Material/Map Browser where you can select the map type.

 Find out more about maps in Chapter 15, "Adding Material Details with Maps."

mental ray Connection rollout

The mental ray Connection rollout includes options for enabling different properties that are used by the mental ray rendering engine. The properties include Surface and Shadow Shaders, Photon and Photon Volume, and Extended Shaders and Advanced Shaders, including Contour and Light Map.

The mental ray rendering engine and its properties are covered in Chapter 22, "Rendering with mental ray and iray."

Tutorial: Coloring a dolphin

As a quick example of applying materials, you'll take a dolphin model created by Zygote Media and position it over a watery plane. You then apply custom materials to both objects.

To add materials to a dolphin, follow these steps:

1. Open the Dolphin.max file from the Chap 14 directory on the CD.

   This file contains a simple plane object and a dolphin mesh.

2. Open the Material Editor by choosing Rendering ⇨ Material Editor ⇨ Slate Material Editor, clicking the Material Editor button on the main toolbar, or pressing the M key.

3. In the Material/Map Browser panel, double-click the Standard material; then double-click the Standard material node and, in the Name field in the Parameter Editor panel, rename the material **Dolphin Skin**. Click the Diffuse color swatch, and select a light gray color. Then click the Specular color swatch, and select a light yellow color. Click the OK button to exit the Color Selector. In the Specular Highlights section, increase the Specular Level to **45**.

4. Double-click the Standard material in the Material/Map Browser again, double-click this new node to access its parameters, and name it **Ocean Surface**. Click the Diffuse color swatch, and select a light blue color. Set the Specular Level and Opacity values to **80**. In the Maps rollout, click the None button to the right of the Bump option. In the Material/Map Browser that opens, double-click the Noise selection in the Maps rollout. Double click the Noise map

button to access the Noise parameters, and then enable the Fractal option and set the Size value to **15** in the Noise Parameters rollout.

5. Select the dolphin body in the viewport and, with the Dolphin Skin material selected in the Material Editor, click the Assign Material to Selection button in the Material Editor toolbar. Then do the same for the ocean surface.

> **NOTE**
> This model also includes separate objects for the eyes, mouth, and tongue. These objects could have different materials applied to them, but they are so small in this image that you won't worry about them.

6. Choose Rendering ⇨ Environment (keyboard shortcut, 8), click the Background Color swatch, and change it to a light sky blue.

Figure 14.19 shows the resulting rendered image.

FIGURE 14.19

A dolphin over the water with applied materials

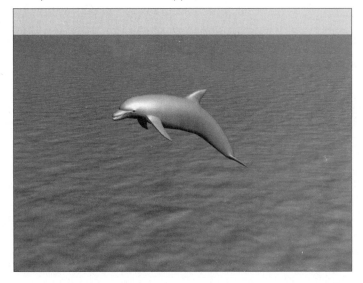

14

Summary

Materials can add much to the realism of your models. Learning to use the Material Editor enables you to work with materials. This chapter covered the following topics:

- Understanding various material properties
- Working with the Slate Material Editor buttons and material nodes

- Using various material types
- Using the various material parameters
- Understanding the basics of using Standard materials
- Learning to use the various shaders
- Exploring the other material rollouts
- Applying materials to a model

This chapter should have been enough to whet your appetite for materials, and yet it really covered only one part of the equation. The other critical piece for materials is maps, and you'll dive into those in the next chapter.

CHAPTER

15

Adding Material Details with Maps

IN THIS CHAPTER

Understanding mapping

Connecting maps to material nodes

Applying maps to material properties using the Maps rollout

Using the Bitmap Path Editor

Creating textures with Photoshop

In addition to using materials, another way to enhance an object is to use a map—but not a roadmap. In the Autodesk® 3ds Max® 2013 software, maps are bitmaps that can be applied to the surface of an object. Some maps wrap an image onto objects, but others, such as displacement and bump maps, modify the surface based on the map's intensity. For example, you can use a diffuse map to add a label to a soup can, or a bump map to add some texture to the surface of an orange.

Several external tools can be very helpful when you create texture maps. These tools include an image-editing package such as Photoshop, a digital camera, and a scanner. With these tools, you can create and capture bitmap images that can be applied as materials to the surface of the object. Maps are great, but with these maps, you'll still need to stop and ask for directions.

Understanding Maps

To understand a material map, think of this example. Cut the label off of a soup can, scan it into the computer, and save the image as a bitmap. You can then create a cylinder with roughly the same dimensions as the can, load the scanned label image as a material map, and apply it to the cylinder object to simulate the original soup can. This is exactly how maps work in 3ds Max.

Different map types

Different types of maps exist. Some maps wrap images about objects, while others define areas to be modified by comparing the intensity of the pixels in the map. An example of this is a *bump map*. A standard bump map would be a grayscale image; when mapped onto an object, those areas of the object that are beneath the lighter-colored sections of the bump map would be raised to show a bump when rendered,

361

and those areas on the object beneath a darker sections would show no bump when rendered. The highest raised bumps match the areas where the map is white, the lowest areas are black, and everything in between is a gradient of gray. This enables you to easily create surface textures, such as the rivets on the side of machine, without having to model them.

Still other uses for maps include environment maps for backgrounds and projection maps that are used with lights.

For information on environment maps, see Chapter 20, "Rendering a Scene and Enabling Quicksilver." Chapter 19, "Using Lights and Basic Lighting Techniques," covers projector maps.

Maps that are used to create materials are all applied using the Material Editor. The Material/Map Browser provides access to all the available maps. These maps have many common features.

Enabling the global viewport rendering setting

To see applied maps in the viewports, select the Views ⇨ Show Materials in Viewport As ⇨ Shaded Materials with Maps menu command.

For more accurate maps that show highlights, you can enable the Views ⇨ Show Materials in Viewport As ⇨ Realistic Materials with Maps option. This is especially helpful when the scene objects use the Arch & Design materials.

Using Real-World maps

When maps are applied to scene objects, they are applied based on the object's UV coordinates, which control the scale, orientation, and position of the applied map. But, each bitmap can be sized along each axis to stretch the map over the surface. Another way to stretch a texture map is to resize the geometric object that the map is applied to. This is the default behavior of maps, but another option is available.

When a geometric object is created, you can enable the Real-World Map Size parameter in the Modify panel, which is generally near the Generate Mapping Coords option. This option is also available when the UVW Mapping modifier is applied to an object. When enabled, this option lets you specify the size of the applied texture using Width and Height values. When this option is enabled, it causes the texture maps to maintain their sizes as geometry objects are resized. You can set the dimensions of applied texture maps in the Coordinates rollout in the Material Editor.

> **TIP**
> You can select to have Real-World mapping enabled for all new objects by default by enabling the Use Real-World Texture Coordinates option in the General panel of the Preference Settings dialog box.

Working with Maps

Maps are used along with materials and are not applied to objects by themselves. You can access material maps from the Material/Map Browser. To open the Material/Map Browser if it isn't visible in the Slate Material Editor, select the Tools ⇨ Material/Map Browser menu or press the 0 key in the Slate

Material Editor. You also can open the Material/Map Browser by clicking any of the map buttons found throughout the Parameter Editor panel, including those found in the Maps rollout. Figure 15.1 shows the Material/Map browser with some of its available standard maps.

FIGURE 15.1

Use the Material/Map Browser to list all the maps available for assigning to materials.

In the Material/Map Browser all available maps are displayed by default in the Maps/Standard rollout, but if you have the Quicksilver Hardware or the mental ray renderer enabled, rollouts for mental ray maps and MetaSL maps are also displayed. If you right-click within the Material/Map Browser and the scroll bar and choose the Show Incompatible option from the pop-up menu, all map rollouts including mental ray maps are displayed even if the mental ray renderer isn't enabled.

To load a map node into the Node View panel of the Material Editor, simply double-click on it or drag the material from the Material/Map Browser to the Node View panel. All map nodes are easily identified by their green title bars in the Node View and Navigator panels.

Connecting maps to materials

A map by itself in the Node View panel cannot be applied to objects in the scene. To add a map to a material it must be connected to one of the material properties. This is done by dragging on the map node's output socket and dropping the connecting line on the input socket for the material property where the map is being applied. For example, Figure 15.2 shows a connection between the Checker map node and the Standard material node's Diffuse Color. Once a connection is made, the material preview is updated to show that the applied map and the sockets at either end of the connection are highlighted green.

> **TIP**
> If you drag from a map node's output socket and drop anywhere on the blank Node View, a pop-up menu lets you choose to select and create a material, map, controller, or sample slot material node.

15

FIGURE 15.2

Map nodes need to be connected to material properties in order to show up in the material.

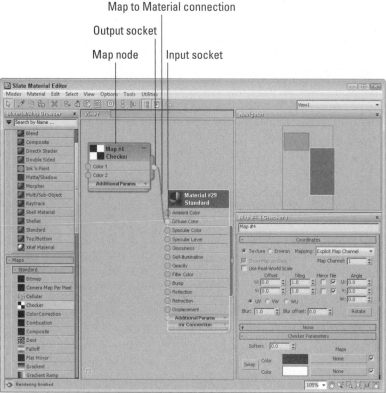

Double-clicking the map node's title opens the map's parameters in the Parameter Editor. Maps also can be applied by clicking on a map button in the Parameter Editor and selecting a map type from the Material/Map Browser that opens.

A single map node can be connected to several different material parameters on the same or on different nodes. Map nodes can also be connected to other map nodes. For example, Figure 15.3 shows a Marble and a Noise map connected to a Checker map node, which is connected to a standard material node.

FIGURE 15.3

Map nodes also can be connected to other map nodes.

To disconnect a map from a material node, simply select the connection line and press the Delete key. This removes the connection but leaves both the map and material nodes in place.

Using the Maps rollout

You can quickly see all the maps that are connected to the current material in the Maps rollout, shown in Figure 15.4, and cover it in more detail.

When a material node is selected, the Maps rollout is available in the Parameters panel. The Maps rollout is where you can see all the different maps available for the given material. To add a map, click the Map button; this opens the Material/Map Browser where you can select the map to use. The selected map appears as a node and is automatically connected to the material. The Amount spinner sets the intensity of the map, and an option to enable or disable the map is available. For example, if a bump map is applied to an object, you can reduce the height of the bumps with the Amount value.

15

FIGURE 15.4

The Maps rollout can turn maps on or off.

The available maps in the Maps rollout depend on the type of material and the Shader that you are using. Raytrace materials have many more available maps than the Standard material. Some of the common mapping types found in the Maps rollout are discussed in Table 15.1.

TABLE 15.1   Material Properties for Maps

Material Property	Description
Ambient Color	Replaces the ambient color component of the base material. You can use this feature to make an object's shadow appear as a map. Diffuse Color mapping (discussed next) also affects the Ambient color. A lock button in the Maps rollout enables you to lock these two mappings together.
Diffuse Color	Replaces the diffuse color component of the base material. This is the main color used for the object. When you select a map such as Wood, the object appears to be created out of wood. As mentioned previously, Diffuse Color mapping also can affect the Ambient color if the lock button is selected.
Diffuse Level	Changes the diffuse color level from 0, where the map is black, to a maximum, where the map is white. This mapping is available only with the Anisotropic, Oren-Nayar-Blinn, and Multi-Level Shaders.
Diffuse Roughness	Sets the roughness value of the material from 0, where the map is black, to a maximum, where the map is white. This mapping is available only with the Oren-Nayar-Blinn and Multi-Layer Shaders.
Specular Color	Replaces the specular color component of the base material. This option enables you to include a different color or image in place of the specular color. It is different from the Specular Level and Glossiness mappings, which also affect the specular highlights.

Material Property	Description
Specular Level	Controls the intensity of the specular highlights from 0, where the map is black, to 1, where the map is white. For the best effect, apply this mapping along with the Glossiness mapping.
Glossiness	Defines where the specular highlights will appear. You can use this option to make an object appear older by diminishing certain areas. Black areas on the map show the non-glossy areas, and white areas are where the glossiness is at a maximum.
Self-Illumination	Makes certain areas of an object glow, and because they glow, they won't receive any lighting effects, such as highlights or shadows. Black areas represent areas that have no self-illumination, and white areas receive full self-illumination.
Opacity	Determines which areas are visible and which are transparent. Black areas for this map are transparent, and white areas are opaque. This mapping works in conjunction with the Opacity value in the Basic Parameters rollout. Transparent areas, even if perfectly transparent, still receive specular highlights.
Filter Color	Colors transparent areas for creating materials such as colored glass. White light that is cast through an object using filter color mapping is colored with the filter color.
Anisotropy	Controls the shape of an anisotropy highlight. This mapping is available only with the Anisotropic and Multi-Layer Shaders.
Orientation	Controls an anisotropic highlight's position. Anisotropic highlights are elliptical, and this mapping can position them at a different angle. Orientation mapping is available only with the Anisotropic and Multi-Layer Shaders.
Metalness	Controls how metallic an area looks. It specifies metalness values from 0, where the map is black, to a maximum, where the map is white. This mapping is available only with the Strauss Shader.
Bump	Uses the intensity of the bitmap to raise or indent the surface of an object. The white areas of the map are raised, and darker areas are lowered. Although bump mapping appears to alter the geometry, it actually doesn't affect the surface geometry.
Reflection	Reflects images off the surface as a mirror does. The three types of Reflection mapping are Basic, Automatic, and Flat Mirror. Basic reflection mapping simulates the reflection of an object's surroundings. Automatic reflection mapping projects the map outward from the center of the object. Flat-Mirror reflection mapping reflects a mirror image off a series of coplanar faces. Reflection mapping doesn't need mapping coordinates because the coordinates are based on world coordinates and not on object coordinates. Therefore, the map appears different if the object is moved, which is how reflections work in the real world.
Refraction	Bends light and displays images through a transparent object, in the same way a room appears through a glass of water. The amount of this effect is controlled by a value called the Index of Refraction. This value is set in the parent material's Extended Parameters rollout.
Displacement	Changes the geometry of an object. The white areas of the map are pushed outward, and the dark areas are pushed in. The amount of the surface displaced is based on a percentage of the diagonal that makes up the bounding box of the object. Displacement mapping isn't visible in the viewports unless the Displace NURBS (for NURBS, or Non-Uniform Rational B-Splines, objects) or the Displace Mesh (for Editable Meshes) modifiers have been applied.

15

Tutorial: Aging objects for realism

I don't know whether your toolbox is well worn like mine; it must be the hostile environment that it is always in (or all the things I keep dropping in and on it). Rendering a toolbox with nice specular highlights just doesn't feel right. This tutorial shows a few ways to age an object so that it looks older and worn.

To add maps to make an object look old, follow these steps:

1. Open the Toolbox.max file from the Chap 15 directory on the website.

   This file contains a simple toolbox mesh created using extruded splines.

2. Press the M key to open the Slate Material Editor. Locate and double-click the Standard material in the Material/Map Browser, and then double-click the material node to open its parameters. Select the Metal shader from the drop-down list in the Shader Basic Parameters rollout. In the Metal Basic Parameters rollout, set the Diffuse color to a nice, shiny red and increase the Specular Level to **97** and the Glossiness value to **59**. Name the material **Toolbox**.

3. In the Maps rollout of the Material/Map Browser, double-click the option for the Splat map and connect this node to the Glossiness parameter. Double-click the Splat map node, and in the Splat Parameters rollout, set the Size value to **100** and change Color #1 to a rust color and Color #2 to white.

4. Double-click the Dent option in the Material/Map Browser and connect its node to the Bump parameter. Double-click the Dent map node, and in the Dent Parameters rollout, set the Size value to **200**, Color #1 to black, and Color #2 to white.

5. Create another standard material node and name it **Hinge**. Select the Metal shader from the Shader Basic Parameters rollout for this material also, and increase the Specular Level in the Metal Basic Parameters rollout to **26** and the Glossiness value to **71**. Also change the Diffuse color to a light gray. Click the map button next to the Glossiness value, and double-click the Noise map in the Material/Map Browser. This automatically creates and connects the Noise map node. Double-click the Noise map node, and in the Noise Parameters rollout, set the Noise map to Fractal with a Size of **10**.

6. Drag the output socket for the "Toolbox" material to the toolbox object and the "Hinge" material to the hinge and the handle objects.

> **NOTE**
> Bump and glossiness mappings are not visible until the scene is rendered. To see the material's results, choose Rendering ⟹ Render.

Figure 15.5 shows the well-used toolbox.

Understanding map types

Within the Material/Map Browser is a wide variety of map types. Table 15.2 lists the common standard maps and briefly explains their features. Each of these maps has multiple parameters that you can change to alter the look of the map. For example, the Checker map includes color swatches for changing the colors or the checkerboard and a Soften value to blur the lines between.

FIGURE 15.5

This toolbox shows its age with Glossiness and Bump mappings.

TABLE 15.2   Standard Maps

Material Property	Description
Bitmap	A bitmap image file. A large variety of formats are supported.
Camera Map Per Pixel	Project a map from the location of a camera.
Cellular	A 3D image composed of patterns of small objects referred to as *cells*.
Checker	A 2D checkerboard image with two colors that alternate every row and column.
Color Correction	Used to color correct and change the colors of a map.
Composite	Combines a specified number of maps into a single map using the alpha channel.
Dent	A 3D map that works as a bump map to create indentations across the surface of an object.
Falloff	A 3D map that creates a grayscale image based on the direction of the surface normals.
Flat Mirror	Reflects the surroundings using a coplanar group of faces.
Gradient	A 2D gradient image using three colors where the color gradually shifts to each color.
Gradient Ramp	A 2D gradient image using multiple selected colors.

continued

15

TABLE 15.2   (continued)

Material Property	Description
Marble/Perlin Marble	A marbled material with random colored veins; a second alternative with a different look.
Mask	Used to select one map to use as a mask for another one to display holes.
Mix	Used to combine two maps or colors.
Noise	A 3D map that randomly alters the surface of an object using two colors.
Normal Bump	Lets you alter the appearance of the details on the surface using a Normal map.
Output	Provides a way to add the functions of the Output rollout to maps that don't include an Output rollout.
Particle Age/ Particle MBlur	Works with particle systems to change the particles' color as they age or blur them as they increase in velocity.
Raytrace	Used as an alternative to the raytrace material.
Reflect/Refract	Provides another way to create reflections and refractions on objects.
RGB Multiply	Multiplies the RGB values for two separate maps and combines them to create a single map.
RGB Tint	Includes color swatches for tinting the red, green, and blue channel values of a map.
Smoke	A map that creates random fractal-based patterns such as those you would see in smoke.
Speckle	Produces small, randomly positioned specks.
Splat	Used to create the look of covering an object with splattered paint.
Stucco	Generates random patches of gradients that create the look of a stucco surface.
Substance	Procedural map generation that creates textures with small file sizes.
Swirl	A 2D image that swirls two colors into a whirlpool effect.
Thin Wall Refraction	Simulates the refraction caused by a piece of glass, such as a magnifying glass.
Tiles	A 2D image that creates patterns of bricks and tiles.
Vertex Color	Makes the vertex colors assigned to an Editable Poly objects visible when the object is rendered.
Waves	Creates wavy, watery-looking maps.
Wood	Produces a two-color wood grain.

Accessing Map parameters

Many maps have several rollouts in common. These include Coordinates, Noise, and Time. In addition to these rollouts, each individual map type has its own parameters rollout.

The Coordinates rollout

Every map that is applied to an object needs to have mapping coordinates that define how the map lines up with the object. For example, with the soup can label example mentioned earlier, you probably would want to align the top edge of the label with the top edge of the can, but you could position the top edge of the map at the middle of the can. Mapping coordinates define where the map's upper-right corner is located on the object.

All map coordinates are based on a UVW coordinate system that equates to the familiar XYZ coordinate system, except that it is named uniquely so it's not confused with transformation coordinates. For UVW coordinates, U represents the horizontal coordinate, V is the vertical coordinate, and W is along the surface normal. To keep them straight, remember that the UVW coordinate system applies to surfaces and the XYZ coordinate system applies to spatial objects. These coordinates are required for every object to which a map is applied. In most cases, you can generate these coordinates automatically when you create an object by selecting the Generate Mapping Coordinates option in the object's Parameter rollout.

> **NOTE**
> Editable meshes don't have any default mapping coordinates, but you can generate mapping coordinates using the UVW Map modifier.

In the Coordinates rollout for 2D Maps, shown in Figure 15.6, you can specify whether the map will be a texture map or an environment map. The Texture option applies the map to the surface of an object as a texture. This texture moves with the object as the object moves. The Environ option creates an environment map, which often shows up on the object as reflections. Environment maps are locked to the world and not to an object. This causes the texture to change as the object is moved. Moving an object with an environment map applied to it scrolls the map across the surface of the object.

FIGURE 15.6

The Coordinates rollout lets you offset and tile a map.

Different mapping types are available for both the Texture and Environ options. Mapping types for the Texture option include Explicit Map Channel, Vertex Color Channel, Planar from Object XYZ, and Planar from World XYZ. The Explicit Map Channel option is the default. It applies the map using the designated Map Channel. The Vertex Color Channel uses specified vertex colors as its channel. The two planar mapping types place the map in a plane based on the Local or World coordinate systems.

The Environ option includes Spherical Environment, Cylindrical Environment, Shrink-Wrap Environment, and Screen mapping types. The Spherical Environment mapping type is applied as if the entire scene were contained within a giant sphere. The same applies for the Cylindrical Environment mapping type, except that the shape is a cylinder. The Shrink-Wrap Environment plasters the map directly on the scene as if it were covering it like a blanket. All four corners of the bitmap are pulled together to the back of the wrapped object. The Screen mapping type just projects the map flatly on the background.

15

The Show Map on Back option causes planar maps to project through the object and be rendered on the object's back.

The U and V coordinates define the X and Y positions for the map. For each coordinate, you can specify an Offset value, which is the distance from the origin. The Tiling value is the number of times to repeat the image and is used only if the Tile option is selected. If the Use Real-World Scale option is selected, the Offset fields change to Height and Width and the Tiling fields change to Size. The Mirror option inverts the map. The UV, VW, and WU options apply the map onto different planes.

Tiling is the process of placing a copy of the applied map next to the current one and so on until the entire surface is covered with the map placed edge to edge. You often will want to use tiled images that are seamless or that repeat from edge to edge.

TIP

Tiling can be enabled within the material itself or in the UVW Map modifier.

Figure 15.7 shows an image tile that is seamless. Notice how the horizontal and vertical seams line up. This figure shows three tiles positioned side by side, but because the opposite edges line up, the seams between the tiles aren't evident.

FIGURE 15.7

Seamless image tiles are a useful way to cover an entire surface with a small map.

The Material Editor includes an option in the Preview window that you can use to check the Tiling and Mirror settings. The Preview UV Tiling option is available in the right-click pop-up menu. You can switch to 2×2, 3×3, or 4×4.

You also can rotate the map about each of the U, V, and W axes by entering values in the respective fields, or by clicking the Rotate button, which opens the Rotate Mapping Coordinates dialog box, shown in Figure 15.8. Using this dialog box, you can drag the mouse to rotate the mapping coordinates. Dragging within the circle rotates about all three coordinates, and dragging outside the circle rotates the mapping coordinates about their center point.

FIGURE 15.8

The Rotate Mapping Coordinates dialog box appears when you click the Rotate button in the Coordinates rollout.

The Blur and Blur Offset values affect the blurriness of the image. The Blur value blurs the image based on its distance from the view, whereas the Blur Offset value blurs the image regardless of its distance.

> **TIP**
> You can use the Blur setting to help make tile seams less noticeable.

The Noise rollout

You can use the Noise rollout to randomly alter the map settings in a predefined manner. Noise can be thought of as static you see on the television added to a bitmap. This feature is helpful for making textures more grainy, which is useful for certain materials.

The Amount value is the strength of the noise function applied; the value ranges from 0 for no noise to 100 for maximum noise. You can disable this noise function at any time, using the On option.

The Levels value defines the number of times the noise function is applied. The Size value determines the extent of the noise function based on the geometry. You also can Animate the noise. The Phase value controls how quickly the noise changes over time.

The Time rollout

Maps, such as bitmaps, that can load animations also include a Time rollout for controlling animation files. In this rollout, you can choose a Start Frame and the Playback Rate. The default Playback Rate is 1.0; higher values run the animation faster, and lower values run it slower. You also can set the animation to Loop, Ping-Pong, or Hold on the last frame.

The Output rollout

The Output rollout includes settings for controlling the final look of the map. The Invert option creates a negative version of the bitmap. The Clamp option prevents any colors from exceeding a value of 1.0 and prevents maps from becoming self-illuminating if the brightness is increased.

The Alpha From RGB Intensity option generates an alpha channel based on the intensity of the map. Black areas become transparent and white areas opaque.

15

> **NOTE**
> For materials that don't include an Output rollout, you can apply an Output map, which accepts a submaterial.

The Output Amount value controls how much of the map should be mixed when it is part of a composite material. You use the RGB Offset value to increase or decrease the map's tonal values. Use the RGB Level value to increase or decrease the saturation level of the map. The Bump Amount value is used only if the map is being used as a bump map; it determines the height of the bumps.

The Enable Color Map option enables the Color Map graph at the bottom of the Output rollout. This graph displays the tonal range of the map. Adjusting this graph affects the highlights, midtones, and shadows of the map. Figure 15.9 shows a Color Map graph.

FIGURE 15.9

The Color Map graph enables you to adjust the highlights, midtones, and shadows of a map.

Reset Curves
Delete Point
Add Point
Scale Point
Move

The left end of the graph equates to the shadows, and the right end is for the highlights. The RGB and Mono options let you display the graphs as independent red, green, and blue curves or as a single monocolor curve. The Copy CurvePoints option copies any existing points from Mono mode over to RGB mode, and vice versa. The buttons across the top of the graph are used to manage the graph points.

The buttons above the graph include Move (with flyout buttons for Move Horizontally and Move Vertically), Scale Point, Add Point (with a flyout button for adding a point with handles), Delete Point, and Reset Curves. Along the bottom of the graph are buttons for managing the graph view. The two fields at the bottom left contain the horizontal and vertical values for the current selected point. The other buttons are to Pan and Zoom the graph.

Creating Textures with External Tools

Several external tools can be valuable when you create material textures. These tools can include an image-editing program like Photoshop, a digital camera or camcorder, and a scanner. With these tools, you can create or capture images that can be applied as maps to a material using the map channels.

After the image is created or captured, you can apply it to a material by clicking a map shortcut button or by selecting a map in the Maps rollout. This opens the Material/Map Browser, where you can select the Bitmap map type and load the image file from the File dialog box that appears.

Creating material textures using Photoshop

When you begin creating texture images, Photoshop becomes your best friend. Using Photoshop's filters enables you to quickly create a huge variety of textures that add life and realism to your textures.

Table 15.3 is a recipe book of several common textures that you can create in Photoshop. The table provides only a quick sampling of some simple textures. Many other features and effects are possible with Photoshop.

TABLE 15.3   Photoshop Texture Recipes

Texture	Technique	Create in Photoshop	Apply in 3ds Max as
	Faded color	Decrease the image saturation value (Image ⇨ Adjustments ⇨ Hue/Saturation) by 20 to 30%.	Diffuse map
	Surface scratches	Apply the Chalk & Charcoal filter (Filter ⇨ Sketch ⇨ Chalk & Charcoal) with a Stroke Pressure of 2, to a blank white image, and then apply the Film Grain (Filter ⇨ Artistic ⇨ Film Grain) filter with maximum Grain and Intensity.	Bump map
	Stains on fabric	Use the Dodge and Burn tools to add stains to a fabric bitmap.	Diffuse map
	Surface relief texture	Apply Dark Strokes filter (Filter ⇨ Brush Strokes ⇨ Dark Strokes) to a texture bitmap, and save the image as a separate bump image.	Diffuse map (original texture), Bump map (Dark Strokes version)
	Planar hair	Apply the Fibers filter (Filter ⇨ Render ⇨ Fibers).	Diffuse, Bump, and Specular maps
	Clouds or fog background	Apply the Clouds filter (Filter ⇨ Render ⇨ Clouds).	Diffuse map
	Nebula or plasma cloud	Apply the Difference Clouds filter (Filter ⇨ Render ⇨ Difference Clouds). Then switch black and white color positions, and apply the Difference Clouds filter again.	Diffuse map

continued

15

375

TABLE 15.3 *(continued)*

Texture	Technique	Create in Photoshop	Apply in 3ds Max as
	Rock wall	Apply the Clouds filter (Filter ➪ Render ➪ Clouds), and then apply the Bas Relief (Filter ➪ Sketch ➪ Bas Relief) filter.	Diffuse and Bump maps
	Burlap sack	Apply the Add Noise filter (Filter ➪ Noise ➪ Add Noise), followed by the Texturizer filter (Filter ➪ Texture ➪ Texturizer) with the Burlap setting.	Diffuse and Bump maps
	Tile floor	Apply the Add Noise filter (Filter ➪ Noise ➪ Add Noise), followed by the Stained Glass filter (Filter ➪ Texture ➪ Stained Glass).	Diffuse map
	Brushed metal	Apply the Add Noise filter (Filter ➪ Noise ➪ Add Noise), followed by the Angled Strokes filter (Filter ➪ Brush Strokes ➪ Angled Strokes).	Diffuse and Bump maps
	Frosted glass	Apply the Clouds filter (Filter ➪ Render ➪ Clouds), and then apply the Glass (Filter ➪ Distort ➪ Glass) filter and select the Frosted option.	Diffuse map
	Pumice stone	Apply the Add Noise filter (Filter ➪ Noise ➪ Add Noise), followed by the Chalk & Charcoal filter (Filter ➪ Sketch ➪ Chalk & Charcoal).	Diffuse and Bump maps
	Planet islands	Apply the Difference Clouds filter (Filter ➪ Render ➪ Difference Clouds), and then apply the Note Paper (Filter ➪ Sketch ➪ Note Paper) filter.	Diffuse and Shininess maps
	Netting	Apply the Mosaic Tiles filter (Filter ➪ Texture ➪ Mosaic Tiles), followed by the Stamp (Filter ➪ Sketch ➪ Stamp) filter.	Diffuse and Opacity maps
	Leopard skin	Apply the Grain filter (Filter ➪ Texture ➪ Grain) with the Clumped option, followed by the Poster Edges (Filter ➪ Artistic ➪ Poster Edges) filter applied twice.	Diffuse and Opacity maps

Capturing digital images

Digital cameras and camcorders are inexpensive enough that they really are necessary items when creating material textures. Although Photoshop can be used to create many unique and interesting textures, a digital image of riverbed stones is much more realistic than anything that can be created with Photoshop. The world is full of interesting textures that can be used when creating images.

Avoiding specular highlights

Nothing can ruin a good texture taken with a digital camera faster than the camera's flash. Taking a picture of a highly reflective surface like the surface of a table can reflect back to the camera, thereby ruining the texture.

You can counter this in several ways. One technique is to block the flash and make sure that you have enough ambient light to capture the texture. Taking pictures outside can help with this because they don't need the flash. Another technique is to take the image at an angle, but this might skew the texture. A third technique is to take the image and then crop away the unwanted highlights.

> **TIP**
>
> The best time to take outdoor photos that are to be used for materials is on an overcast day. This eliminates the direct shadows from the sun, which are very difficult to remove. It also makes the light gradient across the surface much cleaner for tiling the photo.

Adjusting brightness

Digital images that are taken with a digital camera are typically pre-lit, meaning that they already have a light source lighting them. When these pre-lit images are added to a 3ds Max scene that includes lights, the image gets a double dose of light that typically washes out the images.

You can remedy this problem by adjusting the brightness of the image prior to loading it into 3ds Max. For images taken in normal indoor light, you'll want to decrease the brightness value by 10 to 20 percent. For outdoor scenes in full sunlight, you may want to decrease the brightness even more.

You can find the Brightness/Contrast control in Photoshop in the Image ➪ Adjustments ➪ Brightness/Contrast menu.

Scanning images

In addition to taking digital images with a digital camera, you can scan images from other sources. For example, the maple leaf tutorial was scanned from a real leaf found in my yard.

When scanning images, use the scanner's descreen option to remove any dithering from the printed image. If you place the image on a piece of matte black construction paper, then the internal glare from the scanning bulb gets a more uniform light distribution.

> **CAUTION**
>
> Most magazine and book images are copyrighted and cannot be scanned and used without permission.

15

Tutorial: Creating a fishing net

Some modeling tasks can be solved more easily with a material than with geometry changes. A fishing net is a good example. Using geometry to create the holes in the net would be tricky, but a simple Opacity map makes this complex modeling task easy.

To create a fishing net, follow these steps:

1. Before working in 3ds Max, create the needed texture in Photoshop. In Photoshop, select File ⇨ New, enter the dimensions of 512 pixels × 512 pixels in the New dialog box, and click OK to create a new image file.

2. Select the Filter ⇨ Texture ⇨ Mosaic Tiles menu command to apply the Mosaic Tiles filter. Set the Tile Size to **30** and the Grout Width to **3**, and click OK. Then select the Filter ⇨ Sketch ⇨ Stamp menu command to apply the Stamp filter with a Light/Dark Balance value of **49** and a Smoothness value of **50**.

3. Choose File ⇨ Save As, and save the file as **Netting.tif**.

   A copy of this file is available in the Chap 15 directory on the CD.

4. Open the Fish net.max file from the Chap 15 directory on the CD.

   This file includes a fishing net model created by stretching half a sphere with the Shell modifier applied.

5. Select the Rendering ⇨ Material Editor ⇨ Slate Material Editor menu command (or press the M key) to open the Material Editor. Double-click the Standard option in the Material/Map Browser to create a material node. Name the material **net**.

6. Locate and double-click the Bitmap option in the Material/Map Browser to add a node to the Node View. In the Select Image Bitmap File dialog box that opens, locate and select the Netting.tif image file. Drag a connection wire from the output socket of the Bitmap node and drop it on the input node of the Opacity parameter of the material node. Then drag the output socket for the material node and drop it on the net object in the viewports.

7. If you were to render the viewport, the net would look rather funny because the black lines are transparent instead of the white spaces. To fix this, double click the Bitmap node, open the Output rollout, and enable the Invert option. This inverts the texture image.

> **NOTE**
> Although you can enable the maps to display in the viewport, the transparency of the map is not displayed until you render the scene.

Figure 15.10 shows the rendered net.

FIGURE 15.10

A fishing net, completed easily with the net texture applied as an Opacity map

Summary

Now that you know about maps, you have a one-two punch in your materials corner. Learning to use these maps will make a big difference in the realism of your materials.

In this chapter, you learned about the following:

- Connecting map nodes in the Slate Material Editor to material nodes
- The various mapping possibilities provided in the Maps rollout
- How to create materials using external tools such as Photoshop and a digital camera

By combining materials and maps, you can create an infinite number of material combinations, but 3ds Max has even more ways to build and apply materials. In the next chapter, you learn how complex materials and material modifiers are used.

15

CHAPTER

16

Creating Compound Materials and Using Material Modifiers

IN THIS CHAPTER

Creating and using compound materials

Using material IDs to apply multiple materials

Using Matte/Shadow materials

Working with material modifiers

Displacing surface with a bitmap

Now that you've learned to create materials using the Standard material type, you get a chance to see the variety of material types that you can create in the Autodesk® 3ds Max2013® software. You can select all the various 3ds Max materials from the Material/Map Browser. Open this browser automatically by selecting Rendering ⇨ Material/Map Browser.

Although many of these materials are called compound materials, they are really just collections of materials that work together as one. Just like a mesh object can include multiple elements, materials also can be made up of several materials. Using material IDs, you can apply multiple materials to the subobject selections of a single mesh object. In this way, you can use a compound material that holds all different materials that a car model needs including glass, rubber, car body, chrome, and so on, and then just apply this one material to the car. The material IDs are used to mark which subobjects get which material.

The chapter concludes with a quick look at the various modifiers that are applied to materials.

Using Compound Materials

Compound materials combine several different materials into one. You select a compound object type by double-clicking the material type from the Material/Map Browser. Most of the entries in the Material/Map Browser are compound objects.

Compound materials usually include several different levels. For example, a Top/Bottom material includes a separate material for the top and the bottom. Each of these submaterials can then include another

381

Top/Bottom material, and so on. The links between these different submaterials are clearly visible in the View Node panel as connected nodes.

Each compound material includes a customized rollout in the Parameter Editor for specifying the submaterials associated with the compound material.

> **NOTE**
> Some of the material types work closely with specific objects and other 3ds Max features such as Advanced Lighting Override, DirectX Shader, Shell and XRef Material. These materials are covered in their respective chapters.

Blend

The Blend material blends two separate materials on a surface. The Blend Basic Parameters rollout, shown in Figure 16.1, includes separate nodes for each of the two submaterials. The check boxes to the right of these buttons enable or disable each submaterial. The Interactive option enables you to select one of the submaterials to be viewed in the viewports.

The Mask button (which appears below the two submaterial buttons) lets you load a map to specify how the submaterials are mixed. Gray areas on the map are well blended, white areas show Material 1, and black areas show Material 2. As an alternative to a mask, the Mix Amount determines how much of each submaterial to display. A value of 0 displays only Material 1, and a value of 100 displays only Material 2. This value can be animated, allowing an object to gradually change between materials.

FIGURE 16.1

The Blend material can include a mask to define the areas that are blended.

The Mixing curve defines the transition between edges of the two materials. The Upper and Lower spinners help you control the curve.

Composite

The Composite material mixes up to ten different materials by adding, subtracting, or mixing the opacity. The Composite Basic Parameters rollout, shown in Figure 16.2, includes buttons for the base material and nine additional materials that can be composited on top of the base material. The materials are applied from top to bottom.

FIGURE 16.2

Composite materials are applied from top to bottom, with the last layer placed on top of the rest.

You enable or disable each material using the check box to its left. The buttons labeled with the letters A, S, and M specify the opacity type: Additive, Subtractive, or Mix. The Additive option brightens the material by adding the background colors to the current material. The Subtractive option has the opposite effect and subtracts the background colors from the current material. The Mix option blends the materials based on their Amount values.

To the right of the A, S, and M buttons is the Mix amount. This value can range from 0 to 200. At 0, none of the materials below it will be visible. At 100, full compositing occurs. Values greater than 100 cause transparent regions to become more opaque.

Double Sided

The Double Sided material specifies different materials for the front and back of object faces. You also have an option to make the material translucent. This material is for objects that have holes in their surface. Typically, objects with surface holes do not appear correctly because only the surfaces with normals pointing outward are visible. Applying the Double Sided material shows the interior and exterior of such an object.

The Double Sided Basic Parameters rollout includes two buttons, one for the Facing material and one for the Back material. The Translucency value sets how much of one material shows through the other.

Multi/Sub-Object

You can use the Multi/Sub-Object material to assign several different materials to a single object via the material IDs. You can use the Mesh or Poly Select modifier to select each subobject area to receive the different materials.

At the top of the Multi/Sub-Object Basic Parameters rollout, shown in Figure 16.3, is a Set Number button that lets you select the number of subobject materials to include. This number is displayed in a text field to the left of the button. Each submaterial is displayed as a separate area on the sample object in the sample slots. Using the Add and Delete buttons, you can selectively add or delete submaterials from the list.

> **TIP**
>
> You can set the number of materials that are included by default in the Multi/Sub-Object material using the Options ⇨ Preferences dialog box in the Slate Material Editor. Nodes for each material are also included by default when a Multi/Sub-Object material node is created, but you can ensure that no extra material nodes are included by enabling the Empty Sub-Material Slots option in the Preferences dialog box.

FIGURE 16.3

The Multi/Sub-Object material defines materials according to material IDs.

Each submaterial includes a sample preview of the submaterial and an index number listed to the left, a Name field where you can type the name of the submaterial, a button for selecting the material, a color swatch for creating solid color materials, and a check box for enabling or disabling the submaterial. You can sort the submaterials by clicking the ID, Name, or Sub-Material buttons at the top of each column.

After you apply a Multi/Sub-Object material to an object, convert the object to an Editable Mesh or Poly, or use the Mesh or Poly Select modifier to make a subobject selection and match the Material IDs in the Surface Properties rollout to the material for the subobject selection. In the Material section for this subobject selection, choose a material ID to associate with a submaterial ID or select the material by name from the drop-down list.

Tutorial: Creating a patchwork quilt

When I think of patches, I think of a 3D 3ds Max object type, but for many people "patches" instead bring to mind small scraps of cloth used to make a quilt. Because they share the same name, this example uses 3ds Max patches to create a quilt. You can then use the Multi/Sub-Object material to color the various patches appropriately.

To create a quilt using patches, follow these steps:

1. Open the Patch quilt.max file from the Chap 16 directory on the website.

   This file contains a quilt made of patch objects that have been combined into one object.

2. Open the Material Editor by choosing Rendering ⇨ Material Editor ⇨ Slate Material Editor (or press M), and double-click on the Multi/Sub-Object material in the Material/Map Browser panel.

   The Multi/Sub-Object material node loads into the Node View, double-click the new node to make the Multi/Sub-Object Basic Parameters rollout appear in the Parameter Editor panel. Click the Set Number button and enter the value of **10**.

3. Double-click the Standard material in the Material/Map Browser to create a separate node for each of the submaterials included in the Multi/Sub-Object material. Then drag from the output socket of each Standard material node to the input socket in the Multi/Sub-Object node for each of the submaterials.

4. In the Multi/Sub-Object Basic Parameters rollout, click the color swatches to the right of the Material button to open the Color Selector. Select different colors for each of the first ten material ID slots.

5. Drag the Multi/Sub-Object material node's output socket and drop it onto the patch object in the viewports. Close the Material Editor. Initially, the entire quilt is only one color because all the Material IDs haven't been set.

6. In the Modify panel, select the Patch subobject and scroll to the bottom of the Modify panel to the Surface Properties rollout.

7. Assign each patch a separate material ID by clicking a patch and changing the ID number in the rollout field.

Figure 16.4 shows the finished quilt. Because it's a patch, you can drape it over objects easily.

FIGURE 16.4

A quilt composed of patches and colored using the Multi/Sub-Object material

Morpher

The Morpher material type works with the Morpher modifier to change materials as an object morphs. For example, you can associate a blushing effect with light red applied to the cheeks of a facial expression to show embarrassment. You can use this material only on an object that has the Morpher modifier in its Stack. The Morpher modifier includes a button called Assign New Material in the Global Parameters rollout for loading the Material Editor with the Morpher material type.

> Discover more about the Morpher modifier in Chapter 26, "Using Animation Layers and Animation Modifiers."

For the Morpher material, the Choose Morph Object button in the Morpher Basic Parameters rollout lets you pick a morpher object in the viewports and then open a dialog box used to bind the Morpher material to an object with the Morpher modifier applied. The Refresh button updates all the channels. The base material is the material used before any channel effects are used.

The Morpher material includes 100 channels that correlate to the channels included in the Morpher modifier. Each channel can be turned on and off. At the bottom of the parameters rollout are three Mixing Calculation options that can be used to determine how often the blending is calculated. The Always setting can consume lots of memory and can slow down the system. Other options are When Rendering and Never Calculate.

Shellac

The Shellac material is added on top of the Base material. The Shellac Basic Parameters rollout includes only two buttons for each material, along with a Color Blend value. The Blend value has no upper limit.

Top/Bottom

The Top/Bottom material assigns different materials to the top and bottom of an object. The Top and Bottom areas are determined by the direction in which the face normals point. These normals can be according to the World or Local Coordinate System. You also can blend the two materials.

The Top/Bottom Basic Parameters rollout includes two buttons for loading the Top and Bottom materials. You can use the Swap button to switch the two materials. Using World coordinates enables you to rotate the object without changing the material positions. Local coordinates tie the material to the object.

The Blend value can range from 0 to 100, with 0 being a hard edge and 100 being a smooth transition. The Position value sets the location where the two materials meet. A value of 0 represents the bottom of the object and displays only the top material. A value of 100 represents the top of the object, and only the Bottom material is displayed.

Tutorial: Surfing the waves

There's nothing like hitting the surf early in the morning, unless you consider hitting the virtual surf early in the morning. As an example of a compound material, you apply the Top/Bottom material to a surfboard.

To apply a Top/Bottom compound material to a surfboard, follow these steps:

1. Open the Surfboard.max file from the Chap 16 directory on the website.

    This file contains a surfboard model and an infinite plane to represent the ocean.

2. Apply the Ocean Surface material, which is already created in the Material Editor, to the plane object by dragging the material node's output socket from the Material Editor to the Plane object.

3. In the Material/Map Browser, select and double-click the Top/Bottom material to create a new material node.

4. Double-click the new material node, and name it **Surfboard**. Then click the Top Material node, name the material **Surfboard Top**, and change the Diffuse color to White. Double-click the Surfboard node again, and then click the Bottom Material node. Give this material the name **Surfboard Bottom**, and change the Diffuse color to Black.

5. Drag this material node's output socket to the surfboard object.

Figure 16.5 shows the resulting image.

FIGURE 16.5

A rendered image of a surfboard with the Top/Bottom compound material applied

Applying Multiple Materials

Most complex models are divided into multiple parts, each distinguished by the material type that is applied to it. For example, a car model would be separated into windows, tires, and the body, so that each part can have a unique material applied to it.

Using material IDs

Sometimes you may want to apply multiple materials to a single part. Selecting subobject areas and using material IDs can help you accomplish this task.

Many of the standard primitives have material IDs automatically assigned: Spheres get a single material ID, boxes get six (one for each side), and cylinders get three (one for the cylinder and one for each end cap). In addition to the standard primitives, you can assign material IDs to Editable Mesh objects. You also can assign these material IDs to any object or subobject using the Material modifier. These material IDs correspond to the various materials specified in the Multi/Sub-Object material.

> **NOTE**
> Don't confuse these material IDs with the material effect IDs, which are selected using the Material Effect flyout buttons under the sample slots. Material IDs are used only with the Multi/Sub-Object material type, whereas the effect IDs are used with the Render Effects and Video Post dialog boxes for adding effects such as glows to a material.

Tutorial: Mapping die faces

As an example of mapping multiple materials to a single object, consider a die. Splitting the cube object that makes up the die into several different parts wouldn't make sense, so you'll use the Multi/Sub-Object material instead.

To create a die model, follow these steps:

1. Open the Pair of dice.max file from the Chap 16 directory on the CD.

   This file contains two simple cube primitives that represent a pair of dice. I also used Adobe Photoshop and created six images with the dots of a die on them. All these images are the same size.

2. Open the Material Editor, and double-click the Multi/Sub-Object material from the Material/Map Browser. Then double-click the material node, and name the material **Die Faces**.

3. In the Multi/Sub-Object Basic Parameters rollout, click the Set Number button and enter a value of **6**.

4. Name the first material **face 1**, and click the material button to the right that is currently labeled None to open the Material/Map Browser. Select the Standard material type, and click OK. Then click the material button again to view the material parameter rollouts for the first material. Then click the map button to the right of the Diffuse color swatch to open the Material/Map Browser again, and double-click the Bitmap map type. In the Select Bitmap Image File dialog box, choose the dieface1.tif image from the Chap 16 directory on the CD, and click Open.

5. Back in the Material Editor, return to the Multi/Sub-Object Basic Parameters rollout by double-clicking the material node and repeat Step 4 for each of the die faces using the bitmap corresponding to each face.

6. When the Multi/Sub-Object material is defined, select the cube object and click the Assign Material to Selection button.

NOTE

Because the cube object used in this example is a box primitive, you didn't need to assign the material IDs to different sub-object selections. The box primitive automatically assigned a different material ID to each face of the cube. When material IDs do need to be assigned, you can specify them in the Surface Properties rollout for editable meshes.

Figure 16.6 shows a rendered image of two dice being rolled.

TIP

If you enable the Views ⇨ Show Materials in Viewports As ⇨ Shaded Materials with Maps menu command, then the sub-object materials are visible.

FIGURE 16.6

These dice have different bitmaps applied to each face.

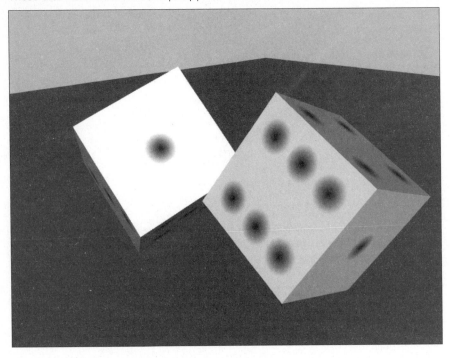

Using the Clean MultiMaterial utility

All compound materials have submaterials that are used to add layers of detail to the material, but if these submaterials aren't used, they can take up memory and disk space. For example, if you have a Multi/Sub-Object material with 10 materials and the scene only uses 3 of the materials, then the other 7 materials aren't needed and can be eliminated.

You can locate and eliminate unused submaterials in the scene using the Clean MultiMaterial utility. This utility can be accessed from the Utilities panel in the Command Panel by clicking the More button or from the Utilities menu in the Material Editor.

Clicking the Find All button finds all submaterials that aren't used and presents them in a list where you can select the ones to clean.

Using the Matte/Shadow Material

Another commonly used material is the Matte/Shadow material. You can apply Matte/Shadow materials to objects to make portions of the model invisible. This lets any objects behind the object or in the background show through. This material also is helpful for compositing 3D objects into a photographic background. Objects with Matte/Shadow materials applied also can cast and receive shadows. The effect of these materials is visible only when the object is rendered.

> **NOTE**
> The Matte/Shadow material type is unavailable if the mental ray renderer is enabled.

Matte/Shadow Basic Parameters rollout

You can apply a Matte/Shadow material by double-clicking Matte/Shadow from the Material/Map Browser. Matte/shadow materials include only a single rollout: the Matte/Shadow Basic Parameters.

The Opaque Alpha option causes the matte material to appear in an alpha channel. This essentially is a switch for turning Matte objects on and off.

You can apply atmospheric effects such as fog and volume light to Matte materials. The At Background Depth option applies the fog to the background image. The At Object Depth option applies the fog as if the object were rendered.

Find out about Atmospheric effects in Chapter 21, "Using Atmospheric and Render Effects."

The Receive Shadows option enables shadows to be cast on a Matte object. You also can specify the Shadow Brightness and color. Increasing Shadow Brightness values makes the shadow more transparent. The Affect Alpha option makes the shadows part of the alpha channel.

Matte objects also can have reflections. The Amount spinner controls how much reflection is used, and the Map button opens the Material/Map Browser.

Tutorial: Adding 3D objects to a scene

A common use of the Matte/Shadow map is to add 3D objects to a background image. For example, if you add a Plane object that is aligned with the ground plane in the background image with a Matte/Shadow material applied to it, the Plane object can capture the shadows of the 3D objects, but the Matte/Shadow material allows the background to be seen through the Plane object. The result is that the 3D object appears added to the background image scene.

To use a Matte/Shadow material to add an object to a background image, follow these steps:

1. Open the Xylophone on shadow matte.max file from the Chap 16 directory on the **website.**

   This file contains a background image of a cow statue taken in front of the Boston Convention Center. The scene also includes a xylophone positioned on the Plane object. The Plane object has a Scale multiplier of 4 to make a complete ground plane when the scene is rendered.

2. Open the Slate Material Editor by pressing the M keyboard shortcut. Double-click the Matte/Shadow option in the Material/Map Browser. Name the material **Shadow plane**, and apply it to the Plane object in the Perspective viewport.

3. Select the Create ⇨ Lights ⇨ Standard Lights ⇨ Omni menu, and click in the Top viewport to create a light. In the General Parameters rollout, enable the Shadows option. Then in the Shadow Parameters rollout, click the Color swatch. In the Color Selector that opens, select the Sample Screen Color eyedropper tool, and click the cow's shadow color to select it. Then adjust the Density setting to 0.7 to make the shadow slightly transparent.

4. Click the Perspective viewport's rendering label in the upper-left corner of the viewport, and select the Lighting and Shadows ➪ Shadows option.

   This makes the shadows appear in the viewport on the Plane object.

5. Move the Omni light in the Left and Top views until the shadows are projected along the same path as the cow's shadows.

> **TIP**
>
> One way to help align the shadows is to make the shadows of parallel geometry objects, like the xylophone's vertical leg and the cow's leg, parallel.

6. To see the final result, you need to render the image. To do this, select Rendering ➪ Render Setup (or press F10) to open the Render Setup dialog box. Click the Render button at the bottom of the dialog box, or press the F9 key.

   The image is rendered in the Rendered Frame Window.

Figure 16.7 shows the resulting rendered image.

FIGURE 16.7

A rendered xylophone fits into the scene because its shadows are cast on an object with a Matte/Shadow material applied.

Material Modifiers

Of the many available modifiers, most modifiers change the geometry of an object, but several work specifically with materials and maps, including the Material, MaterialByElement, Disp Approx, and Displace Mesh (WSM) modifiers in the Surface category. In this section, you get a chance to use several material-specific modifiers.

Material modifier

The Material modifier lets you change the material ID of an object. The only parameter for this modifier is the Material ID. When you select a subobject and apply this modifier, the material ID is applied only to the subobject selection. This modifier is used in conjunction with the Multi/Sub-Object Material type to create a single object with multiple materials.

MaterialByElementmodifier

The MaterialByElement modifier enables you to change material IDs randomly. You can apply this modifier to an object with several elements. The object needs to have the Multi/Sub-Object material applied to it.

The parameters for this modifier can be set to assign material IDs randomly with the Random Distribution option or according to a desired Frequency. The ID Count is the minimum number of material IDs to use. You can specify the percentage of each ID to use in the fields under the List Frequency option. The Seed option alters the randomness of the materials.

Tutorial: Creating random marquee lights with the MaterialByElement modifier

The MaterialByElement modifier enables you to change material IDs randomly. In this tutorial, you reproduce the effect of lights randomly turning a marquee on and off by using the Multi/Sub-Object material together with the MaterialByElement modifier.

To create a randomly lighted marquee, follow these steps:

1. Open the Marquee Lights.max file from the Chap 16 directory on the website.

   This file includes some text displayed on a rectangular object surrounded by spheres that represent lights.

2. Open the Slate Material Editor and double-click the Multi/Sub-Object material from the Material/Map Browser. Give the material the name **Random Lights**.

3. Double-click the Multi/Sub-Object material node and in the Multi/Sub-Object Basic Parameters rollout, click the Set Number button, and change its value to **2**. Then click the Material 1 button and select the Standard material type, and in the Material name field give the material the name **Light On**. Select the material button in the Multi/Sub-Object Basic Parameters rollout and set the Diffuse color to yellow, then enable the Color option next to the Self-Illumination value and set the Self-Illumination color to yellow. Then double-click again on the main material node.

4. Name the second material **Light Off**, and click the material button to right of the name field and select the Standard material type. Then click the material button again and select a gray Diffuse color. Then double-click the Multi/Sub-Object material node.

5. Select all the spheres, and click the Assign Material to Selection button to assign the material to the spheres.

6. With all the spheres selected, open the Modify panel and select the MaterialByElement modifier from the Modifier List drop-down list. In the Parameters rollout, select the Random Distribution option and set the ID Count to **2**.

Figure 16.8 shows the marquee with its random lights. (I've always wanted to see my name in lights!)

TIP

If you want to have the lights randomly flash, then simply animate the changing Seed value.

FIGURE 16.8

This marquee is randomly lighted, thanks to the MaterialByElement modifier.

Comparing Displacement maps and Displace modifiers

You can change the geometry of an object in several ways using a bitmap. One way is to use the Displace modifier (found in the Modifiers ⇨ Parametric Deformers menu). The Displace modifier lets you specify a bitmap and a map to use to alter the object's geometry. Black areas on the bitmap are left unmoved, gray areas are indented, and white areas are indented a greater distance. Several controls are available for specifying how the image is mapped to the object and how it tiles, and buttons are available for setting its alignment, including Fit, Center, Bitmap Fit, Normal Align, View Align, Region Fit, Reset, and Acquire.

NOTE

3ds Max also supports Vector Displacement maps, which are found in the Maps rollout of the Material/Map Browser. Vector Displacement maps require the mental ray renderer and they allow displacement in any direction and not just along surface normals like other displacement methods. Autodesk's Mudbox provides a good way to create this type of map saved using the EXR file format.

Another way to displace geometry with a bitmap is to use a displacement map. Displacement maps can be applied directly to Editable Poly and Mesh, NURBS, and Patch objects. If you want to apply a displacement map to another object type, such as a primitive, you first need to apply the Modifiers ⇨ Surface ⇨ Disp Approx modifier, which is short for Displacement Approximation. This modifier includes three default presets for Low, Medium, and High that make it easy to use.

 More details on working with maps are covered in Chapter 15, "Adding Material Details with Maps."

One drawback to using displacement maps is that you cannot see their result in the viewport, but if you apply the Modifiers ⇨ Surface ⇨ Displace Mesh (WSM) modifier, then the displacement map becomes visible in the viewports. If you change any of the displacement map settings, you can update the results by clicking the Update Mesh button in the Displacement Approx rollout.

> **NOTE**
> The Displace modifier requires a dense mesh in order to see the results of the displacement map, but the Disp Approx modifier creates the required density at render time.

Tutorial: Displacing geometry with a bitmap

When faced with how to displace an object using a bitmap, 3ds Max once again comes through with several ways to accomplish the task. The method you choose depends on the pipeline. You can choose to keep the displacement in the Modifier Stack or on the material level. This simple tutorial compares using both of these methods.

To compare the Displace modifier with a displacement map, follow these steps:

1. Create two square-shaped plane objects side by side in the Top viewport using the Create ⇨ Standard Primitives ⇨ Plane menu command. Then set the Length and Width Segments to **150** for the left plane object and to **20** for the right plane object.

> **TIP**
> When displacing geometry using a bitmap, make sure the object faces that will be displaced have sufficient resolution to represent the displacement.

2. Select the first plane object and apply the Displace modifier with the Modifiers ⇨ Parametric Deformers ⇨ Displace menu command. In the Parameters rollout, set the Strength value to **2** and click the Bitmap button. In the Select Displacement Image dialog box, select the Tulip logo.tif file from the Chap 16 directory on the CD and click Open.

3. Select the second plane object and open the Slate Material Editor by selecting Rendering ⇨ Material Editor ⇨ Slate Material Editor. In the Material Editor, double-click the Standard material in the Material/Map Browser to add a Standard material node to the Node View panel, then double-click the new node to access its parameters. In the Parameter Editor panel, open the Maps rollout, set the Displacement Map Amount value to **10**, and click the Displacement map button. Then double-click the Bitmap option in the Material/Map Browser, and load the same Tulip logo.tif file from the Chap 16 directory on the website. Then apply the material to the second plane object by pressing the Assign Material to Selection button, and close the Material Editor.

4. With the second plane still selected, choose the Modifiers ⇨ Surface ⇨ Displace Mesh (WSM) menu command. In the Displacement Approx. rollout, enable the Custom Settings option and click the High subdivision preset.

Figure 16.9 shows the resulting displacement on both plane objects.

FIGURE 16.9

Objects can be displaced using the Displace modifier or a displacement map.

Summary

This chapter introduced several compound materials that you can create in 3ds Max. The chapter presented various material types, including compound and Multi/Sub-Object materials and the Matte/Shadow material. The chapter also showed off a number of key material modifiers including the Displace Mesh modifier.

The following topics were covered in this chapter:

- Various compound material types
- Applying multiple materials to an object with material IDs
- Using the Matte/Shadow material to hide objects
- Exploring several material modifiers, including the Material and MaterialByElement
- Comparing the different displacement methods

After a map is placed on the surface of an object, you can use the Unwrap UV interface to manipulate how the texture is placed on the surface. This is the topic on the next chapter.

Unwrapping UVs

IN THIS CHAPTER

Working with mapping modifiers

Applying decals with the UVW Map modifier

Using the Unwrap UVW modifier and the Edit UVWs window

Throughout the modeling chapter, as you created objects, the Generate Mapping Coordinates option appeared for almost all objects. Now you find out what mapping coordinates are and how to use them.

Mapping coordinates define how a texture map is aligned to an object. These coordinates are expressed using U, V, and W dimensions. U is a horizontal direction, V is a vertical direction, and W is depth.

When you enable the Generate Mapping Coordinates option for new objects, the Autodesk® 3ds Max® 2013 software takes its best guess at where these coordinates should be located. For example, a Box primitive applies a texture map to each face. This works well in some cases, but you won't have to wait long until you'll want to change the coordinates.

Control over the mapping coordinates is accomplished using many different modifiers, including the granddaddy of them all—UVW Unwrap.

Mapping Modifiers

Among the many modifiers found in the Modifiers menu are several that are specific to material maps. These modifiers are mainly found in the UV Coordinates submenu and are used to define the coordinates for positioning material maps. These modifiers include the UVW Map, UVW Mapping Add, UVW Mapping Clear, UVW XForm, MapScaler (WSM), Projection, Unwrap UVW, Camera Map (WSM), and Camera Map.

UVW Map modifier

The UVW Map modifier lets you specify the mapping coordinates for an object. Primitives, Loft Objects, and NURBS can generate their own mapping coordinates, but you need to use this modifier to apply mapping coordinates to mesh and poly objects and patches.

> **NOTE**
>
> Objects that create their own mapping coordinates apply them to Map Channel 1. If you apply the UVW Map modifier to Map Channel 1 of an object that already has mapping coordinates, then the applied coordinates overwrite the existing ones.

You can apply the UVW Map modifier to different map channels. Applying this modifier places a map gizmo on the object. You can move, scale, or rotate this gizmo. To transform a UVW Map gizmo, you must select it from the subobject list. Gizmos that are scaled smaller than the object can be tiled.

Many different types of mappings exist, and the parameter rollout for this modifier lets you select which one to use. The Length, Width, and Height values are the dimensions for the UVW Map gizmo. You can also set tiling values in all directions.

> **NOTE**
>
> It is better to adjust the tiling within the UVW Map modifier than in the Material Editor because changes in the Material Editor affect all objects that have that material applied, but changes to a modifier affect only the object.

The Alignment section offers eight buttons for controlling the alignment of the gizmo. The Fit button fits the gizmo to the edges of the object. The Center button aligns the gizmo center with the object's center. The Bitmap Fit button opens a File dialog box where you can align the gizmo to the resolution of the selected bitmaps. The Normal Align button lets you drag on the surface of the object, and when you release the mouse button, the gizmo origin is aligned with the normal of the polygon that you are over when you release the mouse. The View Align button aligns the gizmo to match the current viewport. The Region Fit button lets you drag a region in the viewport and match the gizmo to this region. The Reset button moves the gizmo to its original location. The Acquire button aligns the gizmo with the same coordinates as another object.

Figure 17.1 displays a brick map applied to an umbrella using spherical mapping.

Tutorial: Using the UVW Map modifier to apply decals

After mapping coordinates have been applied either automatically or with the UVW Map modifier, you can use the UVW XForm modifier to move, rotate, and scale the mapping coordinates.

Most objects can automatically generate mapping coordinates—with the exception of meshes. For meshes, you need to use the UVW Map modifier. The UVW Map modifier includes seven different mapping options. Each mapping option wraps the map in a different way. The options include Planar, Cylindrical, Spherical, Shrink Wrap, Box, Face, and XYZ to UVW.

In this tutorial, you use the UVW Map modifier to apply a decal to a rocket model. Zygote Media created the rocket model.

FIGURE 17.1

The UVW Map modifier lets you specify various mapping coordinates for material maps.

To use the UVW Map modifier, follow these steps:

1. Open the Nasa decal on rocket.max file from the Chap 17 directory on the CD.

   This file includes a model of a rocket with the appropriate materials applied. The Chap 17 directory on the CD also includes a 300 × 600 image of the word NASA in black capital letters on a white background. The background color of this image was set to be transparent, and the image was saved as a .gif.

> **NOTE**
> The GIF format, typically used for Web pages, can easily make areas of the image transparent. These transparent areas become the alpha channel when loaded into 3ds Max.

2. Open the Slate Material Editor (or press the M key), and double-click on the Standard material in the Material/Map Browser. Double-click the new material node to access its parameters, then name the material **NASA Logo,** click the Diffuse color swatch, and select a white color. Then double-click the Bitmap map button in the Material/Map Browser. Locate the nasa.gif image from the Chap 17 directory on the CD, and click Open, then connect the Bitmap node to the Diffuse Colorchannel of the Standard material. The bitmap image loads. Double-click the new node to view the Bitmap parameters. In the Coordinates rollout, enter a value of **–90** in the W Angle field. The letters rotate vertically. Then, in the Bitmap Parameters rollout, select the Image Alpha option.

3. Select the lower white section of the rocket in the viewport, and open the Modify panel. At the top of the Modify panel, click the Modifier List and select the UVW Map modifier. Select the Cylindrical Mapping option, but don't select the Cap option in the Parameters rollout.

4. With the cylinder section selected, select the logo material in the Material Editor, and click the Assign Material to Selection button or drag from the material's output socket to the rocket cylinder. To see the applied logo, make sure the Views⇨Show Materials in Viewport As⇨Shaded Materials with Maps or the Realistic Materials with Maps menus are enabled.

> **TIP**
>
> When a bitmap is applied to an object using the UVW Map modifier, you can change the length, width, and tiling of the bitmap by using the UVW Map manipulator. If you enable the Select and Manipulate button on the main toolbar, the manipulator appears as green lines. When you move the mouse over the top of these green lines, they turn red, and you can drag them to alter the map dimensions. Use the small green circles at the edges of the map to change the tiling values. As you use the manipulator, the map is updated in real time within the viewports if you have enabled materials to display in the viewport.

Figure 17.2 shows the resulting rendered image.

FIGURE 17.2

You can use the UVW Map modifier to apply decals to objects.

UVW Mapping Add and Clear modifiers

The UVW Mapping Add and the UVW Mapping Clear modifiers are added to the Modifier Stack when you add or clear a channel using the Channel Info utility.

UVW XForm modifier

The UVW XForm modifier enables you to adjust mapping coordinates. It can be applied to mapping coordinates that are automatically created or to mapping coordinates created with the UVW Map modifier. The parameter rollout includes values for the UVW Tile and UVW Offsets. You can also select the Map Channel to use.

Map Scaler modifier

The Map Scaler modifier is available as both an Object-Space modifier and a World-Space modifier. The World-Space version of this modifier maintains the size of all maps applied to an object if the object itself is resized. The Object-Space version ties the map to the object, so the map scales along with the object. The Wrap Texture option wraps the texture around the object by placing it end to end until the whole object is covered.

Camera Map modifier

The Camera Map modifier creates planar mapping coordinates based on the camera's position. It comes in two flavors—one applied using Object-Space and another applied using World-Space.

The single parameter for this modifier is Pick Camera. To use this modifier, click the Pick Camera button and select a camera. The mapping coordinates are applied to the selected object.

Using the Unwrap UVW Modifier

The Unwrap UVW modifier lets you control how a map is applied to a subobject selection. It also can be used to unwrap the existing mapping coordinates of an object. You then can edit these coordinates as needed. This is accomplished by applying a texture map to an object. By selecting each face of the object, you then use the Edit UVWs interface to move and orient the polygon in UVW space to determine how the polygon is set over the applied texture map. For example, imagine a bitmap texture that shows all the different sides of a die. In the UVW Editor, you could select and manipulate each face's UVs to align to the die sides included in the bitmap.

You also can use the Unwrap UVW modifier to apply multiple planar maps to an object. You accomplish this task by creating planar maps for various sides of an object and then editing the mapping coordinates in the Edit UVWs interface.

Another common place where the Edit UVW interface is used is to make game assets. Most game engines like to have all the textures for a model combined into a single bitmap. This efficiently uses memory and eases the loaded time for the assets. To texture a model, a game artist creates a single, high-resolution bitmap that holds the textures for the entire model. Matching bitmaps also are created for specular, bump, and normal channels. The Edit UVWs interface is then used to move and position all the polygons to match the bitmap textures. After the coordinates are positioned correctly, they can be used for the other channels also.

17

Selecting UVW subobjects

The Unwrap UVW modifier lets you control precisely how a map is applied to an object. The Unwrap UVW modifier has Vertex, Edge, and Face subobject modes. In subobject mode, you can select a subobject, and the same selection is displayed in the Edit UVWs interface and vice versa. This synchronization between the Edit UVWs window and the viewports helps to ensure that you're working on the same subobjects all the time.

The Selection rollout, shown in Figure 17.3, includes a button with a plus sign and one with a minus sign. These buttons grow or shrink the current selected subobject selection. When Edge subobjects are selected, the Ring and Loop buttons and the Point-to-Point Edge Selection button become active. The Point-to-Point Edge Selection button is a great way to create seams. When you select two points, all the edges connecting those two points are selected.

In Face subobject mode, the Select by Material ID and Select by Smoothing Group buttons are active. The Select by Element button selects all the subobjects in the current element, which is an easier way to quickly select all subobjects of a defined element. You also can select to Ignore Backfacing and Select by Planar Angle.

FIGURE 17.3

The Selection panel for the UVW Unwrap modifier lets you work with Vertex, Edge, and Face subobjects.

The Select menu commands let you convert selections between vertices, edges, and faces. Additional options in the Select menu let you select all inverted and overlapped faces, allowing you to find potential problem areas.

Accessing the Edit UVWs interface

The Edit UVs rollout includes a button named Open UV Editor. This button opens the Edit UVWs interface. Within the UVW Editor, you have complete control over the various UVs, and the subobject selected in the viewport also is selected within the UVW Editor. The UVW Editor also can select and display the applied texture bitmap; the mapped bitmap also is shown in the viewport.

Tweaking vertices in the viewport

The Edit UVs rollout also includes a Tweak in View button. When this button is enabled, you can drag a single vertex in the viewports to move the texture mapping. This doesn't cause the vertex's actual position in the scene to move, only the mapping. The effects of this mode are apparent only in the viewport when the texture is visible. Texture maps can be made visible in the viewports using the Views ⇨ Show Materials in Viewports As ⇨ Shaded Materials with Maps or Realistic Materials with Maps.

Using the Quick Planar Map

One of the easiest ways to isolate mapping surfaces is with the Quick Planar Map button found in the Edit UVs rollout under the Tweak in View button. If you select a set of faces either in the viewports or in the Edit UVWs window and click this button, a planar map based on the X, Y, Z or an Averaged Normals is separated and the selected area is marked with a map seam. A button to Display Quick Planar Map shows the orientation of the mapping plan when enabled. Quick Planar Maps are one of the easiest ways to select, orient, and group mapping areas together.

Saving and loading mapping coordinates

You also can load and save the edited mapping coordinates using the Save and Load buttons in the Channel rollout, and the Reset UVWs button resets all the mapped coordinates. Saved mapping coordinate files have the .uvw extension and can be loaded for use on another object in another scene. For example, suppose you have a game level with multiple crates. If you create a texture that has all the different sides and correctly map the texture for one cube object, then all other crates in the scene could be correctly mapped by simply saving the mapping coordinates for the completed one and loading them into the others.

Each map can hold up to 99 mapping channels, and the Map Channel value lets you tell them apart. If a single object has multiple instances of the Unwrap UVW modifier applied, then each instance can have a different Map Channel value. Video game objects use these map channels to add wear and tear to a character as the game progresses. Also, the map channel can be a vertex color channel by enabling the Vertex Color Channel option.

The Configure rollout lets you set whether the seams of the planar maps are displayed and their width. The options include Map Seams, Peel Seams, and either Thick or Thin. Map seams mark the different map clusters and show up as green lines. Peel seams mark the edges that get split when a mesh is peeled and show up as blue lines. By making the seams visible, you can easily tell where the textures don't match the object's creases.

Using the Edit UVWs Interface

Although several features for working with UVs are available in the various panels in the main interface, the main work is accomplished in the Edit UVWs interface. All changes made in the Edit UVWs window, shown in Figure 17.4, are automatically reflected in the viewports.

FIGURE 17.4

The Edit UVWs interface lets you control how different planar maps line up with the model.

The Edit UVWs dialog box has multiple icons surrounding the main window. Along the top edge are buttons for selecting and transforming the selected subobjects. Table 17.1 shows and describes the buttons along the top edge.

TABLE 17.1   Top Edit UVW Interface Buttons

Buttons	Name	Description
	Move, Move Horizontal, Move Vertical	Moves the selected vertices when dragged.
	Rotate	Rotates the selected vertices when dragged.
	Scale, Scale Horizontal, Scale Vertical	Scales the selected vertices when dragged.
	Freeform Mode	Displays a gizmo that you can use to transform the subobject selection.

Buttons	Name	Description
	Mirror Horizontal, Mirror Vertical, Flip Horizontal, Flip Vertical	Mirrors or flips the selected vertices about the center of the selection.
	Show Map	Toggles the display of the map in the dialog box.
	Coordinates	Displays the vertices for the UV, UW, and WU axes.
	Show Options	Opens the Options dialog box.
MAP # 1 (CELLULAR)	Pick Texture drop-down list	Displays a drop-down list of all the maps applied to this object. You can display new maps by using the Pick Texture option.

The gizmo is simply a rectangle gizmo that surrounds the current selection. Move the selection by clicking in the gizmo and dragging; Shift+dragging constrains the selection to move horizontally or vertically. The plus sign in the center marks the rotation and scale center point. Scale the selection by dragging one of its handles. Ctrl+dragging a handle maintains the aspect ratio of the selection. Click+dragging the middle handles rotates the selection. Ctrl+dragging snaps to 5-degree positions, and Alt+dragging snaps to 1-degree positions.

Within the Pick Texture drop-down list is a Checker Pattern option. This option applies a checker map to the mesh without having to assign a material. The checker pattern makes easy work of looking for stretching on the model. The drop-down list also includes any textures that are applied to the object. The selected texture appears in the background of the window.

Selecting subobjects within the dialog box

Under the main window in the Edit UVWs dialog box is a toolbar of icons for selecting different subobjects. Table 17.2 shows and describes these buttons.

TABLE 17.2 Selection Buttons

Buttons	Name	Description
	Vertex Subobject mode	Allows Vertex UV selection
	Edge Subobject mode	Allows Edge UV selection
	Polygon Subobject mode	Allows Polygon UV selection
	Select by Element Toggle	Selects all subobjects within the selected element

(continued)

TABLE 17.2   (continued)

Buttons	Name	Description
	Grow Selection	Adds adjacent subobjects to the current selection
	Shrink Selection	Subtracts adjacent subobjects from the current selection
	Loop	Selects a loop of edges placed end to end
	Grow Loop	Adds to the selected edge loop
	Shrink Loop	Subtracts from the selected edge loop
	Ring	Selects a ring of edges parallel to each other
	Grow Ring	Adds to the selected edge ring
	Shrink Ring	Subtracts from the selected edge ring
	Paint Selection	Allows selection by painting over the subobjects
	Enlarge Brush Size	Increases the radius of the selection brush
	Shrink Brush Size	Decreases the radius of the selection brush

Within the Selection toolbar are the Selection modes with buttons for selecting Vertex, Edge, and Face subobjects. Selected subobjects in the Edit UVWs interface are highlighted red. Using the + (plus) and – (minus) buttons, you can expand or contract the current selection. The paintbrush icon button is used to Paint Select subobjects, and the Expand and Shrink Brush buttons to its immediate right allow you to increase and decrease the brush size. The Select Element option selects all subobjects in the given cluster. This happens only when the Select Face subobject mode is enabled.

The Loop button automatically selects all edges that form a loop with the current selected edges. Edge loops are edges that run end to end. You also can use the Ring button to select adjacent edges that are parallel to each other. The Grow and Shrink buttons next to the Loop and Ring buttons are used to select the adjacent edges on either side of the current selection in the loop or ring direction.

TIP

The Loop and Ring buttons also can be used on vertices and faces if two or more are selected.

To the right of the selection buttons located under the main view in the Edit UVWs dialog box are several buttons for enabling and configuring soft selections. Table 17.3 shows and describes these buttons.

TABLE 17.3 **Soft Selection Buttons**

Buttons	Name	Description
	Enable Soft Selection	Toggles Soft Selection on and off
0.0	Soft Selection Falloff value	Sets the amount of falloff for soft selection
	Linear Falloff, Smooth Falloff, Slow Out Falloff, Fast Out Falloff	Changes the falloff type
XY UV	Soft Selection Falloff Space	Switches falloff coordinates between XY and UV space
	Limit Soft Selection by Edges	Limits falloff to a specified number of edges
16	Edge Limit value	Sets the number of edges to include in the falloff

Using these controls, you can enable Soft Selection with a specified Falloff value. The UV and XY options let you switch between texture coordinates and object coordinates for the falloff. The Edge Distance lets you specify the Soft Selection falloff in terms of the number of edges from the selection instead of a falloff value. You also can choose the falloff profile as Smooth, Linear, Slow Out, or Fast Out.

Navigating the main view

Along the bottom edge of the Edit UVWs dialog box are several more buttons for viewing the coordinate values, changing the display options and navigating the main view. Table 17.4 shows and describes these buttons.

TABLE 17.4 **Lower Toolbar Buttons**

Buttons	Name	Description
	Absolute/Relative Toggle	Lets you enter U, V, and W values as absolute values or relative offsets.
U: 0.0 V: 0.0 W: 0.0	U, V, W values	Displays the coordinates of the selected vertex. You can use these values to move a vertex.
	Lock Selected Subobjects	Locks the selected components and prevents additional ones from being selected.
	Display Only Selected Faces	Displays vertices for only the selected faces.
	Hide/Unhide Selected Subobjects	Allows selected subobjects to be hidden and unhidden.

(continued)

TABLE 17.4   *(continued)*

Buttons	Name	Description
	Freeze/Unfreeze Selected Subobjects	Allows selected subobjects to be frozen and unfrozen.
All IDs ▾	All IDs drop-down list	Filters selected material IDs.
	Pan View	Lets you drag to pan the view.
	Zoom View	Lets you drag to zoom in on the view.
	Zoom To Region	Lets you drag to zoom in a specific region.
	Zoom Extents View, Zoom to Selection, Zoom to Subobject Selection	Lets you zoom to include all the mapping coordinates, just the current selection, or any elements with a selected subobject.
	Snap to Pixel, Snap to Grid	Snaps to the closest pixel corner or to the closest grid intersection.

The buttons in the lower-right corner of the Edit UVWs dialog box work just like the Viewport Navigation buttons described in earlier chapters, including buttons to snap to grid and snap to pixel. You also can navigate about the Edit UVWs window using the scroll wheel to zoom in and out of the window and dragging the scroll wheel to pan the view.

Using the Quick Transform buttons

One of the first tasks when unwrapping an object is to select and separate off different areas of polygons that have unique UVs. Each unique set of faces in the Edit UVWs dialog box is called a cluster. For example, if you have a car with a matching texture, then the same texture can be mapped for each of the wheel hubs by placing each of the clusters for the wheel hub on top of each other over the bitmap section that shows the hub details. The same can be done for the side panels on the car, but one of the sides must be flipped horizontally. This is where the Quick Transform functions come in. They allow you to select and manipulate the different clusters.

The Quick Transform rollout, shown in Figure 17.5, in the Edit UVWs dialog box includes buttons for aligning, rotating, and spacing subobjects.

The Set Pivot button includes options as flyouts to set the pivot at the center or at any of the four corners of the selection. You also can move the pivot to a precise location by dragging it when the Freeform Mode button on the top toolbar is selected. The pivot is marked by an orange set of crosshairs, and it is the point about which the selection is rotated and scaled.

The Align feature includes buttons to align the selected vertices or edges to the current pivot or to an average of the selected subobjects. The Align to Pivot option is the default, and the average align is available as a flyout. If you press and hold the Shift key, the entire edge loop is aligned. When used on an edge ring, all the individual edges are oriented to be perfectly parallel. The Linear Align button aligns the vertices or edges to a straight line that stretches between the two endpoints. The Align to Edge button is available only in Edge subobject mode. It rotates the entire cluster until the selected edge is either vertically or horizontally aligned.

FIGURE 17.5

The Quick Transform rollout includes buttons for aligning, rotating, and spacing subobjects.

Linear Align

Align Horizontal | Rotate -90 Around Pivot

Set Pivot | Space Horizontally

Align Vertical | Space Vertically

Aligh to Edge | Rotate 90 Around Pivot

> **CAUTION**
>
> The align features are designed to be used only on vertices and edges, but you can select and use them on faces. However, this only collapses the faces to a single line because it acts to align all vertices in the selection.

The Rotate +90 and Rotate –90 buttons rotate the selected subobjects 90 degrees in the Edit UVW interface. The rotation is about the set pivot. The Space Horizontal and Space Vertical buttons are used to equally space all the selected vertices or edges. The Shift key applies this to the entire edge loop.

Straightening and Relaxing UV clusters

Within the Reshape Elements rollout are three buttons for reshaping the selected cluster of UVs. The Straighten Selection button is available only in Face subobject mode. It realigns the selected polygons into a rectangular grid with all polygons oriented vertically and horizontally.

If your mapping coordinates are too tight, and you're having a tough time moving them, you can use the Relax feature to space the vertices equally. The second button is Relax Until Flat. It causes all vertices within the cluster to move in order to remove any tension from the cluster. It also tries to make all faces in the cluster roughly the same size. Relaxing a cluster removes stretching that occurs across the surface of the area.

If the Relax Until Flat option pushes the cluster too far, the third button allows you to apply a custom set of relax settings. You can access the Relax Tool dialog box using the flyout button under the Relax:Custom button or using the Tools ⇨ Relax menu command. This tool works like the Relax modifier, pushing close vertices away and pulling far vertices closer together. Selecting this menu option opens the Relax Tool dialog box, shown in Figure 17.6, which offers three relax methods: Relax by

Face Angles, Relax by Edge Angles, and Relax by Centers. The Iterations value is the number of times to apply the relax algorithm. The Amount value is how aggressive the movements of the vertices are, and the Stretch value controls how much vertices are allowed to move. You also have options to Keep Boundary Points Fixed and Save Outer Corners.

FIGURE 17.6

The Relax Tool dialog box includes custom settings for the Relax feature.

Stitching and welding

If you select some faces within the Edit UVWs dialog box and drag them away from the other faces, you notice that some edges connecting the selected faces with the non-selected faces remain. You can use the buttons in the Stitch and Explode rollouts, shown in Figure 17.7, to break these remaining edges and to stitch broken clusters back together again.

FIGURE 17.7

The Stitch and Explode rollouts include buttons for breaking, welding, and stitching vertices.

The Stitch button is used in Vertex mode to match the selected vertices along a border to their corresponding vertices. Clicking one of the Stitch buttons moves both faces to a new location, depending on the button you use. The Stitch to Target moves the selected subobjects to the location of their matching subobject. The Stitch to Average moves both to a location midway between each, and the Stitch to Source moves the matching subobjects to the location of the selected subobjects.

If you enable the Display ⇨ Show Shared Sub-objects menu command, the shared edges of the selected vertices are shown as blue lines. This indicates where the subobject face would be moved to when stitched.

The Stitch Custom button moves the subobjects based on the Stitch Settings dialog box's configuration. You can access the Stitch Settings dialog box, shown in Figure 17.8, using the flyout button under the Stitch Custom button or using the Tools⇨Stitch Selected menu command. The Stitch Tool dialog box includes options to align and scale the moved cluster, and the Bias value determines how close the selection moves to or away from the target subobject. A value of 0 moves the target to the source, and a value of 1 moves the source to the target.

FIGURE 17.8

The Stitch Tool dialog box includes a Bias value to determine how far the selected subobjects move.

The Break button in the Explode rollout breaks the selected subobjects from their surrounding faces so they can be moved without stretching out the edges of the adjacent faces. This works best if the Break tool is used before moving the selected faces. When the Break tool is used on vertices or edges, two vertices or edges are created. This allows the independent vertices or edges to be moved away from each other. When Break is used on faces, a new cluster is created.

The opposite of Break is Weld, and the Explode rollout includes several ways to weld subobjects together. The Target Weld button enables a mode that lets you drag vertices or edges and drop them on their matching separated subobject. The cursor changes to a bold set of crosshairs when a matching subobject is under the cursor.

The Weld Selected Subobject button welds selected subobjects only if they are located within the Threshold value, which is found in the Unwrap Options dialog box. You can open the Unwrap Options dialog box using the Options⇨Preferences menu command.

If an edge is selected, its shared edge is highlighted in blue. Click the Weld All Selected Seams button once to automatically select the blue shared edges. If both shared edges are selected, then clicking the Weld All Selected Seams button again welds the two edges by moving both to an average location. The Weld Any Match with Selected button welds the selected subobject without requiring that both shared edges are selected, and it can be used on all vertices, edges, and faces.

The Edit menu also includes Copy, Paste, and Paste Weld commands. The Copy and Paste commands let you copy a mapping and paste it to another set of faces. The Paste Weld command welds vertices as it pastes the mapping.

Separating into clusters using flattening methods

The Explode rollout also includes several methods for automatically separating the object into clusters. This process is called flattening. The Flatten by Face Angle breaks the faces up using an angle threshold of 60 degrees. Any adjacent faces that have normals greater than this threshold are split along the edge they share. This breaks up a cube object into six separate faces.

You also can split up the UVs based on Smoothing Group values and Material IDs. Both of these are helpful if you've already applied smoothing groups or materials to the object. The Flatten Custom breaks the UVs into clusters based on the Flatten Mapping dialog box, which is accessed using the fly-out button under the Flatten: Custom button or with the Mapping ⇨ Flatten Mapping menu.

The Flatten Mapping dialog box, shown in Figure 17.9, lets you break the mesh into clusters based on the angle between adjacent faces. This option is good for objects that have sharp angles like a robot or a machine. The Spacing value sets the distance between adjacent clusters.

FIGURE 17.9

The Flatten Mapping dialog box includes a Face Angle Threshold value for determining how clusters are separated.

Figure 17.10 shows the UVs for a backhoe bucket that was separated into clusters using the Flatten Mapping method. All the clusters have been automatically aligned within the square texture area, and some smaller pieces have been placed within the holes created by the larger pieces. This makes the most of the available texture space.

In addition to the flattening options in the Explode rollout, the Mapping menu includes two additional auto-mapping options: Normal and Unfold Mapping.

The Normal Mapping option lets you select to map a mesh using only specific views, including Top/Bottom, Front/Back, Left/Right, Box, Box No Top, and Diamond. These views are based on the direction of the normals from the faces of the mesh. It is helpful for thin models like butterfly wings or coins.

The Unfold Mapping option is unique because it starts at one face and slowly unwraps all the adjacent faces into a single segment if possible. Figure 17.11 shows a simple cylinder that has been unwrapped using this method. The advantage of this mapping is that it results in a map with no distortions. It includes two options: Walk to Closest Face and Walk to Farthest Face. You almost always want to use the Walk to Closest Face option.

> **NOTE**
> Within a single mesh, multiple different mapping methods can be used. For example, a car's wheel uses cylindrical mapping, but its hood might use planar mapping. Even a subobject selection can use different mapping methods.

Arranging and grouping clusters

Within the Edit UVWs dialog box is a square area that represents the texture bitmap. The goal is to use as much of this texture space as possible to ensure that the maximum amount of detail from the texture is used on the model. The various buttons in the Arrange Elements rollout help with this task.

FIGURE 17.10

The Flatten Mapping method was used to break this backhoe bucket object into several clusters.

After all the various clusters are separated from each other, the Pack Custom button packs all the clusters to fit within the texture space using the settings in the Pack dialog box, shown in Figure 17.12. This dialog box is accessed using the flyout under the Pack Custom button or using the Tools ⇨ Pack UVsmenu command.

The Pack UVs menu command lets you combine UVs into a smaller space. Packed UVs are easy to move and work with because they use a smaller resolution bitmap. Two packing algorithms are available in the Pack dialog box. The Linear Packing method is fast but not very efficient, and the Recursive Packing option is more efficient, although it takes longer. Within the Pack dialog box, the Spacing value sets the amount of space between each segment, and the Normalize Clusters option fits all clusters into the given space. The Rotate Clusters option allows segments to be rotated to fit better, and the Fill Holes option places smaller segments within open larger segments.

The Arrange Elements rollout also includes a Rescale Elements button that scales all clusters relative to each other. The Pack Together button fits all clusters within the texture space without normalizing. The Pack Normalize fits all clusters and allows scaling while fitting. You can select to enable or disable rescaling and rotating, and the padding value is the space between the clusters.

FIGURE 17.11

The Unfold Mapping option splits the model and unfolds it by adjacent faces into a single segment.

FIGURE 17.12

The Pack dialog box includes settings for crunching all clusters within the given texture space.

Within the Element Properties rollout are buttons to create, destroy, and select groups. For each group, you can set a Rescale Priority that determines which groups are rescaled during packing. To create a group of clusters, select two or more clusters using the Face subobject mode and click the Group Selected button. The Selected Groups label identifies each group with a number when selected.

Accessing the Unwrap Options

The Options ➪ Preferences menu command (Ctrl+O) opens the Unwrap Options dialog box, shown in Figure 17.13, and lets you set the Line and Selection Colors as well as the preferences for the Edit UVWs dialog box. You can load and tile background images at a specified map resolution or use the Use Custom Bitmap Size option. It also has a setting for the Weld Threshold and options to constantly update, show selected vertices in the viewport, and snap to the center pixel.

The Bitmap Options section lets you specify the exact size of the loaded bitmap. This only affects how the bitmap is displayed in the interface and doesn't change the actual bitmap file dimensions. The Tile Bitmap option places the bitmap end to end for the specified number of tiles. The Constant Update option causes the viewport to update along with the texture map. The Show Hidden Edges option lets you make the hidden edges visible or invisible. The Center Pixel Snap causes the Pixel Snap button at the bottom right of the interface to snap to the center of the background pixels instead of to its edges.

FIGURE 17.13

In the Unwrap Options dialog box, you can set the preferences for the Edit UVWs dialog box.

Tutorial: Controlling the mapping of a covered wagon

The covered wagon model created by Viewpoint Datalabs is strong enough to carry the pioneers across the plains, but you can add a motivating slogan to the wagon using the Unwrap UVW modifier. In this tutorial, you add and edit the mapping coordinates for the covered wagon using the Unwrap UVW modifier.

415

To control how planar maps are applied to the side of a covered wagon, follow these steps:

1. Open the Covered wagon.max file from the Chap 17 directory on the CD.

   This file includes a covered wagon model. The Chap 17 directory also includes a 256×256 image, created in Photoshop, of the paint that you want to apply to its side. The file is saved as Oregon or bust.tif. (Note that the spelling in the image is rough.)

2. With the covered section selected, choose Modifiers ➪ UV Coordinates ➪ Unwrap UVW. In the Edit UVs rollout, click the Open UV Editor button.

   The Edit UVWs interface opens. In the Modifier Stack, select the Polygon subobject mode.

3. In the Edit UVWs interface, choose Mapping ➪ Normal Mapping. In the NormalMapping dialog box, select the Left/Right Mapping option from the drop-down list and click OK.

   The left and right views of the wagon's top are displayed in the Edit UVWs interface.

4. From the drop-down list at the top of the interface, select the Pick Texture option. The Material/Map Browser opens. Double-click on the Bitmap option, and select the Oregon or bust.tif image from the Chap 17 directory on the CD.

   The texture appears in the window.

5. Drag the mouse over all the faces for the lower half of the wagon's cover, and select the Tools ➪ Flip Horizontal menu command to flip the UVs so they match the top unselected UVs. Then drag and place the selected UVs on top of the unselected ones.

   By matching these two UV sections together, you can apply the same texture to both sides of the covering.

6. Select all the UV faces, and with the Move tool, drag them to the center of the Edit UVWs window. Click and hold over the Scale tool, and select the Vertical Scale tool. Then drag in the window to vertically scale the vertices until they fit over the texture. Then horizontally scale the vertices slightly until the background texture is positioned within the wagon's covering. When you're finished, click the X button in the upper-right corner to close the Edit UVWs window.

   Figure 17.14 shows the covered wagon with the mapped bitmap.

7. Open the Compact Material Editor. Click on the mapping button next to the Diffuse color, and double-click on the Bitmap type in the Material/Map Browser. Then select the Oregon or bust.tif file from the Chap 17 directory on the website. Apply this material to the covered wagon top. Select the Views ➪ Show Materials in Viewport As ➪ Realistic Materials with Maps menu command to see the map on the covered wagon.

Figure 17.15 shows the results of the new mapping coordinates.

Rendering UV templates

After all the UV coordinates are mapped onto a model, you can paint the desired textures in an external paint program like Photoshop and load the texture back into the Edit UVWs window, where they can be aligned to the correct UVs. Using the Tools ➪ Render UVW Template menu command, you can create a template that can be saved and loaded into Photoshop, showing you exactly where the UV boundaries are.

The Tools ➪ Render UVW Template menu command opens the Render UVs dialog box, shown in Figure 17.16. This dialog box lets you set the template's dimensions, set the template's Fill and Edges colors, and show overlaps and seams. The Fill mode can be set to None, Solid, Normals, and Shaded, providing more information about the object.

FIGURE 17.14

The Edit UVWs interface lets you transform the mapping coordinates by moving vertices.

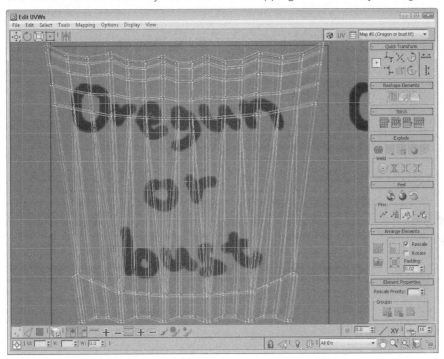

FIGURE 17.15

The position of the covered wagon's texture map has been set using the Unwrap UVW modifier.

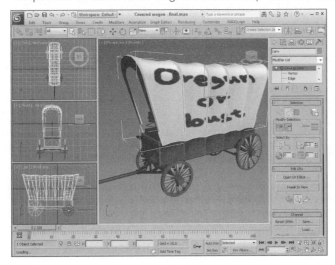

FIGURE 17.16

The Render UVs dialog box lets you render and save a template for painting textures.

Clicking the Render UV Template button renders the template into the Render Frame Buffer window where it can be saved to the needed image format. Then within Photoshop, you can make the template layer a background layer that you can turn on and off to show the lines that you need to stay within when creating a texture.

Mapping multiple objects

If your model is divided into several different pieces, you're in luck because 3ds Max allows you to apply the Unwrap UVW modifier to several pieces at once. When loaded into the Edit UVWs window, the wireframe for each piece is displayed using its object color, which makes identifying the various separate pieces easy.

Tutorial: Creating a mapping for a fighter plane

As a final example of unwrapping, you add a Navy logo to a P-28 Trojan fighter plane. This plane was created by Viewpoint Datalabs. The logo was created and saved as a PNG file, which allowed the background to be saved as transparent. This allows the shiny metallic material to show through the applied logo.

For this tutorial, you add the logo to one of the wings. The tricky part of this tutorial, which you didn't have for the earlier rocket tutorial, is that the wing's ailerons are separated from the wing. This makes it possible to animate the ailerons.

NOTE

I realize that all you military aircraft enthusiasts out there know that the logo actually belongs on the fuselage and not on the wing, but the fuselage isn't divided into separate parts like the wing, so I'm taking creative license for the sake of the tutorial.

To add a texture map to several pieces of an airplane, follow these steps:

1. Open the T-28 Trojan plane.max file from the Chap 17 directory on the CD.

2. In the Perspective viewport, select the wings and the ailerons and flaps. Don't select the molding between the wing and the ailerons.

3. Select the Modifiers ⇨ UV Coordinates ⇨ Unwrap UVW menu to apply the modifier to all the selected pieces. Then click the Open UV Editor button in the Edit UVs rollout to open the Edit UVWs window.

4. From the drop-down list at the top right of the Edit UVWs interface, select the Pick Texture option. The Material/Map Browser opens. Double-click the Bitmap option, and select the T-28 Trojan logo.png image from the Chap 17 directory on the CD.

    The texture appears in the window.

5. Select Face subobject mode in the Modifier Stack and click in the viewport on the center of the right wing. Then click the Grow button (the one with the plus sign) at the bottom of the Edit UVWs window to grow the selection. Keep clicking the Grow button until the entire right half of the wing is selected. Then select the Tools ⇨ Break command. Then zoom out in the Edit UVWs window, and move the separated wing to the top of the window so it doesn't overlap any other sections.

    The selected wing UVs are separated from the rest of the wing object, which includes both wings.

> **TIP**
> Another way to select the faces is to use the Planar Angle value, which selects all the polygons on one side of the wing.

6. Select the center of one of the right ailerons, and click the Grow button until the entire part is selected. Then click the Planar button in the Projection rollout in the Command Panel to orient the part to match the wing. Click the Planar button again to exit Planar mode. Then move the aileron up to the top of the Edit UVWs window near the wing UVs. Repeat this step for the other right aileron.

7. Enable the Select Element option at the bottom of the Edit UVWs window so you can select the entire part by clicking it. Then use the Freeform mode button to move and scale the ailerons UVs to fit next to the wing UVs.

> **TIP**
> If you need to seamlessly fit two separate parts together, you can use the Welding feature in Vertex subobject mode to weld the vertices on each part.

8. Select all the remaining UVs, and move them to the bottom of the window where they don't overlap the logo. Then select the positioned wing and ailerons, and click the Rotate -90 Around Pivot button to rotate the wing to align with the logo. Then scale and position the UVs over the logo, as shown in Figure 17.17. Then close the Edit UVWs window.

9. Press the M key to open the Compact Material Editor. Click the mapping button next to the Diffuse Color, and double-click the Bitmap type in the Material/Map Browser. Then select the T-28 Trojan logo.png file from the Chap 17 directory on the website. Apply this material to the selected wing and ailerons. Select the Views ⇨ Show Materials in Viewport As ⇨ Realistic Materials with Maps menu command to see the map on the plane.

Figure 17.18 shows the results of the plane mapping. After the map is applied to the plane and visible in the viewports, you can open the Edit UVWs window again and tweak the mapping coordinates.

FIGURE 17.17

The UVs are positioned to match the loaded bitmap.

FIGURE 17.18

The logo map is positioned on the wing and spreads over to the ailerons also, even though they are separate parts.

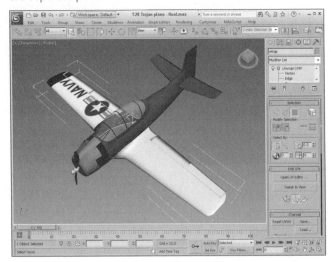

Summary

The Edit UVWs window gives you control over the mapping coordinates for your models so the beautiful texture maps you've created can be placed where they need to be.

In this chapter, you learned about the following:

- Understanding the basics of mapping coordinates
- Using mapping modifiers
- Applying labels with the UVW Map modifier
- Controlling mapping coordinates with the Unwrap UVW modifier
- Rendering a UV template

You don't want to miss any of the action, so it is important that you learn how to point the camera. Cameras are covered in the next chapter.

17

Part V

Working with Cameras, Lighting, and Rendering

IN THIS PART

Configuring and Aiming Cameras

Do you remember as a kid when you first got your own camera? After taking the usual pictures of your dog and the neighbor's fence, you quickly learned how much fun you could have with camera placement, such as a picture of a flagpole from the top of the flagpole or your mom's timeless expression when she found you inside the dryer. Cameras in the Autodesk® 3ds Max® software can also offer all kinds of amusing views of your scene.

The benefit of cameras is that you can position them anywhere within a scene to offer a custom view. Camera views let you see the scene from a different position such as from the top, front, or left. You can open camera views in a viewport, and you can also use them to render images or animated sequences. Cameras in 3ds Max can also be animated (without damaging the camera, even if your mischievous older brother turns on the dryer).

In the Camera Parameters rollout is a section for enabling multi-pass camera effects. These effects include Motion Blur and Depth of Field. Essentially, these effects are accomplished by taking several rendered images of a scene and combining them with some processing.

Learning to Work with Cameras

If you're a photography hobbyist or like to take your video camera out and shoot your own footage, then many of the terms in this section will be familiar to you. The cameras used in 3ds Max to get custom views of a scene behave in many respects just like real-world cameras.

3ds Max and real-world cameras both work with different lens settings, which are measured and defined in millimeters. You can select from a variety of preset stock lenses, including 35mm, 80mm, and even 200mm. 3ds Max cameras also offer complete control over the camera's focal length, field of view, and perspective for wide-angle or telephoto shots. The big difference is that you never have to worry about setting flashes, replacing batteries, or loading film.

Light coming into a camera is bent through the camera lens and focused on the film, where the image is captured. The distance between the film and the lens is known as the *focal length*. This distance is measured in millimeters, and you can change it by switching to a different lens. On a camera that shoots 35mm film, a lens with a focal length of 50mm produces a view similar to what your eyes would see. A lens with a focal length less than 50mm is known as a wide-angle lens because it displays a wider view of the scene. A lens longer than 50mm is called a telephoto lens because it has the ability to give a closer view of objects for more detail, as a telescope does.

Field of view is directly related to focal length and is a measurement of how much of the scene is visible. It is measured in degrees. The shorter the focal length, the wider the field of view.

When you look at a scene, objects appear larger if they are up close than they would be lying at a farther distance. This effect is referred to as *perspective* and helps you interpret distances. As mentioned, a 50mm lens gives a perspective similar to what your eyes give. Images taken with a wide field of view look distorted because the effect of perspective is increased.

Creating a camera object

To create a camera object, you can use the Create ⇨ Cameras menu, or you can open the familiar Create panel and click the Cameras category button. The two types of cameras that you can create are a Free camera and a Target camera.

Camera objects are visible as icons in the viewports, but they aren't rendered. The camera icon looks like a box with a smaller box in front of it, which represents the lens or front end of the camera. Both the Free and Target camera types include a rectangular cone that shows where the camera is pointing.

Free camera

The Free camera object offers a view of the area that is directly in front of the camera and is the better choice if the camera will be animated. When a Free camera is initially created, it points at the negative Z-axis of the active viewport.

Target camera

A Target camera always points at a controllable target point some distance in front of the camera. Target cameras are easy to aim and are useful for situations where the camera won't move. To create this type of camera, click a viewport to position the camera and drag to the location of its target. The target can be named along with the camera. When a target is created, 3ds Max automatically names the target by attaching ".target" to the end of the camera name. You can change this default name by typing a different name in the Name field. Both the target and the camera can be selected and transformed independently of each other.

Creating a camera view

You can change any viewport to show a camera's viewpoint. To do so, click the viewport's Point-of-View label, and select Cameras and the camera's name from the pop-up menu. Any movements done to the camera are reflected immediately in the viewport.

Another way to select a camera for a viewport is to press the C key. This keyboard shortcut makes the active viewport into a camera view. If several cameras exist in a scene, then the Select Camera dialog box appears, from which you can select a camera to use. You also can select a camera and press the C key to make that camera's view appear in the active viewport. Figure 18.1 shows two Target cameras pointing at a car. The two viewports on the right are the views from these cameras.

FIGURE 18.1

A car as seen by two different cameras

You can turn off the camera object icons using the Display panel. In the Display panel, under the Hide by Category rollout, select the Cameras option. When selected, the camera icons are not visible in the viewports.

> **NOTE**
>
> Cameras are usually positioned at some distance from the rest of the scene. Their distant position can make scene objects appear very small when the Zoom Extents button is used. If the visibility of the camera icons is turned off, Zoom Extents does not include them in the zoom. You can also enable the Ignore Extents option in the camera's Object Properties dialog box.

Tutorial: Setting up an opponent's view

There is no limit to the number of cameras that you can place in a scene. Placing two cameras in a scene showing a game of checkers lets you see the game from the perspective of either player.

To create a new aligned view from the opponent's perspective, follow these steps:

1. Open the Checkers game.max file from the Chap 18 directory on the CD.
2. Select Create ⇨ Cameras ⇨ Target Camera, and drag in the Top viewport to create the camera. Then give the new camera the name **Opponents Camera**.

3. Position the new target camera behind the opponent's pieces roughly symmetrical to the other camera by dragging the camera upward in the Front viewport.

4. With the new camera selected, select and drag the target point and position it near the other camera's target point somewhere below the center of the board.

To see the new camera view, click the Point-of-View label in the Perspective viewport and choose Cameras ⇨ Opponents Camera (or select the camera and the Perspective viewport, and press the C key). Figure 18.2 shows the view from this camera.

FIGURE 18.2

Positioning an additional camera behind the opponent's player's pieces offers a view from their perspective.

> **TIP**
>
> Because viewports can be resized, the view you see in the viewport isn't necessarily the view that will be rendered. Using the Safe Frames feature found in the Safe Frames panel of the Viewport Configuration dialog box, you can see a border around exactly what will be rendered.

Controlling a camera

I was once on a ride at Disneyland when a person behind me decided to blatantly disregard the signs not to take photographs. As he leaned over to snap another picture, I heard a fumbling noise, a faint, "Oh no," and then the distinct sound of his camera falling into the depths of the ride. (That was actually more enjoyable than the ride. It served him right.) As this example shows, controlling a camera can be difficult. This chapter offers many tips and tricks for dealing with the cameras in 3ds Max, and you won't have to worry about dropping them.

You control the camera view in a viewport by means of the Camera Navigation controls located in the lower-right corner of the screen. These controls replace the viewport controls when a camera view is selected and are different from the normal Viewport Navigation controls. The Camera Navigation controls are identified and defined in Table 18.1.

> **NOTE**
> Many of these controls are identical to the controls for lights.

You can constrain the movements when panning a camera view to a single axis when dragging with the middle mouse button by holding down the Shift key. Dragging with the Ctrl key causes the movements to increase rapidly and with the Alt key causes the view slowly. For example, holding down the Ctrl key while dragging the Perspective tool magnifies the amount of perspective applied to the viewport.

You can undo changes in the normal viewports using the Views ⇨ Undo View Change (Shift+Z) command, but you undo camera object changes with the regular Edit ⇨ Undo command because it involves the movement of an object.

TABLE 18.1 Camera Navigation Control Buttons

Control Button	Name	Description
	Dolly Camera, Dolly Target, Dolly Camera + Target	Moves the camera, its target, or both the camera and its target closer to or farther away from the scene in the direction it is pointing.
	Perspective	Increases or decreases the viewport's perspective by dollying the camera and altering its field of view.
	Roll Camera	Spins the camera about its local Z-axis.
	Zoom Extents All, Zoom Extents All Selected	Zooms in on all objects or the selected objects by reducing the field of view until the objects fill the viewport.
	Field of View	Changes the width of the view, similar to changing the camera lens or zooming without moving the camera.
	Truck Camera, Walk Through	The Truck Camera button moves the camera perpendicular to the line of sight, and the Walk Through button enables a mode in which you can control the camera using the arrow keys and the mouse.
	Orbit Camera, Pan Camera	The Orbit Camera button rotates the camera around the target, and the Pan Camera button rotates the target around the camera.
	Maximize Viewport T Toggle	Makes the current viewport fill the viewport area. Clicking this button a second time returns the display to several viewports.

> **NOTE**
> If a Free camera is selected, then the Dolly Target and Dolly Camera + Target buttons are not available.

Aiming a camera

In addition to the Camera Navigation buttons, you can use the Transformation buttons on the main toolbar to reposition the camera object. To move a camera, select the camera object and click the Select and Move button (W). Then drag the Move gizmo to move the camera.

Using the Select and Rotate (E) button changes the direction in which a camera points, but only Free cameras rotate in all directions. When applied to a Target camera, the rotate transformation spins only the camera about the axis pointing to the target. You aim Target cameras by moving their targets.

> **CAUTION**
> Don't try to rotate a Target camera so that it is pointing directly up or down, or the camera will flip.

Select the target for a Target camera by selecting its camera object, right-clicking to open the pop-up menu, and selecting Select Camera Target.

Tutorial: Watching a rocket

Because cameras can be transformed like any other geometry, they can also be set to watch the movements of any other geometry. In this tutorial, you aim a camera at a distant rocket and watch it as it flies past us and on into the sky. Zygote Media created the rocket model used in this tutorial.

To aim a camera at a rocket as it hurtles into the sky, follow these steps:

1. Open the Following a rocket.max file from the Chap 18 directory on the CD.

   This file includes a rocket mesh.

2. Select Create ⇨ Cameras ⇨ Target Camera, and drag in the Front viewport from the middle to the bottom of the viewport to create a camera. Then select the camera's target and move it in the Left viewport to be positioned right on the rocket. Set the Field of View value to **2.0** degrees. The corresponding Lens value is around 1031mm.

3. With the camera target selected, click the Select and Link button in the main toolbar, and drag from the target to the rocket object.

4. To view the scene from the camera's viewpoint, click the Point-of-View viewport label for the Perspective viewport and choose Cameras ⇨ Camera01 from the pop-up menu (or press the C button). Then click the Play Animation button to see how well the camera follows the target.

Figure 18.3 shows some frames from this animation.

Aligning cameras

Another way to aim a camera is with the Tools ⇨ Align ⇨ Align Camera menu command or by clicking the Align Camera button on the main toolbar (under the Align flyout). After selecting this command, click an object face and hold down the mouse button; the normal to the object face that is currently under the cursor icon is displayed as a blue arrow. When you've located the point at which you want the camera to point, release the mouse button. The camera is repositioned to point directly at the selected point on the selected face along the normal. The Align Camera command requires that a camera be selected before the command is used.

The Align Camera command does the same thing for cameras that the Place Highlight command does for lights. A discussion of the Place Highlight command appears in Chapter 19, "Using Lights and Basic Lighting Techniques."

FIGURE 18.3

Positioning the camera's target on the rocket enables the camera to follow the rocket's ascent.

Cameras can be positioned automatically to match any Perspective view that a viewport can display, including light views. The Views ⇨ Create Camera From View (Ctrl+C) menu command creates a new Free camera if one doesn't already exist, matches the view of the current active Perspective viewport, and makes the active viewport a camera view. This provides you with the ability to position the view using the Viewport Navigation Controls, and it automatically makes a camera that shows that view. If a camera already exists in the scene and is selected, this command uses the selected camera for the view.

CAUTION

The Create Camera View command doesn't work on Orthogonal views like Top, Front and Left.

Tutorial: Seeing the dinosaur's good side

Using the Align Camera tool, you can place a camera so that it points directly at an item or the face of an object, such as the dinosaur's good side (if a dinosaur has a good side). To align a camera with an object point, follow these steps:

1. Open the Dinosaur.max file from the Chap 18 directory on the CD.

   This file includes a dinosaur model created by Viewpoint Datalabs.

18

431

2. Select Create ⇨ Cameras ⇨ Free Camera, and click in the Top viewport to create a new Free Camera in the scene.

3. With the camera selected, choose Tools ⇨ Align ⇨ Align Camera or click the Align Camera flyout button on the main toolbar.

   The cursor changes to a small camera icon.

4. Right click to select the Perspective viewport and click the cursor on the dinosaur's face just under its eye in the Perspective viewport.

   This point is where the camera will point.

5. To see the new camera view, click the Point-of-View viewport label and choose Cameras ⇨ Camera01 (or press C).

   Although the camera is pointing at the selected point, you may need to change the field of view or dolly the camera to correct the zoom ratios.

Figure 18.4 shows your dinosaur from the newly aligned camera.

FIGURE 18.4

This new camera view of the dinosaur shows his best side.

The Align Camera command points a camera at an object only for the current frame. It does not follow an object if it moves during an animation. To have a camera follow an object, you need to use the Look At Constraint, which is covered in Chapter 25, "Animating with Constraints and Simple Controllers."

Setting Camera Parameters

When a camera is first created, you can modify the camera parameters directly in the Create panel as long as the new camera is selected. After the camera object has been deselected, you can make modifications in the Modify panel's Parameters rollout for the camera.

Lens settings and field of view

The first parameter in the Parameters rollout sets the Lens value or, more simply, the camera's focal length in millimeters.

The second parameter, FOV (which stands for Field of View), sets the width of the area that the camera displays. The value is specified in degrees and can be set to represent a Horizontal, Vertical, or Diagonal distance using the flyout button to its left, as shown in Table 18.2.

TABLE 18.2 **Field of View Buttons**

Button	Description
↔	Horizontal distance
↕	Vertical distance
↗	Diagonal distance

The Orthographic Projection option displays the camera view in a manner similar to any of the orthographic viewports such as Top, Left, or Front. This eliminates any perspective distortion of objects farther back in the scene and displays true dimensions for all edges in the scene. This type of view is used heavily in architecture.

Professional photographers and film crews use standard stock lenses in the course of their work. These lenses can be simulated in 3ds Max by clicking one of the Stock Lens buttons. Preset stock lenses include 15, 20, 24, 28, 35, 50, 85, 135, and 200mm lengths. The Lens and FOV fields are automatically updated on stock lens selection.

TIP
On cameras that use 35mm film, the typical default lens is 50mm.

Camera type and display options

The Type option enables you to change a Free Camera to a Target Camera and then change back at any time.

The Show Cone option enables you to display the camera's cone, showing the boundaries of the camera view when the camera isn't selected. (The camera cone is always visible when a camera is selected.) The Show Horizon option sets a horizon line within the camera view, which is a dark gray line where the horizon is located.

Environment ranges and clipping planes

You use the Near and Far Range values to specify the volume within which atmospheric effects like fog and volume lights are to be contained. The Show option causes these limits to be displayed as yellow rectangles within the camera's cone.

You use clipping planes to designate the closest and farthest object that the camera can see. In 3ds Max, they are displayed as red rectangles with crossing diagonals in the camera cone. If the Clip Manually option is disabled, then the clipping planes are set automatically with the Near Clip Plane set to 3 units. Figure 18.5 shows a camera with Clipping Planes specified. The front Clipping Plane intersects the car and chops off its front end. The far Clipping Plane is far behind the car.

> **TIP**
> Clipping planes can be used to create a cutaway view of your model.

FIGURE 18.5

A camera cone displaying Clipping Planes

Camera Correction modifier

To understand the Camera Correction modifier, you first need to understand what two-point perspective is. Default cameras in 3ds Max use three-point perspective, which causes all lines to converge to a vanishing point off in the distance, but two-point perspective causes all vertical lines to remain vertical.

The visual effect of this modifier is that extra-tall objects appear to bend toward the camera when corrected. For example, if you have a camera pointed at a skyscraper, then correcting the camera with the Camera Correction modifier makes the top of the building appear closer rather than having it recede away.

The Camera Correction modifier has an Amount value that lets you specify how much correction to apply and a Direction value that orients the angle of vertical lines in the scene. There is also a Guess button, which automatically sets the correction values for you based on the Z-axis vertical.

> **CAUTION**
> The Camera Correction modifier doesn't appear in the Modifier List in the Modifier Stack, but you can select it from the Modifiers ⇨ Cameras menu or from the quad menu when a camera is selected.

Creating multi-pass camera effects

All cameras have the option to enable them to become multi-pass cameras. A multi-pass camera creates and blends several passes of the view from the camera's perspective to create the desired effect. You can find these settings in the Parameters rollout when a camera object is selected. Multi-pass cameras are created by checking the Enable button and selecting the effect from the drop-down list. The current available effects include Depth of Field (mental ray/iray), Depth of Field, and Motion Blur. For each, an associated rollout of parameters opens.

> **CAUTION**
> Preview of the multi-pass camera effects in the viewport does not work when the Nitrous display drivers are enabled.

> **NOTE**
> The Depth of Field multi-pass effect is used with the default Scanline renderer, but the drop-down list also includes an option for enabling this effect for the mental ray or iray renderers.

The Multi-Pass Effect section of the Parameters rollout also includes a Preview button. This button makes the effect visible in the viewports for the current frame. This feature can save you a significant amount of time that normally would be spent test-rendering the scene. The Preview button is worth its weight in render speed. Using this button, you can preview the effect without having to render the entire sequence.

> **CAUTION**
> The Preview button does not work unless the Camera view is the active viewport.

The Render Effects Per Pass option causes any applied Render Effect to be applied at each pass. If disabled, then any applied Render Effect is applied after the passes are completed.

 You can also apply these multi-pass effects as Render Effects. See Chapter 21, "Using Atmospheric and Render Effects."

Using the Depth of Field effect

The Depth of Field Parameters rollout, shown in Figure 18.6, appears when the Depth of Field option is selected in the Multi-Pass Effect section of the Parameters rollout. It includes settings for controlling the Depth of Field multi-pass effect.

You can select to use the Target Distance (which is the distance to the camera's target), or you can specify a separate Focal Depth distance. This location is the point where the camera is in focus. All scene objects closer and farther from this location are blurred to an extent, depending on their distance from the focal point.

FIGURE 18.6

Use the Depth of Field Parameters rollout to set the number of passes.

Within the Depth of Field Parameters rollout, you also have the option to display each separate pass in the Rendered Frame Window with the Display Passes option and to use the camera's original location for the first rendering pass by enabling the Use Original Location option.

The Total Passes is the number of times the scene is rendered to produce the effect, and the Sample Radius is the potential distance that the scene can move during the passes. By moving the scene about the radius value and re-rendering a pass, the object becomes blurred more away from the focal distance.

The Sample Bias value moves the blurring closer to the focal point (for higher values) or away from the focal point (for lower values). If you want to highlight the focal point and radically blur the other objects in the scene, set the Sample Bias to 1.0. A Sample Bias setting of 0 results in a more even blurring.

The Normalize Weights option allows you to control how the various passes are blended. When enabled, you can avoid streaking along the object edges. The Dither Strength value controls the amount of dither taking place. Higher Dither Strength values make the image grainier. The Tile Size value also controls dither by specifying the dither pattern size.

With lots of passes specified, the render time can be fairly steep. To lower the overall rendering time, you can disable the Anti-alias and filtering computations. These speed up the rendering time at the cost of image quality.

Tutorial: Applying a Depth of Field effect to a row of windmills

In the dry plains of Southwest America, the wind blows fiercely. Rows of windmills are lined up in an effort to harness this energy. For this example, you use the Depth of Field effect to display the windmills.

To apply a Depth of Field effect to a row of windmills, follow these steps:

1. Open the Depth of field windmills.max file from the Chap 18 directory on the CD.

    This file includes a windmill object (created by Viewpoint Datalabs) duplicated multiple times and positioned in a row.

2. Select Create ⇨ Cameras ⇨ Target Camera, and drag in the Top viewport from the lower-left corner to the center of the windmills. In the Left viewpoint, select the camera and move it upward, and then select the Camera Target and also move it upward to the upper third of the windmill's height, so the entire row of windmills can be seen. If the windmills don't fill the camera view, adjust the Field of View (FOV) setting.

> **TIP**
>
> You can select both the camera and its target by clicking on the line that connects them.

3. Select the Perspective viewport, click on the Point-of-View viewport label, and select Cameras ⇨ Camera01 (or just press the C key) to make this viewport the Camera view.

4. With the Camera selected, open the Modify panel, enable the Multi-Pass Effect option, and then select Depth of Field in the drop-down list.

5. In the Depth of Field Parameters rollout, enable the Use Target Distance option and set the Total Passes to **15**, the Sample Radius to **3.0**, and the Sample Bias to **1.0**.

6. Select the Camera viewport, and select the Rendering ⇨ Render command.

    This shows the Depth of Field effect in the viewport.

Figure 18.7 shows the resulting Depth of Field effect in the viewport for the row of windmills.

FIGURE 18.7

Multi-pass camera effects can be viewed in the viewport using the Preview button.

Using the Motion Blur effect

Motion Blur is an effect that shows motion by blurring objects that are moving. If a stationary object is surrounded by several moving objects, the Motion Blur effect blurs the moving objects and the stationary object remains in clear view, regardless of its position in the scene. The faster an object moves, the more blurry it becomes.

This blurring is accomplished in several ways, but with a multi-pass camera, the camera renders subsequent frames of an animation and then blurs the images together.

The Motion Blur Parameters rollout, shown in Figure 18.8, appears when the Motion Blur option is selected in the Multi-Pass Effect section of the Parameters rollout. Many of its parameters work the same as the Depth of Field effect.

FIGURE 18.8

For the Motion Blur effect, you can set the number of frames to include.

The Display Passes option displays the different frames as they are being rendered, and Total Passes is the number of frames that are included in the averaging. You can also select the Duration, which is the number of frames to include in the effect. The Bias option weights the averaging toward the current frame. Higher Bias values weight the average more toward the latter frames, and lower values lean toward the earlier frames.

The remaining options all work the same as for the Depth of Field effect.

Tutorial: Using a Motion Blur multi-pass camera effect

The Motion Blur effect works only on objects that are moving. Applying this effect to a stationary 2D shape does not produce any noticeable results. For this tutorial, you apply this effect to a speeding car model created by Viewpoint Datalabs.

To apply a Motion Blur multi-pass effect to the camera looking at a car mesh, follow these steps:

1. Open the Car at a stop sign.max file from the Chap 18 directory on the CD.

   This file includes a car mesh, a camera, and a simple stop sign made of primitives. The car is animated.

438

2. Click the Select by Name button on the main toolbar to open the Select From Scene dialog box (or press the H key). Double-click the Camera01 object to select it.

3. With the camera object selected, open the Modify panel. In the Multi-Pass Effect section of the Parameters rollout, click the Enable check box and select the Motion Blur effect from the drop-down list.

4. In the Motion Blur Parameters rollout, set the Total Passes to **10**, the Duration to **1.0**, and the Bias to **0.9**.

5. Drag the Time Slider to frame 57. This is the location where the car just passes the stop sign.

6. With the Camera viewport active, select the Rendering ⇨ Render command.

Figure 18.9 shows the results of the Motion Blur effect. This effect has been exaggerated to show its result. Notice that the stop sign isn't blurred. The only problem with this example is that, with the Motion Blur effect enabled, you can't make out the license plate number, so you can't send this speeder a ticket.

FIGURE 18.9

Using the Motion Blur multi-pass effect for a camera, you can blur objects moving in the scene.

Summary

Cameras can offer a unique look at your scene. You can position and move them anywhere. In this chapter, you discovered how cameras work and how to control and aim them at objects. With multi-pass camera effects, you can add Depth of Field and Motion Blur effects.

In this chapter, you've accomplished the following:

- Learned the basics of cameras
- Created a camera object and view
- Discovered how to control a camera
- Aimed a camera at objects

- Changed camera parameters
- Learned to correct camera perspective with the Camera Correction modifier
- Used a multi-pass camera to create a Depth of Field effect
- Used a multi-pass camera to create a Motion Blur effect

Although the director typically says, "Lights, camera, action," you've switched the order to be cameras and then lights (action comes with animation later in the book). You just finished cameras, so next you move on to lights.

Using Lights and Basic Lighting Techniques

L ights play an important part in the visual process. Have you ever looked at a blank page and been told it was a picture of a polar bear in a blizzard or looked at a completely black image and been told it was a rendering of a black spider crawling down a chimney covered in soot? The point of these two examples is that with too much or too little light, you really can't see anything.

Light in the 3D world figures into every rendering calculation, and 3D artists often struggle with the same problem of too much or too little light. This chapter covers creating and controlling lights in the Autodesk® 3ds Max® software.

Understanding the Basics of Lighting

Lighting plays a critical part of any 3ds Max scene. Understanding the basics of lighting can make a big difference in the overall feeling and mood of your rendered scenes. Most 3ds Max scenes typically use one of two types of lighting: natural light or artificial light. *Natural light* is used for outside scenes and uses the sun and moon for its light source. *Artificial light* is usually reserved for indoor scenes where light bulbs provide the light. However, when working with lights, you'll sometimes use natural light indoors, such as sunlight streaming through a window, or artificial light outdoors, such as a streetlight. So, it is important to know how to work with both types.

Natural and artificial light

Natural light is best created using lights that have parallel light rays coming from a single direction: You can create this type of light using a Direct Light. The intensity of natural light is also dependent on the time, date, and location of the sun: You can control this intensity precisely using the software's Sunlight or Daylight systems.

441

The weather also can make a difference in the light color. In clear weather, the color of sunlight is pale yellow; in clouds, sunlight has a blue tint; and in dark, stormy weather, sunlight is dark gray. The colors of light at sunrise and sunset are more orange and red. Moonlight is typically white.

Artificial light is typically produced with multiple lights of lower intensity. The Omni light is usually a good choice for indoor lighting because it casts light rays in all directions from a single source. Standard white fluorescent lights usually have a light green or light blue tint.

A standard lighting method

When lighting a scene, not relying on a single light is best. A good lighting method includes one key light and several secondary lights.

A spotlight is good to use for the main key light. It should be positioned in front of and slightly above the subject, and it should usually be set to cast shadows, because it will be the main shadow-casting light in the scene.

The secondary lights fill in the lighting gaps and holes. You can position these at floor level on either side of the subject, with the intensity set at considerably less than the key light and set to cast no shadows. You can place one additional light behind the scene to backlight the subjects. This light should be very dim and also cast no shadows. From the user's perspective, all the objects in the scene will be illuminated, but the casual user will identify only the main spotlight as the light source because it casts shadows.

Figure 19.1 shows the position of the lights on an elk model that are included in the standard lighting model using a key light, two secondary lights, and a backlight. This model works for most standard scenes, but if you want to highlight a specific object, additional lights are needed.

FIGURE 19.1

A standard lighting model includes a key light, two secondary lights, and a backlight.

Figure 19.2 shows an elk model that was rendered using different levels of the standard lighting model. The upper-left image uses the default lighting with no lights. The upper-right image uses only the key light. This makes a shadow visible, but the details around the head are hard to define. The lower-left image includes the secondary lights, making the head details more easily visible and adding some highlights to the antlers. The bottom-right image includes the backlight, which highlights the back end of the model and casts a halo around the edges if viewed from the front.

FIGURE 19.2

An elk model rendered using default lighting, a single key light, two secondary lights, and a backlight

The final type of light to keep in mind is *ambient light*. Ambient light is not from a direct source, but is created by light that is deflected off walls and objects. It provides overall lighting to the entire scene and keeps shadows from becoming completely black. Global Lighting (including ambient light) is set in the Environment panel.

Shadows

Shadows are the areas behind an object where the light is obscured. 3ds Max supports several types of shadows, including Area Shadows, Shadow Maps, and Ray Traced Shadows.

Area Shadows create shadows based on an area that casts a light. It doesn't require lots of memory and results in a soft shadow that is created from multiple light rays that blur the shadows. Shadow maps are actual bitmaps that the renderer produces and combines with the finished scene to produce an image. These maps can have different resolutions, but higher resolutions require more memory. Shadow maps typically create fairly realistic, softer shadows, but they don't support transparency.

19

3ds Max calculates raytraced shadows by following the path of every light ray striking a scene. This process takes a significant amount of processing cycles, but can produce very accurate, hard-edged shadows. Raytracing enables you to create shadows for objects that shadow maps can't, such as transparent glass. The Shadows drop-down list also includes an option called Advanced Raytraced Shadows, which uses memory more efficiently than the standard Raytraced Shadows. Another option is the mental ray Shadow Map.

You can learn more about raytracing and mental ray in Chapter 22, "Rendering with mental ray and iray."

Figure 19.3 shows several images rendered with the different shadow types. The image in the upper left includes no shadows. The upper-right image uses Area Shadows. The lower-left image uses a Shadow Map, and the lower-right image uses Advanced Ray Traced Shadows. The last two images took considerably longer to create. Viewpoint Datalabs created the elk model shown in this figure.

FIGURE 19.3

Images rendered with different shadow types, including no shadow (upper left), Area Shadows (upper right), a Shadow Map (lower left), and Advanced Ray Traced Shadows (lower right)

Getting to Know the Light Types

3ds Max includes several different types of lights. The main difference in these types is how the light rays are cast into the scene. Light can come from the default lights that are present when no other user-created lights have been added to the scene. Light also can come from ambient light, which is light that bounces off other objects. 3ds Max includes several standard light objects that can be added where needed to a scene, including Omni, Direct, Spot, and Skylights, each having its own characteristics. 3ds Max also includes a category of Photometric lights, which are based on real-world lights and some lights that work with mental ray. Understanding these sources of light will help you know where to look to control the lighting.

Default lighting

So you get 3ds Max installed, and you eagerly start the application, throw some objects in a scene, and render it . . . and you'll be disappointed in the output, because you forgot to put lights in the scene. Right? Wrong! 3ds Max is smart enough to place default lighting in the scene that does not have any light sources.

The default lighting disappears as soon as a light is created in a scene (even if the light is turned off). When all the lights in a scene are deleted, default lighting magically reappears. So you can always be sure that your objects are rendered using some sort of lighting. Default lighting actually consists of two lights: The first light, the key light, is positioned above and to the left, and the bottom light, the fill light, is positioned below and to the right.

The Visual Style & Appearance panel of the Viewport Configuration dialog box has an option to enable default lighting for any viewport or set the default lighting to use only one light, the key light. You can open this dialog box by choosing Views ⇨ Viewport Configuration or by clicking the plus sign viewport label and selecting Configure Viewports from the pop-up menu.

If you want to access the default lights in your scene, you can use the Create ⇨ Lights ⇨ Standard Lights ⇨ Add Default Lights to Scene menu command to convert the default lights into actual light objects that you can control and reposition. This command opens a simple dialog box where you can select which lights to add to the scene and set the Distance Scaling value. This feature lets you start with the default lights and modify them as needed.

> **CAUTION**
> The Create ⇨ Lights ⇨ Standard Lights ⇨ Add Default Lights to Scene menu command is enabled only if the Default Lights and 2 Lights options are selected in the Viewport Configuration dialog box.

Ambient light

Ambient light is general lighting that uniformly illuminates the entire scene. It is caused by light that bounces off other objects. Using the Environment tab of the Environment and Effects dialog box, you can set the ambient light color. You also can set the default ambient light color in the Rendering panel of the Preference Settings dialog box. This is the darkest color that can appear in the scene, generally in the shadows.

In addition to these global ambient settings, each material can have an ambient color selected in the Material Editor.

> **CAUTION**
> Don't rely on ambient light to fill in unlit sections of your scene. If you use a heavy dose of ambient light instead of placing secondary lights, your scene objects appear flat, and you won't get the needed contrast to make your objects stand out.

Standard lights

Within the Create panel, the available lights are split into two subcategories: Standard and Photometric. Each subcategory has its own unique set of properties. The Standard light types include Omni, Spot (Target and Free), Direct (Target and Free), Skylight, and two area lights (Spot and Omni) that work with mental ray.

Omni light

The Omni light is like a light bulb: It casts light rays in all directions. The two default lights are Omni lights.

Spotlight

Spotlights are directional: They can be pointed and sized. The two spotlights available in 3ds Max are a Target Spot and a Free Spot. A Target Spot light consists of a light object and a target marker at which the spotlight points. A Free Spot light has no target, which enables it to be rotated in any direction using the Select and Rotate transform button. Spotlights always are displayed in the viewport as a cone with the light positioned at the cone apex.

 Both Target Spot and Target Direct lights are very similar in functionality to the Target Camera object, which you learn about in Chapter 18, "Configuring and Aiming Cameras."

Direct light

Direct lights cast parallel light rays in a single direction, like the sun. Just like spotlights, direct lights come in two types: a Target Direct light and a Free Direct light. The position of the Target Direct light always points toward the target, which you can move within the scene using the Select and Move button. A Free Direct light can be rotated to determine where it points. Direct lights are always displayed in the viewport as cylinders when selected.

Skylight

The Skylight is like a controllable ambient light. You can move it about the scene just like the other lights, and you can select to use the Scene Environment settings or select a Sky Color.

mr Area Omni and mr Area Spot

The Area lights project light from a defined area instead of from a single point. This has the effect of casting light along a wider area with more cumulative intensity than an Omni light source. Area lights are supported only by the mental ray renderer. If you use the Scanline renderer, these lights behave like simple Omni lights.

The Area Omni light lets you set its shape as a Sphere or a Cylinder in the Area Light Parameters rollout. Area Spot lights can be set to be either Rectangular or Disc-shaped. Be aware that area lights can take significantly longer to render than simple Omni lights.

 For more details on the mental ray renderer, see Chapter 22, "Rendering with mental ray and iray."

Photometric lights

The standard 3ds Max lights rely on parameters like Multiplier, Decay, and Attenuation, but the last time I was in the hardware store looking for a light bulb with a 2.5 Multiplier value, I was disappointed. Lights in the real world have their own set of measurements that define the type of light that is produced. Photometric lights are lights that are based on real-world light measurement values such as Intensity in Lumens and temperatures in degrees Kelvin.

If you select the Lights menu or the Lights category in the Create panel, you'll notice another subcategory called Photometric. Photometric lights are based on photometric values, which are the values of light energy. The lights found in this subcategory include Free and Target lights.

 The Photometric category also includes a mr Sky Portal option that is used to focus lights coming in from an external source. This feature is covered in Chapter 22, "Rendering with mental ray and iray."

To make choosing the right light easier, 3ds Max includes a Templates rollout for photometric lights that lets you set the configuration for a number of different common real-world lights, including 40, 60, 75, and 100W light bulbs, a number of Halogen spotlights, recessed lights, fluorescent lights, and even street and stadium lights.

> **NOTE**
> Whenever a photometric light is created, a warning dialog box appears, informing you that it is recommended that the Logarithmic Exposure Control be enabled. It also offers you an option to enable this setting. You can learn more about this feature in Chapter 21, "Using Atmospheric and Render Effects."

Creating and Positioning Light Objects

3ds Max, in its default setup, can create many different types of light. Each has different properties and features. To create a light, just select Create ➪ Lights and choose the light type or click the Lights category button in the Create panel. Then click the button for the type of light you want to create and drag in a viewport to create it. Most light types are created with a single click, but you create Target lights by clicking at the light's position and dragging to the position of the target.

Transforming lights

Lights can be transformed just like other geometric objects. To transform a light, click one of the transformation buttons and then select and drag the light.

Target lights can have the light and the target transformed independently, or you can select both the light and target by clicking the line that connects them. Target lights can be rotated around the X and Y axes only if the light and target are selected together. A target light can spin about its local Z-axis even if the target isn't selected. Scaling a target light increases its cone or cylinder. Scaling a Target Direct light with only the light selected increases the diameter of the light's beam, but if the light and target are selected, then the diameter and distance are scaled.

An easy way to select or deselect the target is to right-click the light and choose Select Target from the pop-up menu. All transformations work on free lights.

Viewing lights and shadows in the viewport

Lighting effects and shadows can be displayed in the viewports if you are using the Nitrous or the Direct3D display driver. You can check to see if your video card supports interactive lights and shadows using the Help ➪ Diagnose Video Hardware menu command. This command runs a script and returns the results to the MAXScript Listener window.

If your graphics card supports viewport shadows, you can enable them using the Lighting and Shadows submenu under the viewport Shading label or in the Visual Style & Appearance panel of the Viewport Configuration dialog box. If you're using the Nitrous display driver, then the same menu also includes an option for enabling Ambient Occlusion.

The Viewport Lighting and Shadows quad menu and the Views menu also include options to lock and unlock the selected light, and to display the effects of the selected light. Figure 19.4 shows a snowman with shadows enabled in the viewport.

FIGURE 19.4

By enabling viewport shadows, you can view shadows in real time.

Listing lights

The Tools ⇨ Light Lister menu command opens the Light Lister dialog box, shown in Figure 19.5, where you can see at a quick glance all the details for all the lights in the scene. This dialog box also lets you change the light settings. It includes two rollouts: Configuration, which lets you select to see All Lights, the Selected Lights, or the General Settings that apply to all lights; and Lights, which holds details on each individual light.

If the General Settings option is selected, then a separate rollout opens with all the typical settings, including Multiplier, Color, Shadows, Map Size, and so on. You can apply these changes to the Selected Lights or to All Lights. The Light Lister provides an easy way to change the parameters of many lights at once.

If either the All Lights option or the Selected Lights option is selected in the Configuration rollout, then the parameters are listed in the Lights rollout. Using this rollout, you can change the settings for any of the listed lights that affect all lights. The Refresh button updates the Light Lister dialog box if a new light has been added to the scene or if any parameters have been altered in the Modify panel.

FIGURE 19.5

The Light Lister dialog box includes a comprehensive list of light settings in one place.

NOTE

If several lights are instanced, then only one of the instanced lights appears in the Light Lister dialog box, but each of the instanced lights can be selected from a drop-down list.

Placing highlights

The Place Highlight tool enables you to control the position and orientation of a light in order to achieve a highlight in a precise location. To use this tool, you must select a light object in the scene and then choose Tools ⇨ Align ⇨ Place Highlight, or click the Place Highlight flyout button (located under the Align button) on the toolbar. The cursor changes to the Place Highlight icon. Click a point on the object in the scene where you want the highlight to be positioned, and the selected light repositions itself to create a specular highlight at the exact location where you clicked. The light's position is determined by the Angle of Incidence between the highlight point and the light.

TIP

If you click and drag on the object surface, then a small blue vector points from the surface of the object. The light is positioned inline with this vector when the mouse button is released. This is helpful when trying to precisely place a light.

Tutorial: Lighting the snowman's face

You can use the Place Highlight tool to position a light for our snowman. To place a highlight, follow these steps:

1. Open the Snowman.max file from the Chap 19 directory on the CD.

   This file contains a simple snowman created using primitive objects.

2. Select the Create ⇨ Lights ⇨ Standard Lights ⇨ Target Spotlight menu command, and position the spot light below and to the left of the Snowman model in the Top viewport.

3. To place the highlight so it shows the Snowman's face, select the spot light and then choose Tools ⇨ Align ⇨ Place Highlight. Then click and drag on the Snowman's face in the Perspective viewport where the highlight should be located, just above his right eye.

Figure 19.6 shows the results.

FIGURE 19.6

The snowman, after the lights have been automatically repositioned using the Place Highlight command

Viewing a Scene from a Light

You can configure viewports to display the view from any light, with the exception of an Omni light. To do so, click the viewport Point-of-View label and then select Lights and the light name at the top of the pop-up menu.

> **NOTE**
> The keyboard shortcut for making the active viewport a Light view is the $ (the dollar sign that appears above the 4) key. If more than one light exists, and none is selected, then the Select Light dialog box appears and lets you select which light to use. This can be used only on spot and direct lights.

Light viewport controls

When a viewport is changed to show a light view, the Viewport Navigation buttons in the lower-right corner of the screen change into Light Navigation controls. Table 19.1 describes these controls.

> **NOTE**
> Many of these controls are identical for viewports displaying lights or cameras.

TABLE 19.1   **Light Navigation Control Buttons**

Toolbar Button	Name	Description
	Dolly Light, Dolly Target, Dolly Spotlight + Target	Moves the light, its target, or both the light and its target closer to or farther away from the scene in the direction it is pointing.
	Light Hotspot	Adjusts the angle of the light's hotspot, which is displayed as a blue cone.
	Roll Light	Spins the light about its local Z-axis.
	Zoom Extents All, Zoom Extents All Selected	Zooms in on all objects or the selected objects until they fill the viewport.
	Light Falloff	Changes the angle of the light's falloff cone.
	Truck Light	Moves the light perpendicular to the line of sight.
	Orbit Light, Pan Light	Orbit rotates the light around the target. Pan Light rotates the target around the light.
	Maximize Viewport Toggle	Makes the current viewport fill the screen. Clicking this button a second time returns the display to several viewports.

If you hold down the Ctrl key while using the Light Hotspot or Falloff buttons, 3ds Max changes the size at a much faster rate. Holding down the Alt key causes the size to change at a much slower rate. The Hotspot cone cannot grow any larger than the Falloff cone, but if you hold down the Shift key, trying to make the size of the hotspot larger than the falloff causes both to increase, and vice versa.

You can constrain any light movements to a single axis by holding down the Shift key. The Ctrl key causes the movements to increase rapidly.

For Free lights, an invisible target is determined by the distance computed from the other light properties. You can use the Shift key to constrain rotations to be vertical or horizontal.

Manipulating Hotspot/Beam and Falloff/Field cones

When the Select and Manipulate mode is enabled on the main toolbar, the ends of the Hotspot/Beam and Falloff/Field cones appear green for a selected spotlight. When you move the mouse over these lines, the lines turn red, allowing you to drag the lines and make the Hotspot/Beam and/or Falloff/Field angle values greater. These manipulators provide visual feedback as you resize the spotlight cone.

> **NOTE**
> You can undo changes in the normal viewports using the Views ⇨ Undo View Change command, but you undo light viewport changes with the regular Edit ⇨ Undo command.

19

Tutorial: Lighting a lamp

To practice using lights, you'll try to get a lamp model to work as it should.

To add a light to a lamp model, follow these steps:

1. Open the Lamp.max file from the Chap 19 directory on the CD.

   This file includes a lamp mesh surrounded by some plane objects used to create the infinite walls at render time and floor. The lamp model was created by Zygote Media. It looks like a standard living room lamp that you could buy in any department store.

2. Select the Create ⇨ Lights ⇨ Standard Lights ⇨ Omni menu command, and click in the Perspective viewport.

3. Use the Select and Move transform button (W) to position the light object inside the lamp's light bulb.

The resulting image is shown in Figure 19.7. Notice that the light intensity is greater at places closer to the light.

FIGURE 19.7

The rendered lighted-lamp image

Altering Light Parameters

Lights affect every object in a scene and can really make or break a rendered image, so it shouldn't be surprising that each light comes with many controls and parameters. Several different rollouts work with lights.

If you're looking for a light switch to turn lights on and off, look no further than the Modify panel. When a light is selected, several different rollouts appear. The options contained in these rollouts enable you to turn the lights on and off, select a light color and intensity, and determine how a light affects object surfaces.

General parameters

The Light Type drop-down list in the General Parameters rollout lets you change the type of light instantly, so you can switch from Omni light to Spotlight or Directional Light with little effort. You also can switch between targeted and untargeted lights. To the right of the Targeted option is the distance in scene units between the light and the target. This feature provides an easy way to look at the results of using a different type of light. When you change the type of light, you lose the settings for the previous light.

The General Parameters rollout also includes some settings for shadows. Shadows can be turned on or off easily. In this rollout, you can defer to the global settings by selecting the Use Global Settings option. This option helps to maintain consistent settings across several lights. It applies the same settings to all lights, so changing the value for one light changes that same value for all lights that have this option selected.

You also can select whether the shadows are created using Area Shadows, a Shadow Map, regular or advanced Ray Traced shadows, or a mental ray Shadow Map. A new rollout appears, depending on the selection you make.

The Exclude button opens the Exclude/Include dialog box, where you can select objects to be included in or excluded from illumination and/or shadows. The pane on the left includes a list of all the current objects in the scene. To exclude objects from being lit, select the Exclude option, select the objects to be excluded from the pane on the left, and click the double-arrow icon pointing to the right to move the objects to the pane on the right.

Figure 19.8 shows the Exclude/Include dialog box. This dialog box also recognizes any Selection Sets you've previously defined. You select them from the Selection Sets drop-down list.

19

FIGURE 19.8

The Exclude/Include dialog box lets you set which objects are excluded from or included in being illuminated.

As an example of the Exclude/Include feature, Figure 19.9 shows the elk model with the antlers (left) and its body (right) excluded from shadows and illumination.

FIGURE 19.9

Using the Exclude/Include dialog box, you can exclude objects from casting shadows.

The Intensity/Color/Attenuation rollout

In the Intensity/Color/Attenuation rollout, the Multiplier value controls the light intensity. A light with a Multiplier set to 2 is twice as bright as a light with its Multiplier set to 1. Higher Multiplier values make a light appear white regardless of the light color. The Multiplier value also can be negative. A negative value can be used to pull light from a scene but it should be used with caution.

> **TIP**
> Adding and positioning another light typically is better than increasing the multiplier as brighter lights tend to wash out the surface details.

To the right of the Multiplier value is a color swatch. Clicking the color swatch opens a Color Selector where you can choose a new light color.

Attenuation is a property that determines how light fades over distance. An example of this is a candle set in a room. The farther you get from the candle, the less the light shines.

You use three basic parameters to simulate realistic attenuation. Near Attenuation sets the distance at which the light begins to fade, and Far Attenuation sets the distance at which the light falls to 0. Both these properties are ranges that include Start and End values. The third parameter sets the Decay value, which simulates attenuation using a mathematical formula to compute the drop in light intensity over distance.

Selecting the Use option enables the Near and Far Attenuation values; both have Start and End values that set the range for these attenuation types. The Show option makes the attenuation distances and decay values visible in the viewports. The three types of decay from which you can choose are None, Inverse, and Inverse Square. The Inverse type decays linearly with the distance away from the light. The Inverse Square type decays exponentially with distance.

> **NOTE**
> The Inverse Square type approximates real lights the best, but it is often too dim for computer graphic images. You can compensate for this by increasing the Multiplier value.

Spotlight and directional light parameters

The Spotlight Parameters rollout includes values to set the angular distance of both the Hot Spot/Beam and Falloff/Field cones. The Show Cone option makes the Hotspot and Falloff cones visible in the viewport when the light is not selected. The Overshoot option makes the light shine in all directions like an Omni light, but light projection effects and shadows occur only within the Falloff cone. You also can set the light shape to be circular or rectangular. For a rectangular-shaped spotlight, you can control the aspect ratio. You can use the Bitmap Fit button to make the aspect ratio match a particular projection bitmap.

The Directional Light Parameters rollout, which appears for Directional light types, is identical to the Spotlight Parameters rollout and also includes settings for the Hot Spot/Beam and Falloff/Field values.

Advanced Effects

Options in the Affect Surfaces section of the Advanced Effects rollout control how light interacts with an object's surface. The Contrast value alters the contrast between the diffuse and the ambient surface areas. The Soften Diffuse Edge value blurs the edges between the diffuse and ambient areas of a surface. The Diffuse and Specular options let you disable these properties. When the Ambient Only option is turned on, the light affects only the ambient properties of the surface.

 Find more detail on the Diffuse, Specular, and Ambient properties in Chapter 14, "Creating and Applying Standard Materials with the Slate Material Editor."

You can use any light as a projector; you find this option in the Advanced Effects rollouts. Selecting the Map option enables you to use the light as a projector. You can select a map to project by clicking the button to the right of the map option. You can also drag a material map directly from the Material/Map Browser onto the Projector Map button.

Shadow parameters

All light types have a Shadow Parameters rollout that you can use to select a shadow color by clicking the color swatch. The default color is black. The Dens setting stands for "Density" and controls how dark the shadow appears. Lower values produce lighter shadows, and higher values produce dark shadows. This value also can be negative.

The Map option, like the Projection Map, can be used to project a map along with the shadow color. The Light Affects Shadow Color option alters the Shadow Color by blending it with the light color if selected.

In the Atmosphere Shadows section, the On button lets you determine whether atmospheric effects, such as fog, can cast shadows. You also can control the Opacity and the degree to which atmospheric colors blend with the Shadow Color.

When you select a light and open the Modify panel, one additional rollout is available: the Atmospheres & Effects rollout. This rollout is a shortcut to the Add Atmosphere or Effect dialog box, where you can specify atmospheric effects such as fog and volume lights.

NOTE
The only effects that can be used with lights are Volume Light and Lens Effects.

 Chapter 21, "Using Atmospheric and Render Effects," covers atmospheric effects.

If the Area Shadows option is selected in the General Parameters rollout, then the Area Shadows rollout appears, which includes several settings for controlling this shadow type. In the drop-down list at the top of the rollout, you can select from several Basic Options, including Simple, Rectangle Light, Disc Light, Box Light, and Sphere Light. You can select dimensions depending on which option is selected. You also can set the Integrity, Quality, Spread, Bias, and Jitter amounts.

For the Shadow Map option, the Shadow Map Params rollout includes values for the Bias, Size, and Sample Range. The Sample Range value softens the shadow edges. You also can select to use an Absolute Map Bias and 2 Sided Shadows.

If the Ray Traced Shadows option is selected in the Shadow Parameters rollout, the Ray Traced Shadow Parameters rollout appears below it. This simple rollout includes only two values: Bias and 3ds Max Quadtree Depth. The Bias settings cause the shadow to move toward or away from the object that casts the shadow. The 3ds Max Quadtree Depth determines the accuracy of the shadows by controlling how long the ray paths are followed. There is also an option to enable 2 Sided Shadows, which enables both sides of a face to cast shadows, including backfacing objects.

For the Advanced Ray Traced Shadows options, the rollout includes many more options, including Simple, 1-Pass, or 2-Pass Antialias. This rollout also includes the same quality values found in the Area Shadows rollout.

> **NOTE**
> Depending on the number of objects in your scene, shadows can take a long time to render. Enabling Ray Traced shadows for a complex scene can greatly increase the render time.

Optimizing lights

If you select either the Area Shadows type or the Advanced Ray Traced shadow type, then a separate Optimizations rollout appears. This rollout includes settings that help speed up the shadow rendering process. Using this rollout, you can enable Transparent Shadows. You can also specify a color that is used at the Antialiasing Threshold. You can also turn off anti-aliasing for materials that have SuperSampling or Reflection/Refraction enabled. Or you can have the shadow renderer skip coplanar faces with a given threshold.

Photometric light parameters

Several of the light rollouts for photometric lights are the same as those for the standard lights, but several key parameters are unique for photometric lights, such as the ability to choose a light distribution model and a shape type.

Distribution options

The Distribution options are listed in a drop-down list in the General rollout. Both Free and Target photometric lights can be set to one of four distribution types. Each of these types appears as a different icon in the viewports:

- **Uniform Spherical:** This distribution type emanates light equally in all directions from a central point, like the standard Omni light.
- **Uniform Diffuse:** This distribution type spreads light equally in all directions for only one hemisphere, such as when a light is positioned against a wall.
- **Spotlight:** This distribution type spreads the light in a cone shape, like a flashlight or a car's headlight.
- **Photometric Web:** This distribution type can be any arbitrary 3D representation and is defined in a separate file that can be obtained from the light manufacturer and loaded into the light object. Once loaded, the distribution graph is visible in the Distribution (Photometric Web) rollout.

The Uniform Spherical option distributes light equally in all directions. The Uniform Diffuse option has its greatest distribution at right angles to the surface it is emitted from and gradually decreases in intensity at increasing angles from the normal. For both options, the light gradually becomes weaker as the distance from the light increases.

19

The Spotlight option concentrates the light energy into a cone that emits from the light. This cone of light energy is directional and can be controlled with the Hotspot and Falloff values.

The Photometric Web option is a custom option that lets you open a separate file describing the light's emission pattern. These files have the .ies, .cibse, or .ltli extensions. Light manufacturers have this data for the various real-world lights they sell. You load these files using the Choose Photometric File button found in the Distribution (Photometric Web) rollout. You can also specify the X-, Y-, and Z-axis rotation values.

Color options

The Color section of the Intensity/Color/Attenuation rollout, shown in Figure 19.10, includes two ways to specify a light's color. The first is a drop-down list of options. The options found in the list include standard real-world light types such as Fluorescent (Cool White), Mercury, Quartz Metal Halide, and Halogen.

In addition to a list of available light types, you can specify a color based on temperature expressed in degrees Kelvin. Temperature-based colors run from a cool 1,000 degrees, which is a mauve-pink color, through light yellow and white (at 6,000 degrees Kelvin) to a hot light blue at 20,000 degrees Kelvin. Typical indoor lighting is fairly low on the Kelvin scale at around 3,300 degrees K. Direct sunlight is around 5,500 degrees K. Thunderbolts, arc welders, and electric bolts run much hotter, from 10,000 to 20,000 degrees Kelvin.

FIGURE 19.10

The Intensity/Color/Attenuation rollout for photometric lights uses real-world intensity values.

You also can set a Filter Color using the color swatch found in this section. The Filter Color simulates the color caused by colored cellophane or gels placed in front of the light.

Intensity and Attenuation options

The Intensity options can be specified in Lumens, Candelas, or Lux at a given distance. Light manufacturers have this information available. You also can specify a Multiplier value, which determines how effective the light is. There are also settings for specifying the intensity due to a dimming effect, and the Incandescent lamp color shift when dimming option causes the light from an incandescent light to turn more yellow as it is dimmed. This effect is common as you get farther from a light bulb.

All real-world lights have attenuation, and Far attenuation values also can be set for photometric lights. This helps to speed up rendering times for scenes with lots of lights by limiting the extent of the cast light rays.

Light shapes

In addition to the distribution type, you also can select the light shape, which has an impact on how shadows are cast in the scene using the settings in the Shape/Area Shadows rollout. Selecting a different-shaped light causes the light to be spread over a wider area, so in most cases the Point light results in the brightest intensity with sharper shadows, and lights covering a larger area are less intense and have softer shadows. The available photometric light shapes include the following:

- **Point:** This shape emits light from a single point like a light bulb.
- **Line:** This shape emits light from a straight line like a fluorescent tube.
- **Rectangle:** This shape emits light from an area like a bank of fluorescent lights.
- **Disc:** This shape emits light from a circular area like the light out of the top of a shaded lamp.
- **Sphere:** This shape emits light from a spherical shape like a Chinese lantern.
- **Cylinder:** This shape emits light from a cylindrical shape like some kinds of track lighting.

For each shape you can set the shape's dimensions in the Shape/Area Shadows rollout. The rollout also lets you switch between the different shapes. If you need to see the actual light shape, then you can enable the Light Shape Visible in Rendering option in the Shape/Area Shadows rollout.

Summary

I hope you have found this chapter enlightening. (Sorry about the bad pun, but I need to work them in where I can.) 3ds Max has many different lights, each with plenty of controls. Learning to master these controls can take you a long way toward increasing the realism of the scene. In this chapter, you've accomplished the following:

- Learned the basics of lighting
- Discovered the software's standard and photometric light types
- Created and positioned light objects
- Learned to change the viewport view to a light

In the next chapter you finally see the results of your hard work by rendering the scene.

19

Rendering a Scene and Enabling Quicksilver

IN THIS CHAPTER

Setting render parameters and preferences

Using the Rendered Frame Window

Working with the ActiveShade window and the RAM Player

Rendering non-photorealistic scenes

After hours of long, hard work, the next step—rendering—is where the "rubber hits the road" and you get to see what you've worked on so hard. After modeling, applying materials, and positioning lights and cameras, you're finally ready to render the final output. Rendering deals with outputting the objects that make up a scene at various levels of detail.

The Autodesk® 3ds Max® 2013 software includes a Scanline Renderer that is optimized to speed up this process, and several settings exist that you can use to make this process even faster. Understanding the Render Setup dialog box and its functions can save you many headaches and computer cycles. However, other rendering options are available, including Quicksilver and mental ray.

The need for all these different rendering engines comes about because of a trade-off between speed and quality. For example, the renderer used to display objects in the viewports is optimized for speed, but the renderer used to output final images leans toward quality. Each renderer includes many settings that you can use to speed the rendering process or improve the quality of the results.

Working with Render Parameters

Commands and settings for rendering an image are contained within the Render Setup dialog box. This dialog box includes several tabbed panels.

After you're comfortable with the scene file and you're ready to render a file, you need to open the Render Setup dialog box, shown in Figure 20.1, by means of the Rendering ⇨ Render Setup menu command (F10) or by clicking the Render Setup button on the main toolbar. This dialog box has several panels: Common, Renderer, Render Elements, Raytracer, and Advanced Lighting. The Common panel includes commands that are common for all renderers, but the Renderer panel includes specific settings for the selected renderer.

The Common and Renderer panels for the Default Scanline Renderer are covered in this chapter. The Raytracer and Renderer panel for the mental ray renderer are covered in Chapter 22, "Rendering with mental ray and iray," and the Render Elements panel is covered in Chapter 23, "Compositing with Render Elements and the Video Post Interface."

FIGURE 20.1

You use the Render Setup dialog box to render the final output.

Initiating a render job

At the bottom of the Render Setup dialog box are several controls that are visible for all panels; these controls let you initiate a render job. The render modes, available in the drop-down list to the right of the Render button, are Production, Iterative, and Active Shade. A Submit to Network Rendering option, which sends the job to be rendered over the network, is available as well. Each of these modes can use a different renderer with different render settings as defined using the Assign Renderer rollout.

> **NOTE**
>
> If any objects in the rendered scene are missing mapping coordinates, then a dialog box appears as you try to render the scene with options to Continue or Cancel. A similar dialog box appears for any missing external files or any missing XRefs with options to continue, cancel, or browse from the missing file.

Iterative rendering mode is different from production in that it doesn't save the render to a file, use network rendering, or render multiple frames. Using this mode, you can leave the settings in the Render Setup dialog boxes unchanged while still getting a test render out quickly. This makes it a good mode to use for quickly getting test renders.

The Preset drop-down list to the left of the Render button lets you save and load a saved preset of renderer settings. When saving or loading a preset, the Select Preset Categories dialog box, shown in Figure 20.2, opens (after you select a preset file in a file dialog box). In this dialog box, you can select which panels of settings to include in the preset. The panels listed depend on the selected renderer. All presets are saved with the .rps file extension.

FIGURE 20.2

The Select Preset Categories dialog box lets you choose which settings to include in the preset.

The View drop-down list includes all the available viewports and camera views. When the Render Setup dialog box opens, the currently active viewport appears in the View drop-down list. The one selected is the one that gets rendered when you click the Render button (or when you press Shift+Q). The Render button starts the rendering process. You can click the Render button without changing any settings, and the default parameters are used.

TIP

The little lock icon next to the viewport indicates that the selected viewport is always rendered when the Render button is clicked, regardless of the active viewport.

When you click the Render button, the Rendering dialog box appears. This dialog box, shown in Figure 20.3, displays all the settings for the current render job and tracks its progress. The Rendering dialog box also includes Pause and Cancel buttons for halting the rendering process. If the rendering is stopped, the Rendering dialog box disappears, but the Rendered Frame Window stays open.

CAUTION

If you close the Rendered Frame Window, the render job still continues. To cancel the rendering, click the Pause or Cancel button, or press the Esc key on your keyboard.

TIP

After you've set up the render settings for an image, you can re-render an image without opening the Render Setup dialog box by clicking the Render Production button on the main toolbar, by selecting the Rendering⇨Render menu command, by using the Shift+Q keyboard shortcut, or by selecting a render option from the Render Shortcuts toolbar. The F9 shortcut renders the last viewport again.

Common parameters

The Common Parameters rollout in the Render Setup dialog box includes the same controls regardless of the renderer being used.

FIGURE 20.3

The Rendering dialog box displays the current render settings and progress of the render job.

Specifying range and size

The Time Output section defines which animation frames to include in the output. The Single option renders the current frame specified by the Time Slider. The Active Time Segment option renders the range of frames currently shown in the Time Slider. The Range option lets you set a unique range of frames to render by entering the beginning and ending frame numbers. These values can exceed the range of the Time Slider. The last option is Frames, where you can enter individual frames and ranges using commas and hyphens. For example, entering "1, 6, 8-12" renders frames 1, 6, and 8 through 12. The Every Nth Frame value is active for the Active Time Segment and Range options. It renders every nth frame in the active segment. For example, entering 3 would cause every third frame to be rendered. This option is useful for sped-up animations. The File Number Base is the number to add to or subtract from the current frame number for the reference numbers attached to the end of each image file. For example, a File Number Base value of 10 for a Range value of 1–10 would label the files as image0011, image0012, and so on.

> **TIP**
> Don't render long animation sequences using the .avi, .mpeg, or .mov formats. If the rendering has trouble, the entire file will be corrupt. Instead, choose to render the frames as individual images. These individual images can then be reassembled into a video format using the software's RAM Player, the Video Post interface, or an external package like Adobe Premiere.

The Output Size section defines the resolution of the rendered images or animation. The drop-down list includes a list of standard film and video resolutions, including various 35mm and 70mm options, Anamorphic, Panavision, IMAX, VistaVision, NTSC (National Television Standards Committee), PAL (Phase Alternate Line), and HDTV standards. A Custom option allows you to select your own resolution.

> **TIP**
> Setting up the aspect ratio of the final rendering at the start of the project is helpful. Once an aspect ratio is established, you can use the Safe Frames panel in the Viewport Configuration dialog box to display the borders of the render region in the viewport.

Aperture Width is a property of cameras that defines the relationship between the lens and the field of view. Changing the Output Size by using the drop-down list alters the Aperture Value without changing the view by modifying the Lens value in the scene.

For each resolution, you can change the Width and Height values. Each resolution also has several preset buttons for setting these values.

> **TIP**
> You can set the resolutions of any of the preset buttons by right-clicking the button that you want to change. The Configure Preset dialog box opens, where you can set the button's Width, Height, and Pixel Aspect values.

The Image Aspect is the ratio of the image width to its height. You can also set the Pixel Aspect ratio to correct rendering on different devices. Both of these values have lock icons to their left that lock the aspect ratio for the set resolution. Locking the aspect ratio automatically changes the Width dimension whenever the Height value is changed, and vice versa. The Aperture Width, Image Aspect, and Pixel Aspect values can be set only when Custom is selected in the Output Size drop-down list.

Render options

Within the Render Options section are several toggle options that are generally disabled to speed up the rendering. The Options section includes the following options:

- **Atmospherics:** Renders any atmospheric effects that are set up in the Environment dialog box.
- **Effects:** Enables any Render Effects that have been set up.
- **Displacement:** Enables any surface displacement caused by an applied displacement map.
- **Video Color Check:** Displays any colors that cannot be displayed in the HSV (hue, saturation, and value) color space used by television in black.
- **Render to Fields:** Enables animations to be rendered as fields. Fields are used by video formats. Video animations include one field with every odd scan line and one field with every even scan line. These fields are composited when displayed.
- **Render Hidden Geometry:** Renders all objects in the scene, including hidden objects. Using this option, you can hide objects for quick viewport updates and include them in the final rendering.

20

- **Area Lights/Shadows as Points:** Rendering area lights and shadows can be time-consuming, but point lights render much more quickly. By enabling this option, you can speed the rendering process.

- **Force 2-Sided:** Renders both sides of every face. This option essentially doubles the render time and should be used only if singular faces or the inside of an object are visible.

- **Super Black:** Enables Super Black, which is used for video compositing. Rendered images with black backgrounds have trouble in some video formats. The Super Black option prevents these problems.

The Advanced Lighting section offers options to use Advanced Lighting or Compute Advanced Lighting when Required. Advanced lighting can take a long time to compute, so these two options give you the ability to turn advanced lighting on or off.

Bitmap Proxies

The Bitmap Performance and Memory Options section includes a Setup button to enable a feature that can downscale all maps for the current scene. Clicking the Setup button opens the Global Settings and Defaults for Bitmap Proxies dialog box, shown in Figure 20.4.

FIGURE 20.4

The Bitmap Proxies dialog box lets you replace all texture maps with proxy images.

The Downscale map option lets you select to downscale all maps to Half, Third, Quarter, or Eighth, or to their current size. This lets you create your scene with high-quality maps and quickly reduce their sizes as needed without having to open and scale each individual map. The Proxy System lets you select to use a proxy image if the current map is larger than a specified size in pixels.

This dialog box also lets you set the Render Mode to be optimized for performance or memory. The options include Render with Proxies, Render with Full Resolution and Keep them [image maps] In Memory, and Render with Full Resolution and Free up the Memory once Rendered. If you enable the Page Large Images to Disk, large textures and rendered images are split into pages, which frees up memory, but it can make the update of the scene slower when a new page has to be recalled. The page file location can be specified.

Choosing a Render Output option

The Render Output section enables you to output the image or animations to a file, a device, or the Rendered Frame Window. To save the output to a file, enable the Save File option, click the Files button, and select a location in the Render Output File dialog box. Supported formats include AVI, BMP,

DDS, Postscript (EPS), JPEG, Kodak Cineon (CIN), Open EXR, Radiance Image File (HDRI), QuickTime (MOV), PNG, RLA, RPF, SGI's Format (RGB), Targa (TGA), and TIF. The Use Device option and the Devices button can output to a device such as a video recorder. The Rendered Frame Window option displays the render progress in a separate window, which is discussed later in this chapter. The Skip Existing Images option doesn't replace any images with the same filename, a feature that you can use to continue a rendering job that has been canceled.

> **TIP**
>
> Each of these output formats has its advantages. For example, Targa files are good for compositing because they have an alpha channel. TIF and EPS files are good for files to be printed. JPEG and PNG files are used for web images. DDS images are used in many game engines.

You also have an option to Put Image File List in Output Path, which creates a list of image files in the same location as the rendered file. You also have the choice of choosing the software's IFL standard or the Autodesk ME Image Sequence File (IMSQ). The Create Now button creates an image list instantly. This list is helpful to make sure all the image files have been rendered and are accounted for.

E-mail notifications

The process of rendering an animation (or even a single frame) can be brief or it can take several days, depending on the complexity of the scene. For complex scenes that will take a while to render, you can configure 3ds Max to send you an e-mail message when every so many frames are completed, when your entire rendering is complete, or if it fails. These options are in the Email Notifications rollout, shown in Figure 20.5.

In addition to the options, you can enter whom the e-mail is from, whom it is to, and an SMTP Server.

FIGURE 20.5

The Email Notifications rollout includes options for sending an e-mail message to report on rendering status.

Adding pre-render and post-render scripts

The Scripts rollout includes File buttons for adding pre-render and post-render scripts. The scripts must be .ms scripts and are executed before and after the rendering of each file. These scripts can be used to compile information about the render or to do some post-processing work. Above each script file button is an Execute Now button that can be used to check the script before rendering.

Assigning renderers

3ds Max performs rendering operations in several different places: The Render Setup dialog box renders to the Render Frame Window or to files; the material previews in the Material Editor also are rendered; and the ActiveShade windows show another level of rendering.

The plug-in nature of 3ds Max enables you to select the renderer to use to output images. To change the default renderer, look in the Assign Renderers rollout in the Common panel of the Render Setup dialog box (F10). You can select different renderers for the Production, Material Editor, and ActiveShade modes. For each, you can select from the Default Scanline Renderer, mental ray, Quicksilver Hardware Renderer, and the VUE File Renderer. This list also could contain additional renderers if a new render plug-in has been installed.

> **NOTE**
>
> The VUE File Renderer is used to create a VUE file, which is an editable text file that holds all the details of the scene.

The lock next to the Material Editor option indicates that the same renderer is used for both Production and Material Editor.

Default Scanline Renderer

The Default Scanline Renderer rollout, found in the Renderer panel and shown in Figure 20.6, is the default renderer rollout that appears in the Render Setup dialog box. If a different renderer is loaded, then a different rollout for that renderer is displayed in the Renderer panel.

FIGURE 20.6

The Default Scanline Renderer rollout includes settings unique to this renderer.

You can use the Options section at the top of the Default Scanline Renderer rollout to quickly disable various render options for quicker results. These options include Mapping, Shadows, Auto-Reflect/Refract and Mirrors, and Force Wireframe. For the Force Wireframe option, you can define a Wire Thickness value in pixels. The Enabled SSE option uses Streaming SIMD (Single Instruction, Multiple Data) Extensions to speed up the rendering process by processing more data per instruction.

Anti-alias filters

Another way to speed up rendering is to disable the Anti-aliasing and Filter Maps features. Anti-aliasing smoothes jagged edges that appear where colors change. The Filter Maps option allows you to disable the computationally expensive process of filtering material and environment maps. The Filter drop-down list lets you select image filters that are applied at the pixel level during rendering. Below the drop-down list is a description of the current filter. The Filter Size value applies only to the Soften filter. Available filters include the following:

- **Area:** Does an anti-aliasing sweep using the designated area specified by the Filter Size value.
- **Blackman:** Sharpens the image within a 25-pixel area; provides no edge enhancement.
- **Blend:** Somewhere between a sharp and a coarse Soften filter; includes Filter Size and Blend values.
- **Catmull-Rom:** Sharpens with a 25-pixel filter and includes edge enhancement.
- **Cook Variable:** Can produce sharp results for small Filter Size values and blurred images for larger values.
- **Cubic:** Based on cubic-spline curves; produces a blurring effect.
- **Mitchell-Netravali:** Includes Blur and Ringing parameters.
- **Plate Match/MAX R2:** Matches mapped objects against background plates as used in 3ds Max R2.
- **Quadratic:** Based on a quadratic spline; produces blurring within a 9-pixel area.
- **Sharp Quadratic:** Produces sharp effects from a 9-pixel area.
- **Soften:** Causes mild blurring and includes a Filter Size value.
- **Video:** Blurs the image using a 25-pixel filter optimized for NTSC and PAL video.

SuperSampling

Global SuperSampling is an additional anti-aliasing process that you can apply to materials. This process can improve image quality, but it can take a long time to render; you can disable it using the Disable all Samplers option. SuperSampling can be enabled in the Material Editor for specific materials, but the SuperSampling rollout in the Material Editor also includes an option to Use Global Settings. The Global Settings are defined here in the Default Scanline Renderer rollout.

3ds Max includes anti-aliasing filters as part of the rendering process. You have several SuperSampling methods from which to choose.

SuperSampling is disabled if the Antialiasing option is disabled. Global SuperSampling can be enabled using the Enable Global SuperSampler option.

In a SuperSampling pass, the colors at different points around the center of a pixel are sampled. These samples are then used to compute the final color of each pixel. 3ds Max has four available SuperSampling methods: Max 2.5 Star, Hammersley, Adaptive Halton, and Adaptive Uniform.

20

You can find more information on each of these sampling methods in Chapter 14, "Creating and Applying Standard Materials with the Slate Material Editor."

Motion Blur

The Default Scanline Renderer rollout also offers two different types of motion blur: Object Motion Blur and Image Motion Blur. You can enable either of these using the Apply options.

Object Motion Blur is set in the Object Properties dialog box for each object. The renderer completes this blur by rendering the object over several frames. The movement of the camera doesn't affect this type of blur. The Duration value determines how long the object is blurred between frames. The Samples value specifies how many Duration units are sampled. The Duration Subdivision value is the number of copies rendered within each Duration segment. All these values can have a maximum setting of 16. The smoothest blurs occur when the Duration and Samples values are equal.

Image Motion Blur is also set in the Object Properties dialog box for each object. This type of blur is affected by the movement of the camera and is applied after the image has been rendered. You achieve this blur by smearing the image in proportion to the movement of the various objects. The Duration value determines the time length of the blur between frames. The Apply to Environment Map option lets you apply the blurring effect to the background as well as the objects. The Work with Transparency option blurs transparent objects without affecting their transparent regions. Using this option adds time to the rendering process.

 You can add two additional blur effects to a scene: the Blur Render Effect, found in the Rendering Effects dialog box (covered in Chapter 21, "Using Atmospheric and Render Effects") and the Scene Motion Blur effect, available through the Video Post dialog box (covered in Chapter 23, "Compositing with Render Elements and the Video Post Interface").

Other options

The Auto Reflect/Refract Maps section lets you specify a Rendering Iterations value for reflection maps within the scene. The higher the value, the more objects are included in the reflection computations and the longer the rendering time.

Color Range Limiting offers two methods for correcting over-brightness caused by applying filters. The Clamp method lowers any value above a relative ceiling of 1 to 1 and raises any values below 0 to 0. The Scale method scales all colors between the maximum and minimum values.

The Conserve Memory option optimizes the rendering process to use the least amount of memory possible. If you plan on using 3ds Max (or some other program) while it is rendering, you should enable this option.

Quicksilver Hardware Renderer

The Quicksilver Hardware Renderer takes advantage of the advanced graphics processing capabilities found in modern video cards. The advantage of this rendering option is speed. The Quicksilver Hardware Renderer can render scenes much faster than mental ray and at a better quality than the Scanline Renderer.

> **CAUTION**
>
> Some 3ds Max features don't work with Quicksilver including Exclude/Include for lights, Visibility in the Object Properties dialog box, Vertex Colors, multiple layers of transparency, and several map types including cellular, flat mirror, particle age, particle mblur, thin wall refraction, and non-regular noise.

The Quicksilver Hardware Renderer is available only if your video card supports Shader Model 3.0. If you select Help ⇨ Diagnose Video Hardware, 3ds Max runs a utility that checks and reports the capabilities of your current graphics card. Look for the GPU Shader Model Support to be SM3.0 or later.

You can enable the Quicksilver Renderer by clicking the button to the right of the listed Production Renderer in the Assign Renderer rollout of the Common panel. Then select Quicksilver from the list that appears. When the Quicksilver Hardware Renderer is enabled, the Renderer panel displays the options available for this renderer, as shown in Figure 20.7. This renderer supports many of the same options found in the iray Renderer, making it easy to use, but it also includes options for enabling details such as the rendering level, lighting, and shadows. If you use any hardware shaders in the scene, you can specify their directory in the Hardware Shaders Cache Folder located at the bottom of the panel.

 You can learn more about the mental ray rendering options in Chapter 22, "Rendering with mental ray and iray."

FIGURE 20.7

Many of the options for the Quicksilver Hardware Renderer are similar to the iray renderer.

The Quicksilver Renderer is easy to use. You simply tell it how much time to take or how many iterations to make. Quicksilver then continually improves the rendered image until the time or iterations are completed. If the image quality isn't good enough, increase the time and/or iterations and render again.

Rendering stylized scenes

For many years, the goal of 3D graphics has been to make scenes as realistic as possible, but other types of art emphasize style over realism. These stylistic approaches give us the cubes of Picasso, the

20

points of Seurat, and the surreal landscapes of Dali. Although no software title has a button to magically turn your scene into a classic piece of art, the new Nitrous display drivers found in 3ds Max allow you to display your scene as if it were drawn using acrylic, ink, or pastels.

The same stylized display options that are available in the viewports also are available as render options using the Quicksilver rendering engine. After Quicksilver is enabled, you can select one of the stylized render options from the Rendering Level drop-down list in the Visual Style & Appearance rollout.

When a stylized non-photorealistic rendering option is selected, clicking the Render button renders the scene in the Rendered Frame Window, as shown in Figure 20.8.

FIGURE 20.8

Non-photorealistic rendering methods can be specified in the Render Setup dialog box using the Quicksilver renderer.

Using the Rendered Frame Window

The Rendered Frame Window is a temporary window that holds any rendered images. Often when developing a scene, you want to test-render an image to view certain materials or transparency not visible in the viewports. The Rendered Frame Window, shown in Figure 20.9, enables you to view these test renderings without saving any data to the network or hard drive.

FIGURE 20.9

The Rendered Frame Window displays rendered images without saving them to a file.

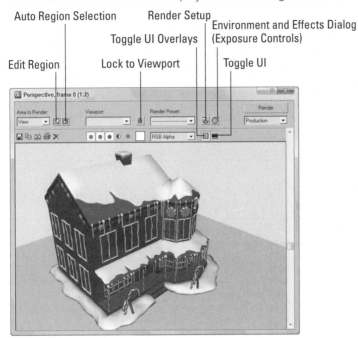

This window opens when you select the Rendered Frame Window option and click the Render button in the Render Setup dialog box. You also can view images from a local hard drive or a network drive in the Rendered Frame Window using the Rendering ➪ View Image File menu command.

To zoom in on the rendered image, hold down the Ctrl key and click the window. Right-click while holding down the Ctrl key to zoom out. The Shift key enables you to drag and pan the image. You also can use the mouse wheel (if you have a scrolling mouse) to zoom and pan within the Rendered Frame Window, just like you can in the viewports.

TIP
You can even zoom and pan the image while it is rendering.

Using the Render Types

From the top of the Rendered Frame Window, the Area to Render drop-down list enables you to render subsections of the scene. The default setting is View. After you pick a selection from the list, click the Render button to begin the rendering. The available Render Types are described in Table 20.1.

20

TABLE 20.1 **Render Type Options**

Render Type	Description
View	Renders the entire view as shown in the active viewport.
Selected	Renders only the selected objects in the active viewport.
Region	Places a frame of dotted lines with handles in the active viewport. This frame lets you define a region to render. You can resize the frame by dragging the handles. When you have defined the region, click OK in the lower-right corner of the active viewport.
Crop	Similar to Region in that it uses a frame to define a region, but the Crop setting doesn't include the areas outside the defined frame.
Blowup	Takes the defined region and increases its size to fill the render window. The frame for Blowup is constrained to the aspect ratio of the final resolution.

At the top of the Rendered Frame Window are several controls and icon buttons.

 The Edit Region button is activated when the Region option is selected. It lets you drag the center of the area to move it around or drag the edge and corner handles of the region to resize the render area. This option lets you precisely define the area that is rendered.

 The Auto Region Selected option automatically sets the render region to the current selection in the viewports.

 The Lock To Viewport causes all renders to be done using the specified viewport, regardless of which viewport is active. Using this option you can lock the renders to the Perspective viewport even if you're using a different viewport.

 The Render Setup button opens the Render Setup dialog box.

 The Environment and Effects Dialog button opens this dialog box, which includes the Exposure Control settings.

The Save Image button enables you to save the current rendered image.

The Copy Image button copies the image in the Rendered Frame Window to the Windows clipboard where you can paste it into another application like Photoshop.

The Clone Rendered Frame Window button creates another frame buffer dialog box. Any new rendering is rendered to this new dialog box, which is useful for comparing two images.

 The Print Image button sends the rendered image to the default printer.

 The Clear button erases the image from the window.

The next five buttons enable the red, green, blue, alpha, and monochrome channels. The alpha channel holds any transparency information for the image. The alpha channel is a grayscale map, with black showing the transparent areas and white showing the opaque areas. Next to the Display Alpha Channel button is the Monochrome button, which displays the image as a grayscale image.

The Channel Display drop-down list lets you select the channel to display. The color swatch at the right shows the color of the currently selected pixel. You can select new pixels by right-clicking and holding on the image. This temporarily displays a small dialog box with the image dimensions and the RGB value of the pixel directly under the cursor. The color in the color swatch can then be dragged and dropped in other dialog boxes such as the Material Editor.

 The Toggle UI Overlays button causes the frame that marks the region area to be visible when rendered.

The Toggle UI button hides the top selection of controls in the Rendered Frame Window.

Previewing with ActiveShade

The ActiveShade window gives a quick semi-rendered look at the current scene. You can open an ActiveShade display within a viewport by clicking the viewport Point-of-View label in the upper-left corner of each viewport and choosing Extended Viewports ⇨ ActiveShade from the pop-up menu. Using the ActiveShade button on the main toolbar (which is a flyout under the Render Production button), you can open a floating ActiveShade window, which is similar to the Rendered Frame Window without all the buttons.

The benefit of ActiveShade is that it shows a rendered view of the scene that is automatically updated every time a change is made. This is helpful when you are tweaking lights or making subtle changes.

NOTE

The ActiveShade window used to be quite valuable, but now that 3ds Max can render lights and shadows in the viewport, the ActiveShade window isn't as helpful.

Only one ActiveShade viewport can be open at a time.

TIP

You can drag materials from the Material Editor and drop them directly on objects in the ActiveShade window.

Summary

This chapter covered the basics of producing output using the Render Setup dialog box. Although rendering a scene can take a long time to complete, 3ds Max includes many settings that can speed up the process and helpful tools such as the Rendered Frame Window and ActiveShade.

In this chapter, you accomplished the following:

- Discovering how to control the various render parameters
- Switching to a different renderer
- Rendering non-photorealistic scenes using the Quicksilver Renderer
- Using the Rendered Frame Window and ActiveShade

The next chapter covers the features found in the Environment and Effects dialog box. These are used to create atmospheric and render effects.

20

CHAPTER

21

Using Atmospheric and Render Effects

IN THIS CHAPTER

Adding an environment background

Using Exposure Controls

Using Atmospheric Apparatus gizmos to position atmospheric effects

Using the Fire effect

Working with fog

Adding render effects

Understanding the other types of render effects

I n the real world, an environment of some kind surrounds all objects. The environment does much to set the ambiance of the scene. For example, an animation set at night in the woods has a very different environment than one set at the horse races during the middle of the day. The Autodesk® 3ds Max® 2013 software includes dialog boxes for setting the color, background images, and lighting environment; these features can help define your scene.

This chapter also covers Exposure Controls and atmospheric effects, including the likes of clouds, fog, and fire. These effects can be seen only when the scene is rendered.

3ds Max also has a class of effects that you can interactively render to the Rendered Frame Window without using any post-production features, such as the Video Post dialog box. These effects are called *render effects*. Render effects can save you lots of time that you would normally spend rendering an image, touching it up, and repeating the process again and again.

The common thread among all these features is their location. All can be found within the Environment and Effects dialog box.

Adding an Environment Background

Whether it's a beautiful landscape or just clouds drifting by, the environment behind the scene can do much to make the scene more believable. In this section, you learn to define an environment using the Rendering ⇨ Environment (8) menu command.

Environment maps are used as background for the scene and can also be used as images reflected off shiny objects in the scene. Environment maps are displayed only in the final rendering and not in the viewports, but you can add a background to any viewport and even set the environment map to be displayed as the viewport backdrop.

Chapter 2, "Controlling the Viewports," covers adding a background image to a viewport.

But there is more to an environment than just a background. It also involves altering the global lighting, controlling exposure, and introducing atmosphere effects.

Defining the rendered environment

You create environments in the Environment and Effects dialog box, shown in Figure 21.1, which you can open by choosing Rendering ➪ Environment (or by pressing the 8 key). Several settings make up an environment, including a background color or image, global lighting, exposure control, and atmospheric effects.

FIGURE 21.1

The Environment and Effects dialog box lets you select a background color or image, define global lighting, control exposure, and work with atmospheric effects.

Setting a background color

The first color swatch in the Environment panel lets you specify a background color. This color appears by default if no environment map is specified or if the Use Map option is disabled (and is black by default). The background color can be animated, so you can set the background color to start black and slowly fade to white.

Using a background image

To select a background image to be used as an environment map, click the Environment Map button in the Environment panel to open the Material/Map Browser. If you want to load a bitmap image as the background image, double-click the Bitmap selection to open the Select Bitmap Image File dialog box. Locate the bitmap to use, and click Open. The bitmap name appears on the Environment Map button.

> **TIP**
>
> If the environment map that you want to use is already displayed in one of the Material Editor sample slots, you can drag it directly from the Material Editor and drop it on the Map button in the Environment panel. You also can drag and drop a filename from Windows Explorer onto the Map button.

To change any of the environment map parameters, you need to load the environment map into the Material Editor. You can do so by dragging the map button from the Environment panel into the Node View panel in the Material Editor. After releasing the material, the Instance (Copy) Map dialog box asks whether you want to create an Instance or a Copy. If you select Instance, any parameter changes that you make to the material automatically update the map in the Environment panel.

Once in the Material Editor, you can use the Environment Map to create a Spherical Environment map that is used to reflect realistically off objects in the scene.

 For more information about the types of available mapping parameters, see Chapter 15, "Adding Material Details with Maps."

The background image doesn't need to be an image: You can also load animations. Supported formats include AVI, MPEG, MOV, and IFL files.

Figure 21.2 shows a scene with an image of the Golden Gate Bridge loaded as the environment map. Viewpoint Datalabs created the airplane model.

FIGURE 21.2

The results of a background image loaded into the Environment panel

Setting global lighting

The Tint color swatch in the Global Lighting section of the Environment panel specifies a color used to tint all lights. The Level value increases or decreases the overall lighting level for all lights in the scene. The Ambient color swatch sets the color for the ambient light in the scene, which is the darkest color that any shadows in the scene can be. You can animate all these settings.

Using Exposure Controls

The Exposure Control rollout of the Environment panel lets you control output levels and color rendering ranges. You can access the Environment panel from the Rendering ⇨ Environment menu command or by pressing the 8 key. Controlling the exposure of film is a common procedure when working with film and can result in a different look for your scene. Enabling the Exposure Controls can add dynamic range to your rendered images that is more comparable to what the eyes actually see. If you've worked with a Histogram in Photoshop, then you'll understand the impact that the Exposure Controls can have.

The Active option lets you turn this feature on and off. The Process Background and Environment Maps option causes the exposure settings to affect the background and environment images. When this option is disabled, only the scene objects are affected by the exposure control settings. The Exposure Control rollout also includes a Render Preview button that displays the rendered scene in a tiny pane. The preview pane is small, but for most types of exposure control settings it is enough. When you click the Render Preview button, the scene is rendered. This preview is then automatically updated whenever a setting is changed.

Automatic, Linear, and Logarithmic Exposure Control

Selecting Automatic Exposure Control from the drop-down list automatically adjusts your rendered output to be closer to what your eyes can detect. Monitors are notoriously bad at reducing the dynamic range of the colors in your rendered image. This setting provides the needed adjustments to match the expanded dynamic range of your eyes.

When the Automatic Exposure Control option is selected, a new rollout appears in the Environment panel. This rollout includes settings for Brightness, Contrast, Exposure Value, and Physical Scale. You also can enable Color Correction, select a color, and select an option to Desaturate Low Levels. The Contrast and Brightness settings can range from 0 to 100. A Contrast value of 0 displays all scene objects with the same flat, gray color, and a Brightness value of 100 displays all scene objects with the same flat, white color. The Exposure Value can range from –5 to 5 and determines the amount of light allowed in the scene.

Another exposure control option is Linear Exposure Control. Although this option presents the same settings as the Automatic Exposure Control, the historgram values are a straight line across the light spectrum.

> **TIP**
> The tricky part is to know when to use which Exposure Control. For still images, the Automatic Exposure Control is your best bet, but for animations, you should use the Logarithmic Exposure Control. Automatic is also a good choice for any scenes that use many lighting effects. Using any of the exposure controls besides the Logarithmic Exposure Control when animating can lead to flickering. The Linear Exposure Control should be used for low dynamic range scenes such as nighttime or cloudy scenes.

The Logarithmic Exposure Control option replaces the Exposure Value setting with a Mid Tones setting. This setting controls the colors between the lowest and highest values. This exposure control option also includes options to Affect Indirect Only and Exterior Daylight. You should enable the Affect Indirect Only option if you use only standard lights in the scene, but if your scene includes an IES Sun light, then enable the Exterior Daylight option to tone down the intensity of the light.

> **NOTE**
> You should always use the Logarithmic Exposure Control setting when enabling the advanced lighting features because it works well with low-level light.

Pseudo Color Exposure Control

As you work with advanced lighting solutions and with radiosity, determining whether interior spaces and objects have too much light or not enough light can be difficult, especially when comparing objects on opposite sides of the scene. This is where the Pseudo Color Exposure Control option comes in handy.

This exposure control option projects a band of colors (or grayscale) in place of the material and object colors that represent the illumination or luminance values for the scene. With these pseudo-colors, you can quickly determine where all the lighting is consistent and where it needs to be addressed.

In the Pseudo Color Exposure Control rollout, shown in Figure 21.3, you can select to apply the colors to show Illumination or Luminance. You also can select to use a Colored or Gray Scale style and to make the Scale Linear or Logarithmic. The Min and Max settings let you control the ranges of the colors, and a Physical Scale setting is included. The color (or grayscale) band is shown across the bottom of the rollout with the values for each color underneath.

FIGURE 21.3

The Pseudo Color Exposure Control rollout can display illumination and luminance values as colors.

When this exposure control is used, the associated render element is automatically set in the Render Elements rollout of the Render Setup dialog box. If the scene is rendered, then the appropriate (Illumination or Luminance) render element is also rendered.

 See Chapter 23, "Compositing with Render Elements and the Video Post Interface," for more on render elements.

Photographic Exposure Control

If you're comfortable working with camera settings such as Shutter Speed, Aperture, and Film Speed, then the mr Photographic Exposure Control puts these settings at your fingertips using real-world values. Even if you're not familiar with camera settings, you can use one of the available presets from the list at the top of the rollout, shown in Figure 21.4.

NOTE

The mr Photographic Exposure Control is available only for the mental ray render engine.

FIGURE 21.4

The mr Photographic Exposure Control rollout works with real-world camera settings.

Tutorial: Using the Logarithmic Exposure Control

As you start to use the new photometric lights, you may find it difficult to get the settings just right. The results are oversaturation or undersaturation, but luckily the Logarithmic Exposure Control can quickly fix any problems that appear.

To adjust the effect of a photometric light using the Logarithmic Exposure Control, follow these steps:

1. Open the Array of chrome spheres.max file from the Chap 21 directory on the CD.

   This file contains lots and lots of chrome mapped spheres with advanced lighting enabled.

2. Choose Rendering ➪ Render (or press the F10 key) to open the Render Setup dialog box, and click the Render button.

   It takes a while to render, but notice the results, shown on the left in Figure 21.3.

3. Choose Rendering ⇨ Environment (or press the 8 key) to open the Environment and Effects dialog box. In the Exposure Control rollout, select Logarithmic Exposure Control from the drop-down list, and enable the Active and Process Background and Environment Maps options. Then click the Render Preview button.

4. In the Logarithmic Exposure Control Parameters rollout, set the Brightness value to **60**, set the Contrast value to **100**, and enable the Desaturate Low Levels option.

5. In the Render Scene dialog box, click the Render button again to see the updated rendering.

The image on the right in Figure 21.5 shows the rendered image with exposure control enabled.

FIGURE 21.5

This rendered image shows an image before and after exposure control was enabled.

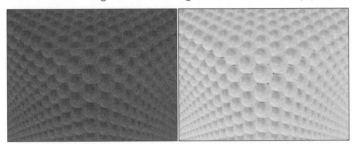

Creating Atmospheric Effects

The Environment and Effects dialog box (keyboard shortcut, 8) contains rollouts for adding atmospheric effects to your scene, but the first question is where. Atmospheric effects are placed within a container called an Atmospheric Apparatus gizmo, which tells the effect where it should be located. However, only the Fire and the Volume Fog effects need Atmospheric Apparatus gizmos. To create an Atmospheric Apparatus gizmo, select Create ⇨ Helpers ⇨ Atmospherics and choose the apparatus type.

The three different Atmospheric Apparatus gizmos are BoxGizmo, SphereGizmo, and CylGizmo. Each has a different shape similar to the primitives.

Working with the Atmospheric Apparatus

Selecting a gizmo and opening the Modify panel reveal two different rollouts: one for defining the basic parameters such as the gizmo dimensions, and another labeled Atmospheres & Effects, which you can use to Add or Delete an Environment Effect to the gizmo. Each gizmo parameters rollout also includes a Seed value and a New Seed button. The Seed value sets a random number used to compute the atmospheric effect, and the New Seed button automatically generates a random seed. Two gizmos with the same seed values have nearly identical results.

Adding effects to a scene

The Add button opens the Add Atmosphere dialog box, where you can select an atmospheric effect. The selected effect is then included in a list in the Atmospheres & Effects rollout. You can delete these atmospheres by selecting them from the list and clicking the Delete button. The Setup button is active if an effect is selected in the list. It opens the Environment and Effects dialog box. Adding Atmospheric Effects in the Modify panel is purely for convenience. They can also be added using the Environment and Effects dialog box.

In addition to the Modify panel, you can add atmospheric effects to the scene using the Atmosphere rollout in the Environment and Effects dialog box, shown in Figure 21.6. This rollout is pretty boring until you add an effect to it. You can add an effect by clicking on the Add button. This opens the Add Atmospheric Effect dialog box, which includes by default four atmospheric effects: Fire Effect, Fog, Volume Fog, and Volume Light. With plug-ins, you can increase the number of effects in this list. The selected effect is added to the Effects list in the Atmosphere rollout.

FIGURE 21.6

The Environment and Effects dialog box lets you select atmospheric effects.

The effects are applied in the order in which they are listed, so the effects at the bottom of the list are layered on top of all other effects. To the right of the Effects pane are the Move Up and Move Down buttons, used to position the effects in the list. Below the Effects pane is a Name field where you can type a new name for any effect in this field. This enables you to use the same effect multiple times. The Merge button opens the Merge Atmospheric Effects dialog box, where you can select a separate 3ds Max file. You can then select and load any render effects contained in the other file.

TIP
The Merge button lets you create and save several different types of fire effects and then quickly merge them into a scene from an external file.

Using the Fire Effect

To add the Fire effect to the scene, select the Rendering ➪ Environment (8) menu command and open the Environment panel; then click the Add button and select the Fire Effect selection. This opens the

Fire Effect Parameters rollout, shown in Figure 21.7. At the top of the Fire Effect Parameters rollout is the Pick Gizmo button; clicking this button lets you select a gizmo in the scene. The selected gizmo appears in the drop-down list to the right. You can select multiple gizmos. To remove a gizmo from the list, select it and click the Remove Gizmo button.

FIGURE 21.7

The Fire Effect Parameters rollout lets you define the look of the effect.

> **NOTE**
> The Fire effect renders only in non-orthographic views such as Perspective or a camera view.

The three color swatches define the color of the fire effect and include an Inner Color, an Outer Color, and a Smoke Color. The Smoke Color is used only when the Explosion option is set. The default red and yellow colors make fairly realistic fire.

The Shape section includes two Flame Type options: Tendril and Fireball. The Tendril shape produces veins of flames, and the Fireball shape is rounder and puffier. Figure 21.8 shows four fire effects. The left two have the Tendril shape, and the two on the right are set to Fireball. The difference is in the Density and Flame Detail settings.

The Stretch value elongates the individual flames along the gizmo's Z-axis. Figure 21.9 shows the results of using the Stretch value. The Stretch values for these gizmos, from left to right, are 0.1, 1.0, 5.0, and 50.

FIGURE 21.8

The Fire atmospheric effect can be either Tendril or Fireball shaped.

FIGURE 21.9

The Stretch value can elongate flames.

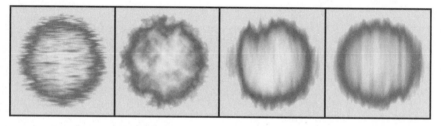

The Regularity value determines how much of the Atmospheric Apparatus is filled. The spherical gizmos in the previous figures were all set to 0.2, so the entire sphere shape wasn't filled. A setting of 1.0 adds a spherical look to the Fire effect because the entire gizmo is filled. For a more random shape, use a small Regularity value.

The Flame Size value affects the overall size of each individual flame (though this is dependent on the gizmo size as well). The Flame Detail value controls the edge sharpness of each flame and can range from 1 to 10. Lower values produce fuzzy, smooth flames, but higher values result in sharper, more distinct flames.

The Density value determines the thickness of each flame in its center; higher Density values result in flames that are brighter at the center, while lower values produce thinner, wispy flames. Figure 21.10 shows the difference caused by Density values of, from left to right, 10, 20, 50, and 100.

The Samples value sets the rate at which the effect is sampled. Higher sample values are required for more detail, but they increase the render time.

The Motion section includes options for setting the Phase and Drift of a fire effect. The Phase value determines how wildly the fire burns. For a wild, out-of-control fire, animate the Phase value to change rapidly. For a constant, steady fire, keep the value constant throughout the frames. The Drift value sets the height of the flames. High Drift values produce high, hot-burning flames.

When the Explosion check box is selected, the fire is set to explode. The Start and End Times for the explosion are set in the Setup Explosion Phase Curve dialog box that opens when the Setup Explosion button is clicked. If the Smoke option is checked, then the fire colors change to the smoke color for

Phase values between 100 and 200. The Fury value varies the churning of the flames. Values greater than 1.0 cause faster churning, and values lower than 1.0 cause slower churning.

FIGURE 21.10

The Fire effect brightness is tied closely to the flame's Density value.

Tutorial: Creating the sun

You can use the Fire effect to create a realistic sun. The modeling part is easy—all it requires is a simple sphere—but the real effects come from the materials and the Fire effect.

To create a sun, follow these steps:

1. Open the Sun.max file from the Chap 21 directory on the CD.

    This file contains a simple sphere with a bright yellow material applied to it.

2. Select Create ⇨ Helpers ⇨ Atmospherics ⇨ Sphere Gizmo, and drag a sphere in the Front viewport that is larger than the "sun" sphere.

3. With the SphereGizmo still selected, open the Modify panel and click the Add button in the Atmospheres & Effects rollout or you can use the Add button located in the Atmosphere rollout in the Environment and Effects dialog box, which is opened using the Rendering ⇨ Environment menu command or by pressing the 8 key. Select Fire Effect from the Add Atmosphere dialog box, and click OK. Then select the Fire effect, and click the Setup button.

    The Environment and Effects dialog box opens.

4. Select the Fire Effect in the Atmosphere rollout, and in the Fire Effects Parameters rollout, leave the default colors as they are—Inner Color yellow, Outer Color red, and Smoke Color black. For the Flame Type, select Tendril with Stretch and Regularity values of **1**. Set the Flame Size to **30**, the Density to **15**, the Flame Detail to **10**, and the Samples to **15**.

Figure 21.11 shows the resulting sun after it's been rendered.

Tutorial: Creating clouds

Sky images are fairly easy to find, or you can just take your camera outside and capture your own. The trick comes when you are trying to weave an object in and out of clouds. Although you can do this with a Shadow/Matte mask, it would be easier if the clouds were actual 3D objects. In this tutorial, you'll create some simple clouds using the Fire effect.

FIGURE 21.11

A sun image created with a simple sphere, a material with a Noise Bump map, and the Fire effect

To create some clouds for a sky backdrop, follow these steps:

1. Open the Clouds.max file from the Chap 21 directory on the CD.

   This file includes several hemispherical-shaped Atmospheric Apparatus gizmos.

2. Choose Rendering ⇨ Environment (or press the 8 key) to open the Environment and Effects dialog box. Click the Background Color swatch, and select a light blue color. In the Atmosphere rollout, click the Add button, select Fire Effect from the Add Atmospheric Effect list, and click OK.

3. Name the effect **Clouds**, click the Pick Gizmo button, and select one of the Sphere Gizmo objects in the viewports. Repeat until all gizmos are selected, and then click on each of the color swatches. Change the Inner Color to a dark gray, the Outer Color to a light gray, and the Smoke Color to white. Set the Flame Type to Fireball with a Stretch of **1** and a Regularity of **0.2**. Set the Flame Size to **35**, the Flame Detail to **3**, the Density to **15**, and the Samples to **15**.

TIP

If you want to add some motion to the clouds, click the Auto Key button, drag the Time Slider to the last frame, and change the Phase value to 45 and the Drift value to 30. The clouds slowly drift through the sky. Disable the Auto Key button when you're finished.

Figure 21.12 shows the resulting rendered sky backdrop. By altering the Fire Effect parameters, you can create different types of clouds.

FIGURE 21.12

You can use the Fire atmospheric effect to create clouds.

Using the Fog Effect

Fog is an atmospheric effect that obscures objects or backgrounds by introducing a hazy layer; objects farther from view are less visible. The normal Fog effect is used without an Atmospheric Apparatus gizmo and appears between the camera's environment range values. The camera's Near and Far Range settings set these values.

In the Environment and Effects dialog box, the Fog Parameters rollout appears when the Fog effect is added to the Effects list. This rollout, shown in Figure 21.13, includes a color swatch for setting the fog color. It also includes an Environment Color Map button for loading a map. If a map is selected, the Use Map option turns it on or off. You can also select a map for the Environment Opacity, which affects the fog density.

The Fog Background option applies fog to the background image. The Type options include Standard and Layered fog. Selecting one of these fog background options enables its corresponding parameters.

The Standard parameters include an Exponential option for increasing density as a function of distance. If this option is disabled, the density is linear with distance. The Near and Far values are used to set the range densities.

FIGURE 21.13

The Fog Parameters rollout lets you use either Standard fog or Layered fog.

Layered fog simulates layers of fog that move from dense areas to light areas. The Top and Bottom values set the limits of the fog, and the Density value sets its thickness. The Falloff option lets you set where the fog density goes to 0. The Horizon Noise option adds noise to the layer of fog at the horizon as determined by the Size, Angle, and Phase values.

Figure 21.14 shows several different fog options. The upper-left image shows the scene with no fog, the upper-right image uses the Standard option, and the lower-left image uses the Layered option with a Density of 50. The lower-right image has the Horizon Noise option enabled.

FIGURE 21.14

A rendered image with several different Fog effect options applied

Using the Volume Fog effect

You can add the Volume Fog effect to a scene by clicking the Add button and selecting the Volume Fog selection. This effect is different from the Fog effect in that it gives you more control over the exact position of the fog. This position is set by an Atmospheric Apparatus gizmo. The Volume Fog Parameters rollout, shown in Figure 21.15, lets you select a gizmo to use with the Pick Gizmo button. The selected gizmo is included in the drop-down list to the right of the buttons. Multiple gizmos can be selected. The Remove Gizmo button removes the selected gizmo from the list.

21

> **NOTE**
> The Atmospheric Apparatus gizmo contains only a portion of the total Volume Fog effect. If the gizmo is moved or scaled it displays a different cropped portion of fog.

FIGURE 21.15

The Volume Fog Parameters rollout includes parameters for controlling the fog density and type.

The Soften Gizmo Edges value feathers the fog effect at each edge. This value can range from 0 to 1.

Many of the settings for Volume Fog are the same as those for the Fog effect, but Volume Fog has several settings that are unique to it. These settings help set the patchy nature of Volume Fog. Step Size determines how small the patches of fog are. The Max Steps value limits the sampling of these small steps to keep the render time in check.

The Noise section settings also help determine the randomness of Volume Fog. Noise types include Regular, Fractal, and Turbulence. You can also select to Invert the noise. The Noise Threshold limits the effect of noise. Wind settings include direction and strength. The Phase value determines how the fog moves.

Tutorial: Creating a swamp scene

When I think of fog, I think of swamps. In this tutorial, you model a swamp scene. To use the Volume Fog effect to create the scene, follow these steps:

1. Open the Dragonfly in a foggy swamp.max file from the Chap 21 directory on the CD.

   This file includes several cattail plants and a dragonfly positioned on top of one of the cattails.

2. Select Create ⇨ Helpers ⇨ Atmospherics ⇨ Box Gizmo, and drag a box that covers the lower half of the cattails in the Left viewport.

3. Choose Rendering ⇨ Environment (or press the 8 key) to open the Environment and Effects dialog box. Click the Add button to open the Add Atmospheric Effect dialog box, and then select Volume Fog. Click OK. In the Volume Fog Parameters rollout, click the Pick Gizmo button and select the BoxGizmo in a viewport.

4. Set the Density to **0.5**, enable the Exponential option and select the Noise Type Turbulence. Then set the Uniformity to **1.0** and the Wind Strength to **10** from the Left.

Figure 21.16 shows the finished rendered image. Using Atmospheric Apparatus gizmos, you can position the fog in the exact place where you want it.

FIGURE 21.16

A rendered image that uses the Volume Fog effect

Using the Volume Light effect

The final Environment option is the Volume Light effect. This effect shares many of the same parameters as the other atmospheric effects. Although this is one of the atmospheric effects, it deals with lights and fits better in that section.

Adding Render Effects

In many cases, rendering a scene is only the start of the work to produce some final output. The post-production process is often used to add lots of different effects, as you'll see when I discuss the Video Post interface. But just because you can add it in post-production doesn't mean you have to add it in post-production. Render effects let you apply certain effects as part of the rendering process.

You can set up all render effects from the Rendering Effects panel, which you open by choosing Rendering ⇨ Effects. Figure 21.17 shows this dialog box. This dialog box also includes a panel with the Environment options.

FIGURE 21.17

The Effects panel lets you apply interactive post-production effects to an image.

The Effects pane displays all the effects that are included in the current scene. To add a new effect, click the Add button to open the Add Effect dialog box, in which you can select from a default list of nine effects: Hair and Fur, Lens Effects, Blur, Brightness and Contrast, Color Balance, Depth of Field, File Output, Film Grain, and Motion Blur. You can delete an effect from the current list by selecting that effect and clicking the Delete button.

Below the Effects pane is a Name field. You can type a new name for any effect in this field; doing so enables you to use the same effect multiple times. The effects are applied in the order in which they are listed in the Effects pane. To the right of the Effects pane are the Move Up and Move Down buttons, which you use to reposition the effects in the list. The effects are added to the scene in the order that they are listed.

CAUTION

It is possible for one effect to cover another effect. Rearranging the order can help resolve this problem.

The Merge button opens a file dialog box, where you can select a separate 3ds Max file. If you select a 3ds Max file and click Open, the Merge Rendering Effects dialog box presents you with a list of render effects used in the opened 3ds Max file. You can then select and load any of these render effects into the current scene.

The Preview section holds the controls for interactively viewing the various effects. Previews are displayed in the Rendered Frame Window and can be set to view All the effects or only the Current one. The Show Original button displays the scene before any effects are applied, and the Update Scene button updates the rendered image if any changes have been made to the scene.

> **NOTE**
>
> If the Rendered Frame Window isn't open, any of these buttons opens it and renders the scene with the current settings in the Render Setup dialog box.

The Interactive option automatically updates the image whenever an effect parameter or scene object is changed. If this option is disabled, you can use the Update Effect button to manually update the image.

> **CAUTION**
>
> If the Interactive option is enabled, the image is re-rendered in the Rendered Frame Window every time a change is made to the scene. This can slow down the system dramatically.

The Currently Updating bar shows the progress of the rendering update.

The remainder of the Effects panel contains global parameters and rollouts for the selected render effect. These rollouts are covered in this chapter, along with their corresponding effects.

Using Render Effects

Within the Add Effect dialog box are several different render effects. Some of these effects are simple, and others are quite complex. If these selections aren't enough, 3ds Max enables you to add even more options to this list via plug-ins.

Blur render effect

The Blur render effect displays three different blurring methods in the Blur Type panel: Uniform, Directional, and Radial. You can find these options in the Blur Type tabbed panel in the Blur Parameters rollout, shown in Figure 21.18.

The Uniform blur method applies the blur evenly across the whole image. The Pixel Radius value defines the amount of the blur. The Directional blur method can be used to blur the image along a certain direction. The U Pixel Radius and U Trail values define the blur in the horizontal direction, and the V Pixel Radius and V Trail values blur in a vertical direction. The Rotation value rotates the axis of the blur.

FIGURE 21.18

The Blur Parameters rollout lets you select a Uniform, Directional, or Radial blur type.

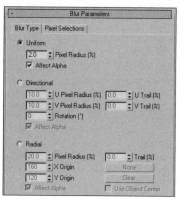

The Radial blur method creates concentric blurred rings determined by the Radius and Trail values. When the Use Object Center option is selected, the None and Clear buttons become active. Clicking the None button lets you select an object about which you want to center the radial blur. The Clear button clears this selection.

Figure 21.19 shows a dinosaur model created by Viewpoint Datalabs. The actual rendered image shows the sharp edges of the polygons. The Blur effect can help this by softening all the hard edges. The left image is the original dinosaur, and the right image has a Directional blur applied.

FIGURE 21.19

The Blur effect can soften an otherwise hard model.

The Blur Parameters rollout also includes a Pixel Selections tabbed panel, shown in Figure 21.20, that contains parameters for specifying which parts of the image get blurred. Options include the Whole Image, Non-Background, Luminance, Map Mask, Object ID, and Material ID.

FIGURE 21.20

The Pixel Selections tabbed panel (shown in two parts) of the Blur Parameters rollout lets you select the parts of the image that get the Blur effect.

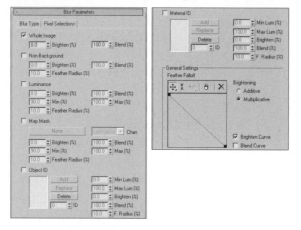

You can use the Feather Falloff curve at the bottom of the Blur Parameters rollout to define the Brighten and Blend curves. The buttons above this curve are for adding points, scaling the points, and moving them within the curve interface.

Brightness and Contrast render effect

The Brightness and Contrast render effect can alter these amounts in the image. The Brightness and Contrast Parameters rollout is a simple rollout with values for both the brightness and contrast that can range from 0 to 1. It also contains an Ignore Background option.

Color Balance render effect

The Color Balance effect enables you to tint the image using separate Cyan/Red, Magenta/Green, and Yellow/Blue channels. To change the color balance, drag the sliders in the Color Balance Parameters rollout. Other options include Preserve Luminosity and Ignore Background. The Preserve Luminosity option tints the image while maintaining the luminosity of the image, and the Ignore Background option tints the rendered objects but not the background image.

File Output render effect

The File Output render effect enables you to save the rendered file to a File or to a Device at any point during the render effect's post-processing. Figure 21.21 shows the File Output Parameters rollout.

FIGURE 21.21

The File Output Parameters rollout lets you save a rendered image before a render effect is applied.

Using the Channel drop-down list in the Parameters section, you can save out Whole Images, as well as grayscale Luminance, Depth, and Alpha images.

Film Grain render effect

The Film Grain effect gives an image a grained look, which hardens the overall look of the image. You can also use this effect to match rendered objects to the grain of the background image. This helps the objects blend into the scene better. Figure 21.22 shows the effect.

The Grain value can range from 0 to 10. The Ignore Background option applies the grain effect only to the objects in the scene and not to the background.

FIGURE 21.22

The Film Grain render effect applies a noise filter to the rendered image.

Motion Blur render effect

The Motion Blur effect applies a simple image motion blur to the rendered output. The Motion Blur Parameters rollout includes settings for working with Transparency and a value for the Duration of the blur. Objects that move rapidly within the scene are blurred.

Depth of Field render effect

The Depth of Field effect enhances the sense of depth by blurring objects close to or far from the camera. The Pick Cam button in the Depth of Field Parameters rollout, shown in Figure 21.23, lets you select a camera in the viewport to use for this effect. Multiple cameras can be selected, and all selected cameras are displayed in the drop-down list. A Remove button lets you remove cameras.

FIGURE 21.23

The Depth of Field Parameters rollout lets you select a camera or a Focal Point to apply the effect to.

In the Focal Point section, the Pick Node button lets you select an object to use as the focal point. This object is where the camera focuses. Objects far from this object are blurred. These nodes are also listed in a drop-down list. You can remove objects from the list by selecting them and clicking the Remove button. The Use Camera option uses the camera's own settings to determine the focal point.

In the Focal Parameters section, if you select the Custom option, then you can specify values for the Horizontal and Vertical Focal Loss, the Focal Range, and the Focal Limit. The Loss values indicate how much blur occurs. The Focal Range is where the image starts to blur, and the Focal Limit is where the image stops blurring.

Figure 21.24 shows a beach scene created by Viewpoint Datalabs. For this figure, I applied the Depth of Field effect using the Pick Node button and selecting some leaves on the tree. Then I set the Focal Range to 100, the Focal Limit to 200, and the Focal Loss values to 10 for both the Horizontal and Vertical.

The Depth of Field and Motion Blur effects can also be applied using a Multi-Pass camera, as discussed in Chapter 18, "Configuring and Aiming Cameras."

FIGURE 21.24

The Depth of Field effect focuses a camera on an object in the middle and blurs objects closer or farther away.

Summary

Creating the right environment can add lots of realism to any rendered scene. Using the Environment and Effects dialog box, you can work with atmospheric effects. Atmospheric effects include Fire, Fog, Volume Fog, and Volume Light.

Render effects are useful because they enable you to create effects and update them interactively. This gives a level of control that was previously unavailable. This chapter explained how to use render elements and render effects and described the various types.

This chapter covered these topics:

- Creating Atmospheric Apparatus gizmos for positioning atmospheric effects
- Working with the Fire atmospheric effects
- Creating fog and volume fog effects
- Applying render effects
- Working with the remaining render effects to control brightness and contrast, film grain, blurs, and more

The next chapter delves into the amazing mental ray rendering engine.

Rendering with mental ray and iray

IN THIS CHAPTER

Enabling the mental ray renderer

Working with iray

Working with mental ray lights

Creating caustic and global illumination lighting

Adding mental ray proxy

Using the specialized mental ray materials

The Autodesk® 3ds Max® 2013 software includes a plug-in architecture that lets you replace or extend any part of the software including the rendering engine. mental ray (actually spelled without capitals) is a plug-in rendering engine that offers many advanced features. This engine takes the rendering in 3ds Max to a new level, enabling you to render your scenes with amazing accuracy. It also includes a host of advanced rendering features including final gather, caustics, and global illumination that are physically realistic.

Final gather, caustics, and global illuminations are features of indirect illumination. Indirect illumination is all the lighting effects caused by bounced and reflected light. Without indirect illumination, only those areas directly in the light's path are illuminated, but using the indirect illumination features, you can illuminate the hidden areas of a scene, much as light does in real life.

Global illumination traces the light photons as they move and bounce from the light to scene objects, and final gather does the reverse, starting from surfaces and moving and bouncing photons back toward the light sources. Caustics are light effects and sparkles added to walls as light is reflected off a shiny surface like glass or water. mental ray creates more realistic rendered images by making these light effects possible.

Although the mental ray renderer is awesome, it can take lots of tweaking to get results to look just right. This is where iray comes in. iray (also spelled without a capital) lets you start a render, and it automatically adjusts the settings to give you great results based on the amount of time you give it. In other words, iray is mental ray for dummies.

Enabling mental ray and iray

If you're accustomed to using the Default Scanline Renderer and you're wondering if the mental ray or iray rendering engines are worth using, the answer is yes. Actually, you should try a couple of test renderings first and play with the different settings, but in working with mental ray I've been amazed at its results. One of the chief benefits of mental ray is its speed. It can render a fully raytraced scene in a fraction of the time without sacrificing quality.

> **NOTE**
> If you need even more speed and don't mind sacrificing a little quality, then try the Quicksilver Hardware renderer. It works with most of the mental ray materials, lights, and settings.

> **NOTE**
> mental ray is an external rendering engine that plugs into 3ds Max. It was developed by a company named mental images, which is now part of NVIDIA, so its development is separate from 3ds Max. Versions of the mental ray rendering engine also can be found in Maya and Softimage as well as a stand-alone version.

mental ray and iray also include support for global illumination without your having to enable the Advanced Lighting settings. In addition, mental ray can use all the software's existing materials without having to use a limited specialized material like the raytrace material. Each material has a new rollout that lets you change the mental ray settings. However, iray requires that you use only a specific set of materials, including the Arch & Design and those materials in the Autodesk Material Library.

> **NOTE**
> mental ray can't use the Advanced Lighting settings. mental ray has its own lighting solution that is independent of Advance Lighting.

Many of the available mental ray materials are covered in Chapter 72, "Using Specialized Material Types."

mental ray also includes native support for Area Lights, Shaders, Depth of Field, and Motion Blur. It also includes some specialized lights that offer functionality, such as caustics, that are unavailable in the Scanline Renderer.

To choose mental ray or iray as the renderer for your scene, simply select it from the list of available renderers in the Assign Renderer rollout of the Common panel of the Render Setup dialog box. You can set a different renderer for Production, the Material Editor, and the ActiveShade viewer. To make mental ray your default renderer, click the Save as Defaults button in this rollout.

Once selected as your Production renderer, you don't need to modify any other settings for the renderer to work. The mental ray settings in the Material Editor, Lights category, and Object Properties dialog box enable additional features that mental ray can take advantage of, but they aren't required to render the scene. The current mental ray version is 3.10.

NOTE

You may have noticed the Raytracer rollout in the Render Setup dialog box when the Scanline Renderer is enabled. There is also a Raytrace material in the Standard set of the materials. These settings and materials are used to enable and configure raytracing in the Default Scanline Renderer, but the mental ray results are much better than these raytrace options, so the focus is to learn mental ray instead of the older raytrace options.

Working with iray

After iray is enabled, you'll notice that the number of panels for configuring it in the Render Setup dialog box has been greatly reduced. The whole idea behind iray is to make the process of configuring the renderer easier. The configuration panel for iray is the Renderer panel, shown in Figure 22.1.

FIGURE 22.1

The iray renderer has only a simplified panel of options in the Render Setup dialog box.

Within iray's Renderer panel, you can set the time for the render to take, choose the number of iterations, or make simply set enable the Unlimited option. The iray renderer then renders and continually refines the given scene. As it renders, the results are shown in the Rendered Frame Window, and the render can be stopped and saved at any time.

The Advanced Parameters rollout includes options for limiting the number of light bounces, options for picking the anti-aliasing filter to use (Box, Gauss, or Triangle), and global settings for handling displacement maps. The Material Override option lets you replace all applied materials with a single designated material that is selected using the button to the right. This lets you see the lighting and shadow effects quickly or get a result if unsupported materials are used in the scene.

One "gotcha" when working with iray is that if a material or map is used that it doesn't support, the object is rendered as flat gray. The supported iray materials are those that have information on how the light interacts with it. For 3ds Max, the Arch & Design materials, the Autodesk Material Library (except for the Metallic Paint material, which isn't supported), Bitmaps, Mix, Noise, Normal Bump, RGB Multiply, and mr Physical Sky are supported. Also, iray supports only Photometric lights.

Figure 22.2 shows a sample scene rendered with iray. The image on the left shows the scene after only a few seconds, and the one on the right shows the scene after a longer render time.

FIGURE 22.2

The iray renderer progressively refines the image for as long as you let it run.

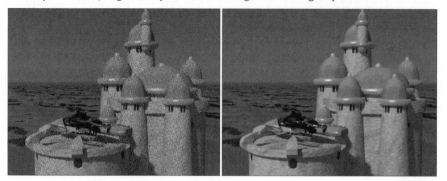

Tutorial: Starting iray

Once you get the hang of using iray, you'll find it is great to start the renderer with the unlimited setting before running off to lunch and check out the results when you get back.

To use the iray renderer to render a scene, follow these steps:

1. Open the Plant in corner.max file from the Chap 22 directory on the CD.

   This file includes several simple objects and a plant. The scene already has materials applied from the Autodesk Material Library.

2. Open the Render Setup dialog box (F10), and switch the Production Renderer in the Assign Renderer rollout of the Common panel to the iray renderer.

3. In the Renderer panel of the Render Setup dialog box, enable the Unlimited option and click the Render button.

4. Let the scene render for a while and when it looks good enough, click the Cancel button in the Rendering dialog box. The rendered results are displayed in the Rendered Frame Window where you can save the image if you desire.

Figure 22.3 shows the scene rendered with iray.

FIGURE 22.3

Using the Unlimited option lets the iray renderer keep running as long as it can.

Working with mental ray

The big difference between iray and mental ray is that mental ray gives you access to all the gritty configuration settings. By tweaking these settings, you can enable specific effects, speed up the render time, and get the exact results you want, but the cost is the time it takes to figure out these settings.

> **TIP**
>
> One way to tell the difference between the Scanline and mental ray rendering is that the Scanline Renderer processes the image in horizontal lines that progress from the top of the image to the bottom, and the mental ray renderer processes square sections of the image (called buckets), usually working on the easiest areas first and the most complex areas last.

mental ray is a complete solution, so it is natural that 3ds Max also includes mental ray-specific lights and materials. Using the lights and materials that are made to work with mental ray gives you access to better results and advanced features like area lights and multi-layer materials.

Using mental ray Lights and Shadows

If you look in the Lights category of the Create ⇨ Lights ⇨ Standard Lights menu, you'll see two mental ray specific lights: mental ray Area Omni and mental ray Area Spot. These area lights spread light from a defined area much like a light card used in filming. When a light is selected, you also can choose to use a mental ray Shadow Map.

Within the Photometric Lights category is a button for creating a mental ray Sky Portal. This light source is used to define the exact area of a window that allows light into an interior scene. Another place mental ray is used is within the Skylight and Daylight systems to define the sun and sky.

Enabling mental ray area lights

If a mental ray area light is added to the scene, you can set the area shape and dimensions in the Area Light Parameters rollout. The Area Omni can be either a sphere or a cylinder, and the Area Spot can be a Rectangle or Disc-shaped. You also can set the light icon to be visible when rendered. This is handy for light bulbs or sun objects that you want visible in the scene. Another benefit of the broader light source is that it creates soft shadows.

For area lights, there also are settings for defining the Indirect Illumination. By default, all mental ray lights use the Global Settings for their illumination values, as defined in the Render Setup dialog box, but you can bump the global values for a particular light using the Energy, Caustic Photons, and GI Photons value in the mental ray Indirect Illumination rollout, shown in Figure 22.4, found in the Modify panel. If you disable the Automatically Calculate Energy and Photons option, then you can override the global settings for the selected light.

FIGURE 22.4

The various rollouts for mental ray area lights let you define the light settings for individual lights including Indirect Illumination.

Each mental ray light also can have a shader applied to it using the buttons in the mental ray Light Shader rollout. The available shaders in the Material/Map Browser include Light Spot, Light Point, Light Infinite, and Ambient/Reflective Occlusion.

Enabling mental ray Shadow Maps

In the Shadows drop-down list of the General Parameters rollout is an option to enable mental ray Shadow Maps. These shadow maps are more accurate than normal shadow maps. These shadows also include an option to make the shadows transparent in the mental ray Shadow Map rollout.

Using mental ray Sky Portal

If you look closely at the Photometric Lights category, you'll notice another light type. The mr Sky Portal provides a way to focus light streaming into an interior space from an external source using a designated portal. Think of this as a sky light that causes all Final Gather light rays to be focused on a specific area. It results in a better Final Gather result with fewer light rays. The Sky Portal is direct light, giving you one bounce for free if Final Gather is disabled.

To use a Sky Portal, you must have mental ray enabled, include a skylight or a Sun & Sky system, and have Final Gather turned on. Then simply drag over the area where the window is located, and all light rays entering the interior space are focused on those areas defined by the Sky Portal. The gizmo for the Sky Portal is a simple rectangular box with an arrow pointing in the direction of the light rays. If the light rays are pointing outward, you can use the Flip Light Flux Direction option to change their direction.

> **TIP**
>
> For better results for interior scenes using exterior lighting, enable the mr Photographic Exposure Control and use the Physically Based Lighting, Indoor Daylight preset in the mr Photographic Exposure Control rollout.

22

Within the mr Skylight Portal Parameters rollout, you can enable or disable the Sky Portal. A Multiplier value and a Filter Color work just like other lights. If the image appears grainy, you can increase the Shadow Samples value to remove any splotchy effect on the walls, but this increases the render time. Within the Advanced Parameters rollout, the Visible to Renderer option makes the Sky Portal visible in the rendered image, causing exterior objects to be blotted out.

You also can set the Color Source to Use the Scene Environment if you want light to be pulled from the environment map. Sky Portals also support HDRI maps as lighting sources. Figure 22.5 shows a house interior lighted using mental ray, Final Gather, and two Sky Portals.

FIGURE 22.5

Sky Portals can focus all rays coming from an external light source to speed up Final Gather passes.

Using mental ray Sun & Sky

If you want to quickly create an outdoor scene and render it using mental ray, then the Daylight system that uses the mr Sun and Sky is an easy quality solution. Before adding the Daylight system to your scene, switch the renderer to mental ray in the Render Setup dialog box. Then add the Daylight system (found in the Create ➪ Lights or the Create ➪ Systems menus) to the scene, and in the Modify panel, select mr Sun in the Sunlight drop-down list and mr Sky in the Skylight drop-down list. When you first select the Daylight system, a dialog box appears recommending that you use the mr Photographic Exposure Control. Click the Yes button to enable this control. When you select the mr Sky option, another dialog box appears, asking if you want to enable the mr Physical Sky environment map. Click Yes to this also.

If you look in the Environment panel of the Environment as Effects dialog box, you can see the mr Physical Sky material applied as an environment map. This material defines how the sky and ground planes look. The default settings look pretty good.

The Daylight system includes controls for positioning the sun in the sky based on a physical location, day of the year, and time of the day. By changing these controls, you can manipulate the sun's position in the sky relative to the scene objects. If the sun appears in the viewport, it is rendered with lens flares, as shown in Figure 22.6.

FIGURE 22.6

The Daylight can be endowed with mr Sun and mr Sky.

When a Sky & Sun system is in place, you can ensure that it displays within the viewport if you select the Views ➪ Viewport Background ➪ Environment Background option. Using this method makes the Sun & Sky system visible.

Selecting the sun light object and moving it about the scene or changing the Time and Date parameters automatically updates the background and the scene. This provides a good way to precisely position the sun where you want it, as shown in Figure 22.7.

FIGURE 22.7

The Sun & Sky system can be viewed and interactively updated in the viewport.

Understanding Caustics and Photons

Light properties for the mental ray renderer include four unique properties: Energy, Decay, Caustic Photons, and Global Illumination (GI) Photons. You can find the settings for these properties in the mental ray Indirect Illumination rollout. Before learning about these properties, you need to understand what caustics and photons are.

Caustics are those strange glowing lines that you see at the bottom of an indoor swimming pool caused by the light refracting through the water. Caustics are common in nature, and now with mental ray you can add these effects to your scenes. *Photons* are small bundles of light energy, and like the raytracing rays, they are emitted from a light source with a given amount of energy. This energy is lost as the photon travels and as it hits objects in the scene. As a render is completed, mental ray keeps track of each photon and bounces it around the scene until all its energy is gone.

The Energy value is the amount of light energy that each photon starts out with, and the Decay value specifies how quickly that energy dissipates. The number of Caustic and GI Photons determines the resulting accuracy of the lighting. More photons yield a better solution, but the greater number also increases the render time substantially. The Multiplier and color swatch lets you set the intensity and color of the caustics.

Figure 22.8 shows a swimming pool with caustics glowing on the side of the wall. The left image shows the pool scene with caustics disabled, and the right image shows them enabled.

FIGURE 22.8

This indoor swimming pool scene is rendered without caustics (left) and with caustics (right).

To get caustics to work in your scene, you need to add a Raytrace, Flat Mirror, or Reflect/Refract map to the Reflection map channel for the material that you want to generate caustics.

Enabling caustics and global illumination for objects

Another "gotcha" when dealing with caustics and global illumination is that each object can be specified to generate and/or receive caustics and global illumination. These settings are found in the mental ray panel of the Object Properties dialog box, shown in Figure 22.9. This dialog box can be opened using the Edit ⇨ Properties menu command. If your scene isn't generating caustics and you can't figure out why, check this dialog box, because the Generate Caustics option is disabled by default. There is also an option to exclude the object from caustics and from GI.

The mental ray panel in the Object Properties dialog box also includes settings so you can configure how the object is treated during the Final Gather pass. Using the Return Black or Pass Through options, you can make the object unshaded or invisible to the final gather.

FIGURE 22.9

The Object Properties dialog box includes options for generating and receiving caustics and global illumination.

> **TIP**
>
> The Indirect Illumination panel of the Render Setup dialog box includes an option that can be used to cause All Objects to Generate and Receive Caustics and GI. Enabling this option enables these options for all objects regardless of their Object Properties settings.

Tutorial: Using Caustic Photons to create a disco ball

When using the mental ray renderer, you can see the results of the caustic photons as they are reflected around the room to help you determine the correct settings you need, but these photons themselves can be used to make a good disco ball effect.

> **TIP**
>
> A common way to get a good, crisp caustic effect is to use significantly more photons than you would need for global illumination—on the order of millions of photons—for good results.

To create a disco ball effect using caustic photons, follow these steps:

1. Open the Disco ball.max file from the Chap 22 directory on the CD.

   This file includes a simple room.

2. Open the Render Setup dialog box (F10), and switch the Production Renderer in the Assign Renderer rollout of the Common panel to the mental ray renderer.

3. Select Create ⇨ Standard Primitives ⇨ Sphere, and click in the Top viewport to create a sphere, and then position it toward the top of the room.

4. Press the M key to open the Slate Material Editor, double-click on the Standard material in the Material/Map Browser, and then double-click on the Raytrace map type in the Material/Map Browser. Then drag on the output socket for the Raytrace map and drop on the Reflection parameter. Then double-click the Standard material node to make its parameters appear, enable the Faceted option in the Shader Basic Parameters rollout; set the Opacity to **50**, the Specular Level to **95**, and the Glossiness to **30**; and drag the standard material's output socket to the sphere object.

5. Select Create Lights ⇨ Standard Lights ⇨ mr Area Omni, and click four times in the Top viewport to create four lights that surround the sphere object. From the main menu, select the Tools ⇨ Light Lister option where you can quickly change the Multiplier value for each of the lights to **0.3**. Then, using the Move tool, offset each light vertically from the others.

6. Select all four light objects and right-click to open the Object Properties dialog box from the pop-up quad menu. Open the mental ray panel in the Object Properties dialog box and enable the Generate Caustics option for each light.

7. Open the Render Setup dialog box (F10). In the Indirect Illumination panel, locate the Caustics section. Enable the Caustics option, set the Multiplier to **10**, enable the Maximum Sampling Radius option, and set the Maximum Sampling Radius value to **1.0**. At the bottom or the Caustics and Global Illumination (GI) rollout, enable the All Objects Generate and Receive GI and Caustics option. Then click the Render button.

22

> **NOTE**
> If the caustics aren't visible, make sure the Use Advanced Lighting option in the Render Setup dialog box is enabled.

Figure 22.10 shows the resulting disco scene with thousands of lights visible on the walls.

FIGURE 22.10

This disco ball simply reflects the caustic photons around the room.

Controlling Indirect Illumination

In addition to the light settings, you can set many of the properties that control how caustics, global illumination, and Final Gather are computed in two rollouts of the Indirect Illumination panel of the Render Setup dialog box, shown in Figure 22.11. These two rollouts are the Final Gather rollout and the Caustics and Global Illumination (GI) rollout.

The Final Gather rollout is split into two parts. The top part features a set of Basic settings with several Presets that take the guesswork out of the settings. Simply choose one of the presets from the drop-down list, and all the key settings are automatically made for you. The preset options include Draft, Low, Medium, High, and Very High. The Multiplier and color swatch changes the intensity and color of the indirect light. The Weight value sets how much indirect light affects the Final Gather solution.

For caustics and for global illumination, the Maximum Number of Photons per Sample value determines how the caustic photons are blended. A higher value results in more blending and softer edges. The Maximum Sampling Radius value sets the size of each photon. This value is set automatically depending on the size of the scene. However, you can enable the Radius value and enter a new value manually.

FIGURE 22.11

The Indirect Illumination panel includes settings for caustics, GI, and Final Gather.

The Volumes setting is used by Volume material shaders to set the photon's size. The Trace Depth settings determine the maximum number of reflections and refractions that a photon can take before it is ignored.

Photon and Final Gather maps can take a while to generate for a complicated scene, but once computed, they can be saved and reloaded. These files are saved using the .pmap and .fgm extensions. To generate a photon map, click the Generate Photon Map Now, or to generate a final gather map, click the Generate Final Gather Map Now button.

Final Gather sends out rays to a scene that has computed caustics and global illumination already and computes the light at that location. All these rays are then combined to produce a total lighting picture of the scene and then blended to help fix any lighting abnormalities that may exist in the scene. The Samples value determines how many rays are cast into the scene. The Final Gather lighting pass can then be saved to a file after it is computed.

Rendering control

The core rendering settings for the mental ray renderer are contained within the Renderer panel of the Render Setup dialog box, shown in Figure 22.12. Using these settings, you can increase the speed of the renderer (at the expense of image quality).

The Sampling settings are used to apply an anti-aliasing pass to the rendered image. These samples can be filtered, and you can control the details of the contrast between the samples. The Bucket Width is the size of the blocks that are identified and rendered. Smaller buckets do not take as long to render and provide quicker feedback in the Render window.

The mental ray renderer uses several different algorithms, and you can specify which ones to ignore in order to speed up the rendering cycle in the Rendering Algorithms rollout. If a needed algorithm is disabled, the features that rely on that algorithm are skipped. You can also set the Trace Depth for Reflections and Refractions and control the Raytrace Acceleration values.

FIGURE 22.12

The Renderer panel includes several rollouts of settings for controlling the mental ray renderer.

When a preview render is rendered in the Rendered Frame Window while mental ray is enabled, an additional panel of options appears below the window as shown in Figure 22.13. The options on this panel let you quickly adjust the precision value for the Antialiasing, Soft Shadows, Final Gather Precision, Reflection, and Refraction settings. You also can speed the re-render by reusing the Geometry and Final Gather solutions if they haven't changed. The Render button lets you re-render the scene immediately.

FIGURE 22.13

When mental ray is rendered in the Rendered Frame Window, a panel of options appears below for tweaking the image.

Advanced mental ray

The mental ray renderer also includes many additional features that you can take advantage of, including Depth of Field, Motion Blur, Contours, Displacement, and Camera Shaders. The settings for these additional features are located in rollouts at the bottom of the Renderer panel. For example, if you add the Glare map to the Output map in the Camera Shader section, then you can get a strong glare from light in the scene, as shown for the house interior in Figure 22.14.

FIGURE 22.14

Placing the Glare map in the Output Camera Shader, you can get a strong glare from the light in the window.

Using mental ray proxies

Complex scenes can have hundreds of objects and when rendered in mental ray, single frames can take several hours to render. This can make it tough to get previews to test lighting and atmospheric effects. If you know that the objects look fine, then you can use the mental ray proxy object to replace multiple objects or a single high-resolution object with a proxy.

To use a mental ray proxy object, add a mr proxy object to the scene using the Create⇨mental ray⇨mr Proxy menu command. Select the Modify panel and click on the Source Object button, then select the object that you want to replace with the proxy.

NOTE
You can select the source object only in the Modify panel.

When the source object is selected, you can save the object to a file. Source objects are saved as .mib files. The object is then displayed within the scene as a point cloud or as a bounding box, and a preview of the source object is displayed in the Parameters rollout. You also can change the number of vertices that are displayed in the viewports.

When the scene is rendered, the source object file is read in and used for the render.

Using mental ray materials

If the mental ray, iray, or the Quicksilver Hardware renderer is enabled, you can open the Material/Map Browser in the Material Editor or separately using the Rendering menu, and be greeted with many additional material and map types and the Autodesk Material Library, which includes hundreds of preset materials organized by category, as shown in Figure 22.15.

> **NOTE**
>
> If you enable the Show Incompatible option in the Material/Map Browser pop-up menu, you can view the list of mental ray materials even if the mental ray renderer isn't enabled.

FIGURE 22.15

The Material/Map Browser includes many additional mental ray materials from the Autodesk Material Library.

Using the Autodesk Material Library and the Arch & Design materials

The Autodesk Material Library and the Arch & Design materials are a set of advanced mental ray materials designed for architects to add to buildings and surfaces found in architectural renderings. These materials are based on physical properties that are typically found in environments lighted with global illumination. For example, the Satin Varnished Wood template includes slightly blurred reflections and a high glossiness to give it a realistic look.

The materials contained in the Autodesk Material Library are categorized into groups and subgroups. Each material has several parameters allowing you to change the color, glossiness, reflectivity, and so on. The available parameters change based on the selected material.

Many of the Arch & Design materials are already defined and available in the Templates rollout. The available presets include Pearl Finish, Satin Varnished Wood, Glazed Ceramic, Glossy Plastic, Masonry, Leather, Frosted Glass, Translucent Plastic Film, Brushed Metal, and Patterned Copper.

For each template, several rollouts of parameters are available for defining the Diffuse, Reflection, Refraction, Translucency, Anisotropy, Fresnel Reflections, Bumps, and Self-Illumination properties along with a full selection of maps. Figure 22.16 shows a sampling of the available materials.

FIGURE 22.16

The materials in the mental ray Arch & Design collection include a broad set of physical properties.

Within the Special Effects rollout are two specialized options that add to the render realism. Ambient Occlusion lights the scene based on how accessible ambient light is to scene objects. It is a material shader solution and is not based on lights. Areas that face a wall or are blocked by other objects are recessed in shadow. Areas facing the lights are highlighted more. Using the Samples and Max Distance, you can control the contrast of the resulting image. By default, ambient occlusion uses black and gray tones to show occluded areas, but if you enable the Use Color From Other Materials (Exact AO), then the object's diffuse color is reflected into the occluded areas. Figure 22.17 shows an example of Ambient Occlusion.

NOTE
The Nitrous display drivers make ambient occlusion effects visible in the viewports.

22

The other useful special effect option is Round Corners. When you apply this option to a mechanical object, the object's edge is rounded so the light source highlights the edge, but no change is made to the object's geometry. This creates a realistic soft edge without the time or extra polygons to create it using geometry.

Using the Self Illumination (Glow) rollout, you can make a material act as a light source to the scene. This rollout includes presets for photometric properties based on real-world values such as degrees Kelvin.

FIGURE 22.17

Ambient Occlusion lets you light the scene by controlling the ambient light that gets bounced around the scene.

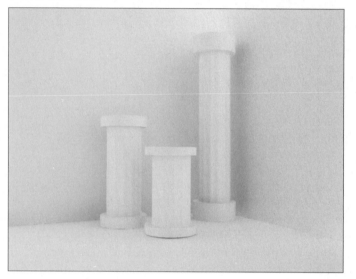

Using the Car Paint material

When cars are painted in the factory, the paint is composed of two layers that give the car its unique look. The undercoat is called the flake layer, and it shines through the top layer. The mental ray Car Paint material includes settings for defining both of these layers. Figure 22.18 shows a car painted with this material.

Using the Subsurface Scattering materials

The four mental ray materials that begin with "SSS" are Subsurface Scattering materials used to shade human skin and other membrane-like objects. Skin has an interesting property that allows it to become slightly translucent when it is placed in front of a strong light source. The ears in particular are a good example of this because they allow light to penetrate and highlight their features. Most organic objects including leaves, rubber, milk, and skin can benefit from these materials.

FIGURE 22.18

Cars rendered with the mental ray Car Paint shader use multiple layers, just like real cars.

Summary

If you're looking for a rendering option that perfectly calculates reflections, refractions, and transparencies, then the mental ray renderer is what you need. iray is another option for rendering when you aren't sure how to configure mental ray.

In this chapter, you accomplished the following:

- Learned to enable the mental ray and iray renderers
- Used the iray renderer to progressively render complex scenes
- Created mental ray lights
- Worked with caustics and photons
- Used mental ray proxies
- Accessed mental ray materials

After you have some great looking renders, you'll need to know how to composite them into a scene. The next chapter covers some simple compositing techniques including 3ds Max's own Video Post.

Compositing with Render Elements and the Video Post Interface

IN THIS CHAPTER

Learning about post-processing

Compositing with Photoshop, Premiere, and After Effects

Using render elements

Working with State Sets

Accessing compositing tools in the State Sets interface

Using the Video Post interface

Working with sequences

Understanding the various filter types

Adding and editing events

Specifying event ranges

After you've completed your scene and rendered it, you're finished, right? Well, not exactly. You still have post-production to complete: That's where you work with the final rendered images to add some additional effects. This phase of production typically takes place in another package, such as Photoshop or After Effects, and understanding how to interact with these packages can be a lifesaver when your client wants some last-minute changes (and they always do).

You can set the Autodesk® 3ds Max 2013® software to render any part in the rendering pipeline individually. These settings are called *render elements*. By rendering out just the Specular layer or just the shadow, you have more control over these elements in your compositor.

If you don't have access to a compositing package, or even if you do, 3ds Max includes a simple interface that can be used to add some post-production effects. This interface is the Video Post interface.

You can use the Video Post window to composite the final rendered image with several other images and filters. These filters let you add lens effects like glows and flares, and other effects like blur and fade, to the final output. The Video Post window provides a post-processing environment within the 3ds Max interface.

> **NOTE**
>
> Many of the post-processing effects, such as glows and blurs, also are available as render effects, but the Video Post window is capable of much more. Render effects are covered in Chapter 21, "Using Atmospheric and Render Effects."

Using External Compositing Packages

Before delving into the Video Post interface, let's take a quick look at some of the available compositing packages. Several of these packages have direct links into 3ds Max that can be used to give you a jump on the post-production process.

Compositing enables motion graphics, editing, and visual effects, which doesn't sound too different from what 3ds Max does, except for that funny word—*compositing*. If you think of the final rendered image produced using 3ds Max as just an image that needs to be combined with other elements such as text, logos, other images, or even a DVD menu, then you're starting to see what post-production teams know. Compositing is the process of combining several different elements into a finished product. Positioning these elements can even be done in 3D by placing images behind or in front of other images or in time by working with animations.

Compositing with Photoshop

Perhaps the most common tool for compositing images is Photoshop. Photoshop can bring multiple images together in a single file and position them relative to one another. Working with layers makes applying simple filters and effects to the various element pieces easy.

Figure 23.1 shows Photoshop with several separate pieces, each on a different layer.

FIGURE 23.1

Photoshop is an important compositing tool for static images.

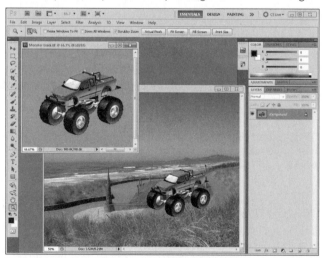

To composite images in Photoshop, you need to load all the separate images into Photoshop and then select the portions of the images that you want to combine. When saving image files in 3ds Max, be sure to include an alpha channel. You can see the alpha channel in the Rendered Frame window if you click the Display Alpha Channel button, as shown in Figure 23.2.

FIGURE 23.2

The Rendered Frame window can display an image's alpha channel.

In Photoshop, you can see an image's alpha channel if you select the Channels panel in the Layers palette. Selecting the alpha channel and using the Magic Wand tool makes selecting the rendered object easy. After it's selected, you can copy and paste the rendered image onto your background image as a new layer.

> **NOTE**
>
> Not all image file formats support an alpha channel. When rendering images to be composited, be sure to use an alpha channel format such as RLA, RPF, PNG, or TGA.

After all your images have been positioned on the background image, you can apply a filter, such as a Gaussian Blur, to smooth the edges between the composite images.

Video editing with Premiere Pro

Photoshop works with still images, but if you work with animations, then Adobe has Premiere Pro to help with your video editing needs. The editing that Premiere Pro makes possible includes patching several animation clips together, adding sound, color-correcting the frames, and adding transitions between animation clips.

Within Premiere Pro, various animation clips can be imported (or dragged directly from Windows Explorer) into the Project panel. From here, the clips can be dropped onto the Timeline in the desired order. The Monitor panel shows the current animation or individual animation clips.

Sound clips can be dropped in the Timeline in the Audio track. The Title menu also can be used to add text to the animation. Another common activity in Premiere Pro is to add transition effects between clips. This is done by clicking the Effects tab in the Project panel, selecting a transition effect, dragging the effect to the Timeline, and dropping it between two animation clips.

When the entire sequence is completed, you can render it using the Sequence ➪ Render Work Area menu command. The completed animation file then can be saved using the File ➪ Export menu command.

Figure 23.3 shows the Premiere Pro interface with the animation clips loaded and positioned in the Timeline panel.

Video compositing with After Effects

If you need to add a little more to your animations than just transitions, you should look into Adobe's After Effects. After Effects lets you composite 2D and 3D clips into a single image or animation. You can paint directly on the animation frames, add lights and cameras, and create visual effects such as Distort, Shatter, and Warp.

After Effects includes a library of resources much like those found in Premiere. These resources can be positioned on a Composition pane. Effects applied to the loaded animation clip are listed in the Effects panel along with all the effects settings.

FIGURE 23.3

Premiere Pro can be used to combine several animation sequences.

After Effects includes many of the same tools used in Photoshop and Illustrator. These tools let you paint and select portions of the animation clip as if it were a still image, but the results can be added or removed over time.

Tutorial: Adding animation effects using After Effects

Some effects are much easier to add using a package like After Effects than to create in 3ds Max. A good example is adding a blurry look and the waves coming from a heat source to the melting snowman animation created earlier.

To add video effects using After Effects, follow these steps:

1. Open After Effects, and drag the Melting snowman.avi file from the Chap 23 directory on the CD to the Project panel.
2. Select Composition ➪ New Composition, select the NTSC DV option from the Preset list, and click OK.
3. Drag the Melting snowman.avi file from the Project panel, and drop it on the Composition pane.
4. With the animation selected in the Composition pane, select Effect ➪ Distort ➪ Wave Warp. The Wave Warp effect appears in a panel. Set the Wave Height to **4**, the Wave Width to **30**, the Direction to **Vertical**, and the Wave Speed to **1**. This adds a heat wave effect to the entire animation.
5. Select Effect ➪ Blur & Sharpen ➪ Gaussian Blur, and set the Blurriness value to **3.0**.
6. In the Timeline panel, drag the Work Area End icon so that it coincides with the end of the animation.
7. Select Composition ➪ Make Movie. In the Render Queue dialog box that opens, click the Render button to render the animation with its effects.

Figure 23.4 shows the After Effects interface with the animation clip loaded.

FIGURE 23.4

After Effects can add special effects to an animation sequence.

Using Render Elements

If your production group includes a strong post-processing team that does compositing, there may be times when you just want to render certain elements of the scene, such as the alpha information or a specific atmospheric effect. Applying individual elements to a composite image gives you better control over the elements. For example, you can reposition or lighten a shadow without having to re-render the entire scene or animation sequence.

Using the Render Elements panel of the Render Setup dialog box, shown in Figure 23.5, you can render a single effect and save it as an image.

You can select and render several render elements at the same time. The available render elements include Alpha, Atmosphere, Background, Blend, Diffuse, Hair and Fur, Illuminance HDR Data, Ink, Lighting, Luminance HDR Data, Material ID, Matte, Object ID, Paint, Reflection, Refraction, Self-Illumination, Shadow, Specular, Velocity, and Z Depth. You also can use the Shift and Ctrl keys to select multiple elements from the list at once.

If the mental ray rendering engine is enabled, then many more Render Elements are also available, including all the parameters that are included as part of the Arch&Design materials, along with a mental ray Shader Element and the mental ray Labeled Element.

The Add button opens the Render Elements dialog box, where you can select the elements to include. The Merge button lets you merge the elements from another 3ds Max scene, and the Delete button lets you delete elements from the list. To be included in the rendered image, the Elements Active option must be checked. The Display Elements option causes the results to be rendered separately and displayed in the Rendered Frame Window.

FIGURE 23.5

You can use the Render Elements rollout to render specific effects.

The Enable check box can turn off individual elements; Enable Filtering enables the anti-aliasing filtering as specified in the 3ds Max Default Scanline A-Buffer rollout. A separate Rendered Frame Window is opened for each render element that is enabled when the rendering starts.

Each element in the list can be given a unique list name, and clicking the Browse button opens a file dialog box where you can give the rendered element a filename. 3ds Max automatically appends an underscore and the name of the element on the end of the filename. For example, if you name the file **myScene** and select to render the Alpha element, the filename for this element is **myScene_alpha**.

When you select the Blend and Z Depth render elements, an additional rollout of parameters appears. You can use the Blend render element to combine several separate elements together. The Blend Element Parameters rollout includes check boxes for each render element type. The Z Depth render element includes parameters for setting Min and Max depth values.

Figure 23.6 shows the resulting image in the Rendered Frame Window for the Alpha render element.

FIGURE 23.6

The Alpha render element shown in the Rendered Frame Window

The Render Elements rollout can also output files that Autodesk's Composite product can use. These files have the .cws extension. Composite is a compositing product that can work with individual elements to increase the highlights, change color hues, darken and blur shadows, and do many other things without having to re-render the scene.

Using State Sets

Another more convenient way to work with render passes is with the State Sets panel, shown in Figure 23.7. This panel is opened using the Rendering ➪ State Sets menu command and includes an interface where you can define a custom state. This state can have some objects hidden, have some lights and shadows disabled, alter the number of frames to display or the rendering method, or specify a specific render element to include.

FIGURE 23.7

The State Sets panel lets you define several individual states, each with unique settings.

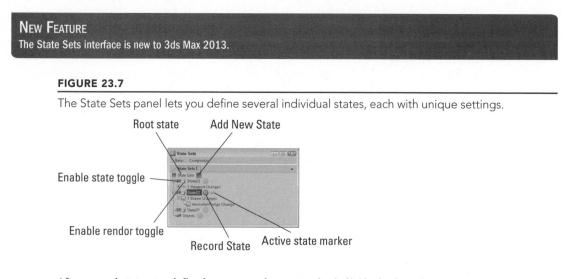

Root state   Add New State

Enable state toggle

Enable rendor toggle

Record State   Active state marker

After several states are defined, you can select to render individual selected states or render them all. For example, suppose you have a single file that includes all the animations for a specific game character one after another, such as a walk cycle in frames 1 through 10 and a run cycle from 11 through 15, and so on. Using the State Sets panel, you can define a separate state for each individual range of frames in the file and then render them all at once using the panel's States ⇨ Render All States menu command.

At the top of the State Sets interface is the root state that includes all states; to its right is the Add New State button. Clicking this button creates a new state that appears under the root state. Initially, new states are simply named State with a number, but you can double-click the state name to change it.

To the left of the state name are two toggle buttons used to enable/disable the state and to enable/disable the rendering of that state. To the right of the state name are buttons to begin/end recording and a green arrow marking the current active state. Only one state can be active at a time.

Recording states

Clicking the Begin Recording State button to the right of the state name begins the recording of any changes made to the scene. The record button turns red when recording is active. Any changes are listed in a hierarchy under the state name where you can expand the list to see the specific commands. Some changes make the new value, such as color swatches and frame number, visible in the State Sets interface where you can easily change them. Clicking the record button again ends the recording of changes. If you want to make some additional changes after the recording has stopped, simply click the Record button again and the new changes are added to the state.

Using templates and nesting states

If a certain state has most of the changes you need, then you can make it into a template with the States ⇨ Create Template menu command. These template states are then available for selection using the States ➪ Add State Template menu command. State templates are added to the bottom of the current hierarchy.

States also can be nested within one another using the States ➪ Add Sub-State menu command. The Delete State menu is used to delete the current selected state. Another option is scripted states, which open a dialog box where you can add a script to be performed when the state is applied and another when the state is disabled.

New states are added to the top of the hierarchy, but you can reorder the states by dragging them above or below their current position. You also can drop a state within another state to nest them.

Rendering states

To render a current state, simply select that state, right-click, and choose the Render Selected State option from the pop-up menu. Several states can be selected at once using the Ctrl and Shift keys. You also can render all states starting at the top of the hierarchy and continuing downward with the States ➪ Render All States menu command. This renders only those states with the Enable Render toggle turned on.

With the States ➪ Render Outputs menu command, a path and naming convention appears at the bottom of the interface. The Browse button is used to change the location where the renders are saved, and using the Set Path button, you can add an output command to all states. The state name typically is included as part of the filename. This is a huge timesaver from saving the file path for each render pass in the Render Setup dialog box.

Tutorial: Presenting several stylized rendered options

Suppose you have a client who wants to have a scene rendered using one of the non-photorealistic rendering options available in 3ds Max, but the client doesn't know which look is right and has asked you to create a rendered copy of the scene using each of the available styles. The client also anticipates that the scene will change, so it would be nice to have a setup that can quickly render all these variants. The answer to this all-too-common problem is using state sets.

To add setup and render images using each of the available render styles, follow these steps:

1. Open the Elk-state sets.max file from the Chap 23 directory on the CD.

   This file contains a simple scene of an elk on a hill.

2. Open the Render Setup dialog box with the Rendering ➪ Render Setup menu command (or by pressing F10), and choose the Quicksilver Hardware Renderer option for the Production render in the Assign Renderer rollout. This sets the root state to use the Quicksilver Renderer.

3. Select the Rendering ➪ State Sets menu to open the State Sets interface. Select State01, rename it **Graphiterender**, and then click the Begin Recording State button.

4. Select the Renderer panel in the Render Setup dialog box, and choose the Graphite option from the Rendering Level drop-down list in the Visual Style & Appearance rollout. Then click the Record State button in the State Sets interface again.

5. Click the Add New State button in the State Sets interface, and rename the state Ink render; then click the Begin Recording State button for this state, change the Rendering Level in the Render Setup dialog box to Ink, and click again on the Recording State button to stop the recording.

23

6. Repeat Step 5 for each of the remaining render styles in the Rendering Level drop-down list, including Color Ink, Acrylic, Tech, Color Pencil, and Pastel.

7. In the State Sets interface, select the States ⇨ Render Outputs menu, set the output path to where you want to save the renders files, and press the Set Path button. This adds the output file changes to each state.

8. Select the States ⇨ Render All States menu command to create and save all the stylized rendered images.

Figure 23.8 shows the State Sets interface with all the different states and one of the resulting rendered images.

FIGURE 23.8

The State Sets interface can automate multiple renders.

Accessing Compositor View

After a state is set up and rendered, you can use the Compositor ⇨ Compositor View menu command to view a node-based hierarchy of the states, as shown in Figure 23.9. All rendered and saved images appear as small thumbnails. If your states include any render elements, you can view those using the Compositor ⇨ Compositor View (RE) menu command.

Navigation about the Compositor window works just like in the Slate Material Editor. Dragging with the scroll button pans the view, the scroll wheel zooms in and out, and a Navigator pane in the upper-right corner shows and lets you move about the entire hierarchy. Additional menu commands in the Compositor menu of the State Sets interface are Select All, Auto-Layout Nodes, Lock View Position, Zoom Extents, Show Connected Inputs Only, and Refresh.

Connection lines are drawn between input and output sockets for each node. You can disconnect any connection line by clicking its input socket and dragging into an open area of the window. Connections are made by dragging from an output socket to an input socket on another node.

530

FIGURE 23.9

The Compositor View includes some basic image-compositing features.

Navigator pane

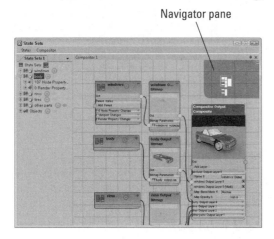

If you need to refresh the Compositor View, you can use the Compositor ⇨ Refresh menu command, or you can close the Compositor View pane by clicking the X in the upper-right corner and reopening it. Any nodes that are not connected are deleted when the Compositor View pane is reopened.

Changing node parameters

Each node that holds a render displays a small thumbnail, but you can increase its size by double-clicking the thumbnail. Clicking the small plus or minus sign in the upper-right corner of each node lets you toggle the node's parameters on and off. For bitmap nodes, the single parameter is the image's filename.

For the composite node, you can click the plus or minus sign to the right of each layer name to open its parameters. For each layer, you can select to turn its layer and its mask on and off, and set its blending mode and opacity. Each of these parameters also has an input socket that you can use.

Adding new nodes

If you drag from any state node's output socket and release it in an open part of the window, an option appears to Create a Render Output Node. Selecting this option opens another node, and using its filename parameter, you can load another bitmap that can be used within the hierarchy as a mask or opacity map.

You also can add a Color Correct node to the hierarchy with the Compositor ⇨ Create Color Correction Node menu command. This node can then be connected between a bitmap and the composite nodes. Its parameters include Hue Shift, Saturation, Contrast, and Brightness. The Hue Shift parameter provides a quick, easy way to change the color of a rendered object.

TIP

Clicking a connection line between a bitmap node and the composite node gives you an option of creating a Color Correction node in between the two.

23

Exporting to Photoshop

The composited results can be exported to Photoshop as a PSD file using the Compositor ➪ Create PSD menu command. This opens a simple dialog box where you can browse to set the save folder and filename. It also includes a Render button to initialize the export. The resulting image can then be opened in Photoshop. Each render state appears in Photoshop as a separate layer, as shown in Figure 23.10.

FIGURE 23.10

Compositor results can be exported to Photoshop, where each render state is a layer.

Linking data to After Effects

Selecting the Compositor ➪ Compositor Link menu command opens a Compositor Link pane at the bottom of the State Sets interface. Clicking the Create Link button opens a file dialog box where you can specify a folder and filename for a file that is shared between 3ds Max and After Effects. This file has an .sof extension.

> **NOTE**
>
> Before a live link between 3ds Max and After Effects can be made, you need to copy the Adobe.AfterFX.dll file and the Autodesk.Plugins.Adobe.AfterFX.SceneIO.dll file from the 3ds Max/ExternalPlugins folder to the After Effects/Support Files folder. You also need to copy the Autodesk.Plugins.Adobe.AfterFX.SceneIO.Loader.aex file from the 3ds Max/ExternalPlugins folder to the After Effects/Support Files/Plug-ins/AEGP folder. Create an AEGP folder if there isn't one already.

Within After Effects, you can access the Open Compositor Link (Autodesk) menu command to open a file dialog box where you can locate the link .sof file created in 3ds Max. This loads the render states into After Effects, where you can edit them as needed. If changes are made in 3ds Max, you can use the Update to Link button in the Compositor Link pane to pass the changes on to After Effects.

Lights, cameras, and objects can be recorded in the Objects state. Any objects identified within this state are transferred to After Effects when a link is created. You can add objects to the Objects state by selecting them and clicking the Record State button or by clicking the Record State button and unhiding those objects that you want to pass on to After Effects. You also can control the type of objects that are passed on using the options listed in the Compositor Link pane. Plane objects are passed as Solids, and all other geometry objects are passed as Null objects.

Completing Post-Production with the Video Post Interface

Post-production is the work that comes after the scene is rendered. It is the time when you add effects, such as glows and highlights, as well as add transitional effects to an animation. For example, if you want to include a logo in the lower-right corner of your animation, you can create and render the logo and composite several rendered images into one during post-production.

Video Post interface is another post-processing interface within 3ds Max that you can use to combine the current scene with different images, effects, and image-processing filters. Compositing is the process of combining several different images into a single image. Each element of the composite is included as a separate event. These events are lined up in a queue and processed in the order in which they appear in the queue. The queue can also include looping events.

The Video Post interface, like the Render Setup dialog box, provides another way to produce final output. You can think of the Video Post process as an artistic assembly line. As the image moves down the line, each item in the queue adds an image, drops a rendered image on the stack, or applies a filter effect. This process continues until the final output event is reached.

The Video Post interface, shown in Figure 23.11, includes a toolbar, a pane of events and ranges, and a status bar. You can open it by choosing Rendering ⇨ Video Post.

FIGURE 23.11

The Video Post interface lets you composite images with your final rendering.

Toolbar   Queue pane   Time bar   Range pane

Within the Video Post interface, each event is displayed as a track in the Queue pane to the left. To the right is the Range pane, where the range for each track is displayed as lines with square boxes at each end. You can edit these ranges by dragging the squares on either end. The time bar, above the Range pane, displays the frames for the current sequence, and the status bar at the bottom of the interface includes information and view buttons.

The Video Post toolbar

At the top of the Video Post interface is a toolbar with several buttons for managing the Video Post features. Table 23.1 shows and explains these buttons.

TABLE 23.1 **Video Post Toolbar Buttons**

Toolbar Button	Name	Description
	New Sequence	Creates a new sequence
	Open Sequence	Opens an existing sequence
	Save Sequence	Saves the current sequence
	Edit Current Event	Opens the Edit Current Event dialog box where you can edit events
	Delete Current Event	Removes the current event from the sequence
	Swap Events	Changes the position in the queue of two selected events
	Execute Sequence	Runs the current sequence
	Edit Range Bar	Enables you to edit the event ranges
	Align Selected Left	Aligns the left ranges of the selected events
	Align Selected Right	Aligns the right ranges of the selected events
	Make Selected Same Size	Makes the ranges for the selected events the same size
	Abut Selected	Places event ranges end-to-end
	Add Scene Event	Adds a rendered scene to the queue

Toolbar Button	Name	Description
	Add Image Input Event	Adds an image to the queue
	Add Image Filter Event	Adds an image filter to the queue
	Add Image Layer Event	Adds a compositing plug-in to the queue when two events are selected
	Add Image Output Event	Sends the final composited image to a file or device
	Add External Event	Adds an external image-processing event to the queue
	Add Loop Event	Causes other events to loop

The Video Post Queue and Range panes

Below the toolbar are the Video Post Queue and Range panes. The Queue pane is on the left; it lists all the events to be included in the post-processing sequence in the order in which they are processed. You can rearrange the order of the events by dragging an event in the queue to its new location.

You can select multiple events by holding down the Ctrl key and clicking the event names, or you can select one event, hold down the Shift key, and click another event to select all events between the two.

Each event has a corresponding range that appears in the Range pane to the right. Each range is shown as a line with a square on each end. The left square marks the first frame of the event, and the right square marks the last frame of the event. You can expand or contract these ranges by dragging the square on either end of the range line.

If you click the line between two squares, you can drag the entire range. If you drag a range beyond the given number of frames, then additional frames are added.

The time bar is at the top of the Range pane. This bar shows the number of total frames included in the animation. You can also slide the time bar up or down to move it closer to a specific track by dragging it.

The Video Post status bar

The status bar includes a prompt line, several value fields, and some navigation buttons. The fields to the right of the prompt line include Start, End, and Total Frames of the selected track, and the Width and Height of the image. The navigation buttons include (in order from left to right) Pan, Zoom Extents, Zoom Time, and Zoom Region.

23

535

Working with Sequences

All the events that are added to the Queue pane make up a *sequence*. You can save these sequences and open them at a later time. The Execute Sequence button (Ctrl+R), found on the toolbar, starts the compositing process.

> **NOTE**
> The keyboard shortcuts for the Video Post interface work only if the Keyboard Shortcut Override Toggle on the main toolbar is enabled.

To save a sequence, click the Save Sequence button on the toolbar to open the Save Sequence dialog box, where you can save the queue sequence. Sequences are saved along with the 3ds Max file when the scene is saved, but they can also be saved independently of the scene. By default, these files are saved with the .vpx extension in the vpost directory.

> **NOTE**
> Saving a sequence as a VPX file maintains the elements of the queue, but it resets all parameter settings. Saving the file as a 3ds Max file maintains the queue order along with the parameter settings.

You can open saved sequences using the Open Sequence button on the toolbar. When a saved sequence is opened, all the current events are deleted. Clicking the New Sequence button also deletes any current events.

The Execute Sequence toolbar button opens the Execute Video Post interface, shown in Figure 23.12. The controls in this dialog box work exactly the way those in the Render Scene dialog box work.

> **NOTE**
> The time and resolution settings in the Execute Video Post dialog box are unique from those in the Render Setup dialog box.

FIGURE 23.12

The Execute Video Post interface includes the controls for producing the queue output.

The Time Output section enables you to specify which frames to render, and the Output Size section lets you specify the size of the output. The Custom selection lets you enter Width and Height values, or you can use one of the presets in the drop-down list or one of the preset resolution buttons. This dialog box also includes controls for entering the Image Aspect and Pixel Aspect ratios.

The Output options let you select to keep the Progress dialog box open, to render to the Rendered Frame Window, and/or to use network rendering. When you're ready to render the queue, click the Render button.

Adding and Editing Events

The seven event types that you can add to the queue are Image Input, Scene, Image Filter, Image Layer, Loop, External, and Image Output. If no events are selected, then adding an event positions the event at the bottom of the list. If an event is selected, the added event becomes a subevent under the selected event.

Every event dialog box, such as the Add Image Input Event dialog box shown in Figure 23.13, includes a Label field where you can name the event. This name shows up in the queue window and is used to identify the event.

FIGURE 23.13

The Add Image Input Event dialog box lets you load an image to add to the queue.

Each event dialog box includes a Video Post Parameters section. This section contains VP Start Time and VP End Time values for defining precisely the length of the Video Post range. It also includes an Enabled option for enabling or disabling an event. Disabled events are grayed out in the queue.

To edit an event, you simply need to double-click its name in the Queue pane (or select it and press Ctrl+E) to open an Edit Event dialog box.

Adding an image input event

The Add Image Input Event dialog box lets you add a simple image to the queue. For example, you can add a background image using this dialog box rather than the Environment dialog box. To open the Add Image Input Event dialog box, click the Add Image Input Event button (Ctrl+I) on the toolbar.

> **TIP**
>
> If you don't name the image event, then the filename appears in the Queue pane as the name for the event.

The Files button in this dialog box opens the Select Image File for Video Post Input dialog box, where you can locate an image file to load from the hard disk or network. The Devices button lets you access an external device such as a video recorder. The Options button becomes enabled when you load an image. The Cache option causes the image to be loaded into memory, which can speed up the Video Post process by not requiring the image to be loaded for every frame.

The Image Driver section of the Add Image Input Event dialog box lets you specify the settings for the image driver, such as the compression settings for an AVI file. Clicking the Setup button opens a dialog box of options available for the selected format, but note that the Setup button is not active for all formats.

Click the Options button open the Image Input Options dialog box, shown in Figure 23.14. This dialog box lets you set the alignment, size, and frames where the image appears. The Alignment section of the Image Input Options dialog box includes nine presets for aligning the image. Preset options include top-left corner, top centered, top-right corner, left centered, centered, right centered, bottom-left corner, bottom centered, and bottom-right corner. You can also use the Coordinates option to specify in pixels the image's upper-left corner.

FIGURE 23.14

The Image Input Options dialog box lets you align and set the size of the image.

In the Size section of this dialog box, you can control the size of the image, using the Do Not Resize, Resize to Fit, or Custom Size options. The Custom Size option lets you enter Width and Height values.

The Frames section applies only to animation files. The From and To values define which frames of the animation to play. The Step value lets you play every nth frame as specified. The Loop at the End value causes the animation to loop back to the beginning when finished.

Adding scene events

A scene event is the rendered scene that you've built in 3ds Max. When you click the Add Scene Event button on the toolbar, the Add Scene Event dialog box shown in Figure 23.15 opens. This dialog box lets you specify the scene ranges and define the render options.

FIGURE 23.15

The Add Scene Event dialog box lets you specify which viewport to use to render your scene.

Below the Label field where you can name the event is a drop-down list that lets you select which viewport to use to render your scene. The active viewport is selected by default. The Render Setup button opens the Render Setup panel, where the Render button has been replaced with OK and Cancel buttons because the rendering is initiated with the Execute Sequence button.

> For more information about the Render Setup panel, see Chapter 20, "Rendering a Scene and Enabling Quicksilver."

The Scene Options section of the Add Scene Event dialog box also includes an option for enabling Scene Motion Blur. This motion blur type is different from the object motion blur that is set in the Object Properties dialog box. Scene motion blur is applied to the entire image and is useful for blurring objects that are moving fast. The Duration (frames) value sets how long the blur effect is computed per frame. The Duration Subdivisions value is how many computations are done for each duration. The Dither % value sets the amount of dithering to use for blurred sections.

In the Scene Range section, the Scene Start and Scene End values let you define the range for the rendered scene. The Lock Range Bar to Scene Range option maintains the range length as defined in the Time Slider, though you can still reposition the start of the rendered scene. The Lock to Video Post Range option sets the range equal to the Video Post range.

Adding image filter events

The Add Image Filter Event button (Ctrl+F) on the toolbar opens the Add Image Filter Event dialog box, shown in Figure 23.16, where you can select from many filter types. The available filters are included in a drop-down list under the Label field.

Below the filter drop-down list are two buttons: About and Setup. The About button gives some details about the creator of the filter. The Setup button opens a separate dialog box that controls the filter. The dialog box that appears depends on the type of filter that you selected in the drop-down list.

FIGURE 23.16

The Add Image Filter Event dialog box lets you select from many filter types.

Several, but not all, filters require a mask such as the Image Alpha filter. To open a bitmap image to use as the mask, click the Files button in the Mask section and select the file in the Select Mask Image dialog box that opens. A drop-down list lets you select the channel to use. Possible channels include Red, Green, Blue, Alpha, Luminance, Z Buffer, Material Effects, and Object. The mask can be Enabled or Inverted. The Options button opens the Image Input Options dialog box for aligning and sizing the mask.

Contrast filter

You use the Contrast filter to adjust the brightness and contrast. Selecting this filter and clicking the Setup button opens the Image Contrast Control dialog box. This simple dialog box includes values for Contrast and Brightness. Both values can be set from 0 to 1. The Absolute option computes the center gray value based on the highest color value. The Derived option uses an average value of the components of all three colors (red, green, and blue).

Fade filter

You can use the Fade filter to fade out the image over time. You can select it from the drop-down list. Clicking the Setup button opens the Fade Image Control dialog box where you select to fade either In or Out. The fade takes place over the length of the range set in the Range pane.

Image Alpha filter

The Image Alpha filter sets the alpha channel as specified by the mask. This filter doesn't have a setup dialog box.

Negative filter

The Negative filter inverts all the colors, as in the negative of a photograph. The Negative Filter dialog box includes a simple Blend value.

Pseudo Alpha filter

The Pseudo Alpha filter sets the alpha channel based on the pixel located in the upper-left corner of the image. This filter can make an unrendered background transparent. When this filter is selected, the Setup button is disabled because it doesn't have a setup dialog box.

Simple Wipe filter

The Simple Wipe filter removes the image by replacing it with a black background. The length of the wipe is determined by the event's time range. The Simple Wipe Control dialog box, shown in Figure 23.17, lets you wipe from the left to the right or from the right to the left. You can also set the mode to Push, which displays the image, or to Pop, which erases it.

FIGURE 23.17

The Simple Wipe Control dialog box lets you select which direction to wipe the image.

Starfield filter

The Starfield filter creates a starfield image. By using a camera, you can motion blur the stars. The Stars Control dialog box, shown in Figure 23.18, includes a Source Camera drop-down list that you can use to select a camera.

The General section sets the brightness and size of the stars. You can specify brightness values for the Dimmest Star and the Brightest Star. The Linear and Logarithmic options use two different algorithms to compute the brightness values of the stars as a function of distance. The Star Size value sets the size of the stars in pixels. Size values can range from 0.001 to 100.

The Motion Blur settings let you enable motion blurring, set the blur Amount, and specify a Dimming value.

The Star Database section includes settings for defining how the stars are to appear. The Random option displays stars based on the Count value, and the random Seed determines the randomness of the star's positions. The Custom option reads a star database specified in the Database field.

> **NOTE**
> 3ds Max includes a starfield database named earth.stb that includes the stars as seen from Earth.

23

FIGURE 23.18

The Stars Control dialog box lets you load a custom database of stars.

You can also specify whether the stars are composited in the background or foreground.

Tutorial: Creating space backdrops

Space backgrounds are popular backdrops, and 3ds Max includes a special Video Post filter for creating starfield backgrounds. You would typically want to use the Video Post interface to render the starfield along with any animation that you've created, but in this tutorial, you render a starfield for a single planet that you've created and outfitted with a planet material.

To create a starfield background, follow these steps:

1. Open the Planet with starfield background.max file from the Chap 23 directory on the CD.

   This file includes a simple space scene with a camera because the Starfield filter requires a camera.

2. Choose Rendering ⇨ Video Post to open the Video Post interface. A Scene Event must be added to the queue in order for the render job to be executed. Click the Add Scene Event button, type **planet scene** in the Label field, Select Camera01 as the Source Camera, and click OK.

   This adds the event to the Queue pane.

3. Click the Add Image Filter Event button (or press Ctrl+F) to open the Add Image Filter Event dialog box, and in the Label field type the name **starfield bg**. Select Starfield from the drop-down list, and click the Setup button to open the Stars Control dialog box, set the Star Size to **3.0** and the Count to **150,000**, and click OK.

4. Click the Execute Sequence button (or press Ctrl+R), select the Single output time option and an Output Size, and click the Render button.

Figure 23.19 shows the resulting space scene.

FIGURE 23.19

A space scene with a background, compliments of the Video Post interface

Adding image layer events

In addition to the standard filters that can be applied to a single image, several more filters, called *layer events*, can be applied to two or more images or rendered scenes. The Add Layer Event button (Ctrl+L) is available on the toolbar only when two image events are selected in the Queue pane. The first image (which is the selected image highest in the queue) becomes the source image, and the second image is the compositor. Both image events become subevents under the layer event.

> **NOTE**
> If the layer event is deleted, the two subevent images remain.

The dialog box for the Add Image Layer Event is the same as the Add Image Filter Event dialog box shown earlier, except that the drop-down list includes filters that work with two images.

Simple Wipe compositor

The Simple Wipe compositor is similar to the Simple Wipe filter, except that it slides the image in or out instead of erasing it. Its setup dialog box looks just like that of the Simple Wipe Control dialog box.

Other layer filters

The remaining layer filters include simple methods for compositing images and some simple transitions. None of these other filters has a Setup dialog box.

You can use the Alpha compositor to composite two images, using the alpha channel of the foreground image. The Cross Fade Transition compositor fades one image out as it fades another image in. You can use the Pseudo Alpha compositor to combine two images if one doesn't have an alpha channel. This compositor uses the upper-left pixel to designate the transparent color for the image. The Simple Additive Compositor combines two images based on the intensity of the second image.

Adding external events

The Add External Event button on the toolbar lets you use an external image-processing program to edit the image. This button is available only when an image event is selected, and the image event becomes a sub-event under the external event. The Add External Event dialog box, shown in Figure 23.20, includes a Browse button for locating the external program. It also includes a Command Line Options field for entering text commands for the external program. Many external programs use the clipboard to do their processing, so the Write image to clipboard and Read image from clipboard options make this possible.

FIGURE 23.20

The Add External Event dialog box lets you access an external program to edit images.

Using loop events

The Add Loop Event button is enabled on the Video Post toolbar when any single event is selected. This button enables an event to be repeated a specified number of times or throughout the Video Post range. The Add Loop Event dialog box, shown in Figure 23.21, includes a value field for the Number of Times to repeat the event, along with Loop and Ping Pong options. The Loop option repeats from beginning to end until the Number of Times value is reached. The Ping Pong option alternates playing the event forward and in reverse. You can name Loop events using the Label field.

FIGURE 23.21

The Add Loop Event dialog box lets you play an event numerous times.

Adding an image output event

If you've added all the events you need and configured them correctly, and you click the Execute Sequence button and nothing happens, then chances are good that you've forgotten to add an Image Output event. This event creates the file that all the events use to output to and should appear last in the queue.

The Add Image Output Event dialog box (Ctrl+O) looks similar to the Add Image Input Event dialog box shown earlier. The output can be saved to a file or to a device using any of the standard file types.

NOTE
If you don't give the output event a name, the filename automatically becomes the event name.

Working with Ranges

The Range pane in the Video Post interface is found to the right of the Queue pane. It displays the ranges for each event. These turn red when selected. The beginning and end points of the range are marked with squares. You can move these points by dragging the squares. This moves the beginning and end points for all selected events.

NOTE
Before you can move the ranges or drag the end points of a range, you need to select the Edit Range Bar button from the toolbar. The button is highlighted yellow when active.

When two or more events are selected, several additional buttons on the toolbar become enabled, including Swap Events, Align Selected Left, Align Selected Right, Make Selected Same Size, and Abut Selected. (These buttons were shown earlier in Table 23.1.)

The Swap Events button is enabled only if two events are selected. When clicked, it changes the position of the two events. Because the order of the events is important, this can alter the final output.

The Align Selected Left and Align Selected Right buttons move the beginning or end points of every selected track until they line up with the first or last points of the top selected event.

The Make Selected Same Size button resizes any bottom events to be the same size as the top selected event. The Abut Selected button moves each selected event under the top event until its first point lines up with the last point of the selected event above it.

Figure 23.22 shows four image events that have been placed end-to-end using the Abut Selected button. Notice that the queue range spans the entire distance.

FIGURE 23.22

You can use the Abut Selected button to position several events end-to-end.

Adding backgrounds and filters using Video Post

As an example of the Video Post interface in action, you'll composite a background image of a waterfall with a rendered scene of an airplane model created by Viewpoint Datalabs. Then you'll add some filter effects.

To composite an image with the Video Post interface, follow these steps:

1. Open the Airplane over waterfall.max file from the Chap 23 directory on the CD.

   This file includes an airplane model. The directory also includes an image called waterfall.tif that is used later.

2. Open the Video Post interface by choosing Rendering ➪ Video Post.

3. Add a background image to the queue by clicking the Add Image Input Event button (or by pressing Ctrl+I). Click the Files button. Locate the waterfall.tif image from the Chap 23 directory on the CD, and click Open. Then click OK again to exit the Add Image Input Event dialog box.

4. Next, add the rendered image by clicking the Add Scene Event button and selecting the Perspective viewport. Name the event **rendered airplane**. Click the Render Setup button to open the Render Setup dialog box, and select the Renderer panel. Disable the Antialiasing option in the Default Scanline Renderer rollout in the Renderer panel, and click OK. Click OK again to exit the Add Scene Event dialog box.

5. Select both the background (waterfall.tif) and the rendered airplane (Perspective) events, and click the Add Image Layer Event button (or press Ctrl+L). Select the Alpha Compositor option, and click OK.

   This composites the background image and the rendered image together by removing all the green background from the rendered scene.

6. To run the processing, click the Execute Sequence button on the toolbar (or press Ctrl+R) to open the Execute Video Post interface, select the Single Time Output range option, click the 640 × 480 size button, and click Render.

Figure 23.23 shows the final composited image.

FIGURE 23.23

The airplane in this image is rendered, and the background is composited.

Summary

Post-production is an important, often overlooked, part of the production pipeline. Using compositing packages, as simple as Photoshop and Premiere Pro or as advanced as After Effects, enables you to make necessary edits after rendering.

The render elements in 3ds Max enable you to pick apart the rendering details of your scene. Rendering using render elements allows you to have more control over individual scene elements in the compositing tool.

Using the State Sets and the Video Post interfaces, you can composite several images, filters, and effects together. All these compositing elements are listed as events in a queue. Using these two interfaces provides, along with the Render Setup dialog box, more ways to create output. In this chapter, you learned about the following:

- The post-production process
- How Photoshop can be used to composite images
- How Premiere and After Effects can be used to composite animations
- How to use render elements
- How to use State Sets
- How to composite with the State Sets interface
- The Video Post interface
- How to work with sequences
- The various filter types
- How to add and edit events and manipulate their ranges

This concludes the Working with Cameras, Lighting, and Rendering part of the book. The next part, "Animating Objects and Scenes," finally gets to the animation portion of the book. We'll begin with a chapter on the basics and understanding keyframes.

Part VI

Animating Objects and Scenes

IN THIS PART

Understanding Animation and Keyframes

IN THIS CHAPTER

Controlling time

Using the animation mode buttons to create keys

Using the Track Bar

Viewing and editing key values

Using the Motion panel and trajectories

Enabling ghosting

Animating cameras, lights, and materials

Creating previews

Using the RAM Player

The Autodesk® 3ds Max® 2013 software can be used to create some really amazing images, but I bet more of you go to the movies than go to see images in a museum. The difference is in seeing moving images versus static images.

In this chapter, I start discussing what is probably one of the main reasons you decided to learn 3ds Max in the first place—animation. 3ds Max includes many different features to create animations. This chapter covers the easiest and most basic of these features—keyframe animation.

Along the way, you'll examine all the various controls that are used to create, edit, and control animation keys, including the Time Controls, the Track Bar, and the Motion panel. Keyframes can be used to animate object transformations, but they also can be used to animate other aspects of the scene, such as materials. If you get finished with this chapter in time, you may have time to watch a movie.

Using the Time Controls

Before jumping into animation, you need to understand the controls that make it possible. These controls collectively are called the Time Controls and can be found on the lower interface bar between the key controls and the Viewport Navigation Controls. The Time Controls also include the Time Slider found directly under the viewports.

The Time Slider provides an easy way to move through the frames of an animation. To do this, just drag the Time Slider button in either direction. The Time Slider button is labeled with the current frame number and the total number of frames. The arrow buttons on either side of this button work the same as the Previous and Next Frame (Key) buttons.

The Time Control buttons include buttons to jump to the Start or End of the animation, or to step forward or back by a single frame. You can also jump to an exact frame by entering the frame number in the frame number field. The Time Controls are presented in Table 24.1.

TABLE 24.1 Time Controls

Toolbar Button	Name	Description
	Go to Start	Sets the time to frame 0.
	Previous Frame/Key	Decreases the time by one frame or selects the previous key.
	Play Animation, Play Selected	Cycles through the frames; this button becomes a Stop Animation button when an animation is playing.
	Next Frame/Key	Advances the time by one frame or selects the next key.
	Go to End	Sets the time to the final frame.
	Key Mode Toggle	Toggles between key and frame modes; with Key Mode on, the icon turns light blue and the Previous Frame and Next Frame buttons change to Previous Key and Next Key.
	Current Frame field	Indicates the current frame; a frame number can be typed in this field for more exact control than the Time Slider.
	Time Configuration	Opens the Time Configuration dialog box where settings like Frame Rate, Time Display, and Animation Length can be set.

The default scene starts with 100 frames, but this is seldom what you actually need. You can change the number of frames at any time by clicking the Time Configuration button, which is to the right of the frame number field. Clicking this button opens the Time Configuration dialog box, shown in Figure 24.1. You can also access this dialog box by right-clicking any of the Time Control buttons.

Setting frame rate

Within this dialog box, you can set several options, including the Frame Rate. *Frame rate* provides the connection between the number of frames and time. It is measured in frames per second. The options include standard frame rates such as NTSC (National Television Standards Committee, around 30 frames per second), Film (around 24 frames per second), and PAL (Phase Alternate Line, used by European countries, around 25 frames per second), or you can select Custom and enter your own frame rate.

FIGURE 24.1

The Time Configuration dialog box lets you set the number of frames to include in a scene.

The Time Display section lets you set how time is displayed on the Time Slider. The options include Frames, SMPTE (Society of Motion Picture Technical Engineers), Frame:Ticks, or MM:SS:Ticks (Minutes and Seconds). *SMPTE* is a standard time measurement used in video and television. A *Tick* is $1/4800$ of a second.

Setting speed and direction

The Playback section sets options for how the animation sequence is played back. The Real Time option skips frames to maintain the specified frame rate. The Active Viewport Only option causes the animation to play only in a single viewport, which speeds up the animation. The Loop option repeats the animation over and over. The Loop option is available only if the Real Time option is disabled. If the Loop option is set, then you can specify the Direction as Forward, Reverse, or Ping-Pong (which repeats, playing forward and then reverse). The Speed setting can be $1/4$, $1/2$, 1, 2, or 4 times normal.

The Time Configuration dialog box also lets you specify the Start Time, End Time, Length, Frame Count, and Current Time values. These values are all interrelated, so setting the Length and the Start Time, for example, automatically changes the End Time. These values can be changed at any time without destroying any keys. For example, if you have an animation of 500 frames and you set the Start and End Time to 30 and 50, the Time Slider controls only those 21 frames. Keys before or after this time are still available and can be accessed by resetting the Start and End Time values to 0 and 500.

The Re-scale Time button fits all the keys into the active time segment by stretching or shrinking the number of frames between keys. You can use this feature to resize the animation to the number of frames defined by Start and End Time values.

The Key Steps group lets you set which key objects are navigated using key mode. If you select Use Track Bar, key mode moves through only the keys on the Track Bar. If you select the Selected Objects Only option, key mode jumps only to the keys for the currently selected object. You can also filter to move between Position, Rotation, and Scale keys. The Use Current Transform option locates only those keys that are the same as the current selected transform button.

Using Time Tags

To the right of the Prompt Line is a field marked Add Time Tag. Clicking this field pops up a menu with options to Add or Edit a Time Tag. Time Tags can be set for each frame in the scene. Once set, the Time Tags are visible in the Time Tag field whenever that time is selected. These are useful for identifying key frames.

Working with Keys

It isn't just a coincidence that the largest button in the entire 3ds Max interface has a key on it. Creating and working with keys is how animations are accomplished. Keys define a particular state of an object at a particular time. Animations are created as the object moves or changes between two different key states. Complex animations can be generated with only a handful of keys.

You can create keys in numerous ways, but the easiest is with the Key Controls found on the lower interface bar. These controls are located to the left of the Time Controls. Table 24.2 displays and explains all these controls. Closely related to the Key Controls is the Track Bar, which is located under the Time Slider.

TABLE 24.2   Key Controls

Toolbar Button	Name	Description
⊙━	Set Keys (K)	Creates animation keys in Set Keys mode.
Auto Key	Toggle Auto Key Mode (N)	Sets keys automatically for the selected object when enabled.
Set Key	Toggle Set Key Mode (')	Sets keys as specified by the key filters for the selected object when enabled.
Selected ▼	Selection Set drop-down list	Specifies a selection set to use for the given keys.
⤢	Default In/Out Tangents for New Keys	Assigns the default tangents that are used on all new keys.
Key Filters...	Open Filters Dialog box	Contains pop-up options for the filtering keys.

3ds Max includes two animation modes: Auto Key (N) and Set Key ('). You can select either of these modes by clicking the respective buttons at the bottom of the interface. When active, the button turns bright red, and the track bar and the border around the active viewport also turns red to remind you that you are in animate mode. Red also appears around a spinner for any animated parameters.

Auto Key mode

With the Auto Key button enabled, every transformation or parameter change creates a key that defines where and how an object should look at that specific frame.

To create a key, drag the Time Slider to a frame where you want to create a key and then move the selected object or change the parameter, and a key is automatically created. When the first key is created, 3ds Max automatically goes back and creates a key for frame 0 that holds the object's original position or parameter. Upon setting the key, 3ds Max then interpolates all the positions and changes between the keys. The keys are displayed in the Track Bar.

Each frame can hold several different keys, but only one for each type of transform and each parameter. For example, if you move, rotate, scale, and change the Radius parameter for a sphere object with the Auto Key mode enabled, then separate keys are created for position, rotation, scaling, and a parameter change.

> **CAUTION**
> Be sure to turn Auto Key mode off when you are finished creating keys; if you leave it on, it automatically creates keys that you didn't mean to set.

Set Key mode

The Set Key button (') offers more control over key creation and sets keys only when you click the Set Key button (K). It also creates keys only for the key types enabled in the Set Key Filters dialog box. You can open the Set Key Filters dialog box, shown in Figure 24.2, by clicking the Key Filters button. Available key types include All, Position, Rotation, Scale, IK Parameters, Object Parameters, Custom Attributes, Modifiers, Materials, and Other (which allows keys to be set for manipulator values).

FIGURE 24.2

Use the Set Key Filters dialog box to specify the types of keys to create.

Tutorial: Rotating a windmill's blades

The best way to learn is to practice, and there's no better time to practice than now. For this quick example, you animate a set of blades on a windmill.

To animate a set of windmill blades rotating, follow these steps:

1. Open the Rotating windmill blades.max file from the Chap 24 directory on the CD.

   This file includes a windmill model created by Viewpoint Datalabs.

2. Click the Auto Key button (or press the N key) at the bottom of the 3ds Max window, and drag the Time Slider to frame 50.

3. Select the "prop" object at the top of the windmill in the Front viewport. The blades are attached to the center prop and rotate a full revolution about its pivot point. Then click the Select and Rotate button on the main toolbar (or press E key), and rotate the "prop" object about its Y-axis.

4. Click the Auto Key button (or press the N key) again to disable animation mode. Select the key in the Track Bar located at frame 0, hold down the Shift key, and drag the key to frame 100 (or press the End key).

   This step copies the key from frame 0 to frame 100. Doing so ensures a smooth looping animation (even though it spins the prop forward and then backward; I guess it must be a strange wind that's blowing).

5. Click the Play Animation button in the Time Controls to see the animation.

Figure 24.3 shows frame 50 of this simple animation.

FIGURE 24.3

Frame 50 of this simple windmill animation

Another way to create keys is to select the object to be animated and right-click the Time Slider button. This opens the Create Key dialog box, shown in Figure 24.4, where you can set Position, Rotation, and Scale keys for the currently selected object. You can use this method only to create transform keys.

FIGURE 24.4

The Create Key dialog box enables you to create a Position, Rotation, or Scale keys quickly.

If a key already exists, you can clone it by dragging the selected key on the Track Bar with the Shift key held down. Dragging the Track Bar with the Ctrl and Alt keys held down changes the active time segment.

Copying parameter animation keys

If a parameter is changed while the Auto Key mode is enabled, then keys are set for that parameter. You can tell when a parameter has a key set because the arrows to the right of its spinner are outlined in red when the Time Slider is on the frame where the key is set. If you change the parameter value when the spinner is highlighted red, then the key value is changed (and the Auto Key mode doesn't need to be enabled).

If you highlight and right-click the parameter value, a pop-up menu of options appears. Using this pop-up menu, you can Cut, Copy, Paste, and Delete the parameter value. You can also select Copy Animation, which copies all the keys associated with this parameter and lets you paste them to another parameter. Pasting the animation keys can be done as a Copy, an Instance, or a Wire. A Copy is independent; an Instance ties the animation keys to the original copy so that they both are changed when either changes; and a Wire lets one parameter control some other parameter.

> **CAUTION**
> To copy a parameter value, be sure to select and right-click the value. If you right-click the parameter's spinner, the value is set to 0.

The right-click pop-up menu also includes commands to let you Edit a wired parameter, show the parameter in the Track View, or show the parameter in the Parameter Wiring dialog box.

 Parameter wiring and the Parameter Wiring dialog box are discussed in more detail in Chapter 27, "Wiring Parameters."

Deleting all object animation keys

Individual keys can be selected and deleted using the Track Bar or the right-click pop-up menu, but if an object has many keys, this can be time consuming. To delete all animation keys for the selected object quickly, choose the Animation ⇨ Delete Selected Animation menu command.

2 4

Using the Track Bar

The 3ds Max interface includes a simple way to work with keys: with the Track Bar, which is situated directly under the Time Slider. The Track Bar displays a rectangular marker for every key for the selected object. These markers are color-coded, depending on the type of key. Position keys are red, rotation keys are green, scale keys are blue, and parameter keys are dark gray.

> **CAUTION**
>
> In the Track View—Dope Sheet interface, position, rotation, and scale keys are red, green, and blue, but parameter keys are yellow.

The current frame also appears in the Track Bar as a light blue, transparent rectangle, as shown in Figure 24.5. The icon at the left end of the Track Bar is the Open Mini Curve Editor button, which opens a mini Track View.

For more on the Track View interface, see Chapter 28, "Editing Animation Curves in the Track View."

FIGURE 24.5

The Track Bar displays all keys for the selected object.

Open Track View Current frame Selected key

Using the Track Bar, you can move, copy, and delete keys. The Track Bar shows key markers only for the currently selected object or objects, and each key marker can represent several different keys. When the mouse is moved over the top of these markers, the cursor changes to a plus sign, and you can select a marker by clicking it (selected key markers turn white). Using the Ctrl key, you can select multiple key markers at the same time. You can also select multiple key markers by clicking an area of the Track Bar that contains no keys and then dragging an outline over all the keys you want to select. If you move the cursor over the top of a selected key, the cursor is displayed as a set of arrows enabling you to drag the selected key to the left or right. Holding down the Shift key while dragging a key creates a copy of the key. Pressing the Delete key deletes the selected key.

> **TIP**
>
> If you drag a key off the end of the Track Bar, the frame number is displayed on the Prompt Line at the bottom of the interface and the key is not included in the current time range. If you ever want to hide a key without deleting it, you can drag it off the end of the Track Bar and recover it by resetting the time in the Time Configuration dialog box.

Because each marker can represent several keys, you can view all the keys associated with the marker in a pop-up menu by right-clicking the marker.

NOTE
In the pop-up menu, a check mark next to a key indicates that the key is shared with another instance.

The marker pop-up menu also offers options for deleting selected keys or filtering the keys. In addition, there is a Go to Time command, which automatically moves the Time Slider to the key's location when selected.

To delete a key marker with all of its keys, right-click to open the pop-up menu and choose Delete Key⇨All, or select the key marker and press the Delete key.

Viewing and Editing Key Values

At the top of the marker's right-click pop-up menu is a list of current keys for the selected object (or if there are too many keys for a marker, they are placed under the Key Properties menu). When you select one of these keys, a key information dialog box opens. This dialog box displays different controls, depending on the type of key selected. Figure 24.6 shows the dialog box for the Position key. There are slight variations in this dialog box, depending on the key type.

FIGURE 24.6

Key dialog boxes enable you to change the key parameters.

NOTE
You can also access key-specific dialog boxes in the Motion panel for a selected object by clicking the Parameters button.

Within each of these key dialog boxes is a Time value that shows the current frame. Next to the Time value are two arrows that enable you to move easily to the other keys in the scene. The dialog box also includes several text fields, where you can change the key parameters.

Most of the key dialog boxes also include flyout buttons for selecting Key Tangents. Key Tangents determine how the animation moves into and out of the key. For example, if the In Key Tangent is set to Slow, and the Out Key Tangent is set to Fast, the object approaches the key position in a slow manner but accelerates as it leaves the key position. The arrow buttons on either side of the Key Tangent buttons can copy the current Key Tangent selection to the previous or next key.

The available types of Tangents are detailed in Table 24.3.

24

TABLE 24.3   **Key Tangents**

Toolbar Button	Name	Description
	Smooth	Produces straight, smooth motion; this is the default type.
	Linear	Moves at a constant rate between keys.
	Step	Causes discontinuous motion between keys; it occurs only between matching In-Out pairs.
	Slow	Decelerates as you approach the key.
	Fast	Accelerates as you approach the key.
	Custom	Lets you control the Tangent handles in function curves mode.
	Custom – Locked Handles	Lets you control the Tangent handles in function curves mode with the handles locked.

Using the Motion Panel

You have yet another way to create keys: by using the Motion panel. The Motion panel in the Command Panel includes settings and controls for animating objects. At the top of the Motion panel are two buttons: Parameters and Trajectories.

Setting parameters

The Parameters button on the Motion panel lets you assign controllers and create and delete keys. *Controllers* are custom key-creating algorithms that can be defined through the Parameters rollout, shown in Figure 24.7. You assign these controllers by selecting the position, rotation, or scaling track and clicking the Assign Controller button to open a list of applicable controllers that you can select.

 For more information on controllers, see Chapter 25, "Animating with Constraints and Simple Controllers."

FIGURE 24.7

The Parameters section of the Motion panel lets you assign controllers and create keys.

Assign Controller

When a keyable object is selected, below the Assign Controller rollout is the PRS Parameters rollout where you can create and delete Position, Rotation, and Scale keys. You can use this rollout to create Position, Rotation, and Scale keys whether or not the Auto Key or Set Key buttons are enabled. Additional rollouts may be available, depending upon the selected controller.

Below the PRS Parameters rollout are two Key Info rollouts: Basic and Advanced. These rollouts include the same key-specific information that you can access using the right-click pop-up menu found in the Track Bar.

Using trajectories

A *trajectory* is the actual path that the animation follows. When you click the Trajectories button in the Motion panel, the animation trajectory is shown as a spline with each key displayed as a node and each frame shown as a white dot. You can then edit the trajectory and its nodes by clicking the Sub-Object button at the top of the Motion panel, shown in Figure 24.8. The only subobject available is Keys. With the Sub-Object button enabled, you can use the transform buttons to move and reposition the trajectory nodes. You can also add and delete keys with the Add Key and Delete Key buttons.

FIGURE 24.8

The Trajectories rollout in the Motion panel enables you to see the animation path as a spline.

For more control over the trajectory path, you can convert the trajectory path to a normal editable spline with the Convert To button. You can also convert an existing spline into a trajectory with the Convert From button.

To use the Convert From button, select an object, click the Convert From button, and then click a spline path in the scene. This creates a new trajectory path for the selected object. The first key of this path is placed at the spline's first vertex, and the final key is placed as the spline's final vertex position. Additional keys are spaced out along the spline based on the spline's curvature as determined by the

Samples value listed in the Sample Range group. All these new keys are roughly spaced between the Start and End times, but smaller Bézier handles result in more closely packed keys.

Click the Collapse button at the bottom of the Trajectories rollout to reduce all transform keys into a single editable path. You can select which transformations to collapse, including Position, Rotation, and Scale, using the options under the Collapse button. For example, an object with several Controllers assigned can be collapsed, thereby reducing the complexity of all the keys.

> **NOTE**
> If you collapse all keys, you cannot alter their parameters via the controller rollouts.

The Views menu includes an option to Show Key Times. The Show Key Times command displays frame numbers along the trajectory path where every animation key is located. Enabling this option displays the frame numbers next to any key along a trajectory path. You can make the trajectory visible for any object by enabling the Trajectory option in the Object Properties dialog box.

Tutorial: Making an airplane follow a looping path

Airplanes that perform aerobatic stunts often follow paths that are smooth. You can see this clearly when watching a sky writer. In this example, I've created a simple looping path using the Line spline primitive, and you'll use this path to make a plane complete an aerobatic loop.

To make an airplane follow a looping path, follow these steps:

1. Open the Looping airplane.max file from the Chap 24 directory on the CD.
   This file includes a simple looping spline path and an airplane created by Viewpoint Datalabs.
2. With the airplane selected, open the Motion panel and click the Trajectories button. Then click the Convert From button in the Trajectories rollout, and select the path in the Front viewport.
3. If you drag the Time Slider, you'll notice that the plane moves along the path, but it doesn't rotate with the path. To fix this, click the Key Mode Toggle button in the Time Controls to easily move from key to key. Click the Key Filters button, select only Rotation, and then click the Set Key button (or press the ' key) to enter Set Key mode.
4. Before moving the Time Slider, click the Set Keys button to create a rotation key at frame 0. Then click the Select and Rotate button, click the Next Key button, rotate the plane in the Front viewport to match the path, and click the large Set Keys button (or press the K key) to create a rotation key. Click the Next Key button to move to the next key, and repeat this step until rotation keys have been set for the entire path.
5. Drag the Time Slider, and watch the airplane circle about the loop.

3ds Max provides an easier way to make the plane follow the path using the Path constraint. To learn more about constraints, see Chapter 25, "Animating with Constraints and Simple Controllers."

Figure 24.9 shows the plane's trajectory.

FIGURE 24.9

When you use a spline path, the position keys are automatically set for this plane.

Using the Follow/Bank utility

When an object travels along a path that defines its trajectory, it maintains its same orientation without rotating. Imagine a roller coaster car; it rotates and banks as it moves around the track. This rotation and banking motion can be added to an object following a path using the Follow/Bank utility. You can access this utility by opening the Utilities panel and clicking the More button. Double-click the Follow/Bank utility to load it into the Utilities panel.

> **CAUTION**
>
> The Follow/Bank utility aligns the local X-axis of the object with the local Z-axis of the spline when the utility is applied, so you need to correctly orient the object's pivot point before applying the utility. If you don't, the object will be aligned at right angles to the path.

The Follow/Bank utility lets you enable a Bank option and set its Amount and Smoothness. Another option allows the object to turn upside down (not recommended for a traditional roller coaster car). Click the Apply Follow button to add the keys to cause the object to follow and bank. The Samples section determines how many keys are created.

Using Ghosting

As you're trying to animate objects, using the ghosting feature can be very helpful. This feature displays a copy of the selected object being animated before and/or after its current position. To enable ghosting, choose Views ⇨ Show Ghosting. The Show Ghosting command displays the position of the selected object in the previous several frames, the next several frames, or both. This command uses the options set in the Preference Settings dialog box. Access this dialog box by choosing Customize ➪ Preferences. In the Viewports panel of this dialog box is a Ghosting section.

You use this Ghosting section to set how many ghosted objects are to appear; whether the ghosted objects appear before, after, or both before and after the current frame; and whether frame numbers should be shown. You can also specify every Nth frame to be displayed. You also have an option to display the ghost object in wireframe (it is displayed as shaded if this option is not enabled) and an option to Show Frame Numbers. Objects before the current frame are colored yellow, and objects after are colored light blue.

Figure 24.10 shows a lion toy object that is animated to travel in a bumpy circle with ghosting enabled. The Preference settings are set to show three ghosting frames at every other frame before and after the current frame.

FIGURE 24.10

Enabling ghosting lets you know where an object is and where it's going.

Animating Objects

Many different objects in 3ds Max can be animated, including geometric objects, cameras, lights, and materials. In this section, you'll look at several types of objects and parameters that can be animated.

Animating cameras

You can animate cameras using the standard transform buttons found on the main toolbar. When animating a camera that actually moves in the scene, using a Free camera is best. A Target camera can be pointed by moving its target, but you risk it being flipped over if the target is ever directly above the camera. If you want to use a Target camera, attach both the camera and its target to a Dummy object using the Select and Link button and move the Dummy object.

Two useful constraints when animating cameras are the Path constraint and the Look At constraint. You can find both of these in the Animation ⇨ Constraints menu. The Path constraint can make a camera follow a spline path, and the Look At constraint can direct the focus of a camera to follow an object as the camera or the object moves through the scene.

> For more on constraints, including these two, see Chapter 25, "Animating with Constraints and Simple Controllers."

Tutorial: Animating darts hitting a dartboard

As a simple example of animating objects using the Auto Key button, you'll animate several darts hitting a dartboard.

To animate darts hitting a dartboard, follow these steps:

1. Open the Dart and dartboard.max file from the Chap 24 directory on the CD.

   This file includes a dart and dartboard objects created by Zygote Media.

2. Click the Auto Key button (or press the N key) to enable animation mode. Drag the Time Slider to frame 25, and click the Select and Move button on the main toolbar (or press the W key).

3. Select the first dart in the Left viewport, and drag it to the left until its tip just touches the dartboard.

   This step creates a key in the Track Bar for frames 0 and 25.

4. Click the Select and Rotate button on the main toolbar, set the reference coordinate system to Local, and constrain the rotation to the Y-axis. Then drag the selected dart in the Front viewport to rotate it about its local Y-axis.

   This step also sets a key in the Track Bar.

5. Select the second dart, and click the Select and Move button again. Right-click the Time Slider to make the Create Key dialog box appear. Make sure that the check boxes for Position and Rotation are selected, and click OK.

   This step creates a key that keeps the second dart from moving before it's ready.

6. With the second dart still selected, drag the Time Slider to frame 50 and move the dart to the dartboard as described in Step 3. Then repeat Step 4 to set the rotation key for the second dart.

7. Repeat Steps 3, 4, and 5 for the last two darts at frames 75 and 100.

8. Click the Auto Key button (or press the N key) again to disable animation mode, maximize the Perspective viewport, and click the Play Animation button to see the animation. Figure 24.11 shows the darts as they're flying toward the dartboard.

24

FIGURE 24.11

One frame of the dart animation

Animating lights

The process for animating lights includes many of the same techniques as those for animating cameras. For moving lights, use a Free Spot light or attach a Target Spot light to a Dummy object. You can also use the Look At and Path controllers with lights.

To flash lights on and off, enable and disable the On parameter at different frames and assign a Step Tangent. To dim lights, just alter the Multiplier value over several frames.

Animating materials

Materials can be animated if their properties are altered while the Auto Key button is active. 3ds Max interpolates between the values as the animation progresses. The material must stay the same for the entire animation: You cannot change materials at different keys; you can only alter the existing material parameters.

If you want to change materials as the animation progresses, you can use a material that combines multiple materials, such as the Blend material. This material includes a Mix Amount value that can change at different keyframes. The next tutorial shows how to use the Blend material in this manner.

Several maps include a Phase value, including all maps that have a Noise rollout. This value provides the means to animate the map. For example, using a Noise map and changing the Phase value over many keys animates the noise effect.

> **NOTE**
>
> Another common way to animate materials is with the Controller nodes that are applied in the Slate Material Editor. Using these Controller nodes, you can alter material parameters for different frames and even access the Curve Editor for these controllers.

Tutorial: Dimming lights

Occasionally, you'll want to change materials in a scene to gradually alter it in some way, such as dimming a light. You can easily accomplish this task with the Blend material.

To create a light that dims with time, follow these steps:

1. Open the Dimming light.max file from the Chap 24 directory on the CD.

   This file contains a simple lamp object with a sphere to represent a light bulb.

2. Open the Slate Material Editor by pressing the M key, and double-click the Blend material in the Material/Map Browser to add a Blend node with two other materials connected to it. Double-click the new Blend node, and give the material the name **Dimming Light**.

3. Double click the first attached material and name the material **Light On.** Set the Diffuse color in the Blinn Basic Parameters rollout to yellow and the Self-Illumination to yellow after enabling the Color option.

4. Double click the second attached material node for the Blend node, name the second material **Light Off**, and select a gray Diffuse color.

5. Select the light bulb object, and click the Assign Material to Selection button to assign the material to the bulb object.

6. With the Time Slider at frame 0, click the Auto Key button (or press the N key). Drag the Time Slider to frame 100, and change the Mix Amount to **100**. Click the Auto Key button again to deactivate it. The material changes gradually from the "Light On" material to the "Light Off" material. When you drag the Time Slider, you won't see the material change, but if you render the scene, you can see the dimming light.

Figure 24.12 shows a simple lamp object with a dimming sphere in its center. The actual dimming effect isn't visible in the viewport—only when the image is rendered.

24

FIGURE 24.12

This lamp object dims as the animation proceeds.

Working with Previews

More than likely, your final output will be rendered using the highest-quality settings with all effects enabled, and you can count on this taking a fair amount of time. After waiting several days for a sequence to render is a terrible time to find out that your animation keys are off. Even viewing animation sequences in the viewports with the Play Animation button cannot catch all problems.

One way to catch potential problems is to create a sample preview animation. Previews are test animation sequences that render quickly to give you an idea of the final output. The Tools ⇨ Views - Grab Viewport menu includes several commands for creating, renaming, and viewing previews. The rendering options available for previews are the same as the shading options available in the viewports, but seeing the animation gives you a sense of the timing.

Creating previews

You create previews by choosing Tools ⇨ Views - Grab Viewport ⇨ Create Animated Sequence File to open the Make Preview dialog box, shown in Figure 24.13. You can also access this command from the viewport General label in the upper-left corner of the viewport.

In the Make Preview dialog box, you can specify what frames to include using the Active Time Segment or Custom Range options. You can also choose Every Nth Frame or select a specific frame rate in the Playback FPS field. The image size is determined by the Percent of Output value, which is a percentage of the final output size. The resolution is also displayed.

FIGURE 24.13

The Make Preview dialog box lets you specify the range, size, and output of a preview file.

The Display Filter section offers a variety of options to include in the preview. These options include Geometry, Shapes, Lights, Cameras, Helpers, Space Warps, Particle Systems, Bone Objects, and Active Grid. Because the preview output is rendered like the viewports, certain selected objects such as Lights and Cameras actually display their icons as part of the file. The Overlay options prints the safe frame borders, frame number and the camera/view name in the upper-left corner of each frame. This is a nice feature that helps in identifying the results.

The Rendering Level drop-down list includes the same shading options used to display objects in the viewports, including Realistic, Shaded, Consistent Colors, Hidden Line, Wireframe, and Bounding Box. It also includes the various Stylized render options including Ink, Color Ink, Acrylic, Tech, Graphite, Color Pencil, and Pastel. There are also options to toggle on or off Edged Faces, Textures, Highlights, and the Background.

If the Camera View uses one of the multi-pass camera effects such as depth-of-field or motion blur, you can enable these effects for the preview also.

Output options include the default AVI option; a Custom File option, which enables you to choose your own format. For the AVI option, you can select a CODEC, which is used to compress the resulting file. Options include Cinepak Codec by Radius, Logitech Video (1420), Intel IYUV, Microsoft Video 1, Intel Indeo Video 4.5, DivX 5.0.5, and Full Frames (uncompressed), depending on the CODECs that are installed on your system.

At the bottom of the dialog box is a Render Viewport drop-down list, where you can select which viewport to use to create your preview file. The Create button starts the rendering process. When a preview is being rendered, the viewports are replaced with a single image of the current render frame, and the Status bar is replaced by a Progress bar and a Cancel button.

> **TIP**
>
> You can use the Esc key on your keyboard to cancel a rendering job.

If you cancel the rendering, the Make Preview alert box offers the options Stop and Play; Stop and Don't Play; and Don't Stop.

Viewing previews

When a preview file is finished rendering, the default Media Player for your system loads and displays the preview file. You can disable this autoplay feature using the Autoplay Preview File option in the General panel of the Preference Settings dialog box.

At any time, you can replay the preview file using the Tools⇨Views- Grab Viewport⇨View Animated Sequence File menu command. This command loads the latest preview file and displays it in the Media Player.

Renaming previews

The preview file is actually saved as a file named _scene.avi and is saved by default in the previews subdirectory. Be aware that this file is automatically overwritten when a new preview is created. To save a preview file by renaming it, choose Tools⇨Views- Grab Viewport⇨Rename Animated Sequence File. This command opens the Save Preview As dialog box, where you can give the preview file a name.

Using the RAM Player

Just as you can use the Rendered Frame Window to view and compare rendered images, the RAM Player enables you to view rendered animations in memory. With animations loaded in memory, you can selectively change the frame rates. Figure 24.14 shows the RAM Player interface, which you open by choosing Rendering⇨RAM Player. You see two images of the rendered gingerbread house placed on top of each other with half of each showing. One was rendered using its default materials; the other was rendered using Ink 'n' Paint materials.

FIGURE 24.14

The RAM Player interface lets you load two different images or animations for comparison.

The buttons at the top of the RAM Player interface window, shown in Table 24.4, enable you to load an image to two different channels named A and B. The two Open Channel buttons open a file dialog box where you can select the file to load. Notice that the image on the right side of the RAM Player is a different frame from the left side.

TABLE 24.4   RAM Player Interface Buttons

Button	Description
	Open Channel
	Open Last Rendered Image
	Close Channel
	Save Channel
	Horizontal/Vertical Split Screen
	Double Buffer

The Open Last Rendered Image button in the RAM Player interface window provides quick access to the last rendered image using the RAM Player Configuration dialog box. The Close Channel button clears the channel. The Save Channel button opens a file dialog box for saving the current file.

CAUTION

All files that load into the RAM Player are converted to 24-bit images.

The Channel A and Channel B (toggle) buttons enable either channel or both. The Horizontal/Vertical Split Screen button switches the dividing line between the two channels to a horizontal or vertical line. When the images are aligned one on top of the other, two small triangles mark where one channel leaves off and the other begins. You can drag these triangles to alter the space for each channel.

The frame controls let you move between the frames. You can move to the first, previous, next, or last frame and play the animation forward or in reverse. The drop-down list to the right of the frame controls displays the current frame rate setting.

You can capture the color of any pixel in the image by holding down the Ctrl key while right-clicking the image. This puts the selected color in the color swatch. The RGB value for this pixel is displayed in the blue title bar.

The Double Buffer button synchronizes the frames of the two channels.

TIP

You can use the arrow keys and Page Up and Page Down keys to move through the frames of the animation. The A and B keys are used to enable the two channels.

24

Tutorial: Using the RAM Player to Combine Rendered Images into a Video File

Not only can the RAM Player be used to load and compare images, but it also can handle animation files. It also can load in multiple frames of an animation that were saved as individual image files and save them back out as an animated file.

To combine multiple rendered image files into a video file using the RAM Player, follow these steps:

1. Select the Rendering ➪ RAM Player menu command to open the RAM Player. Then click the Open Channel A button, and locate and open the Exploding Planet - frame 10.tif file from the Chap 24 directory on the CD.

   This file is the first rendered frame of a ten-frame animation.

2. The Image File List Control dialog box opens. Using this dialog box, you can specify the Start and End Frames to load. You also can select to load every nth frame. Select 0 as the Start Frame and 9 as the End Frame, and click OK.

3. The RAM Player Configuration dialog box opens next, letting you set the Resolution and Memory Usage for the loaded files. Click OK to accept the default values.

   All the image files that share the same base name as the selected file are loaded into the RAM Player sequentially. Press the Play button to see the loaded animation.

4. Click the Save Channel A button to access the file dialog box, where you can save the loaded animation using the AVI, MPEG, or MOV video format.

Figure 24.15 shows one frame of the loaded animation files.

FIGURE 24.15

This rendered image is just one of a series of rendered animation frames that can be viewed in the RAM Player.

Summary

This chapter covered the basics of animating objects in 3ds Max, including working with time and keys. You also learned about the two key creation modes and editing keys. Several animation helps are available, such as trajectories and ghosting. This chapter also discussed how to animate materials and how to create preview animations. In this chapter, you learned how to do the following:

- Control time and work with keys
- Use the two key creation modes
- Work with the Track Bar and the Motion panel
- View and edit key values
- Use trajectories and ghosting
- Animate cameras, lights, and materials
- Create preview animations
- Using the RAM Player

The next chapter shows how to automate the creation of animation keys with constraints and controllers.

24

Animating with Constraints and Simple Controllers

IN THIS CHAPTER

Using constraints

Attaching an object to the surface of an object

Making an object travel along a path with the Path constraint

Controlling the weighted position and orientation of objects

Shifting between two controlling objects using the Link constraint

Following objects with the LookAt constraint

Understanding the controller types

Assigning controllers using the Motion panel and the Track View

Setting default controllers

When you first begin animating and working with keys, having the Autodesk® 3ds Max® 2013 software figure out all the frames between the start and end keys seems amazing, especially if you've ever animated in 2D by drawing every frame. But soon you realize that animating with keys can be time-consuming for complex realistic motions, and again, 3ds Max comes to the rescue. You can use animation constraints and controllers to automate the creation of keys for certain types of motions.

Constraints and controllers store and manage the key values for all animations in 3ds Max. When you animate an object using the Auto Key button, the default controller is automatically assigned. You can change the assigned controller or alter its parameters using the Motion panel or the Track View.

This chapter explains how to work with constraints and some simple controllers. For example, you can use the Noise controller to add random motion to a flag blowing in the wind or use the Surface constraint to keep a bumper car moving over the surface.

Restricting Movement with Constraints

The trick of animating an object is to make it go where you want it to go. Animating objects deals not only with controlling the motion of the object but also with controlling its lack of motion. Constraints are a type of animation controller that you can use to restrict the motion of an object.

Using these constraints, you can force objects to stay attached to another object or follow a path. For example, the Attachment constraint can be used to make a robot's feet stay connected to a ground plane as it moves. The purpose of these constraints is to make animating your objects easier.

Using constraints

You can apply constraints to selected objects using the Animation➪Constraints menu. The constraints contained within this menu include Attachment, Surface, Path, Position, Link, LookAt, and Orientation.

 All constraints have the same controller icon displayed in the Motion panel or the Track View.

After you select one of the constraints from the Animation➪Constraints menu, a dotted link line extends from the current selected object to the mouse cursor. You can select a target object in any of the viewports to apply the constraint. The cursor changes to a plus sign when it is over a target object that can be selected. Selecting a constraint from the Constraints menu also opens the Motion panel, where the settings of the constraint can be modified.

You also can apply constraints using the Assign Controller button found in the Motion panel and in the Track View window.

> Find out more about the Track View window in Chapter 28, "Editing Animation Curves in the Track View."

Working with the constraints

Each constraint is slightly different, but learning how to use these constraints will help you control the animated objects within a scene. You can apply several constraints to a single object. All constraints that are applied to an object are displayed in a list found in the Motion panel. From this list, you can select which constraint to make active and which to delete. You also can cut and paste constraints between objects.

Attachment constraint

The Attachment constraint determines an object's position by attaching it to the face of another object. This constraint lets you attach an object to the surface of another object. For example, you could animate the launch of a rocket ship with booster rockets that are attached with the Attachment constraint. The booster rockets would move along with the ship until the time when they are jettisoned.

The pivot point of the object that the constraint is applied to is attached to the target object. At the top of the Attachment Parameters rollout is a Pick Object button for selecting the target object to attach to. You can use this button to change the target object or to select the target object if the Animation➪Constraints menu wasn't used. There is also an option to align the object to the surface. The Update section enables you to manually or automatically update the attachment values.

NOTE

The Attachment constraint shows up in the Position track of the Assign Controller rollout as the Position List controller. To minimize the effect of other controllers, set their Weight values in the Position List rollout to 0.

The Key Info section of the Attachment Parameters rollout displays the key number and lets you move between the various keys. The Time value is the current key value. In the Face field, you can specify the exact number of the face to attach to. To set this face, click the Set Position button and drag over the target object. The A and B values represent Barycentric coordinates for defining how the object lies on the face. You can change these coordinate values by entering values or by dragging the red cross-hairs in the box below the A and B values. The easiest way to position an object is to use the Set Position button to place the object and then to tweak its position with the A and B values. The Set Position button stays active until you click it again.

The TCB section sets the Tension, Continuity, and Bias values for the constraint. You also can set the Ease To and Ease From values.

Tutorial: Attaching eyes to a melting snowman

When part of a model is deformed, such as applying the Meltmodifier to a snowman's body, smaller parts like the eyes either get left behind or get the full weight of the modifier applied to them. If the Melt modifier weren't applied to these items, they would stay floating in the air while the rest of the snowman melted about them. This problem can be fixed with the Attachment constraint, which causes the eyes to remain attached to the snowball as it melts.

The tutorial where the Melt modifier is applied to the snowman is included in Chapter 26, "Using Animation Layers and Animation Modifiers."

To constrain the solid objects to a melting snowman, follow these steps:

1. Open the Melting snowman.max file from the Chap 25 directory on the CD.

   This file includes the melting snowman file from another chapter with the Melt modifier applied to all objects.

2. Select the left eye object in the scene. In the Modifier Stack, select the Melt modifier and click the Remove Modifier from the Stack button to throw that modifier away.

3. With the left eye still selected, select Animation ⇨ Constraints ⇨ Attachment Constraint. A connecting line appears in the active viewport. Click the top snowball to select it as the attachment object. This moves the eye object to the top of the snowball where the snowball's first face is located.

4. In the Attachment Parameters rollout, change the Face value until the eye is positioned where it should be. This should be around face 315. Then change the A and B values (or drag in the Position graph) to position the eye where it looks good.

5. Repeat Step 5 for the right eye and for any other objects in the scene that you want to attach.

6. Click the Play button (/) and notice that the snow melts, but the eye objects stay the same size.

Figure 25.1 shows the resulting melted snowman.

25

FIGURE 25.1

The Attachment constraint sticks one object to the surface of another.

Surface constraint

The Surface constraint moves an object so that it is on the surface of another object. The object with Surface constraint applied to it is positioned so that its pivot point is on the surface of the target object. You can use this constraint only on certain objects, including spheres, cones, cylinders, toruses, quad patches, loft objects, and NURBS objects.

In the Surface Controller Parameters rollout is the name of the target object that was selected after the menu command. The Pick Surface button enables you to select a different surface to attach to. You also can select specific U and V Position values. Alignment options include No Alignment, Align to U, Align to V, and a Flip toggle.

> **NOTE**
> Don't be confused because the rollout is named Surface Controller Parameters instead of Surface Constraint Parameters. The developers at Autodesk must have missed this one.

Tutorial: Rolling a tire down a hill with the Surface constraint

Moving a vehicle across a landscape can be a difficult procedure if you need to place every rotation and position key, but with the Surface constraint, it becomes easy. In this tutorial, you use the Surface constraint to roll a tire down a hill.

To roll a tire down a hill with the Surface constraint, follow these steps:

1. Open the Tire rolling on a hill.max file from the Chap 25 directory on the CD.

   This file includes a patch grid hill and a wheel object made from primitives.

2. Create a dummy object from the Helpers category, and link the tire object to it as a child. This causes the tire to move along with the dummy object. Position the dummy object's pivot point at the bottom of the tire and the top of the hill. The pivot point can be moved using the Affect Pivot Only button in the Hierarchy panel.

3. Select the dummy object, choose Animation⇨Constraints⇨Surface Constraint, and select the hill object.

4. In the Surface Controller Parameters rollout, select the Align to V and Flip options to position the dummy and tire objects at the top of the hill. Set the V Position value to **50** to move the tire to the center of the hill.

5. Click the Auto Key button (or press the N key), drag the Time Slider to frame 100, and change the U Position to **100**. Click the Auto Key button again to deactivate it, and click the Play Animation button to see the tire move down the hill.

Figure 25.2 shows the tire as it moves down the hill.

FIGURE 25.2

The Surface constraint can animate one object moving across the surface of another.

Path constraint

The Path constraint lets you select a spline path for the object to follow. The object is locked to the path and follows it even if the spline is changed. This is one of the most useful constraints because you can control the exact motion of an object using a spline. With the software's spline features, you can control very precisely the motions of objects that are constrained with the Path constraint. A good example of this constraint is an animated train following a track. Using a spline to create the train tracks, you can easily animate the train using the Path constraint.

When you choose the Animation ⇨ Constraints ⇨ Path Constraint menu command, you can select a single path for the object to follow. This path is added to a list of paths in the Path Parameters rollout.

The Path Parameters rollout also includes Add and Delete Path buttons for adding and deleting paths to and from the list. If two paths are added to the list, then the object follows the position centered between these two paths. By adjusting the Weight value for each path, you can make the object favor a specific path.

The Path Options include a % Along Path value for defining the object's position along the path. This value ranges from 0 at one end to 100 at the other end. The Follow option causes the object to be aligned with the path as it moves, and the Bank option causes the object to rotate to simulate a banking motion.

The Bank Amount value sets the depth of the bank, and the Smoothness value determines how smooth the bank is. The Allow Upside Down option lets the object spin completely about the axis, and the Constant Velocity option keeps the speed regular. The Loop option returns the object to its original position for the last frame of the animation, setting up a looping animation sequence. The Relative option lets the object maintain its current position and does not move the object to the start of the path. From its original position, it follows the path from its relative position. At the bottom of the Path Parameters rollout, you can select the axis to use.

Tutorial: Creating a spaceship flight path

Another way to use splines is to create animation paths. As an example, you use a Line spline to create an animation path. You can use splines for animation paths in two ways. One way is to create a spline and have an object follow it using either the Path constraint or the Path Follow Space Warp. The first vertex of the spline marks the first frame of the animation. The other way is to animate an object and then edit the Trajectory path.

In this tutorial, you use a simple path and attach it to a spaceship model. Viewpoint Datalabs provided the spaceship model.

To attach an object to a spline path, follow these steps:

1. Open the Spaceship and asteroids.max file from the Chap 25 directory on the CD.

    This file contains the spaceship model and several asteroid objects.

2. Select Create ⇨ Shapes ⇨ Line, and click and drag in the Top viewport to create an animation path that moves the spaceship through the asteroids. Right-click when the path is complete. Then select the Modify panel, click the Vertex button in the Selection rollout to enable Vertex subobject mode, and edit several vertices in the Front viewport. Then right-click to exit vertex subobject mode.

3. With the spaceship selected, choose Animation ⇨ Constraints ⇨ Path Constraint. Then click the animation path to select it as the path to follow. Select the Follow option in the Path Parameters rollout, and choose the Y-Axis option.

4. Click the Play Animation button in the Time Controls to see the spaceship follow the path.

Figure 25.3 shows the spaceship as it moves between the asteroids.

FIGURE 25.3

The spaceship object has been attached to a spline path that it follows.

Position constraint

You can use the Position constraint to tie the position of an object to the weighted position of several target objects. For example, you could animate a formation of fighter jets by animating one of the jets and using Position constraints on all adjacent jets.

The Position constraint menu option lets you select a single target object, enabling you to place the pivot points of the two objects on top of one another. To add another target object, click the Add Position Target button in the Position Constraint rollout in the Motion panel. This button enables you to select another target object in the viewports; the target name appears within the target list in the rollout.

If you select a target name in the target list, you can assign a weight to the target. The constrained object is positioned close to the object with the higher weighted value. The Weight value provides a

25

way to center objects between several other objects. The Keep Initial Offset option lets the object stay in its current location, but centers it relative to this position.

Figure 25.4 shows a sled positioned between four tree objects using the Position constraint. Notice how the weight of the downhill tree object is weighted higher than the other targets and the sled is close to it.

FIGURE 25.4

You can use the Position constraint to control the position of an object in relation to its targets.

Link constraint

The Link constraint can transfer hierarchical links between objects. This constraint can cause a child's link to be switched during an animation. Any time you animate a complex model with a dummy object, the Link constraint makes it possible to switch control from one dummy object to another during the animation sequence. This keeps the motions of the dummy objects simple.

The Link Params rollout includes Add Link and Delete Link buttons, a list of linked objects, and the Start Time field. To switch the link of an object, enter for the Start Time the frame where you want the link to switch, or drag the Time Slider and click the Add Link button. Then select the new parent object. The Delete key becomes active when you select a link in the list.

NOTE
If you create a link using the Link constraint, the object is not recognized as a child in any hierarchies.

All links are kept in a list in the Link Params rollout. You can add links to this list with the Add Link button, create a link to the world with the Link to World button, or delete links with the Delete Link button. The Start Time field specifies when the selected object takes control of the link. The object listed in the list is the parent object, so the Start Time setting determines when each parent object takes control.

The Key Mode section lets you choose a No Key option. This option does not write any keyframes for the object. If you want to set keys, you can choose the Key Nodes options and set keys for the object itself (Child option) or for the entire hierarchy (Parent option). The Key Entire Hierarchy sets keys for the object and its parents (Child option) or for the object and its targets and their hierarchies (Parent option).

This constraint also includes the PRS Parameters and Key Info rollouts.

CAUTION
You cannot use Link constraints with Inverse Kinematics systems.

Tutorial: Skating a figure eight

For an animated object to switch its link from one parent to another halfway through an animation, you need to use the Link constraint. Rotating an object about a static point is easy enough: Simply link the object to a dummy object, and rotate the dummy object. The figure-eight motion is more complex, but you can do it with the Link constraint.

To move an object in a figure eight, follow these steps:

1. Open the Figure skater skating a figure eight.max file from the Chap 25 directory on the CD.

   This file includes a figure skater model imported from Poser and two dummy objects. The figure skater is linked to the first dummy object (the one initially closest to the skater).

2. Click the Auto Key button (or press the N key), drag the Time Slider to frame 100, and rotate the first dummy object two full revolutions in the Top viewport.

3. Select the second dummy object, and rotate it two full revolutions in the opposite direction. Click the Auto Key button again to deactivate it.

TIP
If you enable the Angle Snap Toggle button on the main toolbar, then it is easier to rotate objects exactly two revolutions.

4. With the figure skater selected, choose Animation ⇨ Constraints ⇨ Link Constraint. Then click the first dummy object (the top one in the Top viewport).

   The Link constraint is assigned to the figure skater.

25

5. Drag the Time Slider to frame 25, then in the Link Params rollout, click the Add Link button and pick the second dummy object (the bottom one in the Top viewport). This switch control of the skater to the second dummy object. Then drag the Time Slider to frame 75, and with the Add Link button still active, click again on the first dummy object.

6. Click the Play Animation button (or press the / key) to see the animation play.

TIP
Another way to accomplish this same motion is to create a spline of a figure eight and use the Path constraint.

Figure 25.5 shows the skater as she makes her path around the two dummy objects.

FIGURE 25.5

With the Link constraint, the figure skater can move in a figure eight by rotating about two dummy objects.

LookAt constraint

The LookAt constraint won't move an object, but it rotates the object so it is always orientated toward the target object. For example, you could use the LookAt constraint to animate a character's head that is watching a flying bumblebee. It is also very useful to apply to camera objects that follow a specific object throughout the animation.

After you select a target object, a single line extends from the object and points at the target object. This line, called the Viewline, is visible only within the viewports.

The LookAt Constraint rollout, like many of the other constraints, includes a list of targets. With the Add and Delete LookAt Target buttons, you can add and remove targets from the list. If several targets are on the list, the object is centered on a location between them. Using the Weight value, you can cause the various targets to have more of an influence over the orientation of the object. The Keep Initial Offset option prevents the object from reorienting itself when the constraint is applied. Any movement is relative to its original position.

You can set the Viewline Length, which is the distance that the Viewline extends from the object. The Viewline Length Absolute option draws the Viewline from the object to its target, ignoring the length value.

The Set Orientation button lets you change the offset orientation of the object using the Select and Rotation button on the main toolbar. If you get lost, the Reset Orientation button returns the orientation to its original position. You can select which local axis points at the target object.

The Upnode is an object that defines the up direction. If the LookAt axis ever lines up with the Upnode axis, then the object flips upside-down. To prevent this, you can select which local axis is used as the LookAt axis and which axis points at the Upnode. The World is the default Upnode object, but you can select any object as the Upnode object by deselecting the World object and clicking the button to its right.

To control the Upnode, you can select the LookAt option or the Axis Alignment option, which enables the Align to Upnode Axis option. Using this option, you can specify which axis points toward the Upnode.

> **CAUTION**
> The object using the LookAt constraint flips when the target point is positioned directly above or below the object's pivot point.

When you assign the LookAt constraint, the Create Key button for rotation changes to Roll. This is because the camera is locked to point at the assigned object and cannot rotate; rather, it can only roll about the axis.

You can use the LookAt constraint to let cameras follow objects as they move around a scene. It is the default transform controller for Target camera objects.

Orientation constraint

You can use the Orientation constraint to lock the rotation of an object to another object. You can move and scale the objects independently, but the constrained object rotates along with the target object. A good example of an animation that uses this type of constraint is a satellite that orbits the Earth. You can offset the satellite and still constrain it to the Earth's surface. Then, as the Earth moves, the satellite follows.

In the Orientation Constraint rollout, you can select several orientation targets and weight them in the same manner as with the Position constraint. The target with the greatest weight value has the

25

most influence over the object's orientation. You also can constrain an object to the World object. The Keep Initial Offset option maintains the object's original orientation and rotates it relative to this original orientation. The Transform Rule setting determines whether the object rotates using the Local or World Coordinate Systems.

Using the Walkthrough Assistant

One alternative to using the Path and LookAt constraints is to use the Walkthrough Assistant. This tool is accessed from the Animation menu. It opens up a utility panel with several rollouts, as shown in Figure 25.6. Using this panel, you can create a new camera, select a path, and set the viewport to use the created camera. You can then use the View Controls rollout to cause the view to tilt to the left or right as you move through the path. This automates the process of getting a camera to follow a path.

FIGURE 25.6

The Walkthrough Assistant automates several constraints into a single interface.

The Walkthrough Assistant also includes a Render Preview that you use to see the results. If you drag the Time Slider to a different frame and click the Render Preview pane, the preview is updated. At specific frames, you can drag the Turn Head slider to change where the camera is looking. You can even tilt the camera up and down as well as side to side.

In the Advanced Controls rollout (which appears only after a camera has been created) are options for changing the Field of View and the Target Distance, which is useful if you're using a Depth of Field effect. You also can set the camera to move at a constant speed and an option to cause the camera to follow the path.

Understanding Controller Types

Controllers are used to set the keys for animation sequences. Every object and parameter that is animated has a controller assigned, and almost every controller has parameters that you can alter to change its functionality. Some controllers present these parameters as rollouts in the Motion panel, and others use a Properties dialog box.

3ds Max has five basic controller types that work with only a single parameter or track and one specialized controller type that manages several tracks at once (the Transform controllers). The type depends on the type of values the controller works with. The types include the following:

- **Transform controllers:** A special controller type that applies to all transforms (position, rotation, and scale) at the same time, such as the Position, Rotation, Scale (PRS) controllers
- **Position controllers:** Control the position coordinates for objects, consisting of X, Y, and Z values
- **Rotation controllers:** Control the rotation values for objects along all three axes
- **Scale controllers:** Control the scale values for objects as percentages for each axis
- **Float controllers:** Used for all parameters with a single numeric value, such as Wind Strength and Sphere Radius
- **Point3 controllers:** Consist of color components for red, green, and blue, such as Diffuse and Background colors

NOTE

Understanding the different controller types is important. When you copy and paste controller parameters between different tracks, both tracks must have the same controller type.

Float controllers work with parameters that use float values, such as a sphere's Radius or a plane object's Scale Multiplier value. Float values are numbers with a decimal value, such as 2.3 or 10.99. A Float controller is assigned to any parameter that is animated. After it is assigned, you can access the function curves and keys for this controller in the Track View and in the Track Bar. Because Float and Point3 controllers are assigned to parameters and not to objects, they don't appear in the Animation menu.

Assigning Controllers

Any object or parameter that is animated is automatically assigned a controller. The controller that is assigned is the default controller. The Animation panel in the Preference Settings dialog box lists the default controllers and lets you change them. You can also change this automatic default controller using the Track View window or the transformation tracks located in the Motion panel.

Automatically assigned controllers

The default controllers are automatically assigned for an object's transformation tracks when the object is created. For example, if you create a simple sphere and then open the Motion panel (which

25

has the icon that looks like a wheel), you can find the transformation tracks in the Assign Controller rollout. The default Position controller is Position XYZ, the default Rotation controller is Euler XYZ, and the default Scale controller is the Bézier Scale controller.

The default controller depends on the type of object. For example, the Barycentric Morph controller is automatically assigned when you create a Morph compound object, and the Master Point controller is automatically assigned to any vertices or control points subobjects that are animated.

> **NOTE**
> Because controllers are automatically assigned to animation tracks, they cannot be removed; they can only be changed to a different controller. There is no function to delete controllers.

Assigning controllers with the Animation menu

The easiest way to assign a controller to an object is with the Animation menu. Located under the Animation menu are four controller submenus consisting of Transform Controllers, Position Controllers, Rotation Controllers, and Scale Controllers.

> **NOTE**
> Although constraints are contained within a separate menu, they control the animating of keys just like controllers.

When a controller is assigned to an object using the Animation menu, the existing controller is not removed, but the new controller is added as part of a list along with the other controllers. You can see all these controllers in the Motion panel.

For example, Figure 25.7 shows the Motion panel for a sphere object that has the default Position XYZ controller assigned to the Position track. If you choose Animation ⇨ Position Controllers ⇨ Noise, then the Position List controller is added to the Position track, of which Position XYZ and Noise are two available controllers. This lets you animate multiple motions such as the shimmy of a car with a bad carburetor as it moves down the road.

FIGURE 25.7

The Motion panel displays all transform controllers applied to an object.

The List controller makes it possible to add several controllers to a single track. It also allows you to set Weights for each of its controllers. Using the Position List rollout, you can set the active controller and delete controllers from the list. You also can Cut and Paste controllers to other tracks.

Assigning controllers in the Motion panel

The top of the Motion panel includes two buttons: Parameters and Trajectories. Clicking the Parameters button makes the Assign Controller rollout available.

To change a transformation track's controller, select the track and click the Assign Controller button positioned directly above the list. An Assign Controller dialog box opens that is specific to the track you selected.

For more about the Trajectories button, see Chapter 24, "Understanding Animation and Keyframes."

For example, Figure 25.8 shows the Assign Position Controller dialog box for selecting a controller for the Position track. The arrow mark (>) shows the current selected controller. At the bottom of the dialog box, the default controller type is listed. Select a new controller from the list, and click OK. This new controller now is listed in the track, and the controller's rollouts appear beneath the Assign Controller rollout.

FIGURE 25.8

The Assign Position Controller dialog box lets you select a controller to assign.

> **NOTE**
> Transformation controllers can be applied in the Motion panel, but the Track View can be used to apply controllers to all parameters including transforms.

Assigning controllers in the Track View

You also can use the Track View to assign controllers. To do this, locate and select the track to apply a controller to, and then click the Assign Controller button on the Controllers toolbar, choose the Controller ⇨ Assign (keyboard shortcut, C if the Keyboard Shortcut Override Toggle on the main

25

toolbar is enabled) menu command, or right-click the track and select Assign Controller from the pop-up menu. An Assign Controller dialog box opens in which you can select the controller to use.

Chapter 28, "Editing Animation Curves in the Track View," covers the details of the Track View.

You also can use the Controller toolbar to copy and paste controllers between tracks, but you can paste controllers only to similar types of tracks. When you paste controllers, the Paste dialog box lets you choose to paste the controller as a copy or as an instance. Changing an instanced controller's parameters changes the parameters for all instances. The Paste dialog box also includes an option to replace all instances. This option replaces all instances of the controller, whether or not they are selected.

Setting default controllers

When you assign controllers using the Track View, the Assign Controller dialog box includes the option Make Default. With this option, the selected controller becomes the default for the selected track.

You also can set the global default controller for each type of track by choosing Customize ➪ Preferences, selecting the Animation panel, and then clicking the Set Defaults button. The Set Controller Defaults dialog box opens, in which you can set the default parameter settings, such as the In and Out curves for the controller. To set the default controller, select a controller from the list and click the Set Defaults button to open a controller-specific dialog box where you can adjust the controller parameters. The Animation panel also includes a button to revert to the original settings.

> **NOTE**
> Changing a default controller does not change any currently assigned controllers.

Examining Some Simple Controllers

Now that you've learned how to assign controllers, let's look at some simple controllers.

Earlier in the chapter, I mentioned six specific controller types. These types define the type of data that the controller works with. This section covers the various controllers according to the types of tracks with which they work.

> **NOTE**
> Looking at the function curves for a controller provides a good idea of how you can control it, so many of the figures that follow show the various function curves for the different controllers.

Each of these controllers has a unique icon to represent it in the Track View. This makes them easy to identify.

Bézier controller

The Bézier controller is the default controller for many parameters. It enables you to interpolate between values using an adjustable Bézier spline. By dragging its tangent vertex handles, you can control the spline's curvature. Tangent handles produce a smooth transition when they lie on the same line, or you can create an angle between them for a sharp point. Figure 25.9 shows the Bézier controller assigned to a Position track.

FIGURE 25.9

The Bézier controller produces smooth animation curves.

The Bézier controller parameters are displayed in the Motion panel under two rollouts: Key Info (Basic) and Key Info (Advanced).

At the top of the Key Info (Basic) rollout are two arrows and a field that shows the key number. The arrows let you move between the Previous and Next keys. Each vertex shown in the function curve represents a key. The Time field displays the frame number where the key is located. The Time Lock button next to the Time field can be set to prevent the key from being dragged in Track View. The value fields show the values for the selected track; the number of fields changes depending on the type of track that is selected.

At the bottom of the Key Info (Basic) rollout are two flyout buttons for specifying the In and Out curves for the key. The arrows to the sides of these buttons move between the various In/Out curve types. The curve types include Smooth, Linear, Step, Slow, Fast, Custom, and Tangent Copy.

The In and Out values in the Key Info (Advanced) rollout are enabled only when the Custom curve type is selected. These fields let you define the rate applied to each axis of the curve. The Lock button changes the two values by equal and opposite amounts. The Normalize Time button averages the positions of all keys. The Constant Velocity option interpolates the key between its neighboring keys to provide smoother motion.

Linear controller

The Linear controller interpolates between two values to create a straight line by changing its value at a constant rate over time.

The Linear controller doesn't include any parameters and can be applied to time or values. Figure 25.10 shows the curves from the previous example after the Linear controller is assigned—all curves have been replaced with straight lines.

FIGURE 25.10

The Linear controller uses straight lines.

Noise controller

The Noise controller applies random variations in a track's values. In the Noise Controller dialog box, shown in Figure 25.11, the Seed value determines the randomness of the noise and the Frequency value determines how jagged the noise is. You also can set the Strength along each axis: The > (greater than) 0 option for each axis makes the noise values remain positive.

FIGURE 25.11

The Noise controller properties let you set the noise strength for each axis.

You also have an option to enable Fractal Noise with a Roughness setting.

The Ramp in and Ramp out values determine the length of time before or until the noise can reach full value. The Characteristic Graph gives a visual look at the noise over the range. Figure 25.12 shows the Noise controller assigned to the Position track. If you need to change any Noise properties, right-click the Noise track and select Properties from the pop-up menu.

FIGURE 25.12

The Noise controller lets you randomly alter track values.

Spring controller

The Spring controller is similar in many ways to the Flex modifier in that it adds secondary motion associated with the wiggle of a spring after a force has been applied and then removed. When the Spring controller is applied, a panel with two rollouts appears. These rollouts, shown in Figure 25.13, let you control the physical properties of the spring and the forces that influence it.

FIGURE 25.13

The Spring controller rollouts can add additional springs and forces.

In the Spring Dynamics rollout, you can change the Mass and Drag values. Higher mass values result in greater secondary motion as the object is moved, and the Drag value controls how quickly the bouncing motion stops. You can add multiple springs, each with its own Tension and Damping values to be applied Relative or Absolute.

The Forces, Limits, and Precision rollout lets you add forces that affect the spring motion. The Add button lets you identify these forces, which are typically Space Warps, and you can limit the effect to specific axes.

25

Tutorial: Wagging a tail with the Spring controller

One of the best uses of the Spring controller is to gain the secondary motion associated with an existing motion. For example, if a character moves, then an appendage such as a tail can easily follow if you apply a Spring controller to it.

To wag a row of spheres using the Spring controller, follow these steps:

1. Open the Dog wagging tail.max file from the Chap 25 directory on the CD.

   This file contains a dog made of primitives and a linked row of spheres with the top sphere animated rotating back and forth.

2. Select the smallest sphere, and choose the Animation ⇨ Position Controllers ⇨ Spring menu command. This moves the sphere to its parent. Choose the Select and Move button (or press the W key), and return the sphere to its original position.

3. Repeat Step 2 for the remaining spheres, moving from smallest to largest.

4. Click the Play Animation button (or press the / key) to see the resulting motion.

Figure 25.14 shows a frame of the final motion. Notice that the spheres aren't lined up exactly. The smallest sphere is moving the greatest distance because all the springs are adding their effect.

FIGURE 25.14

The Spring controller adds secondary motion to the existing motion of the largest sphere.

Position XYZ controller

The Position XYZ controller splits position transforms into three separate tracks, one for each axis. Each axis has a Bézier controller applied to it, but each component track can be assigned a different controller. The Position XYZ Parameters rollout lets you switch between the component axes.

The Rotation tracks use a variety of controllers, many of them common to the Position track.

Scale XYZ controller

3ds Max has one controller that you can use only in Scale tracks. The Scale XYZ controller breaks scale transforms into three separate tracks, one for each axis. This feature enables you to precisely control the scaling of an object along separate axes. It is a better alternative to using Select and Non-Uniform Scale from the main toolbar because it is independent of the object geometry.

The Scale XYZ Parameters rollout lets you select which axis to work with. This controller works the same way as the other position and rotation XYZ controllers.

Summary

Using the Animation ⇨ Constraints menu, you can apply constraints to objects. This menu also lets you select a target object. You can use the various constraints to limit the motion of objects, which is helpful as you begin to animate. If you're an animator, you should thank your lucky stars for controllers. Controllers offer power flexibility for animating objects—and just think of all those keys that you don't have to set by hand.

In this chapter, you accomplished the following:

- Constrained an object to the surface of another object using the Attachment and Surface constraints
- Forced an object to travel along a path with the Path constraint
- Controlled the position and orientation of objects with weighted Position and Orientation constraints
- Shifted between two different controlling objects using the Link constraint
- Followed objects with the LookAt constraint
- Learned about the various controller types
- Discovered how to assign controllers using the Motion panel and the Track View
- Saw a few examples of using controllers

In the next chapter, you learn about more animation features including animation layers and the various animation modifiers.

25

Using Animation Layers and Animation Modifiers

IN THIS CHAPTER

Using animation layers

Saving and loading animation files

Using the Point Cache modifier

Using the Morpher modifier

Just as layers can be used to organize a scene by placing objects on different layers, you also can separate the various animation motions into different layers. This gives you great control over how motions are organized and blended together.

If you've worked to animate some object in the Autodesk® 3ds Max® 2013 software and are pleased with the result, you can save the animation clip and reuse it on similar objects. Several animation clips can be mixed together to create an entirely new animation sequence.

Another way to work with animations is with the animation modifiers. Modifiers can be used to deform and otherwise alter the geometry of objects, but they also can be used to affect other aspects of an object, including animated changes. One such important animation modifier is the Point Cache modifier. This modifier lets the movement of each vertex in the scene be saved to a cached file for immediate recall and for animating multiple objects simultaneously.

The Modifiers menu also includes an Animation submenu that contains many such modifiers. These modifiers are unique in that each of them changes with time. They can be useful as an alternate to controllers, but their resulting effects are very specific. Included with this submenu are modifiers such as Morpher, which allows an object to move through several different preset shapes.

Using the Animation Layers Toolbar

Behind the scenes, animation layers add several new controller tracks to objects that are visible in the Motion panel and in the Track View interface, but the front end is accessible through a simple toolbar. The Animation Layers toolbar, shown in Figure 26.1, is similar in many ways to the Layers toolbar.

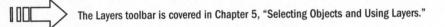

The Layers toolbar is covered in Chapter 5, "Selecting Objects and Using Layers."

FIGURE 26.1

The Animation Layers toolbar includes icons for defining and merging layers.

You can open the Animation Layers toolbar by right-clicking the main toolbar away from the buttons and selecting Animation Layers from the pop-up menu. Each of the toolbar buttons is labeled and explained in Table 26.1.

TABLE 26.1 Animation Layers Toolbar Controls

Toolbar Button	Name	Description
	Enable Animation Layers	Turns the animation layers system on
	Select Active Layer Objects	Selects the objects in the viewport that are on the active animation layer
	Layer Selection drop-down list	Presents a selection list of all the available animation layers
	Animation Layer Weight	Displays the weight value for the current animation layer
	Animation Layer Properties	Opens the Animation Layer Properties dialog box
	Add Animation Layer	Adds another animation layer
	Delete Animation Layer	Deletes the current animation layer
	Copy Animation Layer	Copies the current animation layer
	Paste Active Animation Layer	Pastes the keys from the current animation layer to the selected object
	Paste New Layer	Pastes the copied animation layer keys to a new layer
	Collapse Animation Layer	Combines and deletes the current animation layer with the layer above it
	Disable Animation Layer	Turns the current animation layer off

When a new animation layer is created using the Add Animation Layer button, a dialog box appears where you can name the new layer and select to duplicate the active controller type or use the default controller type. After you click the OK button, a new entry is added to the Animation Layer Selection List. The default name of the animation layer as AnimLayer with a number. The original layer is named Base Layer. To the left of the animation layer name is a small light bulb icon that indicates whether the animation layer is enabled or disabled.

> **CAUTION**
> You cannot rename animation layers after they are created.

Each layer can have a weight assigned to it. These weight values control how much influence the current animation layer has. The weight value also can be animated. For example, if a car is animated moving forward 100 meters over 50 frames, then weighting the animation layer to 30 causes the car to move forward only 30 meters over the 50 frames.

Working with Animation Layers

Animation layers are good for organizing motions into sets that can be easily turned on and off, but you also can use them to blend between motions to create an entirely new set of motions.

> **NOTE**
> Animations can be divided into *primary* motions, which are the major motions, and *secondary* motions, which are derivative motions that depend on the animation of other parts. Using animation layers, you can separate primary motions, like foot placement, from secondary motions, like a swinging arm, and adjust them independently.

Enabling animation layers

The first button on the Animation Layers toolbar is the Enable Animation Layers button. Clicking this button opens a dialog box, shown in Figure 26.2, where you can filter the type of keys to include in the animation layer.

FIGURE 26.2

The Enable Animation Layers dialog box lets you limit which type of keys are included.

The base animation layer can be disabled using the Disable Animation Layer button. This button is available only when you collapse all its layers. This disables the existing animation layer.

Setting animation layers properties

The button to the right of the Weight value opens the Layer Properties dialog box, shown in Figure 26.3. This dialog box lets you specify the type of controller to which the layers are collapsed. The options include Bézier (for Position and Scale tracks) or Euler (for Rotation tracks), Linear or TCB, and Default. You also can specify a range to collapse.

FIGURE 26.3

The Layer Properties dialog box lets you set the controller type to collapse to.

Collapsing animation layers

By collapsing layers, you combine the animation keys on each layer into a single set of keys that includes all the various motions. Be careful when collapsing; the results can be unexpected. Collapsing animation layers is accomplished with the Collapse Animation Layers button.

Tutorial: Using animation layers for a plane takeoff

Have you ever been to a small airport and watched the commuter planes take off? Sometimes they leave the ground and then return to the ground and then finally take off. It's like they need to get a good bounce to overcome gravity. This is a good example of when animation layers come in handy.

To animate a jet's takeoff using animation layers, follow these steps:

1. Open the Mig take-off.max file from the Chap 26 directory on the CD.

    This file includes a detailed Mig-29 jet model created by Viewpoint Datalabs.

2. Open the Animation Layers toolbar by right-clicking the main toolbar away from the buttons and choosing Animation Layers from the pop-up menu.

3. Select the jet object, click the Enable Animation Layers button, enable the Position track, and then click OK to close the pop-up dialog box. This adds a Base Layer to the Selection list of the Animation Layers toolbar.

4. Click the Auto Key button, drag the Time Slider to frame 100, and move the jet to the far end of the runway with the Select and Move tool. Then disable the Auto Key button. Set the Weight value for this layer to **0**.

5. In the Animation Layers toolbar, click the Add Animation Layer button to add a new layer. In the Create New Animation Layer dialog box that appears, select the Duplicate the Active Controller Type option and click OK. A new layer labeled AnimLayer01 is added to the Selection list.

6. Click the Auto Key button again, drag the Time Slider to frame 100, and move the jet upward away from the runway. Then disable the Auto Key button again.

7. Select the Base Layer from the Selection list in the Animation Layers toolbar and set its Weight value to **100**. Then drag the Time Slider, and notice that the jet moves up at an angle over the 100 frames. This motion is caused by blending the two animation layers together.

8. Click the Auto Key button again, drag the Time Slider to frame 0, and set the Weight value for AnimLayer01 to **0**; drag the Time Slider to frame 30, and set the Weight to **60**; drag the Time Slider to frame 50, and set the Weight back to **0**; and finally drag the Time Slider to frame 80, and set the Weight to **80**. Then disable the Auto Key button again.

Dragging the Time Slider shows the jet bounce down the runway before taking off, as shown in Figure 26.4. This gives a single weight value for controlling the vertical height of the airplane as it takes off.

FIGURE 26.4

The Animation Layers feature provides a single parameter for controlling the plane's height.

Saving and Loading Animation Files

Before an animation can be reused on another model, it must be saved. Saving a sequence to the local hard disk makes it accessible for other 3ds Max scenes.

Saving general animations

The animation of objects can be saved using the XML Animation File (XAF) format. To save the animation for the selected object, open the Save XML Animation File dialog box, shown in Figure 26.5, using the Animation ⇨ Save Animation.

FIGURE 26.5

The Save XML Animation File dialog box is used to save animations of the selected object.

For general animations, you can select to include animated tracks, constraints, only keyable tracks, and a specific segment or range. The User Data fields let you enter notes or specific data used by plug-ins about the animation sequence.

The Load XML Animation File dialog box, shown in Figure 26.6, is opened using the Animation ⇨ Load Animation menu command. It looks like a normal file dialog box, but it has some additional features.

The Relative and Absolute options determine whether the animation is loaded relative to the object's current location or whether it is loaded into the frames where it was saved. The Replace and Insert options let the new keys overwrite the existing ones or move them out to insert the loaded keys. You can even select the frame where the new keys are loaded. The Load Motion button lets you load an existing mapping file named the same as the animation file if one exists or lets you create a new one.

FIGURE 26.6

The Load XML Animation File dialog box lets you load animation files from one scene and apply them to another.

Mapping animated objects

Mapping files defines a relationship between objects in the saved animation file and objects in the current 3ds Max file. These relationships allow the animation keys to be transferred from one scene object to another. For example, if you save a dancing robot animation sequence and then want to load it onto a dinosaur model, the mapping file tells the animation that the robot's left arm needs to map to the dinosaur's left arm in the target scene because they might be called by different names in both files. If the objects have the same names in both files, the mapping file isn't needed.

Mapping files are listed in the drop-down list for easy selection, or you can use the Get Mapping button to select a different mapping file to load. Mapping files are saved with the .xmm file extension. The Edit Mapping button is active when a mapping associated with the file in the Load Animation dialog box exists. It opens the Map Animation dialog box, where you can define the mapping between objects in the two scenes.

Using the Map Animation dialog box

The Map Animation dialog box, shown in Figure 26.7, includes several rollouts. The Motion Mapping Parameters rollout includes options for allowing 3ds Max to make its best guess at mapping objects. If the scenes are fairly similar, then this option may be just the ticket. The Exact Names, Closest Names, and Hierarchy buttons allow 3ds Max to attempt the mapping on its own. This works especially well on bipeds that use the default naming conventions. You also can select to have 3ds Max look at the various controllers that are used when trying to match up objects.

FIGURE 26.7

The Map Animation dialog box lets you map objects to receive animation.

The Filters section lets you filter out the tracks that you don't want to see. The Lock button applies the selected filters to both the Current and Incoming lists.

The Map Track to Track rollout consists of three lists. The left list contains all the tracks for the current scene objects, the middle list contains all the mapped tracks, and the right list contains all the tracks from the incoming animation file. Select tracks and click the button with the left-pointing arrow to add tracks to the Mapped list; click the other arrow button to remove them.

At the bottom of the Map Animation dialog box are buttons for saving the current mapping file.

Retargeting animations

The Retargeting rollout, shown in Figure 26.8, lets you specify how the scale changes between certain mapped objects. Scale values can be entered for the mapped nodes as Absolute or Multiply Derived Scale values for each axis. Derived scale values can be obtained from a specific origin object. After the settings are right, the Set button applies the scaling to the selected mapping.

FIGURE 26.8

Use the Retargeting rollout to specify how the scale changes between mapped objects.

Using the Animation Modifiers

Animation is more than just moving an object from here to there. All objects move not only with major transformations but with lots of secondary motions also. When a human character walks, the motions of his arms and legs are major, but the secondary motions of his swinging hips and bobbing shoulders make the walk realistic. Many of the animation modifiers enable these key secondary motions.

All the animation modifiers presented in this chapter are located in the Modifiers ⇨ Animation submenu, except for the Point Cache modifier, which is found in the Cache Tools submenu.

Also included among the Animation modifiers are several Skin modifiers, which are used to make an object move by attaching it to an underlying skeleton. The Skin modifiers are covered in Chapter 30, "Skinning Characters."

Baking Animation Keys with the Point Cache Modifier

When you add keys to an object to control its animation using modifiers, the modifiers remain with the object and can be revisited and altered as needed. However, if you have multiple objects that follow the same set of keys, such as for a crowd scene, then including a set of modifiers for each object can increase the overhead many times over. A simple solution is to bake all the keys into the object, allowing all the keys to be pulled from an external file. This frees the resources required to animate multiple objects and makes the animated keys portable. The Point Cache modifier makes this possible.

You also can use the Point Cache modifier when playback in the viewport is too slow because 3ds Max needs to compute the vertex positions of a huge number of vertices. Reading their position from a separate file increases the playback speed. You also can use the file on a cloned object to control its motion at a different speed.

The Point Cache modifier records the movement of every vertex of an object to a file. Point Cache files have the .xml extension, but they can also be saved using the older .pc2 extension. To create a Point Cache file, apply the Point Cache modifier, click the New button in the Parameters rollout, and name a new file on the hard drive. Then set the range of the animation to capture and click the Record button. Once recorded, the total number of points along with the sample rate and range are displayed for the active cache.

> **CAUTION**
> Point Cache files can be loaded and used only on objects with the same number of vertices as the original used to record the file.

If you select the Disable Modifiers Below button, then all modifiers below the Point Cache in the Modifier Stack are disabled. You can enable the Relative Offset option and set the Strength value to cause the cached animation to be exaggerated or even reversed. In the Playback Type section, you can control the range of the animation.

Tutorial: Trees in a hurricane

As an example of using the Point Cache modifier, you'll use a tree that is bending under violent forces such as a hurricane and duplicate it many times.

To create a forest of trees in a hurricane, follow these steps:

1. Open the Bending tree.max file from the Chap 26 directory on the CD.
   This file includes an animated tree swaying back and forth using the Bend modifier.
2. Select the tree and choose the Modifiers ⇨ Cache Tools ⇨ Point Cache menu to apply the Point Cache modifier to the tree.
3. In the Parameters rollout, click the New button, create a file named "Bending tree.xml," and click the Save button to create the cached animation file. Then click the Record button to save all the animation data to the file.

4. Select the tree and delete its Bend modifier. Then use the Tools ⇨ Array dialog box to create several rows of trees. Be sure to create the trees as copies and not instances.

5. Select a random tree and change the Playback Type to **Custom Start** in the Parameters rollout and change the Start Frame to **–2** to cause some random motion. Then repeat this step for several other trees.

6. Press the Play Animation button to see the results.

Figure 26.9 shows several of the trees being moved about by the storm.

FIGURE 26.9

Using the Point Cache modifier, you can animate a whole forest of trees.

Morpher modifier

The Morpher modifier lets you change a shape from one form into another. You can apply this modifier only to objects with the same number of vertices.

> **TIP**
> In many ways, the Morpher modifier is similar to the Morph compound object, which is covered in Chapter 13, "Working with Compound Objects."

The Morpher modifier can be very useful for creating facial expressions and character lip-synching. 3ds Max makes 100 separate channels available for morph targets, and channels can be mixed. You can use the Morpher modifier in conjunction with the Morph material. For example, you could use the Morpher material to blush a character for an embarrassed expression.

> **TIP**
>
> When it comes to making facial expressions, a mirror and your own face can be the biggest help. Coworkers may look at you funny, but your facial expressions will benefit from the exercise.

The first task before using this modifier is to create all the different morph targets. Because the morph targets need to contain the same number of vertices as the base object, make a copy of the base object for each morph target that you are going to create. As you create these targets, be careful not to add or delete any vertices from the object.

> **NOTE**
>
> Because morph targets deal with each vertex independently, you cannot mirror morph targets, so if you want a morph target for raising the left eyebrow and a morph target for raising the right eyebrow, you need to create each morph target by hand.

After all your morph targets are created, select a channel in the Channel Parameters rollout, shown in Figure 26.10, and use the Pick Object from Scene button to select the morph target for that channel. Another option for picking is to use Capture Current State. After a morph target has been added to a channel, you can view it in the Channel List rollout.

FIGURE 26.10

The Morpher modifier's rollouts

As you animate, you can specify the amount of each morph target to include in the frame using the value to the right of the channel name in the Channel List rollout. The slim color bar to the left of the channel name designates the status of the channel. You can find information on what each color represents in the Channel Color Legend rollout.

The Channel Parameters rollout also includes a Progressive Morph section. This feature lets you define an intermediate step for how the morph is to progress, with the final step being the morph target. Using these intermediate steps, you can control how the object morphs.

Tutorial: Morphing facial expressions

The Morpher modifier is very helpful when you're trying to morph facial expressions, such as those to make a character talk. With the various sounds added to the different channels, you can quickly morph between them. In this example, you use the Morpher modifier to change the facial expressions of the general character.

> **TIP**
> When creating facial expressions, be sure to enable the Use Soft Selection feature, which makes modifying the face meshes much easier.

To change facial expressions using the Morpher modifier, follow these steps:

1. Open the Morphing facial expressions.max file from the Chap 26 directory on the CD.

   This file includes a head model created by Viewpoint Datalabs. The model has been copied twice, and the morph targets have already been created by modifying the subobjects around the mouth.

2. Select the face on the left, and select the Modifiers ⇨ Animation ⇨ Morpher menu command to apply the Morpher modifier.

3. In the Channel List rollout, select channel 1, click the Pick Object from Scene button, and select the middle face object. Then select the second empty channel from the Channel List rollout; in the Channel Parameters rollout, again click the Pick Object from Scene button and select the face on the right.

   If you look in the Channel List rollout, you'll see "cheesy smile" in Channel 1 and "frown" in Channel 2.

4. Click the Auto Key button (or press the N key), drag the Time Slider to frame 50, and then increase the "cheesy smile" channel in the Channel List rollout to **50**. Drag the Time Slider to frame 100, and increase the "frown" channel to **100** and the "cheesy smile" channel to **0**. Then return the Time Slider to **50**, and set the "frown" channel to **0**.

5. Click the Play Animation button in the Time Controls to see the resulting animation.

Figure 26.11 shows the three facial expressions. The Morpher modifier is applied to the left face.

> **TIP**
> Be sure to keep the morph target objects around. You can hide them in the scene or select them and save them to a separate file with the Application Button ⇨ Save As ⇨ Save Selected menu command.

FIGURE 26.11

Using the Morpher modifier, you can morph one facial expression into another.

Summary

The Animation Layers feature provides a simple way to organize animated motions into an easy-to-manage method. The Animation Layers toolbar includes all the tools you need to manage these unique layers. The Animation ➪ Load Animation option, along with its mapping and retargeting features, lets you reuse saved animations by applying them to other scenes. This chapter also introduced several of the available animation modifiers and showed you how to use them. In this chapter, you learned about the following:

- Using the Animation Layers toolbar
- Creating new layers and using weights
- Collapsing animation layers
- Loading saved XML animation files
- Remapping animation tracks between objects
- Retargeting to adjust for a change in scale
- Using the Point Cache modifier
- Using the Morpher modifier to deform a face

The next chapter takes a close look at wiring parameters so that one parameter can control another, and creating custom parameters.

Wiring Parameters

IN THIS CHAPTER

Wiring parameters with manipulator helpers

Collecting parameters

Creating custom parameters

This chapter looks at a unique way to drive animations based on object parameters. Parameters of one object can be wired to parameters of another object so that when one parameter changes, the wired parameter changes with it. For example, you can wire the On/Off parameter of a light to the movement of a switch. All parameters that can be animated can be wired.

As long as you are working with parameters, the Autodesk® 3ds Max® 2013 software includes several helpful tools for viewing and working with the available parameters, including the Parameter Collector. If the Parameter Collector doesn't gather the exact parameters that you need, you can create your own custom parameters also.

Wiring Parameters

When parameters are wired together, the value of one parameter controls the value of the parameter to which it is wired. This is a powerful animation technique that lets a change in one part of the scene control another aspect of the scene. Another way to use wired parameters is to create custom animation controls such as a slider that dims a light source that animators can use as needed.

Using the Parameter Wiring dialog box

You can access the Parameter Wiring dialog box in several places. The Animation ⇨ Wire Parameters ⇨ Wire Parameters (Ctrl+5) menu makes a pop-up menu of parameters appear. Selecting a parameter from the menu changes the cursor to a dotted line (like the one used when linking objects). Click the object that you want to wire to, and another pop-up menu lets you choose the parameter to wire to. The Parameter Wiring dialog box appears with the parameter for each object selected from a hierarchy tree.

You can also wire parameters by selecting an object and right-clicking to access the quad menu and selecting Wire Parameters. The Wire Parameters option is disabled if multiple objects are selected.

The Parameter Wiring dialog box (Alt+5), shown in Figure 27.1, displays two tree lists containing all the available parameters. This tree list looks very similar to the Track View and lets you connect parameters in either direction or to each other. If you used the Wire Parameters feature to open the Parameter Wiring dialog box, then the parameter for each object is already selected and highlighted in yellow.

FIGURE 27.1

The Parameter Wiring dialog box lets you connect parameters so they affect one another.

The three arrow buttons between the two tree lists let you specify the connection direction. These buttons connect the parameter in one pane to the selected parameter in the opposite pane. The direction determines whether the parameter in the left pane controls the parameter in the right pane, or vice versa. You can also select the top bidirectional button to make the parameters mutually affect each other. Below each tree list is a text area where you can enter an expression. An *expression* is a mathematical statement that follows a specific syntax for defining how one parameter controls the other. These expressions can be any valid expression that is accepted in the Animation Controller dialog box or in MAXScript.

After the parameters are selected, click the direction button and enter an expression if needed. Then click the Connect button to complete the wiring. Based on the connection direction, the Master radio button indicates which object controls the other. You can also use this dialog box to disconnect existing wired parameters. You can use the icon buttons at the top of the dialog box, shown in Table 27.1, to Show All Tracks, to find the next wired parameter, and to refresh the tree view.

TABLE 27.1 Parameter Wiring Dialog Box Icons

Button	Description
	Show All Tracks
	Next Wired Parameter
	Refresh Tree View

After the wiring is completed, the Parameter Wiring dialog box remains open. You can try out the wiring by moving the master object. If the results aren't what you wanted, you can edit the expression and click the Update button (the Connect button changes to an Update button).

> **NOTE**
> When you select objects to be wired, the order in which the objects are selected doesn't matter because in the Parameter Wiring dialog box you can select the direction of control.

After you've made a connection in the Parameter Wiring dialog box, the parameter for the controlling object turns green, and the parameter of the object being controlled turns red. If you make a bidirectional connection, then both tracks turn green.

Manipulator helpers

To create general-use controls that can be wired to control various properties, 3ds Max includes three manipulator helpers. These helpers are Cone Angle, Plane Angle, and Slider. They are available as a subcategory under the Helpers category of the Create panel or in the Create ➪ Helpers ➪ Manipulators menu. These manipulators, like Dummy objects, are not rendered along with the scene.

For the Cone Angle helper, you can set the Angle, Distance, and Aspect settings. The default cone base is a circle, but you can make it a square. The Plane Angle helper includes settings for Angle, Distance, and Size. This manipulator is helpful for controlling light and camera parameters.

The Plane Angle helper places a straight line that you can manipulate through an angle. It is useful for rotating objects about a point and makes the rotation angle parameter available.

You can name the Slider helper in the Label field. This name appears in the viewports above the Slider object. You can also set a default value along with maximum and minimum values. To position the object, you can set the X Position, Y Position, and Width settings. You can also set a snap value for the slider. The Hide option lets you hide the Slider if it isn't needed any more.

Once created, you can use these manipulator helpers when the Select and Manipulate button on the main toolbar is enabled (this button must be disabled before the manipulator helpers can be created). The advantage of these helpers is in wiring parameters to be controlled using the helpers.

Tutorial: Controlling a crocodile's bite

One way to use manipulator helpers and wired parameters is to control within limits certain parameters that can be animated. This gives your animation team controls they can use to quickly build animation sequences. In this example, you use a slider to control a crocodile's jaw movement.

To create a slider to control a crocodile's bite, follow these steps:

1. Open the Biting crocodile.max file from the Chap 27 directory on the CD.

    This file includes a crocodile model created by Viewpoint Datalabs. For this model, the head, eyes, and upper teeth have been joined into a single object, and the pivot point for this object has been moved to where the jaw hinges.

2. Select Create ⇨ Helpers ⇨ Manipulators ⇨ Slider, and click in the Perspective view above the crocodile. Name the slider **Croc Bite** in the Label field, and set the Maximum value to **60**.

3. With the Slider selected, choose Animation ⇨ Wire Parameter ⇨ Wire Parameter (or press the Ctrl+5) to access the pop-up menu. Choose Object (Slider) ⇨ value option, drag the dotted line to the crocodile's head object, and click. Choose Transform ⇨ Rotation ⇨ Y Rotation.

   The Parameter Wiring dialog box appears.

4. In the Parameter Wiring dialog box, click the direction arrow that points from the Slider to the head so that the slider is set to control the head. Then click the Connect button. This connects the slider value to the rotation of the crocodile's jaw. Then enable the Select and Manipulate button on the main toolbar, and drag the Slider.

   The crocodile's jaw spins around erratically. This happens because the rotation values are in radians and you need them in degrees.

5. In the expression text area under the head object, enter the expression **degToRad(value)** and click the Update button. Then drag the Slider again.

   Now the values are in degrees, and the range is correct, but the croc's upper jaw rotates unrealistically through the bottom jaw. This can be fixed by multiplying by a negative 1.

6. In the expression text area under the head object, update the expression to be `-1*degToRad (value)` and click the Update button.

7. Click the Select and Manipulate button on the main toolbar if it is not already enabled, and drag the slider to the right.

   The crocodile's mouth opens in proportion to the slider's value.

Figure 27.2 shows the crocodile biting using the slider control.

FIGURE 27.2

A slider control is wired to open the crocodile's mouth.

Collecting Parameters

To help in organizing the various parameters that you use to animate a scene, you can use the Parameter Collector to gather all custom and animated parameters used in the scene. The Parameter Editor can be used to create custom attributes and parameters, but the custom attributes are attached to the specific object or element that was selected when the attribute was created. This can make finding the custom attributes difficult, but 3ds Max includes another tool that you can use to collect all these custom attributes into a single location — the Parameter Collector.

Open the Parameter Collector dialog box, shown in Figure 27.3, with the Animation ➪ Parameter Collector (Alt+2) menu command. This dialog box lets you gather a set of parameters into a custom rollout that can be opened and accessed from anywhere. This provides a convenient way to compile and look at only the parameters that you need to animate a certain task. Under the menus are several toolbar buttons, explained in Table 27.2.

FIGURE 27.3

The Parameter Collector dialog box is used to gather several different parameters into a custom rollout.

TABLE 27.2 Parameter Collector Toolbar Buttons

Toolbar Button	Name	Description
Sphere Collection ▼	Collection Name	Enters a name for the current collection or selects an existing collection.
🗋	New Collection	Creates a new collection of parameters.

continued

TABLE 27.2   *(continued)*

Toolbar Button	Name	Description
	Duplicate Collection	Creates a copy of the existing collection.
	Delete Collection	Deletes the current collection.
	Multiple Edits	Toggle button that allows multiple parameters to be changed at once when enabled.
	Absolute/Relative	Toggle button that maintains the current value in Absolute mode and resets the value to 0 when the mouse is released in Relative mode.
	Key Selected	Creates a key for the selected parameters when the Auto Key mode is enabled.
	Reset Selected	Sets the selected parameter values to 0.
	Move Parameters Down	Moves the selected parameters downward in the rollout order.
	Move Parameters Up	Moves the selected parameters upward in the rollout order.
	Add to Selected Rollout	Opens a Track View Pick dialog box where you can select the parameter to add to the selected rollout.
	Add to New Rollout	Opens a Track View Pick dialog box where you can select the parameter to add to a new rollout.
	Delete Selected	Deletes the selected parameters.
	Delete All	Deletes all parameters in the current collection.
	Properties	Opens the Key Info dialog box for the selected parameter if a key is set. This button is found to the right of a parameter.

Within the Parameter Collection dialog box, you can create and name new rollouts, add parameters to these rollouts using a Track View Pick dialog box, and save multiple rollouts into collections that can be recalled.

Collections are named by typing a new name in the drop-down list located in the upper-left corner of the interface. This drop-down list holds all available collections. The Collection menu (or the toolbar buttons) may be used to create, rename, duplicate, or delete a collection.

A Parameter Collection can include multiple rollouts. The current active rollout is marked with a yellow bar directly under the rollout title and with brackets that surround the rollout name. Using the Rollout menu (or the toolbar buttons) you can create a new rollout, or rename, reorder, or delete existing rollouts.

Parameters are added to the rollouts using the Parameters ⇨ Add to Selected and the Parameters ⇨ Add to New Rollout menu commands. Both of these commands open a Track View Pick dialog box where you can select the specific parameter to add to the current rollout. To the left of each parameter is a small box that you can use to select the parameter. You can also select parameters using the Edit menu commands.

If multiple parameters are selected, then you can change the values for all selected parameters at the same time by enabling the Edit ⇨ Multiple Edits option. With the Multiple Edits option enabled, changing any parameter value also changes all other selected parameters.

CAUTION

Multiple parameters' values can be changed together only if they are of the same type.

At the bottom of the Edit menu is the Edit Notes menu command. Using this menu command, you can change the parameter's name, link it to a URL, and type some notes about how this parameter works.

The Parameter Collector dialog box can also be used to create animation keys. To create a key for the selected parameters, you'll need to enable the Auto Key button and then select the Parameters ⇨ Key Selected or Parameters ⇨ Key All menu commands. If a key exists for the selected parameter, the Properties button to the right of the parameter becomes active and displays the Key Info dialog box when clicked.

Using the Collection ⇨ Show Selected Keys in Track Bar menu command, you can see the keys for the selected parameters regardless of whether the objects are selected in the viewports.

Adding Custom Parameters

Another useful way to expand the number of parameters is to create custom parameters. These custom parameters can define some aspect of the scene that makes sense to you. For example, if you create a model of a bicycle, you can define a custom parameter for the pedal rotation. You can add your own custom parameters using the Parameter Editor dialog box, shown in Figure 27.4. You can open this modeless panel by choosing Animation ⇨ Parameter Editor (or by pressing the Alt+1 keys).

The Add to Type drop-down list at the top of the Attribute rollout in the Parameter Editor dialog box lets you select where the custom attribute shows up. Custom attributes can be created for an object, for the selected modifier, for the object's material, or for any track found in the Track View. The Pick Explicit Track button opens a dialog box where you can select a specific track.

The Add button creates the custom attribute and adds it to a rollout named Custom Attributes for the specified element. If the specified element is selected, you can click the Edit/Delete button to open the Edit Attributes/Parameters dialog box, shown in Figure 27.5. All custom attributes associated with the selected element are displayed.

27

FIGURE 27.4

You can use the Parameter Editor dialog box to create custom parameters.

Pick Explicit Track

FIGURE 27.5

The Edit Attributes/Parameters dialog box lets you edit or delete custom attributes.

> **NOTE**
> Custom attributes show up in a rollout named Custom Attributes positioned beneath all the other rollouts, but if you add the Attribute Holder modifier to the object before creating the new attribute, then the Custom Attributes rollout appears under the Attribute Holder modifier.

The Edit Attributes/Parameters dialog box lets you select and reorder the custom attributes within their rollout. Selecting a custom attribute also loads its settings into the Parameter Editor where they can be changed.

The Parameter Type drop-down list lets you choose the parameter format. Possibilities include Angle, Array, Boolean (true or false), Color, Float (a decimal point number), fRGBA, Integer, Material, Node, Percent, String, TextureMap, and WorldUnits. The UI Type drop-down list defines how the parameter is displayed in the rollout. How the parameter looks depends on the type of parameter. Float and integer values can be spinners or sliders, Boolean values can be check boxes or radio buttons, array values are drop-down lists, nodes are pick buttons (allowing you to select an object in the viewports), color and RGB values are color pickers, and texture maps are map buttons. You can also name the parameter.

The Options rollout changes depending on which parameter type was selected. These rollouts contain settings for the interface's Width, value ranges, default values, Alignment (left, right, or center), and list items.

The Testing Attribute rollout shows what the interface element will look like and lets you change the attribute to see how the custom parameter works.

The value of custom attributes becomes apparent when you start wiring parameters.

Summary

This chapter covered the feature used to wire parameters together in the Parameter Wire dialog box, which opens up a whole new way to control objects. This chapter also covered how you can create new parameters with the Parameter Collector dialog box. All of these tools give you lots of control over the scene using parameters and expressions. In this chapter, you accomplished the following:

- Wired parameters
- Gathered and edited several parameters at once with the Parameter Collector
- Created custom parameters with the Parameter Editor

In the next chapter, you learn to use the Track View to display and manage all the details of the current scene.

Editing Animation Curves in the Track View

IN THIS CHAPTER

Learning the Track View interface

Understanding the Track View Curve Editor and Dope Sheet layouts

Working with keys and time ranges

Adjusting curves

Filtering tracks

Assigning controllers

Optimizing animation keys

Using out-of-range types

Adding notes to a track

Synching animation to a sound track

A s you move objects around in a viewport, you often find yourself eyeballing the precise location of an object in the scene. If you've ever found yourself wishing that you could precisely see all the values behind the scene, then you need to find the Track View. The Track View can be viewed using three different layouts: Curve Editor, Dope Sheet, and Track Bar. Each of these interfaces offers a unique view into the details of the scene.

These Track View layouts can display all the details of the current scene, including all the parameters and keys. This view lets you manage and control all these parameters and keys without having to look in several different places.

The Track View also includes additional features that enable you to edit key ranges, add and synchronize sound to your scene, and work with animation controllers using curves. And, yes, you can precisely change values, giving your eyeballs a rest.

Learning the Track View Interface

Although the Track View can be viewed using different layouts, the basic interface elements are the same. They all have menus, toolbars, a Controller pane, a Key pane, and a Time Ruler. Figure 28.1 shows these interface elements. You can hide any of these interface elements using the Show UI Elements option in the pop-up menu that appears when you right-click the title bar. Also, you can quickly hide the Controller pane by clicking the triangle icon in the upper-left corner of the Key pane.

FIGURE 28.1

The Track View interface offers a complete hierarchical look at your scene.

Time Ruler

The Track View layouts

The Track View includes three different layouts: a Curve Editor, a Dope Sheet, and the Track Bar. The Curve Editor layout displays all parameter and motion changes as graphs that change over time. You manipulate these curves just like normal splines by selecting and dragging the keys marked as small squares. You also can use the Dope Sheet layout to coordinate key ranges between the different parameter tracks. And the Track Bar layout offers a way to quickly view the Track View within the viewports.

You can open the Curve Editor and Dope Sheet layouts using the Graph Editors menu. You can open the Curve Editor window by choosing Graph Editors ⇨ Track View–Curve Editor or by clicking the Curve Editor button on the main toolbar. You open the Dope Sheet interface in a similar manner by choosing Graph Editors ⇨ Track View–Dope Sheet.

After the Track View opens, you can give it a unique name using the Track View–Curve Editor field found on the Name: Track View toolbar. If the Name toolbar isn't visible, right-click the title bar and select Show Toolbars ⇨ Name: Track View from the pop-up menu. These named views are then listed in the Graph Editors ⇨ Saved Track Views menu. Any saved Track Views that are named are saved along with the scene file, and multiple track views can be named and included with the scene.

To open the Track Bar layout in the viewports, expand the Track Bar using the Open Mini Curve Editor button at the left end of the Timeline. Close the Track Bar layout by clicking the Close button on this same toolbar. Figure 28.2 shows this Track View.

FIGURE 28.2

The Track Bar offers quick access to the Track View.

After you open a Track View, you can switch between the Curve Editor and the Dope Sheet using the Editor menu or by right-clicking the menu bar or toolbar (away from the buttons) and selecting a new layout from the Load Layout menu. You also can save customized layouts using the Save Layout or Save Layout As menu commands.

Track View menus and toolbars

In many cases, the menus and the toolbars provide access to the same functionality. One difference is the Editor menu, which lets you switch the current interface between the Curve Editor and the Dope Sheet layouts. The Curve Editor menus include Editor, Edit, View, Curves, Keys, Tangents, and Show. The Dope Sheet menu loses the Tangents menu and adds a Time menu in its place. The Track Bar menus are the same as the Curve Editor menus and can display both the Curve Editor and the Dope Sheet.

The Track View consists of several toolbars. You can open these toolbars by right-clicking the toolbar (away from the buttons) and selecting the Show Toolbars submenu. The available toolbars depend on the layout (Curve Editor or Dope Sheet). All these toolbars can be docked, floated, and hidden. You also can add and delete new toolbars using the right-click pop-up menu.

> **NOTE**
> Depending on the size of the Track View window, you may need to drag the toolbar to the left to see the buttons at the right end of the toolbar.

Key Controls toolbar

The Key Controls toolbar is the first of the default toolbars for the Curve Editor. Table 28.1 describes these buttons.

28

TABLE 28.1 **Key Controls Toolbar Buttons**

Toolbar Button	Name	Description
	Move Keys, Move Keys Horizontal, Move Keys Vertical	Enables you to move the selected keys or limit their movement to horizontal or vertical
	Draw Curves	Creates a curve by dragging the mouse; Curve Editor layout only
	Add Keys	Lets you add new keys to a track
	Region Keys tool	Lets you drag to select move and/or scale multiple keys at once
	Retime tool	Lets you change the timing for selected tracks
	Retime All tool	Lets you change the timing for all tracks

NEW FEATURE

The Retime and Retime All tools are both new to the Autodesk® 3ds Max® 2013 software.

Navigation toolbar

The Navigation toolbar for the Curve Editor lets you pan and zoom to focus on a specific area of the Track View window. Table 28.2 describes these buttons. This same toolbar is available in the Dope Sheet.

TABLE 28.2 **Navigation Toolbar Buttons**

Status Bar Button	Name	Description
	Pan	Pans the view
	Frame Horizontal Extents, Frame Horizontal Extents Keys	Displays the entire horizontal track or keys
	Frame Value Extents, Frame Value Extents Range	Displays the entire vertical track or the range of values
	Zoom, Zoom Time, Zoom Values	Zooms in and out of the view
	Zoom Region	Zooms within a region selected by dragging the mouse
	Isolate Curve	Temporarily hides all curves except for those with selected keys

Key Tangents toolbar

The Key Tangents toolbar is another of the default Curve Editor toolbars. It is used to set the In and Out curve types. Table 28.3 describes these buttons.

TABLE 28.3 Key Tangents Toolbar Buttons

Toolbar Button	Name	Description
	Set Tangents to Auto, Set In Tangents to Auto, Set Out Tangents to Auto	Sets curve to approach and leave the key in an automatic manner
	Set Tangents to Spline, Set In Tangents to Spline, Set Out Tangents to Spline	Sets curve to approach and leave the key in a custom manner defined by the handle positions
	Set Tangents to Fast, Set In Tangents to Fast, Set Out Tangents to Fast	Sets curve to approach and leave the key in an ascending manner
	Set Tangents to Slow, Set In Tangents to Slow, Set Out Tangents to Slow	Sets curve to approach and leave the key in a descending manner
	Set Tangents to Stepped, Set In Tangents to Stepped, Set Out Tangents to Stepped	Sets curve to approach and leave the key in a stepping manner
	Set Tangents to Linear, Set In Tangents to Linear, Set Out Tangents to Linear	Sets curve to approach and leave the key in a linear manner
	Set Tangents to Smooth, Set In Tangents to Smooth, Set Out Tangents to Smooth	Sets curve to approach and leave the key in a smooth manner

Tangent Actions toolbar

The Tangent Actions toolbar is another of the default toolbars in the Curve Editor. It is used to quickly break and unify tangent handles. Table 28.4 describes these buttons.

TABLE 28.4 Tangent Actions Toolbar Buttons

Toolbar Button	Name	Description
	Break Tangents	Allows the tangent handles on either side of the key to move independently
	Unify Tangents	Moves the tangent handles so they form a straight line

Key Entry toolbar

The Key Entry toolbar in the Curve Editor displays the current frame and value for the selected key. If multiple keys are selected, only the frame value is displayed. You also can enter values in these fields to change the current frame and/or value for the selected key or keys. This is a huge timesaver if you want to change multiple keys to the same value.

The same frame and value fields are available in the Dope Sheet in the Key Stats toolbar.

28

Keys toolbar

The Keys toolbar is the first of the default toolbars in the Dope Sheet, but it also exists in the Curve Editor. Table 28.5 describes these buttons.

TABLE 28.5 Keys Toolbar Buttons

Toolbar Button	Name	Description
	Edit Keys	Enables edit keys mode, Dope Sheet layout only
	Edit Ranges	Enables edit ranges mode, Dope Sheet layout only
	Filters	Opens the Filters dialog box, where you can specify which tracks will appear
	Move Keys, Move Keys Horizontal, Move Keys Vertical	Enables you to move the selected keys or limit their movement to horizontal or vertical
	Slide Keys	Enables you to slide the selected keys
	Scale Keys	Enables you to scale the selected keys
	Scale Values	Enables you to scale the selected values, Curve Editor layout only
	Add Keys	Enables you to add new keys to a track
	Draw Curves	Creates a curve by dragging the mouse; Curve Editor layout only
	Simplify Curve	Reduces the complexity of the curve; Curve Editor layout only

Time toolbar

The Time toolbar is another of the default toolbars for the Dope Sheet. It is used to work with time ranges. Table 28.6 describes these buttons.

TABLE 28.6 Time Toolbar Buttons

Toolbar Button	Name	Description
	Select Time	Enables you to select a block of time by clicking and dragging
	Delete Time	Deletes the selected block of time

Toolbar Button	Name	Description
	Reverse Time	Reverses the order of the selected time block
	Scale Time	Scales the current time block
	Insert Time	Inserts an additional amount of time
	Cut Time	Deletes the selected block of time and places it on the clipboard for pasting
	Copy Time	Makes a copy of the selected block of time and places it on the clipboard for pasting
	Paste Time	Inserts the current clipboard time selection

Display toolbar

The Display toolbar is another of the default toolbars for the Dope Sheet. Table 28.7 describes these buttons.

TABLE 28.7 Display Toolbar Buttons

Toolbar Button	Name	Description
	Lock Selection	Prevents any changes to the current selection
	Snap Frames	Causes moved tracks to snap to the nearest frame
	Show Keyable Icons	Displays a key icon next to all tracks that can be animated
	Modify Subtree	Causes changes to a parent to affect all tracks beneath the parent in the hierarchy; Dope Sheet layout only
	Modify Child Keys	Causes changes to child keys when parent keys are changed; Dope Sheet layout only

Track Selection toolbar

At the bottom edge of the Dope Sheet window are three toolbars that appear by default. These toolbars are the Track Selection, Key Stats, and Navigation. Using these toolbars, you can locate specific tracks, see information on the various keys, and navigate the interface.

In the Track Selection toolbar is the Zoom Selected Object button and the Select by Name field, in which you can type a name to locate any tracks with that name.

> **NOTE**
>
> In the Select by Name field, you also can use wildcard characters such as * (asterisk) and ? (question mark) to find several tracks.

The Key Stats toolbar includes Key Time and Value Display fields that display the current time and value. You can enter values in these fields to change the value for the current time. You also can enter an expression in these fields in which the variable *n* equals the key time or value. For example, to specify a key value that is 20 frames from the current frame, enter *n*+20 (where you supply the current value in place of *n*). You also can include any function valid for the Expression controller, such as sin( ) or log( ). Click the Show Selected Key Stats button to display the key value in the Key pane.

Table 28.8 describes the buttons found in the Track Selection and Key Stats toolbars.

TABLE 28.8 Track Selection and Key Stats Toolbar Buttons

Toolbar Button	Name	Description
	Zoom Selected Object	Places current selection at the top of the hierarchy
	Edit Track Set	Opens a dialog box where selected sets of tracks can be edited
	Filter Selected Tracks Toggle	Toggles to show only the selected tracks in the Controller pane
	Filter Selected Objects Toggle	Toggles to show the tracks for the selected objects in the Controller pane
	Filter Animated Tracks Toggle	Toggles to show only the animated tracks in the Controller pane
	Filter Unlocked Attributes Toggle	Toggles to show only the tracks with unlocked attributes in the Controller pane
	Show Selected Key Statistics	Displays the frame number and values next to each key

Other toolbars

The other toolbars provide access to features that also are available through the menus. These toolbars are hidden by default, but they can be made visible using the Show Toolbars menu command in the right-click pop-up menu.

Controller and Key panes

Below the menus (and below the topped docked toolbars) are two panes. The left pane, called the Controller pane, presents a hierarchical list of all the tracks. The right pane is called the Key pane, and it displays the time range, keys, or curves, depending on the layout. You can pan the Controller pane by clicking and dragging on a blank section of the pane: The cursor changes to a hand to indicate when you can pan the pane.

TIP

Using the triangle icon in the upper-left corner of the Key pane, you can quickly hide the Controller pane.

Each track can include several subtracks. To display these subtracks, click the plus sign (+) to the left of the track name. To collapse a track, click the minus sign (–). You also can use the Show menu to Auto Expand a selected hierarchy. Under the Show⇨ Auto Expand menu are options for Selected Objects Only, Transforms, XYZ Components, Limits, Keyable, Animated, Base Objects, Modifiers, Materials, and Children. For example, if the Auto Expand⇨ Transforms option is enabled, then the Transform tracks for all objects is automatically expanded in the Track View. Using these settings can enable you to quickly find the track you're looking for.

The Show⇨ Auto Select⇨ Animated toggle automatically selects all tracks that are animated. You also can auto select Position, Rotation, and/or Scale tracks. The Show⇨ Track View - Auto Scroll menu command can be set for Selected and/or Objects tracks. This command automatically moves either the Selected tracks or the Objects track to the top of the Controller pane.

NOTE

You also can select, expand, and collapse tracks using the right-click pop-up quad menu.

The Controller pane includes many different types of tracks. Every scene includes many global tracks such as World, Sound, Global Tracks, Video Post, Anim Layer Control Manager, SME, Retimer Manager, Environment, Render Effects, Render Elements, Renderer, Global Shadow Parameters, Scene Materials, Medit Materials (for materials in the Material Editor), and Objects, as shown in Figure 28.3. If the global tracks aren't visible, you can enable them in the Filters dialog box.

FIGURE 28.3

Several tracks are available by default.

The Shift, Ctrl, and Alt keys make selecting and deselecting multiple tracks possible. To select a contiguous range of tracks, select a single track and then select another track while holding down the Shift key. This selects the two tracks and all tracks in between. Hold down the Ctrl key while selecting tracks to select multiple tracks that are not contiguous. The Alt key selects all tracks at the same level. If multiple animated tracks are selected, then all the animation curves for the selected tracks are displayed in the Key pane.

Below the Key pane is the Time Ruler, which displays the current frame range as specified in the Time Configuration dialog box. The current frame is marked with a light blue time bar. This time bar is linked to the Time Slider, and moving one updates the other automatically.

At the top right of the Key pane (above the vertical scroll bar) is a split tab that you can use to split the Controller and Key pane into two separate views, as shown in Figure 28.4. Using this feature, you can look at two different sections of the tree at the same time. This makes it easy to copy and paste keys between different tracks.

TIP
You can drag the Time Ruler vertically in the right pane.

FIGURE 28.4

Drag the tab above the vertical scroll bar to split the Track View into two views.

Split tab

Working with Keys

Keys define the main animation points in an animation. 3ds Max interpolates all the positions and values between the key points to generate the animation. Using the Track View, you can edit these animation keys with precision.

 Chapter 24, "Understanding Animation and Keyframes," covers key creation in more detail.

In the Curve Editor, keys are shown as small squares positioned along the curve, and the color of the curves denotes the type of track it represents. Position curves are red, Rotation curves are green, and Scale curves are blue. Parameter curves are gray. In the Dope Sheet, keys are shown as colored boxes that extend across the applicable tracks, as shown in Figure 28.5. Parent tracks (such as an object's name) are colored gray. Selecting a parent key selects all its children keys. Any selected keys appear white. A track title that includes a key is highlighted yellow in the Controller pane.

CAUTION
If the Key pane is not wide enough, then a key is shown as a thick, black line.

FIGURE 28.5

In the Dope Sheet, Position keys are red, Rotation keys are green, Scale keys are blue, and Parameter keys are gray.

Selecting keys

Before you can move and edit keys, you need to be able to select them. Just like selecting keys on the Track Bar, you select keys by clicking them. Selected keys turn white. To select multiple keys, hold down the Ctrl key while clicking several keys, or drag an outline over several keys to select them. Click away from the keys to deselect all the selected keys.

With a key or multiple keys selected, you can lock the selection with the Lock Selection button on the Tools toolbar. The spacebar is the keyboard shortcut for this button. With the selection locked, you cannot select any new keys.

TIP

If you want to access a specific parameter in the Track View, you can right-click the parameter in the Command Panel and select the Show in Track View command from the pop-up menu, and the Track View loads with the parameter visible.

Using soft selection

The Keys menu also includes a Use Soft Select option. This feature is similar to the soft selection found in the Modify panel when working on a subobject selection, except that it works with keys causing adjacent keys to move along with the selected keys, but not as much. The Keys⇨Soft Select Settings menu command opens a simple toolbar where you can enable soft selection and set the Range and Falloff values.

When enabled, all keys within a specified range are also selected and moved to a lesser degree than the selected key. When enabled, the curve is displayed with a gradient for the Curve Editor layout and as a gradient across the key markers in the Dope Sheet layout. This shows the range and falloff for the curve.

The Keys ⇨ Soft Select Settings menu opens a hidden toolbar that lets you enable and disable the soft selection feature with a single button labeled Soft. The Range value sets how many frames the soft selection covers. This toolbar may be docked to the edge of the window.

Adding and deleting keys

You can add a key by clicking the Add Keys button (or pressing the A key) and clicking the location where the new key should appear. Each new key is set with the interpolated value between the existing keys. This can be done whether the Auto Key button at the bottom of the 3ds Max interface is on or off.

To delete keys, select the keys and press the Delete key on the keyboard. If a key is deleted, the curve changes to account for the missing key.

Moving, sliding, and scaling keys

The Move Keys button (keyboard shortcut M) lets you select and move a key to a new location. You can clone keys by pressing and holding the Shift key while moving a key. Using the flyout buttons, you can select to restrict the movement horizontally or vertically. You also can move the selected key to the Time Slider's location (the current frame) with the Keys ⇨ Align to Cursor menu command.

The Slide Keys button in the Dope Sheet lets you select a key and move all adjacent keys in unison to the left or right. If the selected key is moved to the right, all keys from that key to the end of the animation slide to the right. If the key is moved to the left, then all keys to the beginning of the animation slide to the left.

The Scale Keys button, also in the Dope Sheet, lets you move a group of keys closer together or farther apart. The scale center is the current frame. You can use the Shift key to clone keys while dragging.

If the Edit ⇨ Snap Frames menu command or button (keyboard shortcut S) is enabled (found in the Display toolbar in the Dope Sheet and in the Keys toolbar for the Curve Editor), the selected key snaps to the nearest key as it is moved. This makes aligning keys to the same frame easy.

Using the Region tool

Within the Curve Editor, the Region tool is used to move, slide, and scale a set of selected keys. To use this tool, simply drag in the Key pane over the keys you want to select. A box is displayed around all the selected keys with handles at each edge, as shown in Figure 28.6. The selected keys can be moved to a different location by clicking within the region and dragging to a new location. You can drag the selected keys up or down to change their values or left and right to change their frame.

Dragging on either of the side handles scales the range of the selected keys, and dragging on the top or bottom handles scales their values. The side of the selected handle is the side of the region that moves during a scale operation, but if you press and hold the Shift key, the region is scaled equally from both sides. If you scale the region over any non-selected keys, those non-selected keys are simply deleted. The Region Keys tool remains active until another tool, such as the Move tool is selected. If you click and drag outside of the selected region, a new region is selected.

FIGURE 28.6

The Region Keys tool places handles around each side of the selected keys for sliding and scaling keys.

Scaling Handles

Using the Retime tool

As you work with keys and curves, you may want to move and scale only part of a section of a curve without affecting the sections beyond. Suppose you have a top that moves into position as the spinning starts and slowly stops spinning as it falls over. If the keys for the start and the end of the animation are fine, but you need to move the middle keys, you could use the Retime tool to do this easily.

NEW FEATURE
The Retime and Retime All tools are new to 3ds Max 2013.

When the Retime tool is selected, you can double-click any curve to place a retime marker, which appears as a vertical bar. If you place two markers, as shown in Figure 28.7, then all the keys within those two markers scale as you drag either marker left or right, and all keys outside of these markers slide without any change to their scale.

FIGURE 28.7

The Retime tool lets you scale keys within a specific area.

Retime markers

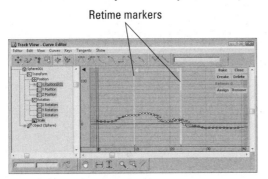

28

In the upper-right corner of the Track View are several yellow buttons that let you control the retime markers. The Bake button commits the current changes and places the keys on the Track Bar. The Close button exits the Retime tool. The Create and Delete buttons add and removes markers, and the Assign and Remove buttons add and remove curves from the current Key pane.

Editing keys

To edit the key parameters for any controller, right-click the key in the Curve Editor or click the Properties button in the Dope Sheet; this opens the Key Info dialog box for most controllers. You also can access this dialog box by right-clicking a track and selecting Properties from the pop-up menu. These commands also can be used when multiple keys on the same or on different tracks are selected.

Using the Randomize Keys utility

The Randomize Keys utility lets you generate random time or key positions with an offset value. To access this utility, select the track of keys that you want to randomize and choose Edit ⇨ Track View Utilities to open the Track View Utilities dialog box. From this dialog box, select Randomize Keys from the list of utilities and click OK; the Randomize Keys utility dialog box opens, as shown in Figure 28.8.

FIGURE 28.8

Use the Randomize Keys utility to create random key positions and values.

In this dialog box, you can specify positive and negative shift values for both Time and Value. Click the Apply button to apply the randomization process.

Using the Euler Filter utility

Euler rotations are easy to understand and use. They provide rotations about each of the three axes or can be thought of as yaw, pitch, and roll, but they have an inherit flaw—they are susceptible to Gimbal flipping and Gimbal lock. Gimbal flipping can occur when the rotation is directed straight up or straight down. This causes the object to instantly flip 180 degrees to continue its rotation. Gimbal lock can occur when two Euler rotation angles are aligned, causing the object to lose a degree of freedom.

To counter these problems, 3ds Max has the ability to use Quaternions instead of Euler angles. Quaternions are vector-based instead of angle-based, so they aren't susceptible to the Gimbal flipping and lock problems, but many animators find Quaternions difficult to understand and use, so they stick to Euler rotations and are watchful for potential problems.

The Track View has a utility that can help if you're dealing with Euler rotations. The Euler Filter utility analyzes the current frame range and corrects any Gimbal flipping that it detects. Selecting this utility from the Track View Utilities dialog box opens a simple dialog box where you can set the range to analyze. You also have an option to Insert Keys if Needed.

Displaying keyable icons

If you're not careful, you could animate a track that you didn't mean to (especially with the Auto Key mode enabled). By marking a track as non-keyable or keyable, you can control which tracks can be animated. To do this, choose the View⇨Keyable Icons menu command. This places a small red key icon to the left of each track that can be animated. You can then click the icon to change it to a non-keyable track. Figure 28.9 shows the Curve Editor with this feature enabled.

FIGURE 28.9

The Keyable Icons feature displays an icon next to all tracks that can be keyed.

Keyable track

Non-keyable track

Editing Time

In some cases, directly working with keys isn't what you want to do. For example, if you need to change the animation length from six seconds to five seconds, you want to work in the Dope Sheet's Edit Ranges mode. To switch to this mode in the Dope Sheet, click the Edit Ranges button on the Keys toolbar. In this mode, the key ranges are displayed as black lines with square markers on either end, as shown in Figure 28.10.

FIGURE 28.10

Click the Edit Ranges button to display the key ranges in the Key pane.

28

Selecting time and the Select Keys by Time utility

Before you can scale, cut, copy, or paste time, you need to select a track and then select a time block. This can be done back in the Edit Keys mode. To select a section of time, click the Select Time button and drag the mouse over the time block.

The Select Keys by Time utility lets you select all the keys within a given time block by entering the frame or time values. To use this utility, click the Track View Utilities button in the Tools toolbar or select the Edit ⇨ Track View Utilities menu command to open the Track View Utilities dialog box, and choose the Select Keys by Time utility from the list. Then in the Select Keys by Time dialog box, enter the Start Time and End Time values to complete the selection.

Deleting, cutting, copying, and pasting time

After you select a block of time, you can delete it by clicking the Delete Time button. Another way to delete a block of time is to use the Cut Time button, which removes the selected time block but places a copy of it on the clipboard for pasting. The Copy Time button also adds the time block to the clipboard for pasting, but it leaves the selected time in the track.

After you copy a time block to the clipboard, you can paste it to a different location within the Track View. The track where you paste it must be of the same type as the one from which you copied it. This is a great way to copy transform keys from one object to another.

All keys within the time block are also pasted, and you can select whether they are pasted relatively or absolutely. *Absolute* pasting adds keys with the exact values as the ones on the clipboard. *Relative* pasting adds the key value to the current initial value at the place where the key is pasted.

You can enable the Exclude Left End Point and Exclude Right End Point buttons on the Extras toolbar when pasting multiple sections next to each other. By excluding either end point, the time block loops seamlessly.

Reversing, inserting, and scaling time

The Reverse Time button flips the keys within the selected time block.

The Insert Time button lets you insert a section of time anywhere within the current track. To insert time, click and drag to specify the amount of time to insert; all keys beyond the current insertion point slide to accommodate the inserted time.

The Scale Time button scales the selected time block. This feature causes all keys to be pushed closer together or farther apart. The scaling takes place around the current frame.

Setting ranges

The Position Ranges button on the Ranges toolbar enables you to move ranges without moving keys. In this mode, you can move and scale a range bar independently of its keys, ignoring any keys that are out of range. For example, this button, when enabled, lets you remove the first several frames of an animation without moving the keys. The Recouple Ranges button (also on the Ranges toolbar) can be used to line up the keys with the range again. The left end of the range aligns with the first key, and the right end aligns with the last key.

Editing Curves

When an object is moving through the scene, estimating the exact point where its position changes direction can sometimes be difficult. Animation curves provide this information by presenting a controller's value as a function of time. The slope of the curve shows the value's rate of change. Steep curves show quick movements. Shallow lines are slow-moving values. Each key is a vertex in the curve. Curves are visible only in the Curve Editor and the Track Bar layout.

Curves mode lets you edit and work with these curves for complete control over the animation parameters.

Inserting new keys and moving keys

Curves with only two keys have slow in and out tangents, making the animation start slow, speed up, and then slow down. You can add more curvature to the line with the addition of another key. To add another key, click the Add Keys button, and then click the curve where you want to place the key.

> **TIP**
> Keep the total number of keys to a minimum. More keys make editing more difficult.

28

If the curve contains multiple curves, such as a curve for the X, Y, and Z Position or RGB color values, then a point is added to each curve. The Move Keys button enables you to move individual keys by dragging them. It also includes flyouts for constraining the key movement to a horizontal or vertical direction.

To scale keys, use the Region Keys tool or the Retime tool.

Tutorial: Animating a monorail

As an example of working with curves, you'll animate a monorail that moves around its track, changing speeds, and stopping for passengers.

To animate the monorail using curves, follow these steps:

1. Open the Monorail.max file from the Chap 28 directory on the CD.

    This file contains a simple monorail setup made from primitives.

2. Click the Play button, and watch the train move around the track.

    As a default, the Path Constraint's Percent track has a Linear Float controller that causes the train to move at a constant speed. To refine the animation, you need to change it.

3. Open the Track View–Curve Editor by first selecting the train object in the scene and then right-clicking and choosing Curve Editor from the pop-up quad menu. The Track View-Curve Editor window opens and shows the Percent track along with a straight linear curve. Select and right-click the Percent track, and select Assign Controller from the pop-up menu to open the Assign Float Controller dialog box. Select the Bézier Float controller, and click OK. Notice how the linear curve changes.

4. Click the Play button. The train starts slowly (represented by the flattish part of the curve), accelerates (the steeper part of the curve), and slows down again (another flattish part).

TIP

When "reading" curves, remember that a steep curve produces fast animation, a shallow curve produces slow animation, a horizontal curve produces no movement or value change, and a straight curve produces a constant animation.

5. You need the train to stop for passengers at the station, so click the Add Keys button and add a key to the curve somewhere around frame 140 when the train is at the dock.

6. Choose the Move Keys Horizontal button from the Move Keys flyout and select the newly created key. Hold down the Shift key, and drag left to copy the key to frame 120.

The curve is flat, so the train stops at the station.

Figure 28.11 shows the final curve after you've completed the editing.

FIGURE 28.11

The finished Percent curve for the train's position along the path

Drawing curves

If you know what the curve you want is supposed to look like, you can actually draw it in the Key pane with the Draw Curves button enabled. This mode adds a key for every change in the curve. You may want to use the Reduce Keys optimization after drawing a curve.

TIP
If you make a mistake, you can just draw over the top of the existing curve to make corrections.

Figure 28.12 shows a curve that was created with the Draw Curves feature.

FIGURE 28.12

Drawing curves results in numerous keys.

Reducing keys

The Curves ⇨ Simplify Curve menu command allows you to optimize the number of keys used in an animation. Certain IK (inverse kinematics) methods and the MassFX system calculate keys for every frame in the scene, which can increase your file size greatly. By optimizing with the Simplify Curve command, you can reduce the file size and complexity of your animations.

Using the Simplify Curve command opens the Simplify Curve dialog box. The threshold value determines how close to the actual position the solution must be to eliminate the key. Figure 28.13 shows the same curve created with the Draw Curves feature after it has been optimized with a Threshold value of 0.5 using the Simplify Curve feature.

FIGURE 28.13

The Simplify Curve feature optimizes the curve by reducing keys.

28

Working with tangents

Animation curves for the Bézier controller have tangents associated with every key. To view and edit these tangents, select the View⇨ All Tangents menu command. These tangents are lines that extend from the key point with a handle on each end. By moving these handles, you can alter the curvature of the curve around the key.

You can select the type of tangent from the Key Tangents toolbar. These can be different for the In and Out portion of the curve. You also can select them using the Key dialog box opened by right-clicking a key. The default tangent type for all new keys is set using the button to the left of the Key Filters button at the bottom of the 3ds Max interface. Using this button, you can quickly select from any of the available tangent types.

You open the Key dialog box, shown in Figure 28.14, by selecting a key and right-clicking it. It lets you specify two different types of tangent points: Continuous and Discontinuous. *Continuous* tangents are points with two handles on the same line. The curvature for continuous tangents is always smooth. *Discontinuous* tangents have any angle between the two handle lines. These tangents form a sharp point.

By default, all tangents are continuous and move together, but you can break them apart to be discontinuous by clicking the Break Tangents button in the Tangent Actions toolbar. This lets each handle be moved independently. Broken tangents can be locked together again with the Unify Tangents button, so they move together. This unifies the tangent handles even if they don't form a straight line.

> ### Tip
> Holding down the Shift key while dragging a handle lets you drag the handle independently of the other handle without having to use the Break Tangents button.

FIGURE 28.14

The Key dialog box lets you change the key's Time, Value, and In and Out tangent curves.

The Lock Tangents button in the Key Info dialog box lets you change the handles of several keys at the same time. If this button is disabled, adjusting a tangent handle affects only the key of that handle.

Tutorial: Animating a flowing river

The default auto-tangent types create a curve that has ease-in and ease-out built into the curve. This causes the animation to start slowly, speed up, and then slow to a stop. While this may be a good starting point for many animations, it won't work for those that should have a constant speed. This example shows how to create a river with a material animated to a constant speed.

To create a flowing river, follow these steps:

1. Open the River.max file from the Chap 28 directory on the CD.

   This file contains a river surface made from a loft. The V Offset for the River Water material's diffuse channel has been animated to simulate flowing water (yes, this river has a checkered past . . .).

2. Click the Play button.

   The river flow starts out slow, speeds up, and then slows to a stop.

> **NOTE**
> The river flows using a checker texture map. Make sure to select a viewport with textures enabled to see the flowing effect.

3. Open the Track View–Curve Editor, and locate and select the V Offset track for the river's material. (You can find this track under the Scene Materials ⇨ River Water ⇨ Maps ⇨ Diffuse Color: Map #2 (Checker) ⇨ Coordinates ⇨ V Offset track.)

4. You have two easy options for creating an animation with a constant speed. The first changes the entire controller type; the second changes the individual key's tangent types.

   Option 1: Right-click over the V Offset track and choose Assign Controller from the pop-up menu to open the Assign Float Controller dialog box. Select Linear Float, and click OK.

   or

   Option 2: Select both keys by clicking one key, holding down the Ctrl button, and clicking the other, or by dragging an outline around both keys. Click the Set Tangents to Linear button.

   Whichever method you use, the line between the two keys is now straight.

5. Click the Play button.

   The river now flows at a constant speed.

6. To increase the speed of the flow, select Move Keys Vertical from the Move Keys button fly-out, and select and move the end key higher in the graph.

   The river flows faster.

Figure 28.15 shows the river as it flows along.

28

FIGURE 28.15

The Checkered River flows evenly.

Applying out-of-range, ease, and multiplier curves

Out-of-range curves define what the curve should do when it is beyond the range of specified keys. For example, you could tell the curve to loop or repeat its previous range of keys. To apply these curves, select a track and select the Out-of-Range Types menu command from the Edit ⇨ Controller menu. This opens a dialog box, shown in Figure 28.16, where you can select from the available curve types.

FIGURE 28.16

The Param Curve Out-of-Range Types dialog box lets you select the type of out-of-range curve to use.

> **NOTE**
>
> You also can apply an out-of-range curve to a select range of frames using the Create Out-of-Range Keys utility. This utility is available via the Edit ⇨ Track View Utilities menu.

By clicking the buttons below the types, you can specify a curve for the beginning and end. This Out-of-Range dialog box includes six options:

- **Constant:** Holds the value constant for all out-of-range frames
- **Cycle:** Repeats the track values as soon as the range ends
- **Loop:** Repeats the range values, like the Cycle option, except that the beginning and end points are interpolated to provide a smooth transition
- **Ping Pong:** Repeats the range values in reverse order after the range end is reached
- **Linear:** Projects the range values in a linear manner when out of range
- **Relative Repeat:** Repeats the range values offset by the distance between the start and end values

You can apply ease curves (choose Curves ➪ Apply Ease Curve, or press Ctrl+E) to smooth the timing of a curve. You can apply multiplier curves (Curves ➪ Apply Multiplier Curve, Ctrl+M) to alter the scaling of a curve. You can use ease and multiplier curves to automatically smooth or scale an animation's motion. Each of these buttons adds a new track and curve to the selected controller track.

Ease and Multiplier curves add another layer of control on top of the existing animation and allow you to edit the existing animation curves without changing the original animation keys. For example, if you have a standard walk cycle, you can use an ease curve to add a limp to the walk cycle or you can reuse the walk cycle for a taller character by adding a multiplier curve.

> **NOTE**
> Not all controllers can have an ease or multiplier curve applied.

You can delete these tracks and curves using the Curves ➪ Remove Ease Curve/Multiplier menu command. You also can enable or disable these curves with the Curves ➪ On/Off Ease Curve/Multiplier menu command.

After you apply an ease or multiplier curve, you can assign the type of curve to use with the Ease Curve Out-of-Range Types button. This button opens the Ease Curve Out-of-Range Types dialog box, which includes the same curve types as the Out-of-Range curves, except for the addition of an Identity curve type.

> **NOTE**
> In the Ease Curve Out-of-Range Types dialog box is an Identity option that isn't present in the Parameter Curve Out-of-Range Types dialog box. The Identity option begins or ends the curve with a linear slope that produces a gradual, constant rate increase.

When editing ranges, you can make the range of a selected track smaller than the range of the whole animation. These tracks then go out of range at some point during the animation. The Ease/Multiplier Curve Out-of-Range Types buttons are used to tell the track how to handle its out-of-range time.

Tutorial: Animating a wind-up teapot

As an example of working with multiplier curves, you'll create a wind-up teapot that vibrates its way across a surface.

28

To animate the vibrations in the Track View, follow these steps:

1. Open the Wind-up teapot.max file from the Chap 28 directory on the CD.

   This file contains a teapot with legs.

2. Click the Play button.

   The teapot's key winds up to about frame 40 and then runs down again as the teapot moves around a bit. To add the random movement and rotation to make the vibrations, you use Noise controllers and Multiplier curves to limit the noise.

3. Open the Track View–Curve Editor, and navigate down to the Wind-up Key's X Rotation track, located at Objects, Teapot Group, Key, Transform, Rotation, X Rotation. Take a moment to observe the shape of the curve, shown in Figure 28.17.

   The key is "wound up" in short spurts and then runs down, slowing until it stops. The vibration, then, should start midway and then taper off as the key runs down.

FIGURE 28.17

The rotation of the Wind-up Key object

When adding the Noise controller, you should assign a List controller first to retain the ability to transform the object independently of the Noise.

NOTE
Assigning controllers through the Animation menu automatically creates a List controller first.

4. Select the Teapot Group's Position track, and click the C key to access the Assign Controller dialog box. Choose Position List and click Ok. Under the Position track are now the X, Y, and Z Position tracks and an Available track. Select the Available track, access the Assign Controller dialog box again, and choose Noise Position and click Ok. The Noise Controller dialog box opens. Close it, and click Play.

NOTE
Remember that the C keyboard shortcut works only if the Keyboard Shortcut Override Toggle button on the main toolbar is enabled.

The teapot vibrates the entire animation. You add a multiplier curve to correct the situation.

5. Select the Noise Position track, and choose Curves ➪ Apply - Multiplier Curve. Select the Multiplier Curve track. Assign the first key a value of **0**. Right-click the first key, and change its Out tangent to Stepped so it holds its value until the next key. Click the Add Keys button, and add a key at frame 50 with a value of **1**. Move the last key to frame 120, and set a value of **0** with Smooth tangents for both In and Out. The Multiplier curve should now look like the curve in Figure 28.18. Select the Noise Position track.

    The noise curve now conforms to the multiplier track with loudest noise where the multiplier curve is at 1.

FIGURE 28.18

The Multiplier curve keeps the Noise track in check.

6. With the Noise Position track still selected, right-click and choose Properties. In the Noise Controller dialog box, set the X and Y Strength to **30**, set the Z strength to **20**, and check the >0 check box for the Z-Strength to keep the teapot from going through the floor. Close the dialog box, and click Play.

    The animation is much better. Next, you add some noise to the Rotation track.

7. Select the Teapot Group's Rotation track, right-click, and choose Assign Controller or press the C key to bring up the Assign Controller dialog box. Select Rotation List, and click OK. Select the Available track, access the Assign Controller dialog box again, and choose Noise Rotation and click Ok.

    Click Play. Again, the noise is out of control.

8. This time, select the Noise Strength track and add a multiplier curve.

    You already have a perfectly good multiplier curve, so you can instance it into the new track.

9. Select the Position Multiplier Curvetrack, right-click, and choose Copy. Now select the rotation Noise Strength Multiplier Curve track, right-click, and choose Paste. Choose Instance, and close the dialog box.

10. Click the Play button, and watch the Teapot wind up and then vibrate itself along until it winds down.

Figure 28.19 shows the teapot as it dances about, compliments of a controlled noise controller.

FIGURE 28.19

The wind-up teapot moves about the scene.

Filtering Tracks and Creating Track Sets

With all the information included in the Track View, finding the exact tracks you need can be difficult. The Filters button on the Controllers toolbar (or in the View menu) can help. Clicking this button (or pressing the Q keyboard shortcut) opens the Filters dialog box, shown in Figure 28.20.

FIGURE 28.20

The Filters dialog box lets you focus on the specific tracks.

TIP

Right-clicking the Filters button reveals a quick list of filter items.

Using the Filters dialog box

Using this dialog box, you can limit the number of tracks that are displayed in the Track View. The Show section contains many display options. The Hide by Controller Type pane lists all the available controllers. Any controller types selected from this list do not show up in the Track View. You also can elect to not display objects by making selections from the check boxes in the Hide By Category section.

The Show Only group includes options for displaying only the Animated Tracks, Selected Objects, Selected Tracks, Visible Objects, Keyable Tracks, Unlocked Attributes, Active Layer, or any combination of these. For example, if you wanted to see the animation track for a selected object, select the Animated Tracks option and click OK; then open the Filters dialog box again, choose Selected Objects, and click OK.

You also can specify whether the curve display includes the Position, Rotation, and Scale components for each axis or the RGB color components.

Creating a track set

A selection of tracks can be saved into a track set by clicking the Edit Track Set button located on the Track Selection toolbar. This button opens the Track Sets Editor, shown in Figure 28.21. Clicking the Create a New Track Set button in the Track Sets Editor creates a new track set containing all the currently selected tracks and lists it in the editor window. Selected tracks can be added, removed, and selected using the other editor buttons.

FIGURE 28.21

The Track Sets Editor dialog box lets you name track selections for easy recall.

Create a new Track Set

Delete Track Sets or Tracks

Add the Track View selection to the current Track Set

Remove the Track View selection from the current Track Set

Highlight tracks selected in the Track View

Select the current track or Track Set in the Track View

After a track set is created, its tracks can be instantly selected by choosing the track set's name from the drop-down list located next to the Edit Track Set button at the bottom of the Track View window.

Working with Controllers

Controllers offer an alternative to positioning keys manually. Each controller can automatically control a key's position or a parameter's value. The Edit ⇨ Controller menu includes several commands for working with controllers. The right-click Copy and Paste commands for controllers let you move existing controllers between different tracks, and the Assign Controller command lets you add a new controller to a track.

Chapter 25, "Animating with Constraints and Simple Controllers," covers all the various controllers used to automate animated sequences.

Although the commands are named Copy and Paste, they can be used to copy different tracks. Tracks can be copied and pasted only if they are of the same type. You can copy only one track at a time, but that single controller can be pasted to multiple tracks. A pasted track can be a copy or an instance, and you have the option to replace all instances. For example, if you have several objects that move together, using the Replace All Instances option when modifying the track for one object modifies the tracks for all objects that share the same motion.

All instanced copies of a track change when any instance of that track is modified. To break the linking between instances, you can use the Edit ⇨ Controller ⇨ Make Unique menu command.

Selecting the Controller ⇨ Assign Controller menu command opens the Assign Controller dialog box, where you can select the controller to apply. If the controller types are similar, the keys are maintained, but a completely different controller replaces any existing keys in the track.

Using visibility tracks

When an object track is selected, you can add a visibility track using the Edit ⇨ Visibility Track ⇨ Add menu command or with the Visibility value in the Object Properties dialog box. This track enables you to make the object visible or invisible. The selected track is automatically assigned the Bézier controller, but you can change it to an On/Off controller if you want that type of control. You can use curves mode to edit the visibility track.

Adding note tracks

You can add note tracks to any track and use them to attach information about the track in the Dope Sheet. The Edit ⇨ Note Track ⇨ Add menu command is used to add a note track, which is marked with a yellow triangle and cannot be animated.

After you've added a note track in the Controller pane, use the Add Keys button to position a note key in the Key pane by clicking in the Note track. This adds a small note icon. Right-clicking the note icon opens the Notes dialog box, where you can enter the notes, as shown in Figure 28.22. Each note track can include several note keys.

The Notes dialog box includes arrow controls that you can use to move between the various notes. The field to the right of the arrows displays the current note key number. The Time value displays the frame where a selected note is located, and the Lock Key option locks the note to the frame so it can't be moved or scaled.

You can use the Tracks ⇨ Note Track ⇨ Remove menu command to delete a selected note track.

FIGURE 28.22

The Notes dialog box lets you enter notes and position them next to keys.

Using the ProSound Plug-in

3ds Max includes an audio plug-in called ProSound for adding multiple audio tracks to a scene. You need to initialize the plug-in before you start, using the Animation panel in the Preference Settings dialog box. You can access this dialog box with the Customize ⇨ Preferences menu.

To select the ProSound plug-in, click the Assign button and select the ProSound option. Once enabled, you can access ProSound by right-clicking the Sound track in the Track View and choosing the Properties menu. This opens the ProSound dialog box, as shown in Figure 28.23.

28

FIGURE 28.23

The ProSound dialog box lets you configure sounds to play during the animation.

Using the ProSound dialog box, you can load and arrange multiple sound files. ProSound supports loading in WAV and AVI sound files. For the selected sound file, you can view its Length, Format, and Statistics. You also can set the sound's Start and End frame. Multiple other options are available for controlling how the audio file plays and how it interacts with other sounds.

The ProSound dialog box also includes some Metronome settings for keeping a defined beat. For a metronome, you can specify the beats per minute and the beats per measure. The first option sets how often the beats occur, and the second option determines how often a different tone is played. This dialog box also contains an Active option for turning the metronome on and off.

Tutorial: Adding sound to an animation

As an example of adding sound to an animation, you'll work with a hyper pogo stick and synchronize its animation to a sound clip.

To synchronize an animation to a sound clip, follow these steps:

1. Open the Hyper pogo stick.max file from the Chap 28 directory on the CD.

2. Open the Preference Settings dialog box with the Customize ⇨ Preferences menu command, and select the Animation panel. Click the Assign button in the Sound Plug-In section, and double-click the ProSound option and click Ok.

3. In the Track View–Dope Sheet window, select and right-click the Sound track and select Properties from the pop-up menu to open the ProSound dialog box. In this dialog box, click the Add button. Then locate the Boing.wav file from the Chap 28 directory on the CD, and click Open. Make sure the Permit Playback option is selected.

4. Expand the Boing.wav track to see the Waveform, as shown in Figure 28.24.

FIGURE 28.24

Sounds loaded into the sound track appear as waveforms.

> **NOTE**
> The ProSound dialog box includes a play button that lets you play the sound before loading it.

5. Enter a Start frame value of **2** in the ProSound dialog box for the audio file to align with the pogo stick's upward motion.

6. Click the Play Animation button, and the sound file plays with the animation.

Figure 28.25 shows the sound track under the Track Bar for this example.

FIGURE 28.25

To help synchronize sound, the audio track can be made visible under the Track Bar.

Summary

Using the Track View, you have access to all the keys, parameters, and tracks in a scene in one convenient location. Different features are available in the different layouts. In this chapter, you accomplished the following:

- Learned the Track View interface elements
- Learned about the different Track View layouts, including the Curve Editor, Dope Sheet, and Track Bar
- Discovered how to work with keys, times, and ranges
- Controlled and adjusted curves
- Selected specific tracks using the Filters dialog box
- Assigned controllers
- Explored the different out-of-range types
- Added notes to a track
- Added multi-track audio with ProSound

The next chapter dives into working with characters, rigging, and bones.

Part VII

Working with Characters

IN THIS PART

29

Understanding Rigging, Kinematics, and Working with Bones

IN THIS CHAPTER

Creating a rigging workflow

Building a bones system

Setting bone parameters and IK Solvers

Making linked objects into a bones system

Understanding Forward and Inverse Kinematics

Learning to work with the available IK solvers

What does a graveyard have in common with animated characters? The answer is bones. Bones are used as an underlying structure attached to a character skin that is to be animated. By using a bones structure, you can produce complex character motions by simply animating the bones and not having to move all the vertices associated with a high-resolution character mesh.

Although the Autodesk® 3ds Max® 2013 software includes a prebuilt skeleton with its Biped and CAT systems, at times you may want to build a custom bones system because not all characters stand on two feet. Have you ever seen a sci-fi movie in which the alien was less than humanlike? If your character skeleton can't be created easily by modifying a biped or CAT skeleton, then you must use the traditional manual methods of rigging by building a skeleton from scratch using bone objects.

This chapter focuses on the process of manually rigging a character that, depending on the complexity of your character, could end up being even easier than working with bipeds. It also gives you a clear idea of what is involved in rigging a character.

Understanding Rigging

A rigged character consists of two parts—an underlying skeleton made of individual linked bones and a high resolution skin mesh that defines how the character looks. The skeleton is the part of the rig that is animated and holds all the animation keys, and the skin is bound to the skeleton and follows the bones as they move. When the animation is complete, the skeleton is hidden and the skin alone is rendered.

The rig's skeleton consists of bones that are organized in a linked hierarchy. A linked hierarchy attaches, or links, one object to another and makes it possible to transform the attached object by moving the one to which it is linked. The arm is a classic example of a linked hierarchy: When the shoulder rotates, so do the elbow, wrist, and fingers. Establishing linked hierarchies can make moving, positioning, and animating many connected objects easy.

A bones system is a unique case of a linked hierarchy that has a specific structure. You can create a structure of bones from an existing hierarchy, or you can create a bones system and attach objects to it. A key advantage of a bones system is that you can use IK (Inverse Kinematics) Solvers to manipulate and animate the structure. These IK Solvers enable the parents to rotate when the children are moved. In this way, the IK Solver maintains the chain integrity.

After the bone structure is created, it needs to be edited to fit the skin mesh that it will control. You also need to define the limits of each bone and joint. This helps prevent the skeleton from moving in unrealistic ways. Applying IK systems is another way to control the motion of the bones and joints. This process of creating a skeleton structure and defining its limits is called *rigging*. Rigging also involves building specialized animation controls.

After you've edited a system of bones, you can cover the bones with objects that have the Skin modifier applied. This modifier lets the covering object move and bend with the bones structure underneath. The process of attaching a model to a bones system and setting the various skin weights is called *skinning*.

The Skin modifier is covered, along with other aspects of skinning a character, in Chapter 30, "Skinning Characters."

After a character is rigged and skinned, the character is ready to be animated.

A typical rigging workflow

The goal of creating a rigged character is that it's easy to animate. In a typical studio environment, this involves several key players. First on the scene is the modeler. The modeler builds the character as a high-resolution mesh complete with materials. This model, which is typically a single object, is known as the skin for the character, and it usually is posed using a standard T-pose, as shown in Figure 29.1, with feet flat at shoulder width, eyes and head looking forward, and arms stretched out straight with palms down.

FIGURE 29.1

The Futureman character displayed in a standard T-pose

The second player in this process is the rigger. This person takes the skin model and builds a skeleton made of bones that is used to control the attached skin. For a standard human character, this skeleton includes a separate bone for every straight section of the character, similar to the way a real set of bones would work. At the places where the model needs to bend, a joint is placed, such as at the knees and elbows. Each bone also can be constrained to allow only proper motion. For example, the elbow joint is limited to bend only within a 180 degree range, which keeps it from bending unrealistically backward.

Another task for the rigger is to build animation controls that let the animator quickly create all the animation keys for specific motions. These controls could include morph targets used to create facial expressions or other special controls for manipulating the hands and feet.

The rigger also attaches the skin to the skeleton and defines the skin weights. Skin weights associate each skin vertex with a specific bone or set of bones. These skin weights determine how the skin moves and bends with the animated bones. For example, the vertices in the center of the thigh are weighted to move with the thigh bone, but vertices near the knee must be weighted to move with the thigh and shin bones, so the weighting is split between those two bones.

After the character is fully rigged and skinned, it is turned over to an animator who uses the skeleton and the animation controls to complete the animations for the character. As the animator is working with the character rig, he or she may request additional controls and adjustments from the rigger, so all team members are still involved until the final animations are completed.

Building a Bones System

To create a skeleton, you need to build a hierarchy of objects that are linked together. This can be done using primitives and the Select and Link tool, but an easier way to build this hierarchy is to use

29

a *bones system*. A bones system consists of many bone objects that are linked together. These bone objects are normally not rendered, but you can set them to be renderable, like splines. You can also assign an IK Solver to the bones system for controlling their motion.

To create a bones system, select Create ⇨ Systems ⇨ Bones IK Chain, click in a viewport at the location for the start of the bone, and click again to place the bone's end. Each successive click adds another bone linked to the bone chain. Each bone has a thick end that represents the bone's head and a tapered small end, which is the tail. When you're finished adding bones, right-click to exit bone creation mode. In this manner, you can create a long chain of bone objects all linked together. Each bone is named simply Bone followed by a three-digit number.

When you right-click to exit bone creation mode, an End bone is added to the bone chain. This End bone doesn't have any length and is used to mark the end of the chain. It also is used by the IK solver and is a necessary part of the bone chain.

These bones are actually linked joints. Moving one bone pulls its neighbors in the chain along with it. Bones can also be rotated, scaled, and stretched. Scaling a bones system affects the distance between the bones. The pivot point for rotating and scaling bones is the bone's head.

CAUTION
Bones should never be scaled after keys are set without the XForm modifier applied, or all animation keys will behave erratically.

To branch the hierarchy of bones, simply click the bone where you want the branch to start while still in bone creation mode (the Bones button in the Command Panel is still highlighted). A new branching bone is created automatically with its head located where the tail of the clicked bone is. Then position and click in the viewport to place the new bone's tail. Continue to click to add new bones to the branch, and right-click to end the new branch. Right-click a second time to turn bone creation mode off.

Assigning an IK Solver

When you first create a bone chain in the IK Chain Assignment rollout of the Create panel, you can select from four IK Solvers: History Dependent, IKHISolver, IKLimb, and SplineIK Solver. You can assign each of these solver types to children and to the root bone using the available options. You need to select both the Assign to Children and the Assign to Root options to assign the IK Solver to all bones in the system. If the Assign to Children option is deselected, then the Assign to Root option is disabled. More on these IK solvers is presented later in this chapter.

Setting bone parameters

The Bone Parameters rollout includes parameters for setting the size of each individual bone, including its Width and Height. You can also set the percentage of Taper applied to the bone. By changing these parameters, you can make the bone appear long and flat, which is helpful for manipulating Plane objects.

> **TIP**
>
> Because bones are simple geometry objects, you can apply an Edit Poly modifier to it and edit the bone shape to be whatever you'd like. However, custom bone geometry doesn't always work with the Bone Tools.

Fins can be displayed on the front, back, and/or sides of each bone by enabling the Fin options. For each fin, you can specify its size and start and end taper values. Including fins on your bones makes correctly positioning and rotating the bone objects easier. It is often helpful to have the Front (or Back) Fin enabled, so you can tell when the bone is upside down. Figure 29.2 shows a simple bones system containing two bones with fins enabled.

FIGURE 29.2

This bone includes fins that make understanding its orientation easier.

At the bottom of the Bone Parameters rollout is an option to Generate Mapping Coordinates. Bones are renderable objects, so this option lets you apply texture maps to them.

> **TIP**
>
> Although bones can be rendered, they are most often hidden for the final render, but applying a bright color or texture to the bones helps them to be seen easily, and it's the sharp reminder to hide all bones when doing final test renders.

Defining joint constraints

The next step is to define the joint constraints, which you specify in the Sliding Joints and Rotational Joints rollouts. These rollouts are found in the Hierarchy panel of the Command Panel if you click the IK button when a bone is selected.

By default, each joint has six degrees of freedom, meaning that the two objects that make up the joint can each move or rotate along the X-, Y-, or Z-axis. The axis settings for all other sliding and rotational joints are identical. Defining joint constraints enables you to constrain these motions to prevent unnatural motions, such as an elbow bending backward. To constrain an axis, select the bone object that includes the pivot point for the joint, locate in the appropriate rollout the section for the axis that you want to restrict, and deselect the Active option. If an axis's Active option is deselected, the axis is constrained. You also can limit the motion of joints by selecting the Limited option.

When the Limited option is selected, the object can move only within the bounds set by the From and To values. The Ease option causes the motion of the object to slow as it approaches either limit. The Spring Back option lets you set a rest position for the object; the object returns to this position when pulled away. The Spring Tension sets the amount of force that the object uses to resist being moved from its rest position. The Damping value sets the friction in the joint, which is the value with which the object resists any motion.

> **NOTE**
> As you enter values in the From and To fields, the object moves to that value to show visually the location specified. You also can press and hold the left mouse button on the From and To values to cause the object to move temporarily to its limits. These settings are based on the current Reference Coordinate system.

Naming bones

A critical, but often forgotten, step in rigging is naming the bones. When bones are created, they are automatically given a name, which is simply "Bone" and a number. As the skeleton gets more complex, these numbered names make it hard to find anything. Naming each bone using the Name field in the Command panel is essential. You also can use the Rename Objects dialog box in the Tools menu to quickly rename multiple bones.

Tutorial: Creating a bones system for an alligator

To practice creating a bones system, you'll take a trip to the Deep South to gator country. The main movement for this gator is going to be in its tail, so you need the most bones there. The front legs are smaller and can be controlled with only two simple bones. You also won't worry about fingers.

To create a bones system for an alligator, follow these steps:

1. Open the Alligator bones.max file from the Chap 29 directory on the CD.

   This file includes an alligator model created by Viewpoint Datalabs.

2. Select Create ⇨ Systems ⇨ Bones IK Chain, and in the IK Chain Assignment rollout, select IK Limb from the IK Solver drop-down list. Then set the Width and Height values to **10**, enable the Side Fins, and set the Size to **5**.

3. In the Top viewport, click once at the top of the tail, again at a spot between the gator's two back legs, again at the mid-abdomen between the two front legs, again at the base of the neck, and finally at the end of the nose. Then right-click to end the bones chain.

4. While still in Bones mode, click below the first bone without clicking on the bone and create an additional five bones that run down the length of tail. Then right-click to end the chain, and right-click again to exit bone creation mode. Select the first bone in the tail chain, and link it to the first joint in the upper bone chain with the Select and Link tool.

TIP

If you can't see the bones to make the link, then hide the body so the bones are clearly visible.

5. Click the Bones button in the Create panel, and select the bone just below the back set of legs in the Top viewport (the cursor changes to a cross-hair when it is over a bone). This creates a new branch from the end of the clicked bone. Then click to place new bones at the gator's knee, ankle, and tip of the foot. Right-click to end the chain. Repeat to create bones for the opposite leg.

6. Click the Select Objects button on the main toolbar to exit Bones mode, and select and name each bone object so it can be easily identified later.

TIP

The Schematic View window is a good interface for quickly labeling bones.

Figure 29.3 shows the completed bones system for the alligator.

FIGURE 29.3

This bones system for an alligator was easy to create.

Using the Bone Tools

After you've created a bones system, you can use the Bone Tools to edit and work with the bones system. You access these tools from a panel that is opened using the Animation ➪ Bone Tools menu command. Figure 29.4 shows this panel of tools, which includes three separate rollouts: Bone Editing Tools, Fin Adjustment Tools, and Object Properties.

FIGURE 29.4

The Bone Tools dialog box includes several buttons for working with bones systems.

Reordering bones

You can use the transform buttons on the main toolbar to move, rotate, and scale a bone along with all its children, but if you want to transform the parent without affecting any of the children, you need to open the Bone Tools panel using the Animation ➪ Bone Tools menu command. Bone Edit Mode lets you move and realign a bone without affecting its children.

Clicking the Remove Bone button removes the selected bone and reconnects the bone chain by stretching the child bone. If you hold down the Shift key while removing a bone, the parent is stretched. Clicking the Delete Bone button deletes the selected bone and adds an End bone to the last child.

> **CAUTION**
> Using the Delete key to delete a bone does not add an End bone, and the bone chain does not work correctly with an IK Solver.

If a bone exists that isn't connected to another bone, you can add an End bone to the bone using the Create End button. The bone chain must end with an End bone in order to be used by an IK Solver.

The Connect Bones button lets you connect the selected bone with another bone. After clicking this button, you can drag a line from the selected bone to another bone to connect the two bones.

Use the Reassign Root button to reverse the chain and move the End bone from the parent to the last child.

Refining and mirroring bones

As you start to work with a bones system that you've created, you may discover that the one long bone for the backbone of your monster is too long to allow the monster to move like you want. If this happens, you can refine individual bones using the Refine button. This button appears at the bottom of the Bone Tools section of the Bone Editing Tools rollout.

Clicking the Refine button enables you to select bones in the viewport. Every bone that you select is divided into two bones at the location where you click. Click on the Refine button again to exit Refine mode.

The Mirror button lets you create a mirror copy of the selected bones. This button makes the Bone Mirror dialog box appear, where you can select the Mirror Axis and the Bone Axis to Flip. You also can specify an Offset value. In the previous example, you easily could have created the arms and legs manually for one side of the gator and then used the Mirror button to create its opposite.

Coloring bones

Bones, like any other objects, are assigned a default object color, and materials can be applied from the Material Editor. For each separate bone, its object color can be changed in the Modify panel or in the Bone Tools dialog box.

You can also apply a gradient to a bone chain using the Bone Tools dialog box. This option is available only if two or more bones are selected. The Start Color is applied to the chain's head, and the End Color is applied to the last selected child. The colors are applied or updated when the Apply Gradient button is clicked. Figure 29.5 shows a long, spiral bone chain with a white-to-black gradient applied.

FIGURE 29.5

A white-to-black gradient was applied to this spiral bone chain.

Adjusting fins

The Fin Adjustment Tools rollout includes the same parameters as those found in the Bone Parameters rollout. You can specify the dimensions and taper of a bone and its fins. But you can also specify that the parameters are applied using Absolute or Relative values. Relative values are based on the parameters of the bone that is above the current bone in the chain.

This rollout also includes Copy and Paste buttons that you can use to copy the bone parameters from one bone to another.

Making objects into bones

You can make any object act like a bone. To make an object into a bone, you need to open the Object Properties rollout in the Bone Tools dialog box. The Object Properties rollout includes a setting for Bone On. If enabled, the object acts like a bone. When the Bone On/Off option is enabled, the remaining Bone controls become available. The Auto-Align option causes the pivot points of adjacent bones to be aligned automatically. The Freeze Length option causes a bone to keep its length as the bones system is moved. If the Freeze Length is disabled, you can specify a Stretch type. None prevents any stretching from occurring, and Scale changes the size along one axis, but Squash causes the bone to get wider as its length is decreased and thinner as it is elongated. You can also select to stretch an axis and choose whether to Flip the axis.

You can use the Realign button to realign a bone to its original orientation. Click the Reset Stretch or Reset Scale button to reset the stretch or scale value to its original value.

Forward Kinematics versus Inverse Kinematics

The biggest advantage of using a bones system is that it moves according to kinematic principles. *Kinematics* is a branch of mechanics that deals with the motions of a system of objects, so *Inverse Kinematics* is its evil twin brother that deals with the non-motion of a system of objects, right? Well, not exactly.

In 3ds Max, a system of objects is a bunch of objects that are linked together. After a system is built and the parameters of the links are defined, the motions of all the pieces below the parent object can be determined as the parent moves, using kinematics formulas. This is called Forward Kinematics.

 Chapter 8, "Grouping, Linking, and Parenting Objects," covers linking objects and creating kinematics chains.

Forward Kinematics is really just a complex word for a simple concept. When a bones system is set up using linked objects, moving any bone in the system automatically affects all its children. For example, when the shoulder bone is rotated, the arm, forearm, and hand bones all move together along with the shoulder. This works great for some motions like walking because you can get all the motions of the legs moving and the arms swinging by simply rotating the top arm and leg bones.

Forward Kinematics works great for some types of motion, but imagine animating a character reaching for light switch. To animate this motion, you'd need to rotate the hip, shoulder, elbow, and wrist to get the hand even close, and then you'd have to work with the fingers until the motion looks good, but it is hard to correctly position the finger even close to the light switch unless multiple bones are rotated. This is a motion where Inverse Kinematics is a better choice.

Inverse Kinematics (IK) is different from Forward Kinematics in that it switches the control of the bones from parent controlling child to child controlling parent. Inverse Kinematics determines all the motions of objects in a system when the last object in the hierarchy chain is moved. The position of the last object, such as a finger or a foot, is typically the one you're concerned with. With IK, you can use these solutions to animate the system of objects by moving the last object in the system. So, using IK, you can drag the hand to the exact position you want, and all other parts in the system follow.

Forward Kinematics is an automatic result of a linked system of bones, so nothing needs to be added to the system to use FK. An IK system, on the other hand, needs to be set up. This is done by simply selecting the start and end bones and then enabling IK for the bone chain that runs between these two. Once established, you use the End Effector object to control the IK system.

Creating an Inverse Kinematics System

Before establishing an IK system, you need to decide where you need one. For human characters, it is helpful to have an IK system for each of the different limbs. IK also is used on long bending extremities like tails and antennae. The spine is another good place to include an IK chain.

3ds Max includes several different IK options, and the one to use depends on the type of motion you need. These IK solvers are set using the drop-down list found in the IK Chain Assignment rollout of the Command Panel when creating a bone chain. To apply the selected IK Solver, make sure the Assign to Children option is enabled.

If you forget to enable the Assign to Children option or if you want to switch the IK solver, you also can apply an IK solver with the selected bone as the root using the Animation ⇨ IK Solvers options. After selecting an option, click the end bone for the IK and an IK chain is created from the initial selection to the picked bone, except for the IK Limb solver, which always is applied to two bones. These are the four available IK solvers:

- **History Independent (HI):** This is the most versatile of the solvers. It can work with a long bone chain, and it uses a Swivel Angle setting to control how the bone chain twists as it moves.
- **History Dependent (HD):** This solver places a point object at each joint in the chain. It isn't as easy to use as the HI solver, but it does allow for sliding joints.
- **IK Limb:** This solver works only on two bones and is good for simple chains such as the upper and lower arm.
- **Spline IK:** This solver lets you select a spline that moves parallel to a bone chain, and it places dummy object handles at regular intervals along the spline.

29

You can tell when an IK solver is applied to a bone chain because a blue point object appears at the pivot point for the end bone. This point is the goal, which is given the name IK Chain and a number. At this same pivot is a green point object called the End Effector. If you select and move the goal object, then the solver works to make the End Effector match the position and orientation of the goal, and the other bones realign to accommodate the motion. When the goal is selected, a white line is displayed between the start and end bones.

When an IK chain is selected, its settings are found in the Motion panel. Using these settings, you can enable or disable the IK chain and change the chain thresholds and iterations. It also lists the Start and End Joints and lets you pick new start and end bones if you wish.

History Independent (HI) IK solver

The History Independent (HI) IK solver is the best option to use when the bone chain you want to control has lots of links. This solver looks at each keyframe independently when making its solution, which makes it speedy. You can animate linked chains with this IK solver applied by positioning the goal object; the solver then inserts a keyframe at the pivot point of the last object in the chain to match the goal object.

The first rollout in the Motion panel after the Assign Controller rollout is the IK Solver rollout. Using this rollout, you can select to switch between the HI IK solver and the IK Limb solver. The Enabled button lets you disable the solver. By disabling the solver, you can use Forward Kinematics to move the objects. To return to the IK solution, simply click the Enabled button again. The IK for FK Pose option enables IK control even if the IK solver is disabled. This lets you manipulate the hierarchy of objects using Forward Kinematics while still working with the IK solution. If both the IK for FK Pose and the Enabled buttons are disabled, then the goal can move without affecting the hierarchy of objects.

If the goal ever gets moved away from the end link, clicking the IK/FK Snap button automatically moves the goal to match the end links position. Auto Snap automatically keeps the goal and the end link together. The Set as Preferred Angle button remembers the angles for the IK system. These angles can be recalled at any time using the Assume Preferred Angle button.

If you want to change the start and end bone objects, you can click the Pick Start Joint or Pick End Joint button and choose the new bone.

CAUTION

If you select a child as the start joint and an object above the child as the end joint, then moving the goal has no effect on the IK chain.

The IK Solver Properties rollout includes the Swivel Angle value. The swivel angle defines the plane that includes the joint objects and the line that connects the starting and ending joints. This plane is key because it defines the direction in which the joint moves when bent. If the IK chain is selected, you also can display and manipulate the swivel angle by enabling the Select and Manipulate button on the main toolbar. By moving the swivel angle control, you can set the direction in which the chain bends as the End Effector is moved. For example, a knee could be set to point outward for a bull-legged cowboy character. Figure 29.6 shows a multi-bone chain with the HI IK solver applied. The chain has been duplicated and shown at different swivel angles.

FIGURE 29.6

Adjusting the swivel angle changes the plane within which the chain moves.

The IK Solver Properties rollout also includes Threshold values. These values determine how close the end joint and the goal must be before the solution is pronounced valid. You can set thresholds for Position and Rotation. The Iterations value sets the number of times the solution is tried.

TIP

Setting the Iterations value to a higher number produces smoother (less jerky) results, but it increases the time required to find a solution.

The IK Display Options rollouts can enable, disable, and set the size of the gizmos used when working with IK solvers. Using this rollout, you can Enable the End Effector, the Goal, the Swivel Angle Manipulator, and the IK solver (which is the line connecting the start and end joints).

History Dependent (HD) IK solver

The History Dependent (HD) IK solver takes into account the previous keyframes as it makes a solution. This solver makes having very smooth motion possible, but the cost of time to compute the solution is increased significantly.

This IK solver places an End Effector at the pivot point of the last bone, but it also places a point object at every bone in the chain. Moving the End Effector changes the position of all the bones in the chain, and you can move the other point objects at each joint to create a sliding effect. This IK solver shows up as a controller in the Motion panel when the IK chain is selected. The settings are contained in a rollout named IK Controller Parameters, which is visible in the Motion panel if you select one of the End Effector gizmos. The End Effector gizmo is the object that you move to control the IK chain. It is displayed as a set of crossing axes.

Any parameter changes affect all bones in the current structure. In the Thresholds section, the Position and Rotation values set how close the End Effector must be to its destination before the solution is complete. In the Solution section, the Iterations value determines the maximum number of times the solution is attempted. The Start Time and End Time values set the frame range for the IK solution.

The Show Initial State option displays the initial state of the linkage and enables you to move it by dragging the End Effector object. The Lock Initial State option prevents any linkage other than the End Effector from moving.

The Update section enables you to set how the IK solution is updated with Precise, Fast, and Manual options. The Precise option solves for every frame, Fast solves for only the current frame, and Manual solves only when the Update button is clicked. The Display Joints options determine whether joints are Always displayed or only When Selected.

When you first create a bones system, an End Effector is set to the last joint automatically. In the End Effectors section, at the bottom of the IK Controller Parameters rollout, you can set any joint to be a Positional or Rotational End Effector. To make a bone an End Effector, select the bone and click the Create button. If the bone is already an End Effector, then the Delete button is active. You also can link the bone to another parent object outside of the linkage with the Link button. The linked object then inherits the transformations of this new parent.

Click the Delete Joint button in the Remove IK section to delete a joint. If a bone is set to be an End Effector, the Position or Rotation button displays the Key Info parameters for the selected bone.

Tutorial: Animating a spyglass with the HD IK solver

A telescoping spyglass is a good example of a kinematics system that you can use to show off the HD solver. The modeling of this example is easy because it consists of a bunch of cylinders that gradually get smaller.

To animate a spyglass with the HD IK solver, follow these steps:

1. Open the Spyglass.max file from the Chap 29 directory on the CD.

   This file includes a simple spyglass made from primitive objects. The pieces of the spyglass are linked from the smallest section to the largest section. At the end of the spyglass is a dummy object linked to the last tube object.

2. To define the joint properties, select the largest tube object, open the Hierarchy panel, and click the IK button. In the Object Parameters rollout, select the Terminator, Bind Position, and Bind Orientation options to keep this joint from moving.

3. With the largest tube section selected, make the Z Axis option active in the Sliding Joints rollout, and disable all the axes in the Rotational Joints rollout. Click the Copy button for both Sliding Joints and Rotational Joints in the Object Parameters rollout.

4. Select each remaining tube object individually, and click the Paste buttons for both the Sliding Joints and Rotational Joints.

   This enables the local Z-axis sliding motion for all tube objects.

5. Select the largest tube section again, and choose Animation ⇨ IK Solvers ⇨ HD Solver. Then drag the dotted line to the dummy object at the end of the spyglass.

6. Select the second largest tube object, and back in the Motion panel for the Sliding Joint Z Axis, select the Limited option with values from **0.0** to **−80**. Click the Copy button for the Sliding Joints in the Object Parameters rollout. Select tubes 3 through 6 individually, and click the Paste button for the Sliding Joints to apply these same limits to the other tube objects.

7. Click the Auto Key button (or press N), drag the Time Slider to frame 100 (or press End), select the Select and Move button on the main toolbar (or press W), and drag the dummy object away from the largest tube object.

Figure 29.7 shows the end tube segment collapsing within the spyglass.

FIGURE 29.7

The HD IK solver is used to control the spyglass.

29

IK Limb solver

The IK Limb solver was specifically created to work with limbs. It is used on chains of two bones such as an upper leg and lower leg. Only two of the bones in the chain actually move. The goal for these joints is located at the pivot point for the second bone. This solver is ideal for game character rigging.

This solver works by considering the first joint as a spherical joint that can rotate along three different axes, such as a hip or shoulder joint. The second joint can bend only in one direction, such as an elbow or knee joint.

The rollouts and controls for the IK Limb solver, including the swivel angle, are exactly the same as those used for the HI solver covered earlier in this chapter.

Tutorial: Animating a spider's leg with the IK Limb solver

As an example of the IK Limb solver, you should probably animate a limb, so I created a simple spider skeleton with not two limbs, but eight. I created this skeleton fairly quickly using four bones for the abdomen; then I created one limb and cloned it three times. Then I used the Bone Tools to connect the leg bones to the abdomen bones, and finally I selected and mirrored the bones on all four legs to get the opposite legs. The hardest part was naming all the bones.

To animate a spider skeleton's leg using the IK Limb solver, follow these steps:

1. Open the Spider skeleton.max file from the Chap 29 directory on the CD.

2. Click the Select by Name button on the main toolbar (or press the H key) to open the Select From Scene dialog box. Double-click the RUpperlegBone0l object to select the upper leg bone object.

3. With the upper leg bone selected, choose Animation ⇨ IK Solvers ⇨ IK Limb Solver. A dotted line appears in the viewport. Press the H key again to open the Pick Object dialog box, and double-click the RFootBone0l object to select it.

   This bone corresponds to the foot bone, which is the end of the limb hierarchy.

4. With the IK Chain01 object selected, click the Auto Key button (or press the N key) and drag the Time Slider to frame 100 (or press End). With the Select and Move button (or by pressing the W key), move the IK chain in the viewport.

   The leg chain bends as you move the End Effector.

Figure 29.8 shows the spider's leg being moved via the IK Limb solver. The IK Limb solver provides a simple and quick way to add an Effector to the end of a limb, giving you good control for animating the spider's walk cycles.

FIGURE 29.8

You can use the IK Limb solver to control limbs such as legs and arms.

Spline IK solver

The IK Limb solver works well for arms and legs that have a joint in the middle, but it doesn't work well for tails. Tails are unique because they require multiple bones to deform correctly. The Spline IK solver works well for tails, but it also works well for rigging tentacles, chains, and rope.

To use the Spline IK solver, you need to create a chain of bones and a spline path. By selecting the first and last bone and then selecting the spline, the bone chain moves to the spline. Each control point on the spline has a dummy object associated with it. By moving these dummy objects, you can control the position of the bones. At either end of the spline are manipulators that you can use to twist and rotate the bones.

The easiest way to use this IK solver is to select SplineIKSolver from the drop-down list in the IK Chain Assignment rollout while you're creating the bone structure. After the bone structure is complete, the Spline IK Solver dialog box, shown in Figure 29.9, appears. If the Auto Create Spline option is enabled, then a spline to match the bone chain is created. With this dialog box, you also can select a name for the IK chain, specify the curve type, and set the number of spline knots. The curve type options include Bézier, NURBS Point, and NURBS CV. You also can select to Create Helpers and to display several options.

29

FIGURE 29.9

The Spline IK Solver dialog box automatically creates the spline for you.

Another way to use this IK solver is with an existing bone structure. To do this, you need a spline curve in the scene that matches how you want the bone chain to look. Select the first bone where you want the solver to be applied, and choose Animation ⇨ IK Solvers ⇨ Spline IK. In the viewports, a dragging line appears; move the line to the last bone that you want to include, and click to pick it; then drag and click a second time to the spline that you want to use.

The bone structure then assumes the shape of the spline curve. A helper object is positioned at the location of each curve vertex. These helper objects let you refine the shape of the curve.

Tutorial: Building an IK Spline alligator

The IK Spline solver is perfect for creating long, winding objects like snakes or an alligator's tail. For this example, you take an existing bone structure and, using the Spline IK solver, make it match a spline.

To create a bone structure for an alligator that follows a spline using the IK Spline solver, follow these steps:

1. Open the Alligator spline IK.max file from the Chap 29 directory on the DVD.

   This file includes an alligator model created by Viewpoint Datalabs, a simple bone chain and a spline.

> **TIP**
>
> If you're having trouble seeing the bones located inside the alligator, select the skin and enable the See-Through option in the Object Properties dialog box or press the Alt+X keyboard shortcut.

2. With the first bone in the tail chain selected, choose Animation ⇨ IK Solvers ⇨ SplineIK Solver.

   A dotted line appears in the viewport extending from the first bone.

3. Drag and click the cursor on the last bone in the bone tail chain.

4. Another dotted line appears; drag and click the spline, and the bone structure moves to match the spline's curve.

Figure 29.10 shows the bone structure for the gator's tail. You can now control the gator's tail by moving the dummy objects along the spline.

FIGURE 29.10

The IK Spline solver is perfect for creating objects such as snakes and animal tails.

Summary

Understanding the benefits of a bones system helps if you ever need to customize a rig or create a new rig from scratch. Inverse Kinematics (IK) provides a unique way to control and animate hierarchical structures by transforming the child node. In this chapter, you learned how to create and work with bones systems and the Bone Tools. This chapter covered the following topics:

- Creating bones systems
- Setting bone parameters and the IK Solver
- Using the Bone Tools
- Making objects into bones systems
- The basic concepts behind IK
- Creating and animating an IK system

Now that you've learned the process for rigging a character and using IK, we look at using the skin modifier to make the character mesh move along with the skeleton.

29

Skinning Characters

IN THIS CHAPTER

Planning your character

Using the Skin modifier

Painting skin weights

Using the Weight Tool

Working with the Skin Wrap and Skin Morph modifiers

I n the taxidermy world, skinning an animal usually involves removing its skin, but in the Autodesk®
3ds Max® 2013 software, skinning a character involves adding a skin mesh to a group of controlling
bones. Skinning a character also involves defining how the skin deforms as the bones are moved using
skin weights.

A character skin created in 3ds Max can be any type of object and is attached to a biped or a bones
skeleton using the Skin modifier. The Skin modifier isn't alone. 3ds Max includes other modifiers like
the Skin Wrap and Skin Morph modifiers that make your skin portable. This chapter covers how the
various Skin modifiers are attached to a skeleton and used to aid in animating your character.

Understanding Your Character

What are the main aspects of your character? Is it strong and upright, or does it hunch over and move with
slow, twisted jerks? Before you begin modeling a character, you need to understand the character. It is helpful to sketch the character before you begin. This step gives you a design that you can return to as needed.

> **TIP**
>
> The sketched design also can be loaded and planar mapped to a plane object to provide a guide to modeling.

You have an infinite number of reference characters available to you (just walk down a city street if you
can't think of anything new). If you don't know where to start, then try starting with a human figure. The
nice thing about modeling a human is that an example is close by (try looking in the mirror).

We all know the basic structure of humans: two arms, two legs, one head, and no tail. If your character is
human, then starting with a human character and changing elements as needed is the easiest way to go.
As you begin to model human figures, being familiar with anatomy is helpful. Understanding the structure

of muscles and skeletal systems helps explain the funny bumps you see in your elbow and why muscles bulge in certain ways.

> **TIP**
>
> If you don't have the ideal physique, then a copy of *Gray's Anatomy* (the book, not the TV show) can help. With its detailed pictures of the underlying muscular and skeletal systems, you'll have all the details you need without having to pull your own skin back.

The curse and blessing of symmetry

The other benefit of the human body is that it is symmetrical. You can use this to your benefit as you build your characters, but be aware that unless you're creating a band of killer robots, it is often the imperfections in the characters that give them, well, character. Positioning an eye a little off normal might give your character that menacing look you need.

Dealing with details

When you start to model a human figure, you quickly realize that the body includes lots of detail, but before you start naming an object "toenail lint on left foot," look for details you won't need. For example, modeling toes is pointless if your character will be wearing shoes and won't be taking them off. (In fact, I think shoes were invented so that modelers wouldn't have to model toes.)

At the same time, details in the right places add to your character. Look for the right details to help give your character life—a pirate with an earring, a clown with a big, red nose, a tiger with claws, a robot with rivets, and so on.

Figure 30.1 shows two good examples. The ninja warrior on the left doesn't need the details of a mouth or teeth because they are hidden behind his mask. In fact, if you were to remove his mask, it would leave a large gaping hole. The Greek woman statue model on the right includes many necessary details including fingernails, toes, a bellybutton, and, uh, well, uh, other details.

> **NOTE**
>
> You can actually find these two character models on the CD at the back of the book, compliments of Viewpoint Datalabs.

FIGURE 30.1

These two characters have details modeled where needed.

Animated Skin Modifiers

Of all the animation modifiers, several specifically are used to deal with skin. The Skin modifier is a key modifier for enabling character animation. The Skin Morph modifier lets you deform a skin object and create a morph target. It is designed to help fix problem areas, such as shoulders and hips, that have trouble with the standard Skin modifier. The Skin Wrap modifier offers a way to animate a low-res proxy and then apply the same animation to a high-res wrapped object.

Understanding the skinning process

Unless you like animating using only a skeleton or a biped by itself, a bones system will have a skin attached to it. Any mesh can be made into a skin using the Skin modifier. The Skin modifier is used to bind a skin mesh to a bones system and to define the associations between the skin vertices and the bones. The first step is to bind the skin mesh to the skeleton object. With a skin attached to a bones system, you can move the bones system and the skin follows, but just how well it follows the skeleton's motion depends on a process called skinning.

 Creating a bones system is covered in more detail in Chapter 29, "Understanding Rigging, Kinematics, and Working with Bones."

Skinning is where you tell which parts of the skin mesh to move with which bones. Obviously, you'd want all the skin vertices in the hand to move with the hand bone, but the skin vertices around the waist and shoulders are trickier.

Each skin area that surrounds a bone gets encompassed by a capsule-shaped envelope. All vertices within this envelope move along with the bone. When two of these envelopes overlap, their surfaces blend together like skin around a bone joint. Most of the skinning process involves getting the skin vertices into the right envelope. The Skin modifier includes several tools to help make this easier, including the Skin Weight table and a painting weights feature.

Binding to a skeleton

After you have both a skeleton and a skin mesh, you need to bind the skin to the skeleton before you can edit the influence envelopes. The binding process is fairly easy: Simply select the skin mesh, and apply the Skin modifier to it using the Modifiers ➪ Animation ➪ Skin menu command.

> **TIP**
>
> Before binding a skeleton to a skin mesh, take some time to match the size and dimensions of the bones close to the skin mesh. When the skin mesh is bound to the skeleton, the envelopes are created automatically. If the bones match the skin, then the new envelopes are pretty close to what they need to be.

In the Parameters rollout, click the Add button above the bones list. This opens a Select Bones dialog box where you can select the bones to use to animate this skin. The selected bones appear in the bones list. The text field directly under the bones list lets you locate specific bones in the list by typing the name. Only one bone at a time may be selected from the list. The Remove button removes the selected bone from the bone list.

Tutorial: Attaching skin to a CAT rig

For human figures, using a biped or Character Animation Toolkit (CAT) skeleton saves lots of time. For this example, because he's close to a human in form, you'll bind a CAT skeleton to the Marvin Moose model.

To bind the skin of a model to a CAT skeleton, follow these steps:

1. Open the Marvin Moose CAT rig - final.max file from the Chap 30 directory on the CD.

   This file includes the CAT rig built in Chapter 31 for the Marvin Moose character.

2. With the CAT rig aligned to the skin mesh, select Unfreeze All from the right-click quad menu. Select the moose model, disable the See-Through option in the Object Properties dialog box, and choose Modifiers ➪ Animation ➪ Skin to apply the Skin modifier.

3. In the Parameters rollout, click the Add button. The Select Bones dialog box opens. Click the Select All button to select all the bones, and click Select. Don't include the Footsteps, Character001, or the Leg Platform objects.

4. In the Parameters rollout, select one of the bones in the list and click the Edit Envelopes button. Zoom in on the highlighted bone, select the cross-section handles for this bone, and adjust them to include all the vertices surrounding the bone. For some bones like the left shin bone, set the Radius values to **0.15** near the body and **0.1** for the other end. Figure 30.2 shows the moose skin with all the CAT rig bones added.

FIGURE 30.2

Bone references are added to the skin modifier.

After the Skin modifier is applied and bound to the skin mesh, every bone includes an area of influence called an envelope that defines the skin vertices that it controls. If any of the skin mesh vertices are outside of the bone's envelope or are included in an envelope for the wrong bone, then the vertices are left behind when the bone is moved. This causes an odd stretching of the skin that is easy to identify.

To check the envelopes, select and rotate several of the skeleton's key bones. If any envelope problems exist, they are easy to spot, as shown in Figure 30.3. The incorrect stretching of the vertices for the boot simply means that the envelopes need to be adjusted.

FIGURE 30.3

If the envelopes are off for any of the skin vertices, the skin stretches incorrectly.

Editing envelopes

When the Skin modifier is selected, the Parameters rollout includes an Edit Envelopes button that places you in a special mode that lets you edit the envelope for the selected bone in the bone list. This mode is also enabled by selecting the Envelope subobject under the Skin modifier at the top of the Modifier Stack.

When the Edit Envelopes mode is enabled, the entire skin mesh is colored with a gradient of colors to visually show the influence of the envelope. Areas of red are completely inside the envelope's influence, areas of green are somewhat affected by the bone, and areas of gray are completely outside the envelope's influence.

Figure 30.4 shows a simple loft object surrounding three bone objects with a Skin modifier applied. The Add Bone button was used to include the three bones within the Skin modifier list. The skin has been set to See Through in the Object Properties dialog box, so the bones are visible. The first bone was selected in the bone list, and the Edit Envelope button was clicked, revealing the envelope for the first bone.

30

FIGURE 30.4

Envelopes define which Skin vertices move with the underlying bone.

An envelope consists of two capsule-shaped volumes within each other called the Inner and Outer Envelopes. Any vertices within the inner envelope are controlled exclusively by that bone. Any vertices positioned between the inner and outer envelopes are controlled by a falloff where the influence is shared between bones.

At either end of these envelopes are four small handles that can be dragged to change the cross-section radius. The cross-section area changes to pink when selected. The radius of the selected cross section is displayed in the Radius field within the Envelope Properties section of the Parameters rollout. The Squash value determines the amount of squash applied to the object for bones that can stretch. You can change an envelope's size by changing its Radius value or by dragging the cross-section handles. Within the Select section of the Parameters rollout, you can choose to select and edit Vertices, Envelopes, and/or Cross Sections. If you choose the Vertices option, selected object vertices are shown as small squares, and the Shrink, Grow, Ring, and Loop buttons become active. These buttons allow you to select a desired set of vertices easily. If the Select Element option is enabled, then all vertices in the element are selected, and the Backface Cull Vertices option prevents vertices on the backside of the object from being selected.

If a cross section is selected, you can add a different cross-section shape using the Add button. This button lets you select a cross-section shape within the viewports. The Remove Cross Section button removes an added cross section from the envelope.

> **NOTE**
> The orientation of the envelope spline is set by the longest dimension of the bone. This works well for arm and leg bones, but the pelvis or clavicle may end up with the wrong orientation.

The Envelope Properties section of the Parameters rollout (just below the Radius and Squash values) includes five icon buttons, shown in Table 30.1. The first toggles between Absolute and Relative. All vertices that fall within the outer envelope are fully weighted when the Absolute toggle is set, but only those within both envelopes are fully weighted when the Relative toggle is selected.

TABLE 30.1 **Envelope Properties**

Button	Name	Description
A R	Absolute/Relative	Toggles between Absolute and Relative
／	Envelope Visibility	Makes envelopes remain visible when another bone is selected
／ ∫ ⌐ ⌐	Falloff Linear, Falloff Sinual, Falloff Fast Out, Falloff Slow Out	Sets Falloff curve shape
▤	Copy Envelope	Copies envelope settings to a temporary buffer
▤ ▤ ▤	Paste Envelope, Paste to All Bones, Paste to Multiple Bones	Pastes envelope settings to the selected bone, to all bones, or to multiple bones chosen from a dialog box

The second icon button enables envelopes to be visible even when not selected. This helps you see how adjacent bones overlap. The third icon button sets the Falloff curve for the envelopes. The options within this flyout are Linear, Sinual, Fast Out, and Slow Out. The last two icon buttons can be used to Copy and Paste envelope settings to other bones. The flyout options for the Paste button include Paste (to a single bone), Paste to All Bones, and Paste to Multiple Bones (which opens a selection dialog box).

Working with weights

For a selection of vertices, you can set its influence value (called its Weight value) between 0 for no influence and 1.0 for maximum influence. This provides a way to blend the motion of vertices between two or more bones. For example, the vertices on the top of a character's shoulder could have a weight value of 1.0 for the shoulder bone, a weight value of 0.5 for the upper arm bone, and a weight value of 0 for all other bones. This lets the shoulder skin area move completely when the shoulder bone moves and only halfway when the upper arm moves.

> **NOTE**
> The shading in the viewport changes as vertices are weighted between 0 and 1. Weight values around 0.125 are colored blue, weight values around 0.25 are colored green, weight values around 0.5 are colored yellow, and weight values around 0.75 are colored orange.

The Absolute Effect field lets you specify a weight value for the selected vertices. The Rigid option makes the selected vertices move only with a single bone. The Rigid Handles causes the handles of the selected vertices for a patch object to move only with a single bone. This is important if the character is wearing a hard item such as armor plates. By enabling this option, you can be sure that the armor plate doesn't deform. The Normalize option requires that all the weights assigned to the selected vertices add up to 1.0.

30

The other buttons found in the Weight Properties section of the Parameters rollout are defined in Table 30.2. Include Vertices and Exclude Vertices buttons let you remove the selected vertices from those being affected by the selected bone. The Select Exclude Verts button selects all excluded vertices.

TABLE 30.2 Envelope Properties

Button	Name	Description
	Exclude Selected Vertices	Excludes the selected vertices from the influence of the current bone.
	Include Selected Vertices	Includes all selected vertices in the bone's influence.
	Select Excluded Vertices	Selects all excluded vertices.
	Bake Selected Verts	Bakes the vertex weights into the model so they aren't changed with the envelope. Baked vertices can be changed using the Weight Table or the Absolute Effect value.
	Weight Tool	Opens the Weight Tool interface.

Using the Weight Tool

The Weight Tool button in the Parameters rollout opens the Weight Tool dialog box, shown in Figure 30.5. The Shrink, Grow, Ring, and Loop buttons work the same as those in the Select section, and they let you quickly select precise groups of vertices. The value buttons on the second row allow you to change weight values with a click of the button or by adding or subtracting from the current value.

FIGURE 30.5

The Weight Tool dialog box includes buttons for quickly altering weight values and for blending the weights of adjacent vertices.

The Copy, Paste, and Paste-Position buttons let you copy weights between vertices quickly. The Paste Position button pastes the given weight to the surrounding vertices based on the Paste Position Tolerance value. The Blend button quickly blends all the surrounding vertices from the current weight value to 0, creating a smooth blend weight. The Weight Tool dialog box also lists the number of vertices in the copy buffer and currently selected. The list at the bottom of the dialog box lists the weight and bone for the selected vertices.

Using the Weight Table

The Weight Table button opens the Weight Table interface, shown in Figure 30.6. This table displays all the vertices for the skinned object by ID in a column on the left side of the interface. All bones are listed in a row along the top. For each vertex and bone, you can set a weight.

FIGURE 30.6

The Weight Table lets you specify weight values for each vertex and for each bone.

The Edit menu includes commands to Copy and Paste weights. It also includes commands to Select All, Select Invert, and Select None. A selection of vertices can be combined into a Vertex Set and named. The Vertex Sets menu lets you create and delete these sets.

The Options menu lets you flip the interface so that bones are displayed in the first column and the vertex IDs are along the top row. The Update On Mouse Up option limits the updates until the mouse is released. Several options for showing and hiding interface elements are included. The Show Affected Bones option lists only the bones that are affected. The Show Attributes option displays a column of attributes labeled S, M, N, R, and H. The Show Exclusions option makes a check box available in each cell. When checked, the vertex is excluded. The Show Global option makes a drop-down list available that enables you to set an attribute for all vertices. The Show Set Sets UI makes available two buttons for creating and deleting vertex sets.

The S attribute is marked if a vertex is selected, the M attribute marks a vertex weight that has been modified, the N attribute marks a normalized weight, the R attribute marks rigid vertices, and an H attribute marks a vertex with rigid handles.

30

To set a weight, just locate the vertex for the bone, click in the cell, and type the new value. If you click a cell and drag to the left or right, the weight value changes. Weight values can be dragged between cells. Right-clicking a cell sets its value to 0, and right-clicking with the Ctrl key held down sets its value to 1.0.

After the vertex weights are set, you can click the Bake Selected Vertices to lock down the weight values. Changes to envelopes do not affect baked vertices.

Painting weights

Using the Paint Weights button, you can paint with a brush over the surface of the skin object. The Paint Strength value (in the Painter Options dialog box) sets the value of each brush stroke. This value can be positive (up to 1.0) for vertices that will move with the bone or negative (to −1.0) for vertices that will not move with the bone.

To the right of the Paint Weights button is the Painter Options button (it has three dots on it), which opens the Painter Options dialog box. Using this dialog box, you can set the brush strength and size.

Tutorial: Applying skin weights

In this example, you change the skin weights of the future man character in an attempt to fix the problem you saw with his boots.

To apply the skin weights to a character, follow these steps:

1. Open the Future man with skin - final.max file from the Chap 30 directory on the CD.

2. With the mesh skin selected, open the Modify panel and choose the Bip01 L Foot bone in the bone list. Then click the Edit Envelopes button at the top of the Parameters rollout. This displays the envelopes around the foot object. Zoom in on the foot object, and change the display option to Realistic or press the F3 key, so you can see the weight shading.

3. Make sure the Cross Sections option in the Select section of the Parameters rollout is selected. Then select the cross-section handles on the outer envelope and pull them in toward the foot. Rotate the view until the side of the foot is visible to make sure that the toe and heel of the boot are still covered.

4. Click the Vertices option in the Parameters rollout, and disable the Backface Cull Vertices option. Drag over all the vertices that are contained in the lower part of the boot, and enable the Rigid option. Then select the vertices above the boot in the shin. You can use the Loop button to select all vertices about the upper part of the boot and press and hold the Alt key to remove any vertices that are part of the lower boot.

5. In the Weight Properties section of the Parameters rollout, click the Weight Tool button. In the Weight Tool dialog box, click the .25 button. This changes the weight of the selected vertices. Then click the Blend button to smooth the transition areas.

6. Click the Edit Envelopes button to exit Edit Envelopes mode. Then select and rotate the upper leg to see whether the problem has been fixed. As I rotated my model, I noticed that some vertices on the back of the boot were left behind, which means that they aren't being influenced by the foot bone.

7. Select the skin object, enter Edit Envelopes mode again, and click the Paint Weights button. The cursor changes to a round brush. Click the Painter Options button (which is next to the Paint Weights button with three dots). This opens the Painter Options dialog box. Set the Max Strength value to **1.0**, and close the dialog box. Then paint in the viewport over the vertices on the back of the boot heel, including those areas that aren't shaded red. Figure 30.7 shows the correct boot with its envelopes.

FIGURE 30.7

Vertices' weights can be fixed with the Weight Tool and by Painting Weights.

8. Exit Edit Envelopes mode again, and check the changes by rotating the upper leg bone.

Mirror settings

Most characters have a natural symmetry, and you can use this symmetry to mirror envelopes and vertex weights between different sides of a model. You can use this feature by clicking the Mirror Mode button in the Mirror Parameters rollout. This button is active only when the Edit Envelopes button is active.

In Mirror Mode, you see an orange plane gizmo that marks the symmetrical line for the model. You can move and orient this plane using the Mirror Offset, Mirror Plane, and Mirror Threshold controls. Once oriented, 3ds Max computes the matching vertices based on the volumes from the mirror plane.

30

All vertices on one half of the character appear blue, and all the matching vertices appear green. All vertices that cannot be matched appear red.

If you drag over bones or vertices in the viewports, you can select them. Clicking the Mirror Paste button pastes the envelopes and vertex weights of the selected vertices to their matches. Or you can select the Paste Green to Blue Bones button or one of its neighbors to copy all the green bones or vertices to their matches, or vice versa.

The Display Projection drop-down list projects the position of the selected vertices onto the Mirror Plane so you can compare their locations relative to each other. With lots of vertices in your skin, you want to enable the Manual Update, or the viewport refreshes become slow.

Tutorial: Mirroring skin weights

Now that you have spent the time correcting the skin weights for the left boot, you use the Mirror Weights feature to apply the same weights to the opposite foot.

To apply the skin weights to a character, follow these steps:

1. Open the Future man with corrected weights - final.max file from the Chap 30 directory on the CD.

2. Select the skinned model and with Edit Envelopes mode turned on, select the Bip01 L Foot bone from the list in the Parameters rollout, and click the Mirror Mode button in the Mirror Parameters rollout. An orange gizmo is added to the viewport that divides the model, as shown in Figure 30.8.

3. Drag over all the vertices that make up the left boot, and then click the Paste Blue to Green Verts button. All the vertex weights on the left side of the model are copied to the right side. The pasted vertices turn yellow once pasted.

FIGURE 30.8

In Mirror mode, matched bones and vertices appear green and blue.

Display and Advanced settings

The Display rollout controls which features are visible within the viewports. Options include Show Colored Vertices, Show Colored Faces, Color All Weights, Show All Envelopes, Show All Vertices, Show All Gizmos, Show No Envelopes, Show Hidden Vertices, Draw On Top Cross Sections, and Draw On Top Envelopes.

With these display options, you can turn on and off the weight color shading on vertices and faces. You can also select to show all envelopes, vertices, and gizmos. The Color All Weights option is unique. It assigns every bone a different color and shows how the weights blend together between bones.

The Advanced Parameters rollout includes an option to Back Transform Vertices. This option avoids applying transform keys to the skin because the bones control the motion. The Rigid Vertices and Rigid Patch Handles options set the vertices so that they are controlled by only one bone. This rollout also includes buttons to Reset Selected Vertices, Reset Selected Bones, and Reset All Bones. This is handy if you really mess up a skinning job, because it gives you a chance to start over. It also includes buttons for saving and loading envelopes. The envelopes are saved as files with the .env extension.

The Animatable Envelopes option lets you create keys for envelopes. Weight All Vertices is a useful option that automatically applies a weight to the nearest bone of all vertices that have no weight. The Remove Zero Weights button removes the vertex weight of any vertex that has a value lower than the Zero Limit. This can be used to remove lots of unnecessary data from your model if you need to put it on a diet.

Using deformers

Below the Advanced Parameters rollout is the Gizmos rollout. You use this rollout to apply deformers to selected skin object vertices. Three deformers are available in the Gizmos rollout: a Joint Angle Deformer, a Bulge Angle Deformer, and a Morph Angle Deformer.

Each of these deformers is unique. They include the following features:

- **Joint Angle Deformer:** Deforms the vertices around the joint between two bones where the skin can bunch up and cause problems. This deformer moves vertices on both the parent and child bones.
- **Bulge Angle Deformer:** Moves vertices away from the bone to simulate a bulging muscle. This deformer works only on the parent bone.
- **Morph Angle Deformer:** Can be used on vertices for both the parent and child bones to move the vertices to a morph position.

All deformers added to a skin object are listed in the Gizmo rollout. You can add deformers to and remove deformers from this list using the Add and Remove Gizmo buttons. You can also Copy and Paste the deformers to other sets of vertices. Before a deformer gizmo can be applied, you need to select vertices within the skin object. To select vertices, enable the Vertices check box of the Parameters rollout and drag over the vertices in the viewport to select the vertices.

The parameters for the deformer selected in the Gizmos rollout's list appear when the deformer is selected in the Deformer Parameters rollout. This rollout lists the Parent and Child bones for the

30

selected vertices and the Angle between them. This rollout changes depending on the type of deformer selected.

For the Joint and Bulge Angle Deformers, a new rollout labeled Gizmo Parameters or Deformer Parameters appears. The Gizmo Parameters rollout includes buttons to edit the control Lattice and to edit the deformer Key Curves. The Edit Lattice button lets you move the lattice control points in the viewports. The Edit Angle Keys Curves opens a Joint Graph window that displays the transformation curves for the deformation.

Using the Skin Wrap modifiers

If you've created a high-resolution model that you want to animate as a skin object, but the mesh is too complex to move around, then the Skin Wrap modifier might be just what you need. The Skin Wrap modifier may be applied to a high-resolution mesh, and with the Parameters rollout you can select a low-resolution control object. Any movements made by the low-resolution control object automatically are applied to high-resolution mesh.

> **TIP**
> Skin Wrap is also very useful for animating clothes on a character.

The Skin Wrap modifier has two available Deformation Engines: Face Deformation and Vertex Deformation. Each vertex contained with the control object acts as a control vertex. The Vertex Deformation option moves the vertices closest to each control vertex when the control vertex is moved, and the Face Deformation option moves the faces that are closest.

For each deformation mode, you can set a Falloff value, which moves vertices farther from the moved control vertex to a lesser extent to ensure a smoother surface. For the Vertex Deformation mode, you can also set a Distance Influence value and Face Limit values to increase the extent of influence for a control vertex.

The Reset button can be used to reset the control object to the high-resolution mesh object. This is useful if you need to realign the control object to the Skin Wrap object. When you're finished animating the control object, the Convert to Skin button may be used to transfer the animation keys to the high-resolution objects.

The Advanced Parameters rollout includes a button for mirroring the selected vertices to the opposite side of the control object.

The Modifiers menu also includes a Skin Wrap Patch modifier, which works the same as the Skin Wrap modifier, but it allows the control object to be a patch.

Tutorial: Making a simple squirt bottle walk

Creating a bones structure and applying a Skin modifier works well for characters with structure, but to animate the motion of an amorphous object such as a squirt bottle, the Skin Wrap modifier works much better than bones.

To animate a squirt bottle object walking using the Skin Wrap modifier, follow these steps:

1. Open the Walking squirt bottle.max file from the Chap 30 directory on the CD.

    This file includes a squirt bottle model with all its parts attached together. The file also includes a simple box object that is roughly the same shape as the squirt bottle. The box object has been animated walking forward.

2. With the squirt bottle object selected, choose the Modifiers ➪ Animation ➪ Skin Wrap menu command to apply the Skin Wrap modifier.

3. In the Parameters rollout, click the Add button and select the Box object. The Box object is added to the Skin Wrap list in the Parameters rollout. Click again on the Add button to disable it.

4. Select the Box object and hide it in the scene.

5. Click the Play Animation button, and the hi-res bottle follows the same animation as the box object.

Figure 30.9 shows the squirt bottle as it moves through the scene.

FIGURE 30.9

Not all animated objects need a bone structure.

Using the Skin Morph modifier

Using the deformation options found in the Skin modifier, you can deform any part of the skin, but this feature relies on using gizmos found in an already complex envelope-editing mode. Skin Morph offers another way to deform a skin object using the underlying bones. The Skin Morph modifier is

30

applied on top of a Skin modifier and lets you pick which bones to use in the deformation. For example, for bulging muscles, the forearm bone is rotated and should be added to the list in the Parameters rollout.

After selecting a bone from the Parameters rollout list, select the frame where the deformation is at a maximum. Then click the Create Morph button in the Local Properties rollout to create the morph target. Morph targets can be given names to make them easy to select later. The Edit button in the Local Properties rollout then lets you move the vertices for the deformation.

Tutorial: Bulging arm muscles

Perhaps the most common bulging deformation for characters is making the bicep muscle bulge as the forearm is raised. This effect can be simplified using the Skin Morph modifier.

To bulge an arm muscle using the Skin Morph modifier, follow these steps:

1. Open the Bulging bicep.max file from the Chap 30 directory on the CD.

   This file includes a rough arm model with a Skin modifier applied attached to a four-bone chain.

2. With the arm skin selected, choose the Modifiers ⇨ Animation ⇨ Skin Morph menu command to apply the Skin Morph modifier on top of the Skin modifier.

3. In the Parameters rollout, click the Add Bone button and select the forearm bone object from the Select Bones dialog box that appears.

   The bone object is added to the Skin Morph list in the Parameters rollout.

4. Select and rotate the forearm bone to the location where the skin deformation is at its maximum. Then select the skin and choose the forearm bone object from the list in the Parameters rollout, and click the Create Morph button in the Local Properties rollout. In the Morph Name field name the morph **Bulging bicep**.

> **TIP**
>
> The forearm bone can be hard to see under the skin, but you can always select the bone using the Select From Scene dialog box, which is opened by pressing H.

5. In the Local Properties rollout, click the Edit button. This enables the Points subobject mode. Then enable the Edge Limit option in the Selection rollout, so the vertices on the forearm aren't accidentally selected. Drag over the points on the front of the bicep muscle in the Left viewport, and enable the Use Soft Selection option in the Selection rollout. Set the Radius value to **0.5**, and scale the points to the right (along the X axis) in the Left viewport to form a bulge. Click the Edit button again to exit Edit mode.

6. Select and rotate the forearm bone to see the bulging bicep muscle.

Figure 30.10 shows the arm muscle as it bulges along with the rotating forearm.

FIGURE 30.10

Using the Skin Morph modifier, you can set a muscle to bulge as the forearm is rotated.

Using Character Animation Techniques

When it comes to character animation, several techniques can really help. Keeping these points in mind as you animate characters can make a difference:

- **Use the Character Animation Toolkit (CAT):** Manual rigging is useful for those cases where CAT won't work, but the tools and features found in CAT make it silly to look elsewhere for human characters.

- **Use dynamics:** Dynamic packages like MassFX can provide incredibly realistic motion based on physical properties. Learning to use this powerful tool for even the most basic animation sequences is worth the effort.

- **Learn by example:** If you're working on a cartoon character, then by all means, watch cartoons. Traditional cartoons understand and invented the language of cartoon motion, including squash and stretch, exaggerated motion, or scaling eyes large to indicate surprise. If your character motion is more realistic, find the motion, videotape it, and watch it over and over to catch the subtle secondary motion.

- **Use background animations:** The viewport background can load animation clips, which can make positioning characters to match real motion easy. This is a poor man's motion capture system.

- **Include secondary motion:** The primary motion of a character is often the main focus, but you can enhance the animation by looking for secondary motion. For example, when a person walks, you see his legs take the steps and his arms moving opposite the legs' motion, but secondary motion includes his hair swishing back and forth and shoelaces flopping about.

30

- **Use the Flex modifier:** The Flex modifier gives soft bodies, such as tails, hair, ears, and clothing, the realistic secondary motion needed to make them believable.
- **Use the Morpher modifier:** The Morpher modifier can be used to morph a character between two poses or to morph its face between the different phonemes as the character talks.
- **Use IK:** Having a character move by positioning its foot or hand is often much easier than pushing it into position.
- **Use the Spring Controller:** Another good way to get secondary motion is to use the Spring Controller. This controller works well with limbs.
- **Add randomness with the Noise Controller:** Often, perfect animation sequences don't look realistic, and using the Noise Controller can help to make a sequence look more realistic, whether the Noise Controller is applied to a walking sequence or to the subtle movement of the eyes.
- **Use manipulators:** Manipulators can be created and wired to give you control over the animation values of a single motion, such as opening and closing the character's eyes.

Summary

Characters are becoming more and more important in the 3ds Max world and can be saved as separate files just like 3ds Max scene files. Combining a detailed skin mesh with a skeleton of bones lets you take advantage of the character animation features. This chapter covered the following topics:

- Designing your character before building
- Working with the Skin modifier
- Reusing animations with Skin Wrap
- Bulging muscles with Skin Morph

The next chapter delves into the Character Animation Toolkit (CAT) and shows how it can be used to quickly create skeletons and animate characters.

CHAPTER

31

Animating Characters with CAT

IN THIS CHAPTER

Learning the basics of creating characters

Creating and editing a CAT preset rig

Creating a custom CAT rig

Animating using CAT

Earlier versions of the Autodesk® 3ds Max® 2013 software have always had a great way to create and animate characters, but until recently, it was available only as a separate plug-in known as Character Studio. Happily, Character Studio has been integrated into 3ds Max to the point that it isn't distinguishable as a separate package. Character Studio was a good first step, and it still exists in 3ds Max, but it has lots of shortcomings that make it difficult to work with.

Another plug-in package known as Character Animation Toolkit, or CAT for short, has been embraced by many 3ds Max animators, and now CAT is embedded within 3ds Max. CAT offers a simple interface that gets great results whether you're building your own custom rig or animating an existing preset rig.

Although 3ds Max includes other features for rigging characters, if you plan on animating a character, then CAT is definitely the way to go. It's an incredible time-saver.

Character Creation Workflow

A typical workflow for creating characters in 3ds Max involves first creating a skin mesh object. After the skin mesh is complete, you can create a skeletal rig to drive its animation. The skeleton consists of a set of bones that provide an underlying structure to the character. Animating these bones provides an easy way to give life to the character.

With a skeletal rig created, position the rig within the skin mesh and match the bone links to the relative size and position inside the skin mesh. The bones do not need to be completely within the skin mesh, but the closer they are to the skin mesh, the more accurate the movements of the character are.

After the rig is sized and matched to the skin mesh, use the Skin modifier to attach the skin mesh to the rig. This automatically sets all the skin weights that govern which skin parts move with which bones. You can also use the Skin modifier settings to deform the skin at certain bone angles, such as bulging a muscle when the arm is flexed.

The next step is to animate the rig using its animation tools, which can include walk, run, and jump cycles using keys. Along the way, you can save, load, and reuse animation sequences, including motion capture files. Animated sequences can be combined and mixed together to form a smooth-flowing animation using the Motion Mixer.

Although this workflow for characters is quite straight-forward, there are many ways to speed it up. Creating a skeletal rig can be time consuming and many days can be shaved off a project if you can use an existing skeletal rig that only needs to be modified. This is one place where CAT comes in. The other huge improvement comes on the animation side. CAT includes several tools for making walk cycles easy.

Creating a CAT Rig

Creating a hierarchical skeleton used to control the animation of the mesh skin draped over it is quite easy using CAT. The skeleton can be set to be invisible in the final render and exists only to make the process of animating easier. Although 3ds Max includes a robust set of tools that can be used to create a skeleton of bones, CAT features automate this entire process and even includes a number of prebuilt skeletons.

> For some characters, modifying a prebuilt skeleton is more work than building a custom skeleton. For these occasions, you can manually create a skeleton structure. Building a rig system by hand is covered in Chapter 29, "Understanding Rigging, Kinematics, and Working with Bones."

Using prebuilt CAT rigs

To add a prebuilt CAT rig to the scene, simply open the Create panel and select the Helpers category. When you choose the CAT Objects subcategory, you have three options: CAT Parent, CAT Muscle, and Muscle Strand. Click the CAT Parent button and drag in the viewport to place the CAT Parent object. This parent is simply an icon used to control the global position of the rig and is not rendered.

TIP
It is best to place the CAT Parent object at the origin of the scene.

While the CAT Parent object is selected, you can choose a preset rig from the list in the CAT Rig Load Save rollout in the Modify panel or you can select a preset before creating a CAT parent to make the specified preset. The size of the rig is determined by how far you drag in the viewport, or you can set the size using the CATUnits Ratio value in the Command Panel. These custom rigs include a variety of human-shaped and animal-shaped rigs, such as the Alien rig shown in Figure 31.1.

FIGURE 31.1

CAT includes several default preset rigs such as this alien character.

One key advantage of CAT rigs over the rigs available in Character Studio and Biped is that they aren't limited in their structure. Although the available CAT rig presets includes a Base Human and even a Bip01 rig that are used for animating human characters, some of the other presets are Dragon, Horse, Lizard, Spider, and Centipede. These different rigs have multiple legs, arms, and wings and all are easily controlled.

Modifying prebuilt CAT rigs

With a prebuilt rig added to the scene, you can use the Transform tools to select and move the bones to match the skin mesh. The arms are automatically set up as a Forward Kinematics (FK) chain, so rotating the upper arm bone automatically rotates the rest of the arm bones with it. The legs are set up with an Inverse Kinematics (IK) chain, so you can position the legs by dragging the feet, and the rest of the leg bones follow. By default, all CAT prebuilt rigs have stretchy bones, so if you select and move a bone, the selected and attached bones stretch to maintain the joint connection.

TIP

If you double-click a bone, the bone and all its children are selected. For example, double-clicking a collar bone selects the entire arm, making it easy to move the whole arm into place.

A CAT rig keeps track of the different types of body parts and presents the appropriate set of parameters depending on which bone is selected. For example, if you select any part of the arm, the Limb Setup rollouts appear in the Modify panel. This rollout has specific parameters for the arms and legs, as shown in Figure 31.2. CAT also recognizes spines, tails, palms, digits (fingers and toes), hubs (head and pelvis), and generic bones.

FIGURE 31.2

The Limb Setup rollout appears when any arm bone is selected.

Copy Limb Settings

  Paste Limb Settings

    Paste/Mirror Limb Settings

Using these settings, you can specify whether the selected arm is the left, middle, or right arm. You also can choose whether this arm has a collarbone or a palm. The Bones value determines the number of bones that make up the arm. The default is 2, but you can change this to be any whole number from 1 to 20. Because arms can be above or below the head, the Up Vector lets you determine which bone points up.

Beneath the Name are three icons used to copy the settings between two bones. The Copy and Paste Settings buttons let you transfer the settings and orientation of one bone to another. The Paste/Mirror Settings mirror the position of one bone to the opposite side. This lets you set up one arm just right and then quickly copy the settings to the opposite arm.

For spines, you can set the number of bones in the chain, the length and size of the spine bones, and the spine curvature using a simple graph. Tails have these same parameters, plus a height and taper value. For palms and ankles, you can specify the length, width, height, and number of digits.

Individual bones that make up the arms and legs also have a Segments value in the Bone Setup rollout that you can set. Within the Limb Setup is a value for setting the number of bones in the limb, but you can use the Segments value to set the number of segments for each individual bone. This allows you to change a long bone, like the thigh bone, into a series of segments that can rotate independent of each other. This allows for twisting bones, as shown for the forearm in Figure 31.3. You also can set the weight curve for bones with many segments.

If you want to save the preset rig after you've made some changes, simply select the CAT Parent object and click the Save Preset Rig button in the CAT Rig Load Save rollout. Rigs are saved by default to the CATRigs folder using the .rg3 extension. Once saved, the rigs appear in the list with the other CAT rig presets for easy recall.

FIGURE 31.3

Increasing the number of bone segments allows the bone to twist like this forearm.

Rigs also are easy to delete. Simply select the CAT Parent object and press the Delete key.

Using custom meshes

The bones that make up a CAT rig by default are simple box objects. This allows them to move quickly with a minimum amount of lag, but the bones don't need to be overly simple. The power of modern computers allows complex scenes to be animated without any lag. If you select a bone and enable the Use Custom Mesh option in the Setup rollout, you can access and modify the existing bone to be more representative of the mesh.

To edit an existing bone, simply apply a modifier to the bone object or an Edit Poly modifier and edit the bone as you wish. You also can attach another mesh to the Edit Poly modifier. After editing is done, simply collapse the changes to the base bone object, and then you can switch back and forth between normal box bones and the custom mesh using the Use Custom Mesh option. Figure 31.4 shows the preset for a gnou.

> **TIP**
>
> If you've gone to all the trouble of building a skin mesh, then you can quickly use the same skin mesh as the skeleton by stripping down its details and using it as a custom mesh.

FIGURE 31.4

Simplified meshes can be used as custom rig bones like this gnou preset.

Tutorial: Editing the head bone

Starting with the alien preset CAT rig, this example edits the alien's head bone to show more character and to demonstrate how custom meshes can be used.

To edit the head bone on a CAT rig, follow these steps:

1. Open the Custom alien head bone.max file from the Chap 31 directory on the CD. This file includes the Alien CAT preset rig.

2. Select the head bone and open the Modify panel. Enable the Use Custom Mesh option in the Hub Setup rollout.

3. Apply the TurboSmooth modifier from the Modifier list and scale the head object up to match the other bones.

4. Open the Create panel and select the Sphere button. Enable the AutoGrid option at the top of the Object Type rollout and drag on the surface of the head to create two eyes and a nose.

5. Open the Modify panel again, select the head bone, and apply the Edit Poly modifier to the object. Then click the Attach button and pick the two eyes and nose objects to combine them to the head object.

6. Right-click in the Modifier Stack, select the Collapse All option from the pop-up menu, and click Yes in the warning dialog box that appears.

Figure 31.5 shows the custom alien head bone. You can switch back to the default box bone by disabling the Use Custom Mesh option.

FIGURE 31.5

Bones can be replaced with custom mesh objects.

Building a custom CAT rig

When building a custom CAT rig, start with the CAT Parent object, but make sure the None option is selected in the CAT Rig Load Save rollout. Then, right-click in the viewport to exit CAT Parent creation mode. This creates the parent without any rig. Position the CAT Parent object so both feet of the skin mesh that you are building the skeleton for are contained within the parent icon's outline.

> **TIP**
>
> If you make the skin mesh object frozen and enable the See-Through option in the Object Properties dialog box, you can easily place the rig bones where they need to be.

The first step in creating a custom CAT rig is to create the pelvis using the Create Pelvis button beneath the list of presets. The pelvis object appears as a simple box object above the CAT Parent object. You can then use the Transform tools to move, scale, and rotate the pelvis into place to match the skin mesh.

With the pelvis object in place and selected, you then have options in the Hub Setup rollout, shown in Figure 31.6, to add legs, arms, and a spine or a tail if you want. The Add Leg button adds to the pelvis a leg with two bones that extends to the floor and an ankle. You can position the leg bones by dragging the foot into position. When one of the legs is in position, you can select the pelvis again and click the Add Leg button again to create the opposite leg. The opposite leg is created using the same settings and position as the first.

FIGURE 31.6

The Hub Setup rollout includes buttons for creating connected legs, arms, and spine.

With the pelvis selected again, click the Add Spine button. This adds a set of spine bones with another hub object on top. The top hub object is used to connect the arms and the neck. The neck is simply another set of spine bones with a hub object on top for the head.

> **NOTE**
> For creatures with multiple arms and legs, the difference between the limbs is that a leg extends from the hub to the ground, and the arm hangs loosely.

You can then select the pelvis, shoulder, or head hub objects and use the Add Tail button to add a tail, wings, or ponytail as needed. Figure 31.7 shows a custom CAT rig created with only a few clicks. The rig includes IK chains on both legs and FK chains on the arms. Fingers and toes could be added easily by selecting the palm or ankle objects and specifying the number of digits.

FIGURE 31.7

Custom CAT rigs are easily created using the CAT tools.

Naming CAT bones

When bones are added to a CAT rig, they are automatically named using the text entered into the Name field. The default name of the entire rig is taken from the name entered into the Name field when the CAT Parent is selected, and names for each body part are associated with the various object parts such as RLeg and LArm. Each bone within a chain is given a default number, so the upper arm object is labeled as 1 and the lower arm is 2.

If you change the name field, all bone names that are affected by the name change are automatically updated, so changing the Name field in the CAT Parent to Reuben automatically changes all bones to start with this name. This makes keeping track of all the various bones much easier and intuitive. It also helps when you start to animate the rig.

Tutorial: Building a custom CAT rig to match a skin mesh

For this example, we use the CAT tools to create a custom rig that matches a mesh skin. The chosen mesh skin is none other than Marvin Moose.

To create a custom CAT rig, follow these steps:

1. Open the Marvin Moose skin.max file from the Chap 31 directory on the CD. This file includes the Marvin Moose skin mesh positioned at the origin.

2. Select and right-click the moose skin mesh object, and select the Object Properties option from the quad menu. Enable the See-Through and Freeze options in the Object Properties dialog box and click OK.

TIP
The keyboard shortcut for making an object see-through is Alt+X.

3. Click the Helpers category, open the CAT Objects subcategory in the Create panel, click the CAT Parent button, select the None option in the CAT Rig Load Save rollout, and drag in the viewport to create the object. Make the CAT Parent just big enough to contain the moose's feet.

4. With the CAT Parent object selected, open the Modify panel and click the Create Pelvis button. Then select and resize the pelvis object and position it to match the skin mesh.

5. With the pelvis object selected, click the Add Leg button to create the left leg. Select and rotate the ankle so the foot is flat against the ground. Scale the foot to roughly match the skin mesh's foot.

6. Select the pelvis, and click Add Leg to create the opposite leg; then click the Add Spine button to create the spine and an object for the shoulders. Position and scale the shoulder hub object. Select the shoulder hub object, and click the Add Arm button. Position the arm bones to match the skin mesh.

7. Select the shoulder hub object, and click Add Arm to create the opposite arm; then click the Add Spine button to create another spine and an object for the head. Select one of the new spine bones, and change the name to **Neck** and the number of bones to **2**. Then scale the head bone to match the moose's head and horns, and name the head bone **Head**.

Figure 31.8 shows the completed custom CAT rig ready to be skinned and animated.

FIGURE 31.8

The moose's skin has been rigged using the CAT tools.

Animating a CAT Rig

The best rig in the world doesn't do you much good if you can't animate it well. Luckily, CAT's animation tools are excellent, just like its rigging tools. CAT uses the concept of animation layers to hold its animation keys. This allows you to blend between different motions.

Animation layers are discussed further in Chapter 26, "Using Animation Layers and Animation Modifiers."

All the animation controls for CAT rigs are found in the Motion panel whenever any of the rig's bones are selected. Within the Layer Manager rollout, shown in Figure 31.9, is a list of the available animation layers. To create a new animation layer, select from four different types, using the Add Layer drop-down list at the bottom right of the list. The four animation layer types include the following:

- **Absolute Layer:** Holds animation key data that defines full motions
- **Local Adjustment Layer:** Holds relative key data relative to the local coordinate system of the above layer
- **World Adjustment Layer:** Applies relative motion in world space that is independent of the previous layers
- **CAT Motion Layer:** Creates procedural-based looping motion such as walk cycles

FIGURE 31.9

The Layer Manager rollout holds the various animation layers.

Setup/Animation Mode Toggle

Layer color

Rig Coloring Mode

Delete Layer

Dope Sheet: Layer Ranges

Move Layer Up
Move Layer Down

Collapse Layers

Paste Layer

Key Pose to Layer

Copy Layer

Display Layer Transform Gizmo

Add Layer

After an animation layer is added and selected, you need to press the Setup/Animation Mode toggle button to begin adding keys to the selected animation layer. You do this using the Auto or Set Key modes to create the keys like normal. Any time a new animation layer is added, it is automatically placed above the currently selected animation layer.

> **TIP**
>
> If you're animating some of the rig bones using Auto Key and the keys don't appear on the Track Bar, check to make sure you have clicked the Setup/Animation Mode toggle button to enable animation.

The selected animation layer can be removed from the list using the Delete Layer button. You also can copy and paste layers between different rigs using the Copy and Paste Layer buttons. The Move Layer Up and Move Layer Down buttons are used to reorder the selected layer. Each layer can be given a unique name using the Name field.

The Ignore option disables the selected animation layer, and the Solo option disables all animation layers except for the current selection.

Blending absolute animation layers

When several absolute animation layers are added, the layers are evaluated according to their order in the Layer Manager list from top to bottom. Each layer can have a Global Weight value that determines how much of the animation layer is blended.

For example, if the top absolute animation layer contains keys for a character raising an arm, and a second absolute animation layer is added that has keys of the character waving its hand, these two can be blended to create the combined motion of the character raising its hand and waving by setting the Global Weight for the second absolute animation layer to 50 percent, as shown in Figure 31.10. If the second layer is set to 0 percent, the character simply raises its arm; if the Global Weight of the second layer is set to 100 percent, the layer takes over the entire animation and the character waves its hand without raising its arm.

FIGURE 31.10

If the Layer Manager contains multiple animation layers, you can blend between them using the Global Weight values.

In addition to the Global Weight value, which affects all parts of the rig, you can also set a Local Weight value for specific bones. For example, if an absolute animation layer is set that moves the rig to a specific pose, you select the left collar bone and set its Local Weight to be a percentage of the final pose. The Local Weight setting lets you control individual bones and limbs differently from the global animation layer.

Another helpful tool as you begin to animate your rig is the Rig Coloring Mode option located to the right of the Setup/Animation Mode toggle button. If you switch the Rig Coloring Mode to display Animation Layer Colors (which is available as a flyout), then the color of the rig matches the color of the animation layer; if two layers are blended together, then the color of the rig also is mixed. If a specific bone is given a different Local Weight, then that bone is colored the same as the animation layer that is controlling it.

TIP

If you plan to blend layers, setting each layer to use a primary color makes it easier to see where layers are blended when the Layer Colors option is enabled.

Clicking the Dope Sheet: Layer Ranges button opens the Dope Sheet with the ranges of the various animation layers displayed. This provides an easy way to modify the ranges for the different animation layers. You also can access the Curve Editor for each of the Global and Local Weights using the button to the right of the respective weight values.

You can use the Display Layer Transform Gizmo button for each layer. This creates a simple helper object that is linked to the character. It can be moved and rotated to control the entire rig. The gizmo is normally placed at floor level between the rig's feet, but if you hold down the Ctrl key while clicking this button, the gizmo is placed at the current bone; if you hold down the Alt key, the gizmo is placed at the world origin. This gizmo is available only for absolute animation layers.

Using adjustment animation layers

If you have your animation layers working just right with the motion you like, but your animation needs a little more exaggeration or a hand needs to reach just a little farther to grab a doorknob, then you can return to the base absolute layer and make the change, or you can apply an adjustment layer.

There are two different adjustment layer types: Local and World. The difference is in how they are affected by the previous animation layer. Local adjustment layers add the adjustment layers changes onto the above layer's motion, so if a local adjustment layer has a hand reach forward a little more, the motion is added to the existing motion.

World adjustment layers work in world space and cause the hand to reach to a specific location in the world. This still blends with the previous layer's motion, but it also moves the selected object to a global position.

Creating a walk cycle with a CAT Motion layer

Keyframing absolute animation layers is okay, but it can be tedious. The CAT Motion layer is where the fun really begins. Adding a CAT Motion layer to the list automatically applies a walk cycle to the rig. This is done without having to create any keys; just press the Play button, and you see the default walk cycle.

When a CAT Motion layer is selected in the Layer Manager rollout, the CAT Motion Editor button appears to the right of the layer color swatch. This button opens the CAT Motion dialog box, shown in Figure 31.11. Using this dialog box, you can adjust the parameters of the walk cycle.

FIGURE 31.11

The CAT Motion dialog box lets you alter the walk cycle parameters.

The first panel (leftmost panel) of the CAT Motion dialog box presents a list of available presets. The buttons at the lower-right corner of the dialog box let you open saved presets. You also can name and save custom presets. The CAT Motion dialog box has its own set of animation layers that are listed in the rightmost pane. Double-clicking a preset in the middle panel, opens a simple dialog box with options to load the preset into a new layer or into the existing layer.

The layers work just like those in the Layer Manager rollout with weights assigned to each layer. For example, if you add the default walk cycle and then a new run cycle set to 50 percent, the run cycle is blended with the walk cycle, creating a slower run cycle. You also can open the Curve Editor to change the shape of the weight curves.

Setting global parameters

Clicking the Globals option in the leftmost pane of the CAT Motion dialog box opens a panel of global CAT motion parameters, shown in Figure 31.12. At the top of the global parameters are settings for changing the Start and End frame of the walk cycle. Note that these settings are different from the Start and End time settings in the Time Configuration dialog box, and they affect only the CAT rig motion.

FIGURE 31.12

The Globals panel of the CAT Motion dialog box lets you change the walk tempo, speed, and direction.

The Max Step Time defines how quickly each step is taken. Low values make the character walk crazy fast, and higher values make a slower, more casual walk. The Max Stride Length sets the distance of each step. These two values together determine the Velocity, but you can't alter the Velocity setting.

The character by default is pointing in the direction indicated on the CAT Parent object, but you can alter the direction that the character is walking by altering the Direction value. A setting of 0 makes the character walk in the direction he is pointing, a value of 90 makes the character shuffle to his right, a value of 180 makes the character walk backward, and a value of 270 makes the character shuffle to the left. The Gradient setting controls the angle that the character is pointing. Negative values make the character point forward as if walking down a hill, and large, positive values make the character walk as if going up a hill.

Walking along a path

The default is to have the character walk in place, but if you select the Walk On Line option, then the character walks forward in a straight line. When the range of frames is reached, the character returns to its starting position and walks the line again. If the Direction value is changed, the character moves straight in the specified direction.

If you click the Path Node button, you can choose a scene object that the character will follow. For example, if you make the Path Node a dummy object, then the character is positioned and walks on top of the dummy object. You can then animate the movement of the dummy object in the scene, and the character follows it.

To make the character walk along a path, you simply need to create a path using the Line tool. Then select the dummy object and use the Animation ⇨ Path Constraint menu command to attach the dummy object to the path. If you enable the Follow option in the Motion panel after making the link, the character turns to stay on the path.

When having a character follow a path with tight corners, the character may become distorted as it attempts to stay on the path. The Preserve Character Shape setting in the CATRig - Globals dialog box lets you minimize the distortion. A setting of 0 allows the distortion caused by tight corners. The Retargeting slider blends the leg motion more or less as you change the slider.

Controlling footsteps and limbs

The Limb Phases panel of the CAT Motion dialog box, shown in Figure 31.13, controls the placement of footsteps and the swing of each leg and arm. The footprints that appear when a character is walking are tied to the rig, so altering the footsteps also alters the rig. If the footsteps don't appear when you select a walk cycle, you can use the Create button to make them appear. You also can delete them with the Delete button. If you move or rotate any of the footsteps, you can use the Reset button to remove any changes for All footsteps or for just the selected footsteps.

FIGURE 31.13

The Limb Phases panel lets you set how the arms and legs swing relative to each other.

The sliders for each leg and arm at the bottom of the Limb Phases panel let you alter how the arms and legs swing relative to each other. By default, the opposite leg and arm swing together, but you can alter these sliders to give the walk cycle a different look.

Matching footsteps to the ground

After footsteps appear, you can select them and use the Pick Ground button. This lets you select a ground plane object. This ground object needs to be a single object, but once selected, the footsteps are moved vertically to align to the ground plane, causing the character to walk along the surface of the ground.

Controlling secondary motions

The remaining panels in the CAT Motion dialog box are used to control the motions of the other rig groups, such as the pelvis, head, and ribcage. If you open the Pelvis group, you see several parameters that you can access including Twist, Roll, Pitch, Lift, Push, Weight Shift, and positional and rotation offsets. Each of these parameters shows an animation curve that you can use to exaggerate or calm the selected motion, such as the Twist parameter shown in Figure 31.14.

FIGURE 31.14

Using the parameter curves in the CAT Motion dialog box, you can control motions such as the twisting of the pelvis.

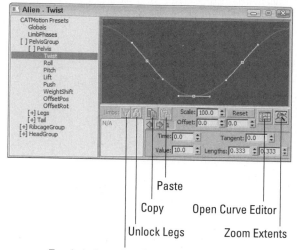

Paste

Copy   Open Curve Editor

Unlock Legs   Zoom Extents

Toggle Independent Leg Settings

Tutorial: Animating a character walking along a path

In this example, you take the default alien character rig and make it walk along a drawn path.

To animate a character walking along a path, follow these steps:

1. Open the Wandering alien.max file from the Chap 31 directory on the CD. This file includes the default CAT alien rig and a random path.

2. With the alien rig's parent object selected, open the Motion panel and add a CAT Motion animation layer to the Layer Manager list by clicking and holding the Add Layers button and selecting the bottom option from the drop-down list. Then click the Animation Mode button. If you click the Play button, you can see the alien walk in place.

3. Click the Helpers category in the Create panel, select the Standard subcategory, and create a dummy object near the alien. Right-click to exit creation mode.

4. Select any part of the rig again, and click the CAT Motion Editor button (it looks like a cat paw print) in the Motion panel. Select the Globals option in the left pane, and click the Path Node button. Then select the dummy object in the scene.

5. Then select the Animation ➪ Constraints ➪ Path Constraint menu command, and click the path. With the dummy object selected, move and rotate the dummy object so the alien is facing the starting end of the path. Open the Motion panel, and enable the Follow option in the Path Parameters rollout.

6. Click the Play button; the character walks along the path, and footsteps mark each step the alien takes.

7. Select the Application Button ⇨ Import ⇨ Merge menu command, and merge the QuadPatch02 object in the Hilly surface.max file into the current scene. Zoom out or click the Zoom Extents All button to see the whole surface. This curvy surface appears as a ground plane. Select the character rig and in the Limb Phases panel of the CAT Motion dialog box, click the Pick Ground button and select the ground plane. The footsteps rise to match the ground plane, as shown in Figure 31.15.

FIGURE 31.15

Constraining the path node to a path makes the character walk along the path.

Summary

This chapter serves as an introduction to CAT and covers all aspects of working with CAT rigs, including its presets, custom rigs, and animation. The following topics were covered:

- Learning the basic workflow for creating characters
- Creating and editing CAT rigs
- Creating a custom CAT rig
- Animating CAT rigs
- Creating walk cycles with the CAT Motion dialog box

Now that you have your characters moving around the scene nicely, the next part looks at several ways to make dynamic animations, starting with particles.

Part VIII

Dynamic Animation

Creating Particles

IN THIS CHAPTER

Understanding the various particle systems

Creating a particle system

Using the Spray and Snow particle systems

Using the Super Spray and Blizzard particle systems

Working with MetaParticles

Using an object as an emitter

Using particle system maps

Every object that you add to the scene slows down the Autodesk® 3ds Max® 2013 software to a small degree because 3ds Max needs to keep track of them all. If you add thousands of objects to a scene, not only does 3ds Max slow down noticeably, but also the objects become difficult to identify. For example, if you had to create thousands of simple snowflakes for a snowstorm scene, the system would become unwieldy, and the number wouldn't get very high before you ran out of memory.

Particle systems are specialized groups of objects that are managed as a single entity. By grouping all the particle objects into a single controllable system, you can easily make modifications to all the objects with a single parameter. This chapter discusses using these special systems to produce rain and snow effects, fireworks sparks, sparkling butterfly wings, and even fire-breathing dragons.

Understanding the Various Particle Systems

A *particle* is a small, simple object that is duplicated en masse, like snow, rain, or dust. Just as in real life, 3ds Max includes many different types of particles that can vary in size, shape, texture, color, and motion. These different particle types are included in various particle systems.

When a particle system is created, all you can see in the viewport is a single gizmo known as an *emitter icon*. An emitter icon is the object (typically a gizmo, but it can be a scene object) where the particles originate. Selecting a particle system gizmo makes the parameters for the particle system appear in the Modify panel.

3ds Max includes the following particle systems:

- **Particle Flow Source:** Particles that can be defined using the Particle Flow window and controlled using actions and events.
- **Spray:** Simulates drops of water. These drops can be Drops, Dots, or Ticks. The particles travel in a straight line from the emitter's surface after they are created.
- **Snow:** Similar to the Spray system, with the addition of some fields to make the particles Tumble as they fall. You also can render the particles as Six Pointed shapes that look like snowflakes.
- **Blizzard:** An advanced version of the Snow system that can use the same mesh object types as the Super Spray system. Binding the system to the Wind Space Warp can create storms.
- **PArray:** Can use a separate distribution object as the source for the particles. For this system, you can set the particle type to Fragment and bind it to the PBomb Space Warp to create explosions.
- **PCloud:** Confines all generated particles to a certain volume. A good use of this system is to reproduce bubbles in a glass or cars on the road.
- **Super Spray:** An advanced version of the Spray system that can use different mesh objects, closely packed particles called MetaParticles, or an instanced object as its particles. Super Spray is useful for rain and fountains. Binding it to the Path Follow Space Warp can create waterfalls.

Creating a Particle System

You can find all the various particle systems under the Create panel and also in the Create menu. To access these systems, click the Geometry category and select the Particle Systems subcategory from the drop-down list. All the particle systems then appear as buttons. Or you can select them from the Create ⇨ Particles menu.

With the Particle Systems subcategory selected, click the button for the type of particle system that you want to use, and then click in a viewport to create the particle system emitter icon. The emitter icon is a gizmo that looks like a simple primitive and that defines the location in the system where the particles all originate. Attached to the icon is a single line that indicates the direction in which the particles move when generated. This line points by default toward the construction grid's negative Z-axis when first created. Figure 32.1 shows the emitter icons for each particle system type including, from left to right, Particle Flow Source; Super Spray; Spray, Snow, and Blizzard (which all have the same emitter icon); PArray; and PCloud.

FIGURE 32.1

The emitter icons for each particle system type

You can transform these icons using the standard transform buttons on the main toolbar. Rotating an emitter changes the direction in which the particles initially move.

After an icon is created, you can set the number, shape, and size of the particles and define their motion in the Parameter rollouts. To apply a material to the particles, simply apply the material to the system's icon. This material is applied to all particles included in the system.

NOTE
Be aware that the particles are displayed as simple objects such as ticks or dots in the viewports. To see the actual resulting particles, you need to render the scene file.

You can set the parameters for the 3ds Max particle systems in the Create panel when they are first created or in the Modify panel at any time. The simpler systems, Spray and Snow, have a single Parameters rollout.

Using the Spray and Snow Particle Systems

All I can say about the Spray and Snow particle systems is that when it rains, it pours. The Spray Parameters rollout includes values for the number of particles to be included in the system. These values can be different for the viewport and the renderer. By limiting the number of particles displayed in the viewport, you can make the viewport updates quicker. You also can specify the drop size, initial speed, and variation. The Variation value alters the spread of the particles' initial speed and direction. A Variation value of 0 makes the particles travel in a straight line away from the emitter.

Spray particles can be Drops, Dots, or Ticks, which affect how the particles look only in the viewport. Drops appear as streaks, Dots are simple points, and Ticks are small plus signs. You also can set how the particles are rendered—as Tetrahedron objects or as Facing objects (square faces that always face the viewer).

The Timing values determine when the particles appear and how long the particles stay around. The Start Frame is the first frame where particles begin to appear, and the Life value determines the number of frames in which the particles are visible. When a particle's lifetime is up, it disappears. The Birth Rate value lets you set how many new particles appear in each frame; you can use this setting or select the Constant option. The Constant option determines the number of particles created at each frame by dividing the total number of particles by the Life value.

The Emitter dimensions specify the width and height of the emitter gizmo. You also can hide the emitter with the Hide option.

NOTE
The Hide option hides the emitter only in the viewports. Emitters are never rendered.

The parameters for the Snow particle system are similar to the Spray particle system, except for a few unique settings. Snow can be set with a Tumble and Tumble Rate. The Tumble value can range from 0 to 1, with 1 causing a maximum amount of rotation. The Tumble Rate determines the speed of the rotation.

The Render options are also different for the Snow particle system. The three options are Six Point, Triangle, and Facing. The Six Point option renders the particle as a six-pointed star. Triangles and Facing objects are single faces.

Tutorial: Creating rain showers

One of the simplest uses for particle systems is to simulate rain or snow. In this tutorial, you use the Spray system to create rain and then learn how to use the Snow system to create snow.

To create a scene with rain using the Spray particle system, follow these steps:

1. Open the Simple rain.max file from the Chap 32 directory on the CD.

   This file includes an umbrella model created by Zygote Media.

2. Select the Create ⇨ Particles ⇨ Spray menu command, and drag the icon in the Top viewport to cover the entire scene. Position the icon above the umbrella object, and make sure the vector is pointing down toward the umbrella.

3. Open the Modify panel, and in the Parameters rollout, set the Render Count to **1000** and the Drop Size to **2**. Keep the default Speed of **10**, and select the **Drops** option; these settings make the particles appear as streaks. Select the Tetrahedron Render method, and set the Start and Life values to **0** and **100**, respectively.

> **NOTE**
> To cover the entire scene with an average downpour, set the number of particles to 1000 for a 100-frame animation.

4. Open the Material Editor (by pressing the M key), and create a material with a light blue Diffuse color and drag this material to the particle system icon.

Figure 32.2 shows the results of this tutorial.

FIGURE 32.2

Rain created with the Spray particle system

Tutorial: Creating a snowstorm

Creating a snowstorm is very similar to what you did in the preceding tutorial. To create a snowstorm, use the Snow particle system with the same number of particles and apply a white material to the particle system.

To create a scene with snow using the Snow particle system, follow these steps:

1. Open the Snowman in snowstorm.max file from the Chap 32 directory on the CD.

   This file includes a snowman created using primitive objects.

2. Select the Create ⇨ Particles ⇨ Snow menu command, and drag the icon in the Top viewport to cover the entire scene. Position the icon above the objects, and make sure that the vector is pointing down toward the scene objects.

3. Open the Modify panel, and in the Parameters rollout, set the Render Count to **1000** and the Flake Size to **6**, and use the Six Point Render option. Set the Start and Life values to **0** and **100**, respectively.

4. Open the Material Editor (by pressing the M key), and create a material with a white Diffuse color with some self-illumination and drag this material to the particle system gizmo.

Figure 32.3 shows the results of this tutorial.

FIGURE 32.3

A simple snowstorm created with the Snow particle system

Using the Super Spray Particle System

If you think of the Spray particle system as a light summer rain shower, then the Super Spray particle system is like a fire hose. The Super Spray particle system is considerably more complex than its Spray and Snow counterparts. With this complexity comes a host of features that make this one of the most robust effects creation tools in 3ds Max.

Unlike the Spray and Snow particle systems, the Super Spray particle system includes several rollouts.

Super Spray Basic Parameters rollout

The Super Spray particle system emits all particles from the center of the emitter icon. The emitter icon is a simple circle set in a plane with an arrow that points in the direction in which the particles will travel. In the Basic Parameters rollout, shown in Figure 32.4, the Off Axis value sets how far away from the icon's arrow the stream of particles will travel. A value of 0 lines up the particle stream with the icon's arrow, and a value of 180 emits particles in the opposite direction. The Spread value can range from 0 to 180 degrees and fans the particles equally about the specified axis. The Off Plane value spins the particles about its center axis, and the Spread value sets the distance from this center axis that particles can be created. If all these values are left at 0, then the particle system emits a single, straight stream of particles, and if all values are 180, then particles go in all directions from the center of the emitter icon.

> **NOTE**
> To actually see the particles in the viewport, you need to drag the Time Slider or press the Play button.

FIGURE 32.4

The Basic Parameters rollout lets you specify where and how the particles appear in the viewports.

The emitter icon size can be set or the emitter icon can be hidden in the viewport. You also can set the particles to be displayed in the viewport as Dots, Ticks, Meshes, or Bounding Boxes. The Percentage of Particles value is the number of the total particles that are visible in the viewport and should be kept low to ensure rapid viewport updates.

Particle Generation rollout

The Particle Generation rollout, shown in Figure 32.5, is where you set the number of particles to include in a system as either a Rate or Total value. The Use Rate value is the number of particles per frame that are generated. The Use Total value is the number of particles generated over the total number of frames. Set the Use Rate value if you want the animation to have a steady stream of particles throughout the animation; use the Use Total value if you want to set the total number of particles that will appear throughout the entire range of frames.

FIGURE 32.5

The Particle Generation rollout lets you control the particle motion.

In the Particle Motion group, the Speed value determines the initial speed of particles. The Variation value alters this initial speed as a percentage of the Speed value. A high Variation value results in particles with all sorts of different speeds.

> **NOTE**
> Be sure to use the Variation values liberally to get more realistic particle behavior.

In the Particle Timing group, you can set when the emitting process starts and stops. Using the Display Until value, you also can cause the particles to continue displaying after the emitting has stopped. The Life value is how long particles stay around, which can vary based on another Variation setting.

When an emitter is animated (such as moving back and forth), the particles can clump together where the system changes direction. This clumping effect is called *puffing*. The Subframe Sampling options help reduce this effect. The three options are Creation Time (which controls emitting particles over time), Emitter Translation (which controls emitting particles as the emitter is moved), and Emitter Rotation (which controls emitting particles as the emitter is rotated). All three options can be enabled, but each one that is enabled adds the computation time required to the render.

> **NOTE**
> The Subframe Sampling options increase the rendering time and should be used only if necessary.

You can specify the particle size along with a Variation value. You also can cause the particles to grow and fade for a certain number of frames.

The Seed value helps determine the randomness of the particles. Clicking the New button automatically generates a new Seed value.

Particle Type rollout

The Particle Type rollout, shown in Figure 32.6, lets you define the look of the particles. At the top of the rollout are three Particle Type options: Standard Particles, MetaParticles, and Instanced Geometry.

FIGURE 32.6

The Particle Type rollout (shown in four parts) lets you define how the particles look.

If you select Standard Particles as the particle type, you can select which geometric shape you want to use from the Standard Particles section. The options are Triangle, Special, Constant, SixPoint, Cube, Facing, Tetra, and Sphere.

The Special type consists of three intersecting planes, which are useful if you apply maps to them. The Facing type is also useful with maps; it creates a simple square face that always faces the viewer. The Constant type maintains the same pixel size, regardless of the distance from the camera or viewer. The Six Point option renders each particle as a 2D six-pointed star. All other types are common geometric objects.

Tutorial: Creating a fireworks fountain

For an example of the Super Spray particle system, you create a fireworks fountain. Fireworks are essentially just lots of particles with a short life span and a high amount of self-illumination. (Tell yourself that the next time you watch a fireworks display.)

To create a fireworks fountain using a particle system, follow these steps:

1. Open the Fireworks fountain.max file from the Chap 32 directory on the CD.

    This file includes a simple fountain base and the Gravity space warp to cause the particles to curve back toward the ground.

2. Select the Create ⇨ Particles ⇨ Super Spray menu command, drag in the Top viewport, and position the system at the top of the fireworks cylinder with the direction arrow pointing toward the sky.

3. Open the Modify panel, and set the Off Axis Spread to **45** and the Off Plane Spread to **90**. In the Particle Generation rollout, select the Use Total option, set the Total number of particles to **2000** with a Speed of **20** and a Variation of **100**. Set the Emit Start to **0** and the Emit Stop to **100**. Set the Display Until to **100** and the Life to **25** with a Variation of **20**. The Size of the particles should be **5**.

4. Open the Material Editor (by pressing the M key), double-click the Standard material in the Material/Map Browser, and then double-click the Standard node to access its parameters. Name the material **Spark** set its Diffuse color to yellow, and set its Self-Illumination color to yellow as well. Then drag the material from the Material Editor to the particle system's icon.

5. Select the Super Spray icon, right-click it to open the pop-up quad menu, and select the Object Properties menu option. In the Object Properties dialog box, select the Object Motion Blur option.

32

> **CAUTION**
> When viewing the animation, maximize a single viewport. If 3ds Max tries to update all four viewports at once with this many particle objects, the update is slow. The shortcut to maximize the viewport is Alt+W.

Figure 32.7 shows sparks emitting from the fireworks fountain.

FIGURE 32.7

The Super Spray particle system is used to create fireworks sparks.

Tutorial: Adding spray to a spray can

The Super Spray particle system is complex enough to warrant another example. What good is a spray can without any spray? In this tutorial, you create a spray can model and then use the Super Spray particle system to create the spray coming from it.

To create a stream of spray for a spray can, follow these steps:

1. Open the Spray can.max file from the Chap 32 directory on the CD.

   This file includes a simple spray can object created using a cylinder for the can base and the nozzle and a lathed spline for the top of the can.

2. Select the Particle Systems subcategory button from the drop-down list in the Create panel, and click the Super Spray button. Drag in the Top viewport to create the Super Spray icon, and position it at the mouth of the nozzle.

3. In the Basic Parameters rollout, set the Off Axis Spread to **20** and the Off Plane Spread to **90**. In the Particle Generation rollout, set the Use Rate to **1000**, the Speed to **20**, and the Life to **30**. Set the Size of the particles to **5**.

4. Open the Material Editor (by pressing M), and locate the Spray Mist material already created in the Sample Slots rollout in the Material/Map Browser. Then drag this material onto the Super Spray icon to apply this material to the Super Spray particle system.

Figure 32.8 shows the fine spray from an aerosol can.

FIGURE 32.8

Using a mostly transparent material, you can create a fine mist spray.

Using the MetaParticles option

The MetaParticles option in the Particle Type rollout makes the particle system release Metaball objects. *Metaballs* are viscous spheres that, like mercury, flow into each other when near. These particles take a little longer to render but are effective for simulating water and liquids. The MetaParticles type is available for the Super Spray, Blizzard, PArray, and PCloud particle systems.

Selecting the MetaParticles option in the Particle Types section enables the MetaParticle Parameters group. In this group are options for controlling how the MetaParticles behave. The Tension value determines how easily objects blend together. MetaParticles with a high tension resist merging with other particles. You can vary the amount of tension with the Variation value. The Tension value can range between 0.1 and 10, and the Variation can range from 0 to 100 percent.

Because MetaParticles can take a long time to render, the Evaluation Coarseness settings enable you to set how computationally intensive the rendering process is. This can be set differently for the viewport and the renderer—the higher the value, the quicker the results. You also can set this to Automatic Coarseness, which automatically controls the coarseness settings based on the speed and ability of the renderer. The One Connected Blob option speeds the rendering process by ignoring all particles that aren't connected.

Tutorial: Spilling soda from a can

MetaParticles are a good option to use to create drops of liquid, like those from a soda can.

To create liquid flowing from a can, follow these steps:

1. Open the MetaParticles from a soda can.max file from the Chap 32 directory on the CD.
   This file includes a soda can model created by Zygote Media positioned with the can on its side.
2. Select the Create ⇨ Particles ⇨ Super Spray menu command, and drag the icon in the Left viewport. Position the icon so that its origin is at the opening of the can and the directional vector is pointing outward.
3. With the Super Spray icon selected, open the Modify panel, and in the Basic Parameters rollout, set the Off Axis and Off Plane Spread values to **40**.
4. In the Particle Generation rollout, keep the default Rate and Speed values, but set the Speed Variation to **50** to alter the speed of the various particles. Set the Particle Size to **20**.
5. In the Particle Type rollout, select the MetaParticles option, set the Tension value to **1**, and make sure that the Automatic Coarseness option is selected.
6. Open the Material Editor (by pressing the M key), and drag the previously created Purple Soda material from the Sample Slots rollout in the Material/Map Browser to the particle system icon.

Figure 32.9 shows a rendered image of the MetaParticles spilling from a soda can at frame 25.

FIGURE 32.9

MetaParticles emitting from the opening of a soda can

Instanced Geometry

Using the Particle Type rollout, you can select any existing scene object to use as the particle with the Instanced Geometry option. To choose an object to use as a particle, click the Pick Object button and select an object from the viewport. If the Use Subtree Also option is selected, then all child objects are also included.

> **CAUTION**
> Using complicated objects as particles can slow down a system and increase the rendering time.

The Animation Offset Keying options determine how an animated object that is selected as the particle is animated. The None option animates all objects the same, regardless of when they are born. The Birth option starts the animation for each object when it is created, and the Random option offsets the timing randomly based on the Frame Offset value. For example, if you have selected an animated bee that flaps its wings as the particle, and you select None as the Animation Offset Keying option, all the bees flap their wings in concert. Selecting the Birth option instead starts them flapping their wings when they are born, and selecting Random offsets each instance differently.

For materials, the Time and Distance values determine the number of frames or the distance traveled before a particle is completely mapped. You can apply materials to the icon that appears when the particle system is created. The Get Material From button lets you select the object from which to get the material. The options include the emitter icon and the Instanced Geometry.

Rotation and Collision rollout

In the Rotation and Collision rollout is an option to enable interparticle collisions. This option causes objects to bounce away from one another when their object boundaries overlap.

The Rotation and Collision rollout, shown in Figure 32.10, contains several controls to alter the rotation of individual particles. The Spin Time is the number of frames required to rotate a full revolution. The Phase value is the initial rotation of the particle. You can vary both of these values with Variation values.

> **NOTE**
> The Rotation and Collision rollout options also can increase the rendering time of a scene.

FIGURE 32.10

The Rotation and Collision rollout options can control how objects collide with one another.

You also can set the axis about which the particles rotate. Options include Random, Direction of Travel/MBlur, and User Defined. The Stretch value under the Direction of Travel option causes the object to elongate in the direction of travel. The User Defined option lets you specify the degrees of rotation about each axis.

Interparticle collisions are computationally intensive and can easily be enabled or disabled with the Enable option. You also can set how often the collisions are calculated. The Bounce value determines the speed of particles after collisions as a percentage of their collision speed. You can vary the amount of Bounce with the Variation value.

Tutorial: Basketball shooting practice

When an entire team is warming up before a basketball game, the space around the basketball hoop is quite chaotic—with basketballs flying in all directions. In this tutorial, you use a basketball object as a particle and spread it around a hoop. (Watch out for flying basketballs!)

To use a basketball object as a particle, follow these steps:

1. Open the Basketballs at a hoop.max file from the Chap 32 directory on the CD.

   This file includes basketball and basketball hoop models created by Zygote Media.

2. Select the Create ⇨ Particles ⇨ Super Spray menu command, and drag the icon in the viewport. Position the icon in the Front view so that its origin is above and slightly in front of the hoop and the directional vector is pointing down. (You need to rotate the emitter icon.)

3. Open the Modify panel, and in the Basic Parameters rollout, set the Off Axis Spread value to **90** and the Off Plane Spread value to **40**; this randomly spreads the basketballs around the hoop. In the Viewport Display group of the Basic Parameters rollout, select the Mesh option. Set the Percentage of Particles to **100** percent to see the position of each basketball object in the viewport.

> **CAUTION**
> Because the basketball is a fairly complex model, using the Mesh option severely slows down the viewport update. You can speed the viewport display using the BBox (Bounding Box) option, but you'll need to choose it after selecting the Instanced Geometry option.

4. In the Particle Generation rollout, select the Use Total option, and enter **30** for the value. (This number is reasonable and not uncommon during warm-ups.) Set the Speed value to **0.2** and the Life value to **100** because you don't want basketballs to disappear. Because of the low number of particles, you can disable the Subframe Sampling options. Set the Grow For and Fade For values to **0**.

5. In the Particle Type rollout, select the Instanced Geometry option and click the Pick Object button. Make sure that the Use Subtree Also option is selected to get the entire group, and then select the basketball group in the viewport. At the bottom of this rollout, select the Instanced Geometry option and click the Get Material From button to give all the particles the same material as the original object.

6. In the Rotation and Collision rollout, set the Spin Time to **100** to make the basketballs spin as they move about the scene. Set the Spin Axis Controls to Random. Also enable the Interparticle Collisions option, and set the Calculation Interval per Frame to **1** and the Bounce value to **100**.

   With the Interparticle Collisions option enabled, the basketballs are prevented from overlapping one another.

7. At the floor of the basketball hoop is a Deflector Space Warp. Move this deflector vertically upward about half the radius of the basketball to prevent the balls from sinking into the floor. Click the Bind to Space Warp button on the main toolbar, and drag from this floor deflector to the Super Spray icon.

   This makes the basketballs bounce off the floor.

Figure 32.11 shows a rendered image of the scene at frame 30 with several basketballs bouncing chaotically around a hoop.

FIGURE 32.11

Multiple basketball particles flying around a hoop

Object Motion Inheritance rollout

The settings on the Object Motion Inheritance rollout, shown in Figure 32.12, determine how the particles move when the emitter is moving. The Influence value defines how closely the particles follow the emitter's motion; a value of 100 has particles follow exactly, and a value of 0 means they don't follow at all.

FIGURE 32.12

The Object Motion Inheritance rollout sets how the particles inherit the motion of their emitter, and the Bubble Motion rollout defines how particles act like bubbles.

The Multiplier value can exaggerate or diminish the effect of the emitter's motion. Particles with a high multiplier can actually precede the emitter.

Bubble Motionrollout

The Bubble Motion rollout, also shown in Figure 32.12, simulates the wobbling motion of bubbles as they rise in a liquid. Three values define this motion, each with variation values. Amplitude is the distance that the particle moves from side to side. Period is the time that it takes to complete one side-to-side motion cycle. Phase defines where the particle starts along the amplitude curve.

Particle Spawn rollout

The Particle Spawn rollout, shown in Figure 32.13, sets options for spawning new particles when a particle dies or collides with another particle. If the setting is None, colliding particles bounce off one another and dying particles simply disappear. The Die After Collision option causes a particle to disappear after it collides. The Persist value sets how long the particle stays around before disappearing. The Variation value causes the Persist value to vary by a defined percentage.

FIGURE 32.13

The Particle Spawn rollout (shown in two parts) can cause particles to spawn new particles.

The Spawn on Collision, Spawn on Death, and Spawn Trails options all enable the spawn controls and define when particles spawn new particles. The Spawns value is the number of times a particle can spawn other particles. The Affects value is the percentage of particles that can spawn new particles; lowering this value creates some duds that do not spawn. The Multiplier value determines the number of new particles created.

> **NOTE**
>
> The Spawn Trails option causes every particle to spawn a new particle at every frame. This option can quickly create an enormous number of particles and should be used with caution.

The Chaos settings define the direction and speed of the spawned particles. A Direction Chaos value of 100 gives the spawned particles the freedom to travel in any direction, whereas a setting of 0 moves them in the same direction as their originator.

The Speed Chaos Factor is the difference in speed between the spawned particle and its originator. This factor can be faster or slower than the original. Selecting the Both option speeds up some particles and slows others randomly. You also can choose to have spawned particles use their parent's velocity or use the factor value as a fixed value.

The Scale Chaos Factor works similarly to the Speed Chaos Factor, except that it scales particles to be larger or smaller than their originator.

The Lifespan Value Queue lets you define different lifespan levels. Original particles have a lifespan equal to the first entry in the queue. The particles that are spawned from those spawned particles last as long as the second value, and so on. To add a value to the list, enter the value in the Lifespan spinner and click the Add button. The Delete button removes the selected value from the list, and the Replace button switches value positions.

If Instanced Geometry is the selected particle type, you can fill the Object Mutation Queue with additional objects to use at each spawn level. These objects appear after a particle is spawned. To pick a new object to add to the queue, use the Pick button. You can select several objects, and they are used in the order in which they are listed.

Load/Save Presets rollout

You can save and load each particle configuration using the Load/Save Presets rollout, shown in Figure 32.14. To save a configuration, type a name in the Preset Name field and click the Save button. All saved presets are displayed in the list. To use one of these preset configurations, select it and click the Load button.

FIGURE 32.14

The Load/Save Presets rollout enables you to save different parameter settings.

3ds Max includes several default presets that can be used as you get started. These presets include Bubbles, Fireworks, Hose, Shockwave, Trail, Welding Sparks, and Default (which produces a straight line of particles).

Using the Blizzard Particle System

The Blizzard particle system uses the same rollouts as the Super Spray system, with some slightly different options. The Blizzard emitter icon is a plane with a line pointing in the direction of the particles (similar to the Spray and Snow particle systems). Particles are emitted across the entire plane surface.

The differences between the Blizzard and Super Spray parameters include dimensions for the Blizzard icon. In the Particle Generation rollout, you'll find values for Tumble and Tumble Rate. Another difference is the Emitter Fit Planar option under the Material Mapping group of the Particle Type rollout. This option sets particles to be mapped at birth, depending on where they appear on the emitter. The other big difference is that the Blizzard particle system has no Bubble Motion rollout, because snowflakes don't make very good bubbles. Finally, you'll find a different set of presets in the Load/Save Presets rollout, including Blizzard, Rain, Mist, and Snowfall.

Using the PArray Particle System

The PArray particle system is a unique particle system. It emits particles from the surface of a selected object. These particles can be emitted from the object's surface, edges, or vertices. The particles are emitted from an object separate from the emitter icon.

The PArray particle system includes many of the same rollouts as the Super Spray particle system. The PArray particle system's emitter icon is a cube with three tetrahedron objects inside it. This system has some interesting parameter differences, starting with the Basic Parameters rollout, shown in Figure 32.15.

In the PArray system, you can select separate objects as emitters with the Pick Object button. You also can select the location on the object where the particles are formed. Options include Over Entire Surface, Along Visible Edges, At All Vertices, At Distinct Points, and At Face Centers. For the At Distinct Points option, you can select the number of points to use.

The Use Selected SubObject option forms particles in the locations selected with the Pick Object button, but only within the subobject selection passed up the Stack. This is useful if you want to emit particles only from a certain selection of a mesh, such as a dragon's mouth or the end of a fire hose. The other options in the PArray system's Basic Parameters rollout are the same as in the other systems.

The Particle Generation rollout includes a Divergence value. This value is the angular variation of the velocity of each particle from the emitter's normal.

FIGURE 32.15

The Basic Parameters rollout for the PArray particle system lets you select the location where the particles form.

Splitting an object into fragments

The Particle Type rollout for the PArray system contains a unique particle type: Object Fragments. This type breaks the selected object into several fragments. Object Fragment settings include a Thickness value. This value gives each fragment a depth. If the value is set to 0, the fragments are all single-sided polygons.

Also in the Particle Type rollout, the All Faces option separates each individual triangular face into a separate fragment. An alternative to this option is to use the Number of Chunks option, which enables you to divide the object into chunks and define how many chunks to use. A third option splits up an object based on the smoothing angle, which can be specified.

In the Material section of the Particle Type rollout, you can select material IDs to use for the fragment's inside, outside, and backside.

The Load/Save Presets rollout includes a host of interesting presets, including the likes of Blast, Disintegrate, Geyser, and Comet.

Tutorial: Creating rising steam

In this tutorial, you create the effect of steam rising from a street vent. Using the PArray particle system, you can control the precise location of the steam.

To create the effect of steam rising from a vent, follow these steps:

1. Open the Street vent.max file from the Chap 32 directory on the CD.

   This file includes a street scene with a vent. The car model was created by Viewpoint Datalabs.

2. Select the Create ⇨ Particles ⇨ PArray menu command, and drag in the Front viewport to create the system.

3. In the Basic Parameters rollout, click the Pick Object button and select the Quadpatch object that is positioned directly beneath the vent object. Set the Particle Formation option to Over Entire Surface.

   Because the Plane object only has a single face, the particles travel in the direction of the Plane's normal.

4. In the Particle Generation rollout, set the Emit Stop value to **100** and the Life value to **60** with a Variation of **50**. Set the Particle Size value to **5.0** with a Variation of **30**.

5. In the Particle Type rollout, select the Standard Particles and the Constant options.

6. Open the Material Editor (by selecting the M key), double-click the Standard material in the Material/Map Browser, and then double-click the new node to access its parameters. Name the selected sample slot **steam**. Click the map button to the right of the Opacity value, and double-click the Mask map type from the Material/Map Browser. Double-click the new node and in the Mask Parameters rollout, click the map button and select the Noise map type. Then double-click the Mask node again, click the Mask button, and select the Gradient map type. Then, double-click the Gradient node, drag the black color swatch to the white color swatch, select Swap in the dialog box that appears, and enable the Radial option. Finally, drag the steam material to the PArray icon.

Figure 32.16 shows the steam vent at frame 60.

FIGURE 32.16

A Plane object positioned beneath the vent is an emitter for the particle system.

Using the PCloud Particle System

The PCloud particle system keeps all emitted particles within a selected volume. This volume can be a box, sphere, cylinder, or a selected object. The emitter icon is shaped as the selected volume. This particle system includes the same rollouts as the Super Spray system, with some subtle differences.

The options on the Basic Parameters rollout are unique to this system. This system can use a separate mesh object as an emitter. To select this emitter object, click the Pick Object button and select the object to use. Other options include Box, Sphere, and Cylinder Emitter. For these emitters, the Rad/Len, Width, and Height values are active for defining its dimensions.

In addition to these differences in the Basic Parameters rollout, several Particle Motion options in the Particle Generation rollout are different for the PCloud system as well. Particle Motion can be set to a random direction, a specified vector, or in the direction of a reference object's Z-axis.

The only two presets for this particle system in the Load/Save Presets rollout are Cloud/Smoke and Default.

Using Particle System Maps

Using material maps on particles is another way to add detail to a particle system without increasing its geometric complexity. You can apply all materials and maps available in the Material Editor to particle systems. To apply them, select the particle system icon and click the Assign Material to Selection button in the Material Editor.

For more details on using maps, see Chapter 15, "Adding Material Details with Maps."

Two map types are specifically designed to work with particle systems: Particle Age and Particle MBlur. You can find these maps in the Material/Map Browser. You can access the Material/Map Browser using the Rendering ⇨ Material/Map Browser menu command or from the Material Editor by clicking the Get Material button.

Using the Particle Age map

The Particle Age map parameters include three different colors that can be applied at different times, depending on the Life value of the particles. Each color includes a color swatch, a map button, an Enable check box, and an Age value for when this color should appear.

This map typically is applied as a Diffuse map because it affects the color.

Using the Particle MBlur map

The Particle MBlur map changes the opacity of the front and back of a particle, depending on the color values and sharpness specified in its parameters rollout. This results in an effect of blurred motion if applied as an Opacity map.

> **NOTE**
> MBlur does not work with the Constant, Facing, MetaParticles, or PArray object fragments.

Tutorial: Creating jet engine flames

The Particle Age and MBlur maps work well for adding opacity and colors that change over time, such as hot jets of flames, to a particle system.

To create jet engine flames, follow these steps:

1. Open the Jet airplane flames.max file from the Chap 32 directory on the CD.

    This file includes an A-10 airplane model created by Viewpoint Datalabs.

2. Select the Create ⇨ Particles ⇨ Super Spray menu command, and drag the icon in the view-port. Rotate and position the emitter icon so that its origin is right in one of the jet's exhaust port and the directional vector is pointing outward, away from the jet.

3. Open the Modify panel, and in the Basic Parameters rollout, set the Off Axis Spread value to **20** and the Off Plane Spread value to **90**.

    These settings focus the flames shooting from the jet's exhaust.

4. In the Particle Generation rollout, select the Use Rate option, set the Rate to 1000, set the Speed to 2, set the Emit Stop to **100**, the Life value to **30**, and the Particle Size to **5.0**.

5. In the Particle Type rollout, select the Standard Particles option and select the Sphere type.

6. Open the Material Editor by pressing the M key, double-click the Standard material in the Material/Map Browser, and then double-click the new node to access its parameters. Name this material **Jet's Exhaust**, and click the map button to the right of the Diffuse color swatch.

7. From the Material/Map Browser that opens, select the Particle Age map. Double-click this node and in the Particle Age Parameters rollout, select dark red, dark yellow, and black as colors for the ages 0, 50, and 100.

    You should use darker colors because the scene is lighted.

8. Double-click the Standard node again to access the base material's parameters again, and then click the map button to the right of the Opacity setting. Select the Particle MBlur map.

9. Double-click the Particle MBlur map node and in the Particle MBlur Parameters rollout, make Color #1 white and Color #2 black with a Sharpness value of **0.1**. Then apply this material onto the particle system's icon.

10. With the Shift key held down, drag the Super Spray icon in the Front viewport to the other exhaust port.

Figure 32.17 shows the jet at frame 30 with its fiery exhaust.

FIGURE 32.17

Realistic jet flames created using the Particle Age and MBlur maps

32

Summary

This chapter presented particle systems and showed how you can use them. The chapter also took a close look at each system, including Spray, Snow, Super Spray, Blizzard, PArray, and PCloud. This chapter covered these topics:

- Learning about the various particle systems
- Creating a particle system for producing rain and snow
- Using the Super Spray particle system
- Working with MetaParticles
- Specifying an object to use as a particle and an object to use as an emitter
- Using the PArray and PCloud particle systems
- Using the Particle Age and Particle MBlur maps on particles

The next chapter explains working with Space Warps to add forces to a scene. These forces can be used to control the motion of objects in the scene.

CHAPTER

33

Using Space Warps

IN THIS CHAPTER

Creating and binding Space Warps to objects

Understanding the various Space Warp types

Working with Space Warps and particle systems

S pace Warps sound like a special effect from a science fiction movie, but actually they are nonrenderable objects that let you affect another object in many unique ways to create special effects.

You can think of Space Warps as the unseen forces that control the movement of objects in the scene such as gravity, wind, and waves. Several Space Warps, such as Push and Motor, deal with dynamic simulations and can define forces in real-world units. Some Space Warps can deform an object's surface; others provide the same functionality as certain modifiers.

Space Warps are particularly useful when combined with particle systems. This chapter includes some examples of Space Warps that have been combined with particle systems.

Creating and Binding Space Warps

Space Warps are a way to add forces to the scene that can act on scene objects. Space Warps are not renderable and must be bound to an object to have an effect. A single Space Warp can be bound to several objects, and a single object can be bound to several Space Warps.

In many ways, Space Warps are similar to modifiers, but modifiers typically apply to individual objects, whereas Space Warps can be applied to many objects at the same time and are applied using World Space Coordinates. This ability to work with multiple objects makes Space Warps the preferred way to alter particle systems and to add forces to dynamic hair and cloth systems.

Another nice feature of Space Warps is that they can be animated. Moving the Wave Space Warp gizmo over the surface of a bound plane object lets you control where the waves appear in the plane object. You also can animate its parameters to gradually increase the size of the waves.

Creating a Space Warp

Space Warps are found in the Create⇨Space Warps menu. Selecting a Space Warp opens the Space Warps category (the icon is three wavy lines) in the Create panel. From the subcategory drop-down list, you can select from several different subcategories. Each subcategory has buttons to enable several different Space Warps, or you can select them using the Create⇨Space Warps menu command. To create a Space Warp, click a button or select a menu option and then click and drag in a viewport.

When a Space Warp is created, a gizmo is placed in the scene. This gizmo can be transformed as other objects can: by using the standard transformation buttons. The size and position of the Space Warp gizmo often affect its results. After a Space Warp is created, it affects only the objects to which it is bound.

Binding a Space Warp to an object

 A Space Warp's influence is felt only by its bound objects, so you can selectively apply gravity only to certain objects. For example, binding gravity to the ground plane wouldn't be helpful. The Bind to Space Warp button is on the main toolbar next to the Unlink Selection button. After clicking the Bind to Space Warp button, drag from the Space Warp to the object to which you want to link it, or vice versa.

All Space Warp bindings appear in the Modifier Stack. You can right click on the binding in the Modifier Stack to copy and paste Space Warps between objects, or you can drag the binding from the Modifier Stack and drop it on other scene objects.

Some Space Warps can be bound only to certain types of objects. Each Space Warp has a Supports Objects of Type rollout that lists the supported objects. If you're having trouble binding a Space Warp to an object, check this rollout to see whether the object is supported.

Understanding Space Warp Types

Just as many different types of forces exist in nature, many different Space Warp types exist. These appear in several different subcategories, based on their function. The subcategories are Forces, Deflectors, Geometric/Deformable, Modifier-Based, and Particles & Dynamics.

Force Space Warps

The Forces subcategory of Space Warps is mainly used with particle systems and dynamic simulations. Space Warps in this subcategory include Motor, Vortex, Path Follow, Displace, Wind, Push, Drag, PBomb, and Gravity. Figure 33.1 shows the gizmos for these Space Warps.

FIGURE 33.1

The Force Space Warps: Motor, Vortex, Path Follow, Displace, Wind, Push, Drag, PBomb, and Gravity

Motor

The Motor Space Warp applies a rotational torque to objects. This force accelerates objects radially instead of linearly. The Basic Torque value is a measurement of torque in Newton-meters, foot-pounds, or inch-pounds.

The On Time and Off Time options set the frames where the force is applied and disabled, respectively. Many of the Space Warps have these same values.

The Feedback On option causes the force to change as the object's speed changes. When this option is off, the force stays constant. You can also set Target Revolution units in revolutions per hour (RPH), revolutions per minute (RPM), or revolutions per second (RPS), which is the speed at which the force begins to change if the Feedback option is enabled. The Reversible option causes the force to change directions if the Target Speed is reached, and the Gain value is how quickly the force adjusts.

The motor force can also be adjusted with Periodic Variations, which cause the motor force to increase and then decrease in a regular pattern. You can define two different sets of Periodic Variation parameters: Period 1, Amplitude 1, Phase 1; and Period 2, Amplitude 2, Phase 2.

For particle systems, you can enable and set a Range value. The Motor Space Warp doesn't affect particles outside this distance. At the bottom of the Parameters rollout, you can set the size of the gizmo icon. You can find this same value for all Space Warps.

Figure 33.2 shows the Motor Space Warp twisting the particles being emitted from the Super Spray particle system in the direction of the icon's arrow.

FIGURE 33.2

You can use the Motor Space Warp to apply a twisting force to particles and dynamic objects.

Push

The Push Space Warp accelerates objects in the direction of the Space Warp's icon from the large cylinder to the small cylinder. Many of the parameters for the Push Space Warp are similar to those for the Motor Space Warp. Using the Parameters rollout, you can specify the force Strength in units of Newtons or pounds.

The Feedback On option causes the force to change as the object's speed changes, except that it deals with Target Speed instead of Target Revolution like the Motor Space Warp does.

The push force can also be set to include Periodic Variations that are the same as with the Motor Space Warp. Figure 33.3 shows the Push Space Warp pushing the particles being emitted from the Super Spray particle system.

FIGURE 33.3

You can use the Push Space Warp to apply a controlled force to particles and dynamic objects.

Vortex

You can use the Vortex Space Warp on particle systems to make particles spin around in a spiral like going down a whirlpool. You can use the Timing settings to set the beginning and ending frames where the effect takes place.

You can also specify Taper Length and Taper values, which determine the shape of the vortex. Lower Taper Length values wind the vortex tighter, and the Taper values can range between 1.0 and 4.0 and control the ratio between the spiral diameter at the top of the vortex versus the bottom of the vortex.

The Axial Drop value specifies how far each turn of the spiral is from the adjacent turn. The Damping value sets how quickly the Axial Drop value takes effect. The Orbital Speed is how fast the particles rotate away from the center. The Radial Pull value is the distance from the center of each spiral path that the particles can rotate. If the Unlimited Range option is disabled, Range and Falloff values are included for each setting. Both Orbital Speed and Radial Pull also have a Damping value. You can also specify whether the vortex spins clockwise or counterclockwise.

Figure 33.4 shows a Vortex Space Warp that is bound to a particle system.

33

FIGURE 33.4

You can use the Vortex Space Warp to force a particle system into a spiral like a whirlpool.

Drag

Drag is another common force that can be simulated with a Space Warp. The Drag Space Warp can be Linear, Spherical, or Cylindrical. This Space Warp causes particle velocity to be decreased, such as when simulating air resistance or fluid viscosity. Use the Time On and Time Off options to set the frame where the Space Warp is in effect.

For each of the Damping shape types—Linear, Spherical, and Cylindrical—you can set the drag, which can be along each axis for the Linear shape or in the Radial, Tangential, and Axial direction for the Spherical and Cylindrical shapes. If the Unlimited Range option is not selected, then the Range and Falloff values are available.

Figure 33.5 shows a Drag Space Warp surrounding a particle system. Notice how the particles are slowed and moved to the side as they pass through the Drag space warp.

FIGURE 33.5

You can use the Drag Space Warp to slow the velocity of particles.

PBomb

The PBomb (particle bomb) Space Warp was designed specifically for the PArray particle system, but it can be used with any particle system. To blow up an object with the PBomb Space Warp, create an object, make it a PArray emitter, and then bind the PBomb Space Warp to the PArray.

 You can find more information on the PArray particle system in Chapter 32, "Creating Particles."

Basic parameters for this Space Warp include three blast symmetry types: Spherical, Cylindrical, and Planar. You also can set the Chaos value as a percentage, which defines how erratically the pieces move.

In the Explosion Parameters section, the Start Time is the frame where the explosion takes place, and the Duration defines how long the explosion forces are applied. The Strength value is the power of the explosion.

A Range value can be set to determine the extent of the explosion. It is measured from the center of the Space Warp icon. If the Unlimited Range option is selected, the Range value is disabled. The Linear and Exponential options change how the explosion forces die out. The Range Indicator option displays the effective blast range of the PBomb.

Figure 33.6 shows a box selected as an emitter for a PArray. The PBomb is bound to the PArray and not to the box object. The Speed value for the PArray has been set to 0, and the Particle Type is set to Fragments. Notice that the PBomb's icon determines the center of the blast.

FIGURE 33.6

You can use the PBomb Space Warp with the PArray particle system to create explosions.

Path Follow

The Path Follow Space Warp causes particles to follow a path defined by a spline. The Basic Parameters rollout for this Space Warp includes a Pick Shape Object button for selecting the spline path to use. You can also specify a Range value or the Unlimited Range option. The Range distance is measured from the path to the particles.

The Path Follow Space Warp is similar to the Path Constraint, which is discussed in Chapter 25, "Animating with Constraints and Simple Controllers."

In the Motion Timing section, the Start Frame value is the frame where the particles start following the path, the Travel Time is the number of frames required to travel the entire path, and the Last Frame is where the particles no longer follow the path. There is also a Variation value to add some randomness to the movement of the particles.

The Basic Parameters rollout also includes a Particle Motion section with two options for controlling how the particles proceed down the path: Along Offset Splines and Along Parallel Splines. The first causes the particles to move along splines that are offset from the original, and the second moves all particles from their initial location along parallel path splines. The Constant Speed option makes all particles move at the same speed.

Also in the Particle Motion section is the Stream Taper value. This value is the amount by which the particles move away from the path over time. Options include Converge, Diverge, or Both. Converging streams move all particles closer to the path, and diverging streams do the opposite. The Stream Swirl value is the number of spiral turns that the particles take along the path. This swirling motion can be

Clockwise, Counterclockwise, or Bidirectional. The Seed value determines the randomness of the stream settings.

Figure 33.7 shows a Path Follow Space Warp bound to a Super Spray particle system. A Helix shape has been selected as the path.

FIGURE 33.7

A Path Follow Space Warp bound to an emitter from the Super Spray particle system and following a Helix path

Gravity

The Gravity Space Warp adds the effect of gravity to a scene. This causes objects to accelerate in the direction specified by the Gravity Space Warp, like the Wind Space Warp. The Parameters rollout includes Strength and Decay values. Additional options make the gravity planar or spherical. You can turn on the Range Indicators to display a plane or sphere where the gravity is half its maximum value.

Wind

The Wind Space Warp causes objects to accelerate. The Parameters rollout includes Strength and Decay values. Additional options make the gravity planar or spherical. The Turbulence value randomly moves the objects in different directions, and the Frequency value controls how often these random turbulent changes occur. Larger Scale values cause turbulence to affect larger areas, but smaller values are wilder and more chaotic.

You can turn on the Range Indicators just like the Gravity Space Warp. Figure 33.8 shows the Wind Space Warp pushing the particles being emitted from a Super Spray particle system.

FIGURE 33.8

You can use the Wind Space Warp to blow particles and dynamic objects.

Displace

The Displace Space Warp is like a force field: It pushes objects and is useful when applied to a particle system. It can also work on any deformable object in addition to particle systems. The strength of the displacement can be defined with Strength and Decay values or with a grayscale bitmap.

The Strength value is the distance that the geometry is displaced and can be positive or negative. The Decay value causes the displacement to decrease as the distance increases. The Luminance Center is the grayscale point where no displacement occurs; any color darker than this center value is moved away, and any brighter areas move closer.

The Bitmap and Map buttons let you load images to use as a displacement map; the amount of displacement corresponds with the brightness of the image. The Bitmap option loads an image file, but the Map button can load any map type from the Material Editor. A Blur setting blurs the image. You can apply these maps with different mapping options, including Planar, Cylindrical, Spherical, and Shrink Wrap. You can also adjust the Length, Width, and Height dimensions and the U, V, and W Tile values.

The Displace Space Warp is similar in function to the Displace modifier. The Displace modifier is discussed in Chapter 15, "Adding Material Details with Maps."

Figure 33.9 shows two Displace Space Warps with opposite Strength values.

FIGURE 33.9

The Displace Space Warp can raise or indent the surface of a patch object.

Deflector Space Warps

The Deflectors subcategory of Space Warps includes POmniFlect, SOmniFlect, UOmniFlect, Deflector, SDeflector, and UDeflector. You use them all with particle systems. This category includes several different types of deflectors starting with P, S, and U. The difference between these types is their shape. P-type (planar) deflectors are box shaped, S-type (spherical) deflectors are spherical, and U-type (universal) deflectors include a Pick Object button that you can use to select any object as a deflector.

> **TIP**
>
> When you use a custom deflector object, the number of polygons makes a big difference. The deflector object uses the normal to calculate the bounce direction, so if the deflector object includes lots of polygon faces, then the system slows way down. A solution to this, especially if you're using a simple plane deflector, because all its polygon normals are the same, anyway, is to use a simplified proxy object as the deflector and hide it so the particles look like they are hitting the complex object.

POmniFlect, SOmniFlect, and UOmniFlect

The POmniFlect Space Warp is a planar deflector that defines how particles reflect and bounce off other objects. The SOmniFlect Space Warp is just like the POmniFlect Space Warp, except that it is spherical in shape. The UOmniFlect Space Warp is another deflector, but this one can assume the shape of another object using the Pick Object button in the Parameters rollout. Its Parameters rollout includes a Timing section with Time On and Time Off values and a Reflection section.

The difference between this type of Space Warp and the other deflector Space Warps is the addition of refraction. Particles bound to this Space Warp can be refracted through an object. The values entered in the Refraction section of the Parameters rollout change the velocity and direction of a particle. The Refracts value is the percentage of particles that are refracted. The Pass Vel (velocity) is the amount that the particle speed changes when entering the object; a value of 100 maintains the same speed. The Distortion value affects the angle of refraction; a value of 0 maintains the same angle, and a value of 100 causes the particle to move along the surface of the struck object. The Diffusion value spreads the particles throughout the struck object. You can vary each of these values by using its respective Variation value.

> **NOTE**
>
> If the Refracts value is set to 100 percent, no particles are refracted.

You can also specify Friction and Inherit Velocity values. In the Spawn Effects Only section, the Spawns and Pass Velocity values control how many particle spawns are available and their velocity upon entering the struck object. Figure 33.10 shows each of these Space Warps bound to a Super Spray particle system. The Reflects value for each of the Space Warps is set to 50, and the remaining particles are refracted through the Space Warp's plane. Notice that the particles are also reflecting off the opposite side of the refracting object.

FIGURE 33.10

The POmniFlect, SOmniFlect, and UOmniFlect Space Warps reflecting and refracting particles emitted from the Super Spray particle system

Deflector, SDeflector, and UDeflector

The Deflector and SDeflector Space Warps are simplified versions of the POmniFlect and SOmniFlect Space Warps. Their parameters include values for Bounce, Variation, Chaos, Friction, and Inherit

Velocity. The UDeflector Space Warp is a simplified version of the UOmniFlect Space Warp. It has a Pick Object button for selecting the object to act as the deflector and all the same parameters as the SDeflector Space Warp.

Geometric/Deformable Space Warps

You use Geometric/Deformable Space Warps to deform the geometry of an object. Space Warps in this subcategory include FFD (Box), FFD (Cyl), Wave, Ripple, Displace, Conform, and Bomb. These Space Warps can be applied to any deformable object. Figure 33.11 shows the icons for each of these Space Warps.

FIGURE 33.11

The Geometric/Deformable Space Warps: FFD (Box), FFD (Cyl), Wave, Ripple, Displace, Conform, and Bomb

FFD (Box) and FFD (Cyl)

The FFD (Box) and FFD (Cyl) Space Warps show up as a lattice of control points in the shape of a box and a cylinder; you can select and move the control points that make up the Space Warp to deform an object that is bound to the Space Warp. The object is deformed only if the bound object is within the volume of the Space Warp.

These Space Warps have the same parameters as the modifiers with the same name found in the Modifiers ⇨ Free Form Deformers menu. The difference is that the Space Warps act in World coordinates and aren't tied to a specific object. This allows a single FFD Space Warp to affect multiple objects.

To move the control points, select the Space Warp object, open the Modify panel, and select the Control Points subobject, which lets you alter the control points individually.

FFD Select modifier

The FFD Select modifier is another unique selection modifier. It enables you to select a group of control point subobjects for the FFD (Box) or the FFD (Cyl) Space Warps and apply additional modifiers to the selection. When an FFD Space Warp is applied to an object, you can select the Control Points subobjects and apply modifiers to the selection. The FFD Select modifier lets you select a different set of control points for a different modifier.

Wave and Ripple

The Wave and Ripple Space Warps create linear and radial waves in the objects to which they are bound. Parameters in the rollout help define the shape of the wave. Amplitude 1 is the wave's height along the X-axis, and Amplitude 2 is the wave's height along its Y-axis. The Wave Length value defines the distance from one wave peak to the next wave peak. The Phase value determines how the wave starts at its origin. The Decay value sets how quickly the wave dies out. A Decay value of 0 maintains the same amplitude for the entire wave.

The Sides (Circles) and Segments values determine the number of segments for the X- and Y-axes. The Division value changes the icon's size without altering the wave effect. Figure 33.12 shows a Wave Space Warp applied to a simple Box primitive. Notice that the Space Warp icon is smaller than the box, yet it affects the entire object.

FIGURE 33.12

The Wave and Ripple Space Warps applied to a patch grid object

> **NOTE**
> Be sure to include enough segments in the bound object, or the effect won't be visible.

Tutorial: Creating pond ripples

For this tutorial, you position a patch object so it aligns with a background image and apply the Ripple Space Warp to it.

To add ripples to a pond, follow these steps:

1. Open the Pond ripple.max file from the Chap 33 directory on the CD.

   This file includes a background image of a bridge matched to a patch grid where the pond is located with a reflective material assigned to it.

> **TIP**
> If you're having trouble locating the patch grid, press F3 to switch to Wireframe mode.

2. Select the Create ⇨ Space Warps ⇨ Geometric/Deformable ⇨ Ripple menu command. Drag in the Perspective viewport to create a Space Warp object. In the Parameters rollout, set the Amplitudes to **4** and the Wave Length to **30**.

3. Click the Bind to Space Warp button, and drag from the patch object to the Space Warp.

Figure 33.13 shows the resulting image.

FIGURE 33.13

A ripple in a pond produced using the Ripple Space Warp

Conform

The Conform Space Warp pushes all object vertices until they hit another target object called the Wrap To Object, or until they've moved a preset distance. The Conform Parameters rollout includes a Pick Object button that lets you pick the Wrap To Object. The object vertices move no farther than this Wrap To Object.

You can also specify a Default Projection Distance and a Standoff Distance. The Default Projection Distance is the maximum distance that the vertices move if they don't intersect with the Wrap To

Object. The Standoff Distance is the separation amount maintained between the Wrap To Object and the moved vertices. Another option, Use Selected Vertices, moves only a subobject selection.

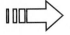 The Conform Space Warp is similar in function to the Conform compound object that is covered in Chapter 13, "Working with Compound Objects."

Figure 33.14 shows some text being deformed with the Conform Space Warp. A warped quad patch has been selected as the Wrap To object.

FIGURE 33.14

The Conform Space Warp wraps the surface of one object around another object.

Bomb

The Bomb Space Warp causes an object to explode to its individual faces. The Strength value is the power of the bomb and determines how far objects travel when exploded. The Spin value is the rate at which the individual pieces rotate. The Falloff value defines the boundaries of faces affected by the bomb. Object faces beyond this distance remain unaffected. You must select Falloff On for the Falloff value to work.

The Min and Max Fragment Size values set the minimum and maximum number of faces caused by the explosion.

The Gravity value determines the strength of gravity and can be positive or negative. Gravity always points toward the world's Z-axis. The Chaos value can range between 0 and 10 to add variety to the explosion. The Detonation value is the number of the frame where the explosion should take place, and the Seed value alters the randomness of the event. Figure 33.15 shows a frame of an explosion produced by the Bomb Space Warp.

FIGURE 33.15

The Bomb Space Warp causes an object to explode.

> **NOTE**
> The Bomb Space Warp's effect is seen over time. At frame 0, the object shows no effect.

Tutorial: Blowing a dandelion puff

You can use Space Warps with other types of objects besides particle systems. The Scatter compound object, for example, can quickly create many unique objects that can be controlled by a Space Warp. In this tutorial, you create a simple dandelion puff that can blow away in the wind.

To create and blow away a dandelion puff, follow these steps:

1. Open the Dandelion puff.max file from the Chap 33 directory on the CD.

   This file includes a sphere covered with a Scatter compound object representing the seeds of a dandelion.

2. Select the Create ⇨ Space Warps ⇨ Geometric/Deformable ⇨ Bomb menu command.Click in the Front viewport, and position the Bomb icon to the left and slightly below the dandelion object. In the Bomb Parameters rollout, set the Strength to **10**, the Spin to **0.5**, the Min and Max Fragment Size values to **24**, the Gravity to **0.2**, and the Chaos to **2.0**.

3. Click the Bind to Space Warp button on the main toolbar, and drag from the dandelion object to the Space Warp. Then press the Play button to see the animation.

Figure 33.16 shows one frame of the dandelion puff being blown away.

FIGURE 33.16

You can use Space Warps on Scatter objects as well as particle systems.

Modifier-Based Space Warps

Modifier-Based Space Warps produce the same effects as many of the standard modifiers, but because they are Space Warps, they can be applied to many objects simultaneously. Space Warps in this subcategory include Bend, Noise, Skew, Taper, Twist, and Stretch, as shown in Figure 33.17. All Modifier-Based Space Warp gizmos are simple box shapes. The parameters for all Modifier-Based Space Warps are identical to the modifiers (found in the Parametric Deformers category) of the same name. These Space Warps don't include a Supports Objects of Type rollout because they can be applied to all objects.

FIGURE 33.17

The Modifier-Based Space Warps: Bend, Noise, Skew, Taper, Twist, and Stretch

These Space Warps include a Gizmo Parameters rollout with values for the Length, Width, and Height of the gizmo. You can also specify the deformation decay. The Decay value causes the Space Warp's effect to diminish with distance from the bound object.

You can reposition the Modifier-Based Space Warp's gizmo as a separate object, but the normal modifiers require that you select the gizmo subobject to reposition it. Unlike modifiers, Space Warps don't have any subobjects.

Combining Particle Systems with Space Warps

To conclude this chapter, you'll look at some examples that use Space Warps along with particle systems. With all these Space Warps and their various parameters combined with particle systems, the possibilities are endless. These examples are only a small representation of what is possible.

Tutorial: Shattering glass

When glass shatters, it is very chaotic, sending pieces in every direction. For this tutorial, you shatter a glass mirror on a wall. The wall keeps the pieces from flying off, and most pieces fall straight to the floor.

To shatter glass, follow these steps:

1. Open the Shattering glass.max file from the Chap 33 directory on the CD.

   This file includes a simple mirror created from patch grid objects. The file also includes a simple sphere that is animated striking the mirror.

2. Select the Create ⇨ Particles ⇨ PArray menu command. Then drag in the Front viewport to create the PArray icon. In the Basic Parameters rollout, click the Pick Object button and select the first patch object representing the glass mirror. In the Viewport Display section, select the Mesh option. In the Particle Generation rollout, set the Speed and Divergence to 0. Also set the Emit Start to 30 and the Life value to 100, so it matches the last frame. In the Particle Type rollout, select the Object Fragments option, and set the Thickness to 1.0. Then in the Object Fragment Controls section, select the Number of Chunks option with a Minimum value of 30. In the Rotation and Collision rollout, set the Spin Time to 100 and the Variation to 50.

   These settings cause the patch to emit 30 object fragments with a slow, gradual rotation.

3. Select the Space Warps category button, and choose the Forces subcategory from the drop-down list. Click the PBomb button, and create a PBomb Space Warp in the Top viewport; then center it above the Mirror object. In the Modify panel, set the Blast Symmetry option to Spherical with a Chaos value of 50 percent. Set the Start Time to 30 with a Strength value of 0.2. Then click the Bind to Space Warp button, and drag from the PBomb Space Warp to the PArray icon.

4. Select the Create ⇨ Space Warps ⇨ Forces ⇨ Gravity menu command, and drag in the Top viewport to create a Gravity Space Warp. Make sure the Gravity Space Warp icon arrow is pointing down in the Front viewport. In the Modify panel, set the Strength value to 0.1. Then bind this Space Warp to the PArray icon.

5. Select the Create ⇨ Space Warps ⇨ Deflectors ⇨ POmniFlect menu command. Drag this Space Warp in the Top viewport, and make it wide enough to be completely under the mirror object. Rotate the POmniFlect Space Warp so that its arrows are pointing up at the mirror. Position it so that it lies in the same plane as the plane object that makes up the floor. In the Modify panel, set the Reflects value to **100** percent and the Bounce value to **0**. Bind this Space Warp to the PArray as well; this keeps the pieces from falling through the floor. Press Play to see the results.

Figure 33.18 shows the mirror immediately after being struck by a ball.

FIGURE 33.18

A shattering mirror

Tutorial: Making water flow down a trough

That should be enough destruction for a while. In this final example, you'll make some water particles flow down a trough. You accomplish this using the Path Follow Space Warp.

To make water flow down a trough, follow these steps:

1. Open the Water flowing down a trough.max file from the Chap 33 directory on the CD.

   This file includes a simple trough made from primitives and a spline path that the water will follow.

2. Select the Create ⇨ Particles ⇨ Super Spray menu command. Create a Super Spray object in the Left viewport and position its pointer where you want the particles to first appear. In the Viewport Display section, select the Ticks option. In the Particle Generation rollout, set the Speed to **10** and the Variation to **100**. Then set the Emit Start to **0** and the Display Until and Life values to **100** and the Size to **20**. In the Particle Type rollout, select MetaParticles and enable the Automatic Coarseness option.

3. Select the Space Warps category button, and choose Forces from the subcategory drop-down list. Click the Path Follow button, and create a Path Follow object; then click the Bind to Space Warp button on the main toolbar, and drag from the Path Follow icon to the Super Spray icon. Open the Modify panel, select the Path Follow icon, click the Pick Shape Object button, and select the path in the viewports. Set the Start Frame to **0** and the Travel Time to **100**.

Figure 33.19 shows the rendered result.

FIGURE 33.19

Water flowing down a trough using the Path Follow Space Warp

Summary

Space Warps are useful for adding forces and effects to objects in the scene. The Autodesk® 3ds Max® 2013 software has several different types of Space Warps, and most of them can be applied only to certain object types. In this chapter, you learned the following:

- How to create Space Warps
- How to bind Space Warps to objects
- How to use all the various Space Warps in several subcategories
- How to combine Space Warps with particle systems

Next up are some helpful appendixes.

What's New with Autodesk 3ds Max 2013

IN THIS APPENDIX

Finding the new features in 3ds Max

Enjoying the minor enhancements that 3ds Max has to offer

The Autodesk® 3ds Max® 2013 software is as astonishing as its predecessors. With each revision of 3ds Max, I'm always amazed at the new features that are included. 3ds Max is a large and complex piece of software, and just when I think it can't hold anything more, a new revision with a host of new features appears. 3ds Max 2013 is no different.

You can find in-depth coverage of the new features in the various chapters, but this appendix provides a quick overview of these new features, along with references on where to learn more about them. Throughout the book, the New Feature icon identifies the features that are new to 3ds Max 2013.

> **NOTE**
> If 3ds Max needs some improvements that haven't made it into the latest release, you can join Autodesk's Customer Involvement Program using the Help ⟳ Customer Involvement Program menu command. This program lets you provide feedback and suggestions to the 3ds Max team.

Major Improvements

3ds Max 2013 includes lots of new improvements. Some are considered major because they likely will affect every user's workflow, and others are minor because they are smaller in scope. However, an improvement listed as minor may be the one you've been waiting for.

> **NOTE**
> Within the Introduction section of the 3ds Max Help file is a What's New in Autodesk 3ds Max 2013 page. You also can access the What's New link in the Help menu.

State Sets

The new State Sets interface lets you save the state of a current scene. This lets you easily create several different versions of a scene that you can quickly review with a client. It also provides a great render pass management system. You can learn more about this system in Chapter 23, "Compositing with Render Elements and the Video Post Interface."

Compact Track View

The Track View interface has been overhauled and redesigned. The result is a simpler, more compact interface that still has all the helpful tools you need. The new interface also more closely matches the curve editors found in other Autodesk products like Maya and MotionBuilder. You can see more of the Track View changes in Chapter 28, "Editing Animation Curves in the Track View."

Viewport Layouts toolbar

Located to the left of the viewports is a new toolbar that holds different layout configurations. This toolbar lets you quickly change between several viewport layouts with a single click. The Viewport Layouts toolbar is covered in Chapter 2, "Controlling the Viewports."

Gradient background

The viewport background can be set to show a linear gradient. Using the Background tab in the Viewport Configuration dialog box, you can change the gradient colors. The Perspective viewport uses gradients by default, but any viewport can be set to display a background gradient. These background options are covered in Chapter 2, "Controlling the Viewports."

Autodesk DirectConnect support

Using Autodesk DirectConnect makes it possible to import several additional CAD formats including CATIA, IGES, JT Open, Pro/ENGINEER, SolidWorks, STEP, and UG-NX files. These formats are imported as Body Objects.

Maya Navigation mode

A setting within the Interaction mode of the Preference Settings dialog box lets you switch the mouse and keyboard controls to use the same settings used by Maya. This lets you navigate objects in both software packages using the same set of commands.

gPoly Modeling Format

The gPoly Modifier lets mesh objects be converted to the raw format that 3ds Max uses internally. This provides better performance for objects that are smoothed or deformed without having to use the Editable modeling formats. More on this unique format is covered in Chapter 11, "Modeling with Polygons."

MassFX improvements

The latest version of MassFX includes several key improvements, including the ability to edit several constraint settings at once. You also can use the Gravity Space Warp within your physics simulations including multiple instances.

Skin improvements

A key improvement when working with the Skin Modifier is that bones applied to a skin object are easier to search. You can list the bones in alphabetical order or set to show only the matching bones. The Skin Modifier is covered in Chapter 30, "Skinning Characters."

Workspaces

Selecting a custom workspace is now easier than ever with the Workspaces drop-down list at the top of the interface. Different custom interface layouts can be defined for each task and switched between as the task changes. Chapter 1, "Exploring the Interface," shows how workspaces work.

Nitrous improvements

The Nitrous display drivers offer some additional display options, including Facets and Clay styles. Settings for better control over lights, shadows, reflections, and Depth-of-Field also are available. Some of these improvements are covered in Chapter 2, "Controlling the Viewports."

iray and mental ray improvements

The iray and mental ray rendering systems also have been improved. iray can now be set up as an ActiveShade renderer providing immediate feedback. Other improvements include support for Motion Blur, a round corner effect, glossy refractions, and translucency. More on the iray improvements is covered in Chapter 22, "Rendering with mental ray and iray."

Minor Improvements

In addition to the major improvements, many minor improvements make working with objects, materials, and other facets of 3ds Max easier. Minor improvements found in version 2013 include the following:

- **Modeless Array dialog box:** The Array dialog box is now modeless, so you can work and reposition scene objects without having to close the dialog box.
- **Egg Spline:** With the Spline primitives menu is a new spline primitive for creating egg-shaped splines.
- **Retimer tool:** The Track View has a new Retimer tool for changing the timing of a section or for the entire animation without losing any frames.
- **Sky Color maps for Skylights:** A Skylight system can use a new Sky Color map for defining the lighting for the scene including support for HDR images.

A

What's on the CD-ROM

IN THIS APPENDIX

System requirements

Using the CD with Windows

What's on the CD

Troubleshooting

Throughout this book, you'll find many tutorials that help you understand the principles being discussed. All the example files used to create these tutorials are included on the CD that comes with this book. In addition to these files, you'll find sample 3D models.

This appendix provides you with information on the contents of the CD. For the latest and greatest information, please refer to the Readme file located at the root of the CD.

System Requirements

Make sure that your computer meets the minimum system requirements listed in this section. If your computer doesn't match up to most of these requirements, you may have a problem using the contents of the CD.

For Windows 7 (recommended), Windows Vista, Windows XP Professional SP2, or Windows XP Home Edition SP2:

- Intel® Pentium® III or AMD® processor, 500 MHz or higher (dual Intel)
- Xeon® or dual AMD Athlon® or Opteron® (32-bit system recommended)
- 512MB RAM (1GB recommended)
- 500MB swap space (2GB recommended)
- Graphics card supporting 1024 × 768 × 16-bit color with 64MB RAM (OpenGL® and Direct3D® hardware acceleration supported; 3D graphics accelerator 1280 × 1024 × 32-bit color with 256MB RAM recommended)
- Microsoft® Windows®–compliant pointing device (optimized for Microsoft IntelliMouse®)
- Microsoft Internet Explorer 6
- A CD drive

Using the CD with Windows

To install the items from the CD to your hard drive, follow these steps:

1. Insert the CD into your computer's CD drive. The license agreement appears.

NOTE

The interface won't launch if you have autorun disabled. In that case, click Start ⇨ Run. In the dialog box that appears, type D:\start.exe. (Replace D with the proper letter if your CD drive uses a different letter. If you don't know the letter, see how your CD drive is listed under My Computer.) Click OK.

2. Read through the license agreement, and then click the Accept button if you want to use the CD. After you click Accept, the License Agreement window won't appear again.

The CD interface appears. The interface allows you to install the programs and run the demos with just a click of a button (or two).

What's on the CD

The following sections provide a summary of the materials you'll find on the CD.

Author-created materials

The example files used in the tutorials throughout the book are included in the "Chapter Example Files" directory. Within this directory are separate subdirectories for each chapter. Supplemental files such as models and images are also included in these directories. Animated scenes include a rendered AVI file of the animation. For each tutorial, the resulting example after all steps are completed has the word "final" in the filename. Using these final examples, you can compare the results to your own work.

Shareware programs are fully functional, free, trial versions of copyrighted programs. If you like particular programs, register with their authors for a nominal fee and receive licenses, enhanced versions, and technical support.

Freeware programs are free, copyrighted games, applications, and utilities. You can copy them to as many PCs as you like—for free—but they offer no technical support.

GNU software is governed by its own license, which is included inside the folder of the GNU software. There are no restrictions on distribution of GNU software. See the GNU license at the root of the CD for more details.

Trial, demo, or *evaluation* versions of software are usually limited either in terms of the time you can use them or the functionality they offer (such as not letting you save a project after you create it).

3D models

Viewpoint Datalabs and Zygote Media have provided sample 3D models. Many of these models were used in the tutorials, and you can find the complete set of models in the "3D Models" directory.

Viewpoint 3D models are copyright Digimation, Inc. All rights reserved.

Troubleshooting

If you have difficulty installing or using any of the materials on the companion CD, try the following solutions:

- **Turn off any anti-virus software that you may have running.** Installers sometimes mimic virus activity and can make your computer incorrectly believe that it is being infected by a virus. (Be sure to turn the anti-virus software back on later.)
- **Close all running programs.** The more programs you're running, the less memory is available to other programs. Installers also typically update files and programs; if you keep other programs running, installation may not work properly.
- **See the ReadMe file.** Please refer to the ReadMe file located at the root of the CD for the latest product information at the time of publication.

Customer Care

If you still have trouble with the CD, please call the Wiley Product Technical Support telephone number: (800) 762-2974. Outside the United States, call 1 (317) 572-3994. You can also contact Wiley Product Technical Support at `http://support.wiley.com`. John Wiley & Sons will provide technical support only for installation and other general quality control items. For technical support on the applications themselves, consult the program's vendor or author.

To place additional orders or to request information about other Wiley products, please call (877) 762-2974.

B

Index

Symbols and Numerics

Index

Index

N

T

John Wiley & Sons, Inc.
End-User License Agreement

READ THIS. You should carefully read these terms and conditions before opening the software packet(s) included with this book "Book". This is a license agreement "Agreement" between you and Wiley Publishing, Inc. "Wiley". By opening the accompanying software packet(s), you acknowledge that you have read and accept the following terms and conditions. If you do not agree and do not want to be bound by such terms and conditions, promptly return the Book and the unopened software packet(s) to the place you obtained them for a full refund.

1. **License Grant.** Wiley grants to you (either an individual or entity) a nonexclusive license to use one copy of the enclosed software program(s) (collectively, the "Software") solely for your own personal or business purposes on a single computer (whether a standard computer or a workstation component of a multi-user network). The Software is in use on a computer when it is loaded into temporary memory (RAM) or installed into permanent memory (hard disk, CD-ROM, or other storage device). Wiley reserves all rights not expressly granted herein.

2. **Ownership.** Wiley is the owner of all right, title, and interest, including copyright, in and to the compilation of the Software recorded on the disk(s) or CD-ROM "Software Media". Copyright to the individual programs recorded on the Software Media is owned by the author or other authorized copyright owner of each program. Ownership of the Software and all proprietary rights relating thereto remain with Wiley and its licensers.

3. **Restrictions On Use and Transfer.**

    (a) You may only (i) make one copy of the Software for backup or archival purposes, or (ii) transfer the Software to a single hard disk, provided that you keep the original for backup or archival purposes. You may not (i) rent or lease the Software, (ii) copy or reproduce the Software through a LAN or other network system or through any computer subscriber system or bulletin-board system, or (iii) modify, adapt, or create derivative works based on the Software.

    (b) You may not reverse engineer, decompile, or disassemble the Software. You may transfer the Software and user documentation on a permanent basis, provided that the transferee agrees to accept the terms and conditions of this Agreement and you retain no copies. If the Software is an update or has been updated, any transfer must include the most recent update and all prior versions.

4. **Restrictions on Use of Individual Programs.** You must follow the individual requirements and restrictions detailed for each individual program in the "What's on the DVD" appendix of this Book. These limitations are also contained in the individual license agreements recorded on the Software Media. These limitations may include a requirement that after using the program for a specified period of time, the user must pay a registration fee or discontinue use. By opening the Software packet(s), you will be agreeing to abide by the licenses and restrictions for these individual programs that are detailed in the "What's on the DVD" appendix and on the Software Media. None of the material on this Software Media or listed in this Book may ever be redistributed, in original or modified form, for commercial purposes.

5. **Limited Warranty.**

    (a) Wiley warrants that the Software and Software Media are free from defects in materials and workmanship under normal use for a period of sixty (60) days from the date of purchase of this Book. If Wiley receives notification within the warranty period of defects in materials or workmanship, Wiley will replace the defective Software Media.

(b) Wiley AND THE AUTHOR OF THE BOOK DISCLAIM ALL OTHER WARRANTIES, EXPRESS OR IMPLIED, INCLUDING WITHOUT LIMITATION IMPLIED WARRANTIES OF MERCHANTABILITY AND FITNESS FOR A PARTICULAR PURPOSE, WITH RESPECT TO THE SOFTWARE, THE PROGRAMS, THE SOURCE CODE CONTAINED THEREIN, AND/OR THE TECHNIQUES DESCRIBED IN THIS BOOK. Wiley DOES NOT WARRANT THAT THE FUNCTIONS CONTAINED IN THE SOFTWARE WILL MEET YOUR REQUIREMENTS OR THAT THE OPERATION OF THE SOFTWARE WILL BE ERROR FREE.

(c) This limited warranty gives you specific legal rights, and you may have other rights that vary from jurisdiction to jurisdiction.

6. **Remedies.**

   (a) Wiley's entire liability and your exclusive remedy for defects in materials and workmanship shall be limited to replacement of the Software Media, which may be returned to Wiley with a copy of your receipt at the following address: Software Media Fulfillment Department, Attn.: *Autodesk 3ds Max 2013 Bible*, John Wiley & Sons, Inc., 10475 Crosspoint Blvd., Indianapolis, IN 46256, or call 1-877-762-2974. Please allow four to six weeks for delivery. This Limited Warranty is void if failure of the Software Media has resulted from accident, abuse, or misapplication. Any replacement Software Media will be warranted for the remainder of the original warranty period or thirty (30) days, whichever is longer.

   (b) In no event shall Wiley or the author be liable for any damages whatsoever (including without limitation damages for loss of business profits, business interruption, loss of business information, or any other pecuniary loss) arising from the use of or inability to use the Book or the Software, even if Wiley has been advised of the possibility of such damages.

   (c) Because some jurisdictions do not allow the exclusion or limitation of liability for consequential or incidental damages, the above limitation or exclusion may not apply to you.

7. **U.S. Government Restricted Rights.** Use, duplication, or disclosure of the Software for or on behalf of the United States of America, its agencies and/or instrumentalities "U.S. Government" is subject to restrictions as stated in paragraph (c)(1)(ii) of the Rights in Technical Data and Computer Software clause of DFARS 252.227-7013, or subparagraphs (c) (1) and (2) of the Commercial Computer Software - Restricted Rights clause at FAR 52.227-19, and in similar clauses in the NASA FAR supplement, as applicable.

8. **General.** This Agreement constitutes the entire understanding of the parties and revokes and supersedes all prior agreements, oral or written, between them and may not be modified or amended except in a writing signed by both parties hereto that specifically refers to this Agreement. This Agreement shall take precedence over any other documents that may be in conflict herewith. If any one or more provisions contained in this Agreement are held by any court or tribunal to be invalid, illegal, or otherwise unenforceable, each and every other provision shall remain in full force and effect.